THE
unofficial GUIDE®
ᵀᴼUniversal
Orlando®

2021

COME CHECK US OUT!

Supplement your valuable guidebook with tips, news, and deals by visiting our websites:

theunofficialguides.com
touringplans.com

Also, while there, sign up for The Unofficial Guide newsletter for even more travel tips and special offers.

Join the conversation on social media:

 @theUGSeries

 theUnofficialGuides

 theUGSeries

 theUGSeries

 TheUnofficialGuideSeries

Other Unofficial Guides

The Disneyland Story: The Unofficial Guide to the Evolution of Walt Disney's Dream

Universal vs. Disney: The Unofficial Guide to American Theme Parks' Greatest Rivalry

The Unofficial Guide to Disney Cruise Line

The Unofficial Guide to Disneyland

The Unofficial Guide to Las Vegas

The Unofficial Guide to Mall of America

The Unofficial Guide to Walt Disney World

The Unofficial Guide to Walt Disney World with Kids

The Unofficial Guide to Washington, D.C.

THE *unofficial* GUIDE®
TO Universal Orlando®

2021

SETH KUBERSKY *with*
BOB SEHLINGER & LEN TESTA

LIST *of* MAPS

ABOUT *the* AUTHORS

Seth Kubersky is the coauthor of *The Unofficial Guide to Disneyland* and *The Unofficial Guide to Las Vegas* and a contributor to *The Unofficial Guide to Walt Disney World*. A resident of Orlando since 1996, Seth is a former employee of Universal Orlando's entertainment department. He covers arts and attractions for the *Orlando Weekly* newspaper, *Attractions Magazine,* and other publications. You can find Seth online at sethkubersky.com or on Twitter @skubersky.

  Bob Sehlinger is the author of *The Unofficial Guide to Walt Disney World* and *The Unofficial Guide to Las Vegas* and is also the publisher of The Unofficial Guide series.

  Len Testa is the coauthor of *The Unofficial Guide to Walt Disney World* and has contributed to *The Unofficial Guide to Disneyland* and *The Unofficial Guide to Las Vegas*. He is also the webmaster of touringplans.com, the sister website of The Unofficial Guides.

INTRODUCTION

WHY "UNOFFICIAL"?

DECLARATION OF INDEPENDENCE

THE AUTHORS AND RESEARCHERS of this guide specifically and categorically declare that they are and always have been totally independent. The material in this guide originated with the authors and has not been reviewed, edited, or in any way approved by Universal Orlando or any other companies whose travel products are discussed.

The purpose of this guide is to provide you with the information necessary to tour with the greatest efficiency and economy and with the least hassle and stress. In this guide we represent and serve you, the consumer. If a restaurant serves bad food, a gift item is overpriced, or a certain ride isn't worth the wait, we can say so, and in the process we hope to make your visit more fun, efficient, and economical.

A WORD ABOUT THEME PARKS IN THE AGE OF CORONAVIRUS

THE ENTIRE UNOFFICIAL GUIDES TEAM hopes that you and your loved ones have remained healthy and safe throughout the COVID-19 pandemic. Our thoughts are with the victims of the virus, as well as all the brave first responders and essential workers who have sustained our society while we struggled with adapting to social distancing. Without intending to trivialize the current crisis, we have continued to cover Orlando's attractions as they reopened after quarantine and as they welcomed returning guests who desired distractions during these trying times. This edition of the *Unofficial Guide* is dedicated to the frontline employees of Orlando's tourism and hospitality industry (many of whom are struggling to make ends meet) who have risked their personal health to help inject a little magic back into visitors' lives. You'll find detailed information about how COVID-19 has affected Universal Orlando in a new special chapter starting on page 20.

DANCE TO THE MUSIC

A DANCE HAS A BEGINNING and an end. But when you're dancing, you're not concerned about getting to the end or where on the dance floor you might wind up. In other words, you're totally in the moment. That's the way you should be on your Universal Orlando vacation.

You may feel a bit of pressure concerning your holiday. Vacations, after all, are very special events—and expensive ones to boot. So you work hard to make your getaway the best that it can be. Planning and organizing are essential to a successful Universal Orlando vacation, but if they become your focus, you won't be able to hear the music and enjoy the dance.

So think of us as your dancing coaches. We'll teach you the steps to the dance in advance, so that when you're on vacation and the music plays, you'll dance with effortless grace and ease.

A BETTER MOUSETRAP?

DIE-HARD DISNEY DEVOTEES may want to cover their mouse ears because we are about to utter the ultimate blasphemy: it is possible to enjoy an awesome Orlando vacation without spending a single minute in Mickey's world. For much of the past half century, the notion of spending a holiday in Central Florida without seeing Walt Disney's sprawling wonderland seemed silly. While visitors might take a day or two out of their trip to explore independent attractions such as Sea-World, Busch Gardens, or Kennedy Space Center, the Magic Kingdom and its sister parks were seen by most as the area's main draw.

Much to the Mouse House's dismay, that situation is swiftly shifting. While Walt Disney World is in no danger of closing for lack of interest, its share of Orlando's lucrative tourism market has been steadily and significantly swinging in favor of an energetic upstart located a few miles up I-4: the Universal Orlando Resort.

Originally opened in 1990 as a single theme park packed with advanced but unreliable attractions, Universal Orlando has matured into a full-service, fully immersive vacation destination with enough world-class activities to keep a family occupied for four days or more. Universal Studios Florida, a longtime rival of Disney's Hollywood Studios that draws its inspiration from movies and television, has been almost entirely overhauled since its debut, and it now houses one of the world's top collections of cutting-edge attractions. Universal's Islands of Adventure debuted in 1999 as the most modern, high-tech theme park in the United States, featuring an all-star lineup of thrill rides that makes it the best park in town for older kids and young-at-heart adults.

Together, the two parks are home to the game-changing Wizarding World of Harry Potter, a meticulously imagined multilayered experience that's drawing millions of Muggle fans from around the world to the hallowed halls of Hogwarts Castle and Gringotts Bank. Surrounding the two parks are six immaculately appointed on-site resort hotels, the elaborately themed Volcano Bay water park, and the CityWalk complex full of restaurants, nightclubs, and entertainment options appealing to families and adults. And Universal Orlando has begun growing beyond the resort's original boundaries, building a pair of value-priced resort hotels on the former site of Wet 'n Wild and announcing ambitious plans to build a brand-new theme park complex near the Orange County Convention Center; those latter plans are currently paused due to the COVID-19 pandemic.

Universal Orlando's ascendancy is not about to bankrupt Walt Disney World, and likely never will—Disney's nearly unlimited dominion over its vast 43-square-mile kingdom practically ensures its dominance. But those who approach Universal with open eyes will find that the resort can provide just as much magic and fantasy in its own fashion. Universal Orlando has an energy, pace, and attitude all its own that might appeal to the most adamant anti–amusement park person, and could even convert confirmed Disney customers. Instead of opting for the same old rat race, consider spending your next vacation playing Quidditch with Harry, saving New York with Spidey, and drinking a Duff with the Simpsons. You may just find yourself asking, "Mickey who?"

IT TAKES MORE THAN ONE BOOK TO DO THE JOB RIGHT

WE'VE BEEN COVERING CENTRAL FLORIDA tourism for almost 40 years. We began by lumping everything into one guidebook, but that was when the Magic Kingdom and Epcot were the only theme parks at Walt Disney World, at the very beginning of the boom that has made Central Florida one of the most visited tourist destinations on Earth. We now have a few titles that provide specialized information tailored to specific Central Florida visitors. Though some tips (such as arriving at the parks early) are echoed in all the guides, most of the information in each book is unique.

The Unofficial Guide to Walt Disney World is the centerpiece of our Central Florida coverage because, well, Walt Disney World is the centerpiece of most Central Florida vacations. *The Unofficial Guide to Walt Disney World* is evaluative, comprehensive, and instructive—the ultimate planning tool for a successful Disney World vacation, including a condensed version of this book's Universal Orlando information.

The Unofficial Guide to Walt Disney World with Kids, by Bob Sehlinger and Liliane J. Opsomer with Len Testa, offers a wealth of planning and touring tips for a successful Disney family vacation.

Finally, you hold our in-depth guide dedicated to the attractions and amenities of the Universal Orlando Resort. All of the guides are available at most bookstores and in digital ebook editions.

THE DEATH OF SPONTANEITY

ONE OF OUR ALL-TIME favorite letters came from a man in Chapel Hill, North Carolina:

Your book reads like the operations plan for an amphibious landing: Go here, do this, proceed to Step 15. You must think that everyone is a hyperactive, type-A theme park commando. What happened to the satisfaction of self-discovery or the joy of spontaneity? Next you'll be telling us when to empty our bladders.

As it happens, Unofficial Guide researchers are a pretty existential crew who are big on self-discovery. But Universal Orlando—especially for first-time travelers—probably isn't the place you want to "discover" the spontaneity of needless waits in line or mediocre meals when you could be doing better.

In many ways, Central Florida's theme parks are the quintessential system, the ultimate in mass-produced entertainment and the most planned and programmed environment anywhere. Lines for rides form in predictable ways at predictable times, for example, and you can either learn here how to avoid them or "discover" them on your own.

We aren't saying that you can't have a great time at Universal Orlando, and enjoying the resort requires much less advance planning than the equivalent vacation at Walt Disney World. What we *are* saying is that you should think about what you want to do before you go. The time and money you save by planning will help your family have more fun.

THE SUM OF ALL FEARS

EVERY WRITER WHO EXPRESSES an opinion is accustomed to readers who strongly agree or disagree: it comes with the territory. Extremely troubling, however, is the possibility that our efforts to be objective have frightened some readers away from Universal Orlando or made others apprehensive.

For the record, if you love theme parks, Universal Orlando is as good as it gets—absolute nirvana. If you arrive without knowing a thing about the place and make every possible mistake, chances are about 90% that you'll have a wonderful vacation anyway. The job of a guidebook is to give you a heads-up regarding opportunities and potential problems. We're certain that we can help you turn a great vacation into an absolutely *superb* one.

THE UNOFFICIAL TEAM

THIS BOOK WAS AUTHORED by Seth Kubersky, building on decades of research from The Unofficial Guides by Bob Sehlinger, Len Testa, and the rest of the Unofficial team. Derek Burgan, our Universal food consigliere, contributed vital research to this guide's dining chapter. Our prologue is excerpted from Sam Gennawey's *Universal vs. Disney: An Unofficial Guide to American Theme Parks' Greatest Rivalry.* Special thanks to Genevieve Bernard for research assistance, proofreading, and patience. Amber Kaye Henderson edited the book, Chris Eliopoulos and Tami Knight drew the cartoons, Steve Jones and Cassandra Poertner created the maps, and Potomac Indexing LLC indexed the book; thanks go to each of them.

UPDATES AND BREAKING NEWS

LOOK FOR THESE at the Unofficial Guide website, theunofficial guides.com, and at our sister website, touringplans.com. See page 33 for a complete description of the sites.

COMMENTS FROM READERS

MANY OF THOSE WHO USE The Unofficial Guides contact us to share comments or their own strategies for visiting Central Florida. We appreciate all such input, both positive and critical, and encourage our readers to continue writing. Readers' comments and observations are frequently incorporated into revised editions of The Unofficial Guides and have contributed immeasurably to their improvement. If you contact us, you can rest assured that we won't release your name and email address to any mailing lists, advertisers, or other third party.

Reader Survey

After your vacation, please fill out our reader survey by visiting touring plans.com/universal-orlando/survey. Unless you instruct us otherwise, we will assume that you don't object to being quoted in a future edition.

How to Contact the Authors

Seth Kubersky and Bob Sehlinger c/o The Unofficial Guides
2204 First Ave. S, Ste. 102
Birmingham, AL 35233
unofficialguides@menasharidge.com

If you email us, let us know where you're from. And remember, as travel writers, we're often out of the office for long periods of time, so forgive us if our response is slow.

UNIVERSAL ORLANDO:
An Overview

PROLOGUE: AMERICAN THEME PARKS' GREATEST RIVALRY

UNIVERSAL STUDIOS DID NOT SET OUT to challenge The Walt Disney Company in the theme park business. The men who ran the Music Corporation of America (MCA) were quite happy with the industrial tour they created in 1964 at Universal City. The Universal Studio Tour took visitors behind the scenes of the largest and busiest back lot in Hollywood to show how motion pictures and television programs were manufactured. . . .

In 1979 MCA bought land in Orlando 10 miles north of Walt Disney World and later announced that it was going to build a motion picture and television production studio. The new studio would have also featured a tour just like the one in California. Lew Wasserman, MCA's

Universal Orlando

Universal's Islands of Adventure

To Tampa & Walt Disney World →

Turkey Lake Road

Universal's Cabana Bay Beach Resort

Universal's Volcano Bay

Hollywood Way

Universal's Aventura Hotel

Loews Sapphire Falls Resort

Loews Royal Pacific Resort

Main Entrance

Surfside Inn & Suites

Universal Blvd.

Dockside Inn & Suites

American Way

Universal CityWalk

Hollywood Way

Parking Garages

Grand National Dr.

continued from page 7

Comcast—which acquired a majority stake in the NBCUniversal conglomerate in 2011 and purchased full ownership from General Electric in 2013—embarked on an unprecedented wave of expansions, rapidly adding new attractions and extensions, including **The Wizarding World of Harry Potter–Diagon Alley** at USF and additional on-site hotels.

While Disney responded to the Potter phenomenon by slowly building *Avatar* and *Star Wars* attractions, Universal struck another blow in the summer of 2017 with the opening of Volcano Bay, its first highly themed on-site water park. Volcano Bay aims to revolutionize the water park experience through cutting-edge slides and advanced Virtual Line technology. Like USF and IOA, Volcano Bay is a state-of-the-art park vying with Disney parks, whose attractions are decades older on average. Despite Walt Disney World deploying a wave of upgrades ahead of the resort's 50th anniversary in 2021, Universal's ever-accelerating expansion appeared undaunted, with a massive second campus under development a few miles to the south, until the coronavirus-caused economic downturn prompted Comcast to pump the brakes.

The gamble seemed to be paying off for Universal. Comcast's theme parks had reported consistently climbing annual revenues, and the Themed Entertainment Association estimated a 109.7% increase in combined attendance at USF and IOA between 2009 and 2019. That was, until the resort's COVID-caused closures resulted in Universal parks' revenue plummeting 94% in the second quarter of 2020, and dropping 81% in the third. Attendance for all tourist attractions are expected to remain well below 2019 levels for years to come, but Universal Orlando moved more aggressively than its competitors to bring visitors back and has reported record-high guest-satisfaction levels among those who have returned.

Disney and Universal officially downplay their fierce competition, pointing out that any new theme park or attraction makes Central Florida a more marketable destination. Behind closed doors, however, the two companies share a Pepsi-versus-Coke rivalry that keeps both working hard to gain a competitive edge. The good news is that all this translates into better and better attractions for you to enjoy.

THE UNIVERSAL DIFFERENCE

IN MANY WAYS, UNIVERSAL ORLANDO will never achieve parity with Walt Disney World. It's minuscule compared to the 27,000-odd acres of Walt Disney World and will still be significantly smaller even after Universal's 750-acre expansion property is fully developed. And while guest service at Universal is generally exceptional by industry standards, there's something special about the "Disney Way" that some visitors will inevitably prefer. But in the areas where it *can* compete with Disney—namely, in theme park design and attraction quality—Universal has pulled even, if not ahead.

Even hard-core Disney fans, such as this Moncton, Nebraska, reader, are beginning to pay attention:

I'm a huge fan of all things Disney, so it pains me a little to say that the highlight of our most recent trip was actually Universal Orlando. Not because Disney World isn't spectacular—it always is—but because Universal's themed Harry Potter experience is by far the most immersive I've ever had. Disney has to be a little nervous.

From a Scarborough, Maine, reader:

Going to Universal is much less stressful than going to Disney. Even though we could go to the parks early, at Universal we slept in and still walked on most rides.

A reader from Toronto, Canada, wrote:

Reluctantly, I agree the Disney magic is fading. Attention to detail has deteriorated, and bus transport is often (but not always) slow and problematic. Tired hotel rooms (at deluxe prices) are badly in need of refurbishment. It was a stark contrast to the seamless experience we had at Universal's on-site moderate hotel.

A woman from Noblesville, Indiana, says:

This was the first non-Disney theme park that I felt could have been a Disney-owned theme park. It was clean and well themed, with fun rides and wonderful team members. I truly enjoyed Universal as much (and in some ways more) than my trips to Disney World.

A Lake Frederick, Virginia, family agrees:

After being loyal to Disney for years, my family wanted to visit The Wizarding World. I was really impressed with Universal! Everyone we talked to was very nice. It was even more pleasant than dealing with Disney people—pretty surprising. We thoroughly enjoyed our time at Universal and can't wait to go back!

A mom of tweens from Ellicott City, Maryland, compared the two resorts' signature cinematic lands and gave the nod to Universal:

Batuu [at Star Wars Galaxy's Edge] is cool and beautiful, but the cast members seemed lost, somewhat uncertain of their roles, and not at all up to the standard of the immersive experience we had at The Wizarding World of Harry Potter. They would have done better taking a cue from their neighbor down the street. The completely immersive Wizarding World blows Batuu out of the galaxy.

Finally, this father from Rigby, Idaho, cuts to the chase:

Universal was less crowded and less expensive, and frankly, the rides were more fun and appropriate for all but the youngest of kids. EVERYONE, all ages, far preferred Universal over Disney World. That wasn't true 25 years ago, when our then-younger and smaller family first visited these places—but it is certainly true now.

To be fair, we also get occasional missives that dissent from our praise for Universal's product, such as this one from a multigenerational matriarch in New York City:

Universal's attractions were indeed state of the art, and the Harry Potter areas were amazing, but I didn't feel that magic that I did when we visited Disney three years ago. I don't know if my expectations were too high, or if it was because we were with a more diverse group age-wise, or what. Overall, I have no burning desire to return anytime soon, unlike with Disney, when I couldn't wait to go back.

Or this, from a mother of two in Arlington, Virginia:

Some of the rides were super impressive and fun, but too much of it was screen based, and there was very little that all four of us could handle (and therefore do together). I'm sure my teens would like to return, but I'll let them save that for their school band trips; as a family it's WDW all the way.

This father from Lawrenceville, New Jersey, was especially critical of Universal's high-energy atmosphere:

The Marvel area was loud and unpleasant to spend time in. CityWalk was a frenetic nightmare after leaving the parks; trying to find somewhere to eat was crazy. All the noise, blaring music, and GIANT TV screens were not at all easy to take after our day in the parks. Like some ADHD torture chamber.

A handful of readers have criticized this book for mentioning Disney at all, including this online reviewer:

If I wanted a book about Disney, I would have purchased a book about Disney. I'm going to Universal; I don't care about what Disney does or offers.

In our defense, the majority of first-time Universal visitors (and hence, our readers) have previously been to Walt Disney World or another Disney attraction. Disney's product practically defines *theme park* in the public imagination, even among people who have never visited a Disney park, and its Florida resort sets the standard against which the entire industry is judged, not only in Orlando but around the world. So we point out parallels between Disney and Universal where appropriate only to give you a clearer picture of what to expect from your visit and how to spend your time.

We see the three Universal parks and the six Disney World parks (including water parks) as rough equals, and every one is world-class. Both Universal and Disney have splendid on-site hotels, with Universal offering more perks to its guests. There will always be those who miss the indescribable "magic" for which Disney World is famous. But here are five important arenas in which we think Universal currently has an advantage in the Orlando theme park wars:

MOUSE JABS

THERE'S NOTHING WRONG with a little friendly competition, and we've seen plenty of examples of the No. 2 brand poking a little fun at the No. 1 brand. Pepsi and Coke, Marvel and DC, Burger King and McDonald's, and . . . Universal and Disney? While you won't find any references to Universal at Walt Disney World, Derek Burgan—author of the weekly "Saturday Six" column on touringplans.com—has cataloged a whole bunch of funny jabs at the Mouse House down the street.

6. Men in Black Alien Attack The entire attraction is a spoof on Disney's iconic pavilions from the 1964–1965 New York World's Fair, like *Carousel of Progress* and Ford's Magic Skyway.

5. The Simpsons Ride You'll see giant posters outside referencing The Jungle Cruise and Pirates of the Caribbean, and the preshow is filled with nods to Disney attractions, including The Haunted Mansion, *The Hall of Presidents*, and even *Kitchen Kabaret*.

4. Dudley Do-Right's Ripsaw Falls Keep an eye open for the movie posters making fun of such films as *Star Wars* and *Three Men and a Baby*, which was the first hit of former Disney CEO Michael Eisner's reign.

3. Duff Brewery The Seven Duffs are pretty much the exact opposites of Disney's lovable Seven Dwarfs. The topiaries of Dizzy, Tipsy, Sleazy, Queasy, Surly, Edgy, and Remorseful make some of the best photo ops in the park.

2. *Shrek 4-D* The queue is filled with fake attraction posters mocking Disneyland rides, such as *Great Moments with Mr. Farquaad, Enchanted Tick Room*, and Donkbo.

1. Jurassic Park River Adventure In a twist on Walt Disney's most famous quote, the narrator of Jurassic Park's queue video says, "I hope we never lose sight of one thing— that it all started with a mosquito."

MORE ADULT   If there's one distinguishing element that most separates Universal from Disney, it's the distinctly adult attitude that informs the resort's attractions and ambience. While Walt wanted a park that appealed equally to parents and their children, the majority of entertainment in today's Walt Disney World focuses on themes and characters catering to little kids. (That's not to say that there aren't plenty of adults who enjoy singing "Let It Go" at the top of their lungs, but the less said about that the better.) The same goes for most Disney rides, which emphasize visual charm over physical intensity; aside from the half dozen "mountains," you could probably take a nap on any given WDW attraction.

Universal, on the other hand, sets its sights slightly higher demographically, with a much higher proportion of attractions aimed at tweens, teens, and young (or young-at-heart) adults. Many of Universal's properties are based on PG-13 or R-rated movies; even its animated ambassadors, such as Shrek and *Despicable Me*'s Minions, are a bit edgier than Mickey and friends. Don't try to fall asleep on Universal's simulators and scream machines, which range in intensity from pleasantly discombobulating to, "Dear Lord, what have I done?"

This parent from the Dallas area agrees:

Universal is PG-13 regarding its rides, while Disney is PG. Universal's rides are amazing, while Disney's seem dated. We might not have noticed if we had visited Disney first. The thrill rides were the most important experience for my teens, who tremendously enjoyed their time on their own at Universal.

Universal offers the CityWalk nightclub venue, just outside the park gates, for those with the energy to make a night of it; WDW's closest equivalent, the sprawling Disney Springs complex, is far more sedate. And observant audience members will also notice that the scripts at Universal have a subversively snarky, postmodern spin that flies over youngsters' heads but serves as a welcome antidote to pixie-dusted perfection. After all, as the host in *Universal Orlando's Horror Make-Up Show* jokes, "This isn't Disney. We don't have to be nice to you!"

All this isn't to imply that there's nothing for wee tykes to enjoy at Universal; on the contrary, the playgrounds in IOA's Seuss Landing and Jurassic Park are as good as any at WDW, and Universal's child-swap policy is arguably more user-friendly than Disney's. But rather than spending the day focused on fulfilling their offspring's fantasies, parents at Universal get to realize some of their own along the way.

MORE ADVANCED   Universal has been technologically ascendant for several years, introducing revolutionary motion systems and special effects in both rides and theater performances. As a dad from Mount Desert Island, Maine, wrote us:

> Our family toured both Disney and Universal, beginning our stay at Disney. The difference in ride quality and technology was striking. It would've been difficult to go the other way (Universal to Disney), as the rides at Disney seemed dated and carnival-like by comparison.

A father from Conway, Arkansas, agrees, adding:

> Magic Kingdom and Epcot are full of old technology and uninteresting rides. New attractions are badly needed, especially to keep up with Universal.

While Disney relies conservatively on a combination of highly detailed themed areas, beloved characters, and inspiration from classic animated features (that many young people under age 16 have never seen), Universal takes more technological swings for the fences.

Granted, Disney parks do have their share of high-tech attractions—particularly Pandora's Flight of Passage, which outdoes Universal simulators in sheer gee-whiz factor—and not all Universal attractions approach the creative genius of Harry Potter and the Forbidden Journey or Escape from Gringotts. But while guests at both Disney and Universal report high levels of satisfaction, it's the next-gen technology manifested in Universal's headliners that delivers true "Wow!" moments. Plus, **Port of Entry** and **Jurassic Park** at Islands of Adventure—along with **The Wizarding World of Harry Potter,** encompassing both **Hogsmeade** at IOA and **Diagon Alley** at USF—clearly demonstrate that Universal can create exquisitely detailed and totally immersive themed areas.

MORE CURRENT   Doc Brown's time-traveling DeLorean from *Back to the Future* may be parked at USF, but Orlando's real time machine is found at Walt Disney World's theme parks. WDW's recent top attractions are nearly all inspired by intellectual properties that date from the 1930s (Seven Dwarfs Mine Train) through the 1990s (Toy Story Land)—with the exception of *Frozen* and *Avatar,* both of which have cooled in the pop-culture consciousness—and much of its older inventory is even more old-fashioned. Disney's Hollywood Studios' new *Star Wars* expansion is set during the sequel films, but its most recognizable icons (like Chewbacca and the *Millennium Falcon*) date to the 1970s. Epcot is finally sweeping away its detritus of dated celebrities for a future of Pixar and Marvel intellectual properties, but the park is still a work in progress at press time.

Universal, on the other hand, has been relentlessly aggressive about constantly updating its lineup with currently relevant characters. The best example of this is its Wizarding World of Harry Potter, the first phase of which debuted while the record-breaking film franchise was still in theaters. Potter mania has seen a revival thanks to the *Fantastic Beasts* film series and *Harry Potter and the Cursed Child* play, while Marvel's superheroes, *Despicable Me*'s Minions, and *Jurassic Park*'s dinosaurs remain hot box office commodities.

The downside to Universal's obsession with staying on the cultural cutting edge is a sense of impermanence that prevents the resort from retaining its rich history. Disney's blessing of size allows it to preserve the type of long-in-the-tooth attractions that space-squeezed Universal often sacrifices for the next generation. As a result, repeat visitors to WDW develop a sense of nostalgia over a lifetime of revisiting beloved rides, whereas those returning to Universal after a long absence are more likely to be befuddled; for a fun (and dangerous) drinking game, stand outside Diagon Alley and take a sip every time someone asks, "Where's Jaws?"

But Universal's weaker sense of tradition is offset by the thrill of the new; while the Magic Kingdom went more than a quarter century without a brand-new E-ticket, Universal Orlando opened a major new attraction nearly every year for the past decade, and despite the pandemic, some promising projects are still on the horizon.

MORE COMPACT   While the lack of available elbowroom hurts Universal in some ways, it's a huge advantage in others. Anyone who has stayed on-site at WDW (especially in a hotel not serviced by the monorail) can testify how arduous navigating Mickey's vast transportation system can be. Taking the Disney bus to Animal Kingdom sometimes seems to take longer than an actual African safari, and if you want to transfer from Disney Springs to a theme park, you'd better pack a lunch.

At Universal, on the other hand, you can go your whole vacation without ever taking a ride (other than the amusement kind) because everything is within easy walking distance. Even the most remote hotel room is only a 20- or 25-minute walk from the park gates, which are themselves separated by only a few hundred yards, making park-hopping at Universal a no-brainer. If your feet do get tired, a fleet of water taxis, pedicabs, and colorful buses are available to transport you, usually with much less waiting than their WDW equivalents. As one reader put it:

What we appreciated about USF and IOA more than Disney is how compact the entire area is. It was incredibly easy to park in one of the large garages and walk to the theme parks. And they are so close together that you can easily walk from one park to another.

In fact, if Universal Orlando closely compares to any Disney resort, it is not Walt Disney World but Disneyland in California. Both properties boast two first-rate theme parks in close proximity to each other, with an adjoining entertainment complex and nearby hotels for easy pedestrian access. If you've ever enjoyed the Disneyland Resort's intimacy, in contrast to Disney World's overwhelming scale, you'll feel right at home at Universal Orlando.

MORE MANAGEABLE   Universal's smaller scale also has both logistical and psychological benefits. Walt Disney World is so vast that there is no way to do it all, even if you were to stay for weeks. For some travelers, that overabundance of options creates anxiety and a fear of missing out or not getting your money's worth. Universal has plenty to occupy your attention—you could stay for a week without getting bored—but the list of choices is much more manageable.

More important, once you choose what you want to do at Universal, you can usually just go ahead and do it without jumping through the hoops now found at Disney World. Despite Disney's investment of well over a billion dollars, many guests find WDW's MyMagic+ vacation-planning service—and the FastPass+ attraction reservations system—to be a royal hassle. Universal's Express line-cutting service, which is included free with every room at the top three on-site hotels, can be used at any time without prior arrangement, so you don't have to decide what time you want to ride Dudley Do-Right's Ripsaw Falls two months from now.

Universal Express was a big hit with this Texas family:

Universal resort's inclusion of the Express Pass [is] genius. My girls couldn't stop raving about the pass. They had gotten spoiled going to any ride and using the Express Pass with less than 10 minutes of wait time. Disney's FastPass had mixed results with us.

Likewise, WDW may have many more table-service restaurants inside and outside its parks, but good luck getting a seat in a popular eatery without booking your table months in advance; at Universal, walk-ups are often accommodated, or you can simply make a reservation with your smartphone a few days (or even hours) before you want to eat.

SHOULD I GO TO UNIVERSAL ORLANDO IF I'VE SEEN UNIVERSAL HOLLYWOOD?

UNIVERSAL STUDIOS HOLLYWOOD (USH) in California shares much in common with its younger sibling in Orlando, including several headliner attractions. So is it worth visiting UOR if you've already done USH? In a word, "Absolutely!"

The Hollywood park is primarily a working movie studio with a park bolted on, making it less than cohesive as a themed attraction. There's nothing in Orlando that can compare to USH's justly famous Studio Tour, though some of its sights (the 3-D King Kong encounter and the Fast & Furious segment) have stand-alone analogues on the East Coast. But aside from the tram tour, a *Secret Life of Pets* dark ride, and the *WaterWorld* stunt show, the bulk of USH's limited lineup consists of virtual clones of attractions found in Orlando, only in less immersive environments. USH's CityWalk complex is larger than Orlando's, and offerings include copies of several unique restaurants that originated in Orlando, along with a number of familiar chains.

USH is looking better than ever, thanks to an ambitious multiyear expansion plan, which renovated three-quarters of the park during the last decade and will bring new attractions, amenities, and production facilities—including America's first Nintendo-themed land—to the California complex in the coming years. The initial phases of this makeover resulted in colorfully rethemed areas around the *Despicable Me* and *Simpsons* attractions, an Art Deco central plaza, and the 2016 debut of Harry Potter's West Coast digs. But even with USH's Wizarding World open, it only reproduces the Hogsmeade area from IOA; for the full Diagon Alley and Hogwarts Express experience, Orlando continues to be your only option.

The bottom line is that USH makes a fine daylong diversion from a Disneyland vacation, but it is not yet big enough by itself to build a trip around. Universal Orlando, on the other hand, has nearly everything USH has, plus a whole lot more.

Critical Comparison of Attractions Found at Both UNIVERSAL STUDIOS HOLLYWOOD and UNIVERSAL ORLANDO

Animal Actors on Location About the same at both parks.

Despicable Me Minion Mayhem USH has an elaborate interactive exterior and much higher capacity; the ride itself is the same at both parks.

Flight of the Hippogriff Track layout and queue look about the same, but USH's ride feels much smoother.

Harry Potter and the Forbidden Journey The USH version boasts scarier animatronics and enhanced lighting and scenery, but it's essentially the same ride.

Jurassic Park River Adventure USH's version was rethemed in 2019 to the *Jurassic World* franchise, with new dinosaurs and special effects. IOA's drop is slightly taller, but USH's is much wetter in warm weather. Otherwise, the rides are similar.

Revenge of the Mummy—The Ride Much longer with better effects at USF.

The Simpsons Ride Ride is about the same at both parks, but USH has a less claustrophobic queue and an on-ride photo op.

Transformers: The Ride 3-D About the same at both parks.

UNIVERSAL-SPEAK POCKET TRANSLATOR AND GUIDE TO COMMON ABBREVIATIONS

IT MAY COME AS A SURPRISE TO MANY, but Universal Orlando (like Walt Disney World) has its own somewhat peculiar language. The following table lists some terms and abbreviations that you're likely to bump into, both in this guide and in the larger Universal (and Disney) community.

UNIVERSAL LEXICON IN A NUTSHELL
ATTRACTION Ride or show
AUDIENCE Crowd
BACKSTAGE Behind the scenes, out of view of customers
CHARACTER Cartoon or movie character impersonated by an employee
• Animated Character A character who wears a head-covering costume (Scooby-Doo, the Minions, the Simpsons)
• Face Character A "celebrity" character who doesn't wear a head-covering costume (Doc Brown, Marilyn Monroe, and the like)
COSTUME Work attire or uniform
DARK RIDE Indoor ride
DAY GUEST Any customer not staying at a Universal resort
EARLY PARK ADMISSION (EPA) Morning hour at Universal's theme parks for eligible guests (*Early Entry, Magic Morning*, or *Extra Magic Hour* in Disney-speak)
GENERAL PUBLIC Same as day guest
GREETER Employee positioned at an attraction entrance
GUEST Customer
ON-SITE One of the Loews-operated resort hotels located on Universal Orlando property
ONSTAGE In full view of customers
PRESHOW Entertainment at an attraction before the feature presentation
QUICK-SERVICE RESTAURANT Counter-service or fast food–style restaurant
RESORT GUEST A customer staying at a Universal resort hotel
ROLE A team member's job
TEAM MEMBER Employee (*cast member* in Disney-speak)
TECHNICAL REHEARSAL Opening a park or attraction before its stated opening date (*soft opening* in Disney-speak)

COMMON ABBREVIATIONS AND WHAT THEY STAND FOR	
AP Annual pass	TM Team member
EPA Early Park Admission	USF Universal Studios Florida theme park
I-DRIVE International Drive (major Orlando thoroughfare)	UOR Universal Orlando Resort
	UX or UEx Universal Express
IOA Universal's Islands of Adventure theme park	VB Volcano Bay
	WWoHP Wizarding World of Harry Potter

UPCOMING AT UNIVERSAL ORLANDO RESORT

THE DOWNTURN IN GLOBAL TRAVEL derailed Universal Orlando's once-lofty expansion plans, but some new additions to the resort are still moving forward. At Islands of Adventure, a towering high-speed roller coaster themed to velociraptors is expected to open in 2021 behind the Jurassic Park Discovery Center. The Lost Continent lost its *Eighth Voyage of Sindbad Stunt Show* in 2018, and its neighbor, *Poseidon's Fury,* was placed on hiatus, heightening rumors of a future replacement—perhaps Hyrule from Nintendo's Zelda games—for the entire island.

At Universal Studios Florida, a new Jason Bourne stunt show debuted in 2020, replacing the former *Terminator 2: 3-D* attraction. Rumors of replacements for *Fear Factor Live*, *Shrek 4-D*, and Woody Woodpecker's KidZone (including Curious George Goes to Town, *A Day in the Park with Barney,* and Woody Woodpecker's Nuthouse Coaster) have been circulating for years. Likewise, an expansion of Volcano Bay that would add sliding capacity to the water park has been anticipated for several years.

Outside the theme parks, the second phase of Universal's Endless Summer Resort, dubbed the Dockside Inn & Suites, made its belated debut in late 2020 on the former Wet 'n Wild parking lot along International Drive.

Finally, on August 1, 2019, Universal officially announced construction of its second resort campus, which will be called Universal's Epic Universe. Roads and other infrastructure are already being constructed on 750 acres Universal acquired near the Orange County Convention Center, about a 12-minute drive south of the current resort. Early concept art depicted a central hub with fountain-filled lagoons, surrounded by hotels, restaurants, and at least four highly themed attraction areas. Originally anticipated to open in 2023, Epic Universe was delayed by at least a year when the pandemic began, and at press time progress has been paused indefinitely until "the future becomes more certain."

The only featured franchise officially confirmed for the new park was Super Nintendo World, featuring rides based on the video games *Mario Kart, Donkey Kong Country,* and *Yoshi;* a version of that land, which has already been built in Japan, may end up replacing KidZone at USF. The proposed park's other rumored intellectual properties were J. K. Rowling's Wizarding World (with the Ministries of Magic from both Harry Potter's London and *Fantastic Beasts'* Paris), DreamWorks' *How to Train Your Dragon,* and Universal Classic Monsters, such as Dracula and Frankenstein. Of course, all of these plans are now subject to change if and when construction restarts.

COVID-19 *and* UNIVERSAL ORLANDO

THEME PARKS *in the* AGE *of* CORONAVIRUS

THE GLOBAL PANDEMIC caused by COVID-19 (novel coronavirus) has affected every aspect of life as we know it, and theme parks are no exception. Efforts to "flatten the curve" prompted an unprecedented three-month closure of all Central Florida attractions in the spring of 2020. Universal Orlando was the first major resort to emerge from quarantine in early June 2020, and Walt Disney World followed suit more than a month later.

At press time, the majority of the Universal Orlando Resort—including both theme parks, along with CityWalk and most of the on-site hotels—is open for business. However, visiting the attractions is now a much different experience than it was before, thanks to numerous new health protocols that Universal (in cooperation with the Centers for Disease Control and Prevention and local authorities) has implemented across its property. Mandatory temperature checks and face masks, limited attraction capacities, and modified entertainment offerings are only the most visible ways in which the resort is working to balance its responsibility toward public health against getting its employees back to work.

Hopefully, coronavirus will have been conquered by the time you visit Universal Orlando, and the restrictions discussed in this chapter will be little more than a memory. On the other hand, it may still be many months—or even years—before the attractions fully operate as they did prior to the pandemic; just as once-unfamiliar phrases like *social distancing* are now part of our daily vocabulary, we should expect that some of the extraordinary measures implemented to slow the virus's spread might stick around long-term as part of our "new normal."

IS UNIVERSAL ORLANDO WORTH IT?

READING ABOUT ALL THESE new restrictions may make you wonder if a visit to Universal Orlando is even worthwhile under these circumstances. Except for some steep short-term discounts offered to Florida residents, Universal has charged more or less full price for its theme parks and hotels since reopening. Part of that is just pragmatism: it would be bad customer service to sell discounted hotel rooms to people who can't get into the theme parks because of capacity limits. But even if you want to go, you can afford it, and you can get hotel reservations, is what's being offered worth paying nearly full price?

We'll answer that question by asking another: think of your favorite pre-pandemic sit-down restaurant, the one that you're ordering takeout from now. Is the to-go experience you're paying full price for today the same as the in-restaurant experience you had before? Probably not. But you're willing to pay full price because you know that, in normal times, the restaurant offers good value for the money, and you want them to make it through this thing. That's how we feel about theme parks.

If you were in the middle of planning your first and only trip to Orlando, wait to go until a vaccine is widely administered and Universal brings back its parades, nighttime spectaculars, and attraction preshows. Although it's not the ideal time for your once-in-a-lifetime vacation, returning guests who can get accustomed to the alterations will enjoy the benefits of a much more intimate experience, including historically low attraction wait times and additional individual attention from the employees. If you don't mind wearing a face mask all day, then we think it's worth going. You'll be helping to employ thousands of team members who need the paychecks. And the first time you're on a ride where the lights dim, the music starts, and the special effects kick in, you'll forget everything going on in the outside world and simply be entertained.

Even with all the precautions the parks are taking, you may also rightly wonder if visiting Orlando is really safe for your family. Universal Orlando explicitly warns on its website: "Exposure to COVID-19 is an inherent risk in any public location where people are present; we cannot guarantee you will not be exposed during your visit." Obviously, you'll need to evaluate your own tolerance for risk, carefully considering any complicating factors that may put you or a member of your party at heightened risk. We can say that for the most part, Universal has enforced its social-distancing policies with impressive seriousness (at least from the guest's perspective), and this author feels far safer walking around Universal than his neighborhood supermarket.

A reader from The Woodlands, Texas, who stayed at the resort shortly after its reopening wrote us in agreement, saying:

It's wonderful to be back in a theme park, where all the team members and guests are mindful of social distancing and respectful of the mask policy!

Below, you'll find complete details on the coronavirus-related changes you will find at Universal Orlando as long as the current social-distancing protocols remain in effect. We'll also reiterate key information throughout the following chapters and highlight it with our own masked Wuffo character (at left), but we've tried to centralize the essentials here to avoid overloading the remainder of the book with COVID callouts. The following information was accurate as we went to press, but Universal's policies are constantly evolving. Before you visit, be sure to check universalorlando .com/web/en/us/plan-your-visit/safety-faqs for the latest updates on the resort's operations.

COVID-19: KNOW BEFORE YOU GO CHECKLIST

* Bring face coverings to wear at all times, and be prepared for temperature checks upon arrival.
* Be mindful of social-distancing precautions; observe posted safety signs and spacing markers.
* Use hand sanitizer before and after experiencing attractions, and wash your hands frequently.
* Some attractions, restaurants, and amenities may be unavailable, or they may offer modified experiences.
* Anticipate that capacity restrictions will slow down standby queues, and take advantage of Virtual Line options where available.
* Use the Universal app's mobile ordering, contactless payments, and other smartphone features to minimize physical contact.

GENERAL PRECAUTIONS

UNIVERSAL'S COVID-RELATED SAFETY PROCEDURES seem more thorough and more enforced than those of any city in the United States. Mask compliance is nearly 100%, hand sanitizers and cleaning products abound, social-distance cues are everywhere, and team members will politely nudge those who need reminding. We think this is in part due to two things: People really, really want to be in the parks, and few guests are going to pay $120 to get in only to be thrown out for not wearing a 50¢ mask.

First and foremost, all guests and employees will have their temperature checked before being allowed to enter the Universal Orlando Resort. This check will be performed using a touch-free forehead thermometer that gives results in a couple of seconds. Any guests registering 100.4°F (38°C) or above will be escorted to a secure area and given some time to cool off before being retested; if they continue to read hot, they'll be offered medical attention and asked to leave until they have been cleared by a doctor.

For most guests, this temperature check will occur in the parking garage, prior to passing through the security checkpoint in the central parking hub. (On-site hotel guests will be checked at their resort, as described below.) In the mornings, a deceptively long line for temperature checks may form alongside the moving walkways, but it moves very quickly and should usually take no more than 5 minutes to pass through. Grab a handful of sanitizer from the dispensers immediately before the checkpoint (the first of many you'll see throughout the day) and pull your hat up to speed the scanning.

Before reaching that temperature check, you'll want to ensure all members of your party age 3 and older have on their face masks because face coverings must be worn at all times. The only exceptions are while eating and drinking in a stationary spot, on water-based rides and slides, or in pools. Masks should be made of a two-ply material, completely cover your mouth and nose, and have ear loops or otherwise secure snugly around your head. Gaiters (which are disallowed at Disney) are acceptable, but masks with valves, holes, or mesh are prohibited, as are open-chin bandannas. Guests without appropriate masks will be offered a free disposable mask or may purchase Universal-branded reusable masks for $8 each (three for $20), with a portion of the proceeds going toward local charities. We've spent many summer weeks testing different masks in the parks. We think a pack of disposable, three-layer paper masks with elastic ear loops is a good choice. They're reasonably effective and cheap, so you can change them every couple of hours, and they fit most people pretty well. We strongly suggest packing an extra face mask for each member of your party (to swap when soaked with sweat), along with a zip-top bag for storage during meals and water attractions.

If you have a medical condition that makes it impossible for you to wear a face mask, speak to Guest Services or any roving employee wearing a Guest Experience Support shirt. After explaining your situation, they may provide you with a wristband that allows you to wear a full-face shield (which you must provide yourself) instead of the standard face mask. However, be aware that face shields are not permitted on most attractions, so you'll need to switch to an approved face mask in order to ride.

U-Rest outdoor break areas are provided around the resort where unmasking is permitted at your own risk. At each, you'll find seating, shade, and plenty of space to socially distance. There are two U-Rest locations in Universal Studios Florida (in Central Park and at the *Fear Factor Live* stadium) and three in Islands of Adventure (lagoonside in Port of Entry, behind Cat and the Hat, and in the former *The Eighth Voyage of Sindbad* stadium), plus one in CityWalk outside the Hard Rock Cafe.

Universal's staff may evict unmasked guests who refuse to observe park policy, or at least direct them to a break area, but we don't recommend directly confronting fellow visitors who violate the rules; simply give them a wide berth, and notify an employee if necessary.

Throughout Universal property, you'll see and hear reminders to maintain a distance of at least 6 feet (2 meters) between your party and others at all times. Blue lines delineating proper spacing have sprouted like mushrooms anywhere a queue might form, and round markers are placed to designate safe standing spaces for street shows and similar gatherings. Social-distancing measures also extend to selected sinks, water fountains, and other facilities being marked off-limits. If you have an especially big group, you might even have to social distance from yourselves; parties of 10 or more guests must split up at rides and restaurants.

You'll also see Universal's stepped-up sanitation efforts in effect across the property, in the form of an army of employees who incessantly sanitizes every handrail and other high-touch surface. As far as personal hygiene goes, hand sanitizer dispensers are found in virtually every building, and you can purchase a small bottle of alcohol-based gel in most shops for about $3. It will also be impossible to avoid the audio announcements and signage encouraging frequent handwashing. Universal team members take frequent breaks to wash their own hands.

Government travel restrictions may require visitors from certain states and foreign countries to undergo mandatory quarantines upon entering or returning from Florida; check your state's health department guidelines at tinyurl.com/USHealthDepts.

Prior to arriving at the resort, we strongly recommend installing the latest version of the Universal Orlando smartphone app from the App or Play stores. Make sure you enable location services and notifications, which are needed to use the mobile ordering and Virtual Line features. It's also helpful to set up and sign in with your universalorlando.com login, and attach your credit card and admission media to your account. Read more about Universal Orlando's app on page 34.

PARKING AND TRANSPORTATION

SELF-PARKING IN THE CENTRAL GARAGES is available for the standard fees. Valet parking is not available, but a small screening checkpoint in the valet circle still allows guests to walk to and from the hotels along Major Boulevard near Kirkman Road.

Inside the parking garage, employees will direct drivers to leave an empty row between cars, a courtesy we wish would be implemented permanently. Those empty spots will be filled in by later arrivals as needed.

Animal care kennels are temporarily closed.

THEME PARKS

Arrival and Entry

Although the Universal Orlando Resort remains open 365 days a year, operating hours for the theme parks and CityWalk may be drastically reduced. Park openings and closings may be staggered, with Universal Studios Florida (USF) open 9 a.m.–5 p.m. and Islands of Adventure (IOA) operating 10 a.m.–6 p.m. (with Early Park Admission beginning at 9 a.m.). Volcano Bay is only open 10 a.m.–5 p.m. (6 p.m. on weekends); it closed November 2020–March 2021, and may not open on Tuesday and Thursday, while CityWalk's venues shut down by 10 p.m. (midnight on some weekends).

During times of social distancing, Universal will cap the maximum number of guests at a level far below its normal capacity and may halt ticket sales and/or stop admitting new day guests to prevent overcrowding. On-site hotel guests with valid tickets will be guaranteed park admission. Unlike at Walt Disney World, no advance reservations or time-specific tickets are required, and all existing tickets and annual passes will be honored (blackouts and standard limitations still apply), but a date-specific admission ticket does NOT guarantee admission if the maximum occupancy is reached.

On-site ticket booths and automated will-call kiosks are still available, but visitors are strongly encouraged to buy tickets in advance, or use the mobile app to purchase admission.

On busier weekends, a line may form outside the theme parks up to an hour prior to admission and can extend along the entire CityWalk waterfront. Much like the temperature check queue, it will look worse than it really is, as Universal's staff directs guests to keep the line moving efficiently in the morning. Arrive later in the morning or afternoon, and you're likely to find little or no line to enter the parks.

The total number of operating turnstiles has been reduced, with spacing markers indicating proper distancing as you wait your turn to enter. Universal's often-unreliable finger-scanning devices on the turnstiles are supposedly cleaned between each guest, but you can ask to show your photo ID instead.

Once through the gates, you'll see that the racks that formerly held paper park maps have been replaced by a sign with a scannable QR code linked to Universal's app. When paper maps are available, some key information such as operating hours and entertainment schedules may be missing from the printed maps, so you'll still want to refer to the Universal app for the day's details.

If you need to stash your bags, note that some of the rental locker banks will be disabled, and access to the locker banks may be controlled to prevent overcrowding. For example, at Universal Studios Florida, the large family lockers closest to the Studio Audience Center may be off-limits, but other lockers will be open near the park exit. Talk to a team member at the rental counter if you have trouble finding an available locker. Paid hourly lockers are also still available in Islands of Adventure at select water rides such as Jurassic Park River Adventure.

Rest assured that all rental items such as wheelchairs, electric convenience vehicles, and strollers are sanitized after every guest.

VIP tours are still available, but some behind-the-scenes experiences may be off-limits.

Rides and Attractions

Universal Orlando has temporarily closed some of its less-popular attractions, including Fast & Furious: Supercharged, Kang & Kodos'

Twirl 'n' Hurl, *Poseidon's Fury,* and Storm Force Accelatron. These experiences may reopen during peak attendance periods.

To reduce the number of people standing in each attraction queue at any one time, Universal Orlando has expanded the use of the Virtual Line system. Free Virtual Line reservations are available for popular attractions through the Universal Orlando app; the exact lineup will vary but often features Hagrid's Magical Creatures Motorbike Adventure and may include the other Harry Potter headliners, along with Revenge of the Mummy, Despicable Me Minion Mayhem, and Skull Island: Reign of Kong. At busier times, use of Virtual Line may be mandatory at certain attractions for all or part of the day, while others will also offer a standby option. During days of lower attendance, Virtual Lines may not be offered at all. Please see page 75 for more details on how to take advantage of Virtual Lines.

Unfortunately, Virtual Line does nothing to alleviate queuing for the mandatory lockers found at many of Universal's thrill rides. To promote distancing in the often-claustrophobic locker banks, employees enforce a "one person in/one person out" rule that can make the lines to stow and retrieve your baggage far longer than your wait for the rides themselves. By only bringing what you can securely fit in your pockets or a hip pack, or by having a nonrider play designated bag carrier for your party, you can avoid wasting significant time waiting for the lockers.

At some attractions using Virtual Lines, Universal Express affords instant access to the Virtual Line entrance. At other attractions, Express may be rerouted through the single-rider queue or another alternate entrance.

Attraction queues have been reconfigured with spacing markers to ensure that all parties remain at least 6 feet apart. As a result, even modest queues can spill outside the attraction entrance, often making waits look more intimidating than they actually are. That reconfiguration also requires some preshow elements to be disabled or bypassed. For example, guests at Harry Potter and the Escape from Gringotts will not experience the holographic encounter with Bill Weasley, nor the simulated elevator plunge; future Men in Black agents skip the "secret" entryway's faux introduction; the Green Planet abandoned its passports, leaving E.T. to call everyone "friend"; and the stage where Jimmy Fallon's Ragtime Gals usually sing is silent and dark, as are the waiting area's interactive tables. Any preshow video imparting important safety information, such as The Simpsons Ride's *Itchy & Scratchy* cartoon, is still played in full, and new recordings reiterating social-distancing rules have replaced the usual announcements in a few queues.

Upon arriving at a ride's loading station, you'll notice that many ride vehicles have had their capacity significantly reduced to maintain distance between unrelated groups. A three-row car capable of holding 12 guests (such as The Amazing Adventures of Spider-Man's SCOOP or Transformers' EVAC) now only holds groups of 4 or fewer guests in the front and back rows, leaving the middle row unused; any party larger than 4 gets a whole vehicle to themselves. In other cases, such as Reign of Kong and The Incredible Hulk Coaster, plexiglass walls have been added to the boarding stations and/or ride vehicles to utilize all rows, but each party still has a row to themselves. Similar reductions in carrying capacity continue across all the resort's attractions, causing queues to move at between one-half and one-quarter of their usual pace. This restriction of guests throughout is balanced by a corresponding reduction in park attendance, and somewhat mitigated by use of Virtual Lines. At peak times on weekends, the slower boarding process may test your patience, but many weekdays we've been able to walk onto rides, receiving an entire ride vehicle to ourselves.

Social distancing also means a suspension of single-rider access, since pairing lone travelers with unrelated parties is the exact opposite of what the safety policies are trying to achieve. Parties of one may still use the other queues and will likely get a row (or even an entire ride vehicle) all to themselves.

When your turn to ride arrives, you'll be given a mandatory squirt of hand sanitizer immediately before stepping on board. This is in lieu of employees wiping down the cars after every guest; vehicles are also periodically cleaned and cycled without riders. Additional hand sanitizer dispensers are also located at the exit of nearly every ride, usually hiding discreetly in a corner along the hallway leading to the gift shop.

On the attraction itself, some mist and fog effects—such as the blast of dragon's breath in Harry Potter and the Forbidden Journey and the sprays of water used to simulate breaking glass in Revenge of the Mummy—are disabled. Curiously, these changes aren't consistent; you may still see blasts of fog in Transformers and get spritzed by Hydro on The Amazing Adventures of Spider-Man. Water-based rides using bromine or chlorine filtering—such as Popeye & Bluto's Bilge-Rat Barges, Dudley Do-Right's Ripsaw Falls, and Jurassic Park River Adventure—are still allowed to operate.

Perhaps the biggest problem for pandemic-era parkgoers are 3-D and 4-D attractions. The 3-D glasses are cleaned after each guest, as always, and are handed out individually by an attendant rather than being set on a self-service rack. However, mask-wearing guests may find their 3-D goggles fogging up almost immediately. It helps to have a face mask that fits firmly along your nose and cheeks, preferably using a flexible wire. If the gap beside your nose is still allowing warm air to travel up behind the lenses, try pulling your mask up higher on your nose, and pinch down on the fabric using the bridge of your glasses.

As inconvenient as they can feel, remember that face masks are required at all times while riding, even on high-speed roller coasters (hey, at least you won't swallow a bug). The only exception is while on water-based flume or raft rides where you're liable to get soaked. Keep in mind that if your mask "accidentally" slips off mid-ride, the staff will have to remove that vehicle from circulation until it can be disinfected, lengthening the wait for everyone behind you.

Finally, the free "secret" tours offered at select attractions (like the Men in Black Immigration Tour) may not be available.

Shows and Entertainment

Although much of Universal's live entertainment is still offered, the operations are restricted in ways similar to the moving attractions. Seated shows are running at reduced capacity, with every other row left empty, and at least three unoccupied seats left between unrelated parties. Venues that were previously self seated instead have ushers directing attendees, and at the conclusion of performances, the audience is called to exit one section at a time. To accommodate the extra time needed to seat guests, performers improvise preshows that are almost as entertaining as the shows themselves. For example, Beetlejuice sometimes haunts the *Horror Make-Up Show,* hurling humorous insults at arriving audience members.

Performances may be modified with new choreography, costuming, and stage blocking to accommodate social distancing. Segments requiring contact with an audience volunteer may be cut or altered, along with any utilizing water-based special effects. In a few extreme cases, a show may be downsized into a photo opportunity or suspended entirely. Postshow meet and greets with performers are suspended, but you can snap a picture of the cast on stage during the curtain call instead.

Street shows enforce social distancing using temporary markers designating appropriate viewing positions on the pavement; you may be asked to move if caught standing between spots, even if there's nobody else around within arm's length. Some outdoor shows previously performed at ground level—such as Marilyn Monroe and the Diamond Bellas—may move to an elevated location, and performers who normally mingle with the crowd (like the Blues Brothers) will instead keep their distance.

Parades may be on hold. Throughout the day, individual floats from Universal's Superstar Parade are brought out with costumed characters, who pose for photos from a distance but don't mingle with guests. Nighttime spectaculars, such as IOA's Hogwarts Castle light displays and USF's *Cinematic Celebration* lagoon show, are suspended or only run on select nights.

The Blue Man Group in CityWalk may be closed, and Universal Cinemark is operating with reduced seating capacity. CityWalk nightclubs and hotel dinner shows are also closed. However, you may find stilt walkers in the streets and live musicians or dancers on the waterside stage. You'll also hear live music at select restaurants like Jimmy Buffett's Margaritaville.

Universal With Kids

First and foremost, keep in mind that all guests age 3 and older must have their temperature checked upon arrival and wear a face covering at all times. Signage and audio announcements around the resort will also remind you to reinforce good handwashing hygiene with your kids. Employees are constantly cleaning high-touch areas, but you should still do your best to dissuade your darlings from dragging their hands along railings, clinging to queue walls, or otherwise making unnecessary contact with indoor surfaces.

Inside the theme parks, the biggest sacrifices to social distancing are the lineup of attractions aimed at little ones. All interactive playgrounds are unavailable, including Me Ship, *The Olive*; Camp Jurassic; and If I Ran the Zoo in IOA, along with Curious George's and Fievel's areas in USF. *A Day in the Park with Barney*, along with several kid-friendly spinning rides, may be temporarily closed.

Child-swap rooms at attractions with minimum height requirements may not be available. Instead, the first guardian will use the standard queue, while their partner waits outside the attraction with the kids, then the second adult will be granted immediate access to the Express entrance when it's their turn. Ask the ride's greeter for alternatives before joining the queue if you need to switch off guardians for a small fry.

All character meet and greets have been transformed into photo opportunities, with characters posing at least 6 feet away from guests and each other, and "face" performers sporting masks. Alternatively, you may catch unmasked "celebrities" like Marilyn Monroe cruising past the crowds in a convertible. Guests are not allowed to make physical contact with characters—no hugs or autographs—but can wave hello and take distanced selfies. You may briefly lower your mask while taking a snapshot, as long as you are at least 6 feet from the performers. Employees are no longer able to take pictures using guests' cameras or phones, but My Universal Photos photographers are still available. These restrictions apply both within the parks and during character meals (when available).

Video arcades and carnival booths are still operating, but some game machines or playing positions have been disabled to maintain distance between participants; see a games attendant if you need assistance. Extra-cost outdoor climbing walls are not available.

DINING AND SHOPPING

SOCIAL-DISTANCING POLICIES extend to Universal Orlando Resort's restaurants, which have reduced capacity and provided spacing markers for all queues. Restaurants may serve limited menus or modify certain offerings due to supply chain restraints, making some ingredients unavailable, and select venues—especially outdoor vending carts—may be closed entirely. Some seating sections are blocked off, and tables are sanitized after every guest. Select third-party locations (specifically the Hard Rock Cafe) may require an additional temperature check before entering.

At many quick-service restaurants, mobile ordering via the Universal app has been implemented to avoid crowding at the cash registers. At some locations (like the Leaky Cauldron and Fast Food Boulevard) parties are seated before placing their mobile order, which is delivered to the table by a server. At other locations, guests are asked to place their mobile order before entering the venue and will be notified when their food is ready to pick up from the designated window. You need to set up your credit card in the Universal app ahead of time and cannot use mobile ordering with prepaid dining plans. Annual pass holder discounts are available directly through the app by scanning your pass barcode during checkout. See page 218 for more information about mobile ordering.

At table-service restaurants, laminated menus replace single-use paper printouts. Quick-service restaurants rely on digital menu screens and QR codes that link guests to online menus. While guests are permitted to remove their masks while seated (and may be provided with complimentary plastic bags for storage), servers wear masks and gloves. Everything is delivered on trays, and your server will ask you to take your food rather than touching the plates themselves.

All utensils and condiments are prerolled or individually packaged. Self-service food options and buffets are suspended. Coke Freestyle beverage dispensers are still available, but some machines are disabled to promote distancing.

When it's time to pay your bill, cash is still accepted, but using contactless payment methods (like ApplePay and Google Wallet) is encouraged. Some restaurants have deployed mobile payment terminals for table-side charging, so your credit card won't disappear into a back room.

Guests inside restaurants can remove their masks when actively eating and drinking at their table but should leave them on while moving around the room. If you get your food and drinks to go, remember not to just walk around munching without your mask on. Instead, find a spot to stop and socially distance while you snack. Remember, holding a drink in your hand doesn't grant you license to wander unmasked at will.

Some indoor bars may close, although select outdoor bars and those attached to table-service restaurants should remain open. At Finnegan's, for example, guests queue outside while waiting to order drinks rather than crowding against the bar.

Shops also control capacity, with queues to corral prospective shoppers outside and additional socially distanced lines to complete purchases. Select smaller shops may be closed entirely. Contactless payments are encouraged, although cash is still accepted. Annual pass holders and other guests may be offered additional discounts to encourage spending. If you want to avoid crowded stores, many souvenirs can be ordered online at shop.universalorlando.com.

RESORT HOTELS

UNIVERSAL'S SAPPHIRE FALLS RESORT and Aventura Hotel were closed at press time but were accepting reservations for early 2021.

All guests entering Universal's on-site hotels will have their temperature taken upon arrival and before using the resort transportation system to visit the parks. Hotel guests who pass the temperature check will receive a wristband good for the rest of the day and will not need to be rechecked again until the following day. (Wristband colors change daily, so they can't be reused.) Guests who register a temperature of 100.4°F or higher will not be allowed to check-in until receiving medical clearance, but the rest of their party will be allowed to check-in. If you run a fever after checking in, you'll be required to seek medical attention and self-quarantine; your traveling companions may be moved to another room and allowed to continue their vacation as long as they pass their temperature checks.

Guests age 3 or older and employees are required to wear face coverings at all times while in hotel public areas, including in the lobby and while using resort transportation. Masks are not required while dining or drinking, at the pool, or inside guest rooms. Social distancing is promoted in public areas by blocking off some furniture, disabling self-service touch screen kiosks, and placing markers on the floors.

Universal's upgraded cleaning measures include leaving guest rooms vacant for 24–48 hours upon checkout for cleaning, wherever possible. You'll see nonstop sanitation of high-contact surfaces (think phones, remote controls, door handles, and light switches) throughout the hotel, along with social-distancing reminder signs and hand sanitizer stations in public areas and elevator landings.

Guests can reduce their contact with hotel staff by using texting services, express checkout, and contactless room deliveries. Some hotel amenities—including food and beverage service, pools, game rooms, and fitness centers—might have limited hours to comply with stepped-up sanitation schedules.

Early Park Admission and Universal Express benefits are still available to hotel guests, who are provided priority park admission in case capacity caps are reached. Resort water taxis and shuttle buses operate as usual, but reduced seating capacity and frequent cleaning means that your wait time might increase. Walking paths around the resort are still open.

VOLCANO BAY WATER PARK AND RESORT POOLS

TRANSPORTATION TO VOLCANO BAY water park is available from the lowest level of the parking garage, or direct from resort hotels, on days when the park is operating. All guests will have their temperature checked before boarding. While traveling to the park, TVs previously used to explain the TapuTapu system instead display safety information.

Whether you are relaxing in the pool or braving the slides, you won't be permitted to wear a face mask while in the water. However, face masks are still required outside the water whenever you visit a shop, restaurant, or restroom, or otherwise can't socially distance.

Rider capacity is reduced on raft rides to avoid grouping unrelated parties. This means that single riders will not be able to enjoy certain slides that require multiple passengers, including Honu ika Moana and Maku Puihi, unless they can find willing strangers to team up with.

The number of tubes in the lazy and fast rivers has also been reduced, and chlorinated water is used to clean rafts and life vests after guests. TapuTapu wristbands are also disinfected between users.

Some lounge chairs have been removed, and the remainder are grouped into clusters so that your party can sit together with at least 6-foot spacing between strangers.

Select locker facilities are closed, and employees regulate access to those that are open. Select restaurants and bars at Volcano Bay are also closed, and mobile ordering is strongly encouraged at those that are operating.

PART ONE

PLANNING *Before* YOU LEAVE HOME

GATHERING INFORMATION

IN ADDITION TO READING THIS GUIDE, we recommend you visit our website, theunofficialguides.com, which is dedicated to news about our guidebooks and also has a blog with posts from Unofficial Guide authors. You can also sign up for the "Unofficial Guide Newsletter," containing even more travel tips and special offers.

Our sister website, touringplans.com, offers essential tools for planning your trip and saving you time and money. At blog.touringplans .com you will find breaking news for the Universal Orlando Resort (UOR) and Universal theme parks worldwide. The site also offers computer-optimized touring plans for Universal Studios Florida (USF) and Islands of Adventure (IOA), as well as complete dining menus, including wine lists, for every food cart, stand, kiosk, counter-service restaurant, and sit-down restaurant in the resort.

Another really popular part of touringplans.com is the Crowd Calendar, which shows crowd projections for USF and IOA for every day of the year. Look up the dates of your visit, and the calendar will not only show the projected wait times for each day but will also indicate for each day which theme park will be the least crowded. Historical wait times are also available, so you can see how crowded the parks were last year for your upcoming trip dates.

Much of the content on touringplans.com—including the menus and resort photos and videos—is completely free for anyone to use. Access to part of the site, most notably the Crowd Calendar, additional touring plans, and in-park wait times, requires a small subscription fee (owners of this book's current edition get a substantial discount). This nominal charge helps keep the site online and costs less than lunch at the Leaky Cauldron restaurant in Diagon Alley. Plus touringplans.com offers a 45-day money-back guarantee.

UNIVERSAL ON THE WEB

THOUGH SOME DISNEY-CENTRIC SITES cover Universal in some (usually minimal) way, independent sites dedicated to Universal Orlando are much rarer. Of the independent Disney sites that deal with Universal, we recommend mousesavers.com for hotel and admission bargains.

For the latest Universal updates and rumors, try orlandoinformer .com, orlandoparkstop.com, parkscope.net, and the discussion boards at insideuniversal.net. For crowd projections and touring tips, check touringplans.com. Attractionsmagazine.com, themeparkinsider.com, screamscape.com, and orlandoparksnews.com are all reliable sites covering Central Florida attractions, including Universal. Local news and theme park developments are available at orlandosentinel.com, orlando.bizjournals.com, and orlandoweekly.com. Jimhillmedia.com offers insider information on attractions, new technologies, and changes in the parks. Finally, there's the official Universal Orlando website, universalorlando.com. Annual pass holders may want to visit uoapfb.com to join the official UOAP Facebook group, which is a rich source of both breaking news and petty griping.

BEST UNIVERSAL MOBILE APPS **Universal** offers a free smartphone app for Apple and Android devices that displays wait times and interactive maps while you're inside the parks, using the resort's free Wi-Fi (connect to "Universal" and accept the legal terms to access). Park admission can also be purchased through the app and stored in a digital wallet. You'll need the app to secure Virtual Line ride reservations, place mobile dining orders, or to set up your TapuTapu account before visiting Volcano Bay, so be sure to install it before your arrival.

We also recommend **Lines,** the mobile app of touringplans.com, available for the Apple iPhone and iPad at the iTunes Store (search for "TouringPlans") and for Android devices at the Google Play Store. Owners of other phones can use the web-based version at m.touringplans .com. The app is free to download, but you'll need to log in with a paid TouringPlans subscription to access most of its features.

IMPORTANT UNIVERSAL ADDRESSES

- **THEME PARKS & CITYWALK PARKING GARAGE ADDRESS** 6000 Universal Blvd., Orlando, FL 32819 **GPS COORDINATES: N28° 28.439′ W81° 27.737′**
- **GUEST SERVICES & CORPORATE OFFICES** Universal Orlando Resort, 1000 Universal Studios Pl., Orlando, FL 32819
- **HARD ROCK HOTEL** 5800 Universal Blvd., Orlando, FL 32819
- **LOEWS PORTOFINO BAY HOTEL** 5601 Universal Blvd., Orlando, FL 32819
- **LOEWS ROYAL PACIFIC RESORT** 6300 Hollywood Way, Orlando, FL 32819
- **LOEWS SAPPHIRE FALLS RESORT** 6601 Adventure Way, Orlando, FL 32819
- **UNIVERSAL'S AVENTURA HOTEL** 6725 Adventure Way, Orlando, FL 32819
- **UNIVERSAL'S CABANA BAY BEACH RESORT** 6550 Adventure Way, Orlando, FL 32819
- **UNIVERSAL'S ENDLESS SUMMER RESORT, DOCKSIDE INN & SUITES** 7125 Universal Blvd., Orlando, FL 32819
- **UNIVERSAL'S ENDLESS SUMMER RESORT, SURFSIDE INN & SUITES** 7000 Universal Blvd., Orlando, FL 32819

UNIVERSAL ORLANDO PHONE NUMBERS	
Universal Orlando Main Information	☎ 407-363-8000
Guest Relations	☎ 407-224-4233 (press 2 for Lost and Found)
Tickets by Mail	☎ 407-224-7840
Merchandise	☎ 888-762-0820
Vacation Packages	☎ 877-801-9720
Vacation Packages Deaf or Hard of Hearing TDD	☎ 800-447-0672
On-Site Hotel Reservations	☎ 888-273-1311
Meeting Attendees/Individual Call-In for Group Blocks	☎ 866-360-7395
Universal In-Park Dining and Character Meals	☎ 407-224-3663
Universal Resort Dining and Character Meals	☎ 407-503-3463
Mandara Spa at Portofino Bay	☎ 407-503-1244
Hard Rock Hotel	☎ 407-503-ROCK (2000)
Loews Portofino Bay Hotel	☎ 407-503-1000
Loews Royal Pacific Resort	☎ 407-503-3000
Loews Sapphire Falls Resort	☎ 407-503-5000
Universal's Aventura Hotel	☎ 407-503-6000
Universal's Cabana Bay Beach Resort	☎ 407-503-4000
Universal's Endless Summer Resort, Dockside Inn & Suites	☎ 407-503-8000
Universal's Endless Summer Resort, Surfside Inn & Suites	☎ 407-503-7000

The touringplans.com website's touring plans, menus, Crowd Calendar, and more are available in Lines, which provides continuous real-time updates on wait times at Universal Orlando. Using in-park staff and updates sent in by readers, Lines shows you the current wait times at every attraction in every park, as well as estimated actual waits for these attractions for the rest of today. For example, Lines will tell you that the posted wait time for Harry Potter and the Escape from Gringotts is 60 minutes, and that based on what they know about how Universal manages Gringotts's queue, the actual time you'll probably wait in line is 48 minutes. Lines is the only Universal app that shows you both posted and actual wait times.

You can update the touring plans when you're in the parks too. The ability to redo your plan allows you to recover from any situation while still minimizing your waits for the rest of the day. Lines also has an online chat feature, where folks can ask questions and give travel tips. Hundreds of "Liners" interact every day in discussions that stay remarkably on-topic for an internet forum.

As long as you have that smartphone handy while visiting the parks, we and your fellow Unofficial Guide readers would love it if you could report on the actual wait times you get while you're there. Run Lines, log in to your user account, and click "+time" in the upper right corner to help everyone out. We'll use that information to update the wait times for everyone in the park and make everyone's lives just a little bit better.

BEST UNIVERSAL PODCASTS The best podcast devoted to Universal is **"UUOP: The Unofficial Universal Orlando Podcast"** (uuopodcast .com), which features regular reports from this book's author on "all the little things" that are new around the resort; ironically, the podcast is based not in Orlando but in the United Kingdom. **Parkscope** and **Inside Universal** also produce irreverent podcasts focusing on UOR. **"Orlando Tourism Report"** (orlandotourismreport.com) often breaks local attraction news. **Seasonpasspodcast.com** and **coasterradio.com** have breaking news and in-depth interviews with theme park designers and executives from parks around the world.

BEST UNIVERSAL TWITTER FEEDS If you want your Universal news and rumors in 280 character bites, follow these prolific park Tweeters: @theugseries, @universalorl, @parkscope, @insideuniversal, @themepark, @themeparks, @attractions, @horrornightsorl, @alicia stella, @orlandoparkstop, @orlandoinformer, @thrillgeek, @richobj, @bioreconstruct, @derekburgan, @touringplans, and @skubersky.

TIMING YOUR VISIT

TRYING TO REASON WITH THE TOURIST SEASON

PRIOR TO THE PANDEMIC, Central Florida theme parks and attractions were traditionally busiest the last week or so of December and the first few days of January. Next busiest is the spring break period from mid-March through the week of Easter, then Thanksgiving week. Following those are June–mid-July, when summer vacation is at its peak, and the week of Presidents' Day.

The least busy time is from the middle of August through the beginning of October. Next slowest are the weeks in mid-January after the Martin Luther King Jr. holiday weekend up to Presidents' Day in February. The weeks after Thanksgiving and before Christmas are less crowded than average, as is mid-April–mid-May, after spring break and before Memorial Day.

unofficial **TIP**
Though crowds have grown in September and October as a result of promotions aimed at the international market and families without school-age children, these months continue to be good for touring.

Late February, March, and early April are dicey. Crowds ebb and flow according to spring break schedules and the timing of Presidents' Day weekend. Besides being asphalt-melting hot, July brings throngs of South American tourists on their winter holiday, when international travel is allowed.

Of course, the coronavirus upended all historical attendance patterns, so although the previously mentioned peak periods will remain relatively busier, you should experience crowds throughout 2021 that are significantly smaller compared to prior years.

THE DOWNSIDE OF OFF-SEASON TOURING

THOUGH WE STRONGLY RECOMMEND going to Universal Orlando in the fall, winter, or spring, there are a few trade-offs. The parks often close early during the off-season, either because of low crowds or special events such as the Halloween and Rock the Universe events at Universal Studios Florida. This drastically reduces touring hours. Even when crowds are small, it can be challenging to see everything at USF or IOA between 9 a.m. and 6 p.m. Early closing also usually means no evening entertainment. And because these are slow times, some rides and attractions may be closed. Finally, Central Florida temperatures fluctuate wildly during late fall, winter, and early spring; daytime highs in the 40s and 50s aren't uncommon.

Given the choice, however, smaller crowds, bargain prices, and stress-free touring are worth risking cold weather or closed attractions. Touring in fall and other off periods is so much easier that our research team, at the risk of being blasphemous, would advise taking children out of school for an Orlando visit.

Most readers who have tried Central Florida's attractions at various times agree. A New Hampshire parent writes:

> I took my grade-school children out of school for a few days to go during a slow time and would highly recommend it. We communicated with the teachers about a month before traveling to seek their preference for whether classwork and homework should be completed before, during, or after our trip. It's so much more enjoyable to be [in Orlando] when your children can experience rides and attractions . . . rather than standing in line. And traveling at a time of year when it's not unbearably hot makes such a difference as well. I would be hard-pressed to go during a hot or busy time ever again.

There's another side to this story, and we've received some well-considered letters from parents and teachers who don't think taking kids out of school is such a hot idea. From a father in Fairfax, Virginia:

> My wife and I are disappointed that you seem to be encouraging families to take their children out of school to avoid the crowds [in Orlando] during the summer months. My wife is an eighth-grade teacher of chemistry and physics. She has parents pull their children, some honor roll students, out of school for vacations, only to discover when they return that the students are unable to comprehend the material. Parents' suspicions about the quality of their children's education should be raised when children go to school for 6 hours a day yet supposedly can complete this same instruction with less than an hour of homework each night.

A Martinez, California, teacher offers this compelling analogy:

> There are a precious 180 days for us as teachers to instruct our students, and there are 185 days during the year for [vacation]. I have seen countless students during my 14 years of teaching struggle to

catch up the rest of the year due to a week of vacation during critical instructional periods. It's like walking out of a movie after watching the first 5 minutes, and then returning for the last 5 minutes and trying to figure out what happened.

But a teacher from Penn Yan, New York, sees things differently:

I've read the comments from teachers saying that they all think it's horrible for a parent to take a child out of school for a vacation. As a teacher and a parent, I disagree. If a parent takes the time to let us know a child is going to be out, we help them get ready for upcoming homework the best we can. If the child is a good student, why shouldn't they go have a wonderful experience with their family? I also don't understand when teachers say they can't get something together for the time the student will be out. We all have to plan ahead, and we know what we are teaching days, if not weeks, in advance. Take 20 minutes out of your day and set something up. Learn to be flexible!

BE UNCONVENTIONAL Orlando's Orange County Convention Center (OCCC) hosts some of the largest conventions and trade shows in the world. Universal is far enough from the OCCC that it isn't usually affected by events, but hotel rooms anywhere around International Drive can be hard to find (and expensive) when there's a big convention. You can check the convention schedule at the OCCC for the next six months at calendar.occc.net/calendar.

DON'T FORGET AUGUST Kids go back to school pretty early in Florida (and in many other places too). This makes mid- to late August a good time to visit Universal Orlando for families who can't vacation during the fall. A New Jersey mother of two school-age children spells it out:

The end of August is the PERFECT time to go (just watch out for hurricanes; it's the season). There were virtually no wait times, 20 minutes at the most.

A mom from Rapid City, South Dakota, agrees:

School starts very early in Florida, so our mid-August visit was great for crowds but not for heat.

And from a family from Roxbury, New Jersey:

I recommend the last two weeks of August for anyone traveling there during the summer. We have visited twice during this time of year and have had great success touring the parks.

Though we recommend off-season touring, we realize it's not possible for many families. We want to make it clear, therefore, that you can have a wonderful experience regardless of when you go. Our advice, irrespective of season, is to arrive early at the parks and avoid the crowds by using one of our touring plans. If attendance is light, kick back and forget the touring plans.

WE'VE GOT WEATHER! Long before theme parks, tourists visited Florida year-round to enjoy the temperate tropical and subtropical climates. The best weather months generally are October, November, March, and April. Fall is usually dry, whereas spring is wetter. December, January, and February vary, with average highs of 72°–73°F intermixed with highs in the 50°–65°F range. May is hot but tolerable. June, July, August, and September are the warmest months. Rain, usually in the form of scattered thunderstorms, is possible anytime. An entire day of rain is unusual, but midafternoon downfalls occur so regularly during the summer that you can practically set your watch by them. These squalls, with lightning and gale-force winds, can temporarily shutter attractions but typically disperse in under an hour. Immediately after a storm is an ideal time to experience rides with little wait, especially at Volcano Bay.

Although everybody talks about Orlando's heat, it can also get quite cold here on rare occasions. You're never going to see real snow sticking to Hogwarts Castle, and during even the most frigid Florida winter, you'll spot Midwesterners walking around wearing shorts. But the temperatures do drop low enough to keep the water park closed, and to confound operations of some theme park attractions, as this reader from Baltimore, Maryland, discovered:

Some of the big thrill rides in Universal (including The Incredible Hulk Coaster, Hollywood Rip Ride Rockit, and Hagrid's Magical Creatures Motorbike Adventure) have trouble in cold weather (I am guessing because of outdoor tracks). We happened to be there during the coldest days of the year in January but didn't know this would be an issue. There were a couple of days that Hulk and Hollywood Rip Ride Rockit didn't operate at all.

UNIVERSAL ORLANDO CLIMATE

	JAN	FEB	MAR	APR	MAY	JUN	JUL	AUG	SEP	OCT	NOV	DEC
Average Daily heat index (temperature + humidity)												
	76°F	75°F	80°F	88°F	104°F	109°F	116°F	117°F	110°F	92°F	80°F	74°F
Average Daily Low												
	50°F	53°F	57°F	62°F	68°F	73°F	76°F	76°F	74°F	68°F	60°F	54°F
Average Rainfall per Month												
	2.9"	2.7"	4.0"	2.3"	3.1"	8.3"	7.0"	7.7"	5.1"	2.5"	2.1"	2.9"
Number of Days of Rain per Month												
	6	6	7	5	8	14	16	16	13	8	5	6

Source: U.S. Climate Data

SUMMER TEMPERATURES CAN FEEL LIKE 120°F Did you know that air temperature is measured in the shade? So if your phone's weather app says it's 95°F in Orlando, it's warmer if you're standing in the sun, and hotter still if you're wearing dark-colored clothing. Florida's notorious humidity makes the heat feel worse because it prevents your perspiration from evaporating to cool you off. The heat index expresses the combined effect of heat and humidity as a temperature reading we can understand. During summer at Universal Orlando, you'll commonly see heat index values above 110°F, and we've measured highs of up to 122°F. How hot is that? A steak cooked rare is considered done at 130°F. If you aren't used to it, don't discount the impact of Orlando's humidity even after the peak of summer, says this couple from Syracuse, New York:

> *We chose September for our trip because of the low crowd levels. We managed to avoid hurricanes, but goodness was it hot and humid. Being from upstate New York (where we are settling in to a lovely autumn this time of year), we were melting by 8:30 in the morning. I think we'll try early December next time!*

HOW MUCH TIME TO ALLOCATE

PRIOR TO THE DEBUT of The Wizarding Worlds, some visitors found that they could see everything of note at both Universal parks within a single day. Not anymore: Touring Universal Studios Florida, including one meal and a visit to Diagon Alley, takes about 8–10 hours, while a comprehensive tour of Islands of Adventure will take a couple hours less.

For that reason, we recommend devoting a minimum of a full day to each Universal Orlando theme park, especially if this is your first visit. Three days is ideal, particularly with a park-to-park pass, as it will allow you to fully explore each park and revisit your favorite attractions. Add an extra day to your trip if you plan on going to Volcano Bay, which you'll want to visit both during early morning and after sunset. An on-site stay of four or more days will allow you to sample the parks in smaller bites while taking full advantage of the resort's other amenities.

unofficial **TIP**
Get to the park with your admission already purchased about 30-45 minutes before official opening time. Arrive 45-60 minutes before official opening time if you need to buy admission. Be aware that you can't do a comprehensive tour of both Universal theme parks in a single day.

Some Universal Orlando attractions don't open until 10 a.m. or later. Most theater attractions don't schedule performances until 11 a.m. or after. This means that early in the day, all park guests are concentrated among the limited number of attractions in operation.

As a postscript, you won't have to worry about any of this if you use our Universal Orlando touring plans. We'll keep you one jump ahead of the crowd and make sure that any given attraction is running by the time you get there.

SELECTING THE DAY OF THE WEEK FOR YOUR VISIT

WHEN READERS ASKED, "What is the best day to visit Universal Orlando?," we used to reply that Sunday was the least crowded day at the resort (presumably because people are starting their vacations at Walt Disney World [WDW]), followed by Monday and Saturday, and that Thursday was the most crowded. However, there are too many other variables—including weather and special events—to make this a reliable rule of thumb. At press time, at least half of Universal's attendance consists of locals and annual pass holders, so crowds are currently far larger on weekends than on weekdays. Some restaurants and other venues are operating only on the weekends (or Thursday–Sunday), and the Volcano Bay water park may be closed on Tuesday and Thursday.

The best way to know which day to visit Universal Orlando is with the Crowd Calendar at touringplans.com/universal-orlando /crowd-calendar. No matter which day you visit, arriving early and following a touring plan makes a much bigger difference than what day of the week it is.

INTEGRATING A UNIVERSAL ORLANDO VISIT WITH A WDW VACATION

WHILE UNIVERSAL ORLANDO has recently made strides in convincing visitors to make UOR their primary destination, for many travelers a stop at Universal is a side trip in their Walt Disney World–centric vacation. If you are devoting the bulk of your Orlando holiday to Disney but still want to make a detour to Universal, you have three primary options:

THE DAY TRIP   Most Disney guests who want to sample Universal take a single day out of their vacation to visit USF and/or IOA. This solution is simplest for guests with their own cars, or shuttle transportation between the resorts can be arranged (see page 151). The day trip has a couple of drawbacks: the per-day cost can be high, especially if you want to visit both UOR theme parks, and (depending on transportation arrangements) you may be unable to arrive before rope drop (essential for optimal touring) or have to depart before closing time.

THE WDW/UOR/WDW SANDWICH   An increasing number of guests take a night or two out of the middle of their WDW trip and stay on property at Universal. Again, transportation can be handled through a private car or shuttle bus. This method allows you to explore Universal over the course of two or three days and enjoy the perks of staying on-site, such as Early Park Admission to The Wizarding World. You can also use Disney's Magical Express for free transfers from and to the airport at the beginning and end of your trip. The main drawback is that you must check in and out (and back in again) at your Disney hotel, or pay for nights in a WDW bed you won't be using.

THE SPLIT TRIP   The best option if you want to divide your vacation roughly equally between Disney and Universal is a split trip, where you stay at one resort for the first half of your visit, and then transfer to the other for the remainder. You'll only be able to use Disney's Magical Express on one end of your vacation (arriving or departing), so look into the three-way transportation offered by outfits such as Quicksilver (see page 150). If Disney is requiring advance park reservations, plan your days around Disney's availability. Otherwise, to decide which resort to visit first, check Touring Plans' Crowd Calendars for both properties, and visit Disney on the days it will be less busy, because crowds can make a bigger difference there than at Universal. If possible, this reader from upstate New York suggests saving your Universal visit for last to diminish disappointment:

> *We visited Universal Orlando first and were blown away by the technology of the rides and the quality of the attractions, especially in the Harry Potter sections. When we got to Disney, we had fun, but we weren't nearly as impressed. We enjoyed the attractions, but some of them seemed dated and a little less than spectacular.*

A mom from Missouri City, Texas, reported a similar experience:

> *For families planning a combined UOR/Disney trip, especially for those who like thrill rides but whose kids are older and the Disney magic may not be as exciting as it used to be, I recommend going to WDW parks before UOR. For my 13-year-old, it seemed like the Disney rides were too tame after having done two days first at UOR. He specifically called out Space Mountain for not being as thrilling as he remembered.*

WHICH PARK TO VISIT?

UNIVERSAL ORLANDO'S TWO THEME PARKS are both spectacular, so if you can only visit one, you can't really go wrong. If you've visited Universal since 2010, when the first Wizarding World opened, but have not yet seen Diagon Alley, you'll want to go to Universal Studios Florida; if you've experienced Harry Potter and the Escape from Gringotts but not Hagrid's Magical Creatures Motorbike Adventure, go to Islands of Adventure. For those who have never been to Universal Orlando, or at least not in the past decade, the decision is down to what type of attractions you prefer. If you are a fan of simulators, screen-based experiences, and live shows, then USF is right for you. If you prefer big outdoor roller coasters and wild water rides, IOA is your destination. Of course, if you are a Harry Potter devotee, you're going to have to visit both parks to get the full Wizarding World experience. Incidentally, USF is a much better park to visit during inclement weather, due to its larger percentage of indoor attractions. Finally, waterslide enthusiasts will want to spend at least one full day of their vacation at Volcano Bay.

ARRIVAL AND DEPARTURE DAY ACTIVITIES

GUESTS STAYING AT UNIVERSAL'S ON-SITE RESORTS can take advantage of all provided theme park perks—including early admission and Express Passes—from dawn on their arrival day until midnight on their day of departure. However, that requires using a full day's park admission for what may be only a few hours of entertainment, depending on your travel plans. Here are some suggestions on how to spend that spare half-day at the start or end of your vacation:

- Explore Universal's resort hotels using the garden walking paths and free water taxis.
- Relax at your hotel pool if the weather is clear, or spend some quarters inside the game room if it's inclement.

- Knock down some pins at Cabana Bay Beach Resort's Galaxy Bowl (see page 252).
- Play a round at the Hollywood Drive-In Mini-Golf, or catch a first-run flick at the Universal Cinemark at CityWalk (see pages 378 and 375).
- Take the free Vibe tour of musical memorabilia at the Hard Rock Cafe (see page 252).
- Enjoy a character breakfast (see page 213) or a musical dinner show (see page 265) at the resort hotels (when available).
- Drive to the nearby Fun Spot America amusement park (fun-spot.com) for a few laps around the multilevel go-cart tracks, then ride the White Lightning and Freedom Flyer roller coasters.
- Indulge in some retail therapy at the Orlando Premium Outlets shopping mall on International Drive (see page 273).
- Try an escape room game on International Drive, like The Bureau (the bureauorlando.com), which features performers from Universal Orlando.
- Visit the Icon Orlando 360 complex (iconorlando.com) on International Drive, home to the world's tallest StarFlyer swing ride and an enormous observation wheel, as well as a wax museum and an aquarium.

OPERATING HOURS

THE UNIVERSAL ORLANDO WEBSITE publishes preliminary park hours up to six months in advance, but schedule adjustments can happen at any time, including the day of your visit. Check tinyurl.com /unihrs or call ☎ 407-363-8000 for the exact hours before you arrive. Off-season, parks may be open as few as 8 hours (9 a.m.–5 p.m.). At busy times (particularly holidays), they may operate 8 a.m.–10 p.m., while 9 a.m.–9 p.m. was the standard summer schedule (prior to 2020).

Volcano Bay opens at 10 a.m. (8:30 or 9 a.m. in the peak season) and may stay open as late as 9 p.m. in the summer. While closing time can be as early as 5 p.m. during the off-season, Volcano Bay was designed for nighttime operation, with the majestic waterfalls cascading down the park's centerpiece transforming into blazing lava after sunset. If the park is open late during your visit, even if you exit during the afternoon, try to return during the closing hours to experience Volcano Bay's beauty after dark. Note that Volcano Bay may not operate on Tuesday and Thursday during slower seasons and was closed for the winter from November 2020 through at least March 1, 2021.

Universal's website publishes the official operating hours, but on most days, the parks open earlier. If the official hours for both theme parks are 9 a.m.–9 p.m., for instance, turnstiles for the park (or parks) participating in Early Park Admission will open between 7:30 a.m. and 8 a.m., and the one not offering early entry may still open its gates as early as 8:30 a.m.

Queues to attractions usually close to new guests at exactly the park's official closing time; if you are already in line at closing, you will be permitted to stay as long as it takes for you to ride, barring technical malfunctions. (Exceptions are popular rides such as Hagrid's Magical Creatures Motorbike Adventure, which may close its queue before the rest of the park if the estimated wait significantly exceeds the time remaining in the operating day.) The main gift shops near the front of each park remain open 30 minutes to an hour after the rest of the park has closed.

ALLOCATING MONEY

UNIVERSAL ORLANDO TICKETS

UNIVERSAL OFFERS TICKETS good for one to five days of admission to its theme parks. The **1-Day Base Ticket** includes entry to one theme park per day. If you buy a 2-Day Base Ticket, you can visit IOA on one day and USF on the next. You may not use a 2-Day Base Ticket to visit both parks in one day, but you can exit and return to the same park on the same day, in case you want to head back to your hotel for a nap.

If you want to visit both USF and IOA on the same day, purchase the **Park-to-Park admission** option, which allows you to move freely between both parks on the same day. It takes about 12–15 minutes to walk from the entrance of one park to the next, or you can take the 4-minute Hogwarts Express trip between The Wizarding Worlds. Be aware that you *must* have park-to-park admission to ride the Hogwarts Express train between IOA and USF; you can upgrade single-park tickets at Guest Services or at the King's Cross (USF) or Hogsmeade (IOA) train stations. (See below for more about Park-to-Park admission.)

In 2020 Universal Orlando shifted from a ticket pricing system based on three tiers of seasonal demand to date-specific pricing. All single and multiday tickets are date-specific, and prices can vary by up to $30 depending on the date you select during purchase for its first use. Flexible date tickets that can be activated on any day are still available for the cost of the most expensive date-specific passes. Examine Universal's online ticket pricing calendar carefully, because in certain seasons you may save a few dollars by shifting your first usage date forward or back by a few days, or by buying multiple one-day tickets instead of a multiday pass. Unlike Walt Disney World, Universal Orlando does not require advance reservations to visit its parks, although the turnstiles may close if the capacity limit is reached; date-specific tickets do not guarantee admission.

Admission to the Volcano Bay water park costs $80–$85 per day for adults ($5 cheaper for kids ages 3–9) depending on the season; Florida residents can save up to $10 on select days during the off-season. Volcano Bay access can be added to multiday 1-Park and Park-to-Park tickets for $40–$60, depending on ticket length.

A 1-Park, 1-Day Base Ticket to Universal is on par with those at the Disney parks, but multiday tickets can be much more expensive at Disney, where, for example, a 2-Day ticket costs about $50–$100 more than what you'd pay at Universal; Disney's 4-Day admission is $155–$240 more than Universal's equivalent 2-Park pass.

UNIVERSAL ORLANDO ADMISSIONS		
TICKET TYPE	ADULTS	CHILDREN (Ages 3-9)
1-Day Single-Park (USF/IOA)	$109.00-$139.00	$104.00-$134.00
1-Day Volcano Bay	$80.00-$85.00	$75.00-$80.00
1-Day Park-to-Park (USF/IOA)	$164.00-$194.00	$159.00-$189.00
2-Day Single-Park (USF/IOA)	$218.99-$246.99	$208.99-$236.99
2-Day Park-to-Park (USF/IOA)	$278.99-$306.99	$268.99-$296.99
2-Day Park-to-Park (USF/IOA/VB)	$318.99-$361.99	$308.99-$351.99
3-Day Single-Park (USF/IOA)	$241.99-$267.99	$231.99-$257.99
3-Day Single-Park (USF/IOA/VB)	$279.99-$322.99	$269.99-$312.99
3-Day Park-to-Park (USF/IOA)	$301.99-$327.99	$291.99-$317.99
3-Day Park-to-Park (USF/IOA/VB)	$339.99-$382.99	$329.99-$372.99
4-Day Single-Park (USF/IOA)	$254.99-$277.99	$244.99-$267.99
4-Day Single-Park (USF/IOA/VB)	$301.99-$342.99	$291.99-$332.99
4-Day Park-to-Park (USF/IOA)	$319.99-$342.99	$309.99-$332.99
4-Day Park-to-Park (USF/IOA/VB)	$366.99-$407.99	$356.99-$397.99
5-Day Single-Park (USF/IOA)	$261.99-$288.99	$251.99-$278.99
5-Day Single-Park (USF/IOA/VB)	$320.99-$363.99	$310.99-$353.99
5-Day Park-to-Park (USF/IOA)	$331.99-$358.99	$321.99-$348.99
5-Day Park-to-Park (USF/IOA/VB)	$390.99-$433.99	$380.99-$423.99
2-Park Seasonal Annual Pass	$304.99	$304.99
2-Park Power Annual Pass	$354.99	$354.99
2-Park Preferred Annual Pass	$394.99	$394.99
2-Park Premier Annual Pass	$559.99	$559.99
3-Park Seasonal Annual Pass	$403.99	$403.99
3-Park Power Annual Pass	$463.99	$463.99
3-Park Preferred Annual Pass	$503.99	$503.99
3-Park Premier Annual Pass	$733.99	$733.99

All multiday tickets expire five to eight days after their first use (up to seven days for flexible date tickets), depending on pass type and length. Kids under age 3 are free, but tickets for ages 3–9 are discounted only $5–$10 from the adult prices, despite the large number of rides with height requirements at Universal. Prices listed in the table above are what you'll pay online, not including 6.5% sales tax; gate prices for multiday tickets are $20 higher.

Park-to-Park: Worth the Price?

Many readers ask us if it's really worth the extra expense of $60–$70 per ticket (depending on length) for park-to-park access, often phrased as "Why spend so much more just to ride a train?" For visits of one or two days, you can easily make do with a base ticket, but we strongly suggest park-to-park admission for anyone who is a) visiting Universal Orlando for three or more days, b) staying at an on-site hotel, or c) a big Harry Potter fan. If you fall into one or more of those categories, here are some key reasons why it doesn't pay to economize on park-to-park access:

1. Hogwarts Express is among Universal Orlando Resort's top-rated attractions on our reader surveys, and we consider it not to be missed.

2. The Early Park Admission perk included with on-site hotel stays is usually valid at only one theme park; with park-hopping privileges, you can take advantage of early entry but spend the rest of the day elsewhere.

3. Park-to-park-access allows you to visit Volcano Bay in the early morning and evening when it's pleasant, and spend the crowded middle part of the day in another park.

4. During inclement weather, park-to-park access lets you hop over to USF when most of the other parks' outdoor attractions are shut down.

If you're anxious to trim admission costs, consider reducing your pass length by a day while keeping the park-to-park option. If you're staying for four days/three nights, a 3-Day park pass—rather than 4—allows you to use your arrival or departure half-day to explore alternative attractions (as suggested on page 42).

UNIVERSAL ORLANDO ANNUAL PASSES

UNIVERSAL ORLANDO offers some of the best deals on annual passes in town, not only for locals but also for anyone visiting the resort more than four days out of the year. The entry-level 2-Park Seasonal Pass costs about the same as a 4-Day Park-to-Park ticket, and Universal's most expensive 3-Park Premier Annual Pass is about the price of two 3-Park, 3-Day Park-to-Park tickets. The 3-Park Premier Pass is also about 25% cheaper than Walt Disney World's Platinum Plus Annual Pass, and while Disney has several more parks included in its annual passes, Universal throws in some great perks (depending on pass level) to compensate.

Universal annual passes include park-to-park admission to USF and IOA, including special events that don't require a separate ticket, such as Mardi Gras (except Seasonal Pass holders on concert nights), Grinchmas, and Universal's Holiday Parade, as well as discounts on those that cost extra, such as Halloween Horror Nights and Rock the Universe.

Any annual pass can be purchased with access to all three parks, which includes Volcano Bay water park. Three-Park Annual Passes cost $99 more than 2-Park passes at the Seasonal level, an additional $109 for Power and Preferred Passes, and $174 more for Premier. Current 2-Park pass holders can upgrade to 3-Park access for the same prices, but no prorated discounts are given. All annual passes except 3-Park Premier are blocked from entry into the water park during select dates; see below for details.

A lounge in the Hollywood section of USF is open to all annual pass holders daily, 11 a.m.–4 p.m. The lounge doesn't offer free snacks like the AmEx one does (see page 160), but it does have air-conditioning, phone charging ports, and the opportunity to purchase ice-cold Coke products. At press time the UOAP lounge was scheduled to close December 31, 2020, but its operations have been extended before.

All annual pass holders receive up to 30% off room rates at on-site hotels, 20% off up to six select Blue Man Group Orlando adult tickets, 25% off Budget rental car base rates and free upgrades, $3 off evening admission for yourself and one guest at Universal Cinemark, $1 off daily Coca-Cola Freestyle souvenir cup refills, and other discounts as detailed below. Here are the four types of annual passes offered by Universal:

Seasonal Pass

- Valid for one year, but with about 8 weeks of block-out dates, including spring break, July, and Christmas week at USF and IOA, and all concert nights at USF only; Volcano Bay block-outs in April and mid-June–August
- No free parking
- No food or merchandise discounts at parks or CityWalk; 10%–15% off at select resort hotel locations
- 10% off gate prices for additional multiday park tickets

Power Pass

- Valid for one year, but with about four weeks of block-out dates at USF and IOA, including spring break and Christmas week; Volcano Bay block-outs before 4 p.m. mid-June–August
- 50% discount on self-parking (after the first visit)
- No food or merchandise discounts at parks or CityWalk; 10%–15% off at select resort hotel locations
- 15% off gate prices for additional multiday park tickets

Preferred Annual Pass

- Valid 365 days at USF and IOA; Volcano Bay block-outs before 4 p.m. July–August
- Early Park Admission 1 hour before official opening to USF and/or IOA; not valid on mornings listed at tinyurl.com/UOAPEPA, including spring break, Thanksgiving, Christmas week, and select weekends
- Free standard self-parking and discounted prime self-parking and valet (after the first visit)
- 10% off most in-park restaurants and merchandise (outdoor carts and alcohol excluded)
- 10%–15% off food and merchandise at select CityWalk and resort hotel locations
- 15% off gate prices for additional multiday park tickets
- 10% off My Universal Photos
- Additional discounts at CityWalk and the resort hotels

Premier Annual Pass

- Valid 365 days at all parks
- Early Park Admission 1 hour before official opening to USF and/or IOA; valid 365 mornings per year

- Free prime self-parking and valet (after the first visit; when available)
- 15% off most in-park restaurants and merchandise (outdoor carts and alcohol excluded)
- Free Universal Express at USF and IOA after 4 p.m. every day (one time per participating attraction; may start at 2 p.m. when parks close early)
- One free Halloween Horror Nights ticket (valid select off-peak nights only)
- 10%–20% off food and merchandise at select CityWalk and resort hotel locations
- 15% off gate prices for additional multiday park tickets
- 15% off My Universal Photos
- Free admission to CityWalk clubs, and free admission for one guest (excludes concerts and special events)
- Additional discounts at CityWalk and the resort hotels

In addition, all annual pass holders get a quarterly newsletter with announcements of special limited-time perks, such as exclusive merchandise offers and menu items, private parking toll lanes and entrance turnstiles, free buttons and magnets, or pass holder–only events during Passholder Appreciation Days, held in the off-season; see tinyurl.com /uniappdays for details. And if you can't handle the cost of a pass in one big bite, Universal's FlexPay service will (after a substantial down payment) split the remaining bill into interest-free payments as low as $17 a month. Be aware that you'll have to pay off your balance in full before upgrading your pass tier. After the initial yearlong payment contract is complete, FlexPay will automatically renew on a month-to-month basis with a significantly higher monthly payment. FlexPay customers do not get the 20% renewal discount offered to paid-in-full pass holders, but they may be eligible for bonus months during seasonal sales promotions. Annual pass pricing and benefits change regularly, so visit tinyurl.com/UORAnnualPass for the latest offers.

So, should you buy a Universal Orlando annual pass, and if so, which one? If you are making only one trip to Universal within the year, are staying off-site, and plan to spend four days or fewer in the parks, then you should stick with standard tickets. If, however, you plan to spend five or more days at Universal's parks, anticipate returning to Universal within the year, or want to stay at an on-site hotel for even one night, it is well worth your while to run the numbers on an annual pass. Even if you live out of state, Universal's annual passes may entice you to become a repeat visitor, like this family from Taos, New Mexico:

unofficial **TIP**
Visit tinyurl.com/UOR HotelAPH to search Universal's online hotel inventory for available pass holder discounts.

The annual pass is an incredible bargain, and when you combine it with a stay at one of the three resorts that include an Express Pass, it makes for a reasonably priced and super fun short getaway.

As for which one to buy, first double-check the current Seasonal and Power Pass block-out dates at tinyurl.com/UOAPblockout to ensure they don't conflict with your trip. If only the first portion of your visit overlaps with the block-out period, it's possible to buy multiday tickets, then apply their full value to annual passes by upgrading them at Guest Services before they expire. Even if you're in the clear, at least one member of your party will want to pick up at least a Preferred Pass for its discounts, especially if you're driving to the resort; four days of self-parking at $26 per day adds up to $104, which is more than the difference in price between the Seasonal and Preferred Passes. The Power Pass is currently only $40 cheaper than the Preferred Pass ($30 for Florida residents), less than the cost of four visits with discounted self-parking; after factoring in the block-out dates and lack of discounts, the Power Pass is a poor value for most guests. (Note that free or discounted parking only applies after your first visit; you must first activate your annual pass at a park gate before receiving free parking.)

If—and only if—you take advantage of all its amenities, the Premier Annual Pass is an amazing value. At a $13.75-per-month upcharge from the 2-Park Preferred Pass, you can easily get your money's worth in free valet parking alone, and the free Universal Express after 4 p.m. is especially useful when the parks are open late. (See the Universal Express section on page 69 for more details.) The free Halloween Horror Nights pass isn't valid on most nights in October and can't be upgraded or transferred to another person, which limits its value if you are also planning to buy a Frequent Fear Pass. Fortunately, Universal provided Premier Pass holders with additional perks (like free guest admission and earlier Express access) when certain privileges were preempted by the pandemic in 2020.

BUYING ADMISSION TO UNIVERSAL ORLANDO

ONE OF OUR BIG GRIPES ABOUT UNIVERSAL is that there are never enough ticket windows open in the morning to accommodate the crowds. That means that guests wait in long ticket lines during the peak holiday and summer seasons just to reach a sales window before they can enjoy more waits at the turnstiles and attractions. You can purchase Volcano Bay tickets at the Volcano Bay bus stop inside the parking structure or at the park entrance. However, we strongly recommend buying your admission in advance. Passes are available directly from Universal at universalorlando.com or by phone at ☎ 800-711-0080; at the concierge desks or attraction box offices of many Orlando-area hotels; and through Guest Services at the Double-Tree at Universal hotel (☎ 407-351-1000), at the intersection of Major Boulevard and Kirkman Road.

If you download the official Universal Orlando app on your smartphone, you can purchase single or multiday admission directly on your mobile device, which will display a bar code that serves as your ticket, avoiding the need for paper altogether. Prices for passes purchased through the app are the same as on Universal's website.

SAVING MONEY ON ADMISSION
TO UNIVERSAL ORLANDO

UNIVERSAL'S ADMISSION DISCOUNTS change too rapidly to comprehensively cover in this guide. The best online clearinghouse for keeping up with the latest available offers is mousesavers.com/universal -orlando-discounts-and-deals.

Ticket Savings Direct from Universal Orlando

Universal offers discounts when you purchase passes online at universal orlando.com, including $20-per-ticket discounts on multiday tickets plus other time-limited specials. Tickets purchased online can be printed at home and used at the turnstiles without the need to exchange them at a box office, or they can be retrieved using the credit card with which they were purchased from automated will call kiosks outside each park; look for the ATM-like terminals to the right of the Guest Services window at USF, or to the left of Toothsome Chocolate Emporium outside IOA. Tickets purchased online (including annual passes) do not begin expiring until first activated at a park entrance.

Universal offers a best-price guarantee: if you buy park tickets through Universal's website and then find them cheaper online within seven days, Universal Orlando will give you a gift card (good at restaurants and shops around the resort) refunding the price difference. The price guarantee is only on regular admission tickets (not Express or special-event tickets) available to the general public from US-based websites, and it excludes time-share promotions, group rates, or other special discounts. To claim your refund, call ☎ 877-589-4783 or send an email via visitorsatisfaction.com/contactus.

Florida (and sometimes Georgia) residents can take advantage of an ever-changing array of price breaks, often tied to a fast-food chain or soft drink promotion. Local resident tickets expire 59 days after first use for two-day tickets and up to 179 days after for three- to five-day tickets, unlike regular multiday tickets, which expire after a week. These specials require valid photo ID proving residency to redeem, so don't try using one if you aren't eligible. Current annual pass holders get a modest 10%–15% price break when buying additional multiday tickets at the gate but may do better with the standard online discount. Visit universalorlando.com/web/en/us/tickets-packages/park -tickets/flr to see the locals' latest discounts.

Universal Orlando frequently offers online-only specials that are usually superior to any other available discount. For example, in fall 2020 Universal sold 5-Day tickets for the price of a 2-Day pass. These tickets have to be used before a certain expiration date, and block-out days may apply, but the savings can be substantial.

Ticket Savings from Third-Party Vendors

The lowest possible prices on electronically delivered Universal tickets that we're aware of are through **Orlando Ticket Connection** (☎ 855-473-7987; orlandoticketconnection.com), which undercuts Universal's online prices on multiday base tickets by $5–$20 and on park-to-park tickets by $20–$50. Orlando Ticket Connection advertises all its prices inclusive of tax and electronic delivery, and it typically will match or beat the short-term deals Universal offers on its own website. Orlando Ticket Connection gets high marks for customer service from readers like this one:

> *I ordered tickets for SeaWorld and Universal Orlando from Orlando Ticket Connection late on Thursday night (around midnight), and at 9:08 on Friday morning I received my tickets by email. It was quick, and they were actual tickets that you take directly to the turnstile. I used them both at the parks today and had no problems whatsoever. I would order tickets from them again without a second thought.*

Dreams Unlimited Travel (dreamsunlimitedtravel.com) charges the same or more for Universal tickets as the official website, but it does offer exclusive one- and two-day park-to-park tickets bundled with discounted round-trip transportation from Disney-area hotels via Quick Transportation (quicktransportation.com). Its tickets are processed through Universal's secure website and can be printed at home or retrieved from will call kiosks.

Universal charges $14 for domestic FedEx shipping of tickets ($19 for international delivery). If you want physical tickets mailed to you for the cheapest price and can order at least two weeks before your trip, consider using an online ticket wholesaler.

If you are visiting from the United Kingdom, check out **Attraction Tickets Direct** (attraction-tickets-direct.co.uk) for good deals on 14-day tickets.

DISCOUNTS AT UNIVERSAL ORLANDO

UNIVERSAL ORLANDO PROVIDES DISCOUNTS on tickets, dining, and lodging to members of many travel organizations, including automobile clubs such as AAA and CAA. Discounts are also available to Universal Orlando annual pass holders. This section is a guide to finding the best discounts for members of these groups and the general public.

Admission

Universal doesn't offer ticket discounts to AAA or CAA members at the gate, but some regional offices sell discounted passes to members in advance; prices vary by area. The closest Auto Club South office to Universal Orlando is at 7339 W. Sand Lake Road, Ste. 424, in Bay Hill; call ☎ 407-351-5610 for hours and directions. AAA South members can buy discounted tickets, annual passes, and vacation packages online at aaa.com/universal.

Costco Wholesale sometimes sells discounted Universal Orlando tickets to members.

Active duty and retired members of the United States armed forces should visit universalorlando.com/military for exclusive deals on tickets and hotel packages. Service members can buy 4-Day tickets for less than the gate price of a 1-Day Park-to-Park pass. A typical military discount package includes three nights of accommodations in an on-site or partner hotel and a 4-Day, 3-Park Park-to-Park ticket. Universal Orlando tickets are available at most base Leisure Travel offices, as well as at Shades of Green at Disney World.

Resorts

All annual pass holders (including Seasonal and Power Pass holders) receive discounts of up to 30% on resort lodging, depending on availability. If you're staying at a Universal resort for two or more days, you may save enough on lodging to offset the cost of an annual pass for the adult booking the room. Similar (and sometimes superior) seasonal Florida resident discounts are detailed at tinyurl.com/uniflres.

AAA members can book on-site rooms and vacation packages at a modest discount, usually 5%–25%. Packages include $25–$50 activity credit that can be used for vacation add-ons. You must call AAA or Loews directly to get the discount; it cannot be applied online.

Cheaptickets.com and orbitz.com often offer discount codes for up to 20% their already-discounted Universal Orlando room rates; Google "Orlando hotel promo codes" or use a site such as retailmenot.com to find the latest offers.

Check mousesavers.com, which lists seasonal and specialized discounts for Universal's resorts, such as discounts available to residents of certain states.

The Hard Rock Rewards frequent-stay program at Hard Rock Hotel offers free priority late checkout and points toward free stays; you can learn about the program and sign up in advance at members.hardrock.com. Note that the perks sometimes cannot be used in conjunction with discounted rates. (A similar Loews YouFirst loyalty program at the other on-site hotels has been discontinued.)

Dining

See page 46 for discounts offered to annual pass holders.

American Express members periodically receive modest discounts on the Quick-Service Universal Dining Plan with Coca-Cola Freestyle cup; you must buy the dining plan on an American Express card and use your smartphone to show the American Express offer in the Universal Orlando mobile app at the time of purchase to receive the discount.

If you are visiting during late August–September, several Universal resort restaurants participate in Orlando's Magical Dining, when you can order three courses from special prix fixe menus for only $35; visit visitorlando.com/magicaldining for details.

Merchandise

See page 46 for discounts offered to annual pass holders.

American Express members periodically receive modest discounts on select merchandise with a minimum purchase when using their AmEx card at Universal-owned shops (excluding inside The Wizarding Worlds). You must use your smartphone to show the American Express offer in the Universal Orlando mobile app at the time of purchase to receive the discount.

Entertainment and Other Discounts

Preferred Pass holders receive 10% off services at Portofino Bay's Mandara Spa, and Premier Pass holders save 20% (Monday–Thursday only; some services excluded). Discounted Mandara Spa packages are also regularly offered on Groupon.

Preferred Pass holders save 20% on CityWalk Party Passes (up to four per day); Premier Pass holders get Party Passes free for themselves and one guest.

Preferred and Premier Pass holders receive discounts on an 18-hole round at Hollywood Drive-In Golf for up to five players; Preferred Pass holders save 10%, while Premier Pass holders save 15%.

All annual pass holders save $3 off adult admission to any Universal Cinemark showing after 6 p.m. for themselves and one guest.

Preferred and Premier Pass holders get a $5 discount on Classic Albums Live concert tickets at the Hard Rock Live box office.

Preferred Pass holders get 10% off all in-park rock climbing walls; Premier Pass holders save 15% per climb.

All annual pass holders (including Seasonal Pass holders) get 10%–20% off inflatable pool tubes, cabana rentals, and souvenir cups at Cabana Bay Beach Resort, and 50% off virtual reality games at Aventura Hotel's arcade.

All annual pass holders can save up to 25% off base rates and get a free upgrade at Budget rental cars.

AAA members get 10% off select Blue Man Group tickets at the box office or up to 25% off online, while annual pass holders (including Seasonal and Power Pass) receive 20% off; limit six seats per transaction.

Finally, you *might* save money at Universal Orlando Resort by booking a package with tickets and lodging through **Universal Orlando Vacations** (☎ 877-801-9720; universalorlandovacations .com), the official travel company of Universal Orlando Resort. It advertises packages with attractive-sounding rates, like "only $135 per person per night," but you must take full advantage of every package component (including food or photos you may not want) to realize a modest 5% discount over buying each component separately. For a full breakdown of Universal Orlando Vacation bundles, see page 110.

MAKING *the* MOST *of* YOUR TIME *and* MONEY *at* UNIVERSAL ORLANDO

THE CARDINAL RULES FOR SUCCESSFUL TOURING

MANY VISITORS DON'T HAVE three or four days to devote to Universal Orlando. Some are en route to other destinations or are visiting Universal as a sideline to their Disney World vacation. For these visitors, efficient touring is a must.

Even the most time-effective touring plan won't allow you to comprehensively cover more than one Universal theme park in one day. Plan to allocate an entire day to each park. An exception to this is when the parks close at different times, allowing you to tour one park until closing and then proceed to another.

One-Day Touring

A comprehensive tour of *both* Universal Orlando theme parks in one day is virtually impossible. A comprehensive one-day tour of USF *or* IOA is possible but requires knowledge of the park, good planning, good navigation, and plenty of energy and endurance. One-day touring leaves little time for sit-down meals, prolonged browsing in shops, or lengthy breaks. One-day touring can be fun and rewarding, but allocating at least three full days to enjoy the two theme parks is preferable.

We provide one-day plans for each Universal park, plus one- and two-day plans for those with park-to-park access. We also provide touring advice for Volcano Bay, though due to the water park's use of Virtual Line technology, a step-by-step touring plan isn't possible. Guests with three days should use our comprehensive two-day/two-park plan, followed by one of our specialized one-day plans; guests with more than three days can try multiple specialized one-day plans, or spend their additional days at leisure exploring without an itinerary. Even if you're on a relaxed schedule, following a touring plan can still enhance your trip, according to this reader from Rockford, Michigan:

> *While we had four days to explore Universal, we followed the two-day park-to-park plan the first day, and it worked amazingly! It allowed us to get so much in that we could relax the rest of the trip and see and do everything we wanted, plus repeat rides everyone liked.*

Successfully touring USF or IOA in one day hinges on three rules:

1. Determine in Advance What You Really Want to See

Which attractions appeal to you most? Which ones would you like to experience if you have time left? What are you willing to forgo?

To help you set your touring priorities, we describe the theme parks and their attractions in detail in Parts Seven and Eight. In each description, we include the author's evaluation of the attraction and the opinions of Universal Orlando guests expressed as star ratings. Five stars is the highest rating.

Finally, because attractions range from midway-type rides and walk-through exhibits to high-tech extravaganzas, we have developed a hierarchy of categories to pinpoint an attraction's magnitude:

SUPER-HEADLINERS The best attractions the theme park has to offer. Mind-boggling in size, scope, and imagination. Represent the cutting edge of attraction technology and design.

HEADLINERS Multimillion-dollar, themed, full-scale adventures and theater presentations. Modern in technology and design and employing a full range of special effects.

MAJOR ATTRACTIONS More modestly themed adventures, but ones that incorporate state-of-the-art technologies, or larger-scale attractions of older design.

MINOR ATTRACTIONS Midway-type rides, small theater presentations, and elaborate walk-through attractions.

DIVERSIONS Exhibits, both passive and interactive. Includes playgrounds, video arcades, and street theater.

Though not every attraction fits neatly into these descriptions, the categories provide a comparison of size and scope. Remember: bigger and more elaborate doesn't always mean better or more popular. Flight of the Hippogriff, a kiddie coaster in IOA's Hogsmeade, sometimes attracts a longer line than the larger Harry Potter and the Forbidden Journey. Likewise, for many young children, no attraction, regardless of size, surpasses One Fish, Two Fish, Red Fish, Blue Fish, a simple Seussian spinner.

2. Arrive Early! Arrive Early! Arrive Early!

This is the single most important key to efficient touring and avoiding long lines. First thing in the morning, there are no lines and fewer people. The same four rides you experience in 1 hour in early the morning can take as long as 3 hours after 10:30 a.m. Besides that, the parks are now open as few as 8 hours per day during the off-season. Factoring in meals and breaks, that leaves as little as 6–6.5 hours to see the park. Eat breakfast before you arrive; don't waste prime touring time sitting in a restaurant.

The earlier a park opens, the greater your advantage. This is because most vacationers won't rise early and get to a park before it opens. Fewer people are willing to make an 8 a.m. opening than a 9 a.m. opening. If you visit during midsummer, arrive at the turnstile 30–45 minutes before you are eligible to enter. During holiday periods, arrive 45–60 minutes early. If you won't take our word for it, listen to this couple from New Orleans:

> *Your advice to get to the parks 30 minutes before they open (we did not have early admission) was spot on. We could pretty much get on almost any ride with little to no wait until about 10:30–11 a.m. each day we were there.*

3. Avoid Bottlenecks

Helping you avoid bottlenecks is what *The Unofficial Guide* is about. This involves being able to predict where, when, and why bottlenecks occur. Concentrations of hungry people create gridlocks at restaurants during lunch and dinner; concentrations of people moving toward the exit near closing time cause gift shops en route to clog; concentrations of visitors at new and popular rides, and at rides slow to load and unload, create logjams and long lines.

Our solution for avoiding bottlenecks: touring plans for USF and IOA. We also provide detailed information on rides and performances, enabling you to estimate how long you may have to wait in line and allowing you to compare rides for their crowd capacity. All touring plans are in the back of this book, following the index. Plans for Universal Studios Florida begin on page 395, and for Islands of Adventure, on page 398. One- and two-day touring plans for both USF and IOA are provided for those with park-to-park admission.

WHAT'S A QUEUE?

THOUGH IT'S NOT COMMONLY USED in the United States, *queue* (pronounced "cue") is the universal English word for a line, such as one in which you wait to cash a check at the bank or to board a ride at a theme park. Queuing theory, a mathematical area of specialization within the field of operations research, studies and models how lines work. Because *The Unofficial Guide* draws heavily on this discipline, we use some of its terminology. In addition to the noun, the verb *to queue* means "to get in line," and a *queuing area* is "a waiting area that accommodates a line."

TOURING PLANS:
WHAT THEY ARE AND HOW THEY WORK

MINIMIZING OUR READERS' WAITS in line has been a top priority. We know from our research and that of others that theme park patrons measure overall satisfaction based on the number of attractions they're able to experience during a visit: the more attractions, the better. Thus, we developed and offered our readers field-tested touring plans that allow them to experience as many attractions as possible with the least amount of waiting in line.

Even with park attendance at 25%–50% of pre-pandemic capacity, we think the touring plans in this book can save you up to an hour or more of waiting in line during a single day, and they allow you to see many more attractions.

Our touring plans have always been based on theme park traffic flow, attraction capacity, the maximum time a guest is willing to wait, walking distance between attractions, and waiting-time data collected at every attraction in every park, every day of the year.

The Unofficial Guide touring plan program contains patented algorithms that allow it to quickly analyze tens of millions of possible plans in a very short time. The program can analyze standby wait times and estimate the time saved by using Universal Express Passes. The software can also schedule rest breaks throughout the day and estimate walking times to meals if you specify a preferred restaurant. Numerous other features are available, many of which we'll discuss in the next section.

Over the years, this research has been recognized by the travel industry and academe, having been cited by such diverse sources as *The New York Times, USA Today, Travel Weekly, Bottom Line, Money, Operations Research Forum,* CBS News, Fox News, the BBC, the Travel Channel, *The Dallas Morning News,* and *The Atlanta Journal-Constitution.* The methodology behind our touring plans was also used as a case study in the 2010 book *Numbers Rule Your World* by Kaiser Fung, professor of statistics at New York University.

We get a ton of reader mail—98% of it positive—commenting on our touring plans. From an Edmonds, Washington, family who used one of our touring plans for IOA:

> *It worked like a charm! I've always wondered how it feels to follow your plans, not ever having seen the park before, and now I know—it was easy!*

Another reader reports:

> *We didn't have early entry and got there 30 minutes before the official opening time of 9 a.m. and walked on the first three rides on the plan. We spent two days at both parks and got on everything twice. Never waited more than 45 minutes.*

And from a Fruit Cove, Florida, family:

> *We found the touring plans extremely helpful. When we followed the plans exactly, we were able to experience all rides with little to no wait.*

Customize Your Touring Plans

The attractions included in our touring plans are the best and most popular as determined by our expert team and reader surveys. If you've never been to Universal Orlando, we suggest using the plans in this book. They'll ensure that you see the best Universal attractions with as little waiting in line as possible.

If you're a return visitor, your favorite attractions may be different. One way to customize the plans is to go to touringplans.com or use the Lines app to create personalized versions. Tell the software the date, time, and park you've chosen to visit, along with the attractions you want to see. The plan will tell you, for your specific travel date and time, the exact order in which to visit the attractions to minimize your waits in line. Lines also supports child swap (see page 204) on thrill rides. Besides rides, you can schedule shows, meals, breaks, character greetings, and more. You can even tell Lines how fast you plan to walk, and whether or not you'll be using Universal Express, and it will make the necessary adjustments.

Alternatively, some changes are simple enough to make on your own. If a plan calls for an attraction in which you're not interested, simply skip it and move on to the next one. You can also substitute similar attractions in the same area of the park. If a plan calls for, say, riding Cat in the Hat and you'd rather not, but you would enjoy the Caro-Seuss-el (which is not on the plan), then go ahead and substitute that for Cat. As long as the substitution is a similar attraction—substituting a show for a ride won't work—and is pretty close by the attraction called for in the touring plan, you won't compromise the plan's overall effectiveness. If all else fails and you need some extra hand-holding, the author of this book provides personalized tour-planning services for all Universal parks; visit sethkubersky.com for pricing and details.

OVERVIEW OF THE TOURING PLANS

OUR TOURING PLANS ARE STEP-BY-STEP GUIDES for seeing as much as possible with a minimum of standing in line, and without needing Universal Express Passes. They're designed to help you avoid crowds and bottlenecks on any day of the year. The plans will save time on days when attendance is lighter (see "Trying to Reason with the Tourist Season," page 36), but on those days, they won't be as critical to successful touring.

What You Can Realistically Expect from the Touring Plans

Though we present one-day/two-park plans for Universal Orlando, USF and IOA together have more attractions than you can reasonably expect to see in one day. You can either see all of The Wizarding World in depth or highlights of the rest of the resort, but not both in a single visit. Because our two-day plans for Universal Orlando are the most comprehensive, efficient, and relaxing, we strongly recommend them over the one-day/two-park plans. However, if you must cram your visit to both parks into a single day, the one-day plans will allow you to see as much as is humanly possible.

Variables That Affect the Success of the Touring Plans

The plans' success will be affected by how quickly you move from ride to ride; when and how many refreshment and restroom breaks you take; when, where, and how you eat meals; and your ability (or lack thereof) to find your way around. Smaller groups almost always move faster than larger groups, and parties of adults generally cover more ground than families with young children. Child swap (see page 204), also known as rider swap, baby swap, or switching off, inhibits families with little ones from moving as expeditiously as possible among attractions.

Plus, some folks simply cannot conform to the plans' "early to rise" conditions, as this reader from Cleveland Heights, Ohio, recounts:

Our touring plans were thrown totally off by one member who could not be on time for opening. Even in October, this made a huge difference in our ability to see attractions without waiting.

And a family from Centerville, Ohio, says:

The toughest thing about your touring plans was getting the rest of the family to stay with them. Getting them to pass by attractions to hit something across the park was no easy task.

If you have young children, the appearance of a cartoon character (especially Dora the Explorer or the Minions) can stop a touring plan in its tracks, and even adults will detour to snap a selfie with Optimus Prime or the Hogwarts Express conductor. While some characters stroll the parks, it's more common that they assemble in a specific location where families queue up for photos. Meeting characters isn't as popular a pastime at Universal as at Disney but can still burn valuable touring time. If your kids collect character selfies, you need to anticipate these interruptions by including character greetings when creating your online touring plans, or else negotiate some understanding with your children about when you'll stop for photos.

Some things are beyond your control. Chief among these are the manner and timing of bringing a particular ride to capacity. For example, Harry Potter and the Escape from Gringotts, an indoor roller coaster in USF, may begin operation with four or five trains running, and then add two to five more as needed. If the waiting line builds rapidly before operators go to full capacity, you could have a long wait, even in early morning.

A variable that can give your touring plans a boost is the singles line (see page 77), as this English reader explains:

We used the touring plans to the letter and found that not only did they work, but they also worked even better in conjunction with single-rider queues. The only rides we queued up for normally were ones with a 20-minute-or-less queue time and wet rides.

Another variable is your arrival time for a theater show. You'll wait from the time you arrive until the end of the presentation in progress. Thus, if a show starts every 30 minutes and you arrive 1 minute after it has begun, your wait will be 29 minutes. Conversely, if you arrive just before the next show begins, your wait will be only a minute or two.

While we realize that following the touring plans isn't always easy, we nevertheless recommend continuous, expeditious touring until around noon. After that, breaks and diversions won't affect the touring plans significantly.

What to Do if You Lose the Thread

We suggest sticking to the plans religiously, especially in the mornings, if you're visiting during busy times. The consequence of touring spontaneity in peak season is hours of standing in line. When using the plans, however, relax and always be prepared for surprises and setbacks. If unforeseen events interrupt a plan:

1. If you're following a touring plan in the Lines app (touringplans.com/lines), just press OPTIMIZE when you're ready to start touring again. Lines will figure out the best possible plan for the remainder of your day.

2. If you're following a printed touring plan, skip a step on the plan for every 20 minutes' delay. For example, if you lose your wallet and spend an hour hunting for it, skip three steps and pick up from there.

3. Forget the plan and organize the remainder of the day using the standby wait times listed in the Lines app.

Even if you aren't strictly following a touring plan, remember to refresh the Lines app after a detour, as a father of three from Sydney, Australia, advises:

When using Lines and seeing what the attraction wait times are, make sure to refresh it first so you can see the up-to-date wait times, not the wait times from 2 hours ago when you last refreshed it. I may have been guilty of not doing this, as I took the family from one side of the park to the other to go to Transformers, and then waited 40 minutes for the ride when I told everyone it was a 15-minute line. Or it might have been the two restroom stops on the way?

Clip-Out Touring Plans

For your convenience, the touring plans combine itineraries with numbered maps. Select the plan appropriate for your party, and get familiar with it. Then clip the pocket version from the back of this guide and carry it with you as a quick reference at the theme park.

Will the Plans Continue to Work Once the Secret Is Out?

Yes! First, all the plans require that a patron be there when a park opens. Many Universal Orlando patrons simply won't get up early while on vacation. Second, less than 2% of any day's attendance has been exposed to the plans—too few to affect results. Last, most groups tailor the plans, skipping rides or shows according to taste.

Why Do I Need a Touring Plan if I Have Universal's Smartphone App?

You might imagine that the availability of real-time wait times inside Universal Orlando's free app would obviate your need for a touring plan. But in fact, it has the exact opposite effect, as this mom from Athens, Georgia, explains:

I believe the touring plans are even more important now that everyone has a wait-time app from the park on their phone. I would see 10-minute wait times pop up on the Universal app, and if we happened to walk past those rides on our way to another ride, the line would jump up to 20 minutes or more. People are just chasing the shortest lines, but then everyone goes to that ride and the lines increase. We did do this for a few hours when we went to the park late in the day and instantly regretted it.

How Frequently Are the Touring Plans Revised?

We revise them every year, and updates are always available at touring plans.com. Be prepared for surprises, though: opening procedures and showtimes may change, for example, and you can't predict when an attraction might break down.

Tour Groups on Steroids

We've discovered that tour groups of up to 200 people sometimes use our plans. Unless your party is as large as that tour group, this development shouldn't alarm you. Because tour groups are big, they move slowly and have to stop periodically to collect stragglers. The tour guide also has to accommodate the unpredictability of five dozen or so bladders. In short, you should have no problem passing a group after the initial encounter.

"Bouncing Around"

Some readers object to crisscrossing a theme park as our touring plans sometimes require. A woman from Decatur, Georgia, told us she "got dizzy from all the bouncing around." Believe us, we empathize.

We've worked hard over the years to eliminate the need to crisscross a theme park in our touring plans. (In fact, our customized software can minimize walking instead of waiting in line, if that's important to you.) Occasionally, however, it's possible to save a lot of time in line with a few extra minutes of walking.

The reasons for this are varied. Sometimes a park is designed intentionally to require walking. In USF, for example, the most popular attraction (Harry Potter and the Escape from Gringotts in Diagon Alley) is placed at the farthest corner from the front gate, so guests are more evenly distributed throughout the day. Other times, you may be visiting just after a new attraction has opened that everyone wants to try. In that case, a special trip to visit the new attraction may be required earlier in the day than normal to avoid longer waits later.

And live shows, especially at USF, sometimes have performance schedules so at odds with each other (and the rest of the park's schedule) that orderly touring is impossible.

If you want to experience headliner attractions in one day without long waits, you can see those first (which requires crisscrossing the park), use Universal Express and single-rider lines (if available), or hope to squeeze in visits during parades and the last hour the park is open (which may not work).

If you have two days to visit Universal, use the two-day touring plans (see pages 405–408). These spread the popular attractions over two mornings and work great even when the parks close early.

Touring Plan Rejection

Some folks don't respond well to the regimentation of a touring plan. If you encounter this problem with someone in your party, roll with the punches, as this Maryland couple did:

> *The rest of the group was not receptive to the use of the touring plans. I think they all thought I was being a little too regimented about planning this vacation. Rather than argue, I left the touring plans behind as we ventured off to the parks. You can guess the outcome. We took videos and watched them when we returned home. About every 5 minutes or so, there's a shot of us all gathered around a park map trying to decide what to do next.*

This Syracuse, New York, couple compromised by following a plan until early afternoon, but then taking a break:

> *Getting there prior to park opening, touring consistently until about 2 p.m., and then leaving for a nap and a swim was a huge hit with my fiance, who had never been to Disney or Universal before. Sometimes we didn't even need to go back to the park at night because we had accomplished everything we wanted to in the 6 hours or so that we had been in the park.*

Finally, as a Connecticut woman alleges, the touring plans are incompatible with some readers' bladders, as well as their personalities:

> *When you write those plans next year, can you schedule bathroom breaks in there too? You expect us to be at a certain ride at a certain time and with no stops in between. The schedules are a problem if you are a laid-back, slow-moving, careful detail noticer. What were you thinking when you made these schedules?*

Before you injure your urinary tract, feel free to deviate from the touring plan as necessary to heed the call of nature. If you're using a customized plan in Lines, you can build in as many breaks (bathroom or otherwise) as you like, and the optimizer will plan around them.

WHAT TO EXPECT WHEN YOU
ARRIVE AT THE PARKS (ROPE DROP)

BECAUSE MOST TOURING PLANS ARE BASED ON being present when the theme park opens, you need to know about opening procedures. Universal Orlando's on-site resort transportation to the parks via buses and water taxis begins 2 hours before official opening, or 1 hour before Early Park Admission (see page 65). Guests staying on-site during peak periods will want to catch the first ride of the morning (or start walking around the time it leaves) to be the first into The Wizarding World during the early-entry period. Off-season visitors should arrive at the gates 15–30 minutes before Early Park Admission (EPA) begins.

The parking garage also opens 2 hours before official opening, but on days of exceptional attendance (like the grand opening of a new attraction), the garage has opened as early as 3 a.m. If you are driving to the resort and aren't eligible for EPA, plan to arrive at the Universal parking garage 45–60 minutes prior to official opening. If you need to purchase park admission, add another 15 minutes to that. It takes approximately 10–15 minutes to walk from the parking garage to the parks' entrance turnstiles, so you should arrive at the turnstiles 30–45 minutes before the park opens.

Lines tend to be evenly distributed at each turnstile. If you see a shorter line, however, get in it, especially if portable ticket scanners (which are usually faster than the fixed turnstiles) have been set up in front of the center gate.

Universal's turnstiles use biometric scanners that record a grid of intersecting points on your finger (not a fingerprint), for guests age 10 and older only, when using your ticket for the first time. Be sure to remember which finger you use to speed reentry. The scanners are wiped clean between each guest, but you may also request to show a photo ID instead. You'll also be asked to sign your pass, so you don't mix it up with those of other family members. Universal's finger scanners aren't nearly as efficient as the ones Disney uses, so be prepared for slowdowns at entry, as this Orchard Park, New York, family found:

The finger scanning going into the park and at Hogwarts Express did not work well. It randomly did not work for some in our party—very annoying and time-consuming.

Rope Drop at Universal Studios Florida

USF team members select a "first family" from the early risers at the turnstiles each morning and usher them in a few minutes early to open the park with an old-fashioned movie clapboard. It's no Magic Kingdom character welcome, but it's a cute moment worth catching if you can.

Once the gates open, there is no mad dash for Diagon Alley, nor is a literal rope dropped. When USF's turnstiles open for EPA, resort guests walk straight toward Revenge of the Mummy and are escorted to The Wizarding World via San Francisco. Day guests are restricted to the front of the park, where Despicable Me Minion Mayhem opens to all guests 10–15 minutes before the official opening.

On days when USF does not officially offer EPA, the gates may still open up to 15 minutes before opening, with Despicable Me typically running for all early guests. Guests can enter the Harry Potter and the Escape from Gringotts queue before official opening, but the ride may not begin running until park opening (or a few minutes before) on non-EPA mornings.

Most of the crowd will head for The Wizarding World of Harry Potter's Gringotts ride, which usually sees its longest waits between opening and early afternoon. Despicable Me, located a short distance past the entrance, also attracts large crowds, as do Transformers: The Ride 3-D and Hollywood Rip Ride Rockit. A smaller number of visitors will head for The Simpsons Ride or Revenge of the Mummy, but these attractions usually don't get crowded until an hour or two after the park has opened.

Rope Drop at Islands of Adventure

IOA's gates may open up to 15 minutes before the official opening time on days when EPA is not offered. Guests headed to The Wizarding World of Harry Potter–Hogsmeade are held at the bridge to Seuss Landing until 10 minutes before opening, while the remaining guests are sent to Marvel Super Hero Island, where they will be held near Cafe 4 until opening time. Once released into the park, most guests turn counterclockwise through Seuss Landing and make a beeline for Hogsmeade as soon as the park is open. A smaller number of guests will head clockwise for The Incredible Hulk Coaster (which may allow guests to ride a few minutes before the official opening time) and then continue through Toon Lagoon to Skull Island.

When EPA is offered at IOA, eligible guests may visit Marvel Super Hero Island, but most head straight to Hogsmeade as soon as the gates open. Guests without EPA privileges can still enter early but will be held in the Port of Entry and Seuss Landing. If IOA officially opens an hour after USF, only guests eligible for EPA may ride the Hogwarts Express during IOA's early-entry hour.

Unless you have early entry, our advice is to see The Amazing Adventures of Spider-Man and Reign of Kong first and save The Wizarding World until later in the day. Note that when one park opens before the other, guests arriving on the first Hogwarts Express train will reach the opposite Wizarding World at the same time or slightly after those entering from the front gates; therefore, you can't use the train to beat the crowds to Hagrid's. And when EPA hour concludes, guests already inside Hogsmeade have the advantage in queuing for the Jurassic World VelociCoaster and Reign of Kong, reaching Skull Island via Jurassic Park a few moments before the general public is released from the Marvel area.

Rope Drop at Volcano Bay

Arrival for Volcano Bay visitors is complicated by the fact that there is no parking at the water park itself, so all guests must be bused in from the main parking garage or resorts. Guests begin arriving at the turnstiles up to an hour before the park opens, but distribution of the mandatory TapuTapu wristbands doesn't begin until moments before early entry starts. Once it does, hotel guests and off-site visitors alike are allowed in, with those eligible for EPA funneled to the left for admittance to the attractions. Day guests are herded to the right, where they may rent lockers and purchase food while awaiting their release into the rest of the park, which may happen up to 30 minutes before official opening. Upon entering, most bolt for the lockers and beach chairs, with all the prime spots around the wave pool usually snapped up within an hour of opening. Long lines for guests trying to rent cabanas also immediately form at the concierge hut closest to the entrance. All slides start the day with "Ride Now" status, but queues can build swiftly, and Virtual Line waits for popular slides may exceed an hour by 11 a.m.

unofficial **TIP**
Decorative planters inhibit lines from forming at Volcano Bay's center turnstiles, making the outside lines longer. Squeeze through to the middle lanes for quicker entry.

EARLY PARK ADMISSION (EARLY ENTRY)

THE MOST VALUABLE PERK available for free to all Universal on-site resort hotel guests is Early Park Admission (EPA, also sometimes referred to as early entry), which grants entry to The Wizarding World of Harry Potter 1 hour before the general public. Thirty minutes to an hour of early entry is also offered every morning at the Volcano Bay water park. In addition to guests staying at on-site hotels, guests holding certain designated vacation packages—purchased through Universal Orlando Vacations (☎ 877-801-9720; universalorlandovacations.com) and including both accommodations at an off-site Universal partner hotel *and* theme park admission—are allowed in early. Premier Pass holders can take advantage of EPA at USF or IOA on any morning, as can Preferred Pass holders on select days (block-outs apply).

Which park you may enter on any particular day, and which attractions will be operating, are at Universal's discretion and will vary with the attendance seasons. The turnstiles to the park(s) participating in early entry will open 60–90 minutes before the official opening time. Both hotel and day guests will be admitted to the park, and each EPA-eligible guest (including children) will need to show his or her own room key or annual pass to pass beyond the park's entry plaza during the early admission hour. Guests not eligible for EPA will be held in an alternate area to await the official opening time.

During EPA, all of the attractions, shops, and restaurants in the participating Wizarding World area should be open, along with select attractions outside the Harry Potter area. Attractions offer standby queues during EPA (along with single-rider lines and child swap, where available), but Express Passes are valid only during regular operating hours. EPA, when available at USF, allows early birds to ride Escape from Gringotts with a minimal wait, as this father from New York City experienced:

> We got to the USF turnstiles 10 minutes before 6 [for 7 a.m. EPA] and had only five people in front of us. Soon there were plenty behind us, however! They let us in at about 6:20, and we were among the first 100–150 people to enter Diagon Alley and subsequently Gringotts. We essentially walked onto the ride, slowed only by our amazed awe at walking through the Gringotts lobby and seeing all the astonishing attractions in the line. We were through so quickly that we immediately got in the singles line and literally walked on the ride a second time, and then a third time with the singles line, which by this time was backed up a bit toward the steps leading to the loading platform, resulting in about a 20-minute wait. It was now 8 a.m. and we had been on the ride three times. The non-resort guests were now streaming into Diagon Alley to be welcomed by a standby entrance to Gringotts, which was marked 180 minutes.

Most of the feedback we get about EPA at Universal is extremely positive, like this comment from a multigenerational family of seven:

> Early entry to the park was a game changer and gave us enough time to do everything we wanted to do by noon. This allowed us to go back to the hotel and rest. (Best idea ever!)

However, because EPA crowds are concentrated in The Wizarding World, it can quickly become overcrowded, particularly on days when only one park participates. This comment from a Carbondale, Illinois, reader reflects a common criticism of Universal's early entry:

> I wasn't a fan of the early admission at Universal. Most of the rides are not open, and you are shuttled back to Harry Potter with everyone else. The early admission did not seem like a perk.

If you aren't at the front of the pack when the turnstiles open, but you're eligible for Express access, you may be better off riding Gringotts just as EPA ends, according to this reader from Natick, Massachusetts:

> The early-entry hour was a bit disappointing because it was soooo crowded in Diagon Alley. It was absolute gridlock in the wand shop from the moment the park opened. We waited about half an hour for Gringotts during that first hour. Then immediately afterward, at 9 a.m., when we could use Express, we walked right onto Gringotts.

Instead, guests with Universal Express Passes may want to use the early-entry hour to enjoy Ollivanders and the interactive wand effects, as this mom from Dallas suggests:

> If your kids want to cast every spell and wander around Hogsmeade and Diagon Alley for hours, do that first thing in the morning, especially if you have Express Passes to ride the other rides.

Similarly, when IOA opens early, the Forbidden Journey ride typically operates only about 25% of its ride vehicles during EPA, which makes the queue move maddeningly slow. If the queue is backed up beyond the talking portraits, you may want to enjoy the other Hogsmeade attractions and save Forbidden Journey until afternoon, lest you spend most of the hour inching through Hogwarts's boarding area. Also, if the Gringotts or Forbidden Journey attractions are not operational when early entry begins, skip them and try again late in the day; by the time they begin running in the morning, there will be a huge backlog of riders.

Universal publishes its EPA calendar several months in advance at tinyurl.com/UniEPA, but procedures seem to change often and arbitrarily with no warning. Ask at your hotel's front desk to find out what opening procedures are in effect during your visit.

IOA-Only Early Park Admission

At certain off-peak times, only IOA (and not USF) may admit eligible guests for EPA. IOA-only EPA was in effect during the fall of 2020. The following attractions should be available during IOA-only EPA:

• Flight of the Hippogriff	• Hogwarts Express (only if USF is open)
• Hagrid's Magical Creatures Motorbike Adventure	• The Incredible Hulk Coaster
• Harry Potter and the Forbidden Journey	• Ollivanders Wand Shop

On days that only IOA offers EPA, USF may still unofficially open up to 15 minutes early, with Despicable Me Minion Mayhem open for all guests (hotel and off-site alike).

Guests entering USF early may also enter the queue for Escape from Gringotts, though the ride itself usually won't begin running until just before the park officially opens.

No matter which park offers EPA, the Hogwarts Express does not provide a shortcut around the rope drop rush. The first Hogwarts Express train from Hogsmeade Station should depart shortly after both parks have opened their gates for the day. The first trainload of guests riding from IOA will enter Diagon Alley a few minutes after the first guests entering through USF's front gates. Likewise, the day's first train riders coming from USF will find themselves standing in line for Hogsmeade's attractions behind the crowd that came straight into IOA. Early-entry guests at IOA are held at the bridge between Hogsmeade and Jurassic Park or in Marvel near Cafe 4 until the park's official opening time, at which point they may proceed to Skull Island: Reign of Kong or any other attraction.

USF-Only Early Park Admission

For the first half of 2020, EPA was confined to USF, and it may return there in the future. The following attractions should be available during USF-only EPA:

• Despicable Me Minion Mayhem	• Ollivanders Wand Shop
• Harry Potter and the Escape from Gringotts	

In addition, Despicable Me Minion Mayhem usually opens to all park guests 10–15 minutes before EPA ends. Day guests are sometimes also allowed to queue for Transformers: The Ride 3-D and Hollywood Rip Ride Rockit prior to the official park opening time.

The Hogwarts Express train from King's Cross Station will not begin running to The Wizarding World of Harry Potter–Hogsmeade in IOA until both parks have opened their gates to guests. The first trainload of guests riding from USF will enter Hogsmeade shortly after the first guests entering through IOA's front gates.

Two-Park Early Park Admission (Peak Season)

Universal Orlando only guarantees early admission to one park per day, but during the busiest times of the year—primarily the weeks around Easter and Christmas—Universal offers EPA to The Wizarding World of Harry Potter areas at both USF (Diagon Alley) and IOA (Hogsmeade).

When both parks are scheduled to open at the same time, Hogwarts Express will begin running when EPA starts.

The following attractions should be available during peak season early entry:

UNIVERSAL STUDIOS FLORIDA

• Despicable Me Minion Mayhem	• Hogwarts Express (only if IOA is open)
• Harry Potter and the Escape from Gringotts	• Ollivanders Wand Shop

ISLANDS OF ADVENTURE

• Flight of the Hippogriff	• Hogwarts Express (only if USF is open)
• Hagrid's Magical Creatures Motorbike Adventure	• The Incredible Hulk Coaster
• Harry Potter and the Forbidden Journey	• Ollivanders Wand Shop

Volcano Bay Early Park Admission

In addition to the early entry offered at USF and IOA, Volcano Bay also opens 30 minutes–1 hour early every morning for all on-site resort hotel guests, with many of its attractions operating. The following attractions should be available during early entry:

• Honu & ika Moana Raft Slides	• Krakatau Aqua Coaster
• Kala & Tai Nui Body Slides	• Ohyah & Ohno Drop Slides
• Ko'okiri Body Plunge	

While EPA is a wonderful luxury in The Wizarding World, at the water park it's an absolute necessity. Because the park closes when it reaches capacity, which on busy days may be within hours of the official opening time, early admission is the only way to be guaranteed admittance to Volcano Bay, much less have a chance to enjoy most of the slides.

During the early-entry hour, most, if not all, of the slides are kept at "Ride Now" status, allowing guests to take advantage of the relatively short lines. During peak season, using EPA is just about the only way to experience all the slides in one day without purchasing an Express Pass, as one woman from Stamford, Connecticut, found:

You are only able to get the "Ride Now" signs if you come for early admission. The moment the park opens to the public, the waiting times for the attractions increase fast. If you don't have early-admission privileges, you may be able to do three or four rides during the day, as waiting times longer then 100 minutes are typical. We came at 7:30 and did the rides we wanted, then left in the afternoon.

Off-site guests who aren't eligible for early entry should still try to get to the gates at least 30 minutes before official opening, potentially getting a few minutes' head start on the slides. If you aren't able to arrive that early, save yourself a lot of frustration and skip Volcano Bay until you can. Alternatively, use a multiday park-to-park pass to sample some slides in the late afternoon (preferably post-rainstorm) after spending the morning in USF or IOA.

To prevent overcrowding, Universal caps attendance inside Volcano Bay at a maximum of 8,000–10,000 guests (far less during social distancing), a limit that can be reached within hours after opening during the peak summer period. When the park approaches maximum capacity, Universal first restricts day visitors, then on-site guests. The park usually reopens its gates as guests depart in the afternoon, but tickets are not date-specific, so no refunds or rain checks are issued if you are refused entry after capacity is reached.

Annual Pass Holder Early Park Admission

Premier Pass holders may use EPA at USF or IOA on any day of the year, while Preferred Pass holders can enter USF or IOA early on most days (see tinyurl.com/APearly for details). During Annual Passholder Appreciation Days, held in the off-season, Power and Seasonal Pass holders can use EPA at IOA or USF on select dates, and all 3-Park pass holders can take advantage of EPA at Volcano Bay without having to stay on-site.

UNIVERSAL EXPRESS

THIS SYSTEM ALLOWS GUESTS to "skip the line" and experience an attraction via a special queue with little or no waiting. Guests approach the marked Universal Express entrance at participating attractions, present their Universal Express Pass to the greeter for scanning, and proceed to ride with a significantly reduced wait—usually 20% or less of the posted standby time, or no more than a 15- to 20-minute wait. For rides that use a Virtual Line like Race Through New York Starring Jimmy Fallon, you'll be able to enter the attraction lobby whenever you like without a prearranged return time.

Though Disney's FastPass+ and Universal Express both let guests bypass the typical wait, there are three major differences between them. While Disney's system requires scheduling your ride reservation hours or days ahead of time, Universal Express involves no advance planning; simply visit any eligible operating attraction whenever you choose, no return time windows required. Also, FastPass+ is only offered at a select list of designated attractions, while nearly all the attractions at Universal (with a couple exceptions, noted later) accept Express. Finally, unlike FastPass+, Universal Express is not free.

Three versions of Universal Express are available, all of which require you to cough up more money beyond your park admission:

UNIVERSAL EXPRESS PASS   Available for purchase online or in the parks, allowing one person one ride on each attraction that participates in Universal Express. (Note that for single-use Express, each Hogwarts Express station counts as a separate attraction, so you can ride the train once in each direction.)

UNIVERSAL EXPRESS UNLIMITED PASS   Available for purchase online or in the parks (either bundled with admission or separately), allowing one person an unlimited number of rides on any attraction that participates in Universal Express.

ON-SITE HOTEL UNIVERSAL EXPRESS UNLIMITED PASS   Included for all guests at the top three Universal Resort hotels (Hard Rock, Portofino Bay, and Royal Pacific) at no extra cost, allowing each person staying on-site an unlimited number of rides on any attraction that participates in Universal Express. Note that the free Express Passes are not valid at Volcano Bay.

No matter which version of Universal Express you use, it works the same: Present your pass to a greeter at each attraction entrance, get it scanned for verification, and enjoy your expedited entertainment. (Universal has been experimenting with a facial-recognition system for identifying Express Pass holders, but it has not been fully rolled out yet.) At shows, you can produce your pass for priority seating 15 minutes before showtime, but that's less of a perk because Universal's large theaters rarely fill up.

It's worth noting that, while almost all the Express queues are themed, in a few cases (Revenge of the Mummy and Men in Black Alien Attack at USF; Doctor Doom's Fearfall and Skull Island: Reign of Kong at IOA), they sacrifice significant scenic elements and story setup that the standby line sees. We recommend experiencing these attractions using the standard queue for your first time, if time permits. Express Pass users at Harry Potter and the Forbidden Journey and Escape from Gringotts rides get to see nearly all of the same scenery as standby guests, and none of the parks' other Express queues skip anything important.

Finally, be aware that Hagrid's Magical Creatures Motorbike Adventure was not yet accepting Express Passes at press time. Pteranodon

Flyers at IOA, a slow-loading children's ride with limited capacity, also does not accept Universal Express, though it does offer free Virtual Line return times. Neither do the Ollivanders Wandkeeper presentations or the kiddie waterslide in Fievel's Playland at USF. Further, all of the Express types (including the free passes for resort guests) are valid only during regular operating hours and not during separately ticketed events. Separate Express Passes are available at an additional cost for special events such as Rock the Universe and Halloween Horror Nights.

PREMIER PASS UNIVERSAL EXPRESS AFTER 4 P.M. Holders of the top-of-the-line Premier Pass get free Universal Express access at USF and IOA every day from 4 p.m. until park closing (excluding special events like Halloween). Even though it's officially valid only once per attraction per day, we've rarely been denied a re-ride.

COVID *tip*
When parks close early due to restricted operations, Premier Pass holders may be eligible for Express after 2 p.m.

Universal Express and Express Unlimited for Purchase

Anyone can purchase Universal Express for one or both theme parks and for either single (one ride only on each participating attraction) or unlimited use. The number of Express Passes is limited each day, and they can sell out. Increase your chances of securing passes by buying and printing them at home from Universal's website. They are available up to eight months in advance at tinyurl.com/UORExpress. You'll need to know when you plan on using it, though, because prices vary depending on the date.

Universal Express Pass prices range from $59.99 for a one-park single-use pass in slow season to $259.99 for a two-park unlimited pass on a holiday; the top-tier passes are significantly cheaper when bundled with a park-to-park multiday pass. Incidentally, the online calendar of Express Pass prices is a great indicator of how crowded Universal will be on any given day; the more expensive the passes, the more packed the park will be.

You can also buy Universal Express at the theme parks' ticket windows, just outside the front gates, but it's faster to do so inside the parks. Express Passes are sold at the large stores near the front of each park and in most major gift shops. Universal also sells Express from freestanding kiosks that seem to proliferate around the parks like mushrooms during peak seasons. When the park is open late, Universal sometimes sells an unadvertised Express Pass valid after 4 p.m. only for about $35; ask at any Express sales location for details.

Universal Express for Resort Guests

This program allows guests at Universal's three original luxury resorts (Hard Rock, Portofino Bay, and Royal Pacific) to bypass the regular lines at USF and IOA and use the Express entrance anytime and as often as desired. Guests of one of the above-mentioned hotels may simply present their room key card for admission through any Universal Express attraction entrance inside USF or IOA.

Universal Express for resort guests is available from the moment of check-in until park closing time on the day of checkout. And even though check-in time at Universal's on-site hotels isn't until 4 p.m., guests can retrieve room keys and Express Passes as early in the morning as they are able to arrive, and guests may drop their luggage in the lobby and head to the parks until their room is ready. Therefore, a single night's stay on-site yields two full days of Universal Express access. This perk far surpasses any benefit accorded to guests of Disney resorts; combined with the hour of Early Park Admission to The Wizarding World, it helps make touring Universal Orlando a remarkably low-stress experience for on-site guests, even during peak attendance periods.

A father from Snellville, Georgia, did the math and discovered that it was cheaper for his family to stay at a Universal resort than buy Universal Express:

> The benefits of staying on-property are worth it, with early entry to The Wizarding World and Express Unlimited privileges at both parks. We got a room at the Royal Pacific Resort for $349 on a Saturday night, which allowed us to use Universal Express Saturday and Sunday. The room cost $43.63 per person per day, while an [à la carte] Express Pass this same weekend would have cost $56 per person per day, and we still would have had to pay for a hotel.

Universal Express at Volcano Bay

Universal Express Passes valid at Volcano Bay are sold on select days inside the park at the concierge stands or in advance online. Volcano Bay's basic Universal Express Passes cost $19.99–$69.99 (depending on the season). Express Passes are valid for one ride each on select slides, which include the Krakatau Aqua Coaster and Honu & ika Moana but exclude the Kala & Tai Nui body slides, Ohyah & Ohno drop slides, and Ko'okiri Body Plunge. A 1-Day Universal Express Plus Pass costs $39.99–$99.99 for a single trip down every slide in the park; at press time, no unlimited usage Express option was available. Express allows you to act as if participating attractions say "Ride Now," but even though you won't need a TapuTapu return time, you'll still experience some waiting before your slide.

Is Universal Express Worth It?

No matter when you use it, Universal Express will significantly reduce the amount of time you spend waiting in queues at Universal Orlando. But whether or not that time saving is worth it depends on the season you visit, hours of park operation, and crowd levels.

During busy periods, Universal Express users should wait no more than 15–20 minutes for a ride, even when the standby wait is well over an hour. That's a significant time savings and may make the difference between seeing all your favorite headliners in a single day or going home disappointed.

During slow periods, Express users should experience little to no wait at most attractions and can practically walk on to most rides. However, the standby waits will typically top out between 15 and 30 minutes at these times, making the total minutes saved with Express much less impressive.

Universal Express is *not* mandatory for enjoying the parks (as we've heard some claim), just so long as you show up bright and early with a well-organized agenda. If you want to sleep in and arrive at a park after opening, Express is an effective, albeit expensive, way to avoid long lines at the headliner attractions, especially during holidays and busy times. If, however, you arrive at least 30 minutes before park opening and you use our touring plans (see pages 395–408), you should experience the lowest possible waits.

If you aren't eligible for free Express Passes, we encourage you to try the touring plans first, but if waits for rides become intolerable, you can always buy Express in the parks (provided they haven't sold out, an infrequent occurrence).

A New York mom had a trouble-free experience, but she questions the value of the investment:

> *Universal Express was neither necessary nor consistently effective. By arriving at park opening, we were able to see many attractions right away without needing the passes at all. The passes helped on about three attractions between the two parks—a poor return for an investment of $156, but it was like life insurance: good to have just in case. On Dudley Do-Right's Ripsaw Falls, we still had to wait 30 minutes even with Express, whereas with Disney's free FastPass+ we never waited more than 5 minutes for an attraction. The only aspect of UE that was better than FP+ is that touring order was unaffected: UE could be used whenever you first approached an attraction instead of your having to come back later.*

On the other hand, this Kansas City family thought very highly of the Express Unlimited Passes included in their Royal Pacific stay:

> *The free Express Pass you get by staying at one of the top three resorts is a lifesaver. We never waited in line more than 15 minutes, and it was usually closer to 5. For my roller coaster–loving family, this was great. We didn't have a scheduled time to ride anything like at Disney, so we could stray from our plan and re-ride The Incredible Hulk Coaster or Hollywood Rip Ride Rockit over and over again.*

Another reader from San Jose, California, concurred:

> *In 90°F heat and 80% humidity, having an Express Pass by staying at the Royal Pacific made all the difference. The ability to get through the ride queues quickly made up for the higher cost of the room.*

A reader from Moore, Oklahoma, added:

The Unlimited Express Pass was fantastic, especially in a park where I knew nothing about the rides beforehand. I'd still want it if I return.

And this mom from Massachusetts agreed:

Universal Express did not disappoint. We walked on to every ride we wanted to, and we could easily and immediately re-ride our faves with no wait. I would definitely either stay at Royal Pacific or spring for Universal Express on my next trip. It was wonderful to have that flexibility with our kids. We could wait to ride Gringotts the first day, until our 8-year-old had worked up the nerve. Then we could spontaneously ride again—right away with no wait!

Finally, you'll want to devise a convenient way to keep track of your pass, as this Endicott, New York, reader suggests:

The paper Express Passes were not nearly as user friendly as Disney's MagicBands. The lanyard was a lifesaver, or we surely would have lost something.

Universal will happily sell you a souvenir lanyard with a plastic pouch, so you can proudly wear your admission around your neck for all to see. Universal's lanyards start at around $12 for a basic one and come in a variety of character themes, including the colors of each Hogwarts house, for $14. You can also pick up equally usable and far cheaper (though less magical) versions at your local office supply store.

How Universal Express Affects Crowd Conditions at Attractions

Guests using Universal Express don't have to modify their touring behavior in any way; simply visit any attraction at will and enjoy the shorter waits. However, the Express effect can be somewhat less salutatory for guests without Express. The standby and Express queues at each attraction meet up shortly before the boarding area, and attendants are supposed to merge them so that Express guests wait 15 minutes or less, without the standby guests' wait being inflated beyond the estimate posted outside.

Typically, this means about half of each ride's capacity is dedicated to Express guests, which ordinarily keeps both queues flowing smoothly. The catch is that, because Universal Express guests (unlike users of Disney FastPass+) don't schedule ride times in advance, the number of them waiting in a queue at any given time is highly variable and unpredictable, as one Highlands Ranch, Colorado, reader pointed out:

The Universal Express Pass is not the same as Disney's FastPass. If everyone holding an Express Pass decides to use it at the same time on the same ride, wait times can get very long, making the pass seem less of a bargain. That being said, an Express Pass almost seemed a necessity on the day we were there because it was a short day due to Halloween Horror Nights and we weren't able to make it there for park opening.

As a result, an unexpected backlog of Express guests—either because of a sudden influx of pass users or a temporary technical breakdown that pauses the line—can force Universal to increase the ratio of Express to standby, slowing non-Express guests' progress to a crawl.

While that's great news for Universal Express users, this can dramatically affect crowd movement (and touring-plan usage) for those without it, as a woman from Yorktown, Virginia, writes:

People in the Express line were let in at a rate of about 10 to 1 over the regular-line folks. This created bottlenecks and long waits for people who didn't have the Express privilege at the very times when it's supposed to be easier to get around!

A Potter fan from Brevard, North Carolina, didn't appreciate the advantage afforded Express guests:

It was obvious that anyone who paid for an Express Pass had preferential treatment—they let in eight Express guests to one standby guest at the Gringotts ride after I had stood in line for almost 2½ hours. I feel like people who buy "normal" tickets are second-class citizens.

If you encounter this situation while waiting standby, simply grit your teeth and take some deep yoga breaths; the situation normally clears up quickly, and your total wait should still be approximately as originally advertised. In case of a major traffic jam where the standby line stops moving altogether, calculate how much time you've invested already, and consider hopping out of line and returning later when things are running more smoothly. And for those who really can't stand watching Express guests pass them by: If you can't beat 'em, join 'em, like this reader from Doylestown, Pennsylvania:

On the third day we finally bought Express Passes because we were miserable standing in lines for so long and watching Express Pass holders pass us again and again and again. It made a huge difference, and next time, we will absolutely stay on-site for the early admission hours and Express Pass benefits.

VIRTUAL LINES

UNIVERSAL HAS INTRODUCED another line-skipping service to its theme parks, but unlike the aforementioned Express options, Virtual Line is completely free for all park guests, regardless of hotel or ticket type. With Virtual Lines guests may claim time slots for certain rides on a first-come, first-serve basis and can experience the attraction with a minimal wait after returning during their assigned hour. The service is mandatory for most slides at Volcano Bay, where it is tied to the TapuTapu wristbands; see page 359 for a detailed explanation. The method and usefulness of Virtual Lines vary depending on the attraction. In USF, Virtual Line is mandatory at Race Through New York Starring Jimmy Fallon during select times of day and is offered as an option at Fast & Furious: Supercharged; return times are available at kiosks outside each attraction or through the official Universal Orlando mobile app. In IOA, Virtual Line is sometimes available for Pteranodon Flyers at a kiosk outside Camp Jurassic; all riders must be present to make a reservation. Hagrid's Magical Creatures Motorbike Adventure has the capability of offering a Virtual Line when the standby queue grows excessively long, and Virtual Line usage may be mandatory on busier days.

To use Universal's Virtual Line system, make sure that the Universal app is properly installed on your mobile device and that you've given it permission to access your device's location services. You don't actually need to be signed in to your account or have valid admission attached to the app, and you don't even need to be inside the park to join a Virtual Line, but your phone's GPS must register that you are inside the geofence surrounding Universal's property. That means you can access the Virtual Line system from the parking garage, CityWalk, or even your on-site hotel room, but not from off-site hotels or your home.

Get started by tapping the main menu button in the top-left corner of the app, and select "Virtual Line Experience." Tap "Virtual Line Venues" to see a list of rides currently using the system. If an attraction displays a wait time number, then Virtual Line is optional and is usually only useful if times are available immediately or if the posted standby wait is over 20 minutes. If an attraction only says "Virtual Line," then you'll need a return time (or an Express Pass, at participating rides) if you want to experience it.

Tap on the attraction you are interested in, and scroll down to "Virtual Line Pass." When you tap there, if any return times are available, the system will present you with a slider to indicate your party size, followed by a series of bubbles representing available half-hour windows. Pick the number of people in your group (up to eight) and the time slot you wish to secure, then press the button at the bottom of the screen.

If everything works, you'll receive a confirmation screen with a QR code, which you'll need to have scanned when your time to ride arrives. You can retrieve this code again later (or modify or cancel it) through the Virtual Line menu by tapping again on the ride you reserved, but it doesn't hurt to take a screenshot as well.

Unfortunately, many times the Virtual Line system will show a blank screen with no return windows to choose from. Or worse yet, it will present you with times, only to say "sorry, an error has occurred" when you try to confirm your selection. When this happens, tap cancel and refresh the page, or close and restart the Universal app.

Virtual Line passes are first distributed approximately 20–30 minutes before the park's scheduled opening time, with the first return windows beginning 5 or 10 minutes before the official opening. Not all of the day's allocated Virtual Line passes are available at once; rather, small batches of additional time slots are released sporadically throughout the day. So if you don't initially see available Virtual Line passes for a coveted attraction (like Hagrid's coaster), keep trying periodically because persistence usually pays off.

Each user of the Universal app can hold Virtual Line passes for two different attractions at the same time, but you can't reserve the same ride a second time until you've used or canceled your first return time. You may find that Virtual Line passes don't automatically disappear from your app after being scanned at the queue entrance, thereby preventing you from making a new reservation. If this happens, just tap the garbage can icon in the top-right corner of the QR code screen to manually delete the used pass.

Because every Universal app user can reserve two rides for themselves and up to seven others, the Virtual Line system gives larger parties a distinct advantage over solo travelers. A family of five could hold five different five-person reservations for Hagrid's Magical Creatures Motorbike Adventure at once, plus appointments at five other attractions, for a total of 10 rides per person!

Once your Virtual Line return time arrives, proceed to the attraction with your QR code in hand. There may be an initial queue outside for guests needing mandatory lockers, along with another line for postride bag retrieval; if you don't have anything to stow, look for a scanning checkpoint closer to the actual entrance. Once past the locker logjam, you should wait 20 minutes or less before boarding the attraction.

Finally, if something goes wrong and your ride is unavailable when your return time arrives—due to technical difficulties, weather delays, or the like—your Virtual Line pass should automatically convert into a free one-time-use Express Pass, valid any time until the end of that operating day at the original attraction (assuming it starts running again) or select other rides.

SINGLE-RIDER LINES *(temporarily unavailable)*

ONE OTHER TIME-SAVING OPTION available to all Universal Orlando guests without extra charge is the single-rider (or singles) line. Several attractions at USF and IOA have this special line for guests traveling alone, or at least willing to be temporarily separated from their companions. Single riders wait in a separate queue and are slipped into vacant seats left by large groups without (theoretically) impacting the other lines. Singles lines are a great alternative for those unable or unwilling to cough up the dough for Universal Express Passes, as this reader from Portland, Connecticut, points out:

> *Single-rider lines are the key to enjoying the parks. While you may miss some of the theming of the queue areas, it's a terrific trade-off to saving 45 minutes per ride. If on a budget, it's a great alternative to the Universal Express Pass granted to guests of the deluxe resorts.*

The singles line is often just as fast as the Express line. However, because the speed of the singles line is highly dependent on the flow of odd-numbered parties through the other queues, the wait time can be extremely unpredictable. At some times we've walked onto Forbidden Journey via the singles line when the standby wait time was more than an hour; at others we've stood longer in Hollywood Rip Ride Rockit's singles line than the posted standby wait.

Single-rider lines open at the discretion of the ride attendants and may temporarily close if crowds are very light (because they aren't needed) or very heavy (when the singles queue becomes filled to capacity, which happens frequently at Gringotts). In the latter case, try hanging around the entrance for 15 or 20 minutes, which is usually how long it takes for the singles line to shrink enough to be reopened.

Also note that some queues (particularly those of Forbidden Journey and Escape from Gringotts) are attractions in themselves and deserve to be experienced during your first ride. Even so, we strongly recommend using the singles line whenever possible—it will decrease your overall wait and leave more time for repeat rides or just ambling around the parks.

Singles lines are almost always available at the following attractions:

SINGLE-RIDER LINES AT UNIVERSAL STUDIOS FLORIDA	SINGLE-RIDER LINES AT ISLANDS OF ADVENTURE
Despicable Me Minion Mayhem	The Amazing Adventures of Spider-Man
Fast & Furious: Supercharged	Doctor Doom's Fearfall
Harry Potter and the Escape from Gringotts	Hagrid's Magical Creatures Motorbike Adventure
Hollywood Rip Ride Rockit	Harry Potter and the Forbidden Journey
Men in Black Alien Attack	The Incredible Hulk Coaster
Revenge of the Mummy	Jurassic Park River Adventure
Transformers: The Ride 3-D	Skull Island: Reign of Kong

COVID *tip*
Single-rider access may not be available due to social distancing.

In addition, Universal intermittently offers single-rider access at Dudley Do-Right's Ripsaw Falls in IOA, and at The Simpsons Ride and E.T. Adventure in USF.

VIP TOURS

FOR THE ULTIMATE no-expenses-spared Universal Orlando experience, book a VIP tour of one or both parks. VIP guests are given the red-carpet treatment at both parks and never have to worry about waiting in line. And don't worry if you aren't a genuine VIP—or even a social media pseudo-celebrity—because at Universal, anyone can be treated like the rich and famous . . . for a price.

Universal offers two types of VIP tours: nonexclusive and private. On nonexclusive tours, your party of up to 6 guests will be paired with other guests to form a group of up to 12. Nonexclusive tours begin at 11 a.m. and last 5–7 hours. Your guide will expedite you onto a minimum of 8 attractions (10 if you take the two-park option) based on group consensus. On a nonexclusive tour, you're at Universal's mercy as to whom you might be paired up with, but you can indicate your interests to your guide upon arrival; if you are a party of thrill-seeking adults, and you're matched with a family of small children, ask if you can swap before your group gets moving.

Private tours give you free reign to set your start time and make your own itinerary because the guide is dedicated to only your party for a full 8 hours. Private tours are mandatory if your party has seven or more members. You can even ride your favorite ride over and over all day, if you like.

Either way, your VIP experience begins with free valet parking and a complimentary Continental breakfast in the private guest services lounge. In addition to back dooring you into rides—bypassing even the Universal Express queues—and getting you reserved seating at shows, VIP tour guides are a font of trivia about the history and operations of the parks and can even grant backstage access to see how some of the magic is done, like a glimpse underneath Revenge of the Mummy's ride track or inside Transformer's high-tech control booth (not available during social distancing). VIP tours also include access to the American Express lounge in USF and a complimentary midday meal. Nonexclusive one-park tour guests each get a one-day Quick-Service Universal Dining Plan to use where they wish on an entrée and snacks, while two-park nonexclusive VIP tour guests get an exclusive lunch inside USF's Cafe La Bamba, where chefs will prepare a sampling of signature dishes from restaurants around the resort. Private VIP tour guests receive two full-service meals inside the theme parks or at CityWalk, along with a three-day My Universal Photos package (valid starting on their first tour day). At the end of the tour, your souvenir VIP lanyard serves as an Express Unlimited Pass for the rest of the day and offers discounts on food and merchandise.

Perhaps most important, VIP tours are the quickest way to skip the queues at the headlining Harry Potter attractions during peak times, when even the Express entrances can be overwhelmed; during the height of Diagon Alley's opening summer, when guests were waiting more than 4 hours just for Gringotts, Bob and Len were able to experience everything in both Wizarding Worlds (including lunch and ice cream) plus other park highlights in a little more than 5 hours. Currently, a VIP tour is the only way to cut the line at Hagrid's Magical Creatures Motorbike Adventure.

Of course, this kind of star treatment doesn't come cheap. While VIP tours start at $189 on select dates during the slowest seasons, at most times, a one-day, one-park nonexclusive VIP tour of USF or IOA will run you $209–$219 per person. A one-day tour of both parks starts at $199 and is typically $219–$239. However, during peak pricing times (the weeks around Christmas and Easter), those rates jump as high as $429 for one park, and $449 for both.

Private-tour pricing approaches "if you have to ask, you can't afford it" territory, starting at $3,099 for a day in both parks; one-park exclusive tours are available during off-peak periods on special request, but you will only save a couple hundred dollars off the two-park price. That flat rate is good for one to five guests; additional guests (up to a total of 10) cost another $375 each for a two-park tour. During peak times (Christmas and spring break), those base prices increase to $3,999, plus $450 for each additional guest. Finally, if you splurge on the ultimate two-day, two-park private tour, you'll be poorer by $4,899 ($6,699 during peak periods).

Before you break out your credit card, there's one final catch: in addition to not including tax, the aforementioned prices are on top of admission, which is required and not included with any VIP tour.

Whether the VIP tours are worth it depends largely on your net worth and your tolerance for any type of wait. Having taken them many times over the years, we can say that the experience is a dream come true for theme park junkies (who will get their money's worth in insider info alone), as well as anyone allergic to rubbing elbows with unwashed hordes. If you were already planning to pony up for Express Unlimited Passes, the extra couple hundred per person (depending on the season) could seem a bargain in the heat of summer. For most visitors, a stay at a luxury on-site hotel (with free Express Unlimited included) is probably a more economical investment, but no one we know who has taken a VIP tour has regretted it, even if it may forever ruin the regular park-going experience for you.

Nonexclusive tours can be booked online through an interactive calendar with availability and pricing at tinyurl.com/univip, but private tours must be booked by phone at ☎ 866-346-9350. If you want to take a VIP tour, order early because they can fill up quickly at busier times.

Note that all of the previously mentioned tours are offered only during regular daytime operating hours. Different VIP tours with their own pricing may be available during separately ticketed special events such as Halloween Horror Nights (see page 311).

FREE BEHIND-THE-SCENES TOURS *(temporarily unavailable)*

IF YOU WANT TO FEEL LIKE A VIP but can't afford the fare, Universal generously offers unpublicized free backstage tours at several

COVID *tip*
Backstage tours may not be available due to social distancing.

attractions to any guest who inquires (subject to staff availability). For details on these "secret" behind-the-scenes experiences, read the attraction descriptions for Men in Black Alien Attack, Race Through New York Starring Jimmy Fallon, and Revenge of the Mummy at USF in Part Seven; and The Incredible Hulk Coaster, Jurassic Park Discovery Center, and Skull Island: Reign of Kong at IOA in Part Eight.

TECHNICAL REHEARSALS

TECHNICAL REHEARSALS, OR SOFT OPENINGS as they are commonly called, are when Universal uses its paying guests as guinea pigs and allows them to preview an attraction that isn't yet ready for prime time. Technical rehearsals may be held anywhere from a few weeks to a few days before a new ride officially opens, but they are never preannounced or guaranteed; frontline employees may be instructed to deny that any opening is possible until the moment they open the queue. In exchange for bragging rights that they were the first inside a hot new attraction, technical rehearsal participants must accept the possibility of waiting a long time without ever getting to ride, as the soft opening may end at any moment.

For theme park junkies who live in the area, technical rehearsals can be both a blessing and a curse; some folks stood in front of Diagon Alley for more than 30 consecutive days waiting for a soft opening, and even then the Gringotts ride never had a public preview before grand opening. Similar scenes occurred at IOA in the spring of 2019 prior to Hagrid's Magical Creatures Motorbike Adventure's opening, as fans waited fruitlessly for days, fueled by rumors on social media. Unless you're a local with lots of time on your hands, or on an extended vacation and obsessed with the about-to-open attraction, avoid spending any of your valuable time waiting for a ride that may or may not open. Instead, enjoy everything else the parks have to offer, and keep your ears open (and an eye on the @theugseries Twitter feed) just in case.

UNIVERSAL ORLANDO INSIDER HACKS

WANT TO CRUISE THROUGH the Universal Orlando Resort like a local, instead of bumbling about like the typical tourist? Be sure to take advantage of these insider tips, tricks, and hacks to make your vacation friction-free:

- Save time and money by buying tickets in advance online instead of at the gate (see page 50).
- Keep your park admission and hotel key card on a lanyard around your neck instead of in your pocket, especially if you'll be pulling it out frequently for Universal Express.
- Arrive after 6 p.m. or see a matinee movie to get free self-parking (see page 154).
- Use the "secret" side entrance at Universal Studios Florida (see page 278).
- Download the Universal app in advance, and use its mobile ordering feature instead of standing in line for a quick-service dining cashier (see page 218).
- Child swap lets parents experience thrill rides without splitting up the family or waiting in line twice (see page 204).
- If you don't mind sitting separately from your party, the single-rider line is a huge time-saver (see page 77).
- Ask about free backstage tours at select theme park attractions (see the opposite page).
- Save on snacks with refillable cups and popcorn buckets (see page 222).
- If you're interested in buying on-ride pictures, consider investing in a My Universal Photos package (see page 172).

- Always ask about available food and merchandise discounts if you have an American Express card or annual pass (see page 52).
- Visit USF's private VIP lounges for American Express members (see page 160) and annual pass holders (see page 46).
- Hit up the bars in CityWalk and the resort hotels for happy hour drinks (see page 175).

QUITTING TIME

BECAUSE THE DAY PARKING for the Universal theme parks and the CityWalk shopping, dining, and entertainment complex is consolidated in the same parking structures, chaos can ensue on days when both parks close at the same time, resulting in an epic flood of humanity heading to the parking garages.

An Orlando woman, obviously very perturbed, comments:

Both Universal Studios and Islands of Adventure share the same parking lot. IT MAKES NO SENSE for the two theme parks to close at the same time. I cannot even explain the amount of people. It was insane at closing (and other people were coming IN to go to City-Walk, so it was SUCH a big mess)!

If you are unlucky enough to find yourself in such a situation, we suggest taking a side trip to CityWalk and sitting out the stampede with a snack or drink. If you haven't yet exited the park, you can try lingering inside the gates as long as possible, browsing the shops that remain open past closing time. Security guards will eventually gently shoo you out, but not until most of the parking mess has cleared.

PART TWO

ACCOMMODATIONS

The **BASIC CONSIDERATIONS**

WHILE YOU'LL SURELY HAVE FUN inside Universal's parks wherever you spend the night, your choice of hotel is critical to the overall success of your vacation. Visitors to Universal face the basic question of whether to stay inside the resort—where room rates range from around $110 on an off-season weeknight at a Value resort to more than $600 per night for a peak-season luxury property—or outside Universal, where rooms are as low as $80 a night. Affordability and easier access to non-Universal attractions must be weighed against the convenience and comfort of staying on property.

Universal Orlando currently operates eight on-site resorts, including the newly opened Dockside Inn, for a total of 9,000 rooms. Former NBCUniversal CEO Stephen Burke said the resort could someday support up to 20,000 rooms, but ambitious plans for additional hotels on the Epic Universe expansion plot are presently in limbo.

Compared to the more than 30,000 rooms Walt Disney World has spread across nearly 30 hotels, your choice of an on-site hotel at Universal is a lot simpler, but you may find limited room availability during busy times. On the other hand, Universal's hotels (all operated by the highly regarded Loews chain) boast service and amenities equal to or better than the competition, and usually at a lower cost; Universal's Preferred property is often priced like Disney's Moderates, and its Prime Value–priced resorts outshine Disney's All-Star and Pop Century hotels. You should also consider the superior benefits granted to Universal's on-site guests, a couple of which can make the difference between a marvelous vacation and a miserable one.

Whether you decide to stay on-site or off, this chapter will help you get a grip on the multitude of lodging options in the Universal Orlando area and find the property that fits your family's needs.

THE TAX MAN COMETH

SALES AND LODGING TAXES can add a chunk of change to the cost of your hotel room. Cumulative tax in Orange County, which includes the Universal Orlando area and International Drive, is 12.5%.

ABOUT HOTEL RENOVATIONS

WE INSPECT SEVERAL HUNDRED HOTELS in the Orlando area to compile *The Unofficial Guide*'s list of lodging choices. Each year we call each hotel to verify contact information and inquire about renovations or refurbishments. If a hotel has been renovated or has refurbished its guest rooms, we reinspect it, along with any new hotels, for the next edition of the guide. Hotels reporting no improvements are rechecked every two years. We inspect most Universal-owned hotels every 6–12 months and no less than once every two years.

Many hotels more than five years old refurbish 10%–20% of guest rooms each year. This incremental approach minimizes disruption, but it makes your room assignment a crapshoot—you might luck into a newly renovated room, or you might be assigned a threadbare one.

Universal reservationists won't guarantee you a recently refurbished room but will note your request and try to accommodate you. On the other hand, off-site hotels will often guarantee you an updated room when you book.

BENEFITS OF STAYING ON-SITE AT UNIVERSAL ORLANDO

UNIVERSAL OFFERS PERKS to get park visitors into its hotels. All guests at any Universal Orlando Resort on-site hotel can take advantage of the following:

- Early Park Admission to The Wizarding Worlds and Volcano Bay up to 1 hour before the public (see page 65)
- The ability to charge in-park purchases to the hotel-room key
- Free package delivery to the hotel room for items purchased in the parks
- Free parking at the main CityWalk parking garage
- Free transportation to the parks and CityWalk
- Pool-hopping privileges to use any hotel's recreational facilities (excludes Endless Summer Resort)
- Free Wi-Fi in all hotel rooms and public areas (faster speeds available for a fee)
- Free scheduled transportation to SeaWorld and Aquatica (see page 152)
- Preferred tee times and complimentary transportation (for foursomes) to participating golf courses
- Free admission to CityWalk clubs (excludes concerts and special events).

In addition, every guest staying at Portofino Bay, Hard Rock, or Royal Pacific receives the following benefits:

- Free Universal Express Unlimited Passes for both theme parks (see page 69)
- Priority seating at select restaurants in the parks and CityWalk

All these benefits are available from the moment you arrive until midnight on the day you check out. Even if your room won't be ready until the afternoon, you can register at your hotel as early in the morning as you like, leaving your bags and retrieving your Express Passes (if eligible) in time for the Early Park Admission hour. Then linger at the resort after your checkout time, taking advantage of your pool privileges until late in the evening.

The most valuable of these perks is admission to The Wizarding World of Harry Potter and Volcano Bay up to 1 hour before the general public each morning, along with the Universal Express Unlimited Passes for guests of the top three hotels. It's hard to put a dollar value on the Early Park Admission, but two-park Universal Express Unlimited Passes are sold to the general public for $89.99–$259.99 per day, per person, plus tax, depending on the time of year you visit. Universal says the pass is "a value of $129.99 per person, per day," which works out to $520 per day for a family of four. One night at Universal's Royal Pacific hotel costs anywhere from $314 to $463, plus tax, depending on the season. If you were planning on staying at a comparable off-site deluxe hotel anyway, staying at the Royal Pacific gets your family two days of Universal Express Unlimited at no additional cost. During busy season, this can be a huge boon for parties of four or five, though be aware that an additional $40-per-night fee applies to each adult beyond the first two staying in the room at Premier hotels. If you are traveling solo or as a couple, or are visiting at a slow time of year, calculate the cost of staying at one of the Preferred, Prime Value, or Value hotels and buying Express Passes on arrival if they turn out to be necessary.

Some of the benefits are of questionable value. Free parking at the parks, for example, is of little use to anyone staying at the resort because it's probably just as much walking from the resort as it is from the garages.

Having stayed at each of Universal's hotels, we think a sometimes-overlooked benefit is the ability to walk to the parks from your hotel. And it's not just the convenience—the walkways are pretty and almost serene at night, if you can ignore the roars from The Incredible Hulk Coaster. This Dallas-area family found foot accessibility to the parks to be Universal's biggest advantage over Walt Disney World's on-site hotels:

The simple convenience of being able to walk everywhere whenever you wanted was definitely worth the expense. Disney's shuttle and parking systems are extensive. We tried the bus, but it gets bogged down by the stops. Parking your own vehicle meant parking and then using a tram to get to the gate. You can't hop from park to park quickly. At Universal, with one parking area, everything was easily and quickly reachable. The girls could enjoy the park early (with little wait time), walk back to the hotel to nap, and then go back to the park or CityWalk. They felt very grown up being on their own without us adults to slow them down. This was inconvenient at Disney due to the transport time.

Combine the resort's walkability with Express Unlimited access from the luxury hotels, and the result is the perfect recipe for rejuvenation, according to this reader from San Antonio, Texas:

I can't remember how long it's been since we had such a relaxing vacation. That's right, I said it was relaxing, and I credit the hotel location and Express Pass. We got up whenever we wanted and went to whatever park we wanted. It was a 5-minute walk to the front gates of USF. We got tired; we took a nap. We felt too hot; we took a dip in the pool. It was heavenly.

UNIVERSAL ORLANDO RESORT HOTELS 101

UNIVERSAL HAS EIGHT RESORT HOTELS. The 750-room **Portofino Bay Hotel** is a gorgeous property set on an artificial bay and themed like an Italian coastal town. The 650-room **Hard Rock Hotel** is an ultracool "Hotel California" replica, and the 1,000-room, Polynesian-themed **Royal Pacific Resort** is sumptuously decorated and richly appointed. All three of the aforementioned hotels are on the pricey side. The retro-style **Cabana Bay Beach Resort,** Universal's largest hotel, has 2,200 moderate-priced rooms, plus a bowling alley and lazy river not seen at comparable Disney resorts. The Caribbean-styled **Sapphire Falls Resort** offers 1,000 rooms priced between Royal Pacific and Cabana Bay. **Aventura Hotel,** a 600-room property, opened in 2018 next to Sapphire Falls and across from the similarly priced Cabana Bay; it's a Miami-style modern high-rise with a Y-shaped glass tower and rooftop lounge. **Endless Summer Resort,** Universal's new value-priced option, consists of the 750-room Surfside Inn and Suites and the 2,050-room Dockside Inn and Suites, which opened to the public in late 2020.

COVID *tip*

At press time, Sapphire Falls Resort and Aventura Hotel were closed but accepting reservations for early 2021.

Before you make any decisions, understand these basics regarding Universal Orlando Resort hotels.

UNIVERSAL ORLANDO RESORT HOTEL POLICIES

Resort Classifications

Universal's hotels fall into four categories. The three most expensive on-site hotels—**Portofino Bay Resort, Hard Rock Hotel,** and **Royal Pacific Resort**—are called Premier resorts, and their perks include Universal Express Unlimited, priority restaurant seating, and water taxi transportation to CityWalk. **Sapphire Falls Resort** is labeled a Preferred resort; it's a AAA Four Diamond–awarded hotel, just like the Premier properties, and offers water taxi service but lacks free Universal Express or priority restaurant seating.

Cabana Bay Beach Resort and the **Aventura Hotel** represent the Prime Value resorts. Both have bus and pedestrian access to the attractions (including Volcano Bay), but neither is connected to the water taxi system. The **Endless Summer Resort** hotels are the first designated as Value hotels, as well as the first located a brief bus ride across I-4 from Universal proper. Regardless of classification, all on-site Universal guests enjoy amenities that surpass any other value-priced hotels in the area.

Seasonal Rates

Universal uses so many adjectives—*Value, Regular, Summer, Holiday,* and *Peak*—to describe its seasonal calendar that it's hard to keep up. Plus, Universal also changes the price of its hotel rooms with the day of the week, charging more for the same room on Friday and Saturday nights. Each Universal hotel profile (see pages 95–110) includes the lowest rack (nondiscounted) rate (Value season) and the highest rack rate (Holiday season). These prices are for a weeknight stay in a basic room with a standard view, usually of a "garden" or parking lot; upgrades to pool or bay views start at $25–$50. Rates include a maximum of two adults per room, plus any children up to the room's capacity; additional adults each incur a $40-per-night surcharge at Premier hotels, $25 at Preferred, $20 at Prime Value, and $15 at Value. Rack rates do not include taxes or parking, but no hidden resort fees are tacked on at Universal's hotels.

Discounts

Universal hotel rack rates are just the starting point, and most clever visitors can save substantially on their stay with a little legwork because Universal frequently offers sizable percentage-off deals to fill its rooms.

Start by reviewing the resort discount information in Part One (see page 52), and then visit universalorlando.com and click on "Places to Stay" then "Special Offers" to view the latest deals. Next, click on "Book Now" next to the hotel you are interested in, select your travel dates, and append "&promo=APH" (for annual pass holders) or "&promo=FLO" (for Florida residents) to the end of the URL in your browser bar to reveal available discounts. You don't have to prove eligibility to book with these codes, but you will need to show appropriate ID upon check-in; newly purchased annual passes may be used to secure hotel discounts even before they are first activated at the park gates, as long as you show them upon checkout.

If you are staying multiple nights, Universal's "Stay More, Save More" pricing structure kicks in. Stays in any on-site hotel room of four to seven nights save 10%–25% during holiday, peak, and summer seasons, and stays of three to seven nights save 10%–30% during regular and value seasons.

Making Reservations

The easiest way to book a room at Universal Orlando is online through universalorlando.com, or by phone at ☎ 888-273-1311. If you are attending a meeting or event, call ☎ 866-360-7395 for your group block room.

Cancellations

A credit card deposit equal to one night's room rate (plus tax) is required when booking. Cancellations made six or more days prior to check-in receive a full refund. Cancellations five or fewer days before check-in forfeit the deposit. However, Universal's severe-weather cancellation policy says that if you are unable to travel to Orlando due to an "active named storm impacting your travel," you can reschedule your vacation or receive a full refund. This applies only for rooms, park tickets, or vacation packages booked directly with Loews and Universal; if you use a third-party reseller, you'll need to consult its cancellation policy.

Check-In and Checkout

Check-in time at all Universal hotels is 4 p.m., and checkout is 11 a.m.; if you ask nicely, you can usually get a noon checkout for free. Remember that all on-site hotel benefits—including Express Unlimited Passes for guests of the top three hotels and Early Park Admission—begin the first morning of your stay and last until midnight after you check out. So even if you can't get into your room, you can preregister as early as you like, leave your luggage, grab your Express Passes (at the top three hotels), and hit the parks at rope drop. Checkout can be done at the front desk, through the interactive TV, or via express with your bill emailed to you.

Note that upon checking in, you'll be asked to pre-authorize your credit card for $200 per day, so you can use your hotel room key for charges around the resort. You may request to change this authorization amount, or decline it entirely if you don't wish to make charges to your room account.

Age Requirements

The minimum age to book a hotel room at Universal Orlando is 21, and valid ID is required at check-in. At least one guest staying in the room must be age 21 or older.

Accessibility

All Universal Orlando hotels have wheelchair-accessible public areas and offer designated accessible rooms for mobility-, sight-, and/or hearing-impaired guests. Accessibility features include 36-inch-wide entry doors, peepholes at 3½ feet from the floor, closets with rods at 48 inches high, toilets with hand bar, and roll-in shower stalls or combination shower/tubs with adjustable showerheads. Sight- and hearing-impaired features include Braille room numbers, closed-caption TVs, smoke detectors with lights, and Hearing-Impaired Kits, including a TDD-relay service that may be used in any guest room.

Pets

Loews "loves pets" and is one of the few luxury chains to allow cats and dogs in its rooms. It even has a special (and expensive) room service menu for four-legged guests. There are some restrictions, starting with a $100 flat fee per stay for a maximum of two pets per guest room. Guests will be assigned a pet-friendly room category on arrival, which includes garden- and bay-view rooms at the Portofino Bay, garden-view rooms at the Hard Rock, and standard rooms at the Royal Pacific and Sapphire Falls. Club rooms don't participate in the pet program, nor do any of the Prime Value or Value properties, such as Cabana Bay Beach Resort, Aventura Hotel, and Endless Summer Resort.

Dogs may be walked only in designated areas and are not allowed in the pool/lounge or restaurant areas. Arrangements must be made with housekeeping for daily room cleaning, and there is a $10-per-hour "time-out" fee if they find your pet left unattended. If other guests complain about your pet's behavior, you may be asked to board it off-site. You must provide current vaccination records from a licensed veterinarian on request. Read the full Loews Loves Pets policy at tinyurl.com/LoewsPetsRPR.

Smoking

All Universal Orlando Resort hotels are smoke free. Smoking is only permitted outdoors in designated locations. If you light up in your room, you'll be burned with a $250 cleaning fee.

Hard Rock Rewards

Hard Rock Hotel accepts the Hard Rock Rewards loyalty card, which offers free priority late checkout and other perks; visit members .hardrock.com to join. Be warned that discounted room bookings may not qualify for reward program benefits. The similar Loews YouFirst program at the other on-site hotels has been discontinued.

UNIVERSAL ORLANDO RESORT HOTEL SERVICES *and* AMENITIES

DINING

TO KEEP YOU FED, every Universal on-site hotel has multiple restaurants, a spot for coffee and grab-and-go snacks, and at least two bars. The Premier and Preferred properties each have sit-down restaurants, including one family-friendly eatery, while Cabana Bay has a counter-service food court, as well as table-service munchies in the bowling alley. Aventura Hotel has an upscale food court with international dishes and a rooftop bar that serves small plates. The Premier and Preferred hotels also have 24-hour room service menus, while the Value and Prime Value properties offer pizza delivery to the rooms noon–midnight (until 1 a.m. Friday–Saturday at Cabana Bay and Aventura).

The primary downside to staying on-site at Universal is the cost of food at the Premier hotels' restaurants, which seem to be priced as if everyone staying at the hotels is on a corporate expense account. Fortunately, many good, cheaper restaurant choices are within a few minutes' drive of the hotels on Major Boulevard, International Drive, and Sand Lake Road. Hotel guests also have easy access to CityWalk, which has some cheaper choices for dining.

POOLS AND RECREATION

SWIMMING IS MANY GUESTS' NO. 1 priority (after the parks, of course), so you'll find some of Orlando's best pools at Universal's hotels. Each resort has at least one themed swimming facility. The main pool is the more active, family-centric one, where you'll find playground equipment and organized activities, both for kids (water-based games and contests) and adults (free smoothies and cool towels). Most resorts (except Royal Pacific, Endless Summer, and Aventura) have a waterslide, and Cabana Bay has a lazy river. On most nights (weather permitting) a PG or PG-13 "dive-in" movie is projected on an outdoor screen, with the Harry Potter, Marvel, and Transformers flicks in heavy rotation.

The secondary pools at Portofino Bay are usually slightly more sedate and attract a more adult clientele. All pools are staffed with trained lifeguards during operating hours (which vary seasonally, typically 8 a.m.–10 p.m.) and have adjacent hot tubs, changing facilities, and drink services. Towels are free with resort ID , and hotel guests (excluding those at Endless Summer) are free to pool-hop from one resort to another; ask an attendant for access if your room key won't open another hotel's security gate.

Each hotel's main pool (except Endless Summer's and Aventura's) has private cabanas for rent, which start around $100 per day. Aside from providing shade and cushioned lounge chairs, cabanas come with ceiling fans, TVs, a refrigerator, free soft drinks, food and drink delivery, and a personal safe. Reserve a cabana by calling ☎ 407-503-4175 at Cabana Bay, ☎ 407-503-5200 ext. 35235 at Sapphire Falls, ☎ 407-503-3235 at Royal Pacific, ☎ 407-503-2236 at Hard Rock, or ☎ 407-503-1200 at Portofino Bay. Same-day cancellations incur a 50% penalty fee. You'll also find a variety of recreational activities around the pools, from a bocce court at Portofino Bay to a croquet lawn at the Royal Pacific; free equipment can be checked out to play.

KIDS' ACTIVITIES AND KIDS SUITES

THE LOEWS LOVES KIDS PROGRAM means that there's always something at the hotel to keep the rug rats occupied when your family isn't in the parks. Free lending libraries of games and sports equipment are available at every hotel, and a schedule of supervised activities is offered at each main pool (or indoors on rainy days). The Minions (or other Universal characters) make regular meet and greet appearances at Cabana Bay Beach Resort on Friday evenings. In addition, the kids' clubs at the top three hotels offer evening childcare for a fee (see page 208), and every hotel has an arcade with video games; Cabana Bay's Game-O-Rama is the biggest, and Aventura Hotel's arcade includes virtual reality headsets.

If you want to go all out and amaze the kids (at the expense of your bank account), reserve one of the elaborately decorated **Kids Suites.** Portofino Bay's Despicable Me suites look like Gru's laboratory, with missile-shaped beds and vaultlike doors. Royal Pacific's Jurassic World suites have appropriately dinosaurian decor, with high-tech headboards and jungle graphics. The Hard Rock's Future Rock Star suites give kids a pint-size stage to shred on. Aventura's and Sapphire Falls's Kids Suites have a separate kids' room with TV and child-size furniture but no whimsical theming. All the Kids Suites have separate bedrooms for the kids that only open on the parents' room (not the hallway). You'll get some extra privacy but pay a hefty price with the resort's highest room rates (outside the outrageous presidential suites). Cabana Bay and Endless Summer don't offer Kids Suites, but they do have Family Suites, without the private kids' quarters, for a much lower cost.

COVID *tip* Some activities may be temporarily suspended to promote social distancing.

PARKING

COVID *tip* Valet parking was temporarily suspended at press time.

UNIVERSAL'S THREE PREMIER HOTELS all charge a $28-per-night self-parking fee ($37 for valet) for registered guests; day guests pay $30 for self-parking and $42 for valet at Portofino Bay and Hard Rock, while Royal Pacific charges day guests $45 for self-parking longer than 30 minutes and $42 for valet. Sapphire Falls overnight guests pay $26 for self-parking and $45 for valet; day guests pay $45 for self-parking longer than 30 minutes and $37 for valet. Cabana Bay and Aventura charge $18 for overnight guests (self-parking only) and Endless Summer charges $15; all three bill $45 per day for day visitors.

Most of the hotel restaurants (including Bice and Mama Della's at Portofino, Jake's and Islands Dining Room at Royal Pacific, Strong Water Tavern and Amatista Cookhouse at Sapphire Falls, and Bar 17 Bistro at Aventura) will validate diners for free self-parking or a discounted rate of $5 valet parking; The Palm at Hard Rock Hotel offers complimentary valet. You must spend at least $25 on food or beverages to receive parking validation. There are no annual pass discounts on parking at the hotels. The hotels don't charge for another night until midnight, so you can leave your car in the lot long past your checkout time without paying extra.

ATTRACTION TICKET CENTER

LOEWS STAFF HAVE NO AUTHORITY over park tickets or anything else involving the attractions, so if you ask the front desk or concierge about park admission and the like, you'll be directed to the Universal Orlando Attraction Ticket Center. Typically located in the main hotel lobby (though the one at Portofino Bay is tucked around a secluded corner), the Ticket Center can help you purchase park tickets (or pick up ones you preordered), as well as arrange for Universal Express Passes, dining reservations, off-site transportation, and other amenities. The Ticket Center in each hotel is usually open daily, 7 a.m.–9 p.m.

INTERNET

ALL UNIVERSAL ORLANDO HOTELS offer free Wi-Fi in their public areas and guest rooms for up to four devices. The service is somewhat spotty but good enough for email and social media. If you plan to stream videos or upload large photos, you may want to pay $15 per 24 hours for Premium Plus Internet, which affords higher bandwidth (we've achieved more than 30 megabits-per-second downloads) on up to eight devices.

BUSINESS CENTERS

EACH OF THE PREMIER AND PREFERRED HOTELS has a fully equipped business center offering computers with printers, copy and fax services, and mail facilities through FedEx and UPS. Portofino Bay's and Royal Pacific's business centers are open Monday–Friday, 7 a.m.–5:30 p.m., and Saturday, 7 a.m.–noon (closed Sunday). Hard Rock Hotel's and Sapphire Falls's business centers are open 24-7, and the others may be accessed during off-hours by contacting the front desk. Fees apply for certain services such as copying and faxing. Aventura Hotel and Endless Summer Resort have no business center, but their lobbies have touch screens for printing airline boarding passes. Cabana Bay's diner has a quiet corner with phone booths but no printers.

CRIBS AND ROLLAWAY BEDS

COMPLIMENTARY CRIBS ARE AVAILABLE in all rooms. Rollaway beds can be requested at Premier and Preferred hotels on a first-come, first-serve basis for $25 per day, plus 12.5% sales tax; this fee is in addition to any nightly charges for having more than two adults in the room. Only one rollaway per room is allowed, and they are not available at Prime Value or Value hotels.

MICROWAVES AND REFRIGERATORS

ALL HOTEL ROOMS INCLUDE small refrigerators, and the Family Suites at Cabana Bay and Endless Summer have kitchenettes with a microwave and sink. Microwaves are available for rent in rooms that don't include them on a first-come, first-serve basis for $15 each per day, plus 12.5% sales tax.

TRANSPORTATION AND CAR RENTAL

ALL OF UNIVERSAL'S HOTELS OFFER free transportation via bus and/or water taxi to CityWalk and the parks, as well as well-lit landscaped walking paths connecting the resorts. Water taxis depart from each of the Premier and Preferred hotels every 15–20 minutes, while the buses from the Prime Value and Value resorts run almost continuously. Either transportation method takes about 15 minutes to reach the park entrances, while walking takes between less than 5 minutes from the Hard Rock Hotel to 15 or 20 minutes from Cabana Bay and Portofino Bay.

If you are staying at one resort but wish to visit another, ask the concierge to arrange a $10 car service or catch the free hotel shuttle bus, which circulates among the Premier and Preferred properties every 30 minutes. A final alternative to walking are the pedicabs operated by Orient Express Rickshaw (OER). Drivers ply the pathways between the resorts and CityWalk, working for tips ($5 per passenger is typical). You can flag down an empty rickshaw, or call OER at ☎ 407-385-0471 to reserve one. Rickshaws run Monday–Friday, 7 a.m.–midnight, and until 2 a.m. Saturday–Sunday.

Free daily transportation for hotel guests to SeaWorld and Aquatica is available (see page 152). A limited number of seats are available on a first-come, first-serve basis, so check with your hotel's Ticket Center a day in advance for the schedule and boarding passes.

Another free bus from Universal's parking hub to Busch Gardens Tampa is available to anyone holding a paid park ticket; visit buschgardens.mears.com or call ☎ 800-221-1339 for details. For a fee, the concierge desk will arrange for Mears Transportation to take you to Walt Disney World or the airport. If you want to rent a car, Avis rental-car service desks operate inside each hotel daily, 8 a.m.–6 p.m.; call ☎ 407-503-3156 for information and reservations.

COVID *tip* Bus service to Busch Gardens was temporarily suspended at press time.

FITNESS CENTERS AND MANDARA SPA

IF YOU WANT TO STAY IN SHAPE while vacationing, every Universal hotel has a well-appointed fitness center filled with the latest in exercise equipment. The expansive Jack LaLanne–themed workout room at Cabana Bay Beach Resort, as well as the somewhat smaller workout rooms in the other hotels, are free for all hotel guests to use. To promote sanitation, fitness centers may be closed for cleaning every hour or so; see signage posted at the gym entrance for the operating schedule.

Whether you are staying at a Universal hotel or not, you may book services at Portofino Bay's Mandara Spa, which is attached to the hotel's fitness center. Access to the spa's shower and sauna facilities costs $10 per day for guests of any on-site resort and is free for club-level guests or anyone purchasing spa services. If you aren't staying on-site, you can get access to the spa (though not the nearby Beach Pool) with a $25 day pass, which also includes free self-parking or $5 valet parking at the hotel entrance.

Universal Orlando's Mandara Spa was renovated in 2017, enhancing its changing and sauna facilities while retaining its Asian ambience despite its location in an Italy-themed resort. We like the contrast, though, and find it slightly exotic. Waiting areas are decorated in comforting earth tones; treatment rooms feature silk-draped ceilings and additional decorative lighting. Changing and bathroom areas are spacious and clean, but they also include less-than-subtle advertisements for products sold on premises.

The emphasis on tranquility extends to the stellar spa services, which include free self-heating oil for massages. Men and women enjoy separate steam and sauna facilities; the hot tub is unisex. The Portofino's sand-bottom pool is conveniently located near the entrance to the spa, as are nail services. The fitness center is still on the other side of the glass wall, however, so you may feel a bit like that doggy in the window.

We rate the Mandara Spa at Portofino Bay as 4 stars, just behind the spas at Disney's Grand Floridian, the Waldorf Astoria, and the Four Seasons and equivalent to the spas at the Ritz-Carlton, Saratoga Springs, and Gaylord Palms. Prices range from $75 for a 25-minute myofascial release to $390 for an 80-minute couple's massage package. Hair salon and makeup services are also on the menu. A 20% automatic gratuity applies to all services, and Preferred and Premier Annual Pass holders can save 10%–20% on services (Monday–Thursday only). Groupon frequently offers discounted Mandara Spa packages, but you'll be charged gratuity based on the full value. Purchase of most massages and treatments also includes access to the fitness center for the day. Call ☎ 407-503-1244 for reservations, or visit tinyurl.com/PBHMandaraSpa to preview the price list.

COVID *tip*

The Mandara Spa was temporarily closed at press time.

LAUNDRY

ALL THE HOTELS EXCEPT PORTOFINO BAY offer self-service Laundromats. Machines take quarters or credit cards and cost $3 per load to wash, and the same to dry; detergent costs $1. At all the Preferred and Premier hotels, you can also avail yourself of valet laundry, dry cleaning, quick pressing, and shoeshines, with express same-day service available daily, 9 a.m.–7 p.m.; pricing and instructions can be found inside your closet.

CLUB LEVEL

THE THREE TOP HOTELS each offer club-level rooms or suites that allow access to an exclusive lounge, where you'll find a complimentary Continental breakfast, afternoon snacks, hot and cold evening hors d'oeuvres with free beer and wine, and after-dinner desserts. Club-level guests also get free fitness center access, discounted poolside cabana rentals, personal concierge service, evening turndown service, and other luxurious touches. Hard Rock Hotel's Rock Royalty and Royal Pacific's Royal Club Lounges are on the seventh floor, while Portofino Bay's Portofino Club Lounge is in the lobby; all are open daily, 7 a.m.–10 p.m. Most of our readers who stay in a club-level room seem happy with their choice, like this family from Kansas City:

COVID *tip*
To promote social distancing, some club lounges may be temporarily relocated, and self-service buffets may be replaced with individually wrapped items.

> *We stayed on the club level of the Royal Pacific. Absolutely worth the money. It not only includes breakfast every morning but also includes sodas all day and cocktails in the evening with heavy appetizers, which we usually made a meal out of. There was always a salad and then something hot. One night it was beef stew, then fried rice, and then chicken potpie. And if you weren't full, they put out dessert 8–9 p.m. This ended up saving us money, and we were usually tired from the day, so just walking down the hall was fabulous.*

This family from St. Louis also felt that the club level's cost was money well spent:

> *Club level was only $40 more, and we easily had this covered with breakfast and dinner that we didn't eat out, along with soda and water taken into the park. For a family of four, it was well worth it. When my son became ill, the concierge service connected us with an urgent care that stayed open late. Amazing service.*

WEDDINGS

THERE IS NO DEDICATED WEDDING PAVILION at Universal (yet), but each hotel has facilities for staging fairy-tale ceremonies, large or small. Intimate weddings with 50 or fewer guests start at $1,600 for a simple ceremony, plus $300 for a cake or $104 per guest for a 1-hour cocktail reception. A Signature wedding for more than 50 guests starts at $2,600–$4,500 for the ceremony and $168-plus per plate for a dinner reception. To Universal's credit, it doesn't quote an hourly rate for having Minions attend your bachelorette party, but this is Orlando: money talks. Visit tinyurl.com/uniweddings to download brochures with pricing and menus, and start planning your Universal union today.

UNIVERSAL ORLANDO RESORT HOTEL PROFILES

Hard Rock Hotel Orlando ★★★★½

Rate per night $358–$603. **Pool** ★★★★. **Fridge in room** Yes.
Shuttle to parks Yes (Universal, SeaWorld, Aquatica). **Maximum**

5800 Universal Blvd.
Orlando
☎ 407-503-2000 or
888-273-1311
hardrockhotelorlando.com

number of occupants per room 5 (two queens) or 4 (king). Comment Pets welcome (2/room; $100/stay). Survey results 93% of *Unofficial Guide* readers would stay here again; 89% would recommend this resort to a friend.

FOR YOUNGER ADULTS AND FAMILIES with older kids, the Hard Rock Hotel is the hippest place to lay your head. Opened in 2001, it is the closest resort to Universal's theme parks. The exterior has a California Mission theme, with white stucco walls, arched entryways, and rust-colored roof tiles. Inside, the lobby is a tribute to rock-and-roll style, all marble, chrome, and stage lighting. The lobby's walls are decorated with enough concert posters, costumes, and musical instruments to start another wing of Cleveland's Rock and Roll Hall of Fame. Exhibits include outfits from Lady Gaga and Rihanna, and QR codes near each artifact let you take a self-guided memorabilia tour via your smartphone.

The eight floors hold 650 rooms, including 29 suites, with the rooms categorized into standard, deluxe, and Rock Royalty club-level tiers. Standard rooms are 375 square feet, slightly larger than rooms at Disney's Moderate resorts and a bit smaller than most Disney Deluxe rooms. The rooms feature light-gray walls and linens, pastel furniture, and colorful retro-inspired accents, such as throw pillows crocheted with phrases such as "Quiet Please" and "Be Nice." To be frank, the style looks more bubblegum pop than hard rock, but the brighter look is a bit more soothing after you stumble back from a fatiguing day in the parks.

Standard rooms are furnished with two queen beds, with plush, comfortable linens and more pillows than you'll know what to do with. Rooms also include a TV, refrigerator, coffee maker, and an alarm clock with an iPhone docking port.

A six-drawer dresser and separate closet with sliding doors ensure plenty of storage space. In addition, most rooms have a reading chair and a small desk with two chairs. An optional rollaway bed, available at an extra charge, allows standard rooms to sleep up to five people.

Each room's dressing area includes a sink and hair dryer. The bathroom is probably large enough for most adults to get ready in the morning while another person gets ready in the dressing area.

Guests staying in standard rooms can choose from one of three views: standard, which can include anything from walkways and parking lots to lawns and trees; garden view, which includes the lawn, trees, and (in some rooms) the waterway around the resort; and pool view, which includes the Hard Rock's expansive pool.

A step up from standard rooms are deluxe rooms. Deluxe rooms with king beds are around 400 square feet and can accommodate up to four people with a pullout sofa and an optional rollaway bed rental. These rooms feature a U-shaped sitting area in place of the second bed, and the rest of the amenities are the same as in standard rooms. Deluxe queen rooms are 500 square feet and can hold up to five people using a pullout sofa, located in a small cubby just off the room's entrance.

For families, each 800-square-foot Future Rock Star suite features an authentic piece of music memorabilia, along with a simulated stage inside the separate kids' bedroom. Or you can really live like The King in the 2,000-square-foot Graceland Suite, which comes complete with a baby grand piano and fireplace.

Situated in the middle of the resort's C-shaped main building, the 12,000-square-foot zero-entry pool includes a 250-foot waterslide (the longest at any Universal hotel), a sand beach, and underwater speakers so you can hear the music while you swim. Adjacent to the pool are a fountain play area for small children, a sand volleyball court, hot tubs, and a poolside bar. The entire pool area is lined with tall palm trees, and private cabanas are available for rent. The Hard Rock also has a small, functional fitness center, but for spa services you'll have to go to the Mandara Spa at Universal's nearby Portofino Bay. Like all Universal Orlando Resort hotels, the Hard Rock has a business center and video arcade.

On-site dining includes The Kitchen, a casual full-service restaurant open for breakfast, lunch, and dinner that serves American food such as burgers, steaks, and salads. The Kitchen hosts strolling magicians on Wednesday and Friday, Kids Can Cook activities on Tuesday and Thursday, and random celebrity-chef sightings. The Palm Restaurant is an upscale steakhouse available for dinner only. There is also an Emack & Bolio's ice cream shop and grab-and-go marketplace on the lower level; the stylish Velvet Bar in the lobby for drinks after dark and monthly Velvet Sessions rock-and-roll cocktail parties (visit velvetsessions.com for the schedule and to purchase tickets); and the BeachClub bar and grill by the pool. And, of course, the Hard Rock Cafe is just a short distance away at CityWalk. Oenophiles will want to keep an eye on tinyurl.com/HRHWineRiffs for announcements about periodic Wine Riffs events ($125 plus tax and gratuity), which pair five courses of vino and victuals with a carefully curated soundtrack.

Guests can also stream a free personalized playlist at music.hardrock hotels.com, and swap their room key card for a free souvenir guitar pick at checkout. If all that musical immersion puts you in the mood to jam, you can borrow a Crosley turntable with a stack of vinyl records or 1 of 20 Fender guitars—including Stratocasters, Telecasters, and even bass guitars—with amp and headphones for free (after a $1,000 credit card deposit) through the hotel's The Sound of Your Stay program; ask the front desk for details. Alternatively, investigate the Rock Om in-room yoga program (hardrockhotelorlando.com/rock-om.htm) if you yearn to achieve a state of Zen.

The Sound of Your Stay, Rock Om, and similar programs may be suspended due to social distancing.

We rate the rooms at Hard Rock slightly ahead of the more-expensive Portofino Bay. In fact, Hard Rock Hotel is so popular with families that, during certain seasons when school is out of session, it can command a higher nightly rate than Portofino Bay. While not exactly cheap, Hard Rock is a good value compared to, say, Disney's Yacht & Beach Clubs. What you're paying for at the Hard Rock is a short walk to the theme parks and Universal Express Unlimited first, and the room second.

While the hotel can get a bit loud, especially in areas facing the pool, it gets high marks from families with teenagers, like this Texas parent with two daughters ages 15 and 17:

One word: "WOW!" My group loved it! We splurged for a club room. My teenag-
ers liked the club lounge . . . allowing them to pop in for food whenever they
wanted. The beds were super comfortable, soft instead of firm mattresses. The
pool was a big hit with the girls. We all liked the convenience of being so close to
walk to the parks.

Loews Portofino Bay Hotel ★★★★½

5601 Universal Blvd.
Orlando
☎ 407-503-1000 or
888-273-1311
loewshotels.com
/portofino-bay-hotel

Rate per night $374–$618. **Pools** ★★★★. **Fridge in room** Yes.
Shuttle to parks Yes (Universal, SeaWorld, Aquatica). **Maximum
number of occupants per room** 5 (two queens) or 3 (king). **Comment** Pets welcome (2/room; $100/stay). **Survey results** 80% of
Unofficial Guide readers would stay here again; 83% would recommend this resort to a friend.

IF YOU WANT THE ULTIMATE European-style, spare-no-expense on-site
experience, look no further than the Portofino Bay Hotel. Universal's top-
of-the-line hotel evokes the Italian seaside city of Portofino, complete
with a man-made Portofino Bay past the lobby. To Universal's credit, the
layout, color, and theming of the guest room buildings are a good
approximation of the architecture around the harbor in the real Portofino
(Universal's version has fewer yachts, though).

The front of the Portofino continues the theme, with Vespa-like scooters parked around a burbling fountain. Deep-green tapestries hang from
the sand-colored porte cochere, which is flanked by narrower recessed
arches. It's a convincing transition from the nearby parking deck.

Inside, the lobby is decorated with pink marble floors, white wood
columns, and arches. The space is both airy and comfortable, with side
rooms featuring seats and couches done in bold reds and deep blues.

Most guest rooms are 450 square feet and have either one king bed or
two queen beds. King rooms sleep up to three people with an optional
rollaway bed; the same option allows queen rooms to sleep up to five.
Two room-view types are available: garden rooms look out over the land-
scaping and trees (many of these are the east-facing rooms in the resort's
east wing; others face one of the three pools); bay-view rooms face either
west or south and overlook Portofino Bay, with a view of the piazza
behind the lobby too. Rooms in the west wing are closest to the water
taxi dock and resort walking paths. A very small number of rooms have
working balconies; you can't reserve one in advance but may upgrade at
check-in if one is available for $15–$30 extra.

Rooms come furnished with a 42-inch TV, a small refrigerator, a coffee maker, and an alarm clock with an iPhone docking port. Other amenities include a small desk with two chairs, a comfortable reading chair
with lamp, a chest of drawers, and a standing closet. Beds are large and
comfortable. You'll have a hard time in the morning convincing yourself
that getting out of them and going to a theme park is the best option
you have.

Guest bathrooms at Portofino Bay are the best on Universal property.
We've seen smaller New York apartments! Speakers inside the bathroom transmit the audio from whatever is playing on the room's TV. The

best thing is the shower, which has enough water pressure to strip paint from old furniture, not to mention an adjustable spray nozzle that varies the water pulses to simulate everything from monsoon season in the tropics to the rhythmic thumps of wildebeest hooves during migrating season. We love it.

Portofino Bay has three pools, the largest of which is the Beach Pool, on the west side of the resort. The Beach Pool has a zero-entry design and a waterslide themed after a Roman aqueduct, plus a children's play area, hot tubs, and a poolside bar and grill. We like the naturalistic Mediterranean seaside feel of the Beach Pool, but it can be a bit too authentic for some guests, like this mom from St. Louis:

> The biggest disappointment about Portofino Bay was actually the main pool. The kids felt that it was dirty with the sand, and it was nearly impossible to find chairs in the afternoon due to many being "reserved" with towels.

Two smaller quiet pools sit at the far end of the east wing and to the west of the main lobby. The Villa Pool has private cabana rentals for that Italian Riviera feeling and a bocce ball court with free equipment for that Jersey shore feeling, while the smaller Hillside Pool, tucked behind the east wing, is the most secluded. Rounding out the luxuries are the full-service Mandara Spa; a complete fitness center with weight machines, treadmills, and more; a business center; and a video arcade.

On-site dining includes three sit-down restaurants serving Italian cuisine, plus a deli that doubles as a pizzeria, as well as a café serving coffee and gelato. Two bars round out the food offerings at Portofino. The Portofino has 10 separate convention meeting rooms and is a popular destination for small to midsize groups. Perhaps because Universal figures that most guests have an expense account, some of the food prices go well beyond what we'd consider reasonable, even for a theme park hotel.

While we think Portofino Bay has some of Universal's best rooms, certain areas are starting to show their age, and the prices put it on par with the Ritz-Carlton, something its good points can't quite justify. On the other hand, the Ritz isn't a short walk from Harry Potter, and the Portofino is significantly cheaper than the hotels along Disney's monorail, as this Shelby, North Carolina, reader remarked:

> We stayed at Portofino Bay for three nights before transferring to Disney's Contemporary Resort, and we liked the Portofino much better for half the price!

If you can't swing a stay here, at least take a complimentary sunset water taxi ride to the harbor for Musica della Notte, the free mini-concert of romantic operatic pop tunes belted from Portofino's bayside balconies daily at sunset (weather permitting). Four times each year, Harbor Nights are held on the plaza, with free-flowing wine, heavy hors d'oeuvres, and live music. Tickets are $65 (plus tax) for general admission and $95 for VIP admission with reserved seating and private food stations. The experience is like attending an upscale wedding without having to bring a gift, and it makes for a wonderfully romantic date night. See tinyurl.com/PBH HarborNights for details on the next date.

Loews Royal Pacific Resort ★★★★½

Rate per night $314–$463. Pool ★★★★. Fridge in room Yes. Shuttle to parks Yes (Universal, SeaWorld, Aquatica). Maximum number of occupants per room 5 (two queens) or 3 (king). Comments Character breakfast on Saturday (when available). Pets welcome (2/room, $100/stay). Survey results 94% of *Unofficial Guide* readers would stay here again; 92% would recommend this resort to a friend.

6300 Hollywood Way
Orlando
☎ 407-503-1000 or
888-273-1311
loewshotels.com
/royal-pacific-resort

A FAVORITE OF BOTH YOUNG FAMILIES AND SOLO travelers, the Royal Pacific Resort is the least expensive and most relaxing of Universal's top hotels. You may be tempted, as we were initially, to write off the Royal Pacific, which opened in 2002, as a knockoff of Disney's Polynesian Village Resort. There are indeed similarities, but the Royal Pacific is attractive enough, and has enough strengths of its own, for us to recommend that you try a stay there to compare for yourself.

The South Seas–inspired theming is both relaxing and structured. Guests enter the lobby—which received a thorough refurbishment in 2020—from a walkway two stories above an artificial stream that surrounds the resort. Once you're inside, the lobby's dark teakwood accents contrast nicely with the enormous amount of light coming in from the windows and three-story A-frame roof. Palms line the walkway through the lobby, which surrounds an enormous outdoor fountain.

The Royal Pacific's 1,000 guest rooms are spread among three Y-shaped wings attached to the resort's main building. Standard rooms are 335 square feet and have one king or two queen beds. The beds, fitted with 300-thread-count sheets, are very comfortable.

The rooms feature modern monochrome wall treatments and carpets, accented with boldly colored floral graphics. Rooms include a flat-panel TV, a refrigerator, a coffee maker, and an alarm clock with an iPhone docking port, plus several USB-equipped power outlets. Other amenities include a small desk with two chairs, a comfortable reading chair, a chest of drawers, and a large closet.

As at the Hard Rock, rooms at the Royal Pacific have a dressing area with sink, separated from the rest of the room by a wall. Adjacent to the dressing area is the bathroom, with a tub, shower, and toilet. While they're acceptable, the bathroom and dressing areas at the Royal Pacific are our least favorite in the upscale Universal resorts.

The Royal Pacific also offers themed rooms for kids with its Jurassic World Kids Suites, which were refurbished in 2018. These 370-square-foot two-room suites have a door connecting the kids' room to the main hotel room, but only the main room has a door out to the hallway. The kids' room has two twin beds with headboards that look like Gyrospheres, as well as a wall-size mural of dinosaurs.

Some standard-view rooms look out over the Royal Pacific's green landscape, while others see the parking lot or nearby roads. Water-view rooms facing the pool or lagoon are also available, many of which have a great look at Hogwarts Castle. Guests in north- and west-facing rooms in Tower 1 are closest to the walking path to the park but also closest to the attractions at Islands of Adventure (IOA); you can hear the roar from IOA's Incredible Hulk Coaster throughout the day and night. East-facing rooms in Towers 1 and 2 are exposed to traffic noise from Universal Boulevard and, more distantly, I-4. Quietest are south-facing pool-view rooms in Tower 1 and south-facing rooms in Tower 3, which are also nearest to the water taxi dock. Tower 2 is the most remote from amenities and transportation.

Like the Hard Rock Hotel, the Royal Pacific's zero-entry pool includes a sand beach, volleyball court, play area for kids, hot tub, and cabanas for rent, plus a poolside bar and grill. Designed to look like a cross between a tropical island and cruise ship pool (complete with faux exhaust tower and observation deck), the swimming complex pool is huge; it does not, however, have a waterslide. Lounge chairs line most of the walkway around the pool, and portable folding umbrellas provide shade where the palm trees and lush green plants can't. A free torch-lighting ceremony with Polynesian dances, music, and fire juggling is held by the pool around sunset on select nights (usually Tuesday, Friday, and Saturday during the summer). For the full island experience, the *Wantilan Luau* is held every Saturday night year-round; see the review on page 265.

Dinner shows, character meals, and evening entertainment may be suspended to promote social distancing.

The Royal Pacific includes a 5,000-square-foot fitness facility, with free weights and machines, treadmills, stair-climbers, elliptical machines, and exercise bikes, plus separate lockers, dressing areas, and sauna rooms for men and women. The Royal Pacific's expansive convention facilities cover more than 132,000 square feet and connect to the Sapphire Falls Resort via an air-conditioned bridge. A business center and video arcade round out the on-site amenities.

On-site dining includes a full-service restaurant, three bars, and a luau. Islands Dining Room is open daily for breakfast; à la carte options range from steel-cut oatmeal and custom omelets to more exotic eye-openers like Tahitian French toast l'orange. At dinner, Islands has better-than-average international cuisine. Another breakfast option is the grab-and-go Tuk Tuk Market in the lobby, which also serves Starbucks coffee, hot sandwiches, and gelato. Jake's American Bar serves a casual sit-down menu for lunch and dinner, along with late-night bar snacks. On select Saturday mornings, the Tahitian Room opens for a character breakfast with the Minions and their *Despicable Me* pals; see page 213 for details. Several casual bar areas—including Jake's American Bar, the Orchid Court Lounge & Sushi Bar, and the poolside Bula Bar & Grille with neighboring ice cream stand—are located in the resort.

Though nice, the rooms alone aren't worth the rates, but adding in Universal Express Unlimited and a short walk to the parks makes it the best deal among Universal's top hotels.

Loews Sapphire Falls Resort ★★★★ *(temporarily closed)*

6601 Adventure Way
Orlando
☎ 407-503-5000 or
888-273-1311
loewshotels.com
/sapphire-falls-hotel

Rate per night $176–$350. **Pool** ★★★★. **Fridge in room** Yes. **Shuttle to parks** Yes (Universal, SeaWorld, Aquatica). **Maximum number of occupants per room** 5 (two queens) or 3 (king). **Comment** Pets welcome (2/room, $100/stay). **Survey results** 92% of *Unofficial Guide* readers would both stay here again and recommend this resort to a friend.

SAPPHIRE FALLS RESORT brings a sunny Caribbean island vibe to the moderate market with its 1,000 rooms (including 77 suites), which opened in summer 2016. Sandwiched between Royal Pacific and Cabana Bay—both physically and price-wise—Sapphire Falls sports most of the amenities of Universal's three fanciest hotels, including water taxi transportation to the parks, with the crucial exception of complimentary Express Passes.

Rather than replicating the stereotypical pastel palette seen at Disney's Caribbean-themed hotel, Sapphire Falls's designers went with a cooler blue-and-white color scheme for the exterior. The lobby continues the modern reinterpretation of island aesthetics with a playful hanging sculpture of wicker beach balls and a massive floor-to-ceiling window providing a postcard-perfect view of the rear lagoon, with the towers of Doctor Doom's Fearfall posing in the background. Public spaces fuse seemingly ancient structures—such as a stunning stone silo, complete with authentic-looking mill equipment—with starkly minimalist architecture and contemporary artwork. The mix can prove somewhat jarring; we sometimes emerged from a richly detailed space into a barren white hallway and wondered if we'd taken a wrong turn into an employee-only area. But we've come to appreciate the Sapphire Falls Resort's casually sophisticated vibe, which hits a sweet spot between the family-friendly freneticism of Cabana Bay and the elegance of Universal's more upscale hotels.

Water figures heavily at Sapphire Falls, whose namesake waterfalls form the scenic centerpiece of the resort. The 16,000-square-foot main pool boasts 3,500 square feet of sand on which to set your lounger, as well as a 100-foot waterslide, children's play areas, fire pits, a hot tub, and cabanas for rent. There are two zero-entry points near the middle of the pool on opposite sides, which allow you to pretend to walk across the water.

A fitness room holds a sauna. Table tennis (free to use) and a pool table (nominal fee per game) are available outside near the small arcade.

On the lower level, Amatista Cookhouse offers à la carte or buffet American breakfast, followed by table-service Caribbean food for lunch and dinner. Drhum Club Kantine serves tapas-style small plates, sandwiches, and massive bowls of alcohol near the pool bar's fire pit. New Dutch Trading Co., an island-inspired grab-and-go marketplace, has ice cream, coffee, hot entrées and sandwiches, refillable Coke Freestyle cups, and packaged snacks. Strong Water Tavern in the lobby offers rum tastings and freshly made ceviche, and a Universal Studios Store in the lobby sells sundries and resort souvenirs.

The rooms range from 322 square feet in a standard queen or king to 529 square feet in the 36 Kids Suites, and up to 1,353 square feet in the

15 Hospitality Suites, which are appointed with charming rustic light fixtures and are sizable enough to live in long-term. All rooms include a 49-inch TV, an alarm clock with iPhone dock, in-wall USB charging ports, a minifridge, and a coffee maker. The rooms are aesthetically acceptable but a bit antiseptic, aside from a garishly colored mirror frame and metallized photos above the beds, and they are barely bigger than the standard Cabana Bay rooms. We like these rooms a bit better than those at Aventura, but they're more expensive too. The layout is perfectly functional, but there are some odd design quirks, such as a sliding door to the toilet that doesn't latch; don't plan on doing your business in private if you have inquisitive kids.

Sapphire Falls also contains nearly 115,000 square feet of meeting space and a business center. Covered walkways connect to a parking structure, which in turn connects to the meeting facilities at Royal Pacific, making the sister properties ideal for conventions. That also leads us to our main critique of Sapphire Falls: outside of the lobby and pool, the public areas feel a little like a standard convention hotel.

Water taxi transportation to Sapphire Falls takes only a few minutes longer than sailing to Royal Pacific, though boats may be delayed by traffic congestion under the bridge between the hotels and CityWalk. A pedestrian pathway to the parks starts near the boat dock, joining up with the Royal Pacific garden path near that hotel's convention center entrance. If you want to walk from Sapphire Falls to Cabana Bay, note that there's no pedestrian crosswalk at the heavily trafficked intersection that separates the two hotels; instead, walk to the corner of Hollywood Way and use the garden bridge to cross over Adventure Way, or use the path between Aventura and Volcano Bay to walk beneath the busy road.

Sapphire Falls occupies an interesting spot in Universal's hotel spectrum, appealing to people turned off both by the mid-century aesthetics of Cabana Bay (or Aventura's ultramodernism) and the higher price tags of the resort's other properties. If water taxi transportation is important to you, but Express Unlimited access is not, Sapphire Falls is your spot. Otherwise, search for photos online to see if you like the resort's look, and carefully compare the rates to both Cabana Bay and Aventura Hotel for the time of your planned visit.

Universal's Aventura Hotel ★★★½ *(temporarily closed)*

Rate per night $128-$278. Pools ★★★½. Fridge in room Yes. Shuttle to parks Yes (Universal, SeaWorld, Aquatica). Maximum number of occupants per room 4 (two queens or king with pull-out) or 6 (Kids Suites). Comment Pets not permitted. Survey results 86% of *Unofficial Guide* readers would stay here again; 80% would recommend this resort to a friend.

6725 Adventure Way
Orlando
☎ 407-503-6000
or 888-273-1311
loewshotels.com
/universals-aventura-hotel

IN THE SUMMER OF 2018, AVENTURA HOTEL opened as the resort's sixth property and second Prime Value option. Squeezed next to the lushly tropical Sapphire Falls and across the street from the colorfully retro Cabana Bay, Universal's Aventura Hotel may seem a bit under-themed in comparison to its neighbors. But if you've ever seen the luxury skyscrapers lining Miami's waterfronts, this 16-story Y-shaped tower will make you feel right at home with its ultramodern curvilinear glass-covered design (which looks suspiciously similar to a giant fidget spinner).

From the sleek, spacious lobby to the streamlined guest rooms, Aventura embodies that trendy aesthetic that Universal describes as simplified style, and which cynics might describe as IKEA stark; if you've stayed in a European micro-hotel, Aventura's rooms will feel familiar. Standard rooms start at a miniscule 238 square feet—about 22 square feet smaller than Disney's All-Star Resorts—for a king room with a pullout couch, while the standard room (with two queen beds), at 314 square feet, is a smidgen smaller than those at Sapphire Falls next door. Deluxe rooms, available with two queen beds or a single king, have a little more elbow-room at 395 square feet but still sleep a maximum of four. Because the deluxe rooms are located at the ends of the hotel's wings, you'll wake up to a dramatic 180-degree view. If you need more room, 16 Kids Suites are available; at 575 square feet, they have space for six, including a separate interior room with two twin beds and a play area with a pullout couch but no special theming. Unusually, room upgrades are priced not based on direction of view but altitude: "skyline" rooms on the topmost floors charge an extra $25 per night for panoramic views of the City Beautiful from one side of the tower or of Universal Orlando from the others. Odd-numbered rooms XX01–XX15 and even-numbered rooms XX30–XX44 face I-4 and International Drive; odd-numbered rooms XX31–XX45 and even-numbered rooms XX50–XX64 face Cabana Bay and Volcano Bay; and even-numbered rooms XX00–XX14 and odd-numbered rooms XX51–XX65 face toward Sapphire Falls and IOA.

All of the hotel's rooms share the same minimalist design scheme, featuring faux-hardwood tile floors and a monochromatic palette with a noticeable absence of color or artwork. Floor plans are oddly shaped, owing to the hotel's curved footprint, but floor-to-ceiling windows and translucent dividers between the bed and bath help the rooms feel more spacious. The beds are passable, though not plush, and all of the electronics work. However, the shower curtain doesn't extend far enough down, resulting in a wet floor every time.

In addition to the standard amenities, such as separate vanity and toilet areas, a minifridge, a coffee maker, and a 43-inch TV, Aventura's rooms integrate smart home technology. Not only are USB plugs preinstalled in the power outlets for recharging your digital devices, but every room also includes a tablet that you can use to adjust the air-conditioning, tune the TV, or even order a pizza and clean towels. If you have a Chromecast-compatible device or subscribe to Netflix or Amazon Prime, you can stream your own videos on the TV set. The iPad integration is innovative but also annoying if you need to use the sink in the middle of the night; thankfully, there are still physical switches for illuminating the toilet.

The pool at Aventura Hotel is also in the chic South Floridian style, with a compact crescent-shaped main pool surrounded by white decks and strategically placed palm trees. There's a splash pad and underwater speakers (all the better to hear the dive-in movies) for the kids, and a fire pit and hot tub for the grown-ups; anyone with a couple of bucks can enjoy the Foosball and pool tables. Rainy day recreation includes a free fitness room, a Universal Studios Store, and an arcade with HTC Vive virtual reality headsets ($10 for 5 minutes of game play; 50% discount for annual pass holders). Aventura is also home to Universal Orlando's first V-Hub lounge, where Virgin Holidays travelers staying at any on-site hotel can stash their luggage, grab some snacks, and relax on their departure day.

Aventura Hotel doesn't have a full-service restaurant, but that doesn't mean you'll starve. Along with the de rigueur Starbucks in the lobby, you'll also find Urban Pantry, a fast-casual food hall serving international entrées like ramen, artisanal pizza, and rotisserie chicken, plus a rooftop bar that serves craft cocktails and small plates. There are two additional bars, in the lobby and at the pool, but you'll want to take the dedicated elevator up to Bar 17 Bistro on the rooftop for its million-dollar views of Volcano Bay's namesake peak and the surrounding city.

Like Cabana Bay, Aventura lacks direct water taxi service to CityWalk, though you can easily walk over to Sapphire Falls and use its boats. Bus service delivers guests to the parking hub, and there is direct pedestrian access to all three parks, including a dedicated sidewalk past the pool to Volcano Bay. Reader ratings for Aventura are lower than almost all Disney and Universal resorts, with this comment from a Portland, Connecticut, father being fairly representative:

The room itself was very, very small. Go for the deluxe room for any sort of extra space if you have more than two in your party. Nothing about Aventura screamed Universal or Florida. NOTHING. The lobby was as sterile as an office building, and about as colorful.

Aventura and Cabana Bay, both Prime Value properties, include Early Park Admission but not Universal Express, and the rack rates are similar. So the choice between them might come down to whether your preferred style is cutting-edge cool or vibrant vintage. That said, we think Cabana Bay is a better option overall.

Universal's Cabana Bay Beach Resort ★ ★ ★ ★

Rate per night $164–$236; suites $189–$258. **Pools** ★★★★½.
Fridge in room Yes. **Shuttle to parks** Yes (Universal, SeaWorld, Aquatica). **Maximum number of occupants per room** 4 (two queens) or 6 (suites). **Comments** Character greeting in lobby on Friday. Pets not permitted. **Survey results** 87% of *Unofficial Guide* readers would stay here again; 84% would recommend this resort to a friend.

6550 Adventure Way Orlando
☎ 407-503-4000 or 888-273-1311
loewshotels.com /cabana-bay-hotel

IF YOU'RE OBSESSED WITH VINTAGE 1950s and 1960s designs, and with finding a good value (we're guilty on both accounts), you may just fall in love with Cabana Bay Beach Resort, one of Universal's Prime Value hotels. The mid-century modern aesthetic starts with the neon signage that welcomes you outside and continues inside with lots of windows, bright colors, and period-appropriate lighting and furniture. The designers were inspired by classic seaside hotels such as the doo-wop Caribbean

Motel in Wildwood Crest, New Jersey, and the original Americana Hotel in Bal Harbour, Florida. We think the resort would be right at home in the deserts of Palm Springs or Las Vegas, while our British friends say the decor reminds them of Butlin's Bognor Regis resort circa 1985.

Whatever Cabana Bay reminds you of, we think you'll like it. Kids will love the two large and well-themed pools (one with a lazy river), the amount of space they have to run around in, the vintage cars parked outside the hotel lobby, and the video arcade. Adults will appreciate the sophisticated kitsch of the decor, the multiple lounges, and the on-site Starbucks. We think Cabana Bay is an excellent choice for price- and/or space-conscious families visiting Universal.

The hotel's closest competitor in the Orlando area is Disney's Art of Animation Resort, and the two share many similarities. Both have standard rooms and Family Suites. At 430 square feet per suite, Cabana Bay suites are about 135 square feet smaller than comparable suites at Art of Animation and have only one bathroom. We found them well appointed for two to four people per room (though not for the six Loews claims as its capacity). Rates for the suites are about $150–$230 per night less than Art of Animation's. Standard rooms are only 300 square feet but can frequently be had for around $120 a night after discounts, undercutting Disney's cheapest rooms.

Each Family Suite has a small bedroom with two queen beds and a 40-inch TV, divided from the living area and kitchenette by a sliding screen; a pullout sofa in the living area offers additional sleeping space and a second 40-inch TV. The bath is divided into three sections: toilet, sink area, and shower room with additional sink; all are separated by doors, so three people can theoretically get ready at once. Retro theming even extends to the toiletries, which include the fondly remembered Zest and VO5 brands. The kitchenette has a microwave, coffee maker, and minifridge. A bar area allows extra seating for quick meals, and a large closet has enough space to store everyone's luggage. Built-in USB charging outlets for your devices are a thoughtful touch. Standard rooms have the same two queen beds but without the living area, kitchenette, or three-way bathroom. Instead, they get a minifridge with coffee maker and an average-size single bathroom.

Cabana Bay's rooms are divided among five long structures and two towers, arranged around two pool courtyards and connected in the center by the lobby facilities. The Castaway, Thunderbird, and Starlight (designated buildings 1, 2, and 3, respectively, each proudly identified in glowing neon script) are motel-style structures with exterior entrances surrounding the Cabana Courtyard. The Continental (building 4) and Americana (buildings 5 and 6) frame the Lazy River Courtyard and have hotel-style interior hallways. At the far end of the Continental and Americana buildings, Universal built the Bayside (building 7) and Beachside (building 8) expansion towers with 400 additional guest rooms, 20 of which are expansive 772-square-foot two-bedroom suites with stunning views of the Volcano Bay water park; be warned that guests in these rooms may struggle to sleep in once the park's conch horn begins blowing at park opening. Buildings 4 (rooms XX00-XX21) and 5 (rooms XX00-XX24) are closest to the bus loop and cafeteria, while some north-facing rooms in building 2 have a view of Hogwarts Castle.

Cabana Bay's two large pools both have artificial beaches and zero-entry sloping bottoms. The Cabana Courtyard Pool is more active, with a splash-pad playground and 100-foot waterslide wrapped around a central diving tower (which you can't actually dive off of, for safety reasons). The Lazy River Courtyard is a little more laid-back, with classic rock music (as opposed to the Top 40 usually played around the Cabana Courtyard) and a lushly landscaped circular stream in which to relax; flotation toys are sold for $4-$15 plus tax, inflation and deflation included (depending on staff availability, so don't wait until the last second before departing to deflate). Cabana Bay even sells watertight cups at the pool bar, so you can sip your cocktail while circulating in the lazy river.

Indoor recreational options include the Game-O-Rama arcade (well stocked with late-model machines and classic carnival-style redemption games) and the 10-lane Galaxy Bowl, modeled after the Hollywood Star Lanes featured in *The Big Lebowski.* Bowling costs $16.99 per adult, $10.99 per kid age 9 and under, for 45-75 minutes of play with shoe rental. Everyone bowls for $9 with the 20-minute Speed Bowling special. Waits for a lane can get long, especially on rainy days. Other diversions include poolside table tennis and billiards, as well as a large Jack LaLanne fitness center for free. An activity room with board games and beanbag chairs opens on rainy days. Finally, outdoor movies are shown nightly near both pools, and the food court sells $8 s'mores kits to roast over the gas-fueled fire pits.

In addition to the lobby's full-service Starbucks, the cavernous cafeteria-style Bayliner Diner food court serves breakfast, lunch, and dinner, with Coke Freestyle dispensers and giant screens in the seating area showing 1960s TV clips. Swizzle Lounge in the lobby, two pool bars (both with attached counter-service grills), in-room pizza delivery, and table-service snacks and sandwiches at the Galaxy Bowl round out the on-site dining options. The Universal Studios Store is the largest hotel store in the resort and stocks candy and clothes exclusive to Cabana Bay.

Colorful buses head to the parks' main parking hub from outside Cabana Bay's food court. The bus service is amazingly efficient; we've never waited more than 5 minutes for one to arrive, and the total transit time to the attractions is usually less than 15 minutes. It takes about the same amount of time to walk to CityWalk along the landscaped garden walkway, which passes the Sapphire Falls Resort before joining the walking path to Royal Pacific. And with an exclusive on-site entrance into Volcano Bay just for Cabana Bay guests, rolling out of bed just in time for early admission at the water park is a breeze; request the Bayside tower or Americana building 6 for the shortest walk.

Day guests who want to check out Cabana Bay should take the bus there from the parking hub because the garden walk's gate requires a key card for hotel access. Take care when driving into and out of the hotel's driveway on Adventure Way. If you miss the entrance, or make a right when exiting, you'll find yourself on a one-way road to I-4 West toward Disney, and you won't be able to correct course until the FL 528 expressway.

We've received rave reviews of Cabana Bay from our readers, like this mom from Putney, Vermont:

> *I LOVED the hotel. I usually share a standard room with my two children, but after trying the (very reasonably priced) Family Suites, I don't think I can go back! We each had our own bed, and it was wonderful. The pullout bed was hard but perfect for my back. The theming of the hotel is so fun. The kids loved the lazy river. The food court is fun too*

A mother from Overland Park, Kansas, adds:

> *We loved Cabana Bay. It had something for all of my kids (oldest is 17, youngest is 5), so everyone was happy. My husband and I even got some time while the kids were swimming each night to sit at the poolside bar and fire pit to wind down. Our kids didn't need us to entertain them in the pool area because there was so much to do. My 5- and 13-year-olds both enjoyed the waterslide. I loved the layout of the hotel and the quick ride to places like CityWalk (by far our favorite Orlando experience) and the parks.*

And a dad from Colorado Springs, Colorado, raves:

> *The hotel was great! We took the bus, and it was very convenient and fast, getting us there well before the park opened. Our second day, we walked to Sapphire Falls and took the boat to the parks, then walked back to Cabana Bay that night. The hotel gift shop was great too. It had some items you couldn't find in the parks.*

The hotel's only real downsides are that, while Cabana Bay guests are eligible for Early Park Admission at Universal, they do not receive complimentary Express Passes, and the furnishings are showing some wear as the hotel approaches its seventh birthday. Also, housekeeping services can sometimes be inconsistent in comparison to the pricier Loews properties, particularly if you don't depart your room before Early Park Admission begins, as this traveler from the Netherlands learned:

> *Our room was cleaned only two out of the five nights we were there. Mistakes can be made, but when we talked to the staff about it, their attitude was very unfriendly; they blamed us for leaving our room so "late" (at latest around 9 a.m.!)*

Universal's Endless Summer Resort ★ ★ ★ ½

Dockside Inn & Suites
7125 Universal Blvd.
Orlando
☎ 407-503-8000 or
888-430-4999
loewshotels.com
/dockside-inn-and-suites

Surfside Inn & Suites
7000 Universal Blvd.
Orlando
☎ 407-503-7000 or
888-430-4999
loewshotels.com
/surfside-inn-and-suites

Rate per night $109–$223; suites $164–$278. **Pools** ★★★. **Fridge in room** Yes. **Shuttle to parks** Yes (Universal, SeaWorld, Aquatica). **Maximum number of occupants per room** 4 (two queens) or 6 (suites). **Comment** Pets not permitted. **Survey results** 94% of *Unofficial Guide* readers would stay here again; 96% would recommend this resort to a friend. Endless Summer is the highest-rated value-priced resort at both Universal Orlando and Walt Disney World.

FOR ANYONE WHO FONDLY REMEMBERS the eponymous seminal 1966 surfing documentary, the phrase *Endless Summer* conjures images of pristine oceans, epic waves, and limitless freedom. Universal's Endless Summer Resort, a 2,800-room complex of value-priced rooms completed in 2020, is built along an inland lake that was previously home to the Wet 'n Wild water park, so the only waves it has ever known were man-made. But the resort does offer liberation of a sort, both from the traditional boundaries of Universal's property and from the limitation that park-owned hotels must always cost more than their off-site competition.

Endless Summer Resort is actually comprised of two sibling hotels, which sit across from each other on Universal Boulevard. Surfside Inn and Suites, located to the south on the land originally occupied by Wet 'n Wild's attractions, opened in summer 2019 with 750 rooms (360 standard and 390 two-bedroom suites) along the shoreline surrounding a surfboard-shaped pool. Dockside Inn and Suites, situated on the north side of the street in the water park's former parking lot, boasts a substantial 2,050 rooms (937 standard and 1,113 suites), supported by a separate lobby and two organically shaped pools; it opened in late 2020, after COVID-19 delayed its debut by several months. Both properties share a similar sunny aesthetic, with colorful images of seaside fun etched into the hotels' multistory cement towers.

Despite being the first to sport Universal's Value label, the 313-square-foot standard room with two queen beds is slightly larger than those at the Prime Value locations. They're also about the size of a Disney Moderate hotel room, but at Disney Value prices: about $100–$145 per night cheaper than a Moderate. That's quite a savings. And they aren't cheap from an aesthetic perspective either, as long as you appreciate the shabby chic look popular at vintage beachside hotels. In this modernized reinterpretation of a hippie hangout, the floors and furniture resemble reclaimed driftwood, and the tie-dyed curtains and vibrant wall art recall the summer of love. Thankfully, unlike the bohemian beach shacks of yore, at Endless Summer all the modern amenities are included: separate vanity and toilet areas, minifridge, convenient soda can holder, 43-inch TV, smart home controls for the temperature, and built-in high-amperage USB-C charging outlets. Room soundproofing is excellent, which is a surprise at this price, and there are plenty of under-shelf hooks on which to hang things, though only a handful of drawers for stowing your clothes. Our biggest nitpick is the poor quality of the soft goods; foam pillows and polyblend bath towels should be outlawed.

A little more than half the rooms at each Endless Summer complex are 440-square-foot suites with three queen beds, one bathroom, and a kitchenette complete with sink, microwave, low-end coffee maker, and kitschy picnic table for dining alfresco indoors. That's about 65–80 square feet smaller—and one less bathroom than—Disney's Family Suites, but a little roomier than the pricier Family Suites at Cabana Bay. We also like that Endless Summer's suites have a separate private bedroom with a second 49-inch TV for the third bed (as opposed to a pullout sofa), though we prefer Cabana Bay's split toilet/shower setup.

Endless Summer's lobbies, which display colorful surfboard signage and provide wicker swings on which to lounge, aren't as architecturally impressive as those at the upscale hotels, but the whole atmosphere is warmer and cozier than at Aventura or Sapphire Falls. The pools feature small splash pads for the kids and hold organized family activities like bingo and hoop contests, but they are unusually shallow (maximum depth 4 feet) and lack waterslides. Unfortunately, Endless Summer guests are forbidden from crashing the pool at the non-Value resorts. Each hotel also includes a surprisingly well-stocked free fitness room with internet-enabled treadmills that have interactive touch screens, plus a Universal Studios Store and a video arcade. Full-service dining isn't offered, but cafeteria-style food courts, lobby and pool bars, Starbucks cafés, and pizza delivery are all available.

Because it's on the opposite side of International Drive and I-4 from the rest of Universal Orlando, walking to the parks from Endless Summer isn't practical, especially with preschoolers in tow, so a fleet of free buses is provided, servicing both the parking hub (from which you walk to City-Walk and the theme parks) and direct to Volcano Bay. The ride to the parking hub from here is actually slightly shorter than the one from Cabana Bay; travel time is barely 5 minutes each way, and the entire trip (including walking and waiting to depart) takes about 15 minutes. At Surfside Inn, tower 1 is closest to the bus stop; the hotel's hallways are seemingly end-less, and it can be quite a hike to the rooms most distant from the lobby.

Universal advertises Endless Summer's rates as "starting from $79 per night," which is based on a five-night stay during the value season. Even at full rack rate, the hotel's competitive pricing undercuts many of its inde-pendent I-Drive neighbors, whose aging amenities will struggle to com-pete with Universal's 800-pound gorilla. While we still think Cabana Bay delivers more value for your dollar, cost-conscious visitors should think long and hard before booking an off-site hotel that doesn't offer Early Park Admission and easy transportation now that Endless Summer is open.

UNIVERSAL ORLANDO VACATION PACKAGES

UNIVERSAL FREQUENTLY OFFERS VACATION packages includ-ing hotel accommodations and park tickets via its in-house travel company, Universal Orlando Vacations. You can book a package yourself by calling ☎ 877-801-9720 or by visiting universalorlando vacations.com, or you can contact your preferred travel agent. Univer-sal Orlando Vacations booked more than 45 days in advance require only a $50-per-person deposit (airfare fully due at time of booking) that is fully refundable until 45 days out; after that, the penalty is $200 per package, though some event tickets may be nonrefundable.

Universal Orlando Vacations also handles group sales; if you want to organize a family reunion at Cabana Bay, call ☎ 800-224-4489 and choose option 3, or visit res.universalorlandovacations.com/Group /Groups.aspx.

Universal advertises its packages with enticing taglines like, "The Wizarding World from only $119 a night!" You have to do the math, though, because it's difficult for package purchasers to save money over buying à la carte unless they fully exploit every included component.

Here's an example. A Wizarding World of Harry Potter Vacation Package in late 2020 offered a family of four (two adults and two kids under age 10) these components:

1. Five nights at a Universal on-site hotel (or off-site partner hotel)

2. Four days of park-to-park admission to all three parks, including Volcano Bay

3. Breakfast at the Three Broomsticks (one per person)

4. Breakfast at Leaky Cauldron (one per person)

5. Photography session at Shutterbutton's in Diagon Alley, including souvenir DVD in a collectible tin and one exclusive designed 8-by-10-inch photo print

6. Souvenir keepsake box delivered to your home, including a welcome letter, three luggage tags featuring Harry Potter characters, and a Hogwarts Express-themed lanyard for each member of your party

7. Early Park Admission to The Wizarding World of Harry Potter and Volcano Bay 1 hour before the general public

8. CityWalk Party Pass

At Endless Summer Resort, the package started at $1,998.73, including tax, during the value season (September–October). There were significant restrictions, including blackout dates, and the stay had to occur on Sunday–Thursday nights to qualify for that low rate; weekend nights were more expensive.

Here's the first thing to recognize: the last two items—early admission to The Wizarding World and a CityWalk Party Pass—are automatically given to everyone who stays at a Universal resort and purchases a multiday ticket, so they don't have any value by themselves. Universal values the exclusive keepsakes and photo at $138.45, but similar lanyards can be purchased for $12–$14 apiece, and the remaining souvenirs are of nominal worth.

There are only four remaining components to price: the hotel, tickets, the Shutterbutton's session, and the breakfasts at the Three Broomsticks and Leaky Cauldron. We checked Universal's website for the cost of the other components using various dates in late 2020 and ensured those dates would also qualify for the aforementioned package. Here's a typical cost per component:

- $438.75 for five nights at Endless Summer Resort during value season

- $1,337.62 for 4-Day, 3-Park park-to-park tickets from universalorlando.com

- $131.97 for breakfast for four at the Three Broomsticks and Leaky Cauldron, including tax

- $85.19 for the Shutterbutton's DVD, or $53.25 if you purchase a photo package, including tax

Universal Orlando Vacations advertises a "Save & Bundle Discount" that saves $75 off five-night stays (and up to $200 off seven or more nights), but the total cost if you bought each component separately is $1,993.53, which means that shopping à la carte actually saves you about $5. However, if you were to forgo the breakfasts and Shutterbutton's video, you'd save more than $220 by buying separately. You can still reserve breakfast in The Wizarding World through your hotel's Ticket Center without a package, or even just walk up to the restaurants on many mornings. Universal's price for the breakfast is $19.16 per adult and $13.83 per child, including tax, so it's easy enough to figure out what it costs. Unless you're certain that you want the breakfasts and DVD, you're better off having lunch at the Leaky Cauldron with the money you'll save by buying each item of the package separately, as this anonymous reader discovered to their dismay:

> I'm still kicking myself for purchasing the entire package: flights, transfers, meal plan, etc. I was a total sucker and had a good time adding up the numbers for our meals and realizing it was virtually impossible to spend enough money to break even.

Even if it won't save you money, there are a few reasons why you might still want to book a Universal Orlando Vacations package. The first is if you can't afford to stay on-site but still want Early Park Admission to The Wizarding World and Volcano Bay. Booking a room at a Universal-area partner hotel as part of a package through Universal Orlando Vacations is the *only* way to get guaranteed early entry to the Harry Potter attractions and the water park, other than staying in an on-site hotel.

Another reason is if you are attending a special event at Universal Orlando that offers exclusive experiences for package buyers. For example, the now-discontinued Celebration of Harry Potter fan convention held an after-hours party in The Wizarding World just for vacation-package purchasers. Occasionally, packages are offered with truly unique perks: before the openings of Hogsmeade and Diagon Alley, a limited number of package holders were allowed into the new Wizarding Worlds weeks before the general public. These rare opportunities are only for the diehards because uncontrollable technical delays can always preempt previews without refunds.

If you opt to book through Universal Orlando Vacations, be sure to pay very close attention during the confirmation process, as a mom of three from Arlington, Virginia, explains:

> We did not get the package we thought we were getting because we didn't catch the omission when the phone attendant confirmed our travel plans. When we called back about it, they went back to the recording transcripts and said that because we had not caught the omission then, it was our fault, and they didn't have to reinstate that portion of the package. I was miffed.

Also be aware that, in case of a cancellation, Universal Vacations may take a while to refund your payments, as was the case with this reader from Drummond, Wisconsin:

When it was announced that the parks would be closed, I called Universal to cancel the trip and was told that the credit back to my account would take four to six weeks to process. Not having received the credit (after seven weeks and multiple calls), I'm frustrated with the process and the uncertainty as to whether I'll actually receive the refund. I'll certainly never consider booking with Universal again.

Finally, if you insist on prepaying for your table-service meals, the Table-Service Universal Dining Plan is available exclusively as an add-on to any Universal Orlando Vacations package. The adult plan costs $64.99 plus tax per person, per day, and includes one table-service meal (entrée, nonalcoholic beverage, and select dessert), one quick-service meal (entrée and nonalcoholic beverage), one snack, and a third nonalcoholic beverage. The child plan costs $24.99 plus tax and includes one table-service meal and one quick-service meal from the kids' menu, plus a regular snack and soft drink. Neither plan's price includes gratuities, which are expected at table-service restaurants based on the value of your meal. Eligible table-service restaurants are restricted to the two sit-down restaurants at each theme park, plus 10 CityWalk locations, including Bigfire, Toothsome Chocolate Emporium, The Cowfish, Vivo Italian Kitchen, and Antojitos Authentic Mexican Food. Bafflingly, none of the restaurants inside the resort's hotels accept the dining plan, making it even more pointless for on-site guests. Occasionally, Universal will run booking specials offering free dining credit at your resort hotel's restaurants, a much better bargain.

Suffice it to say that there are much better ways to spend $65-plus a day on dining at Universal, and you'll have to order very carefully to get your money's worth from every table-service meal. A quick service–only dining plan ($25.99 for adults, $17.99 for kids, plus tax) is also sold to the general public; there's no real benefit to buying it in advance in a package. For more information on Universal's dining plans, see page 214, and visit tinyurl.com/UODiningPlan.

OFF-SITE LODGING OPTIONS

SELECTING AND BOOKING A HOTEL

LODGING COSTS IN ORLANDO vary incredibly. If you shop around, you can find a clean motel with a pool for as low as $80 a night. Because of hot competition, discounts abound, particularly for AAA and AARP members. There are four primary areas to consider:

1. UNIVERSAL ORLANDO AREA   In the triangular area bordered by I-4 on the southeast, Vineland Road on the north, and Turkey Lake Road on the west are Universal Orlando and the hotels most convenient to it. Running north–south through the middle of the triangle is Kirkman Road, which connects to I-4. On the east side of Kirkman are a number of independent hotels and restaurants. Universal hotels,

Hotel Concentrations Around Universal Orlando

1. Universal Orlando Area
2. International Drive Area
3. Lake Buena Vista Resort Area and the I-4 Corridor
WDW Walt Disney World

parks, and CityWalk are west of Kirkman. Traffic in this area is not nearly as congested as on nearby International Drive, and there are good interstate connections in both directions.

2. INTERNATIONAL DRIVE AREA   This area, about 5 minutes from Universal, parallels I-4 on its eastern side and offers a wide selection of hotels and restaurants. Prices range from $56 to $439 per night. The

International Drive & Universal Areas

Lake Cane

Peregrine Ave.
Windhover Dr.

Florida's Turnpike

4 → East to Downtown Orlando

Vineland Road

Universal Blvd.

435

Major Blvd.

Caravan Ct.

77

Universal Orlando

Orlando Premium Outlets

75AB

W. Oak Ridge Road

Turkey Lake Road

Hollywood Way

Adventure Way

74B

75B

American Way

75A

Grand National Dr.

International Dr.

Kirkman Road

Del Verde Way

International Dr.

Carrier Dr.

Canada Ave.

482

Sand Lake Road

Official Visitor Center

74A →■

Jamaican Ct.

Austrian Ct. →

Austrian Row →

International Dr.

Samoan Ct. →

4

Universal Blvd.

I-4 Exits

77	Florida's Turnpike
75A East	Universal Studios/ International Drive
75AB West	FL 435 North/South
75B East	Kirkman Road
74B	Universal Studios
74A	Sand Lake Road
72	FL 528 (Beachline Expressway)
71	Central Florida Parkway

Pointe Plaza Ave.

Universal Blvd.

Orange County Convention Center

Hawaiian Ct.

Destination Pkwy.

To Orlando International Airport →

72

(no toll)

(no toll)

528

Turkey Lake Road

Westwood Blvd.

Sea Harbor Dr.

Aquatica

International Dr.

Orangewood Blvd.

Beachline Expy. (toll road)

West to Walt Disney World Resort & Tampa ↙

71

SeaWorld Orlando

Central Florida Parkway

Discovery Cove

chief drawbacks of this area are its terribly congested roads, countless traffic signals, and inadequate access to I-4 West. While International's biggest bottleneck is its intersection with Sand Lake Road, the mile between Kirkman and Sand Lake Roads is almost always gridlocked.

Regarding traffic on International Drive (known locally as I-Drive), a conventioneer from Islip, New York, weighed in with this:

> *We wasted huge chunks of time in traffic on International Drive. Our hotel was in the section between Sand Lake Road and Universal Boulevard. There are practically no left-turn lanes in this section, so anyone turning left can hold up traffic for a long time.*

Traffic aside, a man from Ottawa, Ontario, sings the praises of his I-Drive experience:

> *International Drive is the place to stay in Orlando. Your description of this location failed to point out that there are several discount stores, boutiques, restaurants, miniputts, and other entertainment facilities all within walking distance of remarkably inexpensive accommodations and a short drive away from the attractions.*

I-Drive hotels are listed on the Visit Orlando website: visitorlando.com/en/places-to-stay (click "International Drive Area").

3. LAKE BUENA VISTA AND THE I-4 CORRIDOR   A number of hotels are along FL 535 and west of I-4 between Disney World and I-4's intersection with Florida's Turnpike. They're easily reached from the interstate and are near many restaurants, including those on International Drive. Traffic on I-4 can be a real slog, so avoid it during rush hours. (See the map on the opposite page.)

WDW   We've also included a few hotels on the northeast side of Walt Disney World property, due to their proximity to Universal Orlando. We have not included other hotels on Disney property, nor have we included hotels along US 192 or those in Kissimmee.

HOTEL SHOPPING

OTAS AND THE MERCHANT MODEL   **Online travel agencies (OTAs)** sell travel products from a wide assortment of suppliers, often at deep discounts. These sites include such familiar names as **Travelocity, Orbitz, Priceline, Expedia, Hotels.com,** and **Hotwire.** Under a merchant model, hotels provide an OTA with a deeply discounted room rate that the OTA then marks up and sells. The difference between the marked-up price and the discounted rate paid to the hotel is the OTA's gross profit.

MORE POWER TO THE SHOPPER   Understanding the market dynamics we've described gives you a powerful tool for obtaining the best rates for the hotel of your choice. It's why we tell you to shop the web for the lowest price available and then call your travel agent or the hotel itself to ask if they can beat it. Any savvy reservationist knows that selling you the room directly will both cut the hotel's cost and improve gross margin. If the reservationist can't help you, ask to speak to his

Lake Buena Vista Resort Area & the I-4 Corridor

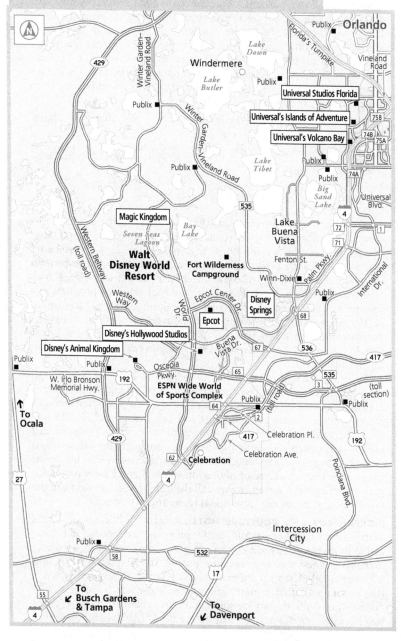

or her supervisor. (We've actually had to explain hotel economics to more than a few clueless reservation agents.)

As for travel agents, they have clout based on the volume of business they send to a particular hotel or chain and can usually negotiate a rate even lower than what you've found online. Even if the agent can't beat the price, he or she can often obtain upgrades, preferred views, free breakfasts, and other deal sweeteners. When we bump into a great deal on the web, we call our agent. Often she can beat the deal or improve on it, perhaps with an upgrade. *Reminder:* Except for special arrangements agreed to by you, the fee or commission due to your travel agent will be paid by the hotel.

THE SECRET When we're really hungry for a deal, there are a number of sites we always check out:

OUR FAVORITE ONLINE HOTEL RESOURCES	
HOTELCOUPONS.COM	Self-explanatory
ORLANDOVACATION.COM	Great rates for condos and home rentals
VISITORLANDO.COM	Good info; not user-friendly for booking

We scour these sites for unusually juicy hotel deals that meet our criteria (location, quality, price, and amenities). If we find a hotel that fills the bill, we check it out at other websites and comparative travel search engines such as **Kayak** (kayak.com), **Hotels.com,** and **Mobissimo** (mobissimo.com) to see who has the best rate. (As an aside, Kayak also sells travel products, raising the issue of whether products not sold by Kayak are equally likely to come up in a search. Mobissimo, on the other hand, only links potential buyers to provider websites.) Another site is **Trivago** (trivago.com). Your initial shopping effort should take about 15–20 minutes, faster if you can zero in quickly on a particular hotel.

Next, armed with your insider knowledge of hotel economics, call the hotel or have your travel agent call. Start by asking about specials. If there are none, or if the hotel can't beat the best price you've found on the internet, share your findings and ask if the hotel can do better. Sometimes you'll be asked for proof of the rate you've discovered online—to be prepared for this, go to the site and enter the dates of your stay, plus the rate you've found to make sure it's available. If it is, print the page or take a screenshot of this information and have it handy for your travel agent or for when you call the hotel. (*Note:* Always call the hotel's local number, not its national reservations number.)

INDEPENDENT AND BOUTIQUE HOTEL DEALS While chain hotels worry about sales costs and profit margins, independent and so-called boutique hotels are concerned about discoverability—making themselves known to the traveling public. The market is huge, and it's increasingly hard for these hotels to get noticed, especially when they're competing with major chains. For these hotels, substantially discounting rates is part of their marketing plan to build a client base. Because such hotels get lost on the big OTA sites and on search engines such as Kayak and Google, they offer almost irresistible rates on daily-coupon sites such as **Groupon** and **LivingSocial,** allowing them to get their product in front of thousands of potential guests.

These offers are very generous but also time-limited. If you're in the market, though, you'll be hard-pressed to find better deals. While an OTA such as Expedia generally obtains rooms at a 20%–35% discount off the hotel's published rate, flash sites cut deals at an extra-deep discount. This allows their subscribers to bid on or secure coupons for rooms that are often as much as 50% lower than the hotel's standard rate, and the coupons frequently include perks such as meals, free parking, waived resort fees, shopping vouchers, spa services, and entertainment. On Groupon's home page, click "Getaways" or just wait for Getaway coupons by email as part of your free subscription. On LivingSocial you have to specifically subscribe to "Travel"; otherwise, you'll receive only non-travel-related offers. We've also had great results using **HotelTonight.com**'s free smartphone app around the country and in Europe. If you don't mind not knowing where you'll rest your head until a few days (or even hours) in advance, you can score tremendous savings on properties near Universal, though not on-site.

NEW IS BETTER—AND SOMETIMES CHEAPER   New hotels rarely burst on the scene at 100% occupancy. During a hotel's first year, when it strives to generate buzz and attract clientele, it often offers deeply discounted rooms. This is true even of prestigious brands. One thing's for sure: a new hotel will charge less the first few months it's open than subsequently, and a hotel that opens during low season will discount more than hotels that open during high season.

AIRBNB   **Airbnb** (airbnb.com) hooks up travelers with owner-hosted alternative lodging all over the world, from spare bedrooms in people's homes to private apartments, vacation homes, and even live-in boats. It's also rattled the hotel industry because it's not subject to most of the regulations and taxes that dedicated hotels must observe.

We use Airbnb extensively in our personal and professional travel, including for most of our work in New York City and Washington, D.C. But we find that Airbnb is not as useful in Orlando for a couple of reasons. One is the enormous supply of vacation home rentals and hotel rooms, which keeps prices down for lodging around Universal. Second are Universal's incentives for staying on property, including extra time in the parks and Universal Express Unlimited. Airbnb users seem to agree: while Orlando is one of the country's biggest travel destinations, it's not one of Airbnb's top 10 markets. However, some of our readers, like this family from Sylva, North Carolina, have had luck with Airbnb in the Universal area:

> We were on a very strict budget. We needed three beds because the teenagers didn't want to sleep in the same bed. After looking at the cost of hotels with sleeper sofas and tickets together, we opted for an inexpensive Airbnb. For the three nights we stayed ($206), I couldn't find a better deal with a hotel.

IS IT WORTH IT? You might be asking yourself if it's worth all this effort to save a few bucks. Saving $10 on a room doesn't sound like a big deal, but if you're staying six nights, that adds up to $60. Earlier we referred to unusually juicy deals, deep discounts predicated by who-knows-what circumstances that add up to big money. They're available every day, and with a little perseverance, you'll find them. Happy hunting!

SCRATCH THAT ITCH . . . FOR INFORMATION

GRANTED, IT WON'T HELP YOU find good deals on hotels, but **The Bedbug Registry** (bedbugregistry.com) is nonetheless a useful resource, allowing you to peruse reports of bedbug and other insect infestations at any hotel in the United States. Simply enter the name, city, and state of the property in question; you can also submit a report of your own. Bedbug outbreaks are usually confined to particular rooms and that the creepy-crawlies were probably brought in by previous guests. If you suspect an infestation, report it to management immediately.

CONDOMINIUMS AND VACATION HOMES

BECAUSE CONDOS TEND TO BE part of large developments (frequently time-shares), amenities such as swimming pools, playgrounds, game arcades, and fitness centers often rival those found in the best hotels. Generally speaking, condo developments don't have restaurants, lounges, or spas. In a condo, if something goes wrong, there will be someone on hand to fix the problem. Vacation homes rented from a property-management company likewise will have someone to come to the rescue, though responsiveness tends to vary vastly from company to company. If you rent directly from an owner, correcting problems is often more difficult, particularly when the owner doesn't live in the same area as the rental home.

In a vacation home, all the amenities are contained in the home (though in planned developments, there may be community amenities available as well). Depending on the specific home, you might find a small swimming pool, hot tub, two-car garage, family room, game room, and even a home theater. Features found in both condos and vacation homes include full kitchens, laundry rooms, TVs, DVD players, and frequently stereos. Interestingly, though almost all freestanding vacation homes have private pools, very few have backyards. This means that, except for swimming, the kids are pretty much relegated to playing in the house.

Time-share condos are clones when it comes to furniture and decor, but single-owner condos and vacation homes are furnished and decorated in a style that reflects the owner's taste. Vacation homes, usually one- to two-story houses in a subdivision, very rarely afford interesting views (though some homes overlook lakes or natural areas), while condos, especially the high-rise variety, sometimes offer exceptional ones.

How the Vacation Home Market Works

In the Orlando area, there are more than 26,000 rental homes, including stand-alone homes, single-owner condos (that is, not time-shares), and townhomes. The same area has more than 129,000 hotel rooms. Some owners deal directly with renters, while others enlist the assistance of a property-management company.

Incredibly, about 700 property-management companies operate in the Orlando market. Most of these are mom-and-pop outfits that manage an inventory of 10 homes or fewer (probably fewer than 70 companies oversee more than 100 rental homes).

Some homes are made available to wholesalers, vacation packagers, and travel agents. A wholesaler or vacation packager will occasionally drop its rates to sell slow-moving inventory, but more commonly the cost to renters is higher than when dealing directly with owners or management companies: because most wholesalers and packagers sell their inventory through travel agents, both the wholesaler/packager's markup and the travel agent's commission are passed along to the renter. These costs are in addition to the owner's cut and/or the fee for the property manager.

Along similar lines, logic may suggest that the lowest rate of all can be obtained by dealing directly with owners, thus eliminating middlemen. Though this is sometimes true, it's more often the case that property-management companies offer the best rates. With their marketing expertise and larger customer base, these companies can produce a higher occupancy rate than the owners themselves can. What's more, management companies, or at least the larger ones, can achieve economies of scale not available to owners regarding maintenance, cleaning, linens, and even acquiring furniture and appliances (if a house is not already furnished). The combination of higher occupancy rates and economies of scale adds up to a win-win situation for owners, management companies, and renters alike.

Location, Location, Location

The best vacation home is one that is within easy commuting distance of the parks. If you plan to spend some time at Walt Disney World and SeaWorld in addition to the Universal parks, you'll want something just to the southwest of Universal Orlando (between Walt Disney World and Orlando).

Zoning laws in Orange County (which also includes most of Orlando, Universal Studios, SeaWorld, Lake Buena Vista, and the International Drive area) only allow short-term rentals of homes and single-owner condos in a few predominantly tourist-oriented areas. Practically all of the vacation-rental homes in Orange County are in the Floridays and Vista Cay developments.

By our reckoning, about half the rental homes in Osceola County and all the rental homes in Polk County are too far away for commuting to be practical. You might be able to save a few bucks by staying farther out, but the most desirable homes to be found are in Vista Cay and in developments no more than 10 miles south of Universal's main entrance, from west of John Young Parkway to east of the FL 429 Western Beltway.

To get the most from a vacation home, you need to be close enough to commute in 20 minutes or less to your Orlando destination. This will allow for naps, quiet time, swimming, and dollar-saving meals you prepare yourself.

Shopping for a Vacation Home

There are three main types of websites in the home-rental game: those for property-management companies, which showcase a given company's homes and are set up for direct bookings; individual owner sites; and third-party listings sites, which advertise properties available through different owners and sometimes management companies as well. Sites in the last category will usually refer prospective renters to an owner's or management company's site for reservations.

We've found that most property-management sites are not very well designed and will test your patience to the max. You can practically click yourself into old age trying to see all the homes available or figure out where on earth they are. Nearly all claim to be "just minutes from Universal [or Disney]." (By that reasoning, we should list Bob's home; it's also just minutes from Universal . . . 570 minutes, to be exact!)

Many websites list homes according to towns (such as Clermont, Lake Buena Vista, Windermere, and Winter Garden) or real estate developments (including Eagle Pointe, Floridays, Golden Oaks, and Vista Cay) in the general Universal area, none of which you're likely to be familiar with. The information that counts is the distance of a home or condo from Universal; for that, you often must look for something like "4 miles from Universal" embedded in the home's description.

The best websites provide the following:

- Numerous photos and in-depth descriptions of individual homes to make comparisons quick and easy
- Overview maps or text descriptions that reflect how far specific homes or developments are from your Orlando destination
- The ability to book the specific rental home of your choice on the site
- An easy-to-find phone number for bookings and questions

The best sites are also easy to navigate, let you see what you're interested in without your having to log in or divulge any personal information, and list memberships in such organizations as the Better Business Bureau and the Florida Vacation Rental Managers Association (visit fvrma.org for the association's code of ethics).

Recommended Websites

After checking out dozens upon dozens of sites, here are the ones we recommend. All of them meet the criteria listed above. If you're stunned that there are so few of them, well, so were we. (For the record, we elected not to list some sites that met our criteria but whose homes are too far away from the Orlando-area attractions.)

#1 Dream Homes (floridadreamhomes.com) has a good reputation for customer service and has photos of and information about the homes in its online inventory.

Vacation Rentals by Owner (vrbo.com) is a nationwide vacation-homes listings service that puts prospective renters in direct contact with owners. The site is straightforward and always lists a large number of rental properties in Celebration, Disney's planned community situated about 15–20 minutes from the Universal theme parks. Two similar listings services with good websites are **Vacation Rentals 411** (vacationrentals411.com) and **Last Minute Villas** (lastminutevillas.net).

The website for **Visit Orlando** (visitorlando.com) is the place to go if you're interested in renting a condo at a time-share development (click on "Places to Stay" at the site's home page). You can call the developments directly, but going through this website allows you to bypass sales departments and escape their high-pressure invitations to sit through sales presentations. The site also lists hotels, vacation homes, and campgrounds. For all types of accommodations, you can sort by distance from where you'll spend your touring time. Distance-sorting categories include Universal, Walt Disney World, the Orange County Convention Center, and downtown Orlando, among others.

Making Contact

Once you've found a vacation home you like, check around the website for a frequently asked questions (FAQ) page. If there's not an FAQ page, here are some of the things you'll want to check out on the phone with the owner or rental company.

1. How close is the property to my vacation destination?
2. Is the home or condominium that I see on the internet the one I'll get?
3. Is the property part of a time-share development?
4. Are there any specials or discounts available?
5. Is everything included in the rental price, or are there additional charges? What about taxes?
6. How old is the house or condo that I'm interested in? When was it last refurbished?
7. What is the view from the property?
8. Is the property near any noisy roads?
9. What is your smoking policy?
10. Are pets allowed? This consideration is as important to those who want to avoid pets as to those who want to bring them.
11. Is the pool heated?
12. Is there a fenced backyard where children can play?
13. How many people can be seated at the main dining table?
14. Is high-speed internet access available?

15. Are linens and towels provided?

16. How far are the nearest supermarket and drugstore?

17. Are childcare services available?

18. Are restaurants nearby?

19. Is transportation to the parks provided?

20. Will we need a car?

21. What is required to make a reservation?

22. What is your change/cancellation policy?

23. When is checkout time?

24. What will we be responsible for when we check out?

25. How will we receive our confirmation and arrival instructions?

26. What are your office hours?

27. What are the directions to your office?

28. What if we arrive after your office has closed?

29. Whom do we contact if something goes wrong during our stay?

30. How long have you been in business?

31. Are you licensed by the state of Florida?

32. Do you belong to the Better Business Bureau and/or the Florida Vacation Rental Managers Association?

We frequently receive letters from readers extolling the virtues of renting a condo or vacation home. This endorsement by a family from Ellington, Connecticut, is typical:

> *Our choice to stay in a vacation home was based on cost and sanity. Our children don't want to share the same bed. We've also gotten tired of turning off the lights at 8 p.m. and lying quietly in the dark waiting for our children to fall asleep. With this in mind, we needed a condo/ suite layout. We decided on the Sheraton Vistana Resort, located on FL 535. We had a two-bedroom villa with a full kitchen, living room, three TVs, and a washer/dryer. I packed for half the trip and did laundry almost every night. The facilities offered a daily children's program and several pools, kiddie pools, and playscapes. We had a 5- to 10-minute drive to most attractions, including SeaWorld, Disney, and Universal.*

THE BEST HOTELS FOR FAMILIES NEAR UNIVERSAL ORLANDO

WHAT MAKES A SUPER FAMILY HOTEL? Roomy accommodations, an in-room fridge, a great pool, complimentary breakfast, childcare options, and programs for kids are a few of the things *The Unofficial Guide* hotel team researched in selecting the top hotels for families from among hundreds of properties in the Universal Orlando area. Some of our picks are expensive, others are more reasonable, and some are a bargain. Regardless of price, be assured that these hotels understand a family's needs.

Though all of the following hotels offer some type of shuttle to the parks, some offer very limited service. Call the hotel before you book and ask what the shuttle schedule will be when you visit. Because families, like individuals, have different wants and needs, we haven't ranked the following properties here; they're listed alphabetically. Most of the properties profiled below, with the exception of Rosen Shingle Creek and Holiday Inn Resort, are along International Drive.

Castle Hotel   ★★★½

Rate per night $110–$332. Pool ★★★. Fridge in room Yes ($15/day). Shuttle to parks Yes (Universal, SeaWorld). Maximum number of occupants per room 4. Comments Pets up to 40 pounds welcome ($150 nonrefundable fee). $15 daily parking fee.

8629 International Dr. Orlando
☎ 407-345-1511 or 877-317-5753
castlehotelorlando.com

YOU CAN'T MISS THIS ONE: it's the only castle on I-Drive and is part of Marriott's Autograph Collection. Inside you'll find royal colors (purple predominates), opulent fixtures (antlers are a recurring motif), European art, and Renaissance music.

The 214 rooms and suites also retain the royal treatment, but the decor is a bit more tasteful and streamlined. All rooms are fairly large and well equipped with a 37-inch TV, free Wi-Fi, coffee maker, iron and board, hair dryer, and safe. The Garden Bistro & Bar off the lobby serves full or Continental breakfast. For lunch or dinner, you might walk next door to Vito's Chop House (dinner only) or Café Tu Tu Tango (an Unofficial favorite). The heated circular pool is 5 feet deep and features a fountain in the center, a poolside bar, and a hot tub. There's no separate kiddie pool. Other amenities include the Poseidon Spa, a fitness center, gift shop, lounge, valet laundry service and facilities, and guest services desk with park passes for sale and babysitting recommendations. Security feature: Elevators require an electronic key card.

CoCo Key Hotel & Water Resort–Orlando   ★★★½

Rate per night $138–$155. Pools ★★★★½. Fridge in room Yes. Shuttle to parks Yes (Universal, Aquatica, SeaWorld: free; Disney: $18/person round-trip). Maximum number of occupants per room 4. Comments $32.95/night resort fee includes use of the water park; day guests may use the water park for $26.95/person.

7400 International Dr. Orlando
☎ 407-351-2626 or 877-875-4681
cocokeyorlando.com

NOT FAR FROM THE UNIVERSAL ORLANDO parks, CoCo Key combines a tropical-themed hotel with a canopied water park featuring three pools and 14 waterslides, as well as poolside food and arcade entertainment. A full-service restaurant serves breakfast and dinner; a food court offers family favorites such as burgers, chicken fingers, and pizza.

A unique feature of the resort is its cashless payment system, much like that on a cruise ship. At check-in, families receive bar-coded wristbands that allow purchased items to be easily charged to their room.

The spacious guest rooms include 37-inch TVs, free Wi-Fi, granite showers and countertops, and plentiful outlets for electronics.

DoubleTree by Hilton Orlando at SeaWorld ★★★★½

10100 International Dr.
Orlando
☎ 407-352-1100 or
800-327-0363
dtresortorlando.com

Rate per night $159–$179. **Pools** ★★★½. **Fridge in room** Standard in some rooms; available in others for a fee. **Shuttle to parks** Yes (Universal, Aquatica, SeaWorld: free; Disney: $8/person). **Maximum number of occupants per room** 4. **Comments** Pets welcome (1/room, 25-pound limit, $75). $19.95/night resort fee. $18/day self-parking. Good option if you're visiting SeaWorld or Aquatica.

ON 28 LUSH, TROPICAL ACRES with a Balinese feel, the DoubleTree is adjacent to SeaWorld and Aquatica water park. The 1,094 rooms and suites—classified as resort or tower—are suitable for business travelers or families. We recommend the tower rooms for good views and the resort rooms for maximum convenience. Laguna serves steak and seafood, along with breakfast; you can also get a quick bite at The Market or the pool bar. Relax and cool off at one of the three pools (there are two more just for kids), or indulge in a spa treatment. A fitness center, minigolf course, children's day camp, and game area afford even more diversions. The resort is about a 12-minute drive to Universal, a 15-minute drive to Walt Disney World, or a short walk to SeaWorld.

Holiday Inn Resort Orlando Suites–Waterpark ★★★½

14500 Continental
Gateway, Orlando
☎ 407-387-5437
hisuitesorlando.com

Rate per night $129–$171. **Pools** ★★★★½. **Fridge in room** Yes. **Shuttle to parks** Yes (Universal, SeaWorld, Disney). **Maximum number of occupants per room** 8. **Comments** $33.75/night resort fee. $12/day self-parking ($17/day for additional vehicle).

FOLLOWING A $30 MILLION RENOVATION IN 2016, the hotel formerly known as the Nickelodeon Suites Resort is now the Holiday Inn Resort Orlando Suites–Waterpark.

The 777 suites come in one-, two-, and three-bedroom varieties and each suite contains a minifridge, microwave, TV, and high-speed internet. The resort also boasts two water parks with 13 slides, a 4-D Experience, Laser Challenge, and a 3,000-square-foot arcade. Kids will love the many free activities at the main pool.

The resort is huge, and the layout of the hotel is somewhat confusing. Unless you prefer the more remote, quiet pool area, we suggest you request a room close to the main pool and The Market Place, the shopping and dining area of the complex. The shuttles to the parks depart from The Market Place.

Rosen Shingle Creek ★★★★

9939 Universal Blvd.
Orlando
☎ 407-996-9939 or
866-996-6338
rosenshinglecreek.com

Rate per night $165–$253. **Pools** ★★★★. **Fridge in room** Yes. **Shuttle to parks** Yes (Universal, SeaWorld, Discovery Cove, Aquatica). **Maximum number of occupants per room** 4. **Comment** Pets welcome ($150 nonrefundable fee). $18/day self-parking; $26/day valet.

BEAUTIFUL ROOMS (east-facing ones have great views) and excellent restaurants distinguish this mostly meeting- and convention-oriented resort. The pools, which are large and lovely, include a lap pool, a family pool, and a kiddie wading pool. There's an 18-hole golf course on-site, as well as a superior spa and an adequate fitness center. Childcare is provided as well.

Though a state-of-the-art video arcade will gobble up your kids' pocket change, the real kicker, especially for the 8-years-and-up crowd, is a natural area encompassing lily ponds, grassy wetlands, Shingle Creek, and an adjacent cypress swamp. Running through the area is a nature trail complete with signs to help you identify wildlife. Great blue herons, wood storks, coots, egrets, mallard ducks, anhingas, and ospreys are common, as are sliders (turtles), chameleons, and skinks (lizards).

If you stay at Shingle Creek and plan to visit the theme parks, you'll want a car. Shuttle service is limited, departing and picking up at rather inconvenient times and stopping at three other hotels before delivering you to your destination.

HOTELS AND MOTELS:
Rated and Ranked

IN THIS SECTION, WE COMPARE HOTELS in four main areas outside Universal Orlando (see page 113) with those inside the resort. Additional hotels can be found at the intersection of US 27 and I-4, on US 441 (Orange Blossom Trail), and in downtown Orlando. Most of these require more than 30 minutes of commuting to the Orlando-area attractions and thus are not rated. We also haven't rated lodging along US 192.

WHAT'S IN A ROOM?
EXCEPT FOR CLEANLINESS, STATE OF REPAIR, and decor, travelers pay little attention to hotel rooms. There is, of course, a clear standard of quality and luxury that differentiates Motel 6 from Holiday Inn, Holiday Inn from Marriott, and so on. Many guests, however, fail to appreciate that some rooms are better engineered than others. Making the room usable to its occupants is an art that combines both form and function.

Decor and taste are important. No one wants to stay in a room that's dated, garish, or ugly. But beyond decor, how "livable" is the room? In Orlando, for example, we've seen some beautifully appointed rooms that aren't well designed for human habitation. Even more than decor, your room's details and design elements are the things that will make you feel comfortable and at home.

ROOM RATINGS
TO EVALUATE PROPERTIES FOR THEIR QUALITY, tastefulness, state of repair, cleanliness, and size of their standard rooms, we have grouped the hotels and motels into classifications denoted by stars—the overall star rating. Star ratings in this guide apply only to Orlando-area properties and don't necessarily correspond to ratings awarded by Frommer's, Forbes, AAA, or other travel critics. Because stars have little

relevance when awarded in the absence of recognized standards of comparison, we have tied our ratings to expected levels of quality established by specific American hotel corporations.

Overall star ratings apply only to room quality and describe the property's standard accommodations. For most hotels, a standard accommodation is a room with one king bed or two queen beds. In an all-suite property, the standard accommodation is either a studio or a one-bedroom suite. In addition to standard accommodations, many hotels offer luxury rooms and special suites, which aren't rated in this guide. Star ratings for rooms are assigned without regard to whether a property has restaurant(s), recreational facilities, entertainment, or other extras.

OVERALL STAR RATINGS		
★★★★★	Superior rooms	Tasteful and luxurious by any standard
★★★★	Extremely nice rooms	What you'd expect at a Hyatt Regency or Marriott
★★★	Nice rooms	Holiday Inn or comparable quality
★★	Adequate rooms	Clean, comfortable, and functional without frills—like a Motel 6
★	Super-budget	These exist but are not included in our coverage

In addition to stars (which delineate broad categories), we use a numerical rating system: the room quality rating. Our scale is 0–100, with 100 being the best possible rating and zero (0) the worst. Numerical ratings show the difference we perceive between one property and another. For instance, rooms at both the Best Western Plus Universal Inn and the Fairfield Inn & Suites Near Universal Orlando Resort are rated 3.5 stars (★★★½). In the supplemental numerical ratings, the former is a 75 and the latter an 80. This means that within the 3.5-star category, Fairfield Inn & Suites has slightly nicer rooms than Best Western Plus.

unofficial **TIP**
The key to avoiding disappointment is to snoop in advance. Ask how old the hotel is and when its guest rooms were last renovated.

The location column identifies the area where you'll find a particular property. A 1 means it's in the Universal Orlando area. A 2 means it's on or near International Drive. All others are marked with 3 and for the most part are along FL 535 and the I-4 corridor, though some are in nearby locations that don't meet any other criteria. WDW, of course, indicates hotels located near Walt Disney World property.

LODGING AREAS *(see map on page 114)*	
1 Universal Orlando Area	**2** International Drive
3 Lake Buena Vista and I-4 Corridor	**WDW** Walt Disney World Resort

Cost estimates are based on the hotel's published rack rates for standard rooms and are rounded to the nearest $50.

We've focused on room quality and excluded consideration of location, services, recreation, or amenities. In some instances, a one- or two-room suite is available for the same price or less than that of a single standard hotel room.

If you've used a previous edition of this guide, you'll notice that new properties have been added and many ratings and rankings have changed, some because of room renovation or improved maintenance or housekeeping. Lax housekeeping or failure to maintain rooms can bring down ratings.

Before you shop for a hotel, consider this letter from a man in Hot Springs, Arkansas:

> *We canceled our room reservations to follow the advice in your book and reserved a hotel highly ranked by* The Unofficial Guide. *We wanted inexpensive but clean and cheerful. We got inexpensive but also dirty, grim, and depressing. The room spoiled the holiday for me aside from our touring.*

This letter was as unsettling to us as the bad room was to the reader—our integrity as travel journalists is based on the quality of the information we provide. When rechecking the hotel, we found our rating was representative, but the reader had been assigned one of a small number of threadbare rooms scheduled for renovation.

Some chains use the same room photo for all their hotels; the rooms at a specific property may bear no resemblance to the photo in question. When you or your travel agent calls, ask how old the property is and when the room you're being assigned was last renovated. If you're assigned a room inferior to your expectations, ask to be moved.

A WORD ABOUT TOLL-FREE TELEPHONE NUMBERS

AS WE'VE REPEATED several times in this chapter, it's essential to communicate with the hotel directly when shopping for deals and stating your room preferences. Most toll-free numbers are routed directly to a hotel chain's central reservations office, and the customer service agents there typically have little or no knowledge of the individual hotels in the chain or of any specials those hotels may be offering. In our Hotel Information Chart (pages 134–139), therefore, we list the toll-free number only if it connects directly to the hotel in question; otherwise, we provide the hotel's local phone number.

The 30 BEST HOTEL VALUES

IN THE CHART ON PAGE 130, we look at the best combinations of quality and value in a room. Rankings are made without consideration for location or the availability of restaurant(s), recreational facilities, entertainment, and/or amenities.

A reader wrote to complain that he had booked one of our top-ranked rooms in terms of value and had been very disappointed in the room. We noticed that the room the reader occupied had a quality rating of ★★½. Remember that the list of top deals is intended to give you some sense of value received for dollars spent. A ★★½ room at $70 may have the same value as a ★★★★ room at $115, but that doesn't mean the rooms will be of comparable quality. Regardless of whether it's a good deal, a ★★½ room is still a ★★½ room.

The 30 Best Hotel Values

HOTEL	LODGING AREA	OVERALL QUALITY	ROOM QUALITY	COST
1. DoubleTree by Hilton Orlando at SeaWorld	2	★★★★½	92	$100+
2. Extended Stay America Convention Center/ Westwood	2	★★★★	84	$100-
3. Extended Stay America Orlando Lake Buena Vista	3	★★★★	83	$100
4. Cypress Pointe Resort by Diamond Resorts	3	★★★★½	90	$150-
5. Quality Suites Turkey Lake South/ Lake Buena Vista	3	★★★½	77	$100-
6. Sheraton Lake Buena Vista Resort	3	★★★★	88	$100+
7. Courtyard Orlando Lake Buena Vista at Vista Centre	3	★★★★	89	$100+
8. Residence Inn Orlando at SeaWorld	3	★★★★	87	$100+
9. Motel 6 Orlando–I-Drive	2	★★★	66	$50+
10. Staybridge Suites Orlando at SeaWorld	2	★★★★½	90	$150
11. Extended Stay America Orlando Theme Parks	1	★★★½	75	$100-
12. Four Points by Sheraton Orlando Studio City	2	★★★★½	90	$150
13. Clarion Inn & Suites Across from Universal Orlando Resort	1	★★★½	82	$100+
14. Hyatt Regency Orlando	2	★★★★½	90	$150+
15. Best Western Plus Universal Inn	1	★★★½	75	$100
16. Marriott's Grande Vista	2	★★★★½	93	$150+
17. Extended Stay America Deluxe Orlando Theme Parks	1	★★★½	75	$100+
18. Quality Inn at International Drive	2	★★★	74	$100-
19. Homewood Suites by Hilton Lake Buena Vista-Orlando	3	★★★★	85	$150-
20. Hilton Grand Vacations Club at SeaWorld	2	★★★★	88	$150-
21. Holiday Inn Resort Orlando-Lake Buena Vista	3	★★★½	82	$100+
22. Renaissance Orlando at SeaWorld	2	★★★★½	90	$150+
23. Rosen Plaza Hotel	2	★★★★½	91	$150+
24. Drury Inn & Suites Orlando	2	★★★★	85	$150+
25. InTown Suites Orlando Universal	2	★★½	63	$50+
26. TownePlace Suites Orlando at SeaWorld	2	★★★★	84	$150-
27. Holiday Inn & Suites Across from Universal Orlando	1	★★★½	75	$100+
28. DoubleTree by Hilton at the Entrance to Universal Orlando	1	★★★★	89	$150+
29. Parc Corniche Condominium Suite Hotel	2	★★★★½	90	$200-
30. Rosen Inn at Pointe Orlando	2	★★★★	84	$150

How the Hotels Compare

HOTEL	LODGING AREA	OVERALL QUALITY	ROOM QUALITY	COST
Four Seasons Resort Orlando at Walt Disney World Resort	WDW	★★★★★	98	$1,000+
Rosen Centre Hotel	2	★★★★½	95	$250–
The Ritz-Carlton Orlando, Grande Lakes	2	★★★★½	94	$450–
Marriott's Grande Vista	2	★★★★½	93	$150+
Waldorf Astoria Orlando	WDW	★★★★½	93	$350–
Hard Rock Hotel Orlando	1	★★★★½	93	$450–
DoubleTree by Hilton Orlando at SeaWorld	2	★★★★½	92	$100+
Hyatt Regency Grand Cypress	3	★★★★½	92	$200–
Loews Portofino Bay Hotel	1	★★★★½	92	$450+
Rosen Plaza Hotel	2	★★★★½	91	$150+
Marriott's Harbour Lake	3	★★★★½	91	$200–
Hyatt House Across from Universal Orlando	1	★★★★½	91	$200+
Four Points by Sheraton Orlando Studio City	2	★★★★½	90	$150
Staybridge Suites Orlando at SeaWorld	2	★★★★½	90	$150
Cypress Pointe Resort by Diamond Resorts	3	★★★★½	90	$150–
Hyatt Regency Orlando	2	★★★★½	90	$150+
Renaissance Orlando at SeaWorld	2	★★★★½	90	$150+
Residence Inn Orlando at SeaWorld	2	★★★★½	90	$150+
Staybridge Suites Lake Buena Vista	3	★★★★½	90	$200–
Orlando World Center Marriott	3	★★★★½	90	$300–
Loews Royal Pacific Resort	1	★★★★½	90	$400–
Courtyard Orlando Lake Buena Vista at Vista Centre	3	★★★★	89	$100+
DoubleTree by Hilton at the Entrance to Universal Orlando	1	★★★★	89	$150+
Sheraton Vistana Resort Villas, Lake Buena Vista/Orlando	3	★★★★	89	$200–
Sheraton Lake Buena Vista Resort	3	★★★★	88	$100+
Hilton Grand Vacations Club at SeaWorld	2	★★★★	88	$150–
Hilton Orlando Bonnet Creek	WDW	★★★★	88	$250–
Rosen Shingle Creek Orlando	2	★★★★	88	$250+
Floridays Resort Orlando	2	★★★★	88	$300–
Hilton Grand Vacations Club at Tuscany Village	2	★★★★	88	$300+
Sheraton Vistana Villages Resort Villas, I-Drive/Orlando	2	★★★★	87	$150+
Hilton Orlando Lake Buena Vista	WDW	★★★★	87	$200–
Las Palmeras by Hilton Grand Vacations	2	★★★★	87	$250–
Marriott's Royal Palms	2	★★★★	86	$250
Marriott's Cypress Harbour	2	★★★★	86	$250+
Marriott's Imperial Palms	2	★★★★	86	$450+
Drury Inn & Suites Orlando	2	★★★★	85	$150–

How the Hotels Compare (continued)

HOTEL	LODGING AREA	OVERALL QUALITY	ROOM QUALITY	COST
Homewood Suites by Hilton Lake Buena Vista-Orlando	3	★★★★	85	$150-
Hawthorn Suites by Wyndham Lake Buena Vista	3	★★★★	85	$150+
Wyndham Orlando Resort International Drive	2	★★★★	85	$150+
Homewood Suites by Hilton Orlando Theme Parks	2	★★★★	85	$200+
Rosen Inn at Pointe Orlando	2	★★★★	84	$150
Extended Stay America Convention Center/ Westwood	2	★★★★	84	$100-
TownePlace Suites Orlando at SeaWorld	2	★★★★	84	$150-
Embassy Suites by Hilton Orlando Lake Buena Vista Resort	3	★★★★	84	$150+
Hyatt Place Orlando/Universal	1	★★★★	84	$200-
Loews Sapphire Falls Resort	1	★★★★	84	$250+
Extended Stay America Orlando Lake Buena Vista	3	★★★★	83	$100
Holiday Inn Express & Suites Orlando at SeaWorld	2	★★★★	83	$150+
Embassy Suites Orlando I-Drive/Jamaican Court	2	★★★★	83	$200+
Residence Inn Orlando Lake Buena Vista	3	★★★★	83	$200+
Universal's Cabana Bay Beach Resort	1	★★★★	83	$200+
Homewood Suites by Hilton Orlando-Nearest to Universal Studios	2	★★★½	82	$250
Clarion Inn & Suites Across from Universal Orlando Resort	1	★★★½	82	$100+
Holiday Inn Resort Orlando-Lake Buena Vista	3	★★★½	82	$100+
CoCo Key Water Resort-Orlando	2	★★★½	82	$150-
Castle Hotel	2	★★★½	82	$150+
Hilton Garden Inn Orlando I-Drive North	2	★★★½	82	$150+
Hilton Orlando	2	★★★½	82	$150+
Hyatt Place Orlando/Lake Buena Vista	3	★★★½	82	$150+
Four Points By Sheraton Orlando Convention Center	2	★★★½	82	$200-
Universal's Aventura Hotel	1	★★★½	82	$200+
Holiday Inn Resort Orlando Suites-Waterpark	2	★★★½	82	$300+
Quality Suites Lake Buena Vista	3	★★★½	81	$150-
Universal's Endless Summer Resort: Dockside Inn and Suites	1	★★★½	81	$150+
Universal's Endless Summer Resort: Surfside Inn and Suites	1	★★★½	81	$150+
Homewood Suites by Hilton Orlando-International Drive/Convention Center	2	★★★½	81	$200-
Hilton Garden Inn Orlando at SeaWorld	2	★★★½	80	$150
Delta Hotels by Marriott Lake Buena Vista	3	★★★½	80	$150-
Fairfield Inn & Suites Near Universal Orlando Resort	1	★★★½	80	$150-
Fairfield Inn & Suites Orlando at SeaWorld	2	★★★½	80	$150-

How the Hotels Compare (continued)

Wingate by Wyndham Universal Studios & Convention Center	1	★★★½	80	$150-
Courtyard Orlando I-Drive	2	★★★½	80	$150+
Courtyard Orlando Lake Buena Vista in Marriott Village	3	★★★½	80	$150+
Residence Inn Orlando Convention Center	2	★★★½	80	$200+
Holiday Inn Orlando–Disney Springs Area	WDW	★★★½	79	$150-
Residence Inn Near Universal Orlando	2	★★★½	78	$200
Hampton Inn & Suites SeaWorld	2	★★★½	78	$150+
Quality Suites Turkey Lake South/ Lake Buena Vista	3	★★★½	77	$100-
Best Western Orlando Gateway Hotel	2	★★★½	77	$150-
Crowne Plaza Universal Orlando	2	★★★½	77	$200-
Holiday Inn Express & Suites International Drive	2	★★★½	76	$100+
Best Western Plus Universal Inn	1	★★★½	75	$100
Extended Stay America Orlando Theme Parks	1	★★★½	75	$100-
Extended Stay America Deluxe Orlando Theme Parks	1	★★★½	75	$100+
Holiday Inn & Suites Across from Universal Orlando	1	★★★½	75	$100+
Wyndham Garden Lake Buena Vista	WDW	★★★½	75	$150-
Embassy Suites Orlando I-Drive	2	★★★½	75	$200+
Ramada Plaza Resort and Suites Orlando I-Drive	2	★★★	74	$150
Quality Inn at International Drive	2	★★★	74	$100-
Hilton Orlando Buena Vista Palace	WDW	★★★	74	$150+
Fairfield Inn & Suites Orlando International Drive	2	★★★	74	$200-
Hampton Inn I-Drive/Convention Center	2	★★★	74	$200-
Hampton Inn South of Universal	2	★★★	74	$200+
Extended Stay America Orlando Convention Center	2	★★★	72	$100
La Quinta Inn & Suites Orlando Universal Area	1	★★★	72	$100+
Rosen Inn near Universal	2	★★★	71	$150-
Comfort Suites Near Universal Orlando Resort	1	★★★	70	$150-
Rosen Inn International Hotel	2	★★★	70	$150-
Westgate Palace	2	★★★	68	$250-
Hampton Inn Universal	1	★★★	67	$150+
Comfort Inn I-Drive	2	★★★	66	$200-
Motel 6 Orlando–I-Drive	2	★★★	66	$50+
Best Western I-Drive	2	★★★	65	$250-
Midpointe Hotel by Rosen	2	★★½	64	$100-
Country Inn & Suites Orlando Universal	2	★★½	63	$200-
InTown Suites Orlando Universal	2	★★½	63	$50+
Extended Stay Orlando Convention Center	2	★★½	58	$100+

Hotels Information Chart

Best Western I-Drive ★★★ 8222 Jamaican Ct. Orlando, FL 32819 ☎ 407-345-1172 tinyurl.com/bwidrive LOCATION 2 ROOM QUALITY 65 COST $250– RESORT FEE $8.95	**Best Western Orlando Gateway Hotel** ★★★½ 7299 Universal Blvd. Orlando, FL 32819 ☎ 407-351-5009 bworlando.com LOCATION 2 ROOM QUALITY 77 COST $150– RESORT FEE $8.00	**Best Western Plus Universal Inn** ★★★½ 5618 Vineland Rd. Orlando, FL 32819 ☎ 407-226-9119 tinyurl.com/bwuniversal LOCATION 1 ROOM QUALITY 75 COST $100 RESORT FEE $2.99
Comfort Inn I-Drive ★★★ 8134 International Dr. Orlando, FL 32819 ☎ 407-313-4000 tinyurl.com/comfortidrive LOCATION 2 ROOM QUALITY 66 COST $200– RESORT FEE $7.95	**Comfort Suites Near Universal Orlando Resort** ★★★ 5617 Major Blvd. Orlando, FL 32819 ☎ 407-363-1967 tinyurl.com/csuniversal LOCATION 1 ROOM QUALITY 70 COST $150– RESORT FEE None	**Country Inn & Suites Orlando Universal** ★★½ 7701 Universal Blvd. Orlando, FL 32819 ☎ 407-313-4200 countryinns.com/orlandofl_universal LOCATION 2 ROOM QUALITY 63 COST $200– RESORT FEE None
Crowne Plaza Universal Orlando ★★★½ 7800 Universal Blvd. Orlando, FL 32819 ☎ 407-355-0550 cporlando.com LOCATION 2 ROOM QUALITY 77 COST $200– RESORT FEE None	**Cypress Pointe Resort by Diamond Resorts** ★★★★½ 8651 Treasure Cay Ln. Orlando, FL 32836 ☎ 407-597-2700 cypresspointe.net LOCATION 3 ROOM QUALITY 90 COST $150– RESORT FEE $15.00	**Delta Hotels by Marriott Lake Buena Vista** ★★★½ 12490 Apopka–Vineland Rd. Lake Buena Vista, FL 32836 ☎ 407-387-9999 tinyurl.com/deltaorlando LOCATION 3 ROOM QUALITY 80 COST $150– RESORT FEE None
Embassy Suites by Hilton Orlando Lake Buena Vista Resort ★★★★ 8100 Lake St. Orlando, FL 32836 ☎ 407-239-1144 embassysuiteslbv.com LOCATION 3 ROOM QUALITY 84 COST $150+ RESORT FEE $20.00	**Embassy Suites Orlando I-Drive** ★★★½ 8978 International Dr. Orlando, FL 32819 ☎ 407-352-1400 embassysuitesorlando.com LOCATION 2 ROOM QUALITY 75 COST $200+ RESORT FEE None	**Embassy Suites Orlando I-Drive/ Jamaican Court** ★★★★ 8250 Jamaican Ct. Orlando, FL 32819 ☎ 407-345-8250 tinyurl.com/jamaicancourt LOCATION 2 ROOM QUALITY 83 COST $200+ RESORT FEE None
Extended Stay America Orlando Lake Buena Vista ★★★★ 8100 Palm Pkwy. Orlando, FL 32836 ☎ 407-239-4300 tinyurl.com/extendedlbv LOCATION 3 ROOM QUALITY 83 COST $100 RESORT FEE None	**Extended Stay America Orlando Theme Parks** ★★★½ 5620 Major Blvd. Orlando, FL 32819 ☎ 407-351-1788 tinyurl.com/extendeduniversal LOCATION 1 ROOM QUALITY 75 COST $100– RESORT FEE None	**Extended Stay Orlando Convention Center** ★★½ 8750 Universal Blvd. Orlando, FL 32819 ☎ 407-903-1500 tinyurl.com/esccuniversal LOCATION 2 ROOM QUALITY 58 COST $100+ RESORT FEE None
Floridays Resort Orlando ★★★★ 12562 International Dr. Orlando, FL 32821 ☎ 407-238-7700 floridaysresortorlando.com LOCATION 2 ROOM QUALITY 88 COST $300– RESORT FEE $18.84	**Four Points By Sheraton Orlando Convention Center** ★★★½ 6435 Westwood Blvd. Orlando, FL 32821 ☎ 407-351-6600 fourpointsorlandocc.com LOCATION 2 ROOM QUALITY 82 COST $200– RESORT FEE None	**Four Points by Sheraton Orlando Studio City** ★★★★½ 5905 International Dr. Orlando, FL 32819 ☎ 407-351-2100 fourpointsorlandostudiocity.com LOCATION 2 ROOM QUALITY 90 COST $150 RESORT FEE None

Castle Hotel ★★★½
8629 International Dr.
Orlando, FL 32819
☎ 407-345-1511
castlehotelorlando.com
LOCATION 2
ROOM QUALITY 82
COST $150+
RESORT FEE None

Clarion Inn & Suites Across from Universal Orlando Resort ★★★½
5829 Grand National Dr.
Orlando, FL 32819
☎ 407-351-3800
tinyurl.com/clarionuniversal
LOCATION 1
ROOM QUALITY 82
COST $100+
RESORT FEE None

CoCo Key Water Resort–Orlando ★★★½
7400 International Dr.
Orlando, FL 32819
☎ 407-351-2626
cocokeyorlando.com
LOCATION 2
ROOM QUALITY 82
COST $150–
RESORT FEE $32.00

Courtyard Orlando I-Drive ★★★½
8600 Austrian Ct.
Orlando, FL 32819
☎ 407-351-2244
tinyurl.com/courtyardidrive
LOCATION 2
ROOM QUALITY 80
COST $150+
RESORT FEE None

Courtyard Orlando Lake Buena Vista at Vista Centre ★★★★
8501 Palm Pkwy.
Lake Buena Vista, FL 32836
☎ 407-239-6900
tinyurl.com/courtyardlbv
LOCATION 3
ROOM QUALITY 89
COST $100+
RESORT FEE None

Courtyard Orlando Lake Buena Vista in Marriott Village ★★★½
8623 Vineland Ave.
Orlando, FL 32821
☎ 407-938-9001
tinyurl.com/courtyardlbvmarriott
village
LOCATION 3
ROOM QUALITY 80
COST $150+
RESORT FEE None

DoubleTree by Hilton at the Entrance to Universal Orlando ★★★★
5780 Major Blvd.
Orlando, FL 32819
☎ 407-351-1000
doubletreeorlando.com
LOCATION 1
ROOM QUALITY 89
COST $150+
RESORT FEE None

DoubleTree by Hilton Orlando at SeaWorld ★★★★½
10100 International Dr.
Orlando, FL 32821
☎ 407-352-1100
dtresortorlando.com
LOCATION 2
ROOM QUALITY 92
COST $100+
RESORT FEE $20.00

Drury Inn & Suites Orlando ★★★★
7301 W. Sand Lake Rd.
Orlando, FL 32819
☎ 407-354-1101
tinyurl.com/druryinnorlando
LOCATION 2
ROOM QUALITY 85
COST $150–
RESORT FEE None

Extended Stay America Convention Center/Westwood ★★★★
6443 Westwood Blvd.
Orlando, FL 32821
☎ 407-351-1982
tinyurl.com/extendedstaywestwood
LOCATION 2
ROOM QUALITY 84
COST $100–
RESORT FEE None

Extended Stay America Deluxe Orlando Theme Parks ★★★½
5610 Vineland Rd.
Orlando, FL 32819
☎ 407-370-4428
tinyurl.com/esvineland
LOCATION 1
ROOM QUALITY 75
COST $100+
RESORT FEE None

Extended Stay America Orlando Convention Center ★★★
6451 Westwood Blvd.
Orlando, FL 32821
☎ 407-352-3454
tinyurl.com/extendedstayocc
LOCATION 2
ROOM QUALITY 72
COST $100
RESORT FEE None

Fairfield Inn & Suites Near Universal Orlando Resort ★★★½
5614 Vineland Rd.
Orlando, FL 32819
☎ 407-581-5600
tinyurl.com/fairfielduniversal
LOCATION 1
ROOM QUALITY 80
COST $150–
RESORT FEE None

Fairfield Inn & Suites Orlando at SeaWorld ★★★½
10815 International Dr.
Orlando, FL 32821
☎ 407-354-1139
tinyurl.com/fairfieldsw
LOCATION 2
ROOM QUALITY 80
COST $150–
RESORT FEE None

Fairfield Inn & Suites Orlando International Drive ★★★
8214 Universal Blvd.
Orlando, FL 32819
☎ 407-581-9001
tinyurl.com/fairfieldidrive
LOCATION 2
ROOM QUALITY 74
COST $200–
RESORT FEE None

Four Seasons Resort Orlando at Walt Disney World Resort ★★★★★
10100 Dream Tree Blvd.
Lake Buena Vista, FL 32836
☎ 407-313-7777
fourseasons.com/orlando
LOCATION WDW
ROOM QUALITY 98
COST $1,000+
RESORT FEE None

Hampton Inn & Suites SeaWorld ★★★½
7003 Sea Harbor Dr.
Orlando, FL 32821
☎ 407-778-5900
tinyurl.com/hamptoninnseaworld
LOCATION 2
ROOM QUALITY 78
COST $150+
RESORT FEE None

Hampton Inn I-Drive/Convention Center ★★★
8900 Universal Blvd.
Orlando, FL 32819
☎ 407-354-4447
tinyurl.com/hamptonocc
LOCATION 2
ROOM QUALITY 74
COST $200–
RESORT FEE None

Hotel Information Chart *(continued)*

Hampton Inn South of Universal ★★★ 7110 S. Kirkman Rd. Orlando, FL 32819 ☎ 407-345-1112 tinyurl.com/hamptonkirkman LOCATION 2 ROOM QUALITY 74 COST $200+ RESORT FEE None	**Hampton Inn Universal** ★★★ 5621 Windhover Dr. Orlando, FL 32819 ☎ 407-351-6716 tinyurl.com/hamptonuniversal LOCATION 1 ROOM QUALITY 67 COST $150+ RESORT FEE None	**Hard Rock Hotel Orlando** ★★★★½ 5800 Universal Blvd. Orlando, FL 32819 ☎ 407-503-2000 hardrockhotels.com/orlando LOCATION 1 ROOM QUALITY 93 COST $450- RESORT FEE None
Hilton Grand Vacations Club at SeaWorld ★★★★ 6924 Grand Vacations Way Orlando, FL 32821 ☎ 407-239-0100 tinyurl.com/hiltongvseaworld LOCATION 2 ROOM QUALITY 88 COST $150- RESORT FEE $25.00	**Hilton Grand Vacations Club at Tuscany Village** ★★★★ 8122 Arrezzo Way Orlando, FL 32821 ☎ 407-465-2600 tinyurl.com/hgvtuscany LOCATION 2 ROOM QUALITY 88 COST $300+ RESORT FEE $25.00	**Hilton Orlando** ★★★½ 6001 Destination Pkwy. Orlando, FL 32819 ☎ 407-313-4300 thehiltonorlando.com LOCATION 2 ROOM QUALITY 82 COST $150+ RESORT FEE $35.00
Holiday Inn & Suites Across from Universal Orlando ★★★½ 5905 Kirkman Rd. Orlando, FL 32819 ☎ 407-351-3333 hiuniversal.com LOCATION 1 ROOM QUALITY 75 COST $100+ RESORT FEE None	**Holiday Inn Express & Suites International Drive** ★★★½ 7276 International Dr. Orlando, FL 32819 ☎ 407-535-4100 tinyurl.com/hiexpressidrive LOCATION 2 ROOM QUALITY 76 COST $100+ RESORT FEE None	**Holiday Inn Express & Suites Orlando at SeaWorld** ★★★★ 10771 International Dr. Orlando, FL 32821 ☎ 407-996-4100 tinyurl.com/holidaysw LOCATION 2 ROOM QUALITY 83 COST $150+ RESORT FEE None
Homewood Suites by Hilton Lake Buena Vista-Orlando ★★★★ 11428 Marbella Palm Ct. Orlando, FL 32836 ☎ 407-239-4540 tinyurl.com/homewoodsuiteslbv LOCATION 3 ROOM QUALITY 85 COST $150- RESORT FEE None	**Homewood Suites by Hilton Orlando Theme Parks** ★★★★ 6940 Westwood Blvd. Orlando, FL 32821 ☎ 407-778-5888 tinyurl.com/homewoodorl LOCATION 2 ROOM QUALITY 85 COST $200+ RESORT FEE None	**Homewood Suites by Hilton Orlando-International Drive/ Convention Center** ★★★½ 8745 International Dr. Orlando, FL 32819 ☎ 407-248-2232 tinyurl.com/homewoodidrive LOCATION 2 ROOM QUALITY 81 COST $200- RESORT FEE None
Hyatt Place Orlando/Universal ★★★★ 5895 Caravan Ct. Orlando, FL 32819 ☎ 407-351-0627 orlandouniversal.place.hyatt.com LOCATION 1 ROOM QUALITY 84 COST $200- RESORT FEE None	**Hyatt Regency Grand Cypress** ★★★★½ 1 Grand Cypress Blvd. Orlando, FL 32836 ☎ 407-239-1234 grandcypress.hyatt.com LOCATION 3 ROOM QUALITY 92 COST $200- RESORT FEE $39.38	**Hyatt Regency Orlando** ★★★★½ 9801 International Dr. Orlando, FL 32819 ☎ 407-284-1234 orlando.regency.hyatt.com LOCATION 2 ROOM QUALITY 90 COST $150+ RESORT FEE $25.00
Loews Portofino Bay Hotel ★★★★½ 5601 Universal Blvd. Orlando, FL 32819 ☎ 407-503-1000 loewshotels.com/portofino-bay-hotel LOCATION 1 ROOM QUALITY 92 COST $450+ RESORT FEE None	**Loews Royal Pacific Resort** ★★★★½ 6300 Hollywood Way Orlando, FL 32819 ☎ 407-503-3000 loewshotels.com/royal-pacific-resort LOCATION 1 ROOM QUALITY 90 COST $400- RESORT FEE None	**Loews Sapphire Falls Resort** ★★★★ 6601 Adventure Way Orlando, FL 32819 ☎ 407-503-5000 loewshotels.com/sapphire-falls-resort LOCATION 1 ROOM QUALITY 84 COST $250+ RESORT FEE None

Hawthorn Suites by Wyndham Lake Buena Vista ★★★★
8303 Palm Pkwy.
Orlando, FL 32836
☎ 407-597-5000
hawthornlakebuenavista.com
LOCATION 3
ROOM QUALITY 85
COST $150+
RESORT FEE None

Hilton Garden Inn Orlando at SeaWorld ★★★½
6850 Westwood Blvd.
Orlando, FL 32821
☎ 407-354-1500
tinyurl.com/hgiseaworld
LOCATION 2
ROOM QUALITY 80
COST $150
RESORT FEE None

Hilton Garden Inn Orlando I-Drive North ★★★½
5877 American Way
Orlando, FL 32819
☎ 407-363-9332
tinyurl.com/hiltonidrive
LOCATION 2
ROOM QUALITY 82
COST $150+
RESORT FEE None

Hilton Orlando Bonnet Creek ★★★★
14100 Bonnet Creek Resort Ln.
Orlando, FL 32821
☎ 407-597-3600
hiltonbonnetcreek.com
LOCATION WDW
ROOM QUALITY 88
COST $250-
RESORT FEE $45.00

Hilton Orlando Buena Vista Palace ★★★
1900 E. Buena Vista Dr.
Lake Buena Vista, FL 32830
☎ 407-827-2727
buenavistapalace.com
LOCATION WDW
ROOM QUALITY 74
COST $150+
RESORT FEE $35.00

Hilton Orlando Lake Buena Vista ★★★★
1751 Hotel Plaza Blvd.
Lake Buena Vista, FL 32830
☎ 407-827-4000
hilton-wdwv.com
LOCATION WDW
ROOM QUALITY 87
COST $200-
RESORT FEE $35.00

Holiday Inn Orlando-Disney Springs Area ★★★½
1805 Hotel Plaza Blvd.
Lake Buena Vista, FL 32830
☎ 407-828-8888
hiorlando.com
LOCATION WDW
ROOM QUALITY 79
COST $150-
RESORT FEE $22.00

Holiday Inn Resort Orlando Suites-Waterpark ★★★
14500 Continental Gateway
Orlando, FL 32821
☎ 407-387-5437
hisuitesorlando.com
LOCATION 2
ROOM QUALITY 82
COST $300+
RESORT FEE $30.00

Holiday Inn Resort Orlando-Lake Buena Vista ★★★½
13351 FL 535
Orlando, FL 32821
☎ 407-239-4500
hiresortlbv.com
LOCATION 3
ROOM QUALITY 82
COST $100+
RESORT FEE $24.95

Homewood Suites by Hilton Orlando-Nearest to Universal Studios ★★★½
5893 American Way
Orlando, FL 32819
☎ 407-226-0669
tinyurl.com/homewoodnearuni
LOCATION 2
ROOM QUALITY 82
COST $250
RESORT FEE None

Hyatt House Across from Universal Orlando ★★★★½
5915 Caravan Ct.
Orlando, FL 32819
☎ 407-352-5660
acrossfromuniversalorlando.house
.hyatt.com
LOCATION 1
ROOM QUALITY 91
COST $200+
RESORT FEE None

Hyatt Place Orlando/ Lake Buena Vista ★★★½
8688 Palm Pkwy.
Orlando, FL 32836
☎ 407-778-5500
orlandolakebuenavista.place
.hyatt.com
LOCATION 3
ROOM QUALITY 82
COST $150+
RESORT FEE None

InTown Suites Orlando Universal ★★½
5615 Major Blvd.
Orlando, FL 32819
☎ 407-370-3734
tinyurl.com/intownsuitesorlando
LOCATION 2
ROOM QUALITY 63
COST $50+
RESORT FEE $1.43

La Quinta Inn & Suites Orlando Universal Area ★★★
5621 Major Blvd.
Orlando, FL 32819
☎ 407-313-3100
laquintaorlandomajorblvd.com
LOCATION 1
ROOM QUALITY 72
COST $100+
RESORT FEE None

Las Palmeras by Hilton Grand Vacations ★★★★
9501 Universal Blvd.
Orlando, FL 32819
☎ 407-233-2200
tinyurl.com/laspalmerashilton
LOCATION 2
ROOM QUALITY 87
COST $250-
RESORT FEE $25.00

Marriott's Cypress Harbour ★★★★
11251 Harbour Villa Rd.
Orlando, FL 32821
☎ 407-238-1300
tinyurl.com/cypressharbourvillas
LOCATION 2
ROOM QUALITY 86
COST $250+
RESORT FEE None

Marriott's Grande Vista ★★★★½
5925 Avenida Vista
Orlando, FL 32821
☎ 407-238-7676
tinyurl.com/marriottsgrandevista
LOCATION 2
ROOM QUALITY 93
COST $150+
RESORT FEE None

Marriott's Harbour Lake ★★★★½
7102 Grand Horizons Blvd.
Orlando, FL 32821
☎ 407-465-6100
tinyurl.com/harbourlake
LOCATION 3
ROOM QUALITY 91
COST $200-
RESORT FEE None

Hotel Information Chart *(continued)*

Marriott's Imperial Palms ★★★★ 8404 Vacation Way Orlando, FL 32821 ☎ 407-238-6200 tinyurl.com/imperialpalmvillas LOCATION 2 ROOM QUALITY 86 COST $450+ RESORT FEE None	**Marriott's Royal Palms** ★★★★ 8404 Vacation Way Orlando, FL 32821 ☎ 407-238-6200 tinyurl.com/marriottsroyalpalms LOCATION 2 ROOM QUALITY 86 COST $250 RESORT FEE None	**Midpointe Hotel by Rosen** ★★½ 9956 Hawaiian Ct. Orlando, FL 32819 ☎ 407-351-5100 midpointehotelorlando.com LOCATION 2 ROOM QUALITY 64 COST $100- RESORT FEE None
Quality Suites Lake Buena Vista ★★★½ 8200 Palm Pkwy. Orlando, FL 32836 ☎ 407-465-8200 qualitysuitesorlandolakebuena vista.com LOCATION 3 ROOM QUALITY 81 COST $150- RESORT FEE $6.95	**Quality Suites Turkey Lake South/ Lake Buena Vista** ★★★½ 9350 Turkey Lake Rd. Orlando, FL 32819 ☎ 407-351-5050 qualitysuitesorlandofl.com LOCATION 3 ROOM QUALITY 77 COST $100- RESORT FEE $4.77	**Ramada Plaza Resort and Suites Orlando I-Drive** ★★★ 6500 International Dr. Orlando, FL 32819 ☎ 407-345-5340 tinyurl.com/ramadaplazaidrive LOCATION 2 ROOM QUALITY 74 COST $150 RESORT FEE None
Residence Inn Orlando Convention Center ★★★½ 8800 Universal Blvd. Orlando, FL 32819 ☎ 407-226-0288 tinyurl.com/resinnconventioncenter LOCATION 2 ROOM QUALITY 80 COST $200+ RESORT FEE None	**Residence Inn Orlando Lake Buena Vista** ★★★★ 11450 Marbella Palm Ct. Orlando, FL 32836 ☎ 407-465-0075 tinyurl.com/residenceinnlbv LOCATION 3 ROOM QUALITY 83 COST $200+ RESORT FEE None	**The Ritz-Carlton Orlando, Grande Lakes** ★★★★½ 4012 Central Florida Pkwy. Orlando, FL 32837 ☎ 407-206-2400 ritzcarlton.com/orlando LOCATION 2 ROOM QUALITY 94 COST $450- RESORT FEE $38.00
Rosen Inn near Universal ★★★ 6327 International Dr. Orlando, FL 32819 ☎ 407-996-4444 roseninn6327.com LOCATION 2 ROOM QUALITY 71 COST $150- RESORT FEE None	**Rosen Plaza Hotel** ★★★★½ 9700 International Dr. Orlando, FL 32819 ☎ 407-996-9700 rosenplaza.com LOCATION 2 ROOM QUALITY 91 COST $150+ RESORT FEE None	**Rosen Shingle Creek Orlando** ★★★★ 9939 Universal Blvd. Orlando, FL 32819 ☎ 407-996-9939 rosenshinglecreek.com LOCATION 2 ROOM QUALITY 88 COST $250+ RESORT FEE None
Staybridge Suites Lake Buena Vista ★★★★½ 8751 Suiteside Dr. Orlando, FL 32836 ☎ 407-238-0777 tinyurl.com/staybridgelbv LOCATION 3 ROOM QUALITY 90 COST $200- RESORT FEE None	**Staybridge Suites Orlando at SeaWorld** ★★★★½ 6985 Sea Harbor Dr. Orlando, FL 32821 ☎ 407-917-9200 tinyurl.com/staybridgeseaworld LOCATION 2 ROOM QUALITY 90 COST $150 RESORT FEE None	**TownePlace Suites Orlando at SeaWorld** ★★★★ 10731 International Dr. Orlando, FL 32821 ☎ 407-996-3400 tinyurl.com/towneplacesw LOCATION 2 ROOM QUALITY 84 COST $150- RESORT FEE None
Universal's Cabana Bay Beach Resort ★★★★ 6550 Adventure Way Orlando, FL 32819 ☎ 407-503-4000 loewshotels.com/cabana-bay-hotel LOCATION 1 ROOM QUALITY 83 COST $200+ RESORT FEE None	**Waldorf Astoria Orlando** ★★★★½ 14200 Bonnet Creek Resort Ln. Orlando, FL 32821 ☎ 407-597-5500 waldorfastoriaorlando.com LOCATION WDW ROOM QUALITY 93 COST $350- RESORT FEE $45.00	**Westgate Palace** ★★★ 6145 Carrier Dr. Orlando, FL 32819 ☎ 407-996-6000 westgateresorts.com/palace LOCATION 2 ROOM QUALITY 68 COST $250- RESORT FEE $10.00

Motel 6 Orlando–I-Drive ★★★
5909 American Way
Orlando, FL 32819
☎ 407-351-6500
tinyurl.com/motel6idrive
LOCATION 2
ROOM QUALITY 66
COST $50+
RESORT FEE None

Orlando World Center Marriott
★★★★½
8701 World Center Dr.
Orlando, FL 32821
☎ 407-239-4200
marriottworldcenter.com
LOCATION 3
ROOM QUALITY 90
COST $300–
RESORT FEE $30.00

Quality Inn at International Drive ★★★
8300 Jamaican Ct.
Orlando, FL 32819
☎ 407-351-1660
tinyurl.com/qualityinndrive
LOCATION 2
ROOM QUALITY 74
COST $100–
RESORT FEE $8.95

Renaissance Orlando at SeaWorld
★★★★½
6677 Sea Harbor Dr.
Orlando, FL 32821
☎ 407-351-5555
tinyurl.com/renorlandoseaworld
LOCATION 2
ROOM QUALITY 90
COST $150+
RESORT FEE $30.00

Residence Inn Near Universal Orlando ★★★½
5614 Major Blvd.
Orlando, FL 32819
☎ 407-313-1234
tinyurl.com/residenceinnuniversal
orlando
LOCATION 2
ROOM QUALITY 78
COST $200
RESORT FEE None

Residence Inn Orlando at SeaWorld ★★★★
11000 Westwood Blvd.
Orlando, FL 32821
☎ 407-313-3600
tinyurl.com/residenceinnseaworld
LOCATION 3
ROOM QUALITY 87
COST $100+
RESORT FEE None

Rosen Centre Hotel ★★★★½
9840 International Dr.
Orlando, FL 32819
☎ 407-996-9840
rosencentre.com
LOCATION 2
ROOM QUALITY 95
COST $250–
RESORT FEE None

Rosen Inn at Pointe Orlando
★★★★
9000 International Dr.
Orlando, FL 32819
☎ 407-996-8585
roseninn9000.com
LOCATION 2
ROOM QUALITY 84
COST $150
RESORT FEE None

Rosen Inn International Hotel
★★★
7600 International Dr.
Orlando, FL 32819
☎ 407-996-1600
roseninn7600.com
LOCATION 2
ROOM QUALITY 70
COST $150–
RESORT FEE None

Sheraton Lake Buena Vista Resort
★★★★
12205 S. Apopka-Vineland Rd.
Orlando, FL 32836
☎ 407-239-0444
sheratonlakebuenavistaresort.com
LOCATION 3
ROOM QUALITY 88
COST $100+
RESORT FEE $24.00

Sheraton Vistana Resort Villas, Lake Buena Vista/Orlando
★★★★
8800 Vistana Centre Dr.
Orlando, FL 32821
☎ 407-239-3100
tinyurl.com/vistanavillas
LOCATION 3
ROOM QUALITY 89
COST $200–
RESORT FEE None

Sheraton Vistana Villages Resort Villas, I-Drive/Orlando ★★★★
12401 International Dr.
Orlando, FL 32821
☎ 407-238-5000
tinyurl.com/sheratonvillages
LOCATION 2
ROOM QUALITY 87
COST $150+
RESORT FEE None

Universal's Aventura Hotel
★★★½
6725 Adventure Way
Orlando, FL 32819
☎ 407-503-6000
loewshotels.com/universals-aventura
-hotel
LOCATION 1
ROOM QUALITY 82
COST $200+
RESORT FEE None

Universal's Endless Summer Resort: Dockside Inn and Suites
★★★½
7125 Universal Blvd.
Orlando, FL 32819; ☎ 407-503-8000
loewshotels.com/dockside-inn-and
-suites
LOCATION 1
ROOM QUALITY 81
COST $150+
RESORT FEE None

Universal's Endless Summer Resort: Surfside Inn and Suites
★★★½
7000 Universal Blvd.
Orlando, FL 32819; ☎ 407-503-7000
loewshotels.com/surfside-inn-and
-suites
LOCATION 1
ROOM QUALITY 81
COST $150+
RESORT FEE None

Wingate by Wyndham Universal Studios & Convention Center
★★★½
5661 Windhover Dr.
Orlando, FL 32819
☎ 407-226-0900
wingateorlando.com
LOCATION 1
ROOM QUALITY 80
COST $150–
RESORT FEE None

Wyndham Garden Lake Buena Vista ★★★½
1850-B Hotel Plaza Blvd.
Lake Buena Vista, FL 32830
☎ 407-842-6644
wyndhamlakebuenavista.com
LOCATION WDW
ROOM QUALITY 75
COST $150–
RESORT FEE $25.00

Wyndham Orlando Resort International Drive ★★★★
8001 International Dr.
Orlando, FL 32819
☎ 407-351-2420
wyndhamorlandoresort.com
LOCATION 2
ROOM QUALITY 85
COST $150+
RESORT FEE $26.00

PART THREE

ARRIVING *and* GETTING AROUND

GETTING THERE

DIRECTIONS TO UNIVERSAL ORLANDO

UNIVERSAL ORLANDO IS LOCATED within Orlando city limits, a short distance from I-4 and Florida's Turnpike. You can access the resort from I-4 East by taking Exit 75A and turning left at the top of the ramp onto Universal Boulevard. From I-4 West, use Exit 74B and then turn right onto Hollywood Way. Entrances are also located off Kirkman Road to the east, Turkey Lake Road to the west, and Vineland Road to the north. Universal Boulevard connects the International Drive area to Universal via an overpass bridging I-4. Grand National Drive has been extended with another I-4 overpass that connects Major Boulevard on the east side of Universal with International Drive's northernmost end. Turkey Lake and Vineland Roads are particularly good alternatives when I-4 is gridlocked. See pages 144–145 and page 147 for maps of the area.

Signs for Universal's hotels and theme parks are easy to find and read as soon as you've left the interstate. Once on Universal property, follow the signs to the parking garage or your hotel.

Tolls

Tolls from the airport to Universal on the Beachline are $2.50 each way. If you take FL 417 to I-4 in the Disney area, you'll need $4.50 each way. Bring a few dollars in quarters if your car doesn't have a SunPass or E-Pass transponder because many exits have no human toll takers to accept bills. Or sign up on paytollo.com via your computer or smartphone for the pay-by-plate system. E-ZPass, available in 18 states on the East Coast, also works at many toll locations in Orlando; bring your transponder from home if you have one (visit e-zpassiag.com for a list of participating systems). You can also pick up a free E-Pass transponder at Orlando International Airport. Go

COVID *tip*
OIA's Visitor Toll Pass service was suspended at press time.

to visitortollpass.com to reserve your pass, which can save you 80% versus paying tolls through your car rental company.

FROM THE ORLANDO INTERNATIONAL AIRPORT (MCO)   Take FL 528/ Beachline Expressway, a toll road, west for about 12 miles to I-4. Bear right and go east 2 miles on I-4 to Exit 75A, marked UNIVERSAL/ INTERNATIONAL DRIVE. Make a left at the end of the exit ramp.

FROM WALT DISNEY WORLD   Go east on I-4, take Exit 75A (marked UNIVERSAL/INTERNATIONAL DRIVE), and make a left at the end of the exit ramp.

FROM DAYTONA, SANFORD INTERNATIONAL AIRPORT (SFB), OR ORLANDO   Head west on I-4 through Orlando. Take Exit 74B toward Universal Orlando.

FROM MIAMI, FORT LAUDERDALE, OR SOUTHEASTERN FLORIDA   Head north on Florida's Turnpike to Exit 259, and merge onto I-4 West toward Tampa. Take Exit 74B toward Universal Orlando.

FROM TAMPA AND SOUTHWESTERN FLORIDA   Take I-75 North to I-4. Go east on I-4, take Exit 75A (marked UNIVERSAL/INTERNATIONAL DRIVE), and make a left at the end of the exit ramp.

FROM FLORIDA'S TURNPIKE SOUTH   Take Exit 259 to merge onto I-4 West toward Tampa; then take Exit 74B toward Universal Orlando.

FROM I-10   Take I-10 East across Florida to I-75 South at Exit 296A/ Tampa; then take Florida's Turnpike (toll road) southbound at Exit 328 (on the left) toward Orlando. Take Exit 259 to merge onto I-4 West toward Tampa; then take Exit 74B toward Universal Orlando.

FROM I-75 SOUTH   Take I-75 South onto Florida's Turnpike via Exit 328 (on the left) toward Orlando. Take Exit 259 to merge onto I-4 West toward Tampa, and then take Exit 74B toward Universal.

FROM I-95 SOUTH   Take Exit 260B to merge onto I-4 West, and then take Exit 74B toward Universal Orlando.

Universal Orlando Exits off I-4

West to east, six I-4 exits serve Universal Orlando.

Exit 74A (Sand Lake Road) serves the southern edge of Universal's property, with access to the resort from Turkey Lake Road, which lies just west of the exit. This exit also provides access to the attractions on the southern end of International Drive, heading toward the Orange County Convention Center, as well as Restaurant Row on West Sand Lake Road. This exit can get quite congested with I-Drive traffic.

Exit 74B (Adventure Way) is only accessible from I-4 West and serves as the primary entrance to Universal from that direction. The exit ramp leads directly to the Cabana Bay Beach and Sapphire Falls Resorts. Make a right at the light past the hotels to reach the Universal parking garage. Note that you can't return to I-4 East via this exit.

Exit 75A (Universal Boulevard/International Drive) serves as the primary entrance to Universal Orlando Resort for visitors coming from Walt Disney World on I-4 East. Make a left at the end of the ramp into Universal property, and the parking garage will be ahead on your right. Make a right off this exit to take Universal Boulevard south across International Drive to the Endless Summer Resort hotels; it then parallels that busy road, making it a perfect bypass to south International Drive and the convention center.

Exit 75BC (Kirkman Road) leads drivers from I-4 East to Kirkman Road on the east side of Universal Orlando. Bearing right on this ramp to 75C leads southbound on Kirkman Road toward International Drive. To enter Universal property, stay in the left lane when exiting for 75B to Kirkman Road northbound, then turn left at the first traffic signal onto Major Boulevard. This is the closest exit to the Portofino Bay and Hard Rock Hotels, as well as most off-site hotels within walking distance.

Exit 75AB (Kirkman Road/International Drive) is the exit from I-4 West to Kirkman Road just south of Universal. Stay to the right after Florida's Turnpike to take Exit 75. Bear left when the exit ramp splits for 75B to Kirkman Road southbound, toward the shopping and attractions on north International Drive, or stay right on Exit 75A to Kirkman Road northbound. You can't make a left turn directly into the resort, but you can make a right at the first intersection onto Major Boulevard, followed by a U-turn at Grand National Drive back toward Universal. Alternatively, make the second left off Kirkman onto Vineland Road, and then turn left onto Universal Boulevard to enter the resort from the north.

Exit 78 (Conroy Road/Millenia) is an option for westbound drivers when traffic is backed up approaching Florida's Turnpike. Make a right off the exit (at the defunct Holy Land Experience theme park), and then make an immediate left onto Vineland Road. Universal Boulevard will be your second left after crossing Kirkman Road.

THE I-4 BLUES

OVER MANY YEARS OF COVERING Orlando's attractions, we've watched I-4 turn from a modern interstate highway into a parking lot. The greatest congestion used to be between the Universal Orlando–International Drive area and downtown Orlando, but the section to the southwest serving the Disney World exits has become the new choke point, seemingly irrespective of the time of day. If you're going from Walt Disney World toward Universal Orlando (east), the jam usually breaks up after you've passed the FL 535 exit. As you head west toward Tampa, traffic calms down after the US 192 interchange.

Ameliorating (or complicating) the situation, the state is renovating a 21-mile stretch of I-4, from FL 434 in the northeast to Kirkman Road in the southwest, to improve traffic flow and capacity in these areas. The construction project will renovate 15 of the busiest interchanges, build 56 new bridges, and replace more than 70 overpasses, plus add four variable-charge toll lanes to help pay for the $2 billion estimated cost. The bad news is that construction, which was supposed to wrap up by 2021, is significantly behind schedule. Lane and exit ramp closures frequently occur between 10 p.m. and 6 a.m., which can snarl night owls exiting from CityWalk or early birds arriving before Early Park Admission. Real-time road conditions are available at i4exitguide .com/i-4-traffic, and an interactive map showing all active construction projects in Florida can be found at data.fdot.gov/road/projects. Info about construction in Orlando and the tourist areas is available at Central Florida Roads (cflroads.com), an FDOT website. For information and current conditions on area toll roads, see cfxway.com.

On long road trips, we always use a GPS device that's smart enough to accept traffic updates and route us around delays. TomTom GPS units, for example, have an accessory cable that picks up traffic signals from HD radio broadcasts. If you have a smartphone, the free mobile app Waze (waze.com; iOS and Android) also does the trick.

If the I-4 traffic becomes intolerable, it's pretty easy to commute from the Universal Orlando–International Drive area to Walt Disney World via Turkey Lake Road, connecting to Palm Parkway and FL 535 on the northwest side of I-4, or on the southernmost section of I-Drive, connecting to FL 536 on the southeast side of the interstate.

SNEAK ROUTES

WE'RE CONSTANTLY LOOKING for ways to avoid traffic snarls. For some roads and areas, there are no alternative routes. For others, we've discovered sneak routes. These suggestions will not only help you avoid congestion, but they're also great ways to discover local restaurants outside the theme park orbit.

International Drive (I-Drive) is by far the most difficult area to navigate without long traffic delays. Most hotels on I-Drive are between Kirkman Road to the north and FL 417 (Central Florida GreeneWay) to the south. Between Kirkman Road and FL 417, three major roads cross I-Drive: From north to south on I-Drive, the first is Universal Boulevard. Next is Sand Lake Road (FL 482), pretty squarely in the middle of the hotel district. Finally, the Beachline Expressway (FL 528) connects I-4 and the airport. The southern third of I-Drive can be accessed via Central Florida Parkway, connecting I-4 and Palm Parkway with the SeaWorld area of I-Drive, and by Daryl Carter Parkway, connecting Palm Parkway with the Orlando Vineland Premium Outlets.

I-Drive is a mess for a number of reasons: scarcity of left-turn lanes, long multidirectional traffic signals, and, most critically, limited access to westbound I-4. From the Orange County Convention Center south to the Beachline Expressway and FL 417/Central Florida GreeneWay, getting on westbound I-4 is easy, but in the stretch where the hotels are concentrated (from Kirkman to about a mile south of Sand Lake),

continued on page 146

South Orlando

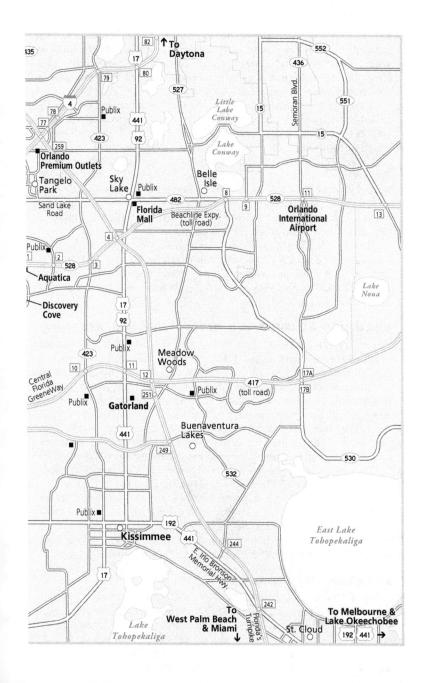

continued from page 143

the only way most visitors know to access I-4 westbound is to slog through the gridlock of the I-Drive–Sand Lake Road intersection en route to the I-4–Sand Lake Road interchange. A combination of a long, long traffic signal; a sea of motorists; and insufficient turn lanes makes this about as much fun as a root canal.

To travel between Universal and the northernmost end of International Drive (near the outlet mall), use the Grand National Drive overpass between Oak Ridge Road and Major Boulevard. If your hotel is north of Sand Lake, access Kirkman Road by going north on I-Drive (in the opposite direction of the heaviest traffic) to the Kirkman Road intersection and turning left, or by cutting over to Kirkman via eastbound Carrier Drive. You can also go north on Universal Boulevard, which parallels I-Drive to the east. After you cross I-4 onto Universal property, stay right and follow the signs for the parking garage, or take two left turns to reach I-4 westbound.

If your hotel is south of Sand Lake Road but north of Austrian Court, use Austrian Row or Jamaican Court to cut over to Universal Boulevard. If south of Austrian Court, continue south until you intersect the Beachline Expressway (FL 528); then take the Beachline west to I-4 (no toll).

SECURITY AT ORLANDO INTERNATIONAL AIRPORT

PRIOR TO THE COVID-19 PANDEMIC, this airport handled about 48 million passengers a year. It wasn't unusual to see lines from the checkpoints snaking out of the terminal and into the main shopping corridor and food court. Airport officials sometimes actually shut down moving sidewalks to use them for more queuing space. A number of passengers have reported missing their flights even when they arrived at the airport 90 minutes before departure. System improvements alleviated some of the congestion, and the drastic drop in tourism has taken care of much of the rest, but social-distancing measures have led to slower security queues. Most waits to clear security are less than 30 minutes on average, compared with as many as 55 minutes before the improvements. Even so, there are substantial fluctuations, with peak waits nearing an hour. Check orlandoairports.net or download the free MCO mobile app for current security wait times.

unofficial **TIP**
We recommend arriving at MCO 90 minutes–2 hours before your scheduled departure.

ALTERNATIVE AIRPORTS

A SHORT DISTANCE NORTHEAST of Orlando is **Sanford International Airport** (SFB; orlandosanfordairport.com). Small, convenient, and easily accessible, it's low hassle compared with the huge Orlando International Airport (MCO) and its block-long security-checkpoint lines.

The primary domestic carrier serving Sanford International is **Allegiant Air** (☎ 702-505-8888; allegiantair.com), with service from large

I-Drive Area Sneak Routes

East to Downtown Orlando

Windover Dr.

Florida's Turnpike

Vineland Road

Universal Blvd.

435

Major Blvd.

Caravan Ct.

Orlando International Premium Outlets

Universal Orlando

75AB

Oak Ridge Road

W. Oak Ridge Road

Turkey Lake Road

Hollywood Way

Adventure Way

75B

74B

American Way

75A

Grand National Dr.

International Dr.

Avoid this intersection

Sneak route (two-way traffic)

International Drive (area to avoid)

Universal's Volcano Bay

International Dr.

Kirkman Road

Del Verde Way

Bridge or overpass

Toll Road

Canada Ave.

Carrier Dr.

Sand Lake Road

482

74A

Universal Blvd.

Jamaican Ct.

Austrian Ct.

Austrian Row

International Dr.

Samoan Ct.

Official Visitor Center

4

Universal Blvd. W.

Orange County Convention Center

Universal Blvd.

Hawaiian Ct.

Destination Pkwy.

I-4 Exits

77	Florida's Turnpike
75A East	Universal Studios/ International Drive/
75AB West	FL 435 North/South
75B East	Kirkman Road
74B	Universal Studios
74A	Sand Lake Road
72	FL 528 (Beachline Expressway)
71	Central Florida Parkway

Turkey Lake Road

72

528

Beachline Expy.

To Orlando → International Airport

Aquatica

West to Walt Disney World Resort & Tampa

71

Westwood Blvd.

Sea Harbor Dr.

International Dr.

SeaWorld Orlando

Central Florida Pkwy.

Discovery Cove

and small airports throughout the Eastern and Midwestern United States. International carriers include **Surinam Airways** (South America: flyslm.com), **TUIFly** (Netherlands, Belgium, UK: ☎ 855-808-4015; en.tuifly.com), and **Wamos Air** (Spain, Mexico: wamosair.com).

A reader from Roanoke, Virginia, uses Sanford frequently, writing:

The 45-minute drive to [Orlando] is more than made up for by avoiding the chaos at Orlando International, and it's stress free.

The downside is that Sanford is 35 miles from Universal Orlando. A one-way taxi ride will cost over $100 with tip, and a ride-share service will charge about $40 or more. One reader recommends **Better Deal Transport** (☎ 407-470-4121; betterdealtransport.com), which advertises $140 round-trip transportation for up to five guests:

I couldn't be happier with our car service out of Sanford. Our driver was great—flexible, patient, and in touch through the day as we dealt with delays. [It] couldn't have been better.

Other readers, like this couple from White Township, New Jersey, prefer flying into Tampa instead:

We've found that flying from Newark to Tampa instead of Orlando saves us money and our sanity. It means significantly lower fares, fewer children on the plane, and shorter security lines.

(Note that it's an 84-mile drive from Tampa International Airport to Universal Orlando—about an hour and 20 minutes.)

GETTING TO UNIVERSAL ORLANDO FROM THE AIRPORT

YOU HAVE FIVE OPTIONS FOR GETTING from Orlando International to Universal Orlando:

1. TAXI **Mears Transportation Group** (☎ 888-983-3346; mearstransportation.com) has a near monopoly on taxi service in Central Florida and operates multiple brands (Yellow Cab, Checker Cab, and City Cab) with identical rates. Taxis carry four to eight passengers (depending on vehicle type). Rates vary according to distance. If your hotel is on Universal property, or nearby on International Drive or Major Boulevard, your fare will be about $45–$50, plus tip. Download the Mears Taxi app for Apple or Android to estimate the cost of your trip, but it's buggy, so don't rely on it to hail your ride. Report to the dispatch stand on level two outside baggage claim.

2. SHUTTLE SERVICE **Mears Transportation Group** (☎ 888-983-3346; mearstransportation.com) also dominates shared shuttle service and provides the transportation for many third-party vacation packages that include airport transfers. Non-package travelers can also use the service. The shuttles collect passengers until a van (or bus) is filled. The vehicles are then dispatched. Mears charges *per-person* rates (children under age 3 ride free). A one-way adult fare is $23 ($18 for children ages 4–11); round-trip is $35 for adults ($27 for children). Reserve online using discount code WEB10 to save 10%.

Universal offers **SuperStar Shuttle** airport transfers only to on-site guests who book their stay through a Universal Vacations package. The shuttle costs $39 per adult, $29 per child ages 3–9 round-trip (kids under age 3 ride free). Guests arriving between 7:30 a.m. and 8:30 p.m. are welcomed at the Hotel Transportation Desk on the first floor of the airport terminal, where they receive a preprinted packet containing any tickets purchased with their vacation package; those with earlier or later flights will need to call ☎ 407-888-9795 for pickup. SuperStar service will not deliver luggage to your room like Disney's Magical Express, so you'll need to retrieve it from baggage claim yourself before checking in, and you'll have to provide your own child car seats. SuperStar airport transfers can be added to an existing Universal Vacations reservation by calling ☎ 800-407-4275. For more information, visit tinyurl.com/unishuttle or call ☎ 866-604-7557 (daily, 8 a.m.–5:30 p.m.). A reader from Exton, Pennsylvania, warns against taking Universal's shuttle service:

The SuperStar Shuttle (which costs extra, although we were staying on-site) was a dark spot on an otherwise great trip. After our arrival in Orlando, we waited over an hour to get picked up. The first shuttle was too small to fit all of the people waiting for it. Why does Universal require advance reservations with flight arrival times if it won't be prepared for the amount of people it needs to transport?

Another dissatisfied SuperStar customer from Tulsa, Oklahoma, comments:

The Universal desk at the airport was very slow and disorganized. The shuttle from the airport to Cabana Bay was a rough ride, it took over 30 minutes for it to show up, it felt like the bus had no shocks, and it about jarred my neck.

When using any shared transportation service, you might have to wait at the airport until a vehicle fills. Once under way, the shuttle will probably stop several times to discharge passengers before reaching your hotel. Obviously, it takes less time to fill a van than a bus, and less time to deliver and unload those passengers.

From your hotel to the airport, you will likely ride in a van (unless you're part of a tour group, for which the company might send a bus). Because shuttles make several pickups, they ask you to leave much earlier than you'd depart if you were taking a cab or returning a rental car.

3. TOWN CAR SERVICE   Like a taxi, a town car service will transport you directly from the airport to your hotel. The driver will usually be waiting for you in your airline's baggage-claim area. If saving time and hassle is worth the money, book a town car.

Each town car service we surveyed offers large, well-appointed late-model sedans, such as the Lincoln Town Car series, or limousines. These hold four persons; trunks easily hold golf bags. Some services also offer roomier luxury SUVs and vans for an extra fee. To reserve a child's car seat, call ahead.

Tiffany Towncar Service (☎ 888-838-2161 or 407-370-2196; tiffanytowncars.com) provides a prompt, clean ride. The round-trip fee to the Universal area in a town car is $135 plus tip; one-way is $75. Tiffany charges an extra $10 for pickups before 6 a.m. or after 11 p.m. but offers a free 30-minute stop at a supermarket en route to your hotel with a round-trip booking.

Quicksilver Tours & Transportation (☎ 888-GO-TO-WDW [468-6939] or 407-299-1434; quicksilver-tours.com) offers 8-person limos and 10-person vans in addition to 4-person town cars. Round-trip in a town car from MCO to the Universal area and back (with a free 30-minute grocery stop on the way) is $125; round-trip in a van costs $140; the round-trip limo rate is $240. Quicksilver also offers a three-way trip from the airport to Walt Disney World, then to Universal Orlando, and finally back to the airport, starting at $170—perfect for those splitting their vacation between the two resorts.

Mears Transportation Group (☎ 407-423-5566; mearstransport ation.com) also offers a town car service from MCO to Universal for $69–$81; the return trip costs $46–$63.

4. RENTAL CARS Short- and long-term rentals are available. Most companies allow drop-off at certain hotels or subsidiary locations in the Universal area if you don't want the vehicle for your entire stay. Likewise, any time during your stay, you can pick up a car at those hotels and locations. Check mousesavers.com for rental-car discount codes.

The preferred routes to Universal Orlando (as well as Walt Disney World, International Drive, and US 192) all involve toll roads. Some roads require exact change to enter or exit via automated gates, and manned tollbooths will not accept any denomination bill higher than $20. So before you leave the airport, make sure you're armed with at least $5 in quarters and some lower-denomination currency if you don't have a toll transponder (see page 140).

5. RIDE-SHARE SERVICES This somewhat controversial option is represented in Orlando by the companies **Uber** and **Lyft.** You start by downloading a service's app to your smartphone (Apple or Android) and registering an account with a form of payment. When you want to hail a ride, the app shows you what available drivers are nearby and estimates the time and cost to your destination. You can follow your car's progress via GPS and add an optional gratuity through the app.

A four-passenger UberX or Lyft from the airport to Universal will cost about $30 (versus more than $45 for a traditional taxi), and UberX will provide a car seat for a few dollars more; a six-passenger UberXL or LyftPlus is around $40. Pickups for most ride-shares are on the airport's second level, the same as where passengers are picked up by family and friends. Luxury ride-shares like UberSelect use the Express Pickup Tunnel near the rental car desks on level one.

We recommend Lyft over Uber. While both companies offer about the same service at about the same cost, Uber's surge pricing policy makes its fare estimates unreliable.

Dollars and Sense

Which option is the best deal depends on how many people are in your party and how much you value your time. If you're traveling solo or have only two in your party and you're pretty sure you won't need a rental car, the shuttle is your least-expensive bet.

A cab for two makes sense if you want to get to your hotel faster than the shuttle can arrange. The cab will cost about $50–$60, including tip. That's $25–$30 per person. The shuttle will cost about $17 each one-way if you buy round-trip transfers, saving $8–$13. You must decide whether the cab's timeliness and convenience are worth the extra bucks.

A one-day car rental costs $40–$70, plus you have to take time to complete the paperwork, get the vehicle, and fill the tank before you return it. The more people you have in your group, the more economical the cab becomes over the shuttle. Likewise with the rental car, though the cab or ride share will get you there faster.

GETTING TO UNIVERSAL ORLANDO FROM WALT DISNEY WORLD

DRIVING FROM WALT DISNEY WORLD to Universal Orlando along I-4 takes about 15 minutes with light traffic, or as much as 40 minutes during rush hour. If you're staying at Walt Disney World and you don't have a car, **Mears Transportation** will shuttle you from your hotel to Universal and back for $23 (free for children age 3 and under). To schedule a shuttle, call ☎ 855-463-2776.

From three Denver college-aged women who tried Mears:

We took a Mears shuttle from Disney to Universal, and we don't recommend it. It takes a very long time to get you there—it stops at Sea-World and a couple of other places before Universal—plus we waited 45 minutes for the shuttle back to the hotel.

Taxis and ride-share services (**Uber** and **Lyft**) are also readily available to and from the resorts. A one-way taxi ride is $35–$45 (plus tip), depending on which Disney hotel you are leaving from, and may be cheaper than a shuttle if you have three to five people. A ride-share will cost about half that, and you can usually get picked up from any WDW hotel in less than 15 minutes. Taxis, as well as shuttle vans and buses, drop off at and pick up from the lower level of Universal's main parking hub, from which you can walk to CityWalk and the parks; ride-share and private cars use a designated drop-off on the garage's roof (see below). This family of five from Texas shares its positive experience getting to Universal from WDW via taxi:

It worked out cheaper for us to get a cab for five people than to hire a service like Mears or to rent a car for two days and pay for parking. We just walked to the front of our resort (Port Orleans Riverside), they hailed a waiting cab/van, and off we went. At the end of the day at Universal, we walked to the cab drop-off and pickup, got right into a cab, and headed back to our resort.

UNIVERSAL PARTNER HOTEL CONNECTOR SHUTTLE

UNIVERSAL OFFERS FREE scheduled transportation to SeaWorld and Aquatica for its on-site hotel guests via the Universal Partner Hotel Connector Shuttle (sometimes referred to as the Super Star Shuttle, not to be confused with the paid SuperStar airport shuttle service previously discussed). Departure and return times are limited and are based on regular park operating hours. Typically there are three outbound trips to SeaWorld and Aquatica in the morning and three returning runs in the evening. Boarding passes are required and available at the Ticket Center in each hotel lobby up to one day in advance and until 30 minutes prior to departure; guests with accessibility needs (including wheelchairs and service animals) must make a reservation 24 hours in advance. The shuttle picks up guests directly at Universal's Premier and Preferred hotels; guests at Value and Prime Value hotels must transfer to the parking hub and catch the shuttle there. As with other free shuttles that service multiple hotels, your free ride may cost you valuable park time with its roundabout route; rope drop enthusiasts may want to rely on ride share or rental cars instead.

OFF-SITE HOTEL SHUTTLES

MANY INDEPENDENT HOTELS AND MOTELS near Universal Orlando provide free shuttle buses to the resort. Some properties participate in the same Universal Partner Hotel Connector Shuttle program that services SeaWorld and Aquatica for Universal's on-site hotel guests, while others operate their own transportation. The shuttles are fairly carefree, depositing you at the parking garages' central hub and saving you parking fees. The rub is that they might not get you there as early as you desire (a critical point if you take our touring advice) or be available when you wish to return to your lodging. Each service is different; check details before you make reservations.

Some shuttles go directly to Universal, while others stop at other hotels en route. This can be a problem if your hotel is the second or third stop on the route. During periods of high demand, buses frequently fill up at the first stop, leaving little or no room for passengers at subsequent stops. Before booking, inquire how many hotels are on the route and the sequence of the stops. The hotels are often so close together that you can easily walk to the first hotel on the route and board there. Similarly, if there's a large hotel nearby, it might have its own dedicated bus service that is more efficient. Use it instead of the service provided by your hotel. The majority of Universal-area shuttles work on a fixed schedule, typically with three or four departures in the morning and a similar or smaller number of returns around closing. Knowing exactly when a bus will depart makes it easier to plan your day.

At closing or during a hard rain, more people will be waiting for the shuttle than it can hold, and some will be left behind. Most shuttles return for stranded guests, but guests may wait 20 minutes to more than an hour.

If you're depending on shuttles, leave the park at least 45 minutes before closing. If you stay until closing and don't want the hassle of the shuttle, take a cab or request a ride share. Cab stands are located on the lower level of the main parking hub, near the bus stops, and at each on-site hotel. Pickup/drop-off for guests and ride share is located on the fifth floor roof of the northern parking garage, in the Jurassic Park section (see page 156).

I-RIDE TROLLEY *(temporarily suspended)*

TROLLEY-SHAPED BUSES, known as the **I-Ride Trolley** (☎ 407-248-9590; iridetrolley.com), offer cheap, convenient transportation servicing the International Drive area. The trolley circulates from the Orlando Vineland Premium Outlets on the south side of town to the hotels near Universal on Major Boulevard, with stops at SeaWorld and the Orange County Convention Center along the way.

COVID *tip*

I-Ride Trolley had temporarily suspended operations at press time.

A single one-way fare costs $2 for adults ($1 for kids ages 3–9; $0.25 for seniors age 65 and older) and must be paid in cash using exact change. You can prepurchase unlimited ride passes for 1 day ($5) to 14 days ($18) via the website or at participating hotels and attractions listed at iridetrolley.com/passes.asp.

The only issue with the I-Ride Trolley is that it doesn't stop at Universal Orlando. The closest stop is at the DoubleTree hotel on the corner of Kirkman Road and Major Boulevard (marked G4 on the trolley route map). From there you can walk to the Universal parks (see below).

WALKING TO UNIVERSAL ORLANDO FROM YOUR HOTEL

UNIVERSAL ORLANDO has a number of nearby off-site hotels within walking distance of the parks. The closest off-site hotels to Universal are along Major Boulevard near the intersection with Kirkman Road, at the eastern entrance to Universal property. The DoubleTree hotel on this corner isn't much farther from Universal's parks than the on-site Portofino Bay. To reach the parks from this area, cross Kirkman at Major from the northeast corner (where a new pedestrian bridge was recently constructed), and follow the sidewalks to Universal Boulevard. Cross Universal Boulevard and turn left, and then walk to the escalators leading up to CityWalk from the valet parking circle. You should be able to walk the 0.5 mile from the DoubleTree to CityWalk in about 15 minutes.

Farther away, but still within walking distance, are the hotels and motels on International Drive near Universal Boulevard, neighboring Universal's Endless Summer Resort. This route requires walking north along Universal Boulevard, over the I-4 overpass, and into the bus and taxi parking loop on the lower level of the parking hub. While there are sidewalks and pedestrian traffic signals the entire way, this is at least a 0.75-mile walk alongside busy traffic and isn't recommended for families with young children.

THE PUBLIC TRANSPORTATION ALTERNATIVE

SOME OFF-SITE HOTEL SHUTTLES don't operate early enough to get you to the parks before opening. An alternative is the **LYNX** public bus system, which costs $2 (exact change required) for a single one-way fare, with discounted all-day, weekly, and monthly passes available for advance purchase online.

If you're staying in downtown Orlando, you can take the LYNX #21 or #40 bus from the central bus station to Universal's parking garage. To reach Walt Disney World, take LYNX #40 from Universal and transfer at Grand National Drive onto #8 (or the I-Ride Trolley from Kirkman and Major) to SeaWorld, and then transfer to LYNX #50 to the Magic Kingdom's Transportation and Ticket Center. The buses begin running daily hours before the parks open to accommodate commuting employees, but service to Universal is limited after 8 p.m. on Fridays, weekends, and holidays. Precise hours of service vary depending on where along the route you are. Use the online trip planner at golynx .com or call ☎ 407-841-LYNX (5969) for travel information.

GETTING ORIENTED

PARKING AT UNIVERSAL ORLANDO

UNIVERSAL IS HOME to two massive multistory parking garages, holding a combined total of 20,000 cars. Signs route you from each of the five resort entrances to the parking structures.

The two rectangular garages lie along a north-south axis, with the pedestrian walkways leading to the theme parks running along the west, or long, side of each building. Sections are named for classic Universal movies and characters found in the parks: Jurassic Park, King Kong, and Jaws in the north garage, and E.T., Spider-Man, and Cat in the Hat in the south structure. The first numeral following the section name tells you on which deck level you are located, and the remaining numbers specify the row. So if a sign tells you that you're on King Kong 409, you're in the King Kong section on the fourth floor in row nine. We strongly recommend taking a photo of the name and number of your section, level, and row.

unofficial **TIP**
When the tollbooths before the garages are backed up, the farthest left one is often the swiftest.

Guests driving to Universal Orlando's attractions have three parking options:

SELF PARKING Parking in the main garage costs $26 for cars and $32 for RVs, trailers, and other large rigs. Regular parking is free for everyone after 6 p.m., except on Halloween Horror Nights when a fee is charged until 10 p.m. Parking is free for Preferred and Premier Annual Pass holders, and half price for Power Pass holders. You can also get free self parking if you buy two or more matinee tickets for any movie starting 11 a.m.–6 p.m. at the Universal Cinemark; show your parking receipt at the box office for reimbursement. Self parking is valid all day long, so if you want to leave the resort and return in the evening, just show your paid receipt at the parking booths for free reentry.

PRIME SELF PARKING   For $36, you will be parked on the garages' central level in the closest available section to the central hub. These spots are supposed to be the second closest to the parks, after the handicapped parking section. However, we've scored spaces just as good or better using the regular parking, especially when we've arrived before 10:30 a.m. Because the garages are two-thirds as wide as they are long, the farther your parking place is from the west side, the worse it will be. This is why prime parking is often not as close as regular parking—with the former, you'll be closer to the covered walkways to the parks, but if your particular space is toward the east side of the garage, you'll end up farther away than a guest who chose regular parking and was assigned a space closer to the west side of the structure.

An advantage of prime parking, however, is that you'll park faster because the ratio of cars choosing prime to regular is about 1 to 13. If you pick prime, a piece of paper will be tucked under your windshield wiper at the tollbooth, and you'll be asked to turn your hazard blinkers on before following signs to the prime parking section. Prime parking is free for Premier Annual Pass holders and costs $9 for Preferred Pass holders. Cars rented from Avis and Budget at Orlando International Airport include vouchers for a free upgrade to prime with paid standard parking.

VOLCANO BAY PARKING   There is no dedicated guest parking at Volcano Bay itself. Instead, visitors pay the usual rates to park on the first level of the southern parking structure used by other Universal theme park guests. Stay in the marked lanes when approaching the parking garage tollbooths and follow the signs for Volcano Bay parking.

Note that parking for oversize vehicles is on the same ground level as Volcano Bay parking, so you may save time by using the Volcano Bay tollbooth lanes to get there.

VALET PARKING *(temporarily suspended)*   In addition to the self-parking garages, valet parking is available at CityWalk for $26 for a visit of up to 2 hours, or $55 for longer than that ($40 if arriving after 6 p.m., except during Halloween Horror Nights and other special events). The entrance to the valet parking circle is on Universal Boulevard, across the street from the parking garages' taxi and bus loop. After dropping off your car, ascend the escalator adjacent to the miniature golf course and turn right to enter the CityWalk complex. Forgo valet parking if you're headed to Volcano Bay because you'll have to backtrack through the parking hub to reach the buses.

Premier Pass holders valet park for free (tip not included); Preferred Pass holders can valet for $20. On July 4, December 31, and Mardi Gras or Halloween event nights, Premier Pass holders are charged $35 ($40 for Preferred Pass holders) if they don't pick up from valet before 7 p.m. Select CityWalk restaurants will validate for up to 2 hours of valet if you eat lunch Monday–Friday, 11 a.m.–2 p.m.

Stay past 2 hours and you'll be charged full freight. And be warned that if you imbibe too much and have to leave your car at valet overnight, you'll have to pay a $75 fine in the morning.

COVID *tip*

Valet parking was temporarily unavailable at press time to promote social distancing, but the valet circle security checkpoint remains open for pedestrian access to Universal Boulevard.

Dropping off your car is usually quick, and our favorite unadvertised feature of the valet circle is its private security checkpoint, which usually has little wait. But beware that retrieving your car at the end of the evening can sometimes take up to half an hour, especially after a concert or special event in CityWalk or the parks. Premier Pass holders and anyone else who prepays can cut the line by using the automated kiosks to the right of the valet windows; just scan your parking ticket and pass or receipt for priority vehicle retrieval.

Guest Drop-Off/Pickup

If you aren't parking at the resort but only dropping off or picking up passengers, stay left when approaching the main Universal Orlando parking garage tollbooths and follow signs to the guest drop-off/ pickup located on the fifth floor roof of the northern parking garage, in the Jurassic Park section. No parking fee is required to access the drop-off area. This is also the designated location for ride-share vehicles like Uber or Lyft, and the best spot to pick up departing guests at the end of the day. Some guests try to use the valet parking circle for this purpose, but it is officially not permitted.

Another option is to drop off at the lobby of the Hard Rock Hotel, which is a short walk from Universal Studios Florida's front gates if you cut through the pool. However, you can't backtrack through the pool at the end of the day without a resort key card.

Speaking of the hotels, don't attempt to save money by parking at one of the resorts. Unless you are eating at a hotel restaurant that validates, off-site guests are charged a hefty fee for parking at the hotels.

Note that Uber tacks on an additional $4 fee for all trips originating from the parking garage pickup area; you can avoid this surcharge by using Lyft instead, or by departing from one of the resort hotels.

SECURITY SCREENINGS AT UNIVERSAL ORLANDO

CENTRAL FLORIDA'S THEME PARKS use uniformed and undercover security to screen and monitor guests entering their parks. In addition to a touchless thermometer temperature check (see page 22), guests arriving at Universal Orlando must either pass through a full-body scanner or be screened with a hand-held detection wand, and also submit any bags for inspection, before continuing on to CityWalk and the parks.

On a busy day, the crowd queuing for inspection in the parking garage rotunda may appear mind-boggling at first glance, but fortunately there is a phalanx of scanning machines, and Universal's security team could teach the TSA a thing or two about courtesy and efficiency.

If you really hate to start your day with waiting, arrive extra early, or opt for valet parking, which has its own dedicated screening checkpoint. Guests staying at the resort hotels will be inspected before boarding the water taxis, and additional security screens pedestrians on the pathways near Margaritaville and Hard Rock Hotel.

Volcano Bay guests get screened at a dedicated security checkpoint on the garage's bottom floor before boarding special shuttle buses that transport them along dedicated lanes to Volcano Bay's entrance. Hotel guests (and day guests on slower days) are screened by security upon arriving at the water park's bus stop. The entire process is not particularly pleasant and can be time-consuming, so arrive on Universal property 45–60 minutes before you want to actually get to Volcano Bay.

We've rarely experienced a serious issue with Universal's security procedures, but some guests (like this reader from Waipahu, Hawaii) found their efforts intrusive:

Security checks at the hotel prior to getting on the boat shuttle are the most thorough I've been through (more than TSA). I encountered an employee who was overzealous in her checks and left me feeling very uncomfortable, and I heard others comment the same.

FINDING YOUR WAY AROUND

THERE ARE NO PARKING TRAMS, so depending on where in the garage your car is parked, you'll have an 8- to 20-minute hike to the theme park entrances. From the garages, (sometimes) moving sidewalks deliver you first to the central hub between the two garages. In this area, you'll find wheelchair rentals, a snack and souvenir stand, and escalators leading down to bus and taxi parking. To proceed to CityWalk and the parks, you'll need to pass through the aforementioned security screening checkpoint. To reach Volcano Bay, follow signs to park on the lowest level of the south garage, where you'll find ticket booths, security screenings, and dedicated shuttle buses that will transport you to and from the water park.

Upon exiting the parking structure, you'll pass Universal Cinemark on your right and Starbucks (always open early for that essential morning caffeine jolt) on your left before reaching CityWalk's central plaza. From here, you walk straight toward the lighthouse to reach the main entrance of Islands of Adventure, or bear right at the Coca-Cola kiosk toward the big globe for Universal Studios Florida's front gate.

TRANSPORTATION BETWEEN UNIVERSAL RESORTS AND PARKS

UNIVERSAL OFFERS WATER TAXI SERVICE between each of its Preferred and Premier hotels and the two theme parks. The boat service uses a dock in CityWalk near the bridge to Universal Studios Florida as a hub, which is great if you're going from one of the hotels to a theme park. If you're traveling between hotels for a meal, however, you'll need to switch boats. Boats depart about every 15 minutes, from 1 hour before Early Park Admission begins until after CityWalk shuts down; allow 20–25 minutes for each leg of your journey by boat.

Universal also offers a shuttle bus service that circulates every 30 minutes between its four Premier and Preferred hotels and the parking garage, from which you may walk to CityWalk or the theme parks. The bus is often faster than transferring between boats for getting from one resort to another at dinnertime; tell the driver your destination when boarding. In addition, colorful character-covered buses run continuously between Cabana Bay Beach Resort and Aventura Hotel and the parking hub, with a separate route servicing the Endless Summer Resort. All of Universal's theme park–bound buses drop off near the same spot, at the base of the escalator leading up to the security checkpoint, which confused one family from Fruit Cove, Florida:

> *We had no idea that you get on the same bus to go to every park. At Disney each park has a separate bus. Also, once we got to the drop off, we didn't see anything that showed us where to go. Luckily, a family had us follow them. It's obvious once you see what's going on, but for someone who hates to be lost or not know where to go, I could feel my anxiety increasing.*

All of the hotels—except for Cabana Bay and Aventura, which provide pedestrian access to the water park—also offer free shuttle buses directly to Volcano Bay. Don't attempt to park at Cabana Bay or Aventura and walk to Volcano Bay if you aren't a registered guest; day visitors are charged $45 for self-parking, and key cards are inspected at the exclusive hotel entrance.

Finally, walking from most resort hotels (except Endless Summer Resort) to either theme park takes a maximum of about 15–20 minutes using the resort's beautifully landscaped (though frustratingly winding) garden pathways. Hard Rock Hotel is the closest to the parks, being only steps away from Universal Studios Florida's front gates, while Portofino and Cabana Bay are the farthest. To walk between Portofino and Cabana Bay takes 30–40 minutes.

You'll find more about Universal Orlando Resort transportation in Part Two (see page 93).

LEAVING UNIVERSAL ORLANDO

AT THE END OF YOUR VISIT, retrace your steps to your vehicle and follow directional signage to depart the resort. From the south garage, you have little option but to follow the arrows to I-4 or International Drive. If you exit the north garage onto Universal Boulevard, you can reach I-4 West by turning right onto Major Boulevard and then right onto Kirkman Road. Reach I-4 East by making a U-turn onto Universal Boulevard southbound at Major Boulevard, and then turn left onto the interstate after passing the garage. Practice deep breathing if you're departing with the masses at park closing on a crowded day because the backups on the parking garages' exit ramps may induce road rage.

PART FOUR

UNIVERSAL ESSENTIALS

MONEY, ETC.

ATMS AND BANKING SERVICES

BANKING AT UNIVERSAL ORLANDO is limited to ATMs, which are marked on the park maps. There are a half dozen ATMs in each theme park, plus three in CityWalk, one in each hotel, and one at Volcano Bay. Most major banking networks are accepted.

The closest full-service bank to Universal Orlando is **Regions** at the corner of Kirkman and Vineland Roads (5401 S. Kirkman Road).

USF ATM LOCATIONS	IOA ATM LOCATIONS
• Outside the park entrance to the right of the Guest Services window	• Outside the park entrance, to the right of the Guest Services window
• Front Lot near First Aid and Lost and Found	• Marvel Super Hero Island near The Amazing Adventures of Spider-Man
• New York near Revenge of the Mummy	• Jurassic Park by the exit of Jurassic Park River Adventure
• Outside Diagon Alley to the right of King's Cross Station	• Hogsmeade outside The Three Broomsticks
• World Expo at the *Fear Factor Live* restrooms	• Lost Continent outside Mythos Restaurant
• Springfield: Home of the Simpsons along Fast Food Boulevard	
CITYWALK ATM LOCATIONS	**VOLCANO BAY ATM LOCATIONS**
• Downstairs to the left of the Guest Services window	• Outside Volcano Bay, to the right of the main entrance
• Upstairs by the second-level exit of the movie theater	
• To the left of The Groove	

CHECKS

UNIVERSAL ORLANDO ACCEPTS ONLY personal checks that are preprinted, drawn on US banks, and made out for the exact amount of the purchase, and they are accepted only at the front gate. Valid photo identification is required, and your check will be submitted to an online verification system.

Traveler's checks in US currency are accepted throughout the resort but must be signed by the bearer in front of the cashier and be presented with photo ID.

Business checks, cashier's checks, and school checks are accepted only if they are preprinted, drawn on US banks, made out for the exact amount of purchase, and presented with photo ID.

CREDIT CARDS

AMERICAN EXPRESS, DINERS CLUB, Discover, MasterCard, and Visa are accepted throughout Universal Orlando; the hotels also accept Japan Credit Bureau and Carte Blanche cards. Most point-of-sale registers at Universal have chip scanners and offer tap-to-pay transactions for mobile devices, such as Apple Pay and Google Pay.

American Express is the official card of Universal Orlando, and members get several discounts and perks, including access to a private **American Express VIP Lounge** hidden behind the Classic Monsters Cafe near the front of Universal Studios Florida (USF); look for the door to the left of the Shrek meet and greet. Inside you'll find free bottled water, chips, granola bars, and phone-charging stations, as well an air-conditioned respite from the crowds. In addition, a full-time concierge inside can assist you with information or reservations. The lounge is open daily, noon–5 p.m., and up to six people may enter per American Express card. Technically, you must have purchased your Universal admission (Park-to-Park tickets or Annual Pass) with your American Express, and your purchase history may be inspected for verification.

If you don't have an AmEx card, you can stop by its membership center (next to security in the parking hub) to receive a $150 bonus statement credit, plus cash back on eligible in-park purchases, in exchange for filling out a card application. For additional details and current discounts, visit tinyurl.com/UniAmEx or select the "AmEx Special Offers" tab inside Universal's mobile app.

CURRENCY EXCHANGE

EXCHANGE YOUR EUROS, KRONER, OR ZLOTYS for good old American greenbacks—the only form of cash accepted at Universal Orlando—at either theme park's Guest Services window or any hotel front desk. There may be a daily limit on how much you can exchange (around $500), and a nominal transaction surcharge applies.

A LICENSE TO PRINT MONEY

AVAILABLE EXCLUSIVELY at the Gringotts Money Exchange shop in USF's Diagon Alley, **Gringotts Wizarding Bank Notes** come in $10 or $20 denominations, and there is no extra fee to exchange your Muggle money for some. The bank notes can be redeemed virtually anywhere on Universal Orlando property (even for valet parking) at a one-for-one exchange rate. While you won't lose any money on Wizarding currency as long as you spend it before you leave the resort, most guests (intentionally or unintentionally) take them home as souvenirs, making a healthy profit for Universal's goblin accountants. Credit card–style Universal

Orlando gift cards with various designs are also sold (in $5 increments up to $500) and accepted throughout the resort; you can buy them at universalorlando.com/web/en/us/gift-cards/purchase.html.

SALES TAX

A COMBINED STATE AND LOCAL SALES TAX of 6.5% applies to all purchases made at Universal Orlando. Hotels also charge a 6% Orange County occupancy tax, for a total of 12.5%. All prices listed in this book are before tax, unless otherwise noted.

PACKING *the* ESSENTIALS

WHAT SHOULD I BRING?

IN ADDITION TO THE BASICS that you would bring along on any vacation—casual clothing, comfortable footwear, bathing attire, necessary medications and toiletries—you'll want to stock up on the following before your Universal Orlando visit:

- Face masks, at least two per person, per day (see page 23)
- Small bottles of hand sanitizer and sunscreen
- Cell phone backup battery or charger with cord and plug (see page 166)
- Lanyard for tickets and hotel key card (see page 74)
- Zip-top plastic or dry bags, to protect electronics and masks on water rides
- A hat with brim and sunglasses (even during the winter)
- Pocket-size umbrella and/or poncho, especially during summer and hurricane season (see page 165)
- Refillable water bottle (if you aren't purchasing unlimited Freestyle drinks; see page 222)

By the same token, there are some items you definitely want to leave behind:

- Alcohol, controlled substances (including medical cannabis), and any illegal drugs
- Weapons, including knives, firearms, and explosives
- Glass containers or glassware
- Large or hard-sided coolers (see page 168)
- Food that requires refrigerating or reheating (bottled water and small snacks are OK)
- Drones, hoverboards, and Segways (except as ADA mobility devices)

PROBLEMS *and* UNUSUAL SITUATIONS

ATTRACTION CLOSURES

FIND OUT IN ADVANCE what attractions are scheduled to be closed for repair during your visit. For complete refurbishment schedules, check Universal's official operating calendar (tinyurl.com/unihrs) or

TouringPlans' Universal Orlando closures page (touringplans.com/uni versal-orlando/closures), or use the mobile app Lines.

Universal's attractions are technically complex, so it's almost inevitable that you will experience some unscheduled downtime during your visit. If a ride is temporarily closed, ask the attendants outside if there is an estimated reopening time (usually they can't tell you) and continue with your touring, returning later if possible. If a ride stops running while you're already in the queue, decide whether to stay based on how long the posted wait was when you entered and how much time you've already invested. Most "brief operational delays" are resolved in about 15 minutes, but there are no guarantees.

If a ride halts unexpectedly while you're on it, remain calm and rest assured that Universal has extremely safe evacuation procedures for every contingency. Stay seated and listen for announcements, and be patient because employees may need to evacuate ride vehicles one at a time in a specific order. On the plus side, you may get an exclusive backstage view of how the ride operates, and you should be offered either an immediate reride (if the attraction resumes operating) or a return ticket to let you skip the standby line later on.

GASOLINE

THERE IS ONE **Speedway** gas station on Universal property. It's on the west side of the resort, adjacent to the corporate offices and employee parking lot. The address is 5981 Turkey Lake Road. From the guest parking garages, take Hollywood Way west to Turkey Lake Road; turn right, and the station will be ahead on your right.

CAR CARE

UNIVERSAL ORLANDO OFFERS free vehicle assistance—including battery jumps—to guests parked in its garage. Raise your car's hood (if possible) and flag down a parking attendant, or use one of the security call boxes located in each parking section.

If you have more-serious car trouble, the nearest repair facility is the **Universal Service Center,** inside the Speedway station above (5989 Turkey Lake Road; ☎ 407-345-4860; universalservicecenter.net).

CELL PHONE SNAFUS

CELL PHONE SERVICE CAN BE SPOTTY at Universal Orlando, especially on days of high attendance. A woman from Leawood, Kansas, tells it like it is:

> In our group, we were using three different carriers, and we all had problems sending and receiving texts and calls.

The problem of signal strength is compounded by crowd noise and the ambient music played throughout the parks. Even if you have a decent signal, it can be challenging to find some place quiet enough to have a conversation. When possible, opt for texting.

Data speeds can be especially sluggish when the park is packed with guests trying to Instagram over LTE. Luckily, Universal's Wi-Fi is free and fairly stable throughout the theme parks and CityWalk; you can even get decent reception inside Gringotts' vaults. In your phone's Wi-Fi settings, choose "Universal" from the list of available networks; then input an email address and accept the user agreement before opening your browser or social media apps. You may have to log in again every day or so.

unofficial **TIP**
Data and Wi-Fi coverage are poor inside Volcano Bay. We suggest that you put away your phone and bring a book for the beach.

LOST AND FOUND

IF YOU LOSE (OR FIND) SOMETHING in USF, go to the **Lost and Found** counter, to the right of the main gate as you enter. At Islands of Adventure (IOA), Lost and Found is near stroller rental to the left of the park's entrance. At Volcano Bay visit **Guest Services** at the front of the park. If you discover your loss after you've left the park(s), call ☎ 407-224-4233 and choose option 2.

It's best not to lose anything in the first place, but if you do, there is hope: we've had an excellent track record with Universal's Lost and Found, which has recovered errant hats and keys for us over the years.

MEDICAL MATTERS

HEADACHE RELIEF   Sample sizes of some over-the-counter medications are available free from the **First Aid Stations** (see page 167 for locations). Aspirin and other sundries are sold at the **Universal Studios Store** in USF, at **Islands of Adventure Trading Company** in IOA, and at **Krakatoa Katy's** in Volcano Bay. Over-the-counter meds are stored behind the counter, so you must ask an employee for them.

ILLNESSES REQUIRING MEDICAL ATTENTION   Off property, the closest walk-in clinic is **AdventHealth Centra Care Dr. Phillips** (8014 Conroy Windermere Road; ☎ 407-291-8975; centracare.advent health.com). The clinic is open Monday–Friday, 8 a.m.–8 p.m., and Saturday–Sunday, 8 a.m.–5 p.m. Centra Care also operates a 24-hour physician house call service and runs a free shuttle (call ☎ 407-938-0650 to arrange pickup).

The Medical Concierge (☎ 855-932-5252; themedicalconcierge .com) has board-certified physicians available 24-7 for house calls to your hotel room. It offers in-room X-rays and IV therapy service, as well as same-day dental and specialist appointments. It also rents medical equipment. Insurance receipts, insurance billing, and foreign-language interpretation are provided. Walk-in clinics are available. You can also inquire about transportation arrangements.

DOCS (Doctors on Call Service; ☎ 407-399-3627; doctorson callservice.com) offers 24-hour house call service. All physicians are certified by the American Board of Medical Specialties. A father of two from O'Fallon, Illinois, gives them a thumbs-up:

My wife's cold developed into an ear infection that required medical attention, and DOCS was able to respond in 40 minutes. The doctor had medicine with him and was very professional and friendly.

Physician Room Service (☎ 407-238-2000; physicianroomservice .com) provides board-certified doctor house calls to Universal Orlando–area guest rooms for adults and children. In case of a life-and-death emergency, the nearest fully equipped ER is at **Dr. Phillips Hospital** (9400 Turkey Lake Road; ☎ 407-351-8500).

DENTAL NEEDS   Call **Advanced Esthetic Dentistry** (6001 Vineland Road, Ste. 106; ☎ 407-874-1546; advancedestheticdentistry.com).

PRESCRIPTION MEDICINE   The nearest pharmacy is **Walgreens** (☎ 407-248-0315) at 5501 Kirkman Road, in the shopping plaza across from the resort. (*Note:* Google indicates a Walgreens at 1000 Universal Studios Plaza, but that's a backstage clinic for Universal employees only.) **Turner Drugs** (☎ 407-828-8125; turnerdrug.com) charges $15 to deliver a prescription to your hotel's front desk ($7.50 for Disney hotels).

Sergeant Blisterblaster's Guide To Happy Feet

1. ON YOUR FEET!   You can easily log 5–10 miles a day at the Universal Orlando parks, and a reader told us she clocked 13.5 (more than a half-marathon!), so shape up beginning a month or two before your visit. Start with short walks around the neighborhood, and gradually increase your distance until you can do 6 miles without CPR.

2. A-TEN-SHUN!   No walking in flip-flops, loafers, or sandals. Wear well-constructed, broken-in running or hiking shoes with a pair of socks (such as Smartwool or Coolmax) that wicks perspiration away from your feet; antifungal powder is optional.

3. WHO DO YOU THINK YOU ARE? JOHN WAYNE?   Don't be a hero. Take care of a foot problem the minute you notice it. Carry a small foot-emergency kit (including gauze, antibiotic ointment, moleskin, and blister bandages) or visit Universal First Aid for supplies if a problem arises. If you develop a hot spot in the same place every time you walk (a clue!), cover it with a blister bandage before set out.

4. BITE THE BULLET!   Check your kids' feet—and your own—several times a day for hot spots, and cover any you find ASAP with a blister bandage. If a blister develops, air out and dry the foot, clean the area with antibiotic ointment, and place a blister bandage over the blister. If you don't have blister bandages, don't cover the hot spot or blister with adhesive bandages; they'll slip and wad up. Moleskin can still be useful for lining the roughened inner surface of shoe heels and toes to prevent further foot damage.

RAIN

WEATHER BAD? Go to the parks anyway. The crowds are lighter, and most attractions and waiting areas are under cover. Showers, especially during warmer months, are usually short and frequently occur in the late afternoon around 4 p.m.

Rainy-Day Touring

When it comes to deciding which park to visit, we think USF is an excellent wet-weather choice—almost all of its headliner attractions (except Hollywood Rip Ride Rockit) are indoors.

While the many outdoor attractions at IOA can operate in a moderate downpour, they must shut down when lightning is in the vicinity and may require safety inspections before restarting. Hagrid's Magical Creatures Motorbike Adventure in particular is notorious for taking up to an hour to reopen after a storm clears. That leaves Harry Potter and the Forbidden Journey, The Amazing Adventures of Spider-Man, Reign of Kong, and Cat in the Hat as virtually the only rides at IOA that can operate during severe weather.

Volcano Bay will let you keep swimming in a moderate rain, but as soon as lightning is detected in the vicinity, everyone must get out of the water. Many guests will flee when a downpour starts, but you should find some shelter and stay put. (Hey, you came here to get wet, right?) Once the weather clears, you'll have the slides to yourself, making poststorm summer afternoons the best time to enjoy the water park without crowds.

unofficial **TIP**
Raingear isn't always displayed in shops, so you may have to ask for it.

Raingear

Ponchos are $12 for adults, $10 for children; umbrellas cost $14–$20. All ponchos sold at Universal Orlando are made of clear plastic (though ones sold within The Wizarding World have a special insignia), so picking out somebody in your party on a rainy day can be tricky. Stores such as Target sell inexpensive solid-color ponchos that will make your family bright beacons in a plastic-covered sea of humanity.

unofficial **TIP**
To keep your head and face as dry as possible, we recommend wearing a cap under the poncho hood.

A Wilmington, North Carolina, mom thinks high-quality raingear is worth the investment:

It rained every day on our trip, driving many people out of the parks and leaving others looking miserable in their ponchos. Meanwhile, we hardly noticed the rain from inside our high-end rain jackets as we walked right on to many of the attractions.

Some unusually heavy rain precipitated (no pun intended) dozens of reader suggestions for dealing with soggy days. The best came from this Memphis, Tennessee, mom:

1. *Raingear should include ponchos and umbrellas. When rain isn't beating down on your ponchoed head, it's easier to ignore.*

2. *Buy blue ponchos at Walgreens. We could keep track of each other more easily because we had blue ponchos instead of clear ones.*

   3. *If you're using a stroller, bring a plastic sheet or extra poncho to protect it from rain. (Ponchos cover only single strollers.) Carry a towel in a plastic bag to wipe off your stroller after experiencing an attraction during a rainfall.*

HOW TO LODGE A COMPLAINT WITH UNIVERSAL

YOU'LL USUALLY FIND Universal folks highly responsive to guests' issues. Guest Services at the front of each Universal park will be happy to listen to any complaints and will be even happier to pass along praise for any exceptional employees you encounter. Minor problems are often addressed with a sincere apology and a pass to skip an attraction queue; on the other hand, a more global gripe, or one beyond an on-site manager's ability to resolve, is likely to founder in the labyrinth of Universal bureaucracy. To contact Guest Services after your trip, use the email contact form at visitorsatisfaction.com/contactus.

SERVICES

CELEBRATION BUTTONS

CELEBRATING A BIRTHDAY, ANNIVERSARY, honeymoon, engagement, or Bat Mitzvah at Universal? Or just celebrating the fact that it's your first visit to the parks? Stop by Guest Services for a free celebration button to wear during your special day. Buttons come in "It's My Birthday!" and more generic "I'm Celebrating!" varieties. At a minimum, you'll have employees (and fellow guests) shouting you warm wishes all day long. If you're lucky, you might find yourself treated to preferred seating, a special meet and greet, or other unexpected perks, as this Endicott, New York, reader happily discovered:

   A birthday button earned many greetings, two free desserts, and a free drink.

CELL PHONE CHARGING

THE AMERICAN EXPRESS VIP LOUNGE and the annual pass holder lounge, both discussed previously, stock charging adapters for most Apple and Android devices (including Micro USB and Lightning). Aside from these locations, however, Universal Orlando has no other designated phone-charging stations in the parks, so pack a power cable and wall plug if you want to steal juice from accessible outlets you find along the way.

   If you prefer to charge on the go, we use **Anker** external batteries for our devices, available at Amazon.

   Another energy option is the **FuelRod,** a precharged battery pack sold from automated kiosks scattered around the parks, CityWalk, and the resort hotels. You can find higher-capacity batteries online for less than the $30 FuelRod—the advantage is that whenever a FuelRod runs out of power, you can simply stop and swap it for a full one at any FuelRod kiosk on Universal property. Kiosks can be found in the following locations:

USF FUELROD ATM LOCATIONS	IOA FUELROD LOCATIONS
• Today Cafe restrooms	• Mulberry Street Store in Seuss Landing
• New York Palace Arcade	• Jurassic Park River Adventure restrooms
• Fast & Furious Custom Gear store	• Marvel Super Hero Island restrooms
• MIB Gear	• Marvel Alterniverse Store
CITYWALK FUELROD LOCATIONS	**RESORT HOTEL FUELROD LOCATIONS**
• Guest Services	• Resort hotel gift shops

The downside: whereas similar kiosks on Disney property provide free unlimited swaps, the ones at Universal charge $3 per exchange, although you can sign into the FuelRod app for a $5 credit; "founders" who purchased one before October 26, 2019, get lifetime free swaps.

You can also save yourself some money by buying FuelRods outside the resort—they're available online and in airports and malls for about $20, and all are compatible with Universal's kiosks. Search online for a discount code to get $3 off your initial purchase.

FIRST AID

EACH UNIVERSAL PARK has a Walgreens-sponsored first aid center. In USF, it's on Canal Street behind Louie's Italian Restaurant, on the border between New York and San Francisco. In IOA, it's in the Lost Continent near The Mystic Fountain; look for the red cross behind the coin vendor. In both parks, the Family Services nursing facilities and companion restroom are right next to First Aid. Volcano Bay's First Aid is just inside the park entrance. CityWalk's First Aid is near Guest Services, at the end of the hallway behind Cold Stone Creamery.

Guests who use the service are generally very positive about it; Seth once sought treatment for a minor flesh wound and was patched up in a matter of minutes.

GROCERIES

EACH UNIVERSAL RESORT HOTEL has a shop or food court selling sundries, snacks, and grab-and-go breakfast foods. While their locations make them convenient, the selection is poor, and you'll find the prices higher and more frightening than Doctor Doom's Fearfall. For down-to-earth prices, try **Publix,** north of Universal at the intersection of Kirkman and Conroy Roads (4606 S. Kirkman Road; ☎ 407-293-7673), or for fancier fare visit **Whole Foods,** southwest of Universal on Sand Lake Road near I-4 (8003 Turkey Lake Road; ☎ 407-355-7100).

If you don't have a car or you just don't feel like going to the supermarket, **WeGoShop.com** will deliver your groceries. WeGoShop takes your typed shopping list to the grocery store you request, buys at market rates, and delivers to your on-site Universal resort. WeGo Shop charges on a sliding scale, from $21 for up to a $50 grocery bill, to 15% of the total for bills over $300; a $3 fuel surcharge is levied on all orders, and a 15% mandatory gratuity is added for deliveries left at bell services. **Instacart.com** will deliver to Universal-area hotels from Publix, Aldi, Costco, and numerous other stores. Delivery fees start at $3.99 with a $10 minimum, but free offers are often available; you must select a 2-hour delivery window and be present to receive your purchases. Finally, Amazon Prime subscribers can order groceries through **Prime Now Pantry** (primenow.amazon.com). The selection is limited, and there's a $35 minimum per order for free 2-hour delivery, but 1-hour delivery and pickup options are also available. You must be present for delivery of perishables, alcohol, or orders over $500.

LOCKERS

WHEN WE VISIT THE UNIVERSAL PARKS, we try to pare down our gear to a bare minimum and bring only those necessities that fit comfortably in our pockets: admission, ID, a credit card or cash, and a cell phone. Many guests keep their tickets handy in a plastic lanyard (readily available around the resort for around $12 and up), and Seth swears by cargo shorts with zippered pockets, for function if not fashion.

But many guests—especially those accompanying young children or those with special needs—find that they simply can't travel that light. When your burden becomes too much to bear, make a beeline for a bank of lockers and lighten your load.

Incidentally, Universal strictly enforces restrictions on the kinds of items guests are allowed to bring into its parks. Obviously, any form of weapon or illegal substance is prohibited, as is clothing with "offensive language or content" or that "represents someone as emergency personnel." You are also disallowed from entering with large duffel bags, folding chairs, beach umbrellas, or hard-sided coolers. Packing picnics is officially prohibited, but you may bring bottled water and small snacks, along with baby food and any medically necessary nutritional items, as long as they are nonalcoholic, are not in glass containers, and are stored in a soft-sided cooler or bag no bigger than 8½ inches by 6 inches by 6 inches.

There are no on-site facilities for refrigerating or reheating food you bring into the parks. Also, be aware that all items are subject to inspection before you enter CityWalk, so come prepared to open your bags at the security checkpoint.

Universal Orlando's lockers are automated and use a computerized locking system. The locker banks are easy to find, and each bank has a small touch screen in the center; hold your physical admission ticket up to the bar code scanner below the screen. If you're using the mobile app to store your admission, ask a locker attendant for a bar code that will work with the scanners.

After you scan your ticket (and swipe your credit card for paid lockers), a nearby locker will pop open for you. Place your stuff (except for your ticket!) in the indicated locker, and press the illuminated button to lock it after you've closed the door. When you're ready to retrieve your belongings, return to the same kiosk and scan your ticket again. The locker should relinquish its contents; if you have any trouble, find a nearby employee to assist.

By default, only the ticket originally used to secure a locker can reopen it, but paid lockers let you attach additional tickets, thus giving other members of your party access. Look for a freestanding assistance kiosk near the lockers, and follow the instructions on the screen.

Universal Orlando Resort offers three types of lockers, described as follows.

Paid All-Day Lockers

These lockers charge one flat rate for a full day and can be opened and relocked as many times as you like during your visit using your ticket. All-day lockers in the theme parks come in two categories: regular (about 12 inches wide by 13 inches high by 16.9 inches deep) for $10 per day, or the roomier family size (about 12 inches wide by 16.25 inches high by 16.9 inches deep) for $15 per day. Lockers inside Volcano Bay cost $9, $13, or $16 per day, depending on size, and are controlled with the TapuTapu wristbands. Volcano Bay has four locker facilities arrayed around the park's perimeter, plus one outside the entrance; see page 361 for details.

All-day lockers can be found in the following locations:

UNIVERSAL STUDIOS FLORIDA ALL-DAY LOCKERS
• Next to the Studio Audience Center inside the front gate (regular size)
• Behind the restrooms near the Studio Audience Center (family size)
• Near the exit turnstiles, next to wheelchair and stroller rental (regular size)

ISLANDS OF ADVENTURE ALL-DAY LOCKERS
• Inside the front gate near wheelchair and stroller rental (regular and family size)

Free and Discounted Short-Term Lockers

Universal enforces a mandatory locker system at its big thrill rides. Lockers outside these attractions come in two varieties. Small lockers (14 inches wide by 5.5 inches high by 16.9 inches deep) are free for an amount of time that varies with the length of the standby line—if the wait in line is 30 minutes, for example, and the ride itself lasts 10 minutes, you get 40 minutes plus a small cushion of about 15 minutes. The lockers then cost $3 for each 30 minutes after that, with a $20 daily maximum.

The free lockers are too small to store souvenir soda cups standing up (empty your drink before stowing it) and are barely large enough for a few cell phones and wallets, as this reader from Brooklyn, New York, was frustrated to find:

I wish I had known how SMALL the mandatory lockers at Universal are. I was very frustrated trying to fit my bag into the lockers, which are seemingly designed to fit only a small backpack or purse.

A limited number of larger lockers (12 inches wide by 13 inches high by 16.9 inches deep) are available, but they cost $2 during the posted wait time and an additional $3 per 30 minutes after. That adds up to the price of an all-day locker after only five attractions, so you may want to weigh that cost before walking too far from the park entrance, as this reader from Nof Ayalon, Israel, advises:

> *We had a medium-size backpack and struggled to stuff it into the lockers. When I reached Men in Black Alien Attack, I decided enough is enough and went to the park entrance to store our knapsack. I only later realized that I picked the farthest point in the park to do this.*

Free short-term lockers are at the following attractions:

UNIVERSAL STUDIOS FLORIDA FREE SHORT-TERM LOCKERS	
• Harry Potter and the Escape from Gringotts	• Hollywood Rip Ride Rockit
• Men in Black Alien Attack • Revenge of the Mummy	

ISLANDS OF ADVENTURE FREE SHORT-TERM LOCKERS	
• Hagrid's Magical Creatures Motorbike Adventure	• Harry Potter and the Forbidden Journey
• The Incredible Hulk Coaster	

On most of the aforementioned rides, all bags, purses, and other objects too large to be secured in a pocket must be placed in a free locker during your ride; wallets, phones, and compact cameras are generally permitted, as are small hip belts or fanny packs that can be securely fastened and tucked beneath a shirt.

Universal strictly enforces a "no loose items" policy at **The Incredible Hulk Coaster** and **Hollywood Rip Ride Rockit.** At these rides, guests are required to undergo an airport-style security screening—complete with walk-through metal detectors and electronic scanning wands—to ensure that no phones, keys, or even spare change enters the queue. You should be permitted to hold on to your prescription eyeglasses and ticket lanyard.

If a ride breaks down while you're in line and you exceed your free usage period through no fault of your own, a locker attendant can override the charge on request. You may need to be firm to avoid paying an overage fee, as this reader found:

> *Watch out for the Men in Black lockers. We went over our allotted time because of ride issues, but the [attendant] kept insisting we had to pay. Only after standing our ground did the attendant finally check with others and confirm that there were ride issues.*

When you want to ride a thrill ride but don't want to bother with a locker, you can use the child-swap area (where available; see page 204) as a bag swap and leave a nonrider with your belongings. This is especially useful for the Harry Potter rides because the free lockers are too small to hold some wand boxes from Ollivanders (at 19 inches, the Rowan, Oak, and Alder boxes are all too long), and the locker banks for Forbidden Journey and Gringotts are frequently overcrowded.

Paid Short-Term Lockers

Universal does not enforce mandatory locker usage on its water rides, but it does conveniently (or capitalistically) provide paid short-term lockers outside each attraction that is likely to soak you and your belongings. The short-term paid lockers come in the same two sizes as the free and discounted ones and operate identically. The difference is that the smaller ones cost $4 for the first 90 minutes and the larger ones are $5; both cost $3 for each additional hour after that, with a $20 daily maximum.

Paid short-term lockers are located only at IOA at the following attractions:

ISLANDS OF ADVENTURE PAID SHORT-TERM LOCKERS

- Dudley Do-Right's Ripsaw Falls • Jurassic Park River Adventure
- Popeye & Bluto's Bilge-Rat Barges

PACKAGE PICKUP AND DELIVERY

FREE PACKAGE PICKUP is available at USF and IOA—ask the salesperson to send your purchases to Package Pickup, and when you leave the park, they'll be waiting for you. At USF, Package Pickup is at **It's a Wrap** gift shop immediately adjacent to the exit turnstiles. At IOA, it's at **Port Provisions** at the park exit. Volcano Bay does not hold packages until the end of the day but will deliver merchandise to on-site hotel rooms.

If you're staying at a Universal Orlando resort, you can also have packages delivered directly to your hotel room by the following day at no charge. If you're leaving within 24 hours, however, take them with you or use the in-park pickup location.

If you get home and realize you missed an essential souvenir, shop for Universal Orlando tchotchkes online at shop.universalorlando.com.

PET CARE

UNIVERSAL ORLANDO'S KENNEL boards dogs and cats (no exotic or native species allowed) on a first-come, first-serve basis. You can find the facility by following the signs to RV and camper parking after passing through the tollbooths; the kennel is located on the corner of the oversize parking lot. It opens at 8 a.m. and does not take reservations. The cost is $15 per pet, per day. Cats, as well as dogs under 39 pounds, are kept indoors in air-conditioning; dogs weighing 39 pounds and up stay outdoors with shade and fans.

COVID *tip*
Universal's kennel was temporarily closed at press time.

An attendant remains on duty at the kennel until 2 hours after the last park closes, but you can retrieve your pet until 3 a.m. by using the phone outside the kennel to call for assistance. The kennel provides water, but you need to bring your own food and toys, and you must return to walk your dog at least once during the day.

Note: You must provide written proof from a veterinarian of current vaccination (rabies, Bordetella, and DHPP for dogs; rabies, calicivirus, panleukopenia, and rhinotracheitis for cats) either at check-in or by fax at ☎ 407-224-9516. Call ☎ 407-224-9509 or visit tinyurl.com /UniServices for more information.

MY UNIVERSAL PHOTOS (MUP)

WHILE SOME GUESTS STILL FIND their point-and-shoot or smartphone sufficient for documenting their vacation, Universal (in partnership with Colorvision's Amazing Pictures) has capitalized on advancing digital photo and social media technology with its My Universal Photos program. All the images captured during your day by Universal—either by roving paparazzi near the park entrances, at organized character meet and greets, or inside attractions—can be collected on plastic cards (distributed free from every photo location) and retrieved at the end of the day at the photography shops at the front of the parks: **On Location** at USF, **DeFotos Expedition Photography** at IOA, or Krakatau Katy's and **Waturi Marketplace** at Volcano Bay.

Photos can be purchased individually, but that quickly gets expensive, at $21 for a single 5-by-7-inch print or $26 for both a print and digital download. The MUP daily packages are a better value, offering 1, 3, or 30 days of unlimited digital photos and a souvenir lanyard to hold your MUP card. With a MUP package, you receive two free printed photos (one 4-by-6-inch and one 5-by-7-inch) as well as deep discounts on videos ($20 for Hollywood Rip Ride Rockit) and additional prints ($2 for 4-by-6-inch; $5 for 5-by-7-inch; $10 for 8-by-10-inch), along with 20% off Amazing Pictures green screen photo ops. MUP packages are valid in all three parks and include all street photographers, on-ride still images, and even unique photo ops such as E.T.'s flying bicycle.

Digital images can be downloaded at myuniversalphotos.com or through the free Apple or Android app (search for "Amazing Pictures Mobile" in your app store or go to amazingpictures.com/app), from which they can be emailed, shared on Facebook and Twitter, or saved at a resolution good enough for printing (though not for poster-size enlargements). You can also purchase an archive disc of all your photos ($59.95) or have your prom picture with Optimus Prime printed on anything from pillows to iPad cases through the website.

To use the MUP package, simply present your card to every Universal photographer you approach, or at the photo counters at the exits of rides. Ride photos can be edited to zoom in on your party, and some photographers can set up special effects shots.

Universal also has automated MUP kiosks at the exits of select attractions, including Men in Black Alien Attack, Revenge of the Mummy, and The Incredible Hulk Coaster, letting you register your photos without waiting in line, though MUP team members are still available to help find and edit your photos if you don't want to use the self-service stations. You get two cards per MUP package, in case your party splits up, and any additional images you get on other photo cards can be added to your MUP account at any photo service center.

In addition to on-ride pictures and wandering photogs, you'll find a few automated photo ops scattered around the parks, including the Back to the Future car in USF, the Jurassic Park spinosaurus in IOA, and several selfie stations at Volcano Bay. Scan your MUP card (or TapuTapu wristband) at the kiosk, then pose at the designated spot while the camera counts down to the flash.

Photo packages also include free poses against green screens that digitally insert you into scenes with the Minions, Transformers, and other Universal characters. Located at **The Darkroom** on USF's Hollywood Boulevard, there are two different green screen photo booths with a total of eight backgrounds, two of which are exclusive to MUP package holders.

If you prepurchase your MUP package online at presale.amazing pictures.com/universalflorida.aspx or tinyurl.com/MyUniversalPhoto, it won't begin expiring until you activate it at the photography shop near the front of each park. Once activated, MUP packages are valid for the purchased number of consecutive days. Online prices (plus tax) are $69.99 for 1 day, $89.99 for 3 days, and $119.99 for 30 days. A full year of MUP service costs $139.99 and is sometimes discounted for annual pass holders. A one-day photo pass valid only at Volcano Bay is $39.99; all other packages are valid in all three parks. Finally, a package combining a three-day MUP package with a video session at Shutterbutton's in Diagon Alley (see page 295) costs $139.99 online. MUP packages cost $20–$30 more if purchased inside the park.

If buying ride and character photos is important to you, you'll save money buying a package versus buying à la carte; if not, the freedom of unlimited snapshots may seduce you. That said, there are some deficits and gotchas to MUP that you should be aware of before buying.

For starters, MUP photographers can be found at each park's entrance, and occasionally at impromptu character greetings, but they aren't on every corner. You can sometimes find an exceptional Universal photographer who will spend time posing with your family in various locations, but you're equally likely to encounter a meet and greet where the photog has gone mysteriously MIA. You certainly shouldn't leave your camera at home expecting that MUP will be able to capture all your vacation memories.

Second, if you want to purchase any photos, you must do so (or buy and activate a MUP package) before you leave the park—once you exit at the end of the day, any photos not paid for or connected to an active MUP account will be erased. Likewise, if a photographers asks you to pose pointing or with your empty palm extended, you should stop by the photo store before leaving to have characters edited into the image; otherwise you'll look pretty silly in the shots. Even if you didn't take any "magic" photos, you should still review your pictures from the day on your phone or at a photo center before you leave, because images occasionally get mysteriously lost on the way to your account.

Finally, a few specific attractions have their own quirks. All digital photos in The Wizarding Worlds are included with MUP, but if you want to use your included free prints for the Forbidden Journey or Escape from Gringotts ride, you must get your photo printed at those attractions. All other attraction pictures may be printed at any photo-service location. For the record, below is where you can always find MUP locations throughout Universal's parks:

MY UNIVERSAL PHOTOS LOCATIONS	
UNIVERSAL STUDIOS FLORIDA	
• Park entrance • Meet and greet near *Shrek 4-D* exit (temporarily closed) • SpongeBob StorePants in Woody Woodpecker's KidZone • Transformers meet and greet • E.T. Toy Closet • Men in Black Alien Attack on-ride photo • Revenge of the Mummy on-ride photo • Hollywood Rip Ride Rockit on-ride photo	• Minions meet and greet at the Despicable Me Minion Mayhem ride exit (temporarily closed) • Harry Potter and the Escape from Gringotts queue photo (temporarily closed) • Back to the Future car automated photo op • The Darkroom green screen photo booths • Roaming photographers during Halloween Horror Nights and other events (seasonal)
ISLANDS OF ADVENTURE	
• Park entrance • The Incredible Hulk Coaster on-ride photo • The Amazing Adventures of Spider-Man on-ride photo • Spider-Man meet and greet (temporarily closed) • Dudley Do-Right's Ripsaw Falls on-ride photo • Jurassic Park spinosaurus automated photo op • Jurassic Park River Adventure on-ride photo	• Harry Potter and the Forbidden Journey on-ride photo • Hagrid's Magical Creatures Motorbike Adventure on-ride photo • The High in the Sky Seuss Trolley Train Ride! queue photo (standby only; temporarily closed) • Raptor Encounter • Grinch meet and greet during Grinchmas (seasonal)
VOLCANO BAY	
• Park entrance • Krakatau Aqua Coaster on-ride photo • Ohyah & Ohno Drop Slides on-ride photo • Tonga and Raki of Taniwha Tubes on-ride photo	• Honu and ika Moana on-ride photo • Punga Racers on-ride photo • Volcano, Family, and Hug a Mo Selfie Station automated photo ops

RELIGIOUS SERVICES

THE CLOSEST CHURCHES TO UNIVERSAL ORLANDO are the nondenominational **I Drive Church** (7440 Universal Blvd.; ☎ 407-573-8743; idrivechurch.org) and the enormous **First Baptist Orlando** (3000 John Young Pkwy.; ☎ 407-425-2555; firstorlando.com). The nearest Catholic Mass is held at **Holy Family Catholic Community** at 5125 S. Apopka-Vineland Road (☎ 407-876-2211; holyfamilyorlando.org), and the nearest synagogue is **Southwest Orlando Jewish Congregation** at 11200 S. Apopka-Vineland Road (☎ 407-239-5444; sojc.org).

For a list of religious services in the Orlando tourist area, check allears.net/btp/church.htm and wdwinfo.com/tips_for_touring/church services.htm. Christian visitors may also be interested in the **Rock the Universe** religious-music weekend, held in late January (see page 308).

VACATION SERVICES

THROUGHOUT THE PARKS, you'll spot stands marked VACATION SER-VICES, staffed by chatty team members who will ask you where you're from as you pass. Most guests hurry by, assuming—correctly—that these outposts serve as sales pitches for time-shares. But Universal's Vacation Services actually serves a number of other useful functions. In addition to selling Universal Orlando gift cards, meal plans, Express Passes, and Blue Man Group tickets, Vacation Services can help you book dining reservations as well as answer other general questions handle by Guest Services, so if you need assistance, stop by one of these locations before you trek back to the front of the park.

WINE, BEER, AND LIQUOR

ALCOHOL IS WIDELY AVAILABLE by the pint, glass, or shot throughout Universal's parks, hotels, and CityWalk. You can also buy wine by the bottle in the resort's table-service restaurants and some hotel shops. Note that while you can walk freely with a drink within the parks or CityWalk, due to liquor-license laws, you may not pass from CityWalk into a park or hotel (or vice versa) with an open container in hand.

To economize on your inebriation, check out one of these happy hours at CityWalk or the resort hotels; better yet, combine a few into an epic Universal bar crawl, as long as you aren't planning on attending early entry the next morning:

- Red Coconut Club at CityWalk (Sunday–Thursday, 8-10 p.m.; Friday–Saturday, 6-9 p.m.; temporarily closed)
- The Palm at Hard Rock Hotel (Sunday–Friday, 5-7 p.m.)
- Velvet Bar at Hard Rock Hotel (daily, 5-7 p.m.)
- The Kitchen at Hard Rock Hotel (Monday–Saturday, 1-5 p.m.)
- Tuk Tuk Market at Royal Pacific Resort (daily, 3-6 p.m.)
- Bar 17 Bistro at Aventura Hotel (daily, 10 p.m.–closing)
- Swizzle Lounge at Cabana Bay Beach Resort (daily, opening-7 p.m.)
- Pool bars at Endless Summer Resort (Monday–Thursday, 5-7 p.m.)

Wine and beer are also sold off property in grocery stores, convenience stores, and liquor stores. The best range of adult beverages is sold by **Grand Liquors** at 5601 International Dr. (☎ 407-751-4517). The **Walgreens** across Kirkman Road from Universal also has a decent, if slightly expensive, liquor selection.

The minimum age to drink or buy booze in Florida is 21, and anyone who looks 30 or younger should plan to present government-issued photo ID (valid driver's license or passport) when purchasing. At CityWalk you'll be tagged with a paper bracelet while drinking, to take home as a hair-snagging reminder of your debauched revels.

UNIVERSAL ORLANDO *for* GUESTS *with* SPECIAL NEEDS

UNIVERSAL ORLANDO STRIVES to accommodate every visitor in accordance with the Americans with Disabilities Act (ADA). The resort offers a free **"Rider's Guide for Rider Safety & Guests with Disabilities,"** describing each attraction's restrictions and requirements in detail at tinyurl.com/UniADA. You can download the booklet for each of the three parks in PDF format before your visit (which we highly recommend) or get printed copies at Guest Services, at resort front desks, or at wheelchair-rental locations inside the parks. The limitations you'll face at Universal Orlando, and the accommodations you can take advantage of, will vary according to the nature of your special needs.

MOBILITY RESTRICTIONS

UNIVERSAL ORLANDO IS FAIRLY FRIENDLY for nonambulatory guests to navigate, and the resort has repaved some bumpy streets (such as the uneven paving stones in USF's San Francisco district) to be more comfortable for wheelchair users.

Universal provides close(r)-in parking for disabled visitors; ask for directions when you pay your parking fee. These spots are on the main level of each parking garage, nearest to the central hub. You'll still have a substantial trip to CityWalk and the parks from even the best handicapped parking spot.

The entire Universal Orlando Resort transportation system is also disabled accessible. Water taxis have roll-on ramps for easy boarding, and bus routes are served by vehicles with wheelchair lifts that can accommodate all but the largest motorized scooters.

Shopping, dining, and restroom facilities at the parks, CityWalk, and hotels are generally ADA compliant for wheelchair access. Some fast-food queues and shop aisles (especially in The Wizarding World of Harry Potter) are too narrow for wheelchairs; at these locations, ask a team member for assistance. All shows and performances (including parades) also have designated disability sections for guests in wheelchairs and their parties.

In addition, attraction queues in USF and IOA (with the exception of Pteranodon Flyers in IOA) are fully wheelchair accessible, so you can enjoy the full preshow experience. Alternative routes are provided wherever necessary—these include elevators to bypass stairs at Harry Potter and the Escape from Gringotts, Revenge of the Mummy, and Men in Black Alien Attack, along with accessible boarding areas such as the stationary loading station at Harry Potter and the Forbidden Journey. You can take advantage of the accessible elevators even if you aren't in a wheelchair. Be sure to read the specific instructions posted outside each attraction, and bring your needs to the attention of the first attendant you see.

At Volcano Bay, only the Krakatau Aqua Coaster and Maku Puihi Round Raft Rides have elevators; for the other slides, you must be able to climb stairs to the top.

Strollers are not normally permitted inside most attractions, so if your child's stroller doubles as his or her wheelchair, swing by Guest Services for a special pass that will allow you to roll it through queues.

Except for the Hogwarts Express trains, Universal ride vehicles are unable to accommodate electric convenience vehicles (ECVs) or motorized wheelchairs, although a handful of rides have special cars that can carry a manual wheelchair. At these rides, guests can transfer from their powered chair to a nonmotorized one that will be provided at each applicable attraction. Be aware that nearly all Universal attractions (including some indoor theater shows like *Shrek 4-D*) require you to transfer from your ECV to a manual wheelchair before you enter the queue, since it's almost impossible to navigate switchbacks in a motorized scooter.

Even if an attraction doesn't accommodate wheelchairs of any kind, nonambulatory guests may ride if they can transfer from their wheelchair to the ride's vehicle. Be aware, though, that Universal staff are neither trained nor permitted to assist with transfers—guests must be able to board the ride unassisted or have a member of their party help them. Either way, members of the nonambulatory guest's party will be permitted to ride with him or her.

Regarding Universal's accessibility for the mobility impaired, a reader from upstate New York wrote:

> My husband used a scooter throughout our trip because, though he can walk short distances, he has leg weakness and balance problems. Whenever we approached a ride or attraction at Universal, the employees were always very attentive and willing to help. When he was using the scooter, they guided him to accessible areas, and when he chose to walk into attractions (with an obvious gait issue), they always very politely showed him the easiest route (avoiding stairs or steep ramps, opening the unused roped-off queuing areas to avoid having to walk around them) or offered wheelchair transport.

Nonetheless, navigating Universal Orlando can be daunting for solo travelers in manual wheelchairs, as this Morristown, New Jersey, visitor shared:

> None of the three parks are wheelchair friendly, with a lot of long uphill areas to battle, and the terrain is not smooth. As well, many of the lines to attractions have long inclines to deal with. When asked, most staff members will decline helping, as they are instructed not to. I found myself asking others in line for help more than I liked. I don't believe Universal considers how physically demanding navigating these parks can be for someone in a wheelchair. Not all of us come with someone to push!

Wheelchair Rentals

Any guest may rent a wheelchair, with no proof of medical need required. Most rides, shows, attractions, restrooms, and restaurants accommodate the nonambulatory disabled. If you're in a park and you need assistance, go to Guest Services. *Note:* Because almost all attraction queues are wheelchair accessible, using a wheelchair doesn't automatically entitle you to skip the standby line or shorten your wait.

Wheelchairs rent for $15 per day (tax included) with a fully refundable $50 deposit (cash or credit card) required. Standard wheelchairs are available at the central parking hub before you reach CityWalk and inside each park near the front gates.

A limited number of ECVs are available for rent at USF and IOA (not Volcano Bay). Easy to drive, they give nonambulatory guests tremendous freedom and mobility. ECVs cost $55 per day (tax inclusive), with no deposit required. An upgraded model with a canopy is $75. ECVs are popular and tend to sell out by midmorning on peak days, so call Guest Services (☎ 407-224-4233, option 3) at least a week in advance to reserve one. ECVs are available only inside the parks; you may rent a standard wheelchair at the parking hub and upgrade to an ECV once you reach the park.

A reader from Newbury, Ohio, found the entire ECV rental process to be user-*un*friendly:

You have to fill out paperwork to rent a wheelchair to get to the ECV rental area, where you have to fill out more paperwork to get the ECV, after traversing a long distance through the entrance terminal, over a long bridge, and through CityWalk. You can't use the ECVs in lines for the attractions, which doesn't matter, I guess, because most attractions are too turbulent for handicapped, older, or larger guests!

If you need an ECV to travel around the resort hotels or CityWalk, consider renting one from a third-party company such as **Walker Mobility** (☎ 407-518-6000; walkermobility.com) or **Scooter Vacations** (☎ 407-362-7745 or 855-939-7266; scootorlando.com). Both will deliver a scooter and all necessary accessories to your hotel (including Universal on-site resorts) for about $25–$40 per day—a worthwhile investment for this reader from Middletown, Delaware:

We rented an ECV for my mother-in-law. We doubled the time we spent in the parks, and she enjoyed the day with dignity. The rental is worth it for the long haul from the parking lot to Diagon Alley alone. The staff on Hogwarts Express are phenomenal with getting the ECV to the queue and help with embarking and disembarking the train.

Finally, those who normally rent ECVs may want to forgo them in favor of manual wheelchairs during evening special events, when the streets are especially dark and densely crowded, as this Illinois reader notes:

Taking an ECV during Halloween Horror Nights became more of a hassle than a help. You can't take the ECV inside the haunted houses—you have to park it at the entrance, sometimes far away from the entrance of the house you just came out of, and then you have to backtrack to get your ECV and then go back to where you exited. It was a pain in the posterior.

MISSING AND PROSTHETIC LIMBS

ALL GUESTS MUST BE ABLE to hold themselves upright and continuously grasp a safety restraint with at least one extremity to experience most rides. Guests with prosthetic limbs may ride with them securely attached on most rides. Those with prosthetic arms or hands may need to demonstrate that they can grip the safety restraints. All prosthetic limbs need to removed before riding Pteranodon Flyers (both natural legs must extend to the edge of your seat or terminate below the knee) or Hollywood Rip Ride Rockit (must have one full natural leg and one natural leg that extends to the edge of the seat or terminates below the knee). Consult the "Rider's Guide" (see page 175) for details.

CASTS AND BOOTS

IF YOUR ARM OR LEG is in a plaster cast or walking boot because of a broken bone, you should still be able to board the rides, provided you can fit comfortably inside the safety restraints. The only exception is **The Incredible Hulk Coaster,** as one young boy from Baltimore, Maryland, was distraught to discover:

Our first ride was The Incredible Hulk Coaster. [All my] kids, except my son, came back ecstatic. He was in tears; he had a hard cast on his arm, and he wasn't allowed on the ride. We were crushed. Thankfully, [Hulk] was the only ride that didn't allow it.

FAMILY RESTROOMS

IF A MEMBER OF YOUR PARTY needs help using the restroom, check the park map for designated family or companion facilities, which are large enough for two adults to access. Family restrooms in USF are near the front of the park near the Studio Audience Center, in Springfield outside Fast Food Boulevard, in San Francisco across from Richter's Burger Co., at First Aid behind Louie's Italian Restaurant in New York, and outside Mel's Drive-In across from the Transformers gift shop. In IOA, the family restrooms are found at Guest Services near the entrance and at First Aid in Lost Continent. In Volcano Bay, family restrooms are at First Aid, under the Ohyah and Ohno slides, and near the entrance to Honu ika Moana.

SERVICE ANIMALS

SERVICE ANIMALS ARE WELCOME at Universal Orlando, and the Premier and Preferred Loews hotels accommodate nonservice pets as well. Working companion animals are allowed inside all Universal restaurant and merchandise locations, attraction queues, and most other locations throughout the resort. Specific guidelines for each attraction are posted at the queue entrance and listed in the "Rider's Guide." For attractions where service animals cannot safely enter, portable kennels are provided.

When nature calls, service-animal relief areas are marked on the park map. There are two designated animal-walking areas in USF

(Woody Woodpecker's KidZone behind the NBC Media Center and World Expo between Men in Black Alien Attack and *Fear Factor Live*) and three in IOA (Marvel Super Hero Island between The Amazing Adventures of Spider-Man and Doctor Doom's Fearfall, Lost Continent behind the Mystic Fountain, and Seuss Landing behind One Fish, Two Fish, Red Fish, Blue Fish). Volcano Bay's service-animal relief areas are near Honu ika Moana and next to Maku Puihi.

DIETARY RESTRICTIONS

UNIVERSAL ORLANDO RESTAURANTS work very hard to accommodate guests' special dietary needs. If properly informed, Universal's chefs can prepare food that is vegetarian or vegan; kosher or halal; or dairy-free, gluten-free, or nut-free. When you make a dining reservation, either online at tinyurl.com/UniDinRes or by phone (☎ 407-224-FOOD [3663] for restaurants in the parks and CityWalk, or ☎ 407-503-DINE [3463] for hotel dining), you'll be asked about food allergies and the like. The host or hostess and your server will also ask about this and send the chef out to discuss the menu; if you're not asked, just talk to your server when you're seated.

Kosher meals ($29.95 plus tax and tip) must be ordered through Guest Services (☎ 407-224-4233) at least 72 hours in advance and can be delivered to Lombard's or Finnegan's in USF, Confisco Grille or Mythos in IOA, or Bambu in Volcano Bay.

At counter-service restaurants, ask to see the menu book with ingredient and allergen info. For those avoiding animal products, plant-based proteins like Beyond Burgers and Gardein Chick'n are now featured on most menus. Unfortunately, one place that does not get high marks for dietary accommodation is the Leaky Cauldron in Diagon Alley—virtually nothing on the menu is vegan, and there's not much more for the gluten-free or lactose intolerant. In general, guests on restricted diets will find many more options at Universal's table-service eateries.

Be aware also that Universal Orlando does not have separate kitchen facilities in which to prepare allergen-free foods, so there is always a slight possibility of inadvertent allergen contamination before or during preparation. You are welcome to bring your own food into the resort, as long as you let security know you have a dietary issue and follow the restrictions on items permitted inside the parks (no glass containers nor large or hard coolers).

For more information, email your specific dietary requests to foodservicecuf@universalorlando.com and visit tinyurl.com/UOAllergies.

HEARING IMPAIRMENT

GUEST SERVICES AT THE PARKS PROVIDES free assistive-technology devices with a refundable deposit (depending on the device) to hearing-impaired guests. Hearing-impaired guests can benefit from amplified audio on many attractions, and closed-captioning is available on request for queue video monitors; select shows offer reflective captioning as well. Guest Services can also provide a printed script to many of the attractions for you to peruse.

In addition, Universal provides complimentary sign language interpretations of live shows at the theme parks daily. There is typically only one interpreted performance of each show per day, so check the show schedule in the park map as soon as you arrive and plan your visit accordingly; additional American Sign Language–interpreted performances can be arranged for free if you email signlanguageservices@universalorlando.com at least a week in advance. Even if you don't understand sign language, it's well worth seeing for how animated and expressive the interpreters are—they truly steal the show.

While we're on the subject of sound, Universal loves to assail its guests with multiple overlapping background tracks, all cranked up to 11 for maximum impact. Even if you didn't have a hearing problem before arriving at Universal Orlando, the overwhelming amplification employed by many of the resort's attractions may leave your eardrums ringing. Anyone with a touch of tinnitus, or who is simply sensitive to loud noise, should heed this advice from a New Orleans parent and pack some hearing protection:

> I recommend earplugs for almost every dark ride, especially for kids. Most of those rides were so loud that earplugs or [noise-canceling] headphones wouldn't lessen the enjoyment.

VISION IMPAIRMENT

PARK INFORMATION GUIDES, restaurant menus, and attraction scripts are available at Guest Services in large print and embossed Braille. Some rides can accommodate guests with white canes (a collapsible cane is recommended), while at others an attendant will hold the cane and return it to the guest immediately at the unload area.

LARGER GUESTS

THRILL-SEEKING GUESTS OF SIZE may discover that several of Universal's rides are unable to accommodate them. The Harry Potter headliners are the most notorious for excluding plus-size riders, although both have certain seats—the outside seats on Harry Potter and the Forbidden Journey, along with rows three and six on Harry Potter and the Escape from Gringotts—that fit a fairly wide variety of body shapes. Likewise, the big roller coasters at IOA have designated seats with double seat belts designed for bigger guests, and row three at Revenge of the Mummy offers extra legroom.

In all cases, these safety restrictions are based less on weight than on torso circumference; some guests with large chests (40" or greater) who would not otherwise be considered overweight may find the restraint harnesses challenging to lock properly. Before getting in line for any attraction, check out the sample ride vehicle at the entrance, and discuss your concerns with the attraction's greeter.

At Volcano Bay, most body slides and raft rides have weight limits posted on each attraction's information sign. Every queue has a scale built into the ground (either at the base of the steps for body slides or at the top for raft slides) that is discreetly checked by an attendant to ensure compliance. Guests weighing more than 300 pounds will find themselves excluded from several slides. Some rafts have an overall weight limit, so even parties of four or more average-size adults may struggle to squeeze everyone into some multirider rafts.

OXYGEN TANKS AND CONCENTRATORS

FOR SAFETY REASONS, oxygen tanks are prohibited on most moving attractions at Universal Orlando, except for **Hogwarts Express** and **Despicable Me Minion Mayhem** (stationary seating only). Oxygen tanks are also permitted inside all shows and playgrounds, and portable oxygen concentrators are allowed on most rides as long as they don't interfere with the safety restraints.

NONAPPARENT DISABILITIES

WE RECEIVE MANY LETTERS from readers whose traveling companion or child requires special assistance but who, unlike a person in a wheelchair, is not visibly disabled. Autism, for example, makes it very difficult or impossible for someone with the disorder to wait in line for more than a few minutes or in queues surrounded by a crowd.

A trip to Universal Orlando can be nonetheless positive and rewarding for guests with autism and similar conditions. And while any theme park vacation requires planning, a little extra effort to accommodate persons with special needs will pay large dividends.

Our first suggestion is to visit Universal's cognitive disabilities page at tinyurl.com/UOCognitive and download a PDF of its comprehensive planning guide. It gives detailed sensory and safety information on every attraction, as well as tips about quieter places in the parks. We also highly recommend exploring the website **Autism at the Parks** (autismattheparks.com) and studying its extensive information on visiting Universal Orlando (the site also covers Walt Disney World and SeaWorld). Filled with practical firsthand advice, Autism at the Parks is the best independent source we know of for dealing with neurosensory issues or developmental disabilities at Universal.

Next, you'll want to familiarize yourself with the following two programs Universal offers to make your visit go more smoothly.

Universal's Attractions Assistance Pass (AAP)

This pass is designed to accommodate guests who can't wait in regular standby lines. You must first obtain an AAP at Guest Services of the first park you visit. Because all Volcano Bay guests are eligible to use the Virtual Line system, no AAPs are available at the water park. AAPs are good for parties of up to six people, but all members of your party who will use the service must have their admission tickets scanned at Guest Services. The same card is valid in the theme parks for the length of your vacation, or up to 14 days for annual pass holders.

When you get to Guest Services, you'll need to present identification and describe your or your family member's limitations. You don't need to disclose a disease or medical condition—by federal privacy law, they are forbidden to ask. Rather than an attempt to have you prove your condition, the goal here is to get you the right level of assistance.

Be as detailed as possible in describing limitations. For instance, if your child is on the autism spectrum, has trouble waiting in long lines, and has sensory issues that make it difficult for him or her to stand or be subjected to loud noises, you need to let the team member know each of these things—"she doesn't wait in lines" isn't enough to go on. A doctor's note explaining the necessary accommodations can be very helpful.

AAPs can be used at any attraction, even if it doesn't have a Universal Express entrance. Present the card to a team member at the attraction you want to ride. If the ride's standby wait time is less than 30 minutes, you'll usually be escorted through the Universal Express entrance. If the standby time is longer than 30 minutes, the team member will enter on the AAP the attraction name, time of day, wait time, and a return time for you to come back to ride. The return time will be based on the current wait time, so if you get to The Amazing Adventures of Spider-Man at 12:20 p.m. and the standby time is 40 minutes, your return time will be 40 minutes later, at 1 p.m.

You may return at the specified time or at any time thereafter, but you can't get another AAP return time until you've used or forfeited the first. When you return, you'll be given access to the Universal Express line, where you should face a wait of 15 minutes or less. The card holder need not be present to obtain a return time but must be present with his or her party for anyone to gain admission.

Universal's Guest Assistance Pass (GAP) Entry Cards

If the AAP doesn't meet your family's needs, Universal makes a small number of these cards available on a strictly limited basis. Basically, a GAP Entry Card is identical to a One-Day/Two-Park Universal Express Unlimited Pass and provides immediate entry to any attraction's Universal Express queue, regardless of the standby wait. Like the Universal Express Pass, GAP Entry is valid only at attractions that offer Universal Express, which excludes Pteranodon Flyers, so you'll still want an AAP or Virtual Line reservation for that attraction.

If you want a GAP because long standby lines make the AAP unworkable for your party, be prepared to plead your case to a Guest Services supervisor and endure some time-consuming scrutiny. If you get turned down or you'd just rather not deal with the hassle, you can always purchase a regular Universal Express Pass (where available).

FRIENDS OF BILL W.

FOR INFORMATION ON THE NEAREST **Alcoholics Anonymous** meetings to Universal Orlando (held daily, except Wednesday), visit cflintergroup.org or call ☎ 407-260-5408 for additional information. For information on **Al-Anon/Alateen** meetings in the area, visit al-anon orlando.org or call ☎ 407-253-9848.

COVID *tip*
International visitors should familiarize themselves with pandemic-related travel restrictions between Florida and their home countries before booking a vacation by visiting floridahealthcovid19.gov /travelers and tinyurl.com /StateDeptCovid, along with their respective governments' health-department websites.

INTERNATIONAL VISITORS

UNIVERSAL ORLANDO PROVIDES park maps in a number of different languages and maintains special websites designed for visitors from Brazil, Latin America, and the United Kingdom. Click the language box at the bottom-right of the universalorlando. com sidebar menu to see the international options.

PART FIVE

UNIVERSAL ORLANDO *with* KIDS

IT'S *a* SMALL UNIVERSE, AFTER ALL

UNIVERSAL ORLANDO RESORT (UOR) has positioned itself as an edgier, more adult alternative to the Mouse. Even Disney diehards will admit that UOR sports more attractions aimed at older teens and young adults than Walt Disney World (WDW) currently does. But the commonly heard rejoinder is that there's "nothing" for little kids to do at Universal's parks.

That stereotype has seeds of truth. While the Magic Kingdom can claim more than a dozen rides with no height restrictions, Universal Studios Florida (USF) and IOA combined have only seven rides that accommodate kids less than 34 inches tall. And as popular as Universal characters like the Minions and SpongeBob are with the single-digit set, it's tough to compete with the multibillion-dollar marketing machine behind Mickey's menagerie. But numbers alone don't tell the tale because a vacation at UOR can actually be a better experience for the youngest visitors (and therefore the family members around them) than the equivalent WDW escape.

For starters, while Universal lacks many moving attractions for tots, it makes up for it with the best themed playgrounds in town, as this family from Lancaster, Pennsylvania, learned:

> We were concerned about the big rides at Universal leaving our youngest child (age 5) bored. In actuality, she had a blast at Fievel's Playland, Seuss Landing, and Camp Jurassic. Even the older kids joined her to play at these areas whenever we got back together.

Second, without theme park reservations and Advanced Dining Reservations to worry about, a stay at UOR requires much less pre-planning, which means less damage to your day when the inevitable toddler tantrum derails your carefully laid touring plans. Universal's parks are more compact than Magic Kingdom and Epcot, which means that little legs won't tire as quickly. Also, on any given day, the crowds are likely to be lighter at UOR, welcome news for anyone shoving a stroller through the streets. Finally, it's far easier to travel from Universal's on-site hotels to its parks and back, a key benefit when heading back to your room for that essential midday nap.

Ideally, your kids should be at least 42 inches tall to experience the bulk of the parks' dark rides and simulators, or 54 inches tall to brave the biggest roller coasters. But traveling to UOR with a toddler, or even infant, can be equally rewarding, as long as you know what you're getting into and prepare thoroughly. The biggest danger is in dealing with a child who's barely under the minimum for something they'll "just die" without riding, so read up on height requirements (see page 202) in advance to avoid disappointment on the day.

When you're planning a UOR vacation with young children, consider the following:

AGE   Though UOR's color and festivity excite all children (with specific attractions that delight toddlers and preschoolers), and there's no admission fee for those under 3 years old, Universal's entertainment is generally oriented to older children and adults. Children should be a fairly mature 8 years old to appreciate USF, and a bit older to tackle the thrill rides in IOA, as this reader recommended:

> *Wait to visit until your children are tall enough, brave enough, and/ or interested enough to ride at least most of the rides. USF and IOA have a much different vibe from the Disney parks. If your children can't or won't ride most of the rides, it will just be a waste of money.*

Note that Universal considers all kids ages 3–9 as children for pricing purposes, regardless of height or ability to experience rides.

WHEN TO VISIT   Avoid the hot, crowded summer months, especially if you have preschoolers. Go in October, November (except Thanksgiving), early December, January, February, or May. If you have children of varied ages and they're good students, take the older ones out of school and visit during the cooler and less congested off-season. Take advantage of the resort's free Wi-Fi to virtually homeschool from your hotel, and arrange special assignments relating to the educational aspects of Universal Orlando. If your children can't afford to miss school, take your vacation as soon as the school year ends.

unofficial **TIP**
Coupled with a sense of humor and a little preparedness on your part, our touring plans and tips for families ensure a super experience at any time of year.

Alternatively, try late August before school starts. Please understand that you don't have to visit during one of the more ideal times of year to have a great vacation.

A Peterborough, England, woman agrees:

> *We visited at the end of August, and we expected that the crowds would be almost unbearable. However, we were surprised to find that*

because most local schools were back in session, we could walk on most headliner rides up until late afternoon, and even then there was only a short wait—some rides at Universal Studios didn't even open until 11 a.m. because we were visiting on a low-attendance day! We'd recommend that more people go this time of year, especially those people whose children don't return to school until later.

BUILD NAPS AND REST INTO YOUR ITINERARY   The parks are huge; don't try to see everything in one day. Tour in the early morning and return to your hotel around 11:30 a.m. for lunch, a swim, and a nap. Even during off-season, when crowds are smaller and the temperature is more pleasant, the size of the parks will exhaust most children younger than age 8 by lunchtime. Return to the park in the late afternoon or early evening and continue touring. A family from Texas underlines the importance of naps and rest:

Probably the most important tip your guide gave us was going to the hotel to swim and regroup during the day. The parks became unbearable by noon—and so did my husband and boys. The hotel was an oasis that calmed our nerves! After about 3 hours of playtime, we headed out to [the other park] for dinner and a cool evening of fun.

Regarding naps, this mom doesn't mince words:

For parents of small kids: Take the book's advice, get out of the park, and take the nap, take the nap, TAKE THE NAP! Never in my life have I seen so many parents screaming at, ridiculing, or slapping their kids. (What a vacation!) [The parks can be] overwhelming for kids and adults.

If you plan to return to your hotel at midday and want your room made up, let housekeeping know.

WHERE TO STAY   The time and hassle involved in commuting to and from the theme parks will be less if your hotel is on Universal property. It's hard to overemphasize how convenient it is to commute between your room and the parks when staying at the top Loews resorts, and even the value-priced Cabana Bay is only a 15-minute stroller push away from IOA's front gates. A number of off-site hotels along Major Boulevard and International Drive (see page 124) are also within walking distance, but you may not feel comfortable crossing busy roads with small kids in tow.

BE IN TOUCH WITH YOUR FEELINGS   When you or your kids get tired and irritable, call a time-out. Trust your instincts. What would feel best? Another ride, an ice cream break, or going back to the room for a nap?

LEAST COMMON DENOMINATORS   Someone is going to run out of steam first, and when he or she does, the whole family will be affected. Sometimes a snack break will revive the flagging member. Sometimes, however, it's better to return to your hotel. Pushing the tired or discontented beyond their capacity will spoil the day for them—and you. Energy levels vary. Be prepared to respond to members of your group who poop out. *Hint:* "We've driven a thousand miles to take you to Harry Potter and now you're ruining everything!" is not an appropriate response.

BUILDING ENDURANCE   Though most children are active, their normal play activities usually don't condition them for the exertion required to tour an Orlando park. Start family walks four to six weeks before your trip to get in shape. A mother from Wescosville, Pennsylvania, reports:

> *We had our 6-year-old begin walking with us a bit every day one month before leaving—when we arrived [in Orlando], her little legs could carry her, and she had a lot of stamina.*

From a Middletown, Delaware, mom:

> *You recommended walking for six weeks prior to the trip, but we began months in advance. My husband lost 10 pounds, and we met a lot of neighbors! We wouldn't have made it without you—thanks!*

SETTING LIMITS AND MAKING PLANS   To avoid arguments and disappointment, establish guidelines for each day and get everybody committed. Include the following:

1. Wake-up time and breakfast plans
2. When to depart for the park
3. What to take with you
4. A policy for splitting the group or for staying together
5. What to do if the group gets separated or someone is lost
6. What you want to see, including plans in the event an attraction is closed or too crowded
7. A policy on what you can afford for snacks
8. How long you plan to tour in the morning and what time you'll return to your hotel to rest
9. When you'll return to the park and how late you'll stay
10. Dinner plans
11. A policy for buying souvenirs, including who pays: Mom and Dad or the kids
12. Bedtimes

BE FLEXIBLE   Any day at Universal Orlando includes surprises; be prepared to adjust your plan. Listen to your intuition, and take advantage of the Lines app's optimization tool to update your itinerary after any unexpected detours.

ABOUT *the* UNOFFICIAL GUIDE TOURING PLANS

PARENTS WHO USE OUR TOURING PLANS are often frustrated by interruptions and delays caused by their young children. Here's what to expect:

1. CHARACTER ENCOUNTERS CAN WREAK HAVOC WITH THE TOURING PLANS. Many children will stop in their tracks whenever they see a cartoon character like Shrek or Scooby-Doo. Attempting to haul your child away before he has satisfied his curiosity is likely to cause anything from whining to a full-scale revolt. Either go with the flow or specify a morning or afternoon for photos. Luckily, queues for characters at Universal aren't nearly as long as at Disney World.

2. OUR TOURING PLANS CALL FOR VISITING ATTRACTIONS IN A SEQUENCE, OFTEN SKIPPING ATTRACTIONS ALONG THE WAY. Children don't like to skip anything! If something catches their eye, they want to see it right then. Some kids can be persuaded to skip attractions if parents explain their plans in advance. Other kids flip out at skipping something, particularly in Seuss Landing and The Wizarding Worlds.

3. IF YOU'RE USING A STROLLER, YOU WON'T BE ABLE TO TAKE IT INTO ATTRACTIONS OR ONTO RIDES. You'll need to leave your stroller (personal or rented) outside each attraction, unless you have a special pass indicating a medical need (see page 182). An exception is the Hogwarts Express train, which provides transportation between the parks and accommodates personal strollers; rentals will be swapped for free at the stations. Well-marked stroller parking is available throughout the parks.

4. YOU PROBABLY WON'T FINISH THE TOURING PLAN. Varying hours of operation, crowds, your group's size, your children's ages, and your stamina will all affect how much of the plan you'll complete. Tailor your expectations to this reality, or you'll be frustrated.

While our touring plans allow you to make the most of your time at the parks, it's impossible to define what *most* will be. It differs from family to family. If you have two young children, you probably won't see as much as two adults will. If you have four children, you probably won't see as much as a couple with only two children.

STUFF *to* THINK ABOUT

BLISTERS AND SORE FEET   In addition to wearing comfortable shoes, bring along some blister bandages if you or your children are susceptible to blisters. These bandages (which are also available at First Aid, if you didn't heed our warnings) offer excellent protection, stick well, and won't sweat off. Remember, a preschooler may not say anything about a blister until it's already formed, so keep an eye on things during the day. For an expanded discussion, see page 164.

OVERHEATING, SUNBURN, AND DEHYDRATION   These are the most common problems of younger children at Universal. Use sunscreen. Apply it on children in strollers, even

unofficial **TIP**
Keep little ones well covered in sunscreen and hydrated with fluids. Don't count on hydrating young children with soft drinks and stops at water fountains. Carry refillable bottles of water. Bottles with screw caps are sold across the resort for about $3.50–$5. *Remember:* Excited kids may not tell you when they're thirsty or hot.

if the stroller has a canopy. To avoid overheating, stop for rest regularly in the shade, in a restaurant, or at a show with air-conditioning.

FIRST AID If you or your children have a medical problem, go to a First Aid Station (see page 167). They're friendlier than most doctor's offices and are accustomed to treating everything from paper cuts to allergic reactions. And if your kid just needs some rehydration and a short nap, they can provide a quiet cot.

CHILDREN ON MEDICATION Some parents of hyperactive children on medication discontinue or decrease the child's dosage at the end of the school year. If you have such a child, be aware that Universal Orlando might overstimulate him or her. Consult your physician before altering your child's medication regimen.

GLASSES AND SUNGLASSES If your kids (or you) wear them, attach a strap to the frames so the glasses will stay on during rides and can hang from the child's neck while indoors.

THINGS YOU FORGOT OR RAN OUT OF Raingear, diapers, baby formula, sunburn treatments, memory cards, and other sundries are sold at the parks and at CityWalk. If you don't see something you need, ask if it's in stock. Basic over-the-counter meds are often available free in small quantities at the First Aid Stations in the parks.

INFANTS AND TODDLERS AT THE THEME PARKS All Universal parks have centralized Family Services facilities for infant and toddler care adjacent to the First Aid Stations. Everything necessary for changing diapers, preparing formula, and warming bottles and food is available. Supplies are for sale, and rockers and special chairs for nursing mothers are provided. In USF, Family Services is in the Front Lot near Lost and Found, and on Canal Street behind Louie's Italian Restaurant, on the border between New York and San Francisco. In IOA, Family Services is in Port of Entry near Guest Services, and in The Lost Continent near the Mystic Fountain; look for the red cross behind the coin vendor. In Volcano Bay, Family Services is immediately on your left as you enter the park. Dads are welcome at the centers and can use most services. In addition, most men's restrooms in the resort have changing tables.

RUNNING OUT OF GAS Hikers preparing for a challenging ascent—such as the 5,000-foot climb from the Colorado River to the rim of the Grand Canyon—are often advised to mix an electrolyte-replacement powder in their water and eat an energy-boosting snack at least twice every hour. While there's not much ascending to do at Universal, battling the heat, humidity, and crowds contributes to pooping out, especially where kids are concerned. Limiting calorie consumption to mealtimes just won't get it, as an experienced and wise grandma points out:

Children who get cranky during a visit often do so from all that time and energy expended without food. Feed them! A snack at any price goes a long way to keeping the little ones happy and parents sane. Oh, and the security people are very nice about you taking snacks or drinks in, but DO NOT bring glass containers!

STROLLERS

STROLLERS ARE AVAILABLE for rent inside USF and IOA but not Volcano Bay, to the left of the front gates as you enter. A single stroller is $17.99 (tax included) per day, and a double stroller is $27.99. A $50 deposit (cash or credit card) is required, which will be fully refunded when you return the stroller. If you leave the park and return, or switch parks during the day, you can get another stroller for free by showing your receipt.

Strollers are a must for infants and toddlers, but we've seen many sharp parents rent strollers for somewhat older children—the stroller spares parents from having to carry kids when they sag, and it provides a convenient place to tote water and snacks.

A family from Tulsa, Oklahoma, recommends a double stroller:

We rented a double for baggage room or in case the older child got tired of walking.

But a New Lenox, Illinois, family advocates not leaving anyone out:

If your kids are 8 or under, rent strollers for all of them! An 8-year-old will fit in a stroller, and you can fit up to four kids in two doubles. My husband suggested getting a stroller for our 6-year-old and the two "babies" (ages 4 and 3). The kids didn't get nearly as tired because they could be seated whenever they wanted.

However, a McKean, Pennsylvania, reader thinks the situation has gotten out of hand:

Please tell parents that their children don't have to be in strollers if a) they're old enough to vote, b) they've served in the armed services, and/or c) they have kids of their own. It's gotten really ridiculous—this last visit we saw more 10-plus-year-olds in strollers than sub-10-year-olds. Strollers add congestion, especially with parents using them to blast through crowds like child-first battering rams. I never knew walking was bad for you.

A Charleston, West Virginia, mom recommends a backup plan:

Strollers are not allowed in lines for rides, so if you have a small child (ours was 4) who needs to be held, you might end up holding him a long time. If I had it to do over, I'd bring along some kind of child carrier for when he was out of the stroller.

Rental strollers are too large for all infants and many toddlers. If you plan to rent a stroller for your infant or toddler, bring pillows, cushions, or rolled towels to buttress him or her in. Bringing your own stroller is permitted. Your stroller is unlikely to be stolen, but mark it with your name.

STROLLER-RENTAL OPTIONS Several Orlando companies are able to undercut the parks' prices, provide more comfortable strollers, and deliver them to your hotel. Most of the larger companies offer the same stroller models (the Baby Jogger City Mini Single, for example), so the primary differences between the companies are price and service.

To rate stroller companies, we had *Unofficial Guide* researchers rent the same strollers from each company, use the strollers in the parks, and return them. Our evaluation covers the overall experience, from the ease with which the stroller was rented to the delivery of the stroller, its condition upon arrival, and the return process.

Kingdom Strollers (☎ 407-271-5301; kingdomstrollers.com) topped our list, getting top marks for website ease of use, stroller selection, condition, and overall service. The stroller was also much easier to use than Universal's standard model, had more storage, and had an easier-to-use braking system. A rental of one to three nights costs $45; four to seven nights is $65. That makes the break-even point for choosing Kingdom Strollers over Universal at three days. At Universal's on-site resorts, you may have to manually enter your hotel name when booking online, and confirm your stroller delivery with the bell services manager on arrival. Alternatively, you can arrange to pick up and return your stroller at Orlando International Airport in Terminal A, Level 1, at the Wrap 'N Fly service counter, near the USO lounge (daily, 5 a.m.–7 p.m.).

We also recommend **Orlando Stroller Rentals, LLC** (☎ 800-281-0884; orlandostrollerrentals.com), which has similar prices ($45 for one to three nights and $65 for four to seven nights), plus an excellent website that allows you to easily compare the features of different strollers. It also requires you to be present to drop off and pick up your stroller (unless you can cajole the bell captain into arranging otherwise) but is more flexible about arranging a meeting time.

STROLLER WARS   Sometimes strollers disappear while you're enjoying a ride or show. Universal staff will often rearrange strollers parked outside an attraction. This may be done to tidy up or to clear a walkway. Don't assume your stroller is stolen because it isn't where you left it. It may be neatly arranged a few feet away—or perhaps more than a few feet away, as this Skokie, Illinois, dad reports:

unofficial **TIP**
Don't try to lock your stroller to a fence, post, or anything else at Universal. You'll get in big trouble.

> *The stroller reorganizations while you're on rides are a bit unnerving. More than once, our stroller was moved out of visible distance from the original spot. On one occasion, it was moved to a completely different stroller-parking area near another ride, and no sign or team member was around to advise where. We had to track down a team member, and she had to call in to find out where it had been moved. Be prepared for this.*

Sometimes, however, strollers are taken by mistake or ripped off by people not wanting to spend time replacing one that's missing. Don't be alarmed if yours disappears. You won't have to buy it, and you'll be issued a new one.

While replacing a stroller is no big deal, it's inconvenient. Through our own experiments and readers' suggestions, we've developed a technique for hanging on to a rented stroller: affix something personal (but expendable) to the handle. Evidently, most strollers are pirated by mistake (they all look alike) or because it's easier to swipe someone else's than to replace one that has disappeared. Because most stroller "theft" results from confusion or laziness, the average pram pincher will hesitate to haul off a stroller containing another person's property. We tried several items and concluded that a bright, inexpensive scarf or bandanna tied to the handle works well as identification. A sock partially stuffed with rags or paper works even better (the weirder and more personal the object, the greater the deterrent). A multigenerational family from Utah went a step further:

We decorated our stroller with electrical tape to make it stand out, and my son added a small cowbell to make it clang if moved.

STROLLERS AS LETHAL WEAPONS   A middle-aged couple from Brunswick, Maine, lobbies for a temporary stroller ban:

As an over-45 couple, we couldn't believe the number and sizes of strollers and those ubiquitous scooters. You had to be constantly vigilant or you would have your foot run over or path slowed down by them. We've decided that one day a week, in one theme park, there should be a "no wheels" day.

You'd be surprised at how many people are injured by strollers pushed by parents who are driving aggressively or in a hurry. Given the number of strollers, pedestrians, and tight spaces, mishaps are inevitable on both sides. A simple apology and a smile are usually the best remediation.

LOST CHILDREN

THOUGH IT'S AMAZINGLY EASY TO LOSE a child (or two) in the parks, it usually isn't a serious problem: Universal employees are schooled in handling the situation. If you lose a child in the resort, report it to the nearest Universal employee, and then check at Guest Services. Paging isn't used, but in an emergency, an all-points bulletin can be issued throughout the park(s) via internal communications.

Iron on or sew a label into each child's shirt that states his or her name, your name, the name of your hotel, and your cell phone number. Accomplish the same thing by writing the information on a strip of masking tape.

An easier and trendier option is a temporary tattoo with your child's name and your phone number. Unlike labels, ID bracelets, or wristbands, the tattoos cannot fall off or be lost. Temporary tattoos last about two weeks, won't wash or sweat off, and are not irritating to the skin. They can be purchased online from new.safetytat.com.

Special tattoos are available for children with food allergies or cognitive impairment such as autism.

A Kingston, Washington, reader recommends recording vital info for each child on a plastic key tag or luggage tag and affixing it to the child's shoe. This reader also snaps a photo of the kids each morning to document what they're wearing. A mother from Rockville, Maryland, reported a strategy one step short of a cattle brand:

Traveling with a 3-year-old, I was very anxious about losing him. I wrote my cell phone number on his leg with a permanent marker and felt much more confident that he'd get back to me quickly if he became lost.

One way to better keep track of your family is to buy each person a Universal uniform—in this case, the same brightly and distinctively colored T-shirt. A Yuma, Arizona, family tried this with great success:

We all got the same shirts (bright red), so we could easily spot each other in case of separation (VERY easy to do). It was a lifesaver when our 18-month-old decided to get out of the stroller and wander off. No matter what precautions you try, it seems there are always opportunities to lose a child, but the recognizable shirts helped tremendously.

HOW KIDS GET LOST

CHILDREN GET SEPARATED FROM THEIR PARENTS every day at Universal Orlando under remarkably similar (and predictable) circumstances:

1. PREOCCUPIED SOLO PARENT   The party's only adult is preoccupied with something like buying refreshments, reading a map, or using the restroom. Junior is there one second and gone the next.

2. THE HIDDEN EXIT   Sometimes parents wait on the sidelines while two or more young children experience a ride together. Parents expect the kids to exit in one place and the youngsters pop out elsewhere. Exits from some attractions are distant from entrances. Know exactly where your children will emerge before letting them ride by themselves.

3. AFTER THE SHOW   At the end of many shows and rides, a Universal staffer announces, "Check for personal belongings and take small children by the hand." When dozens, if not hundreds, of people leave an attraction simultaneously, it's easy for parents to lose their children unless they have direct contact.

4. RESTROOM PROBLEMS   Mom tells 6-year-old Tommy, "I'll be sitting on this bench when you come out of the restroom." Three possibilities: One, Tommy exits through a different door and becomes disoriented (Mom may not know there's another door). Two, Mom decides she also will use the restroom, and Tommy emerges to find her gone. Three, Mom pokes around in a shop while keeping an eye on the bench but misses Tommy when he comes out.

If you can't find a companion- or family-accessible restroom, make sure there's only one exit. Designate a distinctive meeting spot and give clear instructions: "I'll meet you by this flagpole. If you get out first, stay right here." Have your child repeat the directions back to you.

5. PARADES   There are many parades and shows at which the audience stands. Children tend to jockey for a better view. By moving a little this way and that, the child quickly puts distance between you and him before either of you notices.

6. MASS MOVEMENTS   Be on guard when huge crowds disperse after fireworks or a parade, or at park closing. With 20,000–40,000 people at once in an area, it's very easy to get separated from a child or others in your party. Use extra caution after the evening lagoon show in USF or the nighttime light display in Hogsmeade. Plan where to meet in the event you get separated.

7. CHARACTER GREETINGS   When the Universal characters appear, children can slip out of sight.

UNIVERSAL, KIDS, *and* SCARY STUFF

THOUGH THERE'S PLENTY FOR YOUNGER children to enjoy at the Universal parks, most major attractions can potentially make kids under age 8 wig out. To be frank, they freak out a fairly large percentage of adults as well. On average, Universal's rides move more aggressively and feature more intense (some would say assaultive) audiovisual effects than their Disney counterparts. There are attractions with menacing mummies, exploding insects, and man-eating dinosaurs—not to mention demonic soul-sucking Dementors and fire-breathing dragons. And while Walt Disney World rides always end on a happy note, Universal is equally as apt to send you out with a final scare or snarky parting shot, which is less likely to soothe shaken nerves. Universal also sets surprisingly strict minimum height requirements for some kid-centric rides, ruling out attractions such as Cat in the Hat and The High in the Sky Seuss Trolley Train Ride! for the infants who might enjoy them most.

You can reliably predict that a visit to UOR will, at one time or another, send a young child into system overload. Be sensitive, alert, and prepared for almost anything, even behavior that is out of character for your child. Most children take Universal's macabre trappings in stride, and others are easily comforted by an arm around the shoulder or a squeeze of the hand. Parents who know that their children tend to become upset should take it slow and easy, sampling milder adventures like the E.T. Adventure, gauging reactions, and discussing with the

continued on page 199

SMALL-CHILD FRIGHT-POTENTIAL TABLE

This table provides a quick reference to identify attractions to be wary of, and why. It relates specifically to kids ages 3–7. It represents a generalization, and all kids are different. On average, children at the younger end of the range are more likely to be frightened than children in their sixth or seventh year. For more information about ride elements that may induce sensory overload, download Universal's planning guide for cognitive accessibility at tinyurl.com/UOcognitive.

• UNIVERSAL STUDIOS FLORIDA

PRODUCTION CENTRAL

• **DESPICABLE ME MINION MAYHEM**   Universal's mildest simulator motion-wise, but the huge images and loud soundtrack may startle preschoolers. Stationary benches are available in the front row to avoid the moving seats. Child swap available (see page 204).

• **HOLLYWOOD RIP RIDE ROCKIT**   The tallest roller coaster at Universal, with loud music to cover your screams. May terrify guests of any age. Child swap available (see page 204).

• *SHREK 4-D*   Intense, loud, and disrespectful toward beloved fairy-tale icons. Stationary seating is available to avoid the jerky moving chairs. Child swap available (see page 204).

• **TRANSFORMERS: THE RIDE 3-D**   Intense, bloodlessly violent virtual reality simulator may frighten younger children and deafen guests of any age. Child swap available (see page 204).

NEW YORK

• **RACE THROUGH NEW YORK STARRING JIMMY FALLON**   Moderate simulator motion, intense 3-D imagery, loud sounds, and the comedy stylings of Jimmy Fallon may disturb younger kids (and adults who remember Johnny Carson). Child swap available (see page 204).

• **REVENGE OF THE MUMMY**   Very intense roller coaster in the dark with angry mummies, bugs, and fireballs. May frighten guests of any age. Child swap available (see page 204).

SAN FRANCISCO

• **FAST & FURIOUS: SUPERCHARGED**   Parental guidance suggested for intense simulated street-racing action with blasts of fog, loud noises, and improper use of turn signals. The actual motion of the vehicle is very mild. Child swap available (see page 204).

THE WIZARDING WORLD OF HARRY POTTER–DIAGON ALLEY

• **HARRY POTTER AND THE ESCAPE FROM GRINGOTTS**   Visually intimidating with intense 3-D effects and brief moments of moderately fast roller coaster motion. Less frightening than Harry Potter and the Forbidden Journey but may still rattle some riders. Child swap available (see page 204).

• **HOGWARTS EXPRESS: KING'S CROSS STATION**   Brief encounter with Dementors may scare some preschoolers; otherwise, not frightening.

• **OLLIVANDERS**   Not frightening in any respect.

WORLD EXPO

• *FEAR FACTOR LIVE*   An intense stunt show featuring people wearing and/or eating live insects. Explosive ending may startle preschoolers; may nauseate guests of any age.

• **MEN IN BLACK ALIEN ATTACK**   Dark ride with spinning cars and comical aliens may frighten some preschoolers. Child swap available (see page 204).

SPRINGFIELD: HOME OF THE SIMPSONS

• **KANG & KODOS' TWIRL 'N' HURL**   Dumbo-style midway ride. A favorite of many young children. Child swap available (see page 204).

• **THE SIMPSONS RIDE**   Extremely intense visually, with USF's strongest simulated motion. May frighten many adults as well as kids. Child swap available (see page 204).

WOODY WOODPECKER'S KIDZONE

• *ANIMAL ACTORS ON LOCATION!*   Not frightening in any respect, unless you have an animal phobia.

• **CURIOUS GEORGE GOES TO TOWN**   Not frightening in any respect, but your kid may get soaked.

• *A DAY IN THE PARK WITH BARNEY*   Not frightening in any respect, unless you have a purple-dinosaur phobia. Kids typically handle a brief period of darkness, as well as a few seconds of thunder and lightning, well.

• **E.T. ADVENTURE**   Dark ride with simulated flight and psychedelic creatures. A little intense for a few preschoolers, but the end is all happiness and harmony. Child swap available (see page 204).

• **FIEVEL'S PLAYLAND**   Not frightening in any respect, except for the big slide that may scare some preschoolers.

• **WOODY WOODPECKER'S NUTHOUSE COASTER**   A beginner's roller coaster; safe for all but the most timid tykes. Child swap available (see page 204).

HOLLYWOOD

• *THE BOURNE STUNTACULAR*   Intense action-movie fight choreography, including live gunfire and loud explosions, may startle viewers of all ages.

• *UNIVERSAL ORLANDO'S CINEMATIC CELEBRATION*   Oversize images of dinosaurs and Dementors, accompanied by loud fireworks, may startle small children.

• *UNIVERSAL ORLANDO'S HORROR MAKE-UP SHOW*   Gory props and film clips, presented educationally and humorously, may wig out wee ones, but most children seem to handle it disturbingly well. Interestingly, very few families report problems with this show.

ISLANDS OF ADVENTURE

MARVEL SUPER HERO ISLAND

• **THE AMAZING ADVENTURES OF SPIDER-MAN**   Immersive 3-D effects and spinning simulator movement may frighten younger kids, but most take the comic book mayhem in stride. Technically similar to Transformers at USF but significantly less intense. Child swap available (see page 204).

• **DOCTOR DOOM'S FEARFALL**   Visually intimidating to all guests, with an intense launch and brief weightlessness. The actual plummeting is less protracted than on WDW's Tower of Terror. Child swap available (see page 204).

• **THE INCREDIBLE HULK COASTER**   Very intense looping roller coaster with a high-speed launch. This is a scary roller coaster by any standard. Child swap available (see page 204).

• **STORM FORCE ACCELATRON**   Teacups-type midway ride can induce motion sickness in all ages, though most kids seem to love it. Child swap available (see page 204).

TOON LAGOON

• **DUDLEY DO-RIGHT'S RIPSAW FALLS**   Visually intimidating from outside, with several intense, potentially drenching plunges. A toss-up, to be considered only if your kids like water-flume rides. Child swap available (see page 204).

• **ME SHIP,** *THE OLIVE*   Not frightening in any respect.

• **POPEYE & BLUTO'S BILGE-RAT BARGES**   Potentially frightening and certainly soaking for guests of all ages. Most younger children handle it well. Child swap available (see page 204).

SKULL ISLAND

• **SKULL ISLAND: REIGN OF KONG**   The ride vehicle's motion is fairly mild, but don't let the low minimum height fool you: the 3-D visuals of mutant bugs are grosser than anything outside *Fear Factor Live*, and the queue is even more frightening, with sections that resemble a haunted house. Child swap available (see page 204).

JURASSIC PARK

• **CAMP JURASSIC**   Some preschoolers may be spooked by the dark caves and dinosaur sounds; guests who are afraid of heights should avoid the net climb.

• **JURASSIC PARK DISCOVERY CENTER**   Not frightening in any respect.

• **JURASSIC PARK RIVER ADVENTURE**   Visually intimidating boat ride with life-size dinosaurs and an intense flume finale. May frighten and dampen guests of any age. Child swap available (see page 204).

• **JURASSIC WORLD VELOCICOASTER** *(opens 2021)*   An extremely intense roller coaster featuring multiple high-speed launches, stomach-lurching loops, and close encounters with rapacious raptors. Child swap available (see page 204).

• **PTERANODON FLYERS**   A short, slow suspended roller coaster. Frightens some children who are scared of heights.

• **RAPTOR ENCOUNTER**   The velociraptor makes loud, growling noises and sudden, snapping movements that startle even some adults.

THE WIZARDING WORLD OF HARRY POTTER–HOGSMEADE

• **FLIGHT OF THE HIPPOGRIFF**   Another beginner coaster, comparable to The Barnstormer at the Magic Kingdom. May frighten some preschoolers. Child swap available (see page 204).

• **HAGRID'S MAGICAL CREATURES MOTORBIKE ADVENTURE**   A moderately intense outdoor coaster with no loops, but forward and backward launches, dramatic drops, and close encounters with magical creatures may intimidate younger Muggles. Child swap available (see page 204).

SMALL-CHILD FRIGHT-POTENTIAL TABLE *(continued)*

THE WIZARDING WORLD OF HARRY POTTER–HOGSMEADE *(continued)*

• **HARRY POTTER AND THE FORBIDDEN JOURNEY** Extremely intense special effects and macabre visuals with wild simulated movement that may frighten and discombobulate guests of any age. Child swap available (see page 204).

• **HOGWARTS EXPRESS: HOGSMEADE STATION** Not frightening in any respect.

THE LOST CONTINENT

• *POSEIDON'S FURY* Loud explosions, water effects, and brief periods of pitch darkness may scare younger children. You must remain standing through the entire attraction.

SEUSS LANDING

• **CARO-SEUSS-EL** Not frightening in any respect. Child swap available (see page 204).

• **THE CAT IN THE HAT** Mild spinning motion and modest visual effects may frighten a small percentage of preschoolers. Child swap available (see page 204).

• **THE HIGH IN THE SKY SEUSS TROLLEY TRAIN RIDE!** May scare kids who are afraid of heights; otherwise, not frightening in any respect. Child swap available (see page 204).

• **IF I RAN THE ZOO** Not frightening in any respect.

• **ONE FISH, TWO FISH, RED FISH, BLUE FISH** A tame midway ride that's a great favorite of most young children, though they will likely get wet. Child swap available (see page 204).

• VOLCANO BAY

THE VOLCANO

• **VOL'S CAVERNS** Dark pathways may spook sensitive toddlers; otherwise, not frightening.

RAINFOREST VILLAGE

• **KALA & TAI NUI SERPENTINE BODY SLIDES** Even more terrifying than Ko'okiri, with twisting enclosed tubes and extreme g-forces.

• **MAKU ROUND RAFT RIDE** Maku is one of the milder family raft rides in the park, with mostly open troughs and gentle curves. Don't mix it up with Puihi!

• **OHYAH AND OHNO DROP SLIDES** The shortest twisting tube slides in the park, but the final drop of 4-6 feet can knock the wind out of weak swimmers.

• **PUIHI ROUND RAFT RIDE** Puihi is among the scariest family raft rides in the park, with sharp turns that seem to nearly toss you onto the interstate.

• **PUKA ULI LAGOON** Not frightening in any respect.

• **PUNGA RACERS** Enclosed tubes may upset claustrophobes; otherwise, not frightening.

• **TANIWHA TUBES** A moderately fast-moving raft slide with some surprising twists and drops. Each of the four tubes has a different configuration. Accompany smaller kids on a two-seater raft, and ask for a green Tonga slide with more open-air sections if you get claustrophobic.

• **TEAWA THE FEARLESS RIVER** Swift current can swamp smaller swimmers; mandatory life jackets are available in all sizes.

RIVER VILLAGE

• **HONU SLIDE** Honu's hair-raising highly banked walls will wig out almost anyone. Don't confuse it with its sibling, ika Moana.

• **IKA MOANA SLIDE** Ika Moana is a mild raft ride that most kids can handle.

• **KOPIKO WAI WINDING RIVER** A brief segment floats through a dark, foggy cave; otherwise, not frightening in any respect.

• **KRAKATAU AQUA COASTER** Roller coaster–style dips and brief enclosed tunnels may scare younger kids, but most find it thrilling.

• **RUNAMUKKA REEF** Not frightening in any respect.

• **TOT TIKI REEF** Not frightening in any respect.

WAVE VILLAGE

• **KO'OKIRI BODY PLUNGE** High-speed vertical drop slide that will scare anyone silly.

• **THE REEF** Not frightening in any respect.

• **WATURI BEACH** Larger waves may overwhelm little ones; otherwise, not frightening in any respect.

continued from page 195

children how they felt about what they saw. If your child has difficulty coping with the cartoon creatures in Despicable Me Minion Mayhem and Men in Black Alien Attack, you should think twice before exposing him or her to the photo-realistic Lord Voldemort in Harry Potter and the Escape from Gringotts, as this reader from Finstadjordet, Norway, wrote us to emphasize:

> *Please remember: children are different. My 8-year-old boy found Revenge of the Mummy a bit scary and a bit fun, but he was super-scared on both Harry Potter rides because they seemed "too real" compared to the other rides. It can be difficult to tell in advance what will scare your child, but try to read your child while waiting in line. Universal has excellent child-swap systems; if in doubt, use them.*

Sometimes young children will rise above their anxiety in an effort to please their parents or siblings. This doesn't necessarily indicate a mastery of fear, much less enjoyment. If children leave a ride in apparently good shape, ask if they would like to go on it again (not necessarily now but sometime). The response usually will indicate how much they actually enjoyed the experience.

Evaluating a child's capacity to handle the visual and tactile effects of UOR requires patience, understanding, and experimentation. Each of us has our own demons. If a child balks at or is frightened by a ride, respond constructively. Let your children know that lots of people, adults and children, are scared by what they see and feel. Help them understand it's OK if they get frightened and that their fear doesn't lessen your love or respect. Take pains not to compound the discomfort by making a child feel inadequate; try not to undermine self-esteem, impugn courage, or ridicule. Most of all, don't induce guilt by suggesting the child's trepidation might be ruining the family's fun. It's also sometimes necessary to restrain older siblings' taunting.

A visit to UOR is more than an outing or an adventure for a young child. It's a testing experience, a sort of controlled rite of passage. If you help your little one work through the challenges, the time can be immeasurably rewarding and a bonding experience for you both.

THE FRIGHT FACTOR

WHILE EACH YOUNGSTER IS DIFFERENT, following are seven attraction elements that alone or combined could push a child's buttons and indicate that a certain attraction isn't age appropriate for that child:

1. NAME OF THE ATTRACTION Young children will naturally be apprehensive about something called, say, Skull Island or *Horror Make-Up Show.*

2. VISUAL IMPACT OF THE ATTRACTION FROM OUTSIDE Doctor Doom's Fearfall, Dudley Do-Right's Ripsaw Falls, The Incredible Hulk Coaster, Jurassic Park River Adventure, Reign of Kong, and

Hollywood Rip Ride Rockit look scary enough to give adults second thoughts, and they terrify many young children.

3. VISUAL IMPACT OF THE INDOOR-QUEUING AREA The dark forest inside E.T. Adventure and the castle dungeon of Harry Potter and the Forbidden Journey can frighten children, and the creepy creatures lurking inside Skull Island: Reign of Kong's temple ruins may induce an emergency undergarment change.

4. INTENSITY OF THE ATTRACTION Some attractions inundate the senses with sights, sounds, movement, and even smell. USF's *Shrek 4-D*, for example, combines loud sounds, lights, water spray, and moving seats with 3-D cinematography to create a total sensory experience. A Johnston, Iowa, mom describes the situation well:

> *The 3-D and 4-D experiences are way too scary for even a very brave 5-year-old girl. The shows that blew things on her, shot smells in the air, had bugs flying, etc. scared the bejabbers out of her.*

5. VISUAL IMPACT OF THE ATTRACTION Sights in various attractions range from falling fish to flying bats, from grazing dinosaurs to gory body parts. What one child calmly absorbs may scare the bejabbers out of another the same age.

6. DARK Many Universal attractions operate indoors in the dark. For some kids, this triggers fear. A child who gets frightened on one dark ride (E.T. Adventure, for example) may be unwilling to try other indoor rides.

7. THE TACTILE EXPERIENCE Some rides are wild enough to cause motion sickness, wrench backs, and discombobulate guests of any age.

As a footnote, be aware that a kid's courage and confidence in regard to riding attractions doesn't necessarily increase as he or she gets older. A ride that delights a child at age 4 may scare them to death at 5; by 6 years old they may be fine again. As a dad from Maryland explains:

> *Just because a child loves a ride at one age doesn't mean that he or she will love it on the next trip.*

A BIT OF PREPARATION

WE RECEIVE MANY TIPS from parents about how they prepared their young children for their theme park experience. A common strategy is to acquaint children with the characters and stories behind the park attractions by reading Universal-related books and watching movies at home.

USF's attractions prominently feature the family-friendly film series *Despicable Me* and *Shrek* (*E.T.* should already be on your kids' required viewing list), as well as *Men in Black, Transformers, Fast & Furious,* the Jason Bourne franchise, and *The Mummy* (only bother with the Boris Karloff and Brendan Fraser versions) if they are old enough for PG-13 entertainment. *The Simpsons* are in perpetual reruns, so refreshing your memory of Homer and family shouldn't be hard. For extra credit, screen *Jaws* and *Back to the Future* movies, and then hunt for hidden tributes to their extinct attractions.

IOA was inspired by literature, so start by reading the classics before bedtime—Dr. Seuss, Stan Lee's superheroes, ancient mythology, and the Sunday funnies. For Jurassic Park, you can cheat and watch the original Spielberg film; for King Kong (the exception to the literary rule), watch the 2005 Peter Jackson remake, even though the 1933 original is still superior. Of course, you'll want to be well versed in all seven volumes of Harry Potter's academic career (along with the associated films, short stories, and spin-offs) to fully appreciate both Wizarding Worlds; if that's too much work, at a minimum you must watch the first movie before visiting Hogsmeade, and the last one before delving into Diagon Alley.

A more direct approach is to watch videos that show the attractions. Online, you'll find good point of view videos of most Universal attractions from our YouTube channel (youtube.com/theunofficial guideseries), as well as TouringPlans, *Attractions Magazine,* Inside Universal, and other bloggers. Videos of dark indoor rides—especially those that use 3-D glasses—never do the attractions justice, but they usually show enough for you to judge whether your child can comfortably handle the real thing. A Lexington, Kentucky, mom reports:

My timid 7-year-old daughter and I watched rides and shows on You-Tube, and we cut out all the ones that looked too scary.

ATTRACTIONS THAT EAT ADULTS

YOU MAY SPEND SO MUCH ENERGY worrying about Junior that you forget to take care of yourself. The following attractions can cause motion sickness or other problems for older kids and adults:

POTENTIALLY PROBLEMATIC ATTRACTIONS FOR GROWN-UPS

UNIVERSAL STUDIOS FLORIDA

- **NEW YORK** Revenge of the Mummy
- **PRODUCTION CENTRAL** Hollywood Rip Ride Rockit | Transformers: The Ride 3-D
- **SPRINGFIELD: HOME OF THE SIMPSONS** The Simpsons Ride
- **THE WIZARDING WORLD OF HARRY POTTER-DIAGON ALLEY** Harry Potter and the Escape from Gringotts
- **WORLD EXPO** Men in Black Alien Attack

ISLANDS OF ADVENTURE

- **JURASSIC PARK** Jurassic World VelociCoaster
- **MARVEL SUPER HERO ISLAND** The Amazing Adventures of Spider-Man | Doctor Doom's Fearfall | The Incredible Hulk Coaster | Storm Force Accelatron
- **TOON LAGOON** Dudley Do-Right's Ripsaw Falls
- **THE WIZARDING WORLD OF HARRY POTTER-HOGSMEADE** Hagrid's Magical Creatures Motorbike Adventure | Harry Potter and the Forbidden Journey

VOLCANO BAY

- **RAINFOREST VILLAGE** Kala & Tai Nui Serpentine Body Slides | Ohyah & Ohno Drop Slides | Puihi Round Raft Ride
- **RIVER VILLAGE** Honu Raft Slide • **WAVE VILLAGE** Ko'okiri Body Plunge

A WORD ABOUT HEIGHT REQUIREMENTS

ALL ATTRACTIONS AT UOR require that children be at least 48 inches tall to ride without a supervising companion, also known as an older family member or guardian. Most moving attractions at UOR require children to meet additional minimum height requirements. If you have children too short to ride, instead of skipping the ride or splitting up your group, consider using child swap (see page 204). For more information, see the table on the opposite page. Regardless of height requirements, all guests must be able to sit up unassisted on all rides. Handheld infants are welcome in all shows, playgrounds, and walk-through attractions, but the only rides that accommodate handheld infants are Caro-Seuss-el and One Fish, Two Fish, Red Fish, Blue Fish in IOA; Kang & Kodos' Twirl 'n' Hurl and Despicable Me Minion Mayhem (ask for stationary seating) in USF; and Hogwarts Express.

Please note that height requirements only relate to the physical needs of a ride's safety restraints and are not a measure of whether an attraction is intellectually or psychologically appropriate for a given child, as this Illinois parent discovered too late:

It is very important to stress that height requirements are NOT a good indicator for whether a child is ready for a ride. My almost

ATTRACTION HEIGHT REQUIREMENTS

UNIVERSAL STUDIOS FLORIDA

Despicable Me Minion Mayhem	40" minimum height
E.T. Adventure	34" minimum height
Fast & Furious: Supercharged	40" minimum height
Harry Potter and the Escape from Gringotts	42" minimum height
Hollywood Rip Ride Rockit	51" minimum height; 79" maximum height
Men in Black Alien Attack	42" minimum height
Race Through New York Starring Jimmy Fallon	40" minimum height
Revenge of the Mummy	48" minimum height
The Simpsons Ride	40" minimum height
Transformers: The Ride 3-D	40" minimum height
Woody Woodpecker's Nuthouse Coaster	36" minimum height

ISLANDS OF ADVENTURE

The Amazing Adventures of Spider-Man	40" minimum height
The Cat in the Hat	36" minimum height
Doctor Doom's Fearfall	52" minimum height
Dudley Do-Right's Ripsaw Falls	44" minimum height
Flight of the Hippogriff	36" minimum height
Hagrid's Magical Creatures Motorbike Adventure	48" minimum height
Harry Potter and the Forbidden Journey	48" minimum height
The High in the Sky Seuss Trolley Train Ride!	36" minimum height
The Incredible Hulk Coaster	54" minimum height
Jurassic Park River Adventure	42" minimum height
Jurassic World VelociCoaster	51" minimum height
Popeye & Bluto's Bilge-Rat Barges	42" minimum height
Pteranodon Flyers *(Guests taller than 56" must be accompanied by a guest 36"-56".)*	36" minimum height; 56" maximum height
Skull Island: Reign of Kong	36" minimum height

VOLCANO BAY

Honu Raft Slide	48" minimum height
ika Moana Raft Slide	42" minimum height
Kala & Tai Nui Serpentine Body Slides	48" minimum height
Ko'okiri Body Plunge	48" minimum height
Krakatau Aqua Coaster	42" minimum height
Maku Round Raft Ride	42" minimum height
Ohyah and Ohno Drop Slides	48" minimum height
Puihi Round Raft Ride	42" minimum height
Puka Uli Lagoon	under 48" must wear life vest
Punga Racers	42" minimum height
The Reef	under 48" must wear life vest
Taniwha Tubes: Tonga and Raki	42" minimum height
TeAwa the Fearless River	42" minimum height
Waturi Beach	under 48" must wear life vest

4-year-old is a big Harry Potter and Transformers fan and met the height requirements for Transformers and Escape from Gringotts, so we let him go on. He went through the entire ride without crying or screaming, but immediately upon the ride stopping in the bay, he turned to me and said, "I am NOT going on that ride again!" In retrospect, it was waaaay too intense for a child of that age, whether he met the height requirement or not.

Child Swap (also known as Rider Swap, Baby Swap, or Switching Off)

Most Universal Orlando attractions have minimum height requirements. Some couples with children too small or too young forgo these attractions, while others take turns riding. Missing some of Universal's best rides is an unnecessary sacrifice, and waiting in line twice for the same ride is a tremendous waste of time.

Instead, take advantage of child swap, also known as baby swap, rider swap, or switching off. To child swap, there must be at least two adults. When you reach a team member at the entrance of an attraction, say you want to child swap. Child swap at Universal is similar to Disney's version but superior in several respects. Instead of one adult waiting at the exit with the children and returning after through the FastPass+ queue, at Universal the entire family goes through the whole line together before being split into riding and nonriding groups near the loading platform. The nonriding parent and child(ren) wait in a designated room, usually with some sort of entertainment (for example, Harry Potter and the Forbidden Journey at IOA shows the first 20 minutes of *Harry Potter and the Sorcerer's Stone* on a loop), a place to sit down, and sometimes restrooms with changing tables. And nearly every attraction at Universal offers child swap, which can even be used if you don't have children; it works equally well for skittish or infirm adults who don't like thrill rides, or for designated baggage handlers in families who hate to use lockers.

COVID *tip*
To promote social distancing, dedicated child swap rooms may be closed. Instead, the first adult will ride using the standard queue while the rest of the family waits outside the attraction; then the remaining adult will be allowed expedited entry through an alternative queue. Talk to a team member at each attraction entrance for further instructions.

We receive quite a bit of positive feedback from readers who use Universal's child-swap system, such as this mom from Doylestown, Pennsylvania:

I was really happy with the child swap setup. It made it possible for us to stay together most of the trip, as we were traveling with a 1-year-old who couldn't ride anything. It also meant my 6-year-old got to see all the cool preshow stuff in Hogwarts Castle, even though he wasn't big enough to ride Forbidden Journey.

And from a Scarsdale, New York, parent:

There wasn't much for our 3-year-old, and what we took her on terrified her, so she started asking to go in "the room" (child swap room) rather than on the ride. Child swap also meant that her sisters got to ride everything twice.

Attractions where switching off is practiced are oriented to more mature guests. Sometimes it takes a lot of courage for a child just to move through the queue holding Dad's hand, especially in lines like Skull Island with lots of spooky decor. In the boarding area, many children suddenly fear abandonment when one parent leaves to ride. Prepare your children for switching off, or you might have an emotional crisis on your hands. A mom from Edison, New Jersey, writes:

Once my son came to understand that the switch off would not leave him abandoned, he did not seem to mind. Practice the switch off on some dry runs at home, so your child isn't concerned that he will be left behind. At the very least, the procedure should be explained in advance so the little ones know what to expect.

An Ada, Michigan, mother discovered that the child-swap procedure varies among attractions. She says:

Parents need to tell the very first attendant they come to that they would like to switch off. Each attraction has a different procedure for this. Tell every other attendant too because they forget quickly.

As at any theme park, the best tip we can give is to ask the greeter in front of the attraction what you're supposed to do.

UNIVERSAL CHARACTERS

THOUGH OFTEN OVERSHADOWED by the fur-clad cartoon celebrities down the street, Universal Orlando also has a stable of characters to call its own, but the interest in oversize cartoon vermin isn't anywhere near as intense as at Disney World. You'll occasionally see a Minion getting mobbed or a couple dozen families queued to meet SpongeBob, but never anything like the hour-plus waits that Disney's princesses can draw at the Magic Kingdom.

unofficial **TIP** Don't underestimate your child's excitement at meeting the Universal characters—but also be aware that very small children may find the large costumed characters a little frightening.

PREPARING YOUR CHILDREN TO MEET THE CHARACTERS

ALMOST ALL CHARACTERS ARE quite large, and several, like Sideshow Bob, are huge! Small children don't expect this, and preschoolers especially can be intimidated.

Discuss the characters with your children before you go. On first encounter, don't thrust your child at the character. Allow the little one to deal with this big thing from whatever distance feels safe. If two adults are present, one should stay near the youngster while the other approaches the character and demonstrates that it's safe and friendly. Some kids warm to the characters immediately; some never do. Most take a little time and several encounters.

There are two kinds of characters: animated, or those whose costumes include face-covering headpieces (including animal characters and humanlike cartoon characters such as the Simpsons), and celebrities or face characters, those for whom no mask or headpiece is necessary. The latter includes Marilyn Monroe, Doc Brown, and the Knight Bus and Hogwarts Express conductors, among others.

Only face characters speak. Because team members couldn't possibly imitate the animated characters' distinctive cinema voices, Universal has determined that it's more effective to keep such characters silent. Lack of speech notwithstanding, headpiece characters are warm and responsive, and they communicate effectively with gestures. Tell children in advance that these characters don't talk. Exciting exceptions are character encounters such as the Shrek meet and greet with Donkey and the Transformers photo op, where hidden actors or prerecorded audio clips are employed to allow interaction between costumed characters and guests.

Some character costumes are cumbersome and give performers very poor visibility. (Eyeholes frequently are in the mouth of the costume or even on the neck or chest.) Children who approach the character from the back or side may not be noticed, even if the child touches the character. It's possible in this situation for the character to accidentally step on the child or knock him down. A child should approach a character from the front, but occasionally not even this works. If a character appears to be ignoring your child, the character's handler will get its attention.

COVID *tip*

To promote social distancing, guests may be required to remain at least 6 feet away from costumed characters, and autographs may not be available. Guests may not make contact with the characters, so keep a tight grip on little ones lest they sprint in for a forbidden hug.

When social-distancing measures are not being enforced, it's OK for your child to touch, pat, or hug the character. Understanding the unpredictability of children, the character will keep his feet still, particularly refraining from moving backward or sideways. Most characters will pose for pictures or sign autographs. Costumes make it difficult for characters to wield a normal pen, and some characters can't sign autographs at all. If your child collects autographs, carry a pen the width of a Magic Marker.

UNIVERSAL CHARACTER-GREETING LOCATIONS

SOME UNIVERSAL ORLANDO CHARACTERS are confined to a specific location and visit with guests on a schedule. Characters who appear in the Superstar Parade also make daily Character Party Zone appearances in Hollywood, which include a mini-show and meet and greet. Other characters appear at random times in a few regular areas. Most mornings you'll find a rotating collection of characters near the entrance of the park. Not every character will appear every day; the busier the season, the more likely lesser-known characters will come out.

COVID *tip*

Character greetings may be relocated or reduced to promote social distancing.

CHARACTER-GREETING LOCATIONS

UNIVERSAL STUDIOS FLORIDA

CELEBRITIES *(Face Characters)*

- **Beetlejuice** Hollywood; Classic Monsters Café
- **Betty Boop** Hollywood
- **Doc Brown from *Back to the Future*** Hollywood; at the DeLorean outside Fast Food Boulevard
- **Knight Bus Conductor and Talking Head** London Waterfront outside Diagon Alley
- **Marilyn Monroe** Hollywood; New York near Macy's
- **The Men in Black** Hollywood; World Expo outside Men in Black Alien Attack

ANIMATED *(Costumed Characters)*

- **Barney the Dinosaur, BJ, & Baby Bop** Woody Woodpecker's KidZone near *A Day in the Park with Barney*
- ***Despicable Me* Minions** Hollywood; exit of Despicable Me Minion Mayhem ride
- **Dora the Explorer and Diego** Hollywood
- **Gru, Agnes, Edith, Margo, and Vector from *Despicable Me*** Hollywood
- **Hello Kitty** Hollywood outside her store
- **Homer, Marge, Bart, and Lisa Simpson** Hollywood; Springfield outside Kwik-E-Mart
- ***Madagascar* Penguins** Hollywood behind Cafe La Bamba
- **Optimus Prime, Bumblebee, and Megatron from *Transformers*** Eighth Avenue between the *Shrek 4-D* exit and Mel's Drive-In
- **Poppy, Branch, and Guy Diamond from *Trolls*** Woody Woodpecker's KidZone
- **Scooby-Doo, Shaggy, and the Mystery Van** Hollywood; Woody Woodpecker's KidZone
- **Shrek, Donkey, and Princess Fiona** Eighth Avenue across from the *Shrek 4-D* exit
- **Sideshow Bob and Krusty the Clown** Springfield outside Kwik-E-Mart
- **SpongeBob SquarePants, Squidward, and Patrick** Hollywood; Woody Woodpecker's KidZone near SpongeBob StorePants

ISLANDS OF ADVENTURE

CELEBRITIES *(Face Characters)*

- **Betty Boop** Toon Lagoon outside The Betty Boop Store
- **Captain America** Marvel Super Hero Island
- **The Grinch (live-action version)** Seuss Landing inside Mulberry Street (seasonally)
- **Hogwarts Express conductor** Hogsmeade across from Honeydukes

continued on page 208

continued from page 207

CHARACTER-GREETING LOCATIONS *(continued)*

ISLANDS OF ADVENTURE *(continued)*

CELEBRITIES *(Face Characters) (continued)*

- **Popeye and Olive Oyl** Toon Lagoon outside Comic Strip Cafe
- **Rogue, Storm, Wolverine, and Cyclops** Marvel Super Hero Island
- **Spider-Man** Marvel Super Hero Island

ANIMATED *(Costumed Characters)*

- **Alex, Gloria, and King Julien from *Madagascar*** Port of Entry, Lost Continent
- **Beetle Bailey** Toon Lagoon outside Comic Strip Cafe
- **Blue the velociraptor** Jurassic Park at Raptor Encounter
- **Cat in the Hat, Thing 1, and Thing 2** Seuss Landing at *Oh! The Stories You'll Hear!*
- **Green Goblin and Doctor Doom** Marvel Super Hero Island
- **The Grinch (cartoon version)** Seuss Landing at *Oh! The Stories You'll Hear!*
- **The Lorax and Sam-I-Am** Seuss Landing at *Oh! The Stories You'll Hear!*
- **Po and Tigress from *Kung Fu Panda*** Port of Entry, Lost Continent
- **Puss in Boots and Kitty Softpaws** Port of Entry, Lost Continent

See the previous page and above for a guide to the places you're likely to see famous friends in Universal's parks. Refer to Universal's smartphone app for appearance times, which can change daily.

CHARACTER DINING *(temporarily suspended)*

UNIVERSAL ORLANDO OFFERS character meals at both its theme parks and hotels, but unlike Walt Disney World's rodent royalty, you have a reasonable shot of supping with Spider-Man or Gru on short notice.

COVID *tip*
Character dining was suspended at press time to promote social distancing.

A Marvel character dinner, featuring favorites from the Avengers and X-Men, is held in IOA every Thursday–Sunday. The Royal Pacific Resort hosts a *Despicable Me* character breakfast with the Minions every Saturday. During the holiday season, the Grinch hosts a breakfast at IOA. For further details, see page 213.

BABYSITTING

CHILDCARE CENTERS *(temporarily closed)*

CHILDCARE ISN'T AVAILABLE INSIDE THE PARKS, but the top three Loews hotels each offer on-site kids' clubs that operate in the evenings to allow Mom and Dad a night out alone at CityWalk. Only on-site hotel guests may use the clubs, which rotate their days of operation seasonally. Guests of any on-site hotel can register their kids at another hotel's club if the club at their hotel is closed. **Camp**

COVID *tip*
All kids' activity clubs were closed at press time to promote social distancing.

Portofino at Portofino Bay, **Camp Lil' Rock** at Hard Rock Hotel, and **The Mariner's Club** at Royal Pacific all feature story time, arts and crafts, computer games, and a movie room. There is one counselor for every 8–10 children; participants must be toilet-trained and between ages 4 and 14. Childcare costs $15 per hour, per child, and an additional $15 per meal if they stay through dinnertime. The clubs operate Sunday–Thursday, 5–11:30 p.m., and Friday–Saturday, 5 p.m.–midnight; hours vary seasonally and are subject to change. Call ☎ 407-503-1200 for information and reservations.

IN-ROOM BABYSITTING

A COUPLE OF COMPANIES PROVIDE in-room sitting in Universal Orlando and surrounding areas, but **Kid's Nite Out** (☎ 407-828-0920 or 877-749-7594; kidsniteout.com) is the resort's preferred provider, and who the concierge will call if you ask for a babysitter; the company also staffs the hotels' childcare centers. Kid's Nite Out also serves hotels in the greater Orlando area, including downtown. It provides sitters older than age 18 who are insured, bonded, screened, reference-checked, police-checked, and trained in CPR; bilingual sitters are also available. In addition to caring for your kids in your room, the sitters will, if you direct (and pay), take your children to the theme parks or other venues. Kid's Nite Out cares for children as young as six weeks old and can care for kids with special needs as well. Rates start at $20 per hour for one child, up to $29 per hour for four children, plus a $12 transportation fee.

PART SIX

DINING *and* SHOPPING *at* UNIVERSAL ORLANDO

WHEN FOODIES ARE ASKED TO NAME great gourmet vacation spots around the world—New York, Paris, Singapore—Orlando probably doesn't immediately pop to the top of their wish lists. But believe it or not, Central Florida has developed a substantial culinary culture, from the prototype concepts tested by major chains along Sand Lake Road's Restaurant Row and the lauded gastropubs that have sprouted around downtown, to the thriving local community of upscale food trucks.

Even so, while adventurous eaters have always known there's plenty to explore in the greater Orlando area, and even tourist-phobic locals have long been lured to Walt Disney World (WDW) property by its lengthy list of restaurants, Universal has often been left out of the conversation. Thanks to the uniform mediocrity of Universal Studios Florida's (USF's) counter-service food during the resort's formative years, the conventional wisdom was that Universal Orlando's food options simply weren't as delicious or as diverse as those at Disney.

The good news is that, today, food in Universal is almost always on par with, or a step ahead of, what you can find at WDW and other parks. Thanks largely to the efforts of the resort's award-winning executive chef Steven Jayson, more variety, better preparations, and more current trends are generally the rule at Universal. And best of all, a first-class meal at Universal will almost always leave less of a dent in your credit card than the equivalent repast would at Mickey's table.

Quick-service (or counter-service, as it is sometimes called) offerings inside USF and Islands of Adventure (IOA) are largely lackluster, but Harry Potter's **Leaky Cauldron** and **Three Broomsticks,** and The Simpsons' **Fast Food Boulevard,** set a new bar for theme park fast food, and the fare at Volcano Bay is far fresher and more diverse than you'd expect from a water park.

USF's two full-service restaurants are **Finnegan's Bar and Grill** in New York and **Lombard's Seafood Grille** in San Francisco. Finnegan's serves typical bar food—burgers and wings—as well as fresh fish-and-chips and other takes on Irish cuisine. Lombard's is the better restaurant, but it's not in the same stratosphere as Disney's Hollywood Brown Derby (in quality or price).

IOA has two sit-down restaurants: **Confisco Grille** in Port of Entry and **Mythos Restaurant** in The Lost Continent. Confisco is fine for appetizers and drinks. Despite its Hellenic-sounding name, Mythos isn't strictly a Greek restaurant; rather it serves something-for-everyone fusion fare with Mediterranean flair, including Italian risotto, Asian noodles, and Spanish squid, plus steaks and burgers. Diners with dietary restrictions will be happy to see that Mythos has more options for vegetarian, vegan, and gluten-free diners than almost any other in-park Universal restaurant.

For even better eating options, exit the parks into **CityWalk,** Universal's dining, shopping, and entertainment district. CityWalk has seen welcome upgrades to its restaurant lineup in recent years with the addition of **Bigfire, Vivo Italian Kitchen, Toothsome Chocolate Emporium,** and **Antojitos Authentic Mexican Food,** along with **NBC Sports Grill & Brew** and **The Cowfish**'s much-better-than-it-sounds burger/sushi bar. We also like **Bob Marley** and **Pat O'Brien's** for drinks and music.

Many of the older CityWalk restaurants' menus are similar to Applebee's or Chili's. Given the average entrée from **Hard Rock Cafe** or **Jimmy Buffett's Margaritaville,** it would be difficult for a blindfolded diner to be certain from which restaurant it came. That blindfolded diner would probably guess that any plate with shrimp on it had a decent chance of coming from the **Bubba Gump Shrimp Co.,** but there's little else of note on its menu.

Some of Universal's best sit-down restaurants are found at the resort hotels, where the Flavor by Loews program features locally produced ingredients such as bread, honey, and beer. **The Palm Restaurant,** an upscale steakhouse in the Hard Rock Hotel, serves grade A meat at prices to match. If you're in the mood for Italian, try **Bice** (expensive) or **Mama Della's Ristorante** (moderate), both at the Portofino Bay Hotel. Asian food is the specialty at Universal's Royal Pacific, where **Islands Dining Room** is the primary sit-down destination. **Amatista Cookhouse,** the table-service restaurant at Sapphire Falls Resort, leans toward Caribbean comfort food, but the tapas and rum at **Strong Water Tavern**

COVID *tip*
Virtually all of Universal's quick-service and table-service restaurants offer outdoor seating (weather permitting). If you feel more comfortable eating outside, make it known when booking your reservation or upon arriving at the restaurant.

upstairs are top-shelf, as are the small plates and craft cocktails at **Bar 17 Bistro,** on the roof of the neighboring Aventura Hotel. Probably because they handle a lot of convention traffic, menu prices at Universal's Premier and Preferred resorts tend to be higher than you might expect, though they are still easier to swallow than the bill at Disney's top tables.

RESERVATIONS

ONE OF THE BIGGEST DIFFERENCES BETWEEN WDW and Universal Orlando is the ease with which you can secure dining reservations at the latter resort. If you're used to frantically booking your Disney Advance Dining Reservations months before your vacation, you can relax. During much of the year, you can walk up and get a table at most Universal Orlando eateries with only a modest wait; guests staying at an on-site Premier hotel can flash their key card to get seated even sooner.

While reservations are often not needed at Universal, you can use opentable.com or the OpenTable smartphone app to search for a seating at most of the sit-down hotel restaurants. CityWalk locations and in-park table-service restaurants use zomato.com, which also offers an app. If you're not sure which reservation system to use, visit tinyurl.com/unidinres, and click the RESERVE NOW button next to the restaurant where you wish to dine to see availability and make special requests. Alternatively, you can call ☎ 407-224-FOOD (3663) for in-park and CityWalk dining reservations, and ☎ 407-503-DINE (3463) for hotel restaurants. No deposit is necessary to book a Universal restaurant reservation, so there's no penalty when your dinner plans inevitably change. Most of the CityWalk and in-park restaurants only take reservations 30 days in advance, but the hotel restaurants accept bookings 90 days out, and The Palm will let you reserve for next year. If you are visiting at a peak time of the year (such as Thanksgiving or late December) or during a major convention, we suggest making table-service reservations a couple of weeks to a month in advance.

Casting? There's been a mistake. We were supposed to get the Assorted Character Package with one SpongeBob, one Dora, one Gru . . .

DRESS

DRESS IS INFORMAL AT ALL park restaurants and in CityWalk's restaurants. At upscale resort restaurants such as Hard Rock's Palm Restaurant or Portofino Bay's Bice, men are not permitted to wear sleeveless shirts, and resort casual wear is appropriate (but not required) for dinner: khakis, dress slacks, jeans, or dress shorts with a collared shirt for men and Capris, skirts, dresses, jeans, or dress shorts for women.

FOOD ALLERGIES AND SPECIAL REQUESTS

FOR SIT-DOWN MEALS, if you have food allergies or observe a specific diet such as eating kosher or gluten-free, make your needs known when you make your dining reservation and again when your waiter introduces himself at your table. The waitstaff or chef will be able to tell you the kinds of accommodations the kitchen is prepared to make for your meal.

Accommodating dietary needs is more difficult at fast-food places because staff may not be as familiar with the menu's ingredients or preparation. Ask to see the allergen information book, which should be behind the counter at every quick-service location; it lists the menu items that can be made or modified for various diets. Entrées featuring plant-based proteins, such as Beyond burgers or Gardein Chick'n and Saus'age, can be found on the menus of many resort restaurants. When our vegans and vegetarians have doubts about menu descriptions, their strategy is usually to default to the simplest, most-likely-to-be-acceptable item.

See page 180 for additional dietary details.

COVID *tip*
At press time, all character meals were suspended to promote social distancing.

CHARACTER MEALS

(temporarily suspended)

UNIVERSAL OFFERS ONE YEAR-ROUND in-park character dinner, held every Thursday–Sunday starting at 5 p.m. at **Cafe 4** inside IOA. At the **Marvel Character Dinner,** guests dine with characters from the X-Men like Wolverine and Storm, plus Spider-Man and Captain America from the Avengers. The cost is $49.99 for adults and $24.99 for kids; park admission is required and not included, nor is tax or gratuity. A buffet meal with your choice of salads, pastas, pizzas, and Italian entrées, along with soft drinks and dessert, is served. The food is a notch above Cafe 4's standard fare, with shrimp scampi, stuffed pasta shells, and chicken scaloppine on the menu. Attendees also get a digital photo card documenting their Marvel-ous meal. The half dozen heroes circulate among the tables separately, and all excel at interacting with fans of every age. Days and times are subject to change. You can book online at tinyurl.com/marveldinner, but you *must* call ☎ 407-224-3663 at least 24 hours before your meal to reserve your table.

There's also a weekly character breakfast every Saturday morning at the **Tahitian Room** in the Royal Pacific Resort. Gru and his Minions from *Despicable Me,* along with sisters Margo, Edith, and Agnes, are the guests of honor. The cost is $34.99 for adults, $20.99 for kids ages 3–9, plus tax and tip. You don't need theme park admission or have to be staying on-site to attend this breakfast. The meal includes a full breakfast buffet featuring an omelet station and a digital photo of your character encounter. Seatings are at 8, 9:30, and 11 a.m. You must reserve at least 24 hours in advance by visiting loewscharacter breakfast.tix.com or by calling ☎ 407-503-DINE (3463).

During the holiday season, Universal offers a breakfast in IOA's **Seuss Landing** with the Grinch, played by an extremely interactive actor in film-quality prosthetic makeup. This meal (which may include green eggs and ham, if you wish) is held only on select mornings in November and December, 8–10 a.m. Pricing is the same as the Despicable Me breakfast, except theme park admission is required; visit tinyurl.com/UOGrinchBreakfast for booking details.

UNIVERSAL ORLANDO DINING PLANS

UNIVERSAL OFFERS TWO DINING PLANS that allow guests to prepay for their food, and potentially save some money in the process. The **Quick Service Universal Dining Plan** provides one quick-service meal (including an entrée platter and soft drink), another soft drink, and one snack. The cost is $25.99 for adults and $17.99 for kids age 9 and younger. It's valid at most quick-service eateries in all three parks (including Three Broomsticks at The Wizarding World of Harry Potter–Hogsmeade, the Leaky Cauldron in Diagon Alley, and Fast Food Boulevard in Springfield), plus a smattering at Universal City-Walk, but not at any hotel eateries. You can view a complete list of participating restaurants at tinyurl.com/unidineplan.

Virtually every entrée at participating venues can be purchased with a quick-service meal credit, even combo platters that include a side salad or milkshake. A few of the most expensive items, such as whole pizzas, aren't covered. For your nonalcoholic beverages, you can choose from a regular-size fountain beverage; bottled water, juice, or sports drink; or coffee, cocoa, or tea (including tall Starbucks brews). Eligible snacks include churros, pretzels, popcorn, ice cream (regular-size cup or cone, or novelty bar), fruit, cookies, and pastries. Some larger items from snack vendors, such as turkey legs and hot dogs, count as a quick-service meal. Credits can even be used inside The Wizarding Worlds, though the Universal Dining eligibility logo doesn't appear on Potter menus for thematic reasons. However, signature beverages such as Butterbeer will count as a snack, not a drink.

If two sodas a day isn't enough for you, a souvenir Coca-Cola Freestyle cup can be added to any quick-service dining plan for an additional $9, which includes one day of unlimited refills from the Freestyle machines found around the parks (see page 222).

Universal claims the plan can save you up to 25%, but unless you use all your credits and order carefully, adults will probably do as well or better buying à la carte with an annual pass discount (which cannot be applied to purchasing the plan). We're also not big fans in principal of prepaying for meals, but thankfully Universal doesn't force you to book it for every day of your vacation or for every member of your party. It is possible to purchase the quick-service dining plan in advance when reserving your vacation, but there's really no need to.

Instead, take advantage of your ability to buy into the plan on a day-by-day basis at any participating restaurant *after* you've already made your menu selection. If your entrée and drink add up to at least $18 before tax, and you aren't eligible for any discounts, it's probably in your best interest to ask the cashier to sell you a quick-service plan. The extra few dollars will net another beverage (worth about $3–$5) and snack (worth $2.50–$8) for the afternoon, saving you up to $2–$4 on average. Order a ribs platter and pumpkin fizz from Three Broomsticks with a dining plan, and your second drink and snack will add only $3 to your bill. On the other hand, if you order a chicken sandwich, two bottles of juice, and a giant cookie, you'll lose about $5.50 on the deal. As for the kids, the children's plan is almost universally a good deal. Because kids' meals all cost $7.49 without a beverage, even buying bottles of water and a bag of chips puts you in the black. (And there's no law saying that adults with smaller appetites can't order from the children's menu.) Finally, the key to maximizing the value of your dining plan is using the snack credit on a Butterbeer. At $7.99, it's the most expensive eligible snack item in the parks, and arguably the tastiest; order one with the aforementioned ribs and you can save up to $10. Lard Lad's Big Pink Donut from The Simpsons Fast Food Boulevard in USF is another excellent use of your snack credit and can feed a family of four. The dining-plan cards aren't tied to a particular person, so they can be traded among family members, and they don't expire at the end of the day—unused credits hold their value as long as you hold onto the card. Just be aware that if you have a large group, juggling the plan's plastic can become a pain, because each person receives a separate card for every day. One more major minus: at press time, dining plans could not be used with mobile ordering (see page 218).

A **Table Service Universal Dining Plan** is also offered to on-site hotel guests buying vacation packages, but it's a much worse bargain. The full-service plan costs $64.99 per adult per day ($24.99 for kids) and includes everything the quick-service plan does, plus one table-service meal (entrée, soft drink, and select dessert; tax and gratuity not included) per day. Unfortunately, there are only about a dozen participating restaurants on property, none of which are in the resort hotels—which is strange because the only way to buy the table-service plan is as part of a Universal Orlando Vacations hotel package. And if you're visiting during the off-season, eligible table-service locations inside the parks may stop serving before you're hungry for dinner. The table-service plan probably wouldn't be a great deal even if Universal gave it away "free"; at full price, you're basically throwing money away.

FAST FOOD *in* UNIVERSAL ORLANDO'S PARKS

FAST FOOD IS AVAILABLE THROUGHOUT USF, IOA, Volcano Bay, and CityWalk. The food compares in quality to McDonald's, Arby's, or Taco Bell but is more expensive, though often served in larger portions. Quick-service prices are fairly consistent from park to park. Please note that the following menu prices do not include sales tax, unless otherwise noted.

COVID *tip*
Select quick-service locations may operate seasonally, or only open on busier days.

QUICK-SERVICE RECOMMENDATIONS AT UNIVERSAL STUDIOS FLORIDA

MUCH OF THE QUICK SERVICE at USF is utterly unremarkable: burgers, pizza, pasta, chicken fingers, sandwiches, and salads. The mediocre food is matched by the predictable theming in the park's original fast-food joints: American diner? Check. New York Italian? Got it. On the other hand, the more creative menus at the **Today Cafe** and **Universal Studios' Classic Monsters Cafe** prove Universal's quick-service eateries are capable of delivering delicious, memorable meals.

The Springfield: Home of the Simpsons themed area brings a number of wacky *Simpsons*-inspired eateries to life along **Fast Food Boulevard**, including **Krusty Burger, The Frying Dutchman** for seafood, **Cletus' Chicken Shack, Luigi's Pizza, Lard Lad Donuts, Lisa's Teahouse of Horror, Bumblebee Man's Taco Truck, Duff Brewery,** and **Moe's Tavern.** Serving sizes are large, and the food quality is an improvement over your run-of-the-mill theme park fare, with dozens of menu items (including potato barrels and curly fries) that aren't available in any other USF quick-service location.

The best quick-service food in USF can currently be found at the **Leaky Cauldron.** Diagon Alley's flagship restaurant serves authentically hearty British pub fare such as bangers and mash, cottage pie, toad-in-the-hole, Guinness stew, and a ploughman's platter for two of Scotch eggs and imported cheeses. When you're done, head over to **Florean Fortescue's Ice-Cream Parlour** for some delicious Butterbeer ice cream.

QUICK-SERVICE RECOMMENDATIONS AT ISLANDS OF ADVENTURE

OF IOA'S QUICK-SERVICE OFFERINGS, we like **Three Broomsticks,** the counter-service restaurant in The Wizarding World of Harry Potter–Hogsmeade, which serves Boston Market–style rotisserie chicken, plus fish-and-chips, shepherd's pie, and barbecue ribs. The **Hog's Head** pub, attached to Three Broomsticks, serves beer, wine, mixed drinks, and the obligatory Butterbeer (see page 219).

We're also fond of the gyros at **Fire-Eater's Grill,** the kebabs at **Doc Sugrue's Desert Kebab House,** and especially the ribs and roasted corn at **Thunder Falls Terrace**. Almost all of the other IOA counter-service places serve some variation of burgers, chicken, pizza, or pasta, and while your superhero-loving kids are going to be drawn toward Marvel Island's **Cafe 4** and **Captain America Diner** as if the Pied Piper himself was leading them there, avoid both, as there are much better places to eat.

QUICK-SERVICE RECOMMENDATIONS AT VOLCANO BAY

VOLCANO BAY OFFERS exotic, island-inspired fare that far exceeds standard water park counter-service snacks. At **Bambu** in Rainforest Village, we enjoy the creamy coconut chicken salad and chocolate pineapple upside-down cake. Also at Rainforest Village is **The Feasting Frog;** try the ahi tuna poké with plantain chips or carne asada tacos. At River Village, **Whakawaiwai Eats** is home to Hawaiian pizza (with caramelized pineapple, diced ham, and jalapeños) and mac and cheese with jerk shrimp. At **Kohola Reef Restaurant & Social Club** in Wave Village, we love the slow-smoked ribs, the quinoa-edamame burger (topped with roasted shiitake mushrooms and sriracha mayo), and the coconut curry chicken with sweet plantains. For dessert, choose the chocolate lava cake. **Dancing Dragons Boat Bar** (Rainforest Village) and **Kunuku Boat Bar** (Wave Village) serve exotic drinks, but the signature cocktails are far too sugary for our taste. Stick with the locally brewed Volcano Blossom beer instead.

QUICK-SERVICE RECOMMENDATIONS AT CITYWALK AND RESORT HOTELS

DINING OPTIONS AT CITYWALK and the resort hotels are oriented toward sit-down restaurants, but there are some counter-service choices worth considering. The chain franchises on CityWalk's upper floor have a following for their familiarity, but **Hot Dog Hall of Fame, Fusion Bistro Sushi,** and **Bread Box** serve food that's a step above the drive-thru. **Red Oven Pizza** is a fast-casual cross between quick-service and sit-down, and it's delicious no matter how you slice it. For a snack, **Menchie's Frozen Yogurt** and **Voodoo Doughnut** don't disappoint. The best quick-service hotel food is found at **Sal's Market Deli,** whose pies and salads are second only to Red Oven, and at Aventura's **Urban Pantry** food hall; Cabana Bay's **Bayliner Diner** food court has the widest range of selections, while the cafés at Endless Summer offer the lowest prices.

QUICK-SERVICE COURTESY

GETTING YOUR ACT TOGETHER REGARDING quick-service restaurants in the parks is more a matter of courtesy than necessity. Rude guests rank fifth among reader complaints. A mother from Fort Wayne,

Indiana, points out that indecision can be as maddening as outright discourtesy, especially when you're hungry:

Every fast-food restaurant has menu signs the size of billboards, but do you think anybody reads them? People waiting in line spend enough time in front of these signs to memorize them and still don't have a clue what they want when they finally get to the counter. If, by some miracle, they've managed to choose between the hot dog and the hamburger, they then fiddle around another 10 minutes deciding what size Coke to order. Folks, PULEEEZ get your orders together ahead of time!

On that note, it's also courteous to have your form of payment (cash, credit, hotel key, or dining-plan card) in hand by the time you approach the cashier. Better yet, bypass the cashier queue entirely using Universal's mobile ordering option (see below).

A close second on the frustrating scale are folks without food who monopolize restaurant tables while others balance trays, searching for a place to sit and eat. It's polite to wait until you've received your food before claiming a seat, and employees may enforce this policy on busy days, as one family discovered:

Many of the indoor counter-service restaurants require you to purchase your meal before they seat you. We were looking for a break from the sun with our turkey leg and other things bought from a cart. If we had known, we would have bought food from the specific counter-service place with indoor seating. We found that Circus McGurkus was the one place where we could bring in other food.

MOBILE FOOD AND DRINK ORDERING

A GROWING NUMBER of quick-service locations in Universal Orlando offer mobile ordering, which allows guests to select and purchase their meals through the smartphone app. Payment must be made by credit card, but users get to bypass the queue for a cashier. Menu prices are the same as if ordering in person, and you can customize some entrées and side items. Annual pass holders can mobile order exclusive seasonal items and apply their dining discount by scanning the barcode on their pass at checkout. The downsides are that no dining plans may be applied to mobile orders, and kids' meals cannot be ordered through the app at some locations.

COVID *tip*
To promote social distancing, some restaurants may require guests to use mobile ordering; you can still ask for a cashier if you have dietary concerns, or need to pay with cash or a dining plan.

If you haven't already, you'll first need to download Universal's mobile app to set up your account and link your credit card to the digital wallet, ensuring that your associated billing address is also entered correctly. Click "Order Food and Drinks" in the app's main menu to see which dining venues are currently participating (restaurants that usually offer mobile ordering are noted in the reviews beginning on page 225). You can browse the menus and make your selections at any time from anywhere you like; your food won't be prepared until you pay and verify that you are ready to eat.

Outdoor eateries with takeaway windows will have one marked MOBILE ORDER that app users can make a beeline toward once the app announces that their food has been prepared. At some indoor locations, you'll be asked to place your mobile order before entering the venue, then head directly to a designated mobile order window once notified that your meal is ready to pick up. At other indoor restaurants (including Three Broomsticks, Leaky Cauldron, and Fast Food Boulevard), you'll be seated before placing your mobile order; flag down a server once you've made your selections and show them your order number to ensure delivery to your table.

We're huge fans of using mobile ordering, which has saved us up to 30 minutes of standing in line for a register, though you'll still wait a few minutes for your order to be assembled.

THE WIZARDING WORLD OF BEVERAGES: BUTTERBEER AND BEYOND

The Butterbeer Craze

In the fictional Wizarding World, **Butterbeer** is a mildly intoxicating treat favored by Harry Potter and other Hogwarts students. It made its first appearance in the book *Harry Potter and the Prisoner of Azkaban,* and ever since it has made fans' mouths water with dreams of the taste, enticingly described as "a little bit like less-sickly butterscotch."

In the real world, the Butterbeer served at Universal Orlando is a nonalcoholic beverage served from a tap, with a butterscotch-y marshmallow foam head that's added after the drink is poured; it's guaranteed to leave you with a selfie-worthy mustache. Whereas in the books Butterbeer can be bought cold in bottles or hot in "foaming tankards," at Universal there are three liquid varieties, none of which are packaged for taking home, plus three Butterbeer-flavored solid snacks. (Official bottled Butterbeer can be bought from shop.wbstudiotour.co .uk/products/butterbeer, but it only delivers in the United Kingdom.) All were invented by chef Steven Jayson for The Wizarding World and had to meet J. K. Rowling's stringent specifications, which, among other things, required natural sugar (don't ask for Butterbeer Lite). We didn't expect to like it but were pleasantly surprised: it's tasty and refreshing, albeit really sweet.

First, there is the basic **cold Butterbeer,** which is a vanilla cream soda–style liquid with the foam topping. There's also a **frozen Butterbeer** that's sort of like a slushy made from the same cream soda base, again topped with foam. Frozen is the only variety that comes with a straw; beware of putting a straw in the cold kind because stirring the liquid can cause an embarrassing eruption.

Hot Butterbeer is served seasonally during the colder months of October–March. The hot variety eschews the soda base for a rich, creamy beverage that resembles a vanilla chai latte, light on the chai. The signature foam stays on top, natch.

The cold and frozen versions go for $7.99 in a 16-ounce plastic cup. The same drink in a Harry Potter souvenir cup sells for an additional $5.50, but there is no discount on Butterbeer refills. The hot version is sold in a 12-ounce paper cup for $7.99.

Note that while Butterbeer is gluten-free, and the base of cold and frozen Butterbeer has no dairy products, the "nondairy" foam topping contains whey, a protein derived from milk. For licensing reasons, they refuse to serve the drinks without the topping, even if you are vegan or lactose intolerant.

Finally, Diagon Alley introduced the world to soft-serve **Butterbeer ice cream,** which tastes almost exactly like the drinks. You can get it at Florean Fortescue's in a waffle cone ($5.99) or plastic souvenir sundae glass ($7.49). If you want only a cup of Butterbeer ice cream without toppings, the soft-serve is also available off menu at The Hopping Pot and Fountain of Fair Fortune, where you'll find a shorter wait. Three Broomsticks and a cart in Hogsmeade serve hard-packed Butterbeer ice cream in prepackaged cups ($5.99), but it isn't as good as the soft serve. In Diagon Alley you'll find **Butterbeer potted cream** in the Leaky Cauldron (a deliciously light butterscotch mousse) and **Butterbeer fudge** at Sugarplum's (inedibly saccharine with a candy corn–like crust).

If forced to choose among the different types of Butterbeer, Seth's hands-down favorite is the frozen version; the ice crystals seem to dull the overpowering sweetness. That is, unless it's cold out or early in the morning, in which case hot Butterbeer is the clear winner. Lastly, while it's officially forbidden to adulterate your Butterbeer, if you want to order a cup of the frozen stuff at the Hog's Head alongside a shot of, say, Irish cream . . . we won't tell if you pour it in while the barkeep's back is turned.

In IOA's Hogsmeade, the ambrosial liquid is sold only at **Three Broomsticks,** at the **Hog's Head** pub, and by two street vendors. That can mean long waits, as many guests buy from the outside carts, waiting 30 minutes or more in line to be served. We recommend trying your luck at the Hog's Head; the wait here is generally 10 minutes or less, and often there's nobody in line, even when the outdoor carts have lines 30 people deep only 20 feet away. Once served, you can relax with your drink at a table in the pub or out on the rear patio.

In USF's Diagon Alley, Butterbeer flows freely in the **Leaky Cauldron, The Hopping Pot,** and **Fountain of Fair Fortune.** Unfortunately, there's not enough seating to enjoy your drink. Once the picnic tables in Carkitt Market are full, your best bet is to squat on the "stairs to nowhere" next to Harry Potter and the Escape from Gringotts.

Beyond Butterbeer

Though Butterbeer gets most of the press, Hogsmeade and Diagon Alley serve other signature Harry Potter drinks too. You might as well try one because you won't find any Coca-Cola products whatsoever inside The Wizarding Worlds.

Foremost at both parks is **Pumpkin Juice,** which has a slightly pulpy texture and tastes like Thanksgiving dessert. It's available in a cup ($4.99); a sparkling **Pumpkin Fizz** version ($4.99) is served only in Hogsmeade. Refreshing nonalcoholic **Cider** ($3.99) is also on draft in apple or pear flavors. Other exclusive drinks in Diagon Alley include:

TONGUE TYING LEMON SQUASH ($5.49) A tart squeezed-to-order lemonade.

OTTER'S FIZZY ORANGE JUICE ($5.49) Lightly carbonated orange drink with a lip-smacking crust of cinnamon-sugar on the cup's rim; one of our favorites.

FISHY GREEN ALE ($5.49) Green cinnamon-mint boba tea with blueberry "fish eggs" that burst blueberry in your mouth when sucked through a straw. A must-try for the novelty factor but not necessarily a must-finish; many find it downright nasty.

PEACHTREE FIZZING TEA ($5.49) Lightly carbonated sweetened iced tea with peach and ginger flavors.

GILLYWATER ($5.50) A small plastic bottle of filtered water with a Harry Potter label. Seriously! For an extra $4.25 you can get it paired with a vial of flavored "magical elixir" available in four varieties—**Fire Protection** (watermelon, peach, and strawberry), **Babbling Beverage** (fruit punch), **Draught of Peace** (blueberry, blackberry, and cherry), and **Euphoria** (pineapple and mint)—to enhance your water. The most magical thing about the elixirs is how much money Universal has made disappear from Muggles' wallets with fancy punch.

Finally, adults who imbibe shouldn't feel left out of the fun; Universal contracted Florida Beer Company to come up with a trio of exclusive beers served only inside The Wizarding Worlds. In Hogsmeade, Three Broomsticks and Hog's Head pub serve **Hog's Head Brew,** a hoppy Scottish ale. Diagon Alley's Leaky Cauldron, The Hopping Pot, and Fountain of Fair Fortune pour **Wizard's Brew,** a heavy dark porter with chocolate notes, and **Dragon Scale,** a Vienna-style amber lager. All are served in 20-ounce cups for $10.49 (or $14.49 in a stout see-through souvenir stein) and are poured from creative custom-carved taps. Ask your bartender about secret off-menu concoctions, such as the Triple (unofficially known as a Deathly Hallows), made from layers of Strongbow, Hog's Head Brew, and Guinness.

For an added kick, try **Blishen's Fire Whisky,** a 70-proof cinnamon-flavored liquor distilled exclusively for the parks by TerrePURE Spirits of South Carolina. The flavor is warm but wonderfully smooth, and much more drinkable than the superficially similar Fireball whisky. Fire Whisky is available at the Leaky Cauldron and Hopping Pot in USF and at the Hog's Head in IOA. It's served neat or on the rocks for $11 per shot ($16 for a double) and can be mixed in nonalcoholic apple or pear cider for the same price. A pint of Strongbow with a Fire shot is $14 and tastes like apple pie. While Fire Whisky can't officially be served in Butterbeer, we can vouch for a shot snuck into a cup of hot Butterbeer as a breakfast eye-opener.

REFILLABLE DRINKS AND POPCORN

ONE SMART WAY TO CUT snacking costs—if not calories—around Universal Orlando is by investing in refillable souvenir containers. Souvenir cups never expire and can be brought back to the park months or years in the future.

Universal sells two different types of refillable soft drink cups. The standard **collectible souvenir cups,** which are gradually being phased out, can still be found around the resort in various styles for $8–$16, including your first fill-up, and can be refilled at almost any soda fountain in the parks or CityWalk. You won't receive any discount off the regular menu price on refills, but depending on the cup's size, you may get a few bonus ounces of beverage. They can only be refilled with regular fountain flavors—Coke, Diet Coke, Sprite, root beer, or Hi-C—and not with any specialty drinks. Pricier character cups (shaped like Transformers or Minions) and specialty souvenir cups (like Butterbeer mugs) can also be refilled with sodas for the regular price, but you only get as much as those sometimes-skimpy cups can contain.

Universal also sells **Coca-Cola Freestyle souvenir cups** at dining locations with Freestyle soda machines. These massive marvels can mix dozens of different drink brands and additional flavorings together to dispense more than 100 soft drink combinations; you haven't lived until you've had an Orange Coke. The self-service Freestyle fountains can only be activated by the RFID computer chip on the base of the cup. You can purchase a single-use Freestyle cup from select quick-service restaurants for $4.19, or buy a reusable souvenir cup that's valid for unlimited refills (with a 10-minute pause in between pours) for the entire day. Freestyle cups cost $16.99 plus tax for one, $15.99 each for two, or $12.99 each for three or more ($9 each if purchased with a quick-service dining plan online or at participating in-park locations) and can be reactivated for an additional $9.99 per day ($8.99 for annual pass holders); rinse and repeat for as many days as you like. There's also a larger $16 insulated souvenir cup that can either be refilled à la carte at regular prices or optionally activated for unlimited Freestyle refills for $9.99 per day; unlike the standard Freestyle cups, the first day of activation is *not* included with initial purchase. Freestyle cups can also be refilled for free with frozen slushies. (Moose Juice and Goose Juice at IOA's Seuss Landing are eligible, but Springfield Squishees, alas, are not.) Freestyle cups cannot be refilled free at regular soda fountains, but Freestyle machines are now found at nearly every quick-service restaurant, with more than a dozen dispensers in each theme park and a handful at Volcano Bay. You can't get filtered water from Freestyle machines without an activated cup, but any restaurant will give you a cup of free ice water on request, which tastes much better than the sulfurous, lukewarm liquid flowing from the parks' drinking fountains.

A word of warning: If you opt for the Freestyle souvenir cups, you won't be eligible for free refills inside either of the Wizarding Worlds. You can get your cup filled with lemonade, iced tea, or nonalcoholic cider for the regular menu price. But if you don't want to pay extra, you'll have to trek outside the Potter areas, as this reader from Moore, Oklahoma, was disappointed to discover:

> We got to the Leaky Cauldron only to discover that, although I paid for the full dining plan, I couldn't get a drink with my meal because I had the cups, which I had also paid for. When I asked a Universal employee about getting charged for drinks with the dining plan but getting zero drinks with it, they explained that the Freestyle cups were meant to be our drinks for the day.

A related program is the **Souvenir Cup Drink Package** sold exclusively at Aventura Hotel, Endless Summer Resort, Cabana Bay Beach Resort (where it's known as **Sonic Fill**), Royal Pacific Resort, and Sapphire Falls Resort. This cup costs $9.99 plus tax for one day of use, $15.99 for three days, or $18.99 for the entire length of your stay at the resort; prices are $1 cheaper at Endless Summer. A day is considered a calendar day and ends at midnight. Souvenir mugs can be refilled at the Coke Freestyle soda stations in the Bayliner Diner, Galaxy Bowl, and pool areas at Cabana Bay; at Aventura's Urban Pantry; at Endless Summer Resort's Beach Cafe and Pier 8 Market; at Royal Pacific Resort's Tuk Tuk Market; and in New Dutch Trading Co. and the pool area at Sapphire Falls. The cups are only compatible with the Freestyle machines at the hotel they were purchased at and can't be used inside the parks, nor can the parks' Freestyle cups be used at the hotels.

If you're looking for something harder to whet your whistle, all of the hotels' pool bars sell cocktails in souvenir cups for about $15 that can be refilled for only $10 at any of the other hotels, except Cabana Bay, whose refillable cups are larger and cheaper than those at the pricier resorts. Cabana Bay Beach Resort even sells a special watertight "pool cup" that allows you to drink while drifting on the lazy river, which is normally a no-no. Both hotels at Endless Summer Resort have standard drink prices that are cheaper than the other hotels' refills, and Dockside Inn offers upgrades to 32-ounce souvenir buckets. Souvenir cocktail glasses are also available in CityWalk at Fat Tuesday's but are not honored at the freestanding bars. Souvenir beer pilsners are sold inside the parks at select bars (including Moe's Tavern and Chez Alcatraz in USF) for about $13.50; refills cost the same as a regular drink, but you get a couple extra ounces for free. Refillable cocktail cups with blinking lights (in case you get blind drunk?) are sold at a similar price during events like Halloween Horror Nights and Mardi Gras.

Lastly, street-cart vendors in Universal's parks sell fresh popcorn in either $5 single servings or $9.99 **souvenir popcorn buckets** that can be refilled as often as your sodium level can stand for only $2. Flavored varieties such as caramel or cheese can be refilled for $3.69, and (like the soda cups) buckets can be brought back on future trips.

CUTTING YOUR DINING TIME AT THE THEME PARKS

EVEN IF YOU CONFINE YOUR MEALS to vendor and quick-service fast food, you lose a lot of time getting food in the theme parks. Here are some ways to minimize the time you spend hunting and gathering:

1. Eat breakfast before you arrive. Restaurants outside the parks offer some outstanding breakfast specials. Plus, some hotels furnish small refrigerators in their guest rooms, or you can rent a fridge or bring a cooler. If you can get by on cold cereal, rolls, fruit, and juice, this will save a ton of time.

2. After a good breakfast, buy snacks from vendors in the parks as you tour, or stuff some snacks in a fanny pack.

3. All theme park restaurants are busiest between 11:30 a.m. and 2:15 p.m. for lunch and 6 and 9 p.m. for dinner. For shorter lines and faster service, don't eat during these hours, especially 12:30–1:30 p.m.

4. Many quick-service restaurants sell cold sandwiches. Buy a cold lunch minus drinks before 11:30 a.m., and carry it in small plastic bags until you're ready to eat (within an hour or so of purchase). Ditto for dinner. Buy drinks at the appropriate time from any convenient vendor.

5. Whenever possible, use the Universal Orlando app's mobile ordering feature to reduce your wait. Make your selections while queuing for your last attraction before mealtime, so you can confirm your order as soon as you arrive at the restaurant. Skip mobile ordering and ask to see a cashier if you're using a dining plan or have allergy concerns.

6. If you need to order in person, most fast-food eateries have more than one service window. Regardless of the time of day, check the lines at all windows before queuing. Sometimes a window that's staffed but out of the way will have a much shorter line or none at all. Note, however, that some windows may offer only certain items.

7. If you're short on time and the park closes early, stay until closing and eat dinner outside the park before returning to your hotel. If the park stays open late, eat dinner about 4 or 4:30 p.m. at the restaurant of your choice. You should sneak in just ahead of the dinner crowd.

8. Be warned that if you wait until after the dinner rush to eat, you'll discover that most restaurants outside The Wizarding World stop serving at least an hour before the parks close, leaving CityWalk's eateries as your best option for a late supper.

Beyond Quick-Service: Tips for Saving Money on Food

Though buying food from quick-service restaurants and vendors will save time and money (compared with full-service dining), additional strategies can bolster your budget and maintain your waistline.

Our readers offer the following suggestions for stretching food dollars. A Missouri mom writes:

We stocked our steel cooler with milk and sandwich fixings. I froze a block of ice in a milk bottle, and we replenished the cooler daily with ice from the resort ice machine. I also froze small packages of deli meats for later in the week. We ate cereal, milk, and fruit each morning, with boxed juices. I also had a hot pot to boil water for instant coffee, oatmeal, and soup. Each child had a belt bag of his own, which he filled from a special box of goodies each day. Some things were actual food, such as packages of crackers and cheese, peanuts, and raisins. Some were worthless junk, such as candy and gum. Each child also had a small plastic water bottle that could hang on the belt. We filled these at water fountains before getting into lines. We left the park before noon; ate sandwiches, chips, and soda in the room; and napped. We purchased our evening meal in the park at a quick-service eatery. We budgeted for both morning and evening snacks from a vendor but often didn't need them.

A Whiteland, Indiana, mom suggests:

One must-take item if you're traveling with younger kids is a supply of small paper or plastic cups to split drinks, which are both huge and expensive.

The top budget-trimming tip we can offer is to skip the soft drinks and instead order free ice water with every meal. It's far healthier and more hydrating than soda (sugared or artificially sweetened), and at $3.99 per fountain drink, you'll be shocked at how swiftly the savings add up. The parks' drinking fountains are potable in a pinch, but the filtered water that all counter-service restaurants (excluding vending carts) give away tastes as good as the bottled water they sell, which goes for $3.50 from outdoor vending carts and $5 at indoor restaurants.

UNIVERSAL ORLANDO QUICK-SERVICE RESTAURANT MINI-PROFILES

TO HELP YOU FIND FLAVORFUL FAST FOOD while staying fleet of foot, we've developed mini-profiles of Universal Orlando's quick-service restaurants. The restaurants are listed alphabetically by location. Detailed profiles of all Universal Orlando full-service restaurants begin on page 242.

The restaurants profiled in the following pages are rated for quality and portion size as well as value. The value rating ranges from A to F as follows:

A Exceptional value; a real bargain	**D** Somewhat overpriced
B Good value	**F** Extremely overpriced
C Fair value; you get exactly what you pay for	

Note: Because of special or unusual offerings, the three following quick-service restaurants are listed with the full-service restaurants:

• Leaky Cauldron *(Universal Studios Florida)*	• Red Oven Pizza Bakery *(CityWalk)*
• Three Broomsticks *(Islands of Adventure)*	

In addition to the profiled locations, you'll also encounter counter-service kiosks and takeout windows from several familiar franchises—including Auntie Anne's, Ben & Jerry's, Cinnabon, Cold Stone Creamery, Fat Tuesday, and Menchie's—with snack prices only slightly more exorbitant than what you'd pay at your local mall.

UNIVERSAL STUDIOS FLORIDA

Bumblebee Man's Taco Truck

LOCATION Springfield   **QUALITY** Good   **VALUE** B-   **PORTION** Medium
READER-SURVEY RESPONSES 89% 👍 11% 👎

SELECTIONS Chicken and beef soft-shell tacos served with tortilla chips. Coca-Cola fountain products; Buzz Cola; Duff, Duff Lite, and Duff Dry beers.

COMMENTS Capitalizing on the popular trend of food trucks, Bumblebee Man's Taco Truck is the first eatery guests encounter walking into Springfield: Home of the Simpsons from the main gates. The truck is adorned with a huge taco on the front bumper and an even bigger Bumblebee Man head coming out of the roof. Each of the selections is well done. While the guacamole and salsa seem to be off-the-shelf varieties, every other element tastes great. The quality is very competitive with the food at Moe's Southwest Grill in City-Walk. Our favorite picks are the carne asada and the Korean beef.

Central Park Crepes

LOCATION Hollywood   **QUALITY** Good–Excellent   **VALUE** B+   **PORTION** Medium-Large
READER-SURVEY RESPONSES 100% 👍 0% 👎

SELECTIONS Fresh crepes with savory or sweet toppings; Freestyle soda.

COMMENTS This tiny booth outside Cafe La Bamba (home to VIP tour lunches and special events) attracts long lines with the smell of its made-to-order fancy French pancakes. You can make one into a light lunch by filling it with pesto chicken and goat cheese, barbecue brisket and coleslaw, or vegan "sausage" and "cheese." The dessert versions—stuffed with lemon curd and blueberries, Nutella and strawberries, or Oreo mascarpone—are big enough to share. Only soft drinks are served here, so step across the street to the bar on Cafe La Bamba's left side for a mimosa or wine to wash your crepe down.

Chez Alcatraz

LOCATION San Francisco   **QUALITY** Good   **VALUE** B   **PORTION** Medium–Large
READER-SURVEY RESPONSES 94% 👍 6% 👎

SELECTIONS Mixed drinks, beer, soda, and appetizers.

COMMENTS With usually little to no wait and plenty of seating, Chez Alcatraz can be a great place to relax and unwind with an adult beverage and a quick snack (we recommend the seasoned house-made chips with chipotle ketchup). And you just happen to be next to one of the best photo ops in USF: Bruce the shark from Jaws.

Duff Brewery

LOCATION Springfield   **QUALITY** Fair–Good   **VALUE** C   **PORTION** Medium
READER-SURVEY RESPONSES 88% 👍 12% 👎

SELECTIONS Corn dogs, pretzels, and assorted snacks. Beverages include Coca-Cola products, Buzz Cola, Duff beer, and other *Simpsons*-related drinks. In *The Simpsons* TV show, Duff, Duff Lite, and Duff Dry are all the exact same beer, but the Duff beers at Duff Brewery are completely different from each other. Duff beer is most equivalent to Yuengling, Duff Lite is closer to your standard light beer (like Miller Lite), and Duff Dry is a stout dark beer that can be compared to Guinness but has a strong coffee taste. Seasonal brews like Dufftoberfest are periodically poured.

COMMENTS Duff Brewery is an outdoor bar area with plenty of seating nearby to relax. It's part of the larger Duff Gardens, which, in *The Simpsons* TV show, is a theme park run by a beer-brewing company. The character of Duffman is available for photo ops, and there are hilarious topiaries of the Seven Duffs (Tipsy, Queasy, Surly, Sleazy, Edgy, Dizzy, and Remorseful), a parody of Disney's Seven Dwarfs and the mascots of Duff Gardens. Duff beers are brewed exclusively for Universal by the Florida Beer Company, which also brews beers for The Wizarding Worlds of Harry Potter. Because Duff Brewery is out in the open and in view of every guest, it can often attract a big crowd, especially on a hot day. The waterfront-viewing terrace is a fine place to enjoy the evening lagoon show if the Central Park viewing area is overcrowded. Order a drink here (the banana Squishee is especially tasty) with one of the giant Bavarian pretzels.

Fast Food Boulevard *(Mobile Ordering)*

LOCATION Springfield   **QUALITY** Good–Excellent   **VALUE** A-   **PORTION** Large
READER-SURVEY RESPONSES 81% 👍 19% 👎

SELECTIONS Burgers, chicken, pizza, seafood, sandwiches, and salads. Different eateries pulled straight from *The Simpsons* TV series include Krusty Burger, The Frying Dutchman, Flaming Moe's, Cletus' Chicken Shack, Luigi's Pizza, Lard Lad Donuts, and Lisa's Teahouse of Horror.

COMMENTS Besides the hilarious menus themselves (taste-tested by writers of *The Simpsons* TV show), Fast Food Boulevard contains items you can't get anywhere else in the park, including a pulled-pork sandwich, potato barrels, and seasoned curly fries. Our favorites are the gloriously messy Clogger Burger, the tender fried calamari, and the chicken-and-waffle sandwich (with extra maple mayo on the side). And thanks in large part to Lisa's Teahouse of Horror, Fast Food Boulevard also has several options, outside of the ever-present salad, for the vegetarians and vegans in your party. Note that this is a very popular spot for lunch, and a long line can develop. Guests may be required to wait for an employee to find them an empty table before ordering their meal. The process can take a while on busy days, and the TVs broadcast a loop of classic *Simpsons* clips that is maddeningly brief. An Ambler, Pennsylvania, couple sampled the offerings:

> The doughnuts at Lard Lad were fresh, flavorful, and surprisingly delicious. (Mmm . . . doughnuts.) My husband's Krusty Burger was pretty good; my chicken-and-waffle sandwich was excellent but had too much sauce on it.

Florean Fortescue's Ice-Cream Parlour

LOCATION Diagon Alley   **QUALITY** Excellent   **VALUE** B   **PORTION** Medium-Large
READER-SURVEY RESPONSES 98% 👍 2% 👎

SELECTIONS Ice cream is served in waffle cones and plastic souvenir sundae glasses. A single order can contain two different flavors, and you can add unusual toppings such as shortbread crumbles and meringue pieces for about a dollar.

COMMENTS Readers of the Harry Potter books will remember Florean Fortescue's Ice-Cream Parlour for its prominent appearance in *Harry Potter and the Prisoner of Azkaban.* When Harry spent several weeks staying in a room above the Leaky Cauldron, he would spend time there, and Florean himself gave Harry free ice cream sundaes every half hour. Now Muggles can have their own sundaes in this very establishment, with some very "magical" flavors, including Butterbeer-flavored ice cream. Our favorites are the salted caramel blondie and chocolate chili—but be warned, it has a bite!

Fountain of Fair Fortune *(Mobile Ordering; seasonal)*

LOCATION Diagon Alley   **QUALITY** Good-Excellent   **VALUE** B-   **PORTION** Medium
READER-SURVEY RESPONSES 98% 👍 2% 👎

SELECTIONS Potter-themed drinks, both soft and hard.

COMMENTS Named after a short story in *Tales of Beedle the Bard,* this pub sells Fishy Green Ale, Gillywater, Wizard's Brew, and Dragon Scale (see page 221)—and features an exclusive Butterbeer souvenir mug not found in Hogsmeade. You can also get a cup of Butterbeer soft-serve here, usually with a much shorter wait than at the ice cream shop next door.

The Hopping Pot *(Mobile Ordering)*

LOCATION Diagon Alley   **QUALITY** Good-Excellent   **VALUE** B-   **PORTION** Medium
READER-SURVEY RESPONSES 98% 👍 2% 👎

SELECTIONS Potter-themed drinks, including all four varieties of Butterbeer: cold, frozen, hot, or soft-serve. If you're peckish, snack portions of meat pasties and bags of British potato crisps are also available.

COMMENTS Outdoor bar with eight different brews—including Wizard's Brew (a heavy porter) and Dragon Scale (a hoppy amber)—on draft, each with its own customized tap handle, along with the area's most complete selection of signature nonalcoholic drinks. Much better food is available elsewhere in Diagon Alley. Seating is at a limited number of picnic tables, within sight of the Carkitt Market stage.

KidZone Pizza Company *(seasonal)*

LOCATION Woody Woodpecker's KidZone   **QUALITY** Fair   **VALUE** C   **PORTION** Medium
READER-SURVEY RESPONSES 71% 👍 29% 👎

SELECTIONS Pizzas, pizza fries, sweet potato casserole fries, and milkshakes.

COMMENTS Located at the front of Woody Woodpecker's KidZone and directly next to the impressive SpongeBob StorePants, KidZone Pizza is only open during select seasons. There's no indoor seating, and even the few seats outdoors can fill up quickly during the busier times. The only reason to order here is the cult-favorite pizza fries: crinkle-cut fries smothered in pepperoni and mozzarella, or vegan primavera sauce. You can get better pizza at several other locations in the park.

London Taxi Hut *(seasonal)*

LOCATION Outside Diagon Alley	QUALITY Fair-Good	VALUE C	PORTION Medium
READER-SURVEY RESPONSES 92% 👍 8% 👎			

SELECTIONS You can get a jacket potato (baked potato to Americans) smothered with baked beans and cheese, broccoli and cheese, or the salty stuffing from a shepherd's pie. Bags of crisps (British potato chips), hot dogs, and canned European beers fill out the brief menu.

COMMENTS Outside the gorgeous London Waterfront facade in front of Diagon Alley are two "cabman shelter" kiosks. One sells London-themed merchandise such as T-shirts, and this one sells quick-service food and drink items. The signature item is an extralong hot dog in an odd tubelike bun; shape aside, it tastes about the same.

Louie's Italian Restaurant *(Mobile Ordering)*

LOCATION New York	QUALITY Fair-Good	VALUE C	PORTION Medium
READER-SURVEY RESPONSES 89% 👍 11% 👎			

SELECTIONS Spaghetti with meatballs or vegan sausage; fettuccine Alfredo; cheese, pepperoni, or veggie pizza; Caesar salad; soup; cookies; cake; fruit cups; gelato; Italian ices; pizza fries; beer.

COMMENTS One of the largest indoor restaurants in the Studios and a good choice to get out of the hot sun. The name of the restaurant is an homage to the movie *The Godfather,* which had a very famous scene set at Louie's Restaurant. The food is nothing special, and the whole pies are outrageously overpriced at more than $35 apiece, but it's hard to screw up pizza and pasta. Pizza fries are also served here seasonally, sometimes exclusively to annual pass holders. Guido's, a small counter in the corner, offers a limited selection of frozen Italian desserts. Be warned: It can be very crowded throughout the afternoon.

Mel's Drive-In *(Mobile Ordering)*

LOCATION Hollywood	QUALITY Fair	VALUE C	PORTION Medium-Large
READER-SURVEY RESPONSES 81% 👍 19% 👎			

SELECTIONS Hamburgers, cheeseburgers, vegan burgers, chicken fingers, grilled chicken sandwich, grilled chicken salad, fries, onion rings, and ice cream floats.

COMMENTS Based on the diner from the George Lucas movie *American Graffiti,* Mel's has several vintage automobiles in the parking lot for photo ops. Check out the license plates for some fun references. During Halloween Horror Nights, the neon lights in the Mel's Drive-in sign are creatively changed to Mel's Die-in.

Over half the menu lists some combination of hamburger patty, cheese, and bacon, with fries. The food is as bland as the selection. Root beer floats and onion rings are the best bets on the menu, but we wouldn't make a special trip here for anything.

Moe's Tavern

LOCATION Springfield   **QUALITY** Good   **VALUE** C+   **PORTION** Medium
READER-SURVEY RESPONSES 86% 👍 14% 👎

SELECTIONS Duff beer and Flaming Moe.

COMMENTS Grab a Duff beer (regular or Duff Lite on draft or in a bottle; Duff Dry in a bottle only) or a Flaming Moe from this replica of Homer and Barney's haunt from *The Simpsons* TV series. Filled with nods to the TV show, the tavern has a large photo op with Barney, along with a working Love Tester. If you're lucky and sitting by the red phone on the bar top, you may just happen to take a prank phone call. The Flaming Moe is the first signature drink "experience" we have seen to date. Pricey at about $9 each, a Flaming Moe comes in a souvenir cup that does a good job of hiding dry ice via a separate compartment. The orange soda–tasting drink bubbles up with smoke billowing out, giving a really good representation of being on fire. The nonalcoholic Flaming Moe is sure to be a hit with the younger set when they see it for the first time, as it was with this Austin reader:

> *The Flaming Moe tastes like a bubbly orange soda; it really did seem to give me energy! It's only [a few dollars] more than that horrible Fishy Green Ale AND you keep the glass.*

Richter's Burger Co. *(Mobile Ordering)*

LOCATION San Francisco   **QUALITY** Fair   **VALUE** C   **PORTION** Medium-Large
READER-SURVEY RESPONSES 73% 👍 27% 👎

SELECTIONS Burgers, chicken sandwiches, vegan burgers, chili-cheese fries, salads, and milkshakes.

COMMENTS Near the Fast & Furious attraction, Richter's Burger Co. has a theme tied to the 1906 San Francisco earthquake. All of the menu items have earthquake-related names, and the decor around the surprisingly large seating areas includes photos from that era (including some wonderful ads for products that are just hilarious to read with 20/20 hindsight), as well as seismologist props. One of the more impressive elements in the restaurant is the faithful re-creation of the Louis Agassiz statue that fell off a Stanford University building during the 1906 earthquake; the statue lodged itself firmly into the concrete, head first. The food here is nothing to start quaking over, but you can upgrade your sandwich with guacamole or sautéed mushrooms for an additional fee.

San Francisco Pastry Company *(seasonal)*

LOCATION San Francisco   **QUALITY** Fair-Good   **VALUE** C+   **PORTION** Medium-Large
READER-SURVEY RESPONSES 80% 👍 20% 👎

SELECTIONS Soups; caprese, turkey, veggie, or roast beef sandwiches; fruit plates; salads; cookies, cakes, pies, and pastries; espresso, cappuccino, and coffee; beer and wine.

COMMENTS The selection is similar to the Today Cafe at the front of the park but a little less upscale. The pastries and coffee make a good pick-me-up if you're in the area during the afternoon, and the sandwiches are premade but can be served heated up.

Schwab's Pharmacy *(seasonal)*

LOCATION Hollywood   QUALITY Good   VALUE C+   PORTION Medium
READER-SURVEY RESPONSES   88% 👍   12% 👎

SELECTIONS Ice cream sundaes and milkshakes.

COMMENTS Schwab's Pharmacy, modeled after the legendary drugstore counter where Lana Turner was supposedly discovered, serves frozen treats made with Ben & Jerry's ice cream. A wider selection of Ben & Jerry's flavors can be found near the Starbucks in New York. You can also get a famous Dole Whip pineapple soft-serve in a cup or cone here cheaper than at the Magic Kingdom. The medicines here are for display only; if you need a nostrum, head to First Aid. Schwab's is open for only a few hours each afternoon, and it often doesn't open at all in the off-season.

Today Cafe *(Mobile Ordering)*

LOCATION Hollywood   QUALITY Good-Excellent   VALUE B+   PORTION Medium-Large
READER-SURVEY RESPONSES   93% 👍   7% 👎

SELECTIONS Hot breakfast sandwiches, overnight oatmeal; fresh deli sandwiches and gourmet salads; cookies, cakes, and pastries; draft beer, wine, and cold-brew coffee.

COMMENTS Inspired by the studio of its namesake, Today Cafe's white-and-orange color scheme captures the up-and-at-'em cheerfulness of NBC's long-running *Today* show. Located near the park's front gates, Today Cafe, complete with Al Roker and the gang watching over your meal from omnipresent TV screens, is a convenient spot to grab coffee and a breakfast pastry, but don't dally here during rope drop if the lines wrap outside. It's usually not as crowded as other restaurants for lunch. We like The Bulls & The Bears (beef brisket and Cheddar), Mulberry Street (Italian cold cuts and provolone), and Carnegie (pastrami and Swiss) sandwiches the best, especially when served hot with tangy potato salad. Portions aren't huge, but the entrées are filling with unexpectedly elevated ingredients, such as *porchetta* and prosciutto. Be sure to save room for a dessert from the tempting pastry trays; the green matcha tea cream puff is deliciously airy, without too much sugar, and pairs well with an iced nitro coffee.

Universal Studios' Classic Monsters Cafe
(Mobile Ordering; seasonal)

LOCATION Production Central QUALITY Good-Excellent VALUE B+ PORTION Medium-Large
READER-SURVEY RESPONSES   74% 👍   26% 👎

SELECTIONS Smoked brisket, chicken, ribs, and sausage, served with baked beans, mac and cheese, Brussels sprouts, coleslaw, and corn bread; vegan slow-cooked jackfruit sandwich; kale salad with brisket; individual wood-oven pizzas; peach cobbler; s'mores cookies; beer.

COMMENTS With a lot of indoor seating, Universal Studios' Classic Monsters Cafe can be a good place for a meal and to get out of the hot sun. The restaurant is filled with movie props from various monster films, including *The Creature from the Black Lagoon* and *The Mummy,* but also has references from *The Munsters* TV show. Universal remade the Monsters' menu in 2019 with barbecue meat combos and home-style side dishes, making it into one of the park's best non-Potter bets. Chicken and ribs are comparable to those at Three Broomsticks, the brisket runs fatty but has fantastic seasoning on the bark, and the personal pizzas (available with barbecue chicken) are much better than your average theme park pizza. Vegetarians can get a combo of only side dishes, or be adventurous and try the jackfruit (a mild, fleshy cousin of the fig and breadfruit), served hot with crispy onions on a kaiser roll. The signature nonalcoholic beverage here is Sprite with blueberry popping boba, called the Lavender Elixir; it tastes much better than the Fishy Green Ale in Diagon Alley.

ISLANDS OF ADVENTURE

Blondie's *(Mobile Ordering)*

LOCATION Toon Lagoon	QUALITY Fair-Good	VALUE C+	PORTION Large
READER-SURVEY RESPONSES	79% 👍 21% 👎		

SELECTIONS Dagwood deli sandwiches; made-to-order roast beef, turkey, tuna, and ham sandwiches; Nathan's hot dogs; brookies.

COMMENTS Avoid the signature sandwich—the Dagwood—which is premade and refrigerated until needed. It also has more bread than necessary, making it dry. If you're really in the mood for a sandwich, try one of the made-to-order turkey or ham subs; the roast beef is invariably too dry. Blondie's serves subs on white or multigrain rolls, accompanied by a side of potato salad. If you like Nathan's hot dogs, Blondie's serves chili and Chicago styles and pairs them with crinkle-cut fries.

The Burger Digs *(Mobile Ordering)*

LOCATION Jurassic Park	QUALITY Fair	VALUE C	PORTION Medium-Large
READER-SURVEY RESPONSES	82% 👍 18% 👎		

SELECTIONS Double cheeseburger, chicken sandwich, vegan burger, chicken tenders, and milkshakes.

COMMENTS Burger Digs has indoor seating. The burgers and chicken sandwiches are nothing special, though they come on kaiser rolls, and a cold toppings bar allows for customization. The specialty burger is topped with mango barbecue sauce, smoked Gouda, and coleslaw, and it can be ordered with a vegan patty made from brown rice and mushrooms. For a lighter meal, try the chicken spring salad with corn, black beans, and pineapple vinaigrette; the flavorless vegan Chick'n avocado sandwich is best avoided. If you're looking for better food, try Thunder Falls Terrace a little farther along in Jurassic Park.

Cafe 4 *(Mobile Ordering)*

LOCATION Marvel Super Hero Island	QUALITY Fair-Good	VALUE C	PORTION Medium
READER-SURVEY RESPONSES	74% 👍 26% 👎		

SELECTIONS Pizza, pasta, meatball or chicken Parmesan sub, Caesar salad, and breadsticks.

COMMENTS The food is generic and fairly flavorless, but it's served rather speedily. However, Doctor Doom seems to think an average price of $16 for a single slice of pizza and side salad (or a jaw-dropping $35–$40 for a whole pie) is reasonable in a theme park setting. This is not Via Napoli by any "stretch" of the imagination (that one is for the Mr. Fantastic fans), but the café does make specialties such as barbecue chicken pizza. The exact same salads, meatball subs, and basic pastas and sauces that are served at Louie's in USF round out the not-so-Fantastic menu. At 5 p.m. on select nights, this location turns into a Marvel character buffet (see page 213).

Captain America Diner *(Mobile Ordering; seasonal)*

LOCATION Marvel Super Hero Island   QUALITY Fair   VALUE C   PORTION Medium-Large
READER-SURVEY RESPONSES   58% 👍   42% 👎

SELECTIONS Cheeseburgers, chicken sandwiches, vegan burgers, chicken fingers, chicken salad, milkshakes, and onion rings.

COMMENTS The meat is entirely average but comes served on a sesame-seed bun, and the specialty burger is topped with barbecue pulled pork. While the name of the restaurant is Captain America Diner, the air-conditioned inside is themed to the Marvel Comics version of The Avengers, including references to C-level characters in the group such as the Black Knight and Wonder Man—even the flooring is themed. Inside seating features a gorgeous look outside into the lagoon (with a great view of Mythos and Hogwarts Castle).

Circus McGurkus Cafe Stoo-pendous
(Mobile Ordering; seasonal)

LOCATION Seuss Landing   QUALITY Fair-Good   VALUE C+   PORTION Medium-Large
READER-SURVEY RESPONSES   61% 👍   39% 👎

SELECTIONS Fried chicken, pasta, pizza, cheeseburgers, and Caesar salad. Dippin' Dots sundaes and floats for dessert.

COMMENTS Certainly one of the more interesting counter-service venues. The High in the Sky Seuss Trolley Train Ride! passes overhead. During inclement weather *Oh! The Stories You'll Hear!* takes place inside the restaurant. The fried chicken is actually pretty good; it comes in two- or three-piece combos with corn on the cob and mashed potatoes with home-style gravy. The tropical spring mix salad is a refreshing change of pace; ask for a hot grilled chicken breast on top. Everything else on the menu is just average. When this venue is closed, look for pizza at Moose Juice, Goose Juice, and burgers at Green Eggs and Ham Cafe.

Comic Strip Cafe *(Mobile Ordering; seasonal)*

LOCATION Toon Lagoon   QUALITY Poor-Fair   VALUE C-   PORTION Medium-Large
READER-SURVEY RESPONSES   73% 👍   27% 👎

SELECTIONS Asian barbecue chicken, stir-fry, chicken fingers, fish-and-chips, personal pizza, pasta, salads, cheeseburgers, and chili dogs.

COMMENTS Long notorious for serving the worst fast food in IOA, Comic Strip Cafe attempts to serve something for everyone and ends up satisfying no one. The "Chinese" dishes are pretty dire. Better fish-and-chips can be found at Three Broomsticks, and better pizza is at Cafe 4. The least awful entrée is the fresh baked cod on warm pita with tropical salsa, but it takes up to 20 minutes to prepare. If you're hungry for funnel cake, try the bite-size funnel puffs.

Croissant Moon Bakery *(Mobile Ordering; seasonal)*

LOCATION Port of Entry   QUALITY Fair-Good   VALUE B-   PORTION Large
READER-SURVEY RESPONSES   94% 👍   6% 👎

SELECTIONS Hot breakfast sandwiches; deli sandwiches, soups and salads, freshly baked pastries, and Lavazza coffee.

COMMENTS Tucked into the right side of Port of Entry's main walkway as you enter the park, Croissant Moon Bakery is a good place to get a quick breakfast (its "on the run" Continental combo is a great deal) or a pastry and coffee pick-me-up between meals. Prices for fancy flavored lattes are lower here than at the Starbucks across the street. The cold sandwiches tend to be premade and refrigerated, but you can get them heated up on a panini press. The service is fast and friendly, and there's some shaded seating outdoors, where you can people-watch.

Doc Sugrue's Desert Kebab House
(Mobile Ordering; seasonal)

LOCATION The Lost Continent **QUALITY** Good **VALUE** C+ **PORTION** Medium-Small
READER-SURVEY RESPONSES 84% 👍 16% 👎

SELECTIONS Meat and vegetarian kebabs, hummus, Greek salad, yogurt, and beverages.

COMMENTS The stand offers nicely seasoned beef and chicken kebabs, and it's also vegetarian and vegan friendly, with hummus, fruit cups, Greek yogurt, and pretzels on the menu. The skewers are among our favorite light meals. This location also has the closest Coke Freestyle machines to Hogsmeade. Doc Sugrue's is in the unfortunate position of being between the popular eatery Mythos and The Wizarding World of Harry Potter. With many hungry guests making a beeline toward the Potter-themed food in Hogsmeade or the award-winning Mythos, both Doc Sugrue's and Fire-Eater's Grill in Lost Continent are often overlooked.

Fire-Eater's Grill *(Mobile Ordering)*

LOCATION The Lost Continent **QUALITY** Good **VALUE** B- **PORTION** Medium
READER-SURVEY RESPONSES 86% 👍 14% 👎

SELECTIONS Gyros, falafel, chicken tenders, hot dogs, chili-cheese fries, and salads.

COMMENTS The lamb gyro with salad is the best combo here, and also the most popular. Vegetarians can request falafel as a meat substitute, and combo platters include pita with tzatziki, peanut butter hummus, or edible cookie dough. You have to admire Universal's ability to combine the various entrées to make more meal options. One is a plain chicken tenders platter. Add hot sauce, and it becomes the Chicken Stingers platter. Omit the sauce and add lettuce, and it's the Crispy Chicken Salad.

Green Eggs and Ham Cafe

LOCATION Seuss Landing **QUALITY** Good **VALUE** B **PORTION** Medium
READER-SURVEY RESPONSES 83% 👍 17% 👎

SELECTIONS Potato barrels with a variety of toppings, s'mores, soft drinks.

COMMENTS After spending nearly a decade as a perpetually closed photo op, Universal reopened this iconic outdoor eatery with an indulgent new menu revolving around potato barrels. The elementary school cafeteria favorites can be smothered in pepperoni-and-sausage pizza toppings; other offerings include buffalo chicken tenders with mozzarella and ranch dressing, or the namesake combo of green eggs (colored with natural herbs) and diced ham. The menu's artery-clogging star has to be the corned beef Who Hash, served with white cheese sauce and scallions in a souvenir can. For a sweet snack, the s'mores are made with hazelnut-chocolate spread.

Hog's Head

LOCATION Hogsmeade **QUALITY** Good **VALUE** B- **PORTION** Medium
READER-SURVEY RESPONSES 95% 👍 5% 👎

SELECTIONS Butterbeer, Pumpkin Juice, beer, wine, and mixed drinks.

COMMENTS Wonderfully themed pub attached to the Three Broomsticks restaurant that offers both alcoholic and alcohol-free drinks. If you want a Butterbeer, the line is often shorter here than at either of the outdoor carts. A full liquor selection is kept behind the bar, but there are no sodas to mix with (only juice), nor are the bartenders allowed to add alcohol to nonalcoholic Potter drinks (which is not to say that you can't mix them yourself). There are also some potent secret cocktails available off-menu, like Hog's Tea (a raspberry Long Island iced tea) and a triple-layered cider/ale/porter potion that (for trademark reasons) you should definitely *not* refer to as a Deathly Hallows. The animatronic hog hanging behind the bar is known to snort and snarl if you slide the barkeep a tip.

The Mess Tent

LOCATION Skull Island   **QUALITY** Fair-Good   **VALUE** C+   **PORTION** Medium-Large
READER-SURVEY RESPONSES 100% 👍 0% 👎

SELECTIONS Hot dogs, pretzels, churros, frozen slushies, and beer.

COMMENTS Apparently, all an attraction needs to qualify as an entire island on Universal's map is an adjoining souvenir kiosk and snack stand, which explains the presence of this modest mess tent outside Reign of Kong's entrance. The appropriately oversize ⅓-pound foot-long hot dog comes topped with cheese sauce and relish on a pretzel roll in a Kong Combo. The banana slushy tastes suspiciously like the banana Squishee served at USF's Duff Brewery, but it's still darn tasty.

Moose Juice, Goose Juice

LOCATION Seuss Landing   **QUALITY** Good   **VALUE** C   **PORTION** Small-Medium
READER-SURVEY RESPONSES 90% 👍 10% 👎

SELECTIONS Corn dogs, pretzels, cookies, and churros; frozen orange, apple, watermelon, or grape juice.

COMMENTS Cartoon animal rights activists rest easy: no geese nor meese were harmed in the making of these drinks. Moose Juice is actually an orange tangerine-flavored frozen slushy, and Goose Juice is a green sour apple–flavored slushy. Both can hit the spot on a hot Florida day.

Pizza Predattoria *(Mobile Ordering; seasonal)*

LOCATION Jurassic Park   **QUALITY** Fair-Good   **VALUE** C+   **PORTION** Medium
READER-SURVEY RESPONSES 86% 👍 14% 👎

SELECTIONS Personal pizzas, meatball sub, bruschetta chicken sandwich, vegetarian calzone, Caesar salad, and brookies.

COMMENTS The meat-lovers pizza is decent, as far as theme park pizza goes. Stick to that or the salads. The brookie—a cookie-brownie hybrid—is a brilliant development in the history of desserts.

Thunder Falls Terrace *(Mobile Ordering)*

LOCATION Jurassic Park   **QUALITY** Excellent   **VALUE** A-   **PORTION** Large
READER-SURVEY RESPONSES 89% 👍 11% 👎

SELECTIONS Rotisserie chicken, ribs, smoked turkey legs, rice and bean bowl, soups, and salads.

COMMENTS A nice change from the usual theme park hamburgers and pizza served throughout IOA. The roasted corn on the cob and seasoned rice with beans are excellent. Thunder Falls is quite possibly the best bet for a meal in the park. It's not as busy as Three Broomsticks and serves food almost as good, making this location a winner.

Wimpy's *(seasonal)*

LOCATION Toon Lagoon	QUALITY Good	VALUE B-	PORTION Medium-Large
READER-SURVEY RESPONSES 88% 👍 13% 👎			

SELECTIONS Cheeseburgers, vegan burgers, chicken fingers, caprese salad, curly fries, Dole Whip, beer.

COMMENTS This outdoor-only burger stand, themed to Popeye's perpetually indebted pal, was once the white whale of Universal dining, operating so infrequently that it was presumed permanently closed. Just when we'd written it off entirely, Wimpy's reopened with a brand-new menu, featuring a Wellington Cheeseburger and Vegan Supreme Cheeseburger. Neither is life-changing, but they are among the parks' better quick-service burgers and (better yet) are served with seasoned curly fries. Wimpy's other main attraction is Dole Whip, the iconic pineapple sorbet from Disney World's Adventureland, available in cups or cones for less money than at the Mouse.

VOLCANO BAY

Bambu *(Mobile Ordering)*

LOCATION Rainforest Vlg.	QUALITY Good	VALUE B	PORTION Medium-Large
READER-SURVEY RESPONSES 86% 👍 14% 👎			

SELECTIONS Cheeseburgers, chicken sandwiches, chicken tenders, and salads.

COMMENTS Bamboo-shaded patios provide plenty of sheltered seating near the Maku Puihi slides. The coconut chicken salad with grapes and apples is excellent, as is the pineapple upside-down cake.

The Feasting Frog *(Mobile Ordering)*

LOCATION Rainforest Vlg.	QUALITY Good	VALUE B	PORTION Medium
READER-SURVEY RESPONSES 91% 👍 9% 👎			

SELECTIONS Tacos, nachos, and tuna poké.

COMMENTS This charming amphibian-shaped hut serves pretty good carne asada and chicken tacos, though the shells seem to go stale swiftly in the Orlando humidity. Our favorite is the poké bowl, with sashimi-quality ahi tuna and crispy plantain chips. You can grab food and sit at the neighboring Kunuku Boat Bar, which serves a refreshing locally brewed Volcano Blossom beer and an array of supersweet signature cocktails.

Kohola Reef Restaurant & Social Club *(Mobile Ordering)*

LOCATION Wave Vlg.	QUALITY Good-Excellent	VALUE B+	PORTION Medium-Large
READER-SURVEY RESPONSES 82% 👍 18% 👎			

SELECTIONS Hot breakfast sandwiches and breakfast pizza; Hawaiian ribs, burgers, veggie burgers, jerk fish or pulled-pork sandwiches, chicken, pizzas, salads, and sushi.

COMMENTS As Volcano Bay's largest eatery and the one closest to the park's entrance, this is usually the most crowded restaurant at mealtimes. Breakfast items are served here until 10:30 a.m., and this is the park's only eatery that stays open until closing time. The burgers are served on Hawaiian rolls, but you're better off skipping them and the "longboard" pizzas in favor of more exotic entrées, like the braised chicken in green coconut curry, quinoa-edamame burger, smoked ribs, or mango barbecue pulled pork. For lighter fare, we like the jerk-seasoned mahi-mahi with cucumber slaw, and California rolls. Chocolate lava cake is the can't-miss dessert. If you want an adult beverage with your meal, step across the path to the nearby Dancing Dragons Boat Bar.

Whakawaiwai Eats *(Mobile Ordering)*

LOCATION River Vlg.	QUALITY Good	VALUE B	PORTION Medium
READER-SURVEY RESPONSES 90% 👍 10% 👎			

SELECTIONS Pizza, hot dogs, mac and cheese, and salads.

COMMENTS Somewhat isolated in the rear of the park, this is probably your best bet for getting food without a long wait, though the menu isn't particularly innovative. The same "longboard" pizzas served at Kohola Reef are also found here, plus Hawaiian varieties and an island barbecue version (chicken, Gouda, and mango sauce). The hot dogs are served on pretzel buns and topped with bacon and pineapple, and the upscale mac and cheese is stuffed with jerk-seasoned shrimp.

CITYWALK

BK Whopper Bar

LOCATION Upper Level	QUALITY Fair	VALUE C	PORTION Large
READER-SURVEY RESPONSES 67% 👍 33% 👎			

SELECTIONS A Burger King location with Whoppers of all kinds; plant-based Impossible burger; fried chicken sandwich or strips; salads; fries; onion rings; shakes; sundae pie.

COMMENTS Because the menu is so familiar, long lines can develop here during lunchtime. Prices are markedly higher than your local drive-thru, and there's no value menu, but you are getting a double Whopper with unique toppings (such as blue cheese or angry onions), and the "small" fries and drink are the size of a medium elsewhere.

Bread Box Handcrafted Sandwiches *(Mobile Ordering)*

LOCATION Upper Level	QUALITY Good	VALUE C-	PORTION Small-Medium
READER-SURVEY RESPONSES 91% 👍 9% 👎			

SELECTIONS Hot and cold deli sandwiches, grilled cheese, house-made potato chips, soups, salads, milkshakes, beer, and wine.

COMMENTS The Bread Box claims that guests will be "transported back to your childhood kitchen or your favorite street corner deli" through its use of high-quality meats, vegetables, fresh bread, and simple preparation. Sounds good, and the menu indeed has a wide selection of grilled cheeses (stuffed with everything from bacon to pastrami to smoked brisket), along with house-made soups and various sandwiches made fresh to order. And you can't complain about Nutella milkshakes for dessert. The problem is that, while everything we've tasted at Bread Box has been yummy, you can't ignore how outrageously overpriced it is, especially compared to its noble competition; $10–$13 will buy you a sandwich, though at least the fries or potato barrels are included. If you want a high-quality, creative snack and can stomach the price, give one of the grilled cheese creations a go, but save some money for another meal later.

Fusion Bistro Sushi & Sake Bar

LOCATION Upper Level	QUALITY Good	VALUE C-	PORTION Small-Medium
READER-SURVEY RESPONSES 50% 👍 50% 👎			

SELECTIONS Raw and cooked sushi *nigiri* and makimono, sake and Japanese beer, miso soup, edamame, hot appetizers, and salads.

COMMENTS Fusion Bistro's unusual sushi preparations mix traditional Japanese with tastes and ingredients from throughout Eastern Asia and the Pacific Rim, all made in a glassed-in kitchen you can observe from outside. The sushi here ain't cheap, but it's quicker and less expensive than The Cowfish. Because of its extended hours, you can get your fix until the wee hours. Quality is a cut above your local supermarket, but because everything is made from fairly pedestrian fish—tuna, salmon, imitation crab, shrimp, and eel—sushi snobs will want to eat elsewhere. The spicy tuna rolls are acceptable.

Hot Dog Hall of Fame *(Mobile Ordering)*

LOCATION Lower Level	QUALITY Fair-Good	VALUE C	PORTION Medium
READER-SURVEY RESPONSES 89% 👍 11% 👎			

SELECTIONS Nathan's and Vienna hot dogs, bratwurst, and a variety of toppings; potato chips; beer and soda.

COMMENTS Developed by Steven Schussler, the creative force behind Rainforest Cafe and T-REX, Hot Dog Hall of Fame is a tribute to the iconic baseball-park food. Unfortunately, many of the unique touches—from the mustard bar curated by the National Mustard Museum in Wisconsin, to famous dogs from ballparks across the nation—fell by the wayside during the pandemic in favor of a simplified menu. The outdoor venue still features large-screen TVs and bleacher-type seating (from actual Major League Baseball parks) for those interested in catching a game. The sausages, buns, and toppings are all properly prepared, but the value will vary with the variety; a New York–style dog costs double what you'd pay in Times Square, while the Milwaukee bratwurst and grilled onions delivers a decent bang for the buck. Platters include potato chips for an extra $1. There's also a 2-foot dog for just under twice the price, if you want to share.

Moe's Southwest Grill

LOCATION Upper Level	QUALITY Good	VALUE B+	PORTION Large
READER-SURVEY RESPONSES 85% 👍 15% 👎			

SELECTIONS Tacos, burritos, quesadillas, nachos, fajitas, and taco salads made with steak, ground beef, chicken, tofu, or veggies; chips and salsa; cookies; beer.

COMMENTS The Mexican-food equivalent of a Subway sandwich shop. You place your order (for example, steak tacos) at the front of a long assembly line, and then follow your plate down the line as it's passed from worker to worker, each of whom adds whatever garnishes, sides, and sauces you want. We like Moe's quite a bit. The menu is filled with references to TV shows and movies, such as the John Coctostan (from *Fletch*).

Panda Express

LOCATION Upper Level	QUALITY Fair	VALUE C	PORTION Medium-Large
READER-SURVEY RESPONSES 81% 👍 19% 👎			

SELECTIONS Chinese food, including entrées of sweet-and-sour chicken, orange chicken, kung pao chicken, beef and broccoli, beef with mushrooms and asparagus, honey walnut shrimp, and eggplant tofu, with sides of mixed veggies, chow mein, and white or fried rice.

COMMENTS The kung pao chicken has a darker, smoky flavor than most we've tried, and the sauces are heavier than our local Chinese takeouts. Still, Panda

Express is a hit with the kids in our group, who want to eat here every time they see it. Panda Express usually has the longest line of the three fast-food joints on CityWalk's upper level.

Starbucks

LOCATION Lower Level	QUALITY Good	VALUE C	PORTION Medium
READER-SURVEY RESPONSES 94% 👍 6% 👎			

SELECTIONS Coffees and teas in many blends and flavors; espresso, cappuccino, frozen coffees, and smoothies; pastries; cookies; and sodas.

COMMENTS While the Starbucks in IOA, USF, and Cabana Bay Beach Resort feature the chain's full sandwich menu, this particular Starbucks offers a more limited selection of pastries. However, it does provide a large amount of seating (with free Wi-Fi and accessible power ports) both inside and out. Though this handsomely designed coffee shop has much more barista capacity than the average franchise, its ground-central location leads to long lines around park opening. *Note:* Starbucks loyalty stars can be earned at Universal locations, but rewards can't be redeemed here. Starbucks gift cards and Universal annual pass discounts are both honored here.

Voodoo Doughnut *(Mobile Ordering)*

LOCATION Lower Level	QUALITY Good	VALUE B-	PORTION Medium
READER-SURVEY RESPONSES 89% 👍 11% 👎			

SELECTIONS Raised yeast, cake, or vegan doughnuts, topped with everything from fruit cereal or orange powdered-drink mix to bacon, plus coffee to wash them down.

COMMENTS This Portland-based bakery has built a cult following for its outrageously shaped confections. The signature Voodoo Doll (with a pretzel stake through its heart) is Instagram-worthy, and exclusive varieties for annual pass holders arrive regularly, but the original anatomically explicit menu items aren't sold at a family-friendly theme park. The vegan Portland Cream is so delicious that you'd never guess it contains no actual cream. Expect long lines outside the shop at breakfast and as the parks empty. Use mobile ordering to avoid the queue; pickups are made from a pink cart outside the shop. Even if you don't get anything to eat, pose for a photo on the doughnut throne outside.

RESORT HOTELS

Bayliner Diner

LOCATION Cabana Bay Beach	QUALITY Good	VALUE B	PORTION Medium-Large
READER-SURVEY RESPONSES 85% 👍 15% 👎			

SELECTIONS Cheeseburgers, roasted chicken, hot dogs, beef churrasco, pizza, pasta, flatbread, grilled cheese sandwiches, wraps, salads, and pastries.

COMMENTS Cabana Bay's Bayliner Diner is a food court–style cafeteria with several different stations offering a wide range of food options. The preparations are a cut above the counter service found inside the parks. The churrasco-style flat iron with creamy chimichurri is surprisingly tender and tasty for counter-service steak. For breakfast, the diner serves up all the usual suspects. Get waffles or French toast, or wait for a made-to-order omelet, but avoid the precooked eggs on the combo platter and the croissant sandwich. The seating area, filled with booths and tables, is large. Large screens play retro commercials to evoke a feeling of nostalgia. The diner offers a considerable amount of usable outlets to charge your phones and tablets, including one outside every booth. If you prefer to dine poolside, the Hideaway Bar & Grill by the lazy river slings burgers, fish tacos, and Honolulu-style hot dogs, while Atomic Tonic near the waterslide serves *döner* kebabs and falafel wraps.

Beach Break Cafe

LOCATION Surfside Inn   **QUALITY** Fair–Good   **VALUE** B+   **PORTION** Medium
READER-SURVEY RESPONSES 66% 👍 34% 👎

SELECTIONS Rotisserie chicken, baked fish, "power bowls" topped with carne asada or tofu, focaccia sandwiches, Cobb and Caesar salads, pizza by the slice, baked pasta, burgers, chicken sandwiches, and fresh-squeezed juices.

COMMENTS The cafeteria-style food courts at the Endless Summer properties are the humblest eateries at Universal's on-site hotels, but they're better than most of the franchised family restaurants on nearby International Drive and provide better value to boot. For breakfast, try the blueberry pancakes topped with lemon curd, and healthy blends of fresh-pressed juice. At lunch and dinner, the Pipeline burger with caramelized onions and bacon jam costs less than a basic cheeseburger inside the parks, and between the tofu-topped bowls of quinoa and cilantro rice, and the seasoned grilled corn on the cob, there's plenty to satisfy non-carnivores. There's ample seating at communal picnic tables, which surround a self-serve Coca-Cola Freestyle dispenser that allows free refills for 2 hours after any soft drink purchase. Our biggest problem with Beach Break Cafe is the speed of service; our food got cold before our entire order could be assembled, and simple requests prompted employees to disappear for long stretches, suggesting that Universal isn't staffing its budget hotels with the best and brightest.

Emack & Bolio's Marketplace

LOCATION Hard Rock Hotel   **QUALITY** Good   **VALUE** C   **PORTION** Medium
READER-SURVEY RESPONSES 80% 👍 20% 👎

SELECTIONS Ice cream, sorbet, frozen yogurt, sundaes, Starbucks coffee, sandwiches, candy, pizza, snacks, soft drinks, cereal, and pastries.

COMMENTS Boston-based Emack & Bolio's has a long history of associating with rock stars (check out the vintage van doors outside) and naming ice cream flavors after their songs. Here you can have a cone or sundae made from Space Cake, Trippin' on Espresso, or "Deep Purple" Chip. It also has a grab-and-go selection of snacks, cold breakfast foods, and Starbucks drinks to speed you through your morning, plus a decent selection of hot and cold snacks, sandwiches, and takeout pizzas (in 10- or 16-inch pies) after noon.

New Dutch Trading Co. *(temporarily closed)*

LOCATION Sapphire Falls   **QUALITY** Good   **VALUE** C+   **PORTION** Medium
READER-SURVEY RESPONSES 97% 👍 3% 👎

SELECTIONS Hot and cold sandwiches, soups, salads, coffee, pastries, hand-scooped ice cream, and milkshakes.

COMMENTS This white-tiled quick-service marketplace in the Sapphire Falls Resort lobby is far smaller than the food hall at Aventura next door, but it manages to pack a lot of options—including Cuban and grilled veggie sandwiches, tropical salads, specialty smoothies, and lattes blended with the house brew—into a small space. The eatery also doubles as a grab-and-go market for snacks and sundries, where you can secure s'mores kits for the pool's fire pit. About the only thing there isn't space for is seating, with only a handful of stools along a bar, so plan on eating on the run or bringing food back to your room. New Dutch Trading Co. opens at 6 a.m. for breakfast and stays open until 11 p.m., so you can refill the Coke Freestyle mugs available here (see page 222).

Pier 8 Market

LOCATION Dockside Inn   Too new to rate

SELECTIONS Hot breakfast sandwiches, chicken and waffles, fish-and-chips, deli sandwiches, pizza, pasta, pastries, frozen yogurt, and smoothies.

COMMENTS The sister cafeteria to Surfside Inn's Beachside Cafe has its own unique menu with similarly low prices, as well as a seaport-inspired layout featuring five grab-and-go serving windows that resemble open-air market stalls. Breakfast specialties include upscale items like avocado toast and Baja burritos, while the signature lunchtime entrée is a Dockworker Wrap filled with pastrami, Swiss cheese, coleslaw, and fries. Dinner offerings include whole pizzas, stuffed shells, and barbecue-bacon burgers. The best news is that you can have fried chicken and waffles in the morning with maple syrup, and again in the evening with hot sauce and mashed potatoes. Desserts include a panini-pressed s'mores sandwich, Key lime pie, and sugar-dusted zeppole. Dockside Inn also has a full-service Starbucks, an indoor Sunset Lounge lobby bar, and a poolside Oasis Beach Bar that serves drinks named after former Wet 'n Wild waterslides.

Sal's Market Deli

LOCATION Portofino Bay **QUALITY** Good-Excellent **VALUE** C+ **PORTION** Medium-Large
READER-SURVEY RESPONSES   94% 👍   6% 👎

SELECTIONS Pizza, calzones, deli sandwiches, salads, wine, and beer.

COMMENTS This casual counter-service deli and pizzeria is practically the only affordable option on Portofino Bay property. The pizza is the best in Universal outside of Red Oven and can be made with gluten-free dough. Around the corner, a full-service Starbucks with an attached *gelateria* and bakery serves breakfast and desserts. Food can be packaged and taken back to your room, undercutting the expensive room service.

Tuk Tuk Market

LOCATION Royal Pacific   **QUALITY** Good   **VALUE** B-   **PORTION** Medium
READER-SURVEY RESPONSES   71% 👍   29% 👎

SELECTIONS Hot and cold sandwiches, soups, salads, coffee, pastries, hand-scooped ice cream, and milkshakes.

COMMENTS This quick-service convenience store was added to the rear of Royal Pacific's lobby during the hotel's 2020 renovation. It makes it easy for hotel guests to grab a quick meal or snack on their way to and from the parks. The seating area is small but has a lovely view of the luau pavilion. In keeping with the resort's Pacific theme, the standard quick-service menu items—breakfast cereals and pastries, deli sandwiches and salads, pizzas and hot dogs—are supplemented by sushi rolls and stir-fry. If you have a sweet tooth, try the house-made dessert tarts or hand-scooped gelato. Starbucks coffee drinks, along with a selection of wines and liquors, are also served here; buy drinks during happy hour (daily, 3-6 p.m.) and get a free charcuterie platter.

Urban Pantry Food Hall *(temporarily closed)*

LOCATION Aventura	QUALITY Good	VALUE B	PORTION Medium-Large
READER-SURVEY RESPONSES	87% 👍	13% 👎	

SELECTIONS Burgers, pizzas, chicken, Asian dishes, salads, beer, and wine.

COMMENTS In lieu of a full-service restaurant, Aventura Hotel has a fast-casual food court off the main lobby. Inspired by big-city indoor markets, this next-generation food hall follows all the hip foodie trends: individual feeding stations, each with its own open kitchen and cash register, serving healthier and more diverse dining, in a minimalist industrial environment. Unfortunately, the pandemic pushed most of the more upscale items off the menu. In the morning, pancakes, scrambled eggs, and other American breakfast standards—along with Belgian waffles and fresh fruit—are served. For lunch and dinner, start at the stir-fry station for a bowl of beef or chicken lo mein. The burger station grills thick patties, either Black Angus beef, turkey, or the vegan Beyond meat substitute. The roast station serves chicken sandwiches and fish tacos, and pizzas can be topped with cheese or pepperoni. End your meal with a scoop of gelato or a shot glass–size cake. We've found food quality here to generally be above average, but we hear complaints from readers about the hall's confusing layout and slow service.

UNIVERSAL ORLANDO FULL-SERVICE RESTAURANT PROFILES

TO HELP YOU MAKE CHOICES FOR SIT-DOWN MEALS at breakfast, lunch, or dinner, we've provided full profiles of Universal's full-service restaurants, most of which are located in the CityWalk complex. Each profile lets you quickly check the restaurant's cuisine,

COVID *tip*

Table-service restaurants may limit seating capacity and operate on a reduced schedule. Select menu items may be unavailable.

location, star rating, cost range, quality rating, and value rating. Profiles are listed alphabetically by restaurant. In addition to all full-service restaurants, we also list and profile a few quick-service eateries around the resort that transcend basic burgers, hot dogs, and pizza.

STAR RATING

THE STAR RATING REPRESENTS THE ENTIRE DINING experience: style, service, and ambience, in addition to taste, presentation, and food quality. Five stars, the highest rating, indicates that the restaurant offers the best of everything. Four-star restaurants are above average, and three-star restaurants offer good, though not necessarily memorable, meals. Two-star restaurants serve mediocre fare, and one-star restaurants are below par. Our star ratings don't correspond to ratings awarded by AAA, Forbes, Zagat, or other restaurant reviewers.

COST RANGE

Inexpensive	under $15/person
Moderate	$15–$35/person
Expensive	over $35/person

THE NEXT RATING TELLS HOW MUCH an adult full-service entrée will cost. Appetizers, sides, desserts, drinks, taxes, and tips aren't included. We've rated the cost as inexpensive, moderate, or expensive.

QUALITY RATING

THE FOOD QUALITY IS RATED on a scale of one to five stars, five being the best. The quality rating is based on the taste, freshness of ingredients, preparation, presentation, and creativity of food. There is no consideration of price. If you want the best food available and cost is no issue, look no further than the quality ratings.

VALUE RATING

★★★★★	Exceptional value; a real bargain
★★★★	Good value
★★★	Fair value; you get exactly what you pay for
★★	Somewhat overpriced
★	Extremely overpriced

IF, ON THE OTHER HAND, you are looking for both quality *and* value, check the value rating, also expressed as stars:

PAYMENT

ALL UNIVERSAL ORLANDO RESTAURANTS accept American Express, MasterCard, Visa, Discover, Diners Club, and Universal Orlando Resort hotel-room charges.

Amatista Cookhouse ★★★ *(temporarily closed)*

CARIBBEAN	MODERATE	QUALITY ★★★	VALUE ★★★
READER-SURVEY RESPONSES	82% 👍	18% 👎	

Sapphire Falls Resort; ☎ 407-503-DINE (3463)

Customers Hotel guests. Reservations Accepted via OpenTable. When to go Breakfast or dinner. Entrée range $14–$38. Service rating ★★½. Friendliness rating ★★★. Parking $5 valet or free self-parking at hotel with validation. Bar Full service. Wine selection Modest. Dress Resort casual. Disabled access Good. Hours Closed at press time; previously, daily, 7–11 a.m., 11:30 a.m.–2:30 p.m., and 5–10 p.m.

SETTING AND ATMOSPHERE A large, sunny room on Sapphire Falls Resort's lower level features an exhibition kitchen and indoor–outdoor seating with a view of the hotel's lagoon. Seating is in the open main area or one of the private dining rooms.

HOUSE SPECIALTIES Buffet breakfast with waffles and smoked salmon; rotisserie chicken, flatbreads, and sandwiches for lunch; Caribbean seafood paella, chargrilled steak, and vegan curry for dinner.

SUMMARY AND COMMENTS Bright and clean, though a bit too big to be cozy, Amatista is the main table-service restaurant at Sapphire Falls and caters to families and conventioneers by serving comfort food favorites with an abundance of Caribbean creativity. We love the jerk-seasoned chicken wings, flaky empanadas, conch chowder, and juicy Angus burger. Ordering breakfast à la carte quickly adds up, so if you want more than a muffin, spring for

continued on page 245

UNIVERSAL ORLANDO RESTAURANTS BY CUISINE

CUISINE	LOCATION	OVERALL RATING	COST	QUALITY RATING	VALUE RATING
AMERICAN					
Bigfire	CITYWALK	★★★★	MOD	★★★★	★★★★
The Cowfish Sushi Burger Bar	CITYWALK	★★★★	MOD	★★★★	★★★½
Toothsome Chocolate Emporium & Savory Feast Kitchen	CITYWALK	★★★½	MOD	★★★★	★★★
The Kitchen	HARD ROCK HOTEL	★★★½	MOD	★★★½	★★★
Bar 17 Bistro	AVENTURA HOTEL	★★★½	MOD	★★★	★★★
Confisco Grille	ISLANDS OF ADVENTURE	★★★	MOD	★★★	★★★
Hard Rock Cafe	CITYWALK	★★★	MOD	★★★	★★★
Jimmy Buffett's Margaritaville	CITYWALK	★★★	MOD	★★★	★★★
NBC Sports Grill & Brew	CITYWALK	★★★	MOD	★★★	★★★½
Orchid Court Lounge & Sushi Bar	ROYAL PACIFIC RESORT	★★★	MOD-EXP	★★★	★★
Jake's American Bar	ROYAL PACIFIC RESORT	★★★	MOD	★★★	★★½
Galaxy Bowl	CABANA BAY BEACH RESORT	★★	INEXP	★★½	★★½
ASIAN					
Islands Dining Room	ROYAL PACIFIC RESORT	★★★½	MOD	★★★½	★★★
Wantilan Luau	ROYAL PACIFIC RESORT	★★★½	EXP	★★★½	★★★
Orchid Court Lounge & Sushi Bar	ROYAL PACIFIC RESORT	★★★	MOD-EXP	★★★	★★
BRITISH AND IRISH					
Leaky Cauldron	UNIVERSAL STUDIOS FLORIDA	★★★½	INEXP	★★★½	★★★★
Three Broomsticks	ISLANDS OF ADVENTURE	★★★	INEXP	★★★½	★★★
Finnegan's Bar & Grill	UNIVERSAL STUDIOS FLORIDA	★★★	MOD	★★★	★★★
CAJUN/SOUTHERN					
Pat O'Brien's Orlando	CITYWALK	★★★	INEXP	★★★½	★★★½
The Bubba Gump Shrimp Co. Restaurant & Market	CITYWALK	★★½	MOD	★★★	★★
CARIBBEAN/JAMAICAN					
Strong Water Tavern	SAPPHIRE FALLS RESORT	★★★½	MOD	★★★★	★★½
Amatista Cookhouse	SAPPHIRE FALLS RESORT	★★★	MOD	★★★	★★★
Jimmy Buffett's Margaritaville	CITYWALK	★★★	MOD	★★★	★★★
Bob Marley—A Tribute to Freedom	CITYWALK	★★½	INEXP	★★★	★★★

UNIVERSAL ORLANDO RESTAURANTS BY CUISINE

CUISINE	LOCATION	OVERALL RATING	COST	QUALITY RATING	VALUE RATING
ITALIAN					
Bice Ristorante	PORTOFINO BAY HOTEL	★★★★½	EXP	★★★★½	★★★★
Vivo Italian Kitchen	CITYWALK	★★★★	MOD	★★★★	★★★★½
Mama Della's Ristorante	PORTOFINO BAY HOTEL	★★★★	MOD-EXP	★★★★	★★★½
Red Oven Pizza Bakery	CITYWALK	★★★½	INEXP	★★★½	★★★★½
Trattoria del Porto	PORTOFINO BAY HOTEL	★★★	MOD	★★★	★★
MEXICAN					
Antojitos Authentic Mexican food	CITYWALK	★★★½	MOD	★★★½	★★★½
SEAFOOD					
The Cowfish Sushi Burger Bar	CITYWALK	★★★★	MOD	★★★★	★★★½
Mythos Restaurant	ISLANDS OF ADVENTURE	★★★½	MOD	★★★½	★★★★
Lombard's Seafood Grille	UNIVERSAL STUDIOS FLORIDA	★★★	MOD	★★★½	★★★
Orchid Court Lounge & Sushi Bar	ROYAL PACIFIC RESORT	★★★	MOD-EXP	★★★	★★
The Bubba Gump Shrimp Co. Restaurant & Market	CITYWALK	★★½	MOD	★★★	★★
STEAK					
Bigfire	CITYWALK	★★★★	MOD	★★★★	★★★★
The Palm	HARD ROCK HOTEL	★★★★	V. EXP	★★★★	★★½
Mythos Restaurant	ISLANDS OF ADVENTURE	★★★½	MOD	★★★½	★★★★
NBC Sports Grill & Brew	CITYWALK	★★★	MOD	★★★	★★★½

continued from page 243

the buffet (when available). Service, like that on the actual islands, is friendly but inconsistent; at lunch you may have the place all to yourself, but don't count on a quick dinner here if you're on a tight schedule.

Antojitos Authentic Mexican Food   ★★★½

MEXICAN   MODERATE   QUALITY ★★★½   VALUE ★★★½
READER-SURVEY RESPONSES 90% 👍 10% 👎

CityWalk; ☎ 407-224-FOOD (3663)

Customers Locals and tourists. Reservations Accepted via Zomato. When to go Dinner. Entrée range $13–$31. Service rating ★★★. Friendliness rating ★★★★. Parking Universal Orlando garage. Bar Full service. Wine selection Good. Dress Casual; *luchador* masks and sombreros optional. Disabled access Good. Hours Daily, 4–10 p.m.

SETTING AND ATMOSPHERE This festive postmodern tribute to Mexican street culture features a large open kitchen framed by graffiti graphics and eye-catching neon, with the central bar and surrounding booths fashioned from reclaimed wood and metal. The downstairs can get very noisy, so if you want a quieter meal, ask for one of the private rooms upstairs. Or grab a seat on the patio or balcony to watch the CityWalk crowds go by.

HOUSE SPECIALTIES Roasted corn casserole (*esquites*), quesadillas, enchiladas, tacos, fajitas, grilled salmon, churrasco steak, and flan.

ENTERTAINMENT A modern mariachi ensemble plays outside and inside Antojitos on select nights.

SUMMARY AND COMMENTS A Universal Studios concept, the colorful Antojitos offers unique and craveable tapas-style Mexican food, serving handcrafted tortillas, made-while-you-watch guacamole, and fresh sauces for a taste of Mexico City without the high crime rate.

For starters, you'll probably want a drink, and Antojitos has Orlando's best tequila selection this side of Epcot's La Cava. Order from the four-sided bar on the ground floor or from the converted Volkswagen bus outside the entrance. If you don't do straight shots, try a signature drink such as The Horse You Rode In On (garnished with an expensive Amarena black cherry).

When it comes to the food, while it's pricier than your local taco joint, Antojitos prepares familiar plates with exceptionally fresh ingredients. The table-side guacamole is a must-have that will convert the most hardened avocado-hater, and the *esquites* (roasted corn with cotija cheese and jalapeño mayo) is almost a meal in itself. The portion sizes of the enchiladas and tacos aren't enormous, but you'll probably be full after the free chips (served hot with house-made salsa) and the excellent rice and beans accompanying most entrées. The *comidas de la casa* include some holdovers from the short-lived upscale menu briefly served on the second floor; the churrasco steak and orange-marinated salmon are wonderfully seasoned.

Bar 17 Bistro ★ ★ ★ *(temporarily closed)*

AMERICAN	MODERATE		QUALITY ★ ★ ★	VALUE ★ ★ ★
READER-SURVEY RESPONSES	78% 👍	22% 👎		

Aventura Hotel; ☎ 407-503-6000

Customers Locals and hotel guests. Reservations Not accepted. When to go Dinner. Entrée range $7–$15. Service rating ★ ★ ★. Friendliness rating ★ ★ ★½. Parking Free self-parking at hotel with validation. Bar Full service. Wine selection Moderate. Dress Casual. Disabled access Good. Hours Closed at press time; previously, daily, 4–10 p.m.; bar open Sunday–Wednesday, 4 p.m.–midnight, and Thursday–Saturday, 4 p.m.–2 a.m.

SETTING AND ATMOSPHERE Located on the roof of the Aventura Hotel, Bar 17 Bistro boasts a better view than any watering hole at Walt Disney World, with 360-degree views of Universal Orlando—including Volcano Bay—and International Drive.

HOUSE SPECIALTIES Burgers, salads, fried rice, small plates, and tapas-style appetizers.

ENTERTAINMENT DJ on weekend evenings.

SUMMARY AND COMMENTS Even if you aren't staying at Aventura, you'll want to visit the hotel just to ride the dedicated elevator to the 17th floor and take in the picture-postcard panorama from the roof. But the carefully balanced craft cocktails and savory small plates of exotic flavors are what will make you want to linger at Bar 17 Bistro long past sunset.

Begin by picking one of the signature cocktails (Seth recommends the Japanese whisky-based Volcano View) or a draft craft beer. Next, order a couple of appetizers—like the Korean-style spicy fried chicken wings and international cheese plate—or a burger from the short selection of entrées.

A word of warning: Bar 17 Bistro's glorious open-air atmosphere includes complimentary exposure to wind and rain. In case of a severe storm, the entire establishment may temporarily shut down.

Bice Ristorante ★★★★½

ITALIAN	EXPENSIVE	QUALITY ★★★★½	VALUE ★★★★
READER-SURVEY RESPONSES 100% 👍 0% 👎			

Portofino Bay Hotel; ☎ 407-503-1415

Customers Locals and tourists. Reservations Recommended via OpenTable, in person, or over the phone. When to go Dinner. Entrée range $23–$48. Service rating ★★★★★. Friendliness rating ★★★★. Parking $5 valet or free self-parking at hotel with validation. Bar Full service. Wine selection Very good. Dress Resort dressy. Disabled access Good. Hours Daily, 5:30–9 p.m.

SETTING AND ATMOSPHERE Cedarwood and marble floors, crisp white linens, opulent flower arrangements, and waiters in black suits give Bice ("beachay") the feeling of a formal restaurant, but there is nothing stiff or fussy about the space or the staff. It's immaculately clean, beautifully lit, and relatively quiet even when crowded. Outdoor seating overlooking the bay is lovely on spring and fall evenings.

HOUSE SPECIALTIES The menu changes seasonally. Selections may include prosciutto with fresh melon and baby greens, homemade braised beef short rib ravioli in mushroom-Marsala sauce, veal Milanese with an arugula and cherry tomato salad, or risotto of the day.

ENTERTAINMENT Piano in bar.

SUMMARY AND COMMENTS This is part of a chain of very upscale and quite impressive restaurants found in New York, Tokyo, Las Vegas, and other international locales. The food is incredibly fresh, well prepared, and elegant, and the service is top-notch. But be prepared: Even a modest meal will put a dent in your wallet, and even though the food and service are definitely worth it, it may be too expensive for many vacationers. If you want to try a variety of things on the menu, split a salad, appetizer, or pasta dish between two people for a starter; portions are large enough for sharing, and the staff is more than happy to accommodate.

Our favorite appetizer is the fresh *burrata* mozzarella caprese. The other appetizers, mostly salads and antipasti of meats and cheeses, aren't bad, but you've probably had something similar already.

Among the best entrées is the breaded veal, which is pounded so thin that it takes up almost the entire plate. It's served with a small salad on top, and the salad's dressing keeps the veal juicy. The penne *all'arrabbiata* is even spicier than advertised.

We rate Bice as one of the best restaurants in all of Universal Orlando Resort, and it compares favorably to any of the similar restaurants at Walt Disney World. Because the Portofino gets a lot of business-convention traffic, it's probably easier to get a reservation at 5:30 p.m. than 7:30 p.m.

Bigfire ★★★★

AMERICAN/STEAK	EXPENSIVE	QUALITY ★★★★	VALUE ★★★★
READER-SURVEY RESPONSES	96% 👍	4% 👎	

CityWalk; ☎ 407-224-FOOD (3663)

Customers Locals and tourists. Reservations Accepted via Zomato. When to go Dinner. Entrée range $14–$39. Service rating ★★★★. Friendliness rating ★★★★. Parking Universal Orlando garage. Bar Full service. Wine selection Good. Dress Casual. Disabled access Good. Hours Thursday–Sunday, 4–10 p.m.; closed Monday–Wednesday (subject to change).

SETTING AND ATMOSPHERE Bigfire takes its aesthetic cues from tony lakeside summer homes, with blazing fire pits out front, stained shiplap and decorative oars on the walls, and a skeletal boat's hull dramatically suspended from the vaulted ceiling. Hard surfaces can make the downstairs noisy, so request a table on the upper floor overlooking the main dining room. Fortunately, a powerful ventilation system keeps the blazing open kitchen from overheating the hall. You can also eat at the beautiful white marble bar, which boasts its own hand-selected barrel of Woodford Reserve bourbon.

HOUSE SPECIALTIES Fresh baked bread with herb butter, charred Brussels sprouts, and roasted mussels to start off. Flame-grilled meats cooked over a custom blend of oak, pecan wood, and cherrywood is the menu's main focus. In addition to beef and pork, options include lamb, seafood, and vegetarian, as well as conventionally cooked entrées such as fried chicken, pasta, burgers, and salads.

ENTERTAINMENT Prerecorded playlist of baby boomer soft-rock classics from the 1960s and '70s.

SUMMARY AND COMMENTS Bigfire, which opened in the summer of 2019, had big shoes to fill taking over the former home of Emeril's Orlando, but it happily continues the trend set by Vivo and Toothsome of bringing fresh flavors at fair prices to CityWalk's reenergized restaurant lineup. The American Fare subtitle suggests even picky eaters will find something familiar on the menu, though the ingredients and preparations are head and shoulders above a T.G.I. Friday's-style chain restaurant. For beef eaters, Bigfire delivers the best bang for your buck on property; the Creekstone Farms cowboy rib eye is nearly as tender as the steaks served at The Palm but costs a third less and includes two sides (indulge in the mac and cheese with bits of pork belly). But don't have a cow if you don't eat cow; the grilled cauliflower steak is excellent, as are the beer-glazed jumbo scallops. For dessert, the tabletop s'mores for two are overpriced considering the vending machine components but are almost worth the entertainment value from flambéing marshmallows over a miniature campfire. Service is attentive and friendly but not as fussily formal as Emeril's was, making Bigfire feel comfortably balanced between fine and family dining.

Bob Marley—A Tribute to Freedom ★★½

JAMAICAN/CARIBBEAN	INEXPENSIVE	QUALITY ★★★	VALUE ★★★
READER-SURVEY RESPONSES	70% 👍	30% 👎	

CityWalk; ☎ 407-224-FOOD (3663)

Customers Locals and tourists. Reservations Accepted via Zomato. When to go Early evening. Entrée range $12–$22. Service rating ★★. Friendliness rating ★★★. Parking Universal Orlando garage. Bar Full service. Wine selection Poor. Dress Casual.

Disabled access Good. Hours Thursday–Sunday, 4–10 p.m.; closed Monday–Wednesday (subject to change).

SETTING AND ATMOSPHERE Set in a replica of reggae singer Bob Marley's Jamaican home, the building is filled with memorabilia and photos showcasing his career and life. Lots of lions, the colors of the Jamaican flag, and other Rastafarian influences pay tribute to the musician's career. Most of the area is open to the elements, and there's no air-conditioning, though there are shelters from the occasional rainstorm.

HOUSE SPECIALTIES Jerk-marinated chicken breast; smoky white-Cheddar cheese fondue; Jamaican beef or vegetable patties; yucca fries; oxtail stew.

ENTERTAINMENT Live reggae band and DJ in courtyard nightly; cover charge after 10 p.m.

SUMMARY AND COMMENTS None of the food is spectacular or particularly adventurous, but it's worth a visit for the laid-back atmosphere. Feel free to get up and dance.

The Bubba Gump Shrimp Co. Restaurant & Market ★★½

SOUTHERN/SEAFOOD	MODERATE	QUALITY ★★★	VALUE ★★
READER-SURVEY RESPONSES	83% 👍	17% 👎	

CityWalk; ☎ 407-903-0044

Customers Tourists. Reservations Not accepted; waiting list available via Yelp. When to go Anytime. Entrée range $13–$34. Service rating ★★★. Friendliness rating ★★★★. Parking Universal Orlando garage. Bar Full service. Wine selection Minimal. Dress Casual. Disabled access Good. Hours Daily, 11 a.m.–8 p.m. (subject to change).

SETTING AND ATMOSPHERE The movie that inspired the chain, *Forrest Gump,* plays on TVs throughout but without sound, just closed-captioning. Movie memorabilia decorates the wooden walls of this seafood shanty. License plates that say RUN FORREST RUN on one side and STOP FORREST STOP on another help signal a waiter when you need service, and waiters may ask you trivia questions from the movie.

HOUSE SPECIALTIES Fried, stuffed, or grilled shrimp (and shrimp cooked almost every other way); burgers; salads; grilled salmon; fried chicken; baby back ribs. A gluten-free menu is also offered.

SUMMARY AND COMMENTS The theme may seem a little cheesy, but this is a fun and festive atmosphere to bring the kids. The food is no worse than your average seafood chain (think Red Lobster without the cheese biscuits) and is not too spicy.

Confisco Grille ★★★

AMERICAN	MODERATE	QUALITY ★★★	VALUE ★★★
READER-SURVEY RESPONSES	83% 👍	17% 👎	

Islands of Adventure, Port of Entry; ☎ 407-224-4406

Customers Park guests. Reservations Accepted via Zomato. When to go Anytime. Entrée range $14–$21. Service rating ★★★. Friendliness rating ★★★★. Parking Universal Orlando garage. Bar Full service. Wine selection Moderate. Dress Casual. Disabled access Good. Hours Daily, noon–6 p.m. (varies with park closing).

SETTING AND ATMOSPHERE A way station on the road to Morocco, perhaps? Actually, it's meant to look like a customs house. Look for "smuggled goods," representing the park's various islands, decorating the lobby's upper level.

You'll see giant dinosaur skeletons from Jurassic Park, golden urns from the Lost Continent, and even a wand from The Wizarding World of Harry Potter if you look hard enough.

HOUSE SPECIALTIES Sweet and sour chicken wings or smoked ribs; hummus served with a puffy lavash bread larger than most human heads; selection of salads; grilled sandwiches and burgers; pad Thai.

SUMMARY AND COMMENTS Confisco isn't fine dining, but it does fine when you just can't stand in another line. Because of its varied menu of Mediterranean, Italian, Mexican, and Asian dishes, most people should find something to please them at Confisco Grille. More adventurous options include Philippine-style sticky ribs, chilled soba noodle bowls with seared tuna sashimi, and a pork belly banh mi. Several menu items can be made vegetarian and vegan friendly, and annual pass holders get exclusive use of the upstairs dining rooms during select seasons. The adjoining Backwater Bar is a good spot to grab a cool sangria on a hot day.

The Cowfish Sushi Burger Bar ★★★★

AMERICAN/SUSHI	MODERATE	QUALITY ★★★★	VALUE ★★★½
READER-SURVEY RESPONSES	86% 👍	14% 👎	

CityWalk; ☎ 407-224-2690

Customers Locals and park guests. Reservations Accepted via Zomato. When to go Early afternoon or late evening. Entrée range $12–$28. Service rating ★★½. Friendliness rating ★★★★. Parking Universal Orlando garage. Bar Full service. Wine selection Good. Dress Resort casual. Disabled access Good. Hours Thursday–Sunday, 4–10 p.m.; closed Monday–Wednesday (subject to change).

SETTING AND ATMOSPHERE A photo op of this restaurant's mascot—a giant bug-eyed fish with a saddle on its back—should clue you in that this isn't the spot for stuffy food snobs. The Cowfish features colorful Pop Art, larger-than-life displays (including King Kong and a noodle-filled fishbowl), and silly signage—be sure to check out the restrooms. Guests can enter though the small lobby on the ground floor or the patio bar on the upper level; all seating—both indoors and out—is on the second and third floors, offering spectacular views over CityWalk.

Aside from table seating, there are multiple bars at Cowfish. Young children will enjoy the touch screen games and a make-your-own-fish app, which you can then watch swim in a virtual aquarium.

HOUSE SPECIALTIES Crab Rangoon dip, blackened tuna nachos, half-pound burgers, sushi and sashimi combos, fusion and Burgushi rolls and bento boxes, hand-spun milkshakes, specialty cocktails, and spiked shakes.

SUMMARY AND COMMENTS A one-of-a-kind dining concept that melds pan-Asian cuisine with the good ol' American burger, Cowfish brings something completely unique to the table. Like peanut butter and chocolate, The Cowfish's burgers and sushi both taste great, and taste great together.

The voluminous menu starts with familiar-sounding appetizers, such as Parmesan bacon truffle fries and tuna nachos, expertly prepared and presented in generous portions (a recurring theme). Next comes an extensive list of half-pound hormone-free hamburgers, with names such as the Jalapeño Popper Show-Stopper, Big Squeal, and Rise & Swine. Veggie and turkey burgers are also available, and all are served with seasoned fries, which can be substituted with seaweed salad, bacon coleslaw, or edamame. The

Boursin Bacon Burger, with garlic-herb cheese and sautéed mushrooms, is a standout. Traditional sushi selections range from chef combos of sashimi and *nigiri*, classic makimono rolls, and fusion specialties stuffed with tuna, coconut shrimp, shiitake mushrooms, or crabmeat; the premium tuna and salmon on Jen's Fresh Find roll is particularly flavorful.

Finally, we arrive at the creative center of Cowfish's menu: the Burgushi. You can try a sushi roll made with lobster and filet mignon (The Prime Time), Angus beef and applewood bacon (The Taste Explosion), or pulled pork and barbecue sauce (High Class Hillbilly). Despite the bizarro pairing, all the ones we've sampled (with the exception of the What's Shakin' Tuna Bacon Sandwich) have been as delicious as they are odd, which is saying something. Doug's Filet Roll (with ginger dipping sauce for the steak) is a safe bet. If you're still apprehensive, try a bento box, which brings a slider mini-burger, sushi roll, and several side dishes together on a Japanese TV dinner tray.

The extensive craft cocktail list includes a bourbon and candied bacon concoction and old-fashioned mules. Hand-spun milkshakes (nonalcoholic or spiked) headline the dessert menu, which also features sushi-shaped pastries exclusive to the Orlando location.

We love the overall atmosphere, but the time it takes for a meal to come out can be painfully slow because the kitchen is undersized for the multistory dining rooms. The wait can be long on a busy weekend, but the host will take your cell phone number when you check in, allowing them to text you when your table is ready.

Finnegan's Bar & Grill ★★★

IRISH MODERATE QUALITY ★★★ VALUE ★★★
READER-SURVEY RESPONSES 83% 👍 17% 👎

Universal Studios Florida, New York; ☎ 407-363-8757

Customers Park guests. Reservations Accepted via Zomato. When to go Anytime. Entrée range $15-$26. Service rating ★★★. Friendliness rating ★★★★. Parking Universal Orlando garage. Bar Full service. Wine selection Limited. Ireland isn't really known for its wines; good beer selection, though. Dress Casual. Disabled access Good. Hours Daily, 11 a.m.–6 p.m. (varies with park closing).

SETTING AND ATMOSPHERE Fashioned after an Irish bar in New York City, albeit one built as a movie set. Along with the requisite publike accoutrements—such as the tin ceiling and belt-driven paddle fans—are movie lights and half walls that suggest the back of scenery flats. Obligatory references to Guinness beer and New York City abound. The bar area is a popular gathering spot for locals and gets insanely busy during special events like Halloween Horror Nights.

HOUSE SPECIALTIES Shepherd's pie; fish-and-chips; Guinness beef stew; bangers and mash; Kilkenny chicken potpie; Irish coffee.

ENTERTAINMENT Singer/guitarist in the bar.

SUMMARY AND COMMENTS The food is modest, but the entertainment is fun and the beer is cold. Brew fans can happily explore a five-sample flight of international ales as they rest from the park. Add to that the fact that this is one of only two full-service spots in USF, and the average pub fare starts to look a bit more attractive.

The fish-and-chips, which come wrapped in "newspaper," are about the same as those served in The Wizarding World. The shepherd's pie is bland, but the potato-leek soup is good, and the fried potato-onion "web" is addictive. For entrées, burgers, sandwiches, salads, and Guinness stew are safe choices.

Galaxy Bowl ★★

AMERICAN	INEXPENSIVE	QUALITY ★★½	VALUE ★★½
READER-SURVEY RESPONSES 80% 👍 20% 👎			

Cabana Bay Beach Resort; ☎ 407-503-4230

Customers Hotel guests. Reservations Not accepted. When to go Early afternoon or late evening. Entrée range $9–$14. Service rating ★★. Friendliness rating ★★★. Parking Universal Orlando garage or $45 for self-parking at hotel. Bar Full service. Wine selection Limited. Dress Casual. Disabled access Good. Hours Daily, 5–11 p.m. (bar and bowling until midnight).

SETTING AND ATMOSPHERE Galaxy Bowl, on the second floor of the main Cabana Bay building directly above Starbucks, is the only full-service dining option inside the hotel. The 10-lane bowling alley is inspired by Hollywood Star Lanes, made famous in the film *The Big Lebowski.* The lanes are illuminated in trippy colors at night, and large projection screens broadcast sporting events.

HOUSE SPECIALTIES Cheese sticks, chicken wings, salads, sandwiches, burgers, and fried fish.

ENTERTAINMENT Bowling costs $16.99 for adults, $10.99 for kids age 12 and under, including shoe rental; during select times, everyone pays the kids' price. Parties of one to three people get 45 minutes of lane time; four to eight people get 75 minutes.

SUMMARY AND COMMENTS Some people enjoy the athleticism of basketball, while others admire the grace and skill of soccer, but we at the Unofficials favor bowling, as it's the only one in which you can participate while eating chili-cheese fries. Galaxy Bowl has several tables where you can enjoy a meal, but you can also order snacks and drinks while enjoying a game of bowling. When the wait for a lane grows long (as it often does on rainy days), ask for a table, and order drinks and appetizers until your turn arrives.

The limited menu offers fast-food selections similar to items served downstairs in the Bayliner Diner, and quality is about on par for greasy bowling alley grub. Draft beer is served in pitchers, and the list of specialty drinks is nearly as long as the food menu. There are two Coke Freestyle machines at Galaxy Bowl for your Sonic Fill mugs. If you want the alcohol without the ambience of falling pins, the hotel lobby's Swizzle Lounge (Friday–Saturday, 4 p.m.–midnight; hours subject to change) serves craft beers and classic cocktails.

Hard Rock Cafe ★★★

AMERICAN	MODERATE	QUALITY ★★★	VALUE ★★★
READER-SURVEY RESPONSES 87% 👍 13% 👎			

CityWalk; ☎ 407-351-7625

Customers Tourists. Reservations Accepted at hardrockcafe.com/location/orlando or via OpenTable. When to go Afternoon or evening. Entrée range $17–$34. Service rating ★★★. Friendliness rating ★★. Parking Universal Orlando garage. Bar Full service. Wine selection Moderate. Dress Casual. Disabled access Good. Hours Daily, 11 a.m.–10 p.m. (subject to change).

SETTING AND ATMOSPHERE This is the biggest Hard Rock Cafe in the world (or in the Universe, as they like to say in this part of town). Shaped like the Roman Coliseum, the two-story dining room is a massive museum of rock art memorabilia. The circular center bar features a full-size pink 1959 Cadillac spinning overhead. If you need to be told that this is a noisy restaurant, you've never been to a Hard Rock Cafe before.

HOUSE SPECIALTIES Barbecue pork sandwich, charbroiled burgers, barbecue ribs, New York strip steak, hot fudge brownie, and milkshakes.

ENTERTAINMENT Rock-and-roll records and memorabilia, the biggest such collection on display anywhere in the Hard Rock chain. Ask at the check-in podium about free guided Vibe tours of the restaurant; if you're lucky, you may get a glimpse of the VIP-only John Lennon Room upstairs.

SUMMARY AND COMMENTS The best meals we've had here are when we order only appetizers (try the spicy Bangkok shrimp) or only desserts, and drinks. The entrées are average, and you'd be hard-pressed to differentiate them from anything you'd get at, say, Margaritaville. For vegans, the Impossible plant-based burger is nearly indistinguishable from the real thing. We like sitting at the bar, where service can be slow, but the snarky bartenders provide plenty of entertainment.

Hard Rock Cafe offers a 15% discount on food for Preferred and Premier Annual Pass holders and military personnel with ID; 10% AAA discounts also apply. You can sign up for a Hard Rock Rewards membership at members .hardrock.com to get additional offers and earn points on purchases (including alcohol). Be aware that admission to the adjoining Hard Rock Live concert hall is completely separate from the restaurant, though you can sometimes order food from the venue's bar.

Islands Dining Room ★★★½

PAN-ASIAN	MODERATE	QUALITY ★★★½	VALUE ★★★
READER-SURVEY RESPONSES 88% 👍	13% 👎		

Royal Pacific Resort; ☎ 407-503-3410

Customers Hotel guests. Reservations Accepted via OpenTable. When to go Breakfast or dinner. Entrée range Breakfast, $13–$17; dinner, $18–$38. Service rating ★★★. Friendliness rating ★★★. Parking Free self-parking at hotel with validation. Bar Full service. Wine selection Average. Dress Casual. Disabled access Good. Hours Monday–Tuesday, 7–11 a.m. and 6–10 p.m.; Wednesday–Saturday, 7 a.m.–10 p.m.; Sunday, 7 a.m.–noon.

SETTING AND ATMOSPHERE Pretty standard hotel dining room; big and open, and always spotless.

HOUSE SPECIALTIES Breakfast features waffles with mixed berries, Tahitian French toast à l'orange, and pancakes. Dinner options include stir-fry, vegetarian lo mein, honey-glazed salmon, and Korean bulgogi-style rib eye.

SUMMARY AND COMMENTS Breakfast here is a treat—the specialties are all tasty and (surprisingly) moderately priced. Dinner is good too, but with all the other restaurants around, especially if you're spending the day in the parks, we suggest having a hearty breakfast here and an evening meal elsewhere.

Jake's American Bar ★★★

AMERICAN	MODERATE	QUALITY ★★★	VALUE ★★½
READER-SURVEY RESPONSES 82% 👍	18% 👎		

Royal Pacific Resort; ☎ 407-503-DINE (3463)

Customers Hotel guests. Reservations Accepted via OpenTable. When to go Early or late evening. Entrée range $14–$38. Service rating ★★★. Friendliness rating ★★★.

Parking Free self-parking at hotel with validation. Bar Full service. Wine selection Average. Dress Resort casual. Disabled access Good. Hours Daily, 11 a.m.–midnight.

SETTING AND ATMOSPHERE Run-of-the-mill hotel bar and restaurant with a vaguely 1930s "Rick's Cafe" feel. The menu explains the backstory of Captain Jake McNally and his association with Royal Pacific Airways, continuing the overall theme of the resort, which centers on the golden age of travel.

HOUSE SPECIALTIES Homemade pretzel rods, hot wings, Mediterranean meze platter, pizzas, rib eye and *frites,* salmon with wild rice, and grilled tomato-and-mozzarella sandwich.

ENTERTAINMENT Live music on select nights (temporarily suspended at press time).

SUMMARY AND COMMENTS This is a viable option if you're staying in the hotel, but as far as special meals go, this place doesn't deliver—and really isn't meant to.

Beer lovers will want to check out the four-sample flights, as well as the five-course pairing parties held on select nights (visit tinyurl.com/jakesbeer for Jake's Beer Dinner schedule). Jake's serves a limited late-night menu and is usually the only table-service restaurant at the resort serving hot food after 10 p.m.

Jimmy Buffett's Margaritaville ★★★

CARIBBEAN/AMERICAN	MODERATE	QUALITY ★★★	VALUE ★★★
READER-SURVEY RESPONSES	84% 👍	16% 👎	

CityWalk; ☎ 407-224-2155

Customers Local and tourist Parrot Heads. Reservations Accepted via Zomato. When to go Early evening. Entrée range $16–$29. Service rating ★★★. Friendliness rating ★★★★. Parking Universal Orlando garage. Bar Full service. Wine selection Minimal. Dress Floral shirts and flip-flops. Disabled access Good. Hours Daily, 11 a.m.–10 p.m. (subject to change).

SETTING AND ATMOSPHERE A boisterous tribute to the chief Parrot Head, this two-story dining space has many large-screen TVs playing Jimmy Buffett music videos and scenes from his live performances. The focal point is a volcano that erupts occasionally, spewing margarita mix instead of lava.

HOUSE SPECIALTIES Cheeseburgers and margaritas, of course; volcano nachos; fish tacos; jambalaya; coconut shrimp; Key lime pie.

ENTERTAINMENT Live music on the porch early; band on inside stage late evening.

SUMMARY AND COMMENTS This is a relaxing, festive place, but it's not always worth the wait (especially if it's 2 hours, which it's been known to be). This place is wildly popular with Jimmy Buffett fans, who stand in line just to get on the wait list, so they can stand in line some more and wait for a table. The atmosphere, though, is like a taste of the beach without having to travel to the coast.

The food is a mix of Floridian and Caribbean, so expect lots of seafood and Jamaican seasoning. The food is good, but not good enough for non-Buffett fans to make a special trip. If the line for a table is outrageous, see if you can sidle up to the bar for a margarita and appetizers, which is just as much—if not more—fun than actually having a full meal. None of the entrées, including the cheeseburger, will make you think you're in paradise, but fans don't seem to care.

The Lone Palm Airport tiki bar across from the restaurant (home to Buffett's seaplane, the *Hemisphere Dancer*) is a great place to sit back with a drink and people-watch on CityWalk.

The Kitchen ★★★½

AMERICAN	MODERATE	QUALITY ★★★½	VALUE ★★★
READER-SURVEY RESPONSES	80% 👍	20% 👎	

Hard Rock Hotel; ☎ 407-503-2430

Customers Tourists. Reservations Recommended via OpenTable. When to go Breakfast or dinner. Entrée range $15–$39. Service rating ★★★. Friendliness rating ★★★★. Parking $5 valet or free self-parking at hotel with validation. Bar Full service. Wine selection Good. Dress Casual. Disabled access Good. Hours Daily, 7-10 p.m. (may vary seasonally).

SETTING AND ATMOSPHERE With the appearance of a spacious kitchen in a rock megastar's mansion, The Kitchen features walls adorned with culinary-themed memorabilia from the Hard Rock Hotel's many celebrity guests. A colorful "kids' crib" adorned with beanbag chairs and TVs allows the adults to eat in peace.

HOUSE SPECIALTIES Breakfast choices include eggs Benedict, spinach-and-sausage frittata, and custom omelets. The lunch menu has salads, burgers, flatbreads, three-cheese mac and cheese, and chicken potpie. At dinner, grilled Antarctic salmon, filet mignon, shrimp penne, and stir-fried rice cauliflower are served. A gluten-free menu is available.

ENTERTAINMENT Rock stars occasionally visit to cook their specialties at the Chef's Table, so call ahead to see if any rock stars will be in the kitchen—you may find yourself having dinner with Joan Jett or Bob Seger. Signed aprons and rock memorabilia hang on the walls. A magician performs table-side on Wednesdays and Fridays, 6-9 p.m. On Tuesdays and Thursdays at Kids Can Cook, kids create their own pizzas or quesadillas 5-7 p.m. For adults, wine and martini specials Sunday–Thursday (5 p.m.–close) offer discounted flights and bottles. (All entertainment and events were temporarily suspended at press time.)

SUMMARY AND COMMENTS Though we must admit our expectations weren't too high for this Hard Rock venture, we were pleasantly surprised with the food and service here. Though expensive, the food is actually quite good, and the setting is pretty fun. The half-pound Angus beef burger will set you back about $18 but is quite tasty. Brave and/or crazy souls can take part in the Kitchen Sink Challenge, which consists of eating the burger, a pound of fries, a fried pickle, and the humongous Kitchen Sink Cake within a 30-minute time limit (advance reservations required). If dinner is a little out of your price range but you still want the experience, visit at lunchtime or go for the $23 family-style breakfast ($14 for kids ages 10-14, $13 for ages 3-9, and free for those under 3; 7-11 a.m.), which includes pancakes or French toast, plus scrambled eggs, bacon and sausage, and cinnamon rolls.

Leaky Cauldron ★★★½ *(Mobile Ordering)*

BRITISH	INEXPENSIVE	QUALITY ★★★½	VALUE ★★★★
READER-SURVEY RESPONSES	94% 👍	6% 👎	

Universal Studios Florida, The Wizarding World of Harry Potter–Diagon Alley; ☎ 407-224-4233

Customers Park guests. Reservations Breakfast only. When to go Early or late. Entrée range $11–$22. Service rating ★★★. Friendliness rating ★★★★. Parking Universal Orlando garage. Bar Beer, wine, and Fire Whisky. Wine selection Limited. Dress Casual. Disabled access Good. Hours Daily, park opening–park closing.

SETTING AND ATMOSPHERE Modeled after the Leaky Cauldron in the Harry Potter books and films, this table-service restaurant is the flagship diner of Diagon Alley. A haunt of wizards, Leaky Cauldron was located outside The Wizarding World on Charing Cross Road in the novels and movies but is located inside Diagon Alley in the Universal Studios version. (You can find a non-opening replica of the pub door from the original film just outside Diagon Alley, tucked between the bookstore and record shop.) To get a sense of what the restaurant looks like, check out "Prisoner of Azkaban—The Leaky Cauldron" on youtube.com.

HOUSE SPECIALTIES For breakfast, English bacon, black pudding, baked beans, and grilled tomato; pancakes with bacon; and an egg, leek, and mushroom pasty with breakfast potatoes. Lunch and dinner selections include bangers and mash, cottage pie, toad-in-the-hole, Guinness stew, fish-and-chips, shepherd's pie, and a ploughman's platter for two of Scotch eggs and imported cheeses.

SUMMARY AND COMMENTS Diagon Alley's flagship restaurant, the Leaky Cauldron serves hearty British pub fare similar to that of Three Broomsticks but with even more authentically Anglo favorites. You can reserve breakfast by booking through your travel agent or the Ticket Center at your Universal Resort hotel; walk-ins for day guests are also usually available. The morning menu costs $17.99 plus tax for adults ($12.99 for kids) with a small drink and has a similar mix of American and British breakfast foods to Three Broomsticks. The breakfast is fair at best; the blood sausage and beans aren't bad if you have a taste for them, but the scrambled eggs are awful, and the oatmeal is outrageously overpriced, making the quichelike mushroom pasty your best bet. And yes, you can have hot or cold Butterbeer for breakfast. If you want to eat breakfast here, buy it with the Quick-Service Dining Plan for maximum value, and do it as late in the morning as possible; your early-entry time is better spent exploring Diagon Alley or riding Harry Potter and the Escape from Gringotts.

The star of the lunch and dinner menu is the ploughman's platter for two, with an array of gloriously stinky imported cheeses. The bangers are also bang on, whether ordered with mash, in a sandwich, or (best of all) baked into a toad-in-the-hole with Yorkshire pudding. The fish-and-chips are the same as those served in Hogsmeade, as is the soup and salad (which isn't vegan). The fisherman's pie is extremely salty, as is the Guinness stew, which comes in a nearly inedible bread bowl. Top off your meal with chocolate or Butterbeer potted cream or sticky toffee pudding for dessert. Children's menu items include macaroni and cheese, fish-and-chips, and mini meat pies (for your budding *Sweeney Todd* enthusiast).

Leaky Cauldron can be overwhelmed by Diagon Alley crowds. To avoid long waits, eat early or late.

Lombard's Seafood Grille   ★★★

SEAFOOD	MODERATE	QUALITY ★★★½	VALUE ★★★
READER-SURVEY RESPONSES	93% 👍	7% 👎	

Universal Studios Florida, San Francisco; ☎ 407-224-3613

Customers Park guests. Reservations Recommended via Zomato. When to go Anytime. Entrée range $16–$29. Service rating ★★★. Friendliness rating ★★★. Parking Universal Orlando garage. Bar Full service. Wine selection Good. Dress Casual. Disabled access Good. Hours Monday–Thursday, noon–3 p.m.; Friday–Sunday, 11 a.m.–5 p.m. (may vary with park hours).

SETTING AND ATMOSPHERE Situated on the park's main lagoon, Lombard's looks like a converted wharf-side warehouse. The centerpiece of the brick-walled room is a huge aquarium with bubble glass windows, and a fish-sculpture fountain greets guests. Private dining rooms upstairs have balconies that overlook the park.

HOUSE SPECIALTIES Shrimp cocktail, mahi-mahi tacos, fried fisherman's basket, lobster roll, filet mignon, and fresh fish.

SUMMARY AND COMMENTS This is USF's San Francisco–inspired seafood restaurant, where the emphasis is on deep-fried favorites and daily fresh fish specials. Lombard's has a more casual focus, and unfortunately, so does the kitchen. The New England clam chowder is a standout, and the lobster roll is loaded with tender tail and knuckle meat, but the tuna poké is oddly salsa-like with its tomato-heavy garnish. Stick to the grilled or fried fish, and you should be safe. There are arguably better food options in the park, but as one of only two full-service restaurants inside USF, it's your best choice for a quiet meal.

With two floors of seating, it's generally easy to get a table, even during the busier times. Only annual pass holders can request to dine upstairs during select seasons.

Mama Della's Ristorante ★★★★

ITALIAN	MODERATE-EXPENSIVE	QUALITY ★★★★	VALUE ★★★½
READER-SURVEY RESPONSES	93% 👍 7% 👎		

Portofino Bay Hotel; ☎ 407-503-1432

Customers Hotel guests. Reservations Recommended via OpenTable. When to go Dinner. Entrée range $20–$38. Service rating ★★★★. Friendliness rating ★★★★. Parking $5 valet or free self-parking at hotel with validation. Bar Full service. Wine selection Good. Dress Nice casual. Disabled access Good. Hours Daily, 5:30–10 p.m.

SETTING AND ATMOSPHERE Just like being in the dining room of a Tuscan home, with hardwood floors, Provincial printed wallpaper, and wooden furniture. Check out the collection of chicken-themed tchotchkes on the walls.

HOUSE SPECIALTIES Veal picatta, pan-seared branzino, filet mignon with truffled potatoes, and lasagna.

ENTERTAINMENT Strolling musicians perform Italian American standards on select evenings.

SUMMARY AND COMMENTS This restaurant falls on the fancy scale somewhere between Bice and Trattoria del Porto. Traditional Italian food is served in a comfortable atmosphere conducive to a special meal but not quite as extravagant as its lavish neighbor, Bice. If you want food (almost) as tasty but for (a bit) less dough, Mama Della's is a great choice.

Mythos Restaurant ★★★½

STEAK/SEAFOOD	MODERATE	QUALITY ★★★½	VALUE ★★★★
READER-SURVEY RESPONSES	93% 👍 7% 👎		

Islands of Adventure, The Lost Continent; ☎ 407-224-4012

Customers Park guests. Reservations Recommended via Zomato. When to go Early evening. Entrée range $14–$36. Service rating ★★★½. Friendliness rating ★★★. Parking Universal Orlando garage. Bar Full service. Wine selection Good. Dress Casual. Disabled access Good. Hours Daily, 11 a.m.–5 p.m. or later; call ahead for closing time.

SETTING AND ATMOSPHERE A grottolike atmosphere suggests that you're eating in a cave. Large picture windows, framed by water cascading down from waterfalls on top of the restaurant, look out over the central lagoon to The Incredible Hulk Coaster. You can time your meal by coaster launchings.

HOUSE SPECIALTIES Fried calamari, meze platter, Greek salad, pan-roasted salmon, blue cheese–crusted pork, beef medallions, grilled cheese sandwich, Moroccan-spiced lamb chops, and seasonal risotto.

SUMMARY AND COMMENTS Outside the restaurant is a sign proclaiming that Mythos was voted WORLD'S BEST THEME PARK RESTAURANT by visitors to the website themeparkinsider.com, an honor it has earned seven times, most recently in 2019.

The food is well above average for theme park eats, and the setting provides a pleasant retreat. The spanakopita dip isn't far off from T.G.I. Friday's spinach dip, but the meze platter and deep-fried shrimp sushi roll are satisfying. Your best bets among the entrées are the cranberry pork chop (one of Seth's favorite entrées on property); a bacon cheeseburger; the Fork, Knife and Spoon Grilled Cheese (Derek Burgan's recommendation); or the seasonal mushroom risotto. A Big Apple–based friend of the *Unofficial Guide* had this to say:

> *I had a beautiful piece of salmon at Mythos, and while the theme left something to be desired, everything it served was on par with what I would expect at a decent New York restaurant.*

Make an early reservation if you want to dine here on a busy day. During off-season, Mythos may close before dinnertime, as this reader discovered:

> *We were disappointed to find out that Mythos closed at 5 when the park closed at 7 p.m. Due to its popularity, only the Harry Potter area remained completely open until 7 p.m.*

NBC Sports Grill & Brew ★ ★ ★

AMERICAN/STEAK	MODERATE	QUALITY ★ ★ ★	VALUE ★ ★ ★½
READER-SURVEY RESPONSES	82% 👍	18% 👎	

CityWalk; ☎ 407-224-FOOD (3663)

Customers Sports fans. Reservations Accepted via Zomato. When to go When the game is on. Entrée range $13–$30. Service rating ★★★. Friendliness rating ★★★½. Parking Universal Orlando garage. Bar Full service; more than 100 beers. Wine selection Average. Dress Casual. Disabled access Good. Hours Daily, 4–10 p.m. (subject to change).

SETTING AND ATMOSPHERE NBC Sports Grill & Brew has nearly 100 big-screen TVs, so guests will have no problem ignoring their tablemates to watch the latest game. The decor is intended to evoke a luxury skybox (though it's more like sports bar industrial with dark concrete floors and exposed duct-work ceilings painted black), and the central show kitchen contains a signature open-flame kettle grill. Sadly, the giant steel fermenting tanks are only for show, as no brewing takes place on the premises. Bonus: Some dining tables are playable games (such as Foosball) with glass tops for the food. The exterior is distinguished by a supersize video screen that broadcasts games to all of CityWalk; during major events (like the Olympics), bleachers may be erected outside for alfresco viewing.

HOUSE SPECIALTIES Nachos, wraps, grilled wings, flatbreads, salads, ribs, steaks, and burgers.

SUMMARY AND COMMENTS With a large selection of burgers and beers, NBC Sports Grill & Brew is the go-to place at Universal to catch the latest game. The menu is surprisingly deep, and the open kitchen concept allows you to see the chefs in action. Beer lovers will be drawn to the large variety of selections (more than 100), including two brewed exclusively for the restaurant by Florida Beer Company, and a fresh firkin-contained ale that's hand-pumped from the cask.

As for the food, it's decent but not especially memorable. The grilled chicken wings are underwhelming, but the steaks and fresh fish sandwich are unexpectedly excellent, and the monster soft pretzel (served on its own stand with mustard and queso) has a cult following. Otherwise, stick to burgers and beer. On Monday–Wednesday a limited bar bites menu, featuring drinks and appetizers but no entrées, is served.

Orchid Court Lounge & Sushi Bar ★★★

AMERICAN/ASIAN/SUSHI	MODERATE-EXPENSIVE		QUALITY ★★★	VALUE ★★
READER-SURVEY RESPONSES	75% 👍	25% 👎		

Royal Pacific Resort; ☎ 407-503-3200

Customers Hotel guests. Reservations Not accepted. When to go Early or late evening. Entrée range $12–$75. Service rating ★★★. Friendliness rating ★★★. Parking Free self-parking at hotel with validation. Bar Full service. Wine selection Average, but an excellent sake selection. Dress Resort casual. Disabled access Good. Hours Thursday–Sunday, 5 p.m.–midnight.

SETTING AND ATMOSPHERE Located on the lobby level of the Royal Pacific Resort with gorgeous views of the pool and central reflecting fountain, the Orchid Court Lounge was recently refurbished, replacing the heavy hand-carved Balinese furnishings with cooler, more contemporary colors. In the center of the lounge, you'll find a chandelier-crowned bar with both liquor and traditional sushi in see-through cases. Surrounding the four-sided bar, clusters of couches and armchairs form cozy seating areas.

HOUSE SPECIALTIES The sushi bar offers miso soup, seaweed salad, edamame, tuna *tataki*, *nigiri*, sashimi, makimono rolls, and cold and warm sake.

SUMMARY AND COMMENTS The Orchid Court Lounge, which almost exclusively caters to guests staying at the Royal Pacific Resort, has sushi chefs who prepare fishy fare that falls (in terms of quality and creativity) somewhere between The Cowfish and Fusion Bistro at CityWalk. Most of the rolls are adequate executions of Japanese American standards—California, spicy tuna, shrimp tempura, and volcano. Ordering *nigiri* à la carte can quickly add up at $2–$4 a piece, but the combinations aren't cheap either: a 25-piece sashimi combo will set you back more than $60, and a sushi and sashimi combo costs $75.

The Palm ★★★★

STEAK	VERY	EXPENSIVE	QUALITY ★★★★	VALUE ★★½
READER-SURVEY RESPONSES	94% 👍	6% 👎		

Hard Rock Hotel; ☎ 407-503-7256

Customers Tourists. Reservations Recommended via OpenTable. When to go Dinner. Entrée range $36–$99. Service rating ★★★. Friendliness rating ★★★. Parking Free valet at hotel with validation. Bar Full service. Wine selection Very good. Dress Resort, business casual, or smart casual; no sleeveless men's shirts. Disabled access Good. Hours Sunday–Thursday, 5–9 p.m.; Friday–Saturday, 5–10 p.m.

SETTING AND ATMOSPHERE Despite the celebrity caricatures drawn on the wall, the restaurant exudes sophistication due to the dark woods and white table-cloths. The chain's flagship location is in New York, and the decor reflects this. Waiters wear long, white aprons.

HOUSE SPECIALTIES New York strip, bone-in rib eye, lamb chops, veal parmi-giana, whole live lobster, Chilean sea bass, Atlantic salmon, and iceberg let-tuce wedge salad.

SUMMARY AND COMMENTS The crowd here can get noisy, so The Palm may not be the best place for a romantic night out. However, if you're looking to celebrate with friends or family, this is a good, if very expensive, choice. Stick with the sig-nature dishes: the steaks are done well, and the ginormous lobsters are impec-cably prepared, while some of the other dishes could be better. The side dishes are meant for sharing, and the creamed spinach and Brussels sprouts are justly famous. If you want a taste of The Palm on a hamburger budget, drop by the bar during PrimeTime (Sunday–Friday, 5–7 p.m.) for discounted appetizers, or take advantage of the annual $99 summer special on 4-pound lobsters for two. If you dine here more than once a year, look into joining the 837 Club (thepalm .com/837-Club) for discounts and exclusive event invitations.

Pat O'Brien's Orlando ★★★

CAJUN	INEXPENSIVE	QUALITY ★★★½	VALUE ★★★½
READER-SURVEY RESPONSES 96% 👍	4% 👎		

CityWalk; ☎ 407-224-2106

Customers Tourists. Reservations Accepted via Zomato. When to go Anytime. Entrée range $12–$21. Service rating ★★. Friendliness rating ★★★. Parking Uni-versal Orlando garage. Bar Full service. Wine selection Modest. Dress Casual. Dis-abled access Good. Hours Friday–Saturday, 4–10 p.m.; closed Sunday–Thursday (subject to change).

SETTING AND ATMOSPHERE A fairly faithful rendition of the original Pat O'Brien's in New Orleans, from the redbrick facade to the fire-and-water fountain in the courtyard. The outdoor dining area is the most pleasant place to eat. Inside areas include a noisy "locals" bar and a dueling piano bar, featuring some of Orlando's most talented musicians. A cover charge is levied after 9 p.m. when the venue is open late because it's mostly a music venue that also serves food.

HOUSE SPECIALTIES Shrimp gumbo, jambalaya, muffuletta, and red beans and rice.

SUMMARY AND COMMENTS The food is surprisingly good and surprisingly affordable. Be careful about ordering a Hurricane, the restaurant's signature drink. Not only is it deceptively potent, but you are also automatically charged for the souvenir glass, and if you don't want it, you must turn it in at the bar for a refund.

Red Oven Pizza Bakery ★★★½ *(Mobile Ordering)*

ITALIAN	INEXPENSIVE	QUALITY ★★★½	VALUE ★★★★½
READER-SURVEY RESPONSES 91% 👍	9% 👎		

CityWalk; ☎ 407-224-2690

Customers Tourists. Reservations Not accepted. When to go Anytime. Entrée range $11–$16. Service rating ★★. Friendliness rating ★★★. Parking Universal Orlando garage. Bar Wine and beer only. Wine selection Limited. Dress Casual. Disabled access Good. Hours Daily, 11 a.m.–10 p.m. (subject to change).

SETTING AND ATMOSPHERE Hardwood beams, colorful tile, and gleaming countertops make Red Oven look unexpectedly upscale for an open-air pizza joint. You can pose for photos on the red scooter parked out front.

HOUSE SPECIALTIES White and red pizza with gourmet toppings, salads, and imported beer and wine.

SUMMARY AND COMMENTS Red Oven Pizza Bakery may be seen as Universal's answer to Via Napoli in Epcot, which brought high-quality pizza to the theme park world. Only whole pies, not slices, can be ordered at Red Oven. However, with a reasonable price of only $13–$16 per pizza, two people can eat very cheaply. The six white and five red Neapolitan-style artisan pies are made with San Marzano tomatoes, organic extra-virgin olive oil, buffalo mozzarella, fine-ground "00" flour, and filtered water, and then baked in a 900°F oven while you watch. Salads and a limited selection of beer and wine are available, with free refills on soda.

After ordering your food and receiving your drinks, a server will seat you and bring your order once it's ready; a pickup window for mobile orders is also available. Plenty of covered outdoor seating is available, a welcome relief from the Florida sun (and rain). Because of its location in the main hub of CityWalk, Red Oven is a great place to get a bite to eat and people-watch. Red Oven can also be delivered to the freestanding bars along the CityWalk waterfront (when available).

Strong Water Tavern ★ ★ ★½ *(temporarily closed)*

CARIBBEAN	MODERATE	QUALITY ★★★★	VALUE ★★½
READER-SURVEY RESPONSES	100% 👍	0% 👎	

Sapphire Falls Resort; ☎ 407-503-5447

Customers Hotel guests. Reservations Not accepted. When to go Evenings. Entrée range $8–$16. Service rating ★★★. Friendliness rating ★★★. Parking $5 valet or free self-parking at hotel with validation. Bar Full service with extensive rum selection. Wine selection Average. Dress Casual. Disabled access Good. Hours Closed at press time; previously, daily 4 p.m.–2 a.m..

SETTING AND ATMOSPHERE One of the largest lobby bars at any Universal Resort hotel, Strong Water Tavern—like the rest of Sapphire Falls Resort—fuses organically aged objects and sleek modern elements. This New World watering hole sports oversize vintage couches on which to sprawl, faux reclaimed rum barrels forming the ceiling on the inside, and a spectacular view over the hotel's signature waterfalls from the patio. A video display wall, which usually broadcasts sports or a loop of Universal advertisements, dominates one end of the room. The centerpiece of Strong Water Tavern is the massive marble bar, which features a designated seating area for rum-tasting experiences.

HOUSE SPECIALTIES Ceviche, arroz con pollo, *ropa vieja,* empanadas, and rum cocktails.

SUMMARY AND COMMENTS We love almost everything about Strong Water Tavern—the contemporary Caribbean atmosphere, the variety of fresh ceviches, the potent cocktails—except for the prices. Drinks are a bit steep ($14–$16) but not unreasonable considering the top-shelf ingredients. A couple mugs of the Tavern Grog will make you want to join the merchant marines, and the $18 tasting flight lets you sample three rums that normally retail at up to $29 per shot; don't order the Hamilton 151 if you plan on driving home. On the other hand, while those who enjoy authentic West Indian, Cuban, and Puerto Rican recipes will feel right at home, your *abuela* would never dream of charging this much for such tiny tapas-style servings. Pretty much all the savory plates are overpriced, but the beef empanadas are probably the best buy. Periodic rum dinners (temporarily suspended at press time) feature an hors d'oeuvres reception, five culinary courses paired with craft rums, and an after-party with coffee and cigars; visit sapphirefalls.tix.com for details.

Three Broomsticks ★ ★ ★ *(Mobile Ordering)*

BRITISH	INEXPENSIVE	QUALITY ★ ★ ★½	VALUE ★ ★ ★
READER-SURVEY RESPONSES	94% 👍	6% 👎	

Islands of Adventure, The Wizarding World of Harry Potter–Hogsmeade; ☎ 407-224-4012

Customers Park guests. Reservations Breakfast only. When to go Early or late. Entrée range $11–$22. Service rating ★ ★ ★. Friendliness rating ★ ★ ★. Parking Universal Orlando garage. Bar Beer and wine only. Wine selection Limited. Dress Casual. Disabled access Good. Hours Daily, park opening–park closing.

SETTING AND ATMOSPHERE Modeled after the Three Broomsticks inn in the Harry Potter books and films, this buffeteria is the most visually interesting eatery at IOA. Open beams, dark furniture, and the contiguous Hog's Head pub (see page 234) make Three Broomsticks a place to linger and savor. The detail is incredible, and it's one of the best-themed restaurants we've seen. The amazing thing about the decor, aside from the vaulted ceiling, is that Universal's architects managed to hide virtually every modern convenience, such as air-conditioning vents, behind 18th-century facades. Alfresco dining is behind the restaurant.

HOUSE SPECIALTIES Breakfast items include English bacon, black pudding, baked beans, and grilled tomato; pancakes with bacon; and porridge with fruit. Lunch and dinner offerings are fish-and-chips, rotisserie chicken, smoked spareribs, shepherd's pie, Cornish pasty, turkey legs, and nonalcoholic Butterbeer. Children's menu items include chicken, macaroni and cheese, fish-and-chips, and chicken fingers.

SUMMARY AND COMMENTS The menu is very similar to Thunder Falls Terrace in Jurassic Park, with which it shares the title of best counter-service restaurant in IOA. The ribs or chicken, or the combo plate, are your best bets, though the tartar sauce is a tasty side to the fish-and-chips (made from fresh cod). The Great Feast family platter includes ribs, chicken, corn, potatoes, and salad for four for $60.99 ($15.99 each additional portion); even a large family may have leftovers, so bring along doggie bags. As the only dining option in Hogsmeade, Three Broomsticks stays busy all day. Like the Leaky Cauldron, you can reserve breakfast at Three Broomsticks by booking through your travel agent or the Ticket Center at your Universal Resort hotel, and walk-ins for day guests are also usually available, but there are probably better uses of your morning touring time.

Toothsome Chocolate Emporium & Savory Feast Kitchen
★ ★ ★½

CHOCOHOLIC-AMERICAN	MODERATE	QUALITY ★ ★ ★ ★	VALUE ★ ★ ★
READER-SURVEY RESPONSES	90% 👍	10% 👎	

CityWalk; ☎ 407-224-FOOD (3663)

Customers Tourists and locals. Reservations Not accepted. When to go Dinner or late evening dessert. Entrée range $12–$30. Service rating ★★½. Friendliness rating ★★★★. Parking Universal Orlando garage. Bar Full service with craft cocktails. Wine selection Modest. Dress Casual. Disabled access Good. Hours Daily, 4–10 p.m.; candy store and milkshake bar opens at 11 a.m.

SETTING AND ATMOSPHERE Looming across the CityWalk lagoon like Willy Wonka's summer home, Toothsome Chocolate Emporium & Savory Feast Kitchen is an original concept from Universal Creative that draws heavily on both Roald Dahl's crazed confectioner (closer to the Johnny Depp version than Gene Wilder) and steampunk, the Jules Vern–influenced sci-fi style that ditches futuristic chrome for Victorian-era copper. This multistory brick-faced venue seems to be a whimsical factory from the outside, complete with billowing smokestacks, while the inside is a wonderland of imaginative industrial contraptions (both physical and projected on large video screens) adorned with antique doodads. Much of the ground floor is devoted to a takeaway milkshake counter; a glassed-in kitchen where you can watch sweets being assembled; and a shop full of chocolates, candies, and steampunk souvenirs. Upstairs seating includes decadent semicircular booths and a private dining room; make sure to get a good look at the fiber-optic ceiling sculpture near the serpentine second-floor bar.

HOUSE SPECIALTIES Warm chocolate almond bread, baked Brie, pork belly sliders, salads, flatbreads, sandwiches, hamburgers, pasta, steaks, and all-day brunch with quiche and crêpes. And of course, drinks, desserts, and milkshakes with lots and lots of chocolate.

ENTERTAINMENT Actors portraying proprietress Penelope Toothsome and her animatronic assistant Jacques roam the restaurant interacting with guests. Brush up on their backstory (found on the first page of the menu) before they arrive at your table for a more in-depth conversation.

SUMMARY AND COMMENTS Toothsome takes a trendy aesthetic and potentially gut-busting gastronomic concept and combines them into an unexpectedly upscale eating experience. Many (though not all) of the offerings include some form of cocoa, from the old-fashioned cocktails with chocolate bitters to the chocolate mole sauce served on the gnocchi (ask for it as an accompaniment with the brisket and mushroom meat loaf). Prices are moderate, and portions are big enough to share or take home leftovers. Be sure to save room for the dark chocolate mousse, which is richer than any we've tasted outside Paris. A mom from Meridian, Idaho, is one of many readers who raves about Toothsome:

> Great food. The theme is unlike anything we'd ever experienced before. Both of my kids loved the steampunk atmosphere, and if you like chocolate, this is the place to be! A truly unique and fun experience.

Toothsome's signature milkshakes have proved so popular that at peak times they may be unavailable for table service and are only served at the downstairs to-go counter. The $12–$14 price tag may have you quoting John Travolta in *Pulp Fiction,* particularly since the shakes themselves are achingly sweet and not especially thick or large. But they are served in a souvenir Mason jar and crowned with an absurd mountain of toppings, such as an entire cupcake, brownie, or slice of Key lime pie. Be warned that the sour ice cream used in some varieties lives up to its name. Our biggest problem with Toothsome is that it's extremely popular and doesn't accept reservations, leading to hour-plus waits at mealtimes; try to slip in around 4 p.m., or ask if you can sit at the second-floor bar. Once seated, the restaurant often seems understaffed for its size, so come expecting a leisurely meal, this mom from Gurnee, Illinois, warns:

We really like Toothsome, but the service was so slow. It took over 2 hours, and with three kids, that was just too long for them to sit still.

Trattoria del Porto ★★★

ITALIAN	MODERATE	QUALITY ★★★	VALUE ★★
READER-SURVEY RESPONSES 88% 👍 13% 👎			

Portofino Bay Hotel; ☎ 407-503-1430

Customers Hotel guests. Reservations Suggested for dinner via OpenTable. When to go Breakfast or dinner. Entrée range Breakfast, $12–$17; lunch and dinner, $15–$37. Service rating ★★★. Friendliness rating ★★★. Parking $5 valet or free self-parking at hotel with validation. Bar Full service. Wine selection Average. Dress Resort casual. Disabled access Good. Hours Daily, 7–11 a.m. and 5:30–10:30 p.m. Select days, 11 a.m.–2 p.m.

SETTING AND ATMOSPHERE Like a boisterous down-home Italian kitchen. A play area lets kids watch cartoons while the grown-ups eat.

HOUSE SPECIALTIES At breakfast, Belgian waffles, steak and eggs, and eggs Benedetto with prosciutto and arugula. At dinner, pesto flatbread, salads, burgers, steaks, vegan pastas, and make-your-own pasta combos.

SUMMARY AND COMMENTS Where Mama Della's succeeds in not feeling like a hotel restaurant, Trattoria del Porto does not. The food is perfectly fine and moderately priced (relatively speaking). The interactive Pasta Cucina is available every night until 10 p.m., allowing you to create your own entrée from a variety of noodles and sauces ($26.99 adults, $12.99 kids). Omelets at breakfast can set you back more than $14, so opt instead for the buffet (when available) offered in the mornings.

Vivo Italian Kitchen ★★★★

ITALIAN	MODERATE	QUALITY ★★★★	VALUE ★★★★½
READER-SURVEY RESPONSES 94% 👍 6% 👎			

CityWalk; ☎ 407-224-2318

Customers Locals and tourists. Reservations Accepted via Zomato. When to go Dinner. Entrée range $14–$28. Service rating ★★★. Friendliness rating ★★★. Parking Universal Orlando garage. Bar Full service. Wine selection Good. Dress Casual. Disabled access Good. Hours Thursday–Sunday, 4–10 p.m.; closed Monday–Wednesday (subject to change).

SETTING AND ATMOSPHERE Sleek and contemporary without being stuffy, Vivo brings a touch of casual class to CityWalk's central crossroads. There are outdoor tables (with embedded chessboards) and a well-lit bar, along with plush semicircular booths surrounded by sinuous steel cages. But the real action is around the open kitchen; see if you can snag a seat at the food bar in front of the "tree" where fresh pasta is hung.

HOUSE SPECIALTIES Freshly made pasta, homemade mozzarella, pizza, salads, lasagna, chicken Marsala, and risotto.

SUMMARY AND COMMENTS Vivo is Universal's best Italian food outside Portofino Bay. The menu is filled with classic recipes prepared à la minute with the freshest ingredients, such as chicken piccata, veal parmigiana, spinach ravioli, and spaghetti Bolognese. Best of all, you can dine here for half the price of Bice, Mama Della's, or one of Disney's Signature restaurants.

Start by ordering an enormous house-made meatball, hand-pulled mozzarella, or beet-and-Gorgonzola salad. Standout entrées include linguine with seasonal clams, black squid ink pasta with seafood, and risotto with short ribs. On a cost–quality basis, this may be the best table-service meal you'll have on Universal property.

Wantilan Luau ★ ★ ★ ½ *(temporarily closed)*

HAWAIIAN	EXPENSIVE	QUALITY ★ ★ ★ ½	VALUE ★ ★ ★
READER-SURVEY RESPONSES	100% 👍	0% 👎	

Royal Pacific Resort; ☎ 407-503-DINE (3463)

Customers Tourists. Reservations Required via wantilanluau.tix.com. When to go Dinner only. Entrée range Buffet: $75.62 adults, $38.34 children ages 3–9. (Prices include tax and gratuity for everyone, and mai tais, wine, and beer for guests age 21 and older.) Service rating ★ ★ ★. Friendliness rating ★ ★ ★ ★. Parking Free valet or free self-parking at hotel with validation. Bar Mai tais, wine, and beer included. Wine selection Limited. Dress Floral shirts, beachy casual. Disabled access Average. Hours Closed at press time; previously Saturday; seating begins at 6 p.m., with registration starting 30 minutes before.

SETTING AND ATMOSPHERE Typical luau setting with tiki torches and wooden tables.

HOUSE SPECIALTIES Buffet includes pit-roasted suckling pig with spiced rum-soaked pineapple purée; Pacific catch of the day; Hawaiian chicken teriyaki; fire-grilled beef with mushrooms; and chicken fingers, mac and cheese, PB&J, and pizza for kids. Dessert buffet has white chocolate mousse shots, passion fruit crème brûlée, and Kona coffee tarts.

ENTERTAINMENT Polynesian dancing, storytelling, hula dancers, and live music.

SUMMARY AND COMMENTS This is a fun diversion and a change of scenery from the other restaurants on Universal property. Though dinner is a bit expensive, it's the best food of any luau show in the area, and the entertainment is more energetic than *Disney's Spirit of Aloha*. Premium Seating gets you a souvenir tiki mug and a reserved table near the middle of the room for an extra $10.65 per adult ($5.33 per kid), while Priority Seating (for another $10.65 per person on top of Premium) guarantees seats up front. The check-in process can take a while, so send the rest of your party to watch the preshow on the nearby lawn while one member waits in line, but be sure to line up by the open-air venue's entrance before seating starts to get first crack at the buffet. The culinary star of the show is the roast pork, and the seared ahi tuna salad and cedar-plank roasted salmon are also excellent, but the bottomless mai tais are overpoweringly sweet. Food (with musical accompaniment) is served until 7:15 p.m., with the main show cranking up at 7. The hour-long entertainment features grass-skirted dancers paying tribute to the traditions of Hawaiian, Maori, and Tahitian cultures, climaxing in a dazzling display of fire twirling.

DINING *near*
UNIVERSAL ORLANDO

AS WE'VE MENTIONED PREVIOUSLY, guests staying at Universal Orlando's on-site resorts may find their dining options a bit limited and expensive compared to the restaurants found at some Walt Disney World hotels. The flip side is that, while Disney's resorts are largely isolated from the outside world, Universal hotel guests have an array of off-property eateries only a few minutes' drive—or even walk—away. And if you don't feel like leaving your hotel room, most of these restaurants deliver through UberEats, GrubHub, DoorDash, and similar smartphone services.

The closest off-site restaurants to Universal Orlando are found between the hotels along Major Boulevard, just east of the resort entrance on Kirkman Road. **Miller's Ale House** (5573 S. Kirkman Road; ☎ 407-248-0000; millersalehouse.com) is a popular after-hours hangout for Universal employees and serves the largest chicken nachos you'll ever see. Chefs at **Kobe Japanese Steakhouse & Sushi Bar** (5605 S. Kirkman Road; ☎ 407-248-1978; kobesteakhouse.com) perform at teppanyaki tables; ask about early bird and late-night specials. On the opposite side of Major Boulevard, you'll find a run-of-the-mill **T.G.I. Friday's** and **Tabla Restaurant** (5847 Grand National Dr.; ☎ 407-248-9400; tablacuisine.com), an upscale Indian/Thai/Chinese restaurant tucked into the back of a Clarion Inn. A **Wendy's** and **Burger King** round out the block; more fast-food franchises, **Soupa Saiyan** ramen bar (5689 Vineland Road; ☎ 407-930-3396; soupasaiyan.com), and **Carrabba's Italian** are across the street on the north side of Vineland Road. Continue a few lights farther north, and you'll find a strip mall at the corner of Kirkman and Conroy Roads, housing **Karen's Tasty Crabs** (4898 S. Kirkman Road; ☎ 407-293-3036; addicted2karens.com); **Bubbalou's Bodacious Bar-B-Que** (5818 Conroy Road; ☎ 407-295-1212; kirkman.bubbalous.com); **Smashburger** (5812 Conroy Road; ☎ 407-440-3595; smashburger.com); and **Sloppy Taco Palace** (4892 S. Kirkman Road; ☎ 407-574-6474), which lives up to its name.

Slightly farther afield, international treasures near Universal property along International Drive include **Aashirwad Indian Cuisine** (7000 S. Kirkman Road; ☎ 407-370-9830; aashirwadrestaurant.com), **Ichiban** sushi buffet (5529 International Dr.; ☎ 407-930-8889; ichibanbuffet.com), **BoiBrazil Churrascaria** (5668 International Dr.; ☎ 407-354-0260; boibrazil.com), **Thai Silk** (6803 S. Kirkman Road; ☎ 407-226-8997; thaisilkorlando.com), **Nile Ethiopian Restaurant** (7040 International Dr.; ☎ 407-354-0026; nileorlando.com), **World's Magic Indonesian Restaurant** (7044 International Dr.; ☎ 407-203-3330; facebook.com/worldsmagicrestaurant), and **Del Taco** (6855 Grand National Dr.; ☎ 407-363-0738; deltaco.com) for those late-night munchies. If you take Universal Boulevard south past I-Drive and Sand Lake Road, you can access rear entrances for I-Drive restaurants without the traffic, ending up at the **Pointe Orlando** shopping and dining complex. Finally, take Turkey Lake Road south from Universal to Sand Lake Road, and turn right toward Restaurant Row for a plethora of upscale chain restaurants, including **Seasons 52, Bonefish Grill, Ocean Prime,** and many more.

If you want to take a drive to downtown Orlando or beyond in search of a fine meal, we can vouch for **The Ravenous Pig** (565 W. Fairbanks Ave.; ☎ 407-628-2333; theravenouspig.com), **Kabooki Sushi** (7705 Turkey Lake Road; ☎ 407-776-2001; or 3122 E. Colonial Dr.; ☎ 407-228-3839; kabookisushi.com), **Saigon Noodle & Grill** (101 N. Bumby Ave.; ☎ 407-532-7373; sngbumby.com), **Pig Floyd's Urban Barbakoa** (1326 N. Mills Ave.; ☎ 407-203-0866; pigfloyds.com), **The Strand** (807 N. Mills Ave.; ☎ 407-920-7744; strandorlando.com), and **The Artisan's Table** (55 W. Church St.; ☎ 407-730-7499; artisanstableorlando.com).

SHOPPING *at* UNIVERSAL ORLANDO

YOU'LL HAVE PLENTY OF OPPORTUNITIES at Universal Orlando to take home overpriced dust magnets (oops, we meant to say priceless mementos) from your stay. And if you're staying on-site, you can charge them to your room using your hotel key card; just be prepared for the reckoning upon checkout.

If you return home and realize you forgot something, a selection of Universal Orlando merchandise can be ordered online at shop.universal orlando.com.

COVID *tip*
Select stores may not be open, or operate with limited hours and selections. Signage on closed shops should direct you to other locations where similar merchandise is sold.

SHOPPING AT UNIVERSAL STUDIOS FLORIDA

AS KANG AND KODOS OBSERVE at the end of The Simpsons Ride, it's apparently a state law that every Universal attraction must end in (or near) a gift shop. Most of these have the typical T-shirts and toys tied to the experience you just exited, though a few have offerings of note.

The Universal Studios Store sits near the park's entrance: if you forgot to get a gift elsewhere in the park, you can probably find it here. Browse the selection of exclusive character-themed candy bars, including E.T.'s chocolate–peanut butter bar with Reese's Pieces, SpongeBob's white chocolate bar with pineapple bits, and Donkey's maple-flavored waffle bar. **It's A Wrap** straddles the park exit, selling last season's souvenirs at discount prices, as well as serving as the park's package pickup point. If you prepurchased a My Universal Photos package, stop in **On Location** to activate it or pick up prints.

In **Production Central, Super Silly Stuff** at Despicable Me Minion Mayhem is decorated like the candy-colored amusement park from the film. You can access the Minion photo op at the attraction's postshow (when available) from the shop if the ride's queue is too long. There's a magic mirror and some other fun decor in **Shrek's Ye Olde Souvenir Shoppe.** Transformers' **Supply Vault** has pricey collectibles, as well as toy versions of the attraction's cybertronic stars, including exclusive models of Optimus Prime and Megatron. Directly across from the Transformers entrance sits **The Film Vault,** a movie nerd's nirvana with new products tied to vintage Universal films, from *Psycho* and *Scarface* to *Back to the Future* and *The Big Lebowski.* Nearby, the **Park Plaza Holiday Shop** sells hand-painted Universal ornaments, be it October or August. Beware the bins of bulk candies at **Studio Sweets**; they are priced per quarter-pound, and small bags can add up very quickly.

New York's postride shops are fairly pedestrian, though you'll find NBC apparel at **The Tonight Shop** and faux-Egyptian jewelry in Revenge of the Mummy's **Sahara Traders. Rosie's Irish Shop** has everything Emerald Isle expats (or just admirers) need, from coat of arms key chains to football club sweatshirts.

Shopping in **San Francisco** is limited to the **San Francisco Candy Factory** (sadly, Ghirardelli is just a facade) and the **Custom Gear** gift shop at the exit of Fast & Furious: Supercharged, where you can pick out a personalized toy car.

The Wizarding World of Harry Potter–Diagon Alley is groaning with great shopping opportunities, including **Weasleys' Wizard Wheezes** (toys and candy), **Borgin and Burkes** (spooky stuff), **Madam Malkin's Robes for All Occasions** (clothing), **Magical Menagerie** (stuffed animals), **Sugarplum's Sweet Shop** (cakes and candy), **Globus Mundi** (travel-themed tchotchkes), and of course **Ollivanders** (wands). See page 295 for more Diagon Alley shopping details.

In **Springfield: Home of the Simpsons,** the **Kwik-E-Mart** has a great selection of *Simpsons* collectibles and exclusive candy bars, like the Krusty Klump (from the "Homer Badman" episode) and Farmer Billy's Choco-Bacon. **MIB Gear** in **World Expo** has a selection of DC comics and superhero collectibles, along with a custom-printed T-shirt kiosk.

Woody Woodpecker's KidZone is home to **SpongeBob StorePants,** where the big yellow guy himself holds court daily; adults will appreciate the snarky signs inside. **E.T. Toy Closet** has toys from that Spielberg classic and others, plus two adorable photo ops (one on a flying bicycle and the other in a closet full of toys) that are included with My Universal Photos packages. The most notable thing about **The Barney Store,** aside from the world's largest collection of purple-dinosaur videos, is the character meet and greet in the adjoining playground.

Back in **Hollywood,** the **Hello Kitty** shop is as eye-poppingly adorable as the *kawaii* Japanese feline and her cartoon friends, who appear on clothing, housewares, postcards (which you can get stamped with a unique postmark), and countless other Sanrio-sanctioned products. **The Betty Boop Store** stocks Boop-centric accessories and apparel, including nightgowns. **The Bourne Stuntacular Store** (does that make it a storetacular?) stocks hoodies, shirts, and other apparel inspired by the show that exits through it, along with Universal Classic Monsters memorabilia for the *Horror Make-Up Show* next door. Note that in Universal's Hollywood, the **Brown Derby** is a hat shop, not a restaurant.

Williams of Hollywood is perhaps the most special shop in all of Universal because it's the only place where you can purchase an actual piece of the theme parks. Props, posters, and pieces of ride vehicles from *Terminator, Disaster!, Beetlejuice Graveyard Revue,* and even Jaws have been sold to the public, for prices ranging from $50 up to $5,000; Seth took home a door from the *Twister* preshow and a YOU MUST BE THIS TALL TO RIDE sign for a couple Benjamins, but you'll need to drop some big bills if you want to take home a flying cow. Read the price tags carefully; items actually used in the parks will be clearly marked, while others are simply thrift store finds and reproductions used to fill out the shelves. Before buying a large artifact, you may also want to consider how you'll transport your treasure home; Universal will happily mail it for you, but the shipping cost may exceed the sale price. Sadly, the shop was temporarily shuttered at press time, but some of its artifacts are available in other stores. Right next to Williams of Hollywood, you'll find **The Darkroom** green screen photo booths (see page 173) and the **UOAP Lounge,** where annual pass holders can chill out and recharge (see page 46).

Finally, **The NBC Media Center,** inside the Garden of Allah Villas between Hollywood and KidZone, is like a shop in reverse. Instead of spending money, you can volunteer to watch a video—often from a potential NBC TV series—and answer a survey in exchange for a gift card or modest amount of cash. It isn't always available, and you may have to meet certain demographic qualifications, but you can make $20 or more in less than an hour. For guests on a tight schedule, this is a poor use of park time, but if you're a local or you're spending several days at Universal, it can be an interesting experience.

SHOPPING AT ISLANDS OF ADVENTURE

LIKE USF, IOA PLACES ITS BIGGEST RETAIL VENUE venue right near the entrance; **Islands of Adventure Trading Company** in **Port of Entry** has selections from every area of the park, especially The Wizarding World. Next to it sits the open-air **Ocean Trader Market,** which sells exotic clothing and crafts. For Grinch fans, the **Port of Entry Christmas Shoppe** celebrates the holiday season 365 days a year; there's even a section dedicated to Harry Potter–themed Yuletide gifts. **DeFoto's Expedition Photography** is this park's My Universal Photos headquarters, and **Port Provisions** is the last-chance gift discounter and package pickup location at the exit turnstiles.

The **Marvel Alterniverse Store** on **Marvel Super Hero Island** stocks life-size busts of the Avengers (does anyone really put these in their home?), while the **Comic Book Shop** has a good selection of current releases and trade paperback classics, along with collectible figurines. For something superheroic yet still stylish, stop into the small **Marvel Boutique** for on-trend clothes and accessories highlighting edgier characters like Deadpool, Spider-Gwen, and the Guardians of the Galaxy.

The main drag of **Toon Lagoon** is made up of two stores: the **Betty Boop Store** and **Toon Extra**—selling toys and apparel tied to characters no one under age 40 has heard of. **WossaMotta U** sells T-shirts and toys from *The Secret Life of Pets.*

Jurassic Park's post-splashdown shop **Jurassic Outfitters** specializes in beach towels (small wonder), and the Discovery Center's **Dinostore** sells semiprecious gems and semieducational toys. The gift kiosk at the exit of **Skull Island: Reign of Kong** is so small that it doesn't even have a name, though it does have some adorable plush monkey merchandise.

In **The Wizarding World of Harry Potter–Hogsmeade, Honeydukes** (candy), **Dervish and Banges** (toys, apparel), **Ollivanders** (wands), and **Filch's Emporium of Confiscated Goods** at the Forbidden Journey exit will sap your wallet as surely as a Dementor sucks souls. See page 341.

The diminished **Lost Continent** still has a few curiosities in its Arabian bazaar, such as **The Coin Mint,** where you can watch money being made, and a **heraldry shop** with heavy armor. The most eclectic award goes to **Treasures of Poseidon,** where you can pick up a polo shirt, a potted plant, and a $16 pearl that's still inside a live oyster.

If you want a set of the Thing 1 and Thing 2 T-shirts you'll spot around Universal, **Cats, Hats and Things** at The Cat in the Hat ride exit in **Seuss Landing** is the spot. **Mulberry Street** has a small entrance door just for kids, but its limited edition prints and sculptures will appeal to adults. If your Theodor Geisel collection has any gaps, **All the Books You Can Read** can help fill it. And be warned: Upon exiting The High in the Sky Seuss Trolley Train Ride!, you may be forced to pass through **Snookers & Snookers Sweet Candy Cookers,** which is known to cause weight gain simply from staring at its case of fudge and candy apples.

SHOPPING AT VOLCANO BAY

SHOPPING IS PROBABLY THE LAST THING on the minds of most guests splashing at the water park, unless they've forgotten some essential item. That explains why merchandise opportunities in Volcano Bay are minimal and mostly focused on beach apparel—hats, swimsuits, flip-flops—and accessories. **Waturi Marketplace,** next to the ice cream stand to the left of the park entrance, is the main gift store; it consists of two adjoining huts hocking clothing with the park logo, plus live plants and tiki tchotchkes. **Krakatoa Katy's,** a smaller outpost on the beach to the right of the main entrance, has a more limited selection of shirts, focusing instead on towels, bags, and collectible cups. Both locations stock sundries like sunscreen.

SHOPPING AT UNIVERSAL CITYWALK

CITYWALK (citywalk.com) comprises 30 acres in a relatively compact area between the two Universal theme parks. CityWalk's focus is on food and entertainment, rather than high-dollar shopping sprees, so the store lineup is designed for casual browsing and impulse buys. At press time, a large swath of former CityWalk shops were under construction for a currently unannounced upcoming emporium.

Quiet Flight Surf Shop sells merchandise from beachy brands such as Billabong, Hurley, Nixon, Oakley, Quiksilver, Reef, Rip Curl, Roxy, Volcom, and VonZipper. Quiet Flight sports an iconic surfboard photo op outside.

MAGICAL MERCHANDISE

DEREK BURGAN IS BACK AGAIN with a "Saturday Six" list of his favorite magic surprises to be found inside the wonderful shops of Harry Potter's Wizarding Worlds.

6. Professor Umbridge on a Unicycle at Weasleys' Wizard Wheezes (USF) The *Half-Blood Prince* film starts off with our favorite wizarding trio visiting Fred and George Weasley's new store in Diagon Alley. One of the whimsical items they see is a toy featuring the villainous Dolores Umbridge precariously balancing cauldrons of liquid while on a unicycle. At the Weasleys' store, you can not only see a life-size version of this toy working its way across a tight rope up above, but you can even buy a version to take home!

5. Vanishing Cabinet at Borgin and Burkes (USF) Also in *Half-Blood Prince*, Draco Malfoy uses vanishing cabinets to sneak Death Eaters into Hogwarts. In the back corner of the Borgin and Burkes location in Knockturn Alley, there is a vanishing cabinet. If you listen closely, you may just hear a little bird chirp.

4. Mirror at Madame Malkin's Robes For All Occasions (USF) While shopping for their favorite house's gear in Diagon Alley, Muggles can pose or even just pass by this magical contraption and get complimented on their attire (or possibly get some burning critique).

3. Snake at Magical Menagerie (USF) In Diagon Alley's Magical Menagerie, you can practice your Parseltongue on the snake in the window. You can watch the snake move, and if you get real close, you can even hear it hiss. Maybe you can impress your friends by translating what he is saying.

2. *Monster Book of Monsters* at Dervish and Banges (IOA) In *Prisoner of Azkaban*, Hagrid gets his chance at being a professor. One of the required texts is the *Monster Book of Monsters*, a book that spends most of its time attempting to attack anything around it. Don't worry—it has been locked up to protect guests from its occasional attacks!

1. Letter Stamped at Owl Post (IOA/USF) One of the best magical secrets of The Wizarding World is the ability to send regular Muggle mail via "owl." Visit the Owl Post with a letter or postcard and have it stamped by the wizard or witch on hand, and then put it in the drop box for delivery. Please note that standard Muggle mailing is used for all deliveries, as they don't want to alarm your neighbors.

Up for some ink? CityWalk also has a branch of **Hart & Huntington Tattoo Company. The Universal Studios Store** offers one-stop shopping for all theme park merchandise, including the best selection of Harry Potter products outside the parks. Finally, many of the restaurants—including Bubba Gump, Margaritaville, Hard Rock Cafe, Bob Marley, and Pat O'Brien's—have merchandise shops, in case you want memories of your meal to live on forever in your closet.

SHOPPING AT UNIVERSAL ORLANDO RESORT HOTELS

EACH OF THE ON-SITE LOEWS HOTELS has a main store near the central lobby carrying sundries, souvenirs, and branded apparel. **Hard Rock Hotel's Rock Shop** carries hip brands such as Harajuku and English Laundry, sells the bed and bath linens used in guest rooms, and even has a touch screen video wall with info on the hotel's rock memorabilia collection. At **Portofino Bay Hotel,** you'll find resort-specific items in **Le Memories de Portofino** and a full array of Universal merch in the harbor promenade's **Universal Studios Store,** along with **Alta Moda** resort wear and swim clothes, an **art gallery,** and a **family photography studio. Toko Gifts** is a shop just inside the **Royal Pacific Resort**'s entrance that covers

Chris Eliopoulos

all the essentials, while **Treasures of Bali** by the pool carries beach gear and island wear. **Cabana Bay Beach Resort,** the cheapest hotel, actually has one of the best stores, with retro clothes, custom candy, and even Jack LaLanne gear in the **Universal Studios Store. Sapphire Falls Resort, Aventura Hotel,** and **Endless Summer Resort** each has a **Universal Studios Store** of its own; while all have a good selection of sundries and theme park souvenirs, those hotels' branded merchandise isn't nearly as eye-catching as Cabana Bay's.

SHOPPING *near*
UNIVERSAL ORLANDO

IF YOU'VE EXHAUSTED Universal Orlando's shopping venues and want to venture off property, Central Florida's premier shopping experience is found only a couple exits east along I-4 at **The Mall at Millenia** (☎ 407-363-3555; mallatmillenia.com), anchored by **Bloomingdale's, Macy's,** and **Neiman Marcus**. Other stores include **Anthropologie, Burberry, Chanel, Coach, Gucci, Guess, J. Crew, Kate Spade, Louis Vuitton, Lululemon Athletica, Tiffany & Co., Tory Burch, Urban Outfitters,** and **Versace**. Hours are daily, 11 a.m.–7 p.m.

The luxurious **Cinemark movie theater** (5150 International Dr.; ☎ 407-352-1042; cinemark.com) and **Bass Pro Shops** (5156 International Dr.; ☎ 407-563-5200; stores.basspro.com) attached to the former Artegon Marketplace are still in operation. **Gods & Monsters** (5421 International Dr.; ☎ 407-270-6273; godmonsters.com), our favorite former Artegon fixture, relocated its comic books and sci-fi collectibles across the street, adding a retro arcade and postapocalypse-themed pub.

On the south end of International Drive is **Pointe Orlando** (9101 International Dr.; ☎ 407-248-2838; pointeorlando.com), with a handful of stores. This complex gets a lot of its business from the convention center, less than a mile away, rather than from locals. Retail hours are daily, 11 a.m.–6 p.m. (Bars and restaurants stay open later.) I-Drive is the heart of Orlando's tourist district, jammed with hotels, discount stores, and endless traffic; locals generally avoid the area or use Universal Boulevard (on the south end) and Grand National Drive (on the north end) to dodge the worst of the congestion.

OUTLETS NEAR UNIVERSAL ORLANDO

AT MOST OUTLET STORES you'll save about 20% on desirable merchandise and up to 75% on last-season (or older) stock. Some stores in the outlet malls are full retail or sell a few brands at a 20% discount and the rest at full price.

Orlando Premium Outlets–International Drive (4951 International Dr.; ☎ 407-352-9600; premiumoutlets.com/outlet/orlando-international; open daily, 10 a.m.–7 p.m.; select holidays, 9 a.m.–11 p.m.), on the north end of I-Drive, features 180 of the world's hottest designers and brand names, among them **Dooney & Bourke, J. Crew, Kate Spade, Michael Kors, Movado, Saks Fifth Avenue OFF 5TH, St. John, Under Armour, Victoria's Secret,** and **White House Black Market**. There's even a **Disney's Character Warehouse,** where unsold Walt Disney World souvenirs go to die; read Derek Burgan's monthly "Magic, Memories, and Merch" reports at tinyurl.com/burganmerch. You can reach the outlets by car (arrive early for any hope of free parking), taxi, or I-Ride Trolley (when operating; it's stop #1).

PART SEVEN

UNIVERSAL STUDIOS FLORIDA

LIKE ITS ELDER SIBLING in Hollywood, **Universal Studios Florida** (USF) has always offered guests movie- and TV-themed rides and shows, along with limited opportunities to observe actual filming or preview upcoming productions. But if the last time you visited Universal was in the early 2000s, you literally won't recognize the majority of the park. Universal has updated, upgraded, or entirely replaced nearly every attraction that debuted during the park's first decade, replacing Kongfrontation with Revenge of the Mummy, Back to the Future with The Simpsons Ride, Jaws with Harry Potter's Diagon Alley, and *Earthquake* (and its descendant *Disaster!*) with Fast & Furious: Supercharged. With each renovation came groundbreaking advancements in ride hardware and special effects.

Watching USF's constant evolution has been thrilling, but it can also be disconcerting. USF celebrated its 30th anniversary in 2020, but precious little early history is left intact in the park for long-time visitors who loved long gone opening-day attractions such as *Alfred Hitchcock: The Art of Making Movies,* The Funtastic World of Hanna-Barbera, and *Ghostbusters Spooktacular.* (For a trip down memory lane, visit Universal's retired attraction tributes at tinyurl .com/uniretired.)

NOT TO BE MISSED AT UNIVERSAL STUDIOS FLORIDA

PRODUCTION CENTRAL • Transformers: The Ride 3-D

NEW YORK • Revenge of the Mummy

THE WIZARDING WORLD OF HARRY POTTER—DIAGON ALLEY
• Harry Potter and the Escape from Gringotts • Hogwarts Express

WORLD EXPO • Men in Black Alien Attack

SPRINGFIELD: HOME OF THE SIMPSONS • The Simpsons Ride

HOLLYWOOD • *The Bourne Stuntacular* • *Universal Orlando's Horror Make-Up Show*

GETTING ORIENTED *at* UNIVERSAL STUDIOS FLORIDA

USF IS LAID OUT in a P configuration, with the rounded part of the *P* sticking out disproportionately from the stem. Beyond the main entrance plaza (known as the **Front Lot**), a wide boulevard stretches past several shows and rides to the park's New York area. Branching off this pedestrian thoroughfare to the right are four streets that access other areas of the park and intersect a promenade circling a large, oval man-made lake, where the majority of the shows and attractions are located. The area of USF open to visitors is a bit smaller than Epcot.

Beginning at the park entrance and going clockwise, the first area you'll encounter is **Production Central,** which includes Despicable Me Minion Mayhem, Hollywood Rip Ride Rockit, Transformers: The Ride 3-D, and *Shrek 4-D.* At the top of the *P* is the **New York** area, including Race Through New York Starring Jimmy Fallon and Revenge of the Mummy. Next is **San Francisco,** the home of Fast & Furious: Supercharged; **The Wizarding World of Harry Potter—Diagon Alley** with Hogwarts Express–King's Cross Station and Harry Potter and the Escape from Gringotts; **World Expo** with Men in Black Alien Attack; **Springfield: Home of the Simpsons,** featuring, of course, The Simpsons Ride; and **Woody Woodpecker's KidZone,** containing E.T. Adventure, an animal show, and several play areas. The last themed area, back near the front of the park, is **Hollywood,** featuring *Universal Orlando's Horror Make-Up Show* and *The Bourne Stuntacular.*

In most of USF, the line where one themed area begins and another ends is blurry because much of the architecture consists of boring boxlike soundstages barely concealed behind false fronts. No matter; guests orient themselves by the major rides, sets, and landmarks and refer, for instance, to "the waterfront," "over by E.T.," or "by Mel's Drive-In." In diametric contrast, The Wizarding World of Harry Potter—Diagon Alley (and, to a much lesser extent, the Springfield area around The Simpsons Ride) is an immersive themed area whose scope and scale point to the place-making potential of upcoming Universal lands.

Almost all guest services are found in the **Front Lot,** just inside the main entrance. Services and amenities include stroller and wheelchair rentals to the left as you enter; lockers, Lost and Found, and First Aid are to the right. You'll also find the **Studio Audience Center,** where you can sign up to be an audience member at any live TV productions that may be recording that day. Past series taped at USF have included game shows, talk shows, cooking shows, Telemundo's *La Voz Kids,* and TNA's *IMPACT Wrestling.* Call ☎ 407-363-8400 and select option 5 to find out what's scheduled during your visit.

continued on page 278

Universal Studios Florida

Attractions

1. *Animal Actors on Location!* UX
2. *The Bourne Stuntacular* ☑
3. Curious George Goes to Town
4. *A Day in the Park with Barney* (seasonal) UX
5. Despicable Me Minion Mayhem UX
6. E.T. Adventure UX
7. Fast & Furious: Supercharged (seasonal) UX VL
8. *Fear Factor Live* (seasonal) UX
9. Fievel's Playland
10. Harry Potter and the Escape from Gringotts UX ☑
11. Hogwarts Express: King's Cross Station UX ☑
12. Hollywood Rip Ride Rockit UX
13. Kang & Kodos' Twirl 'n' Hurl (seasonal) UX
14. Men in Black Alien Attack UX ☑
15. Ollivanders

16. Race Through New York
    Starring Jimmy Fallon UX VL
17. Revenge of the Mummy UX ☑
18. *Shrek 4-D* UX
19. The Simpsons Ride UX ☑
20. Transformers: The Ride–3-D UX ☑

Counter-Service Res

A. Bumblebee Man's Taco
   Truck
B. Central Park Crepes
C. Chez Alcatraz
D. Duff Brewery
E. Fast Food Boulevard 👍
F. Florean Fortescue's
   Ice-Cream Parlour 👍
G. Fountain of Fair Fortune
   (seasonal)

21. Universal Orlando's Horror Make-Up Show UX ☑
22. Universal Orlando's Cinematic Celebration *(seasonal)*
23. Woody Woodpacker's Nuthouse Coaster UX

Restaurants

H. The Hopping Pot
I. KidZone Pizza Company *(seasonal)*
J. London Taxi Hut *(seasonal)*
K. Louie's Italian Restaurant
L. Mel's Drive-In
M. Moe's Tavern

N. Richter's Burger Co.
O. San Francisco Pastry Company *(seasonal)*
P. Schwab's Pharmacy *(seasonal)*
Q. Today Cafe 👍
R. Universal Studios' Classic Monsters Cafe *(seasonal)*

Table-Service Restaurants

AA. Finnegan's Bar & Grill
BB. Leaky Cauldron (counter service) 👍
CC. Lombard's Seafood Grille

UX Attraction Offers Universal Express   VL Virtual Line   ✚ First Aid Station   🚻 Restrooms

👍 Recommended Dining   ☑ Not to Be Missed   - - - Parade Route

continued from page 275

A "secret" secondary entrance to USF is tucked under the Hollywood Rip Ride Rockit track, between Despicable Me Minion Mayhem and the Universal Studios Store. It doesn't open until late morning (usually around 10:30 a.m.), but it can save you a few minutes entering on a busy afternoon. Follow the signs from CityWalk for the Blue Man Group theater to find it. It also makes an excellent egress when you want to exit toward the Hard Rock Cafe or Islands of Adventure (IOA). On peak days, this gate may provide direct pedestrian access to Seuss Landing in IOA for guests with park-to-park admission, which can be a huge time-saver over taking the Hogwarts Express.

UNIVERSAL STUDIOS FLORIDA ATTRACTIONS

PRODUCTION CENTRAL

AT THE FRONT OF USF, Production Central is the first land guests see upon entering the park and passing through the Front Lot. It's a shame, therefore, that this is one of the most meh main streets of any theme park, with bland beige buildings broken up only by the incongruously colossal coaster tracks. Its underwhelming aesthetics don't seem to hurt the area's attractiveness to guests because Production Central holds three of the park's most popular attractions outside of Diagon Alley.

In addition to the rides, show, and counter-service restaurant, Production Central is home to **Music Plaza Stage,** a Hollywood Bowl–inspired amphitheater with an artificial turf viewing lawn (where you'll often find unconscious tourists sprawled on sunny days) that's used during Mardi Gras concerts and similar special events. There's also access (when applicable) from here to the soundstages used for TV production and Halloween haunted houses.

Despicable Me Minion Mayhem *(Universal Express)* ★★★½

APPEAL BY AGE PRESCHOOL ★★★★ GRADE SCHOOL ★★★★½ TEENS ★★★★ YOUNG ADULTS ★★★★ OVER 30 ★★★★ SENIORS ★★★★

What it is Motion-simulator ride. Scope and scale Major attraction. When to go Immediately after park opening or just before closing. Comments Child swap available (see page 204); single-rider line available. Expect *long* waits in line. Duration of ride 5 minutes. Loading speed Moderate-slow.

DESCRIPTION AND COMMENTS Despicable Me Minion Mayhem is a motion-simulator ride similar to Universal's The Simpsons Ride and Star Tours at Disney's Hollywood Studios. You're seated in a ride vehicle that faces a large video screen, onto which the attraction's story is projected. When the story calls for you to drop down the side of a building, your ride vehicle tilts forward as if you were falling; when you need to swerve left or right, your ride vehicle tilts the same way.

The main difference between Minion Mayhem and other simulators is that most other simulators provide one video screen per ride vehicle, while Minion Mayhem arranges all of its eight-person vehicles in front of one IMAX-size screen. The vehicles are set on raised platforms that get slightly higher toward the back of the theater, affording good views for all guests in the rear. Though the ride debuted with high-definition digital 3-D technology that created a sense of depth and allowed objects to pop out of the screen, Despicable Me ditched its 3-D glasses in 2019 and switched to 2-D projection. The downgrade may agree with guests who are aggravated by 3-D effects, but it also makes the experience much less immersive.

The ride's story serves as a mini sequel to the original animated movie *Despicable Me,* starring Gru, the archvillain, along with his adopted daughters and his diminutive yellow Minions. The preshow area is inside Dr. Gru's house, where you see his unique family tree and other artifacts. Our favorite is the mounted lion's head (in the lion's mouth is a dog, in the dog's mouth is a cat, and in the cat's mouth is a mouse). The premise of the ride is that you're being turned into one of Dr. Gru's Minions. Once converted you must navigate the Minion Training Grounds, where your "speed, strength, and ability not to die" are tested. Something soon goes amiss, though, and your training turns into a frenetic rescue operation. The events of this ride take place exactly one year after the original *Despicable Me* film; a subplot of the ride involves Gru's daughters (Edith, Agnes, and Margo) celebrating the anniversary of their adoption. In a brilliant marketing tie-in, the adorable gift Agnes gives to Gru can be purchased in the Super Silly Stuff gift shop on your way out.

The ride itself is a fast-paced series of dives, climbs, and tight turns through Gru's Rube Goldberg–esque machines. Like The Simpsons Ride, there are more sight gags and interesting things to see here than anyone possibly could in a single ride. Luckily, it's Universal's least intense motion simulator, so re-rides are less likely to make you lose your lunch. Guests exit the ride into a disco party with interactive video screens and a photo op where they can boogie down with a Minion.

TOURING TIPS Despicable Me Minion Mayhem is unfortunately situated at the very front of the park, within a few yards of the entrance turnstiles, and usually begins operating before the official opening time. As a result, long lines develop as soon as the park opens. If you're among the first to enter and the wait is 20 minutes or less, get in line for Despicable Me, and then ride Hollywood Rip Ride Rockit. However, if the line for Despicable Me exceeds 20 minutes, try late afternoon or the hour before the park closes. Note that the posted standby time is just the wait to enter the building; you'll be watching preshows for an additional 10 minutes before you actually ride.

The perspective from simulators on the sides can be skewed, and the vehicles up front are a bit too close. For the best view, you want to be in the middle of one of the center rows. Stationary seating is available for those prone to motion sickness and for children less than 40 inches tall; ask an attendant for directions. On busy days they occasionally open a queue with direct access to stationary seating, which can significantly slash your wait time.

Hollywood Rip Ride Rockit *(Universal Express)*   ★★★★

APPEAL BY AGE   PRESCHOOL ★   GRADE SCHOOL ★★★★   TEENS ★★★★½
YOUNG ADULTS ★★★★½   OVER 30 ★★★★   SENIORS ★★★

What it is High-tech roller coaster. Scope and scale Headliner. When to go The first hour after park opening or late afternoon. Comments 51" minimum height requirement; child swap available (see page 204); single-rider line available. Expect long waits in line. Woo-hoo! (and ouch!). Duration of ride 2½ minutes. Loading speed Moderate.

Motion Sickness

DESCRIPTION AND COMMENTS Let's start with the basics: Rip Ride Rockit is a sit-down X-Car coaster that runs on a 3,800-foot steel track, with a maximum height of 167 feet and a top speed of 65 mph. Manufactured by German coaster maker Maurer AG, X-Car vehicles are more maneuverable than most other kinds and use less restrictive restraints, making for an exhilarating ride.

You ascend—vertically—at 11 feet per second to crest the 17-story-tall first hill, one of the highest points reached by any roller coaster in Orlando. The drop is almost vertical too, launching you into Double Take, a 136-foot-tall loop inversion in which you begin on the inside of the loop, twist to the outside at the top (so you're upright), and then twist back inside the loop for the descent. Other innovative track elements include a treble clef–shaped twist and a spiraling negative-g Jump Cut maneuver.

The ride starts in the Production Central area; weaves into the New York area near Race Through New York Starring Jimmy Fallon, popping out over the heads of guests in the square below; and then storms out toward the lagoon separating USF from CityWalk.

Each train consists of two cars, with riders arranged two across in three rows per car. Each row is outfitted with color-changing LEDs and high-end audio and video technology for each seat. Like Rock 'n' Roller Coaster at Disney's Hollywood Studios, the "Triple R" features a musical soundtrack, but in this case you can choose the genre of music you want to hear as you ride: classic rock, country, disco, pop, or rap. The ride has dozens of hidden songs in its catalog. Press the Rip Ride Rockit logo on the number pad for 10 seconds, then enter 113 to hear Led Zeppelin's "Immigrant Song." Press 902 to hear The Muppets sing "The Rainbow Connection." For the complete list, see tinyurl.com/rockitsongs, or download the Pocket Rockit Setlist app from the Apple or Android stores.

When it's over, Universal flogs both still photos and a DVD video of your ride, which intercuts stock footage of the coaster with clips of you screaming, as recorded by your seat-mounted camera. The DVD costs $35, or $40 with a 5-by-7-inch print; My Universal Photos members pay $20 for just the video.

While perfectly safe, Rip Ride Rockit subjects you to a lot of side-to-side jarring. To crib a phrase from Tina Turner, some folks like it easy . . . and some folks like it *rough.* This reader from Armonk, New York, definitely falls in the former category:

Despite the fact that I love roller coasters and am in good physical shape with no issues, Hollywood Rip Ride Rockit hurt my back. My 17-year-old daughter who also loves all rides didn't love it either.

A Seattle visitor volunteers this visceral warning:

Tell older people not to go on Rip Ride Rockit. I don't know how anyone stands it. I call it the Punisher because it was a minute of sheer pain. It is so incredibly bumpy that I felt like I was being hit on the back of the head with a foam baseball bat for a full minute.

And from another reader in Belgium, Wisconsin:

I've ridden many roller coasters in my 35 years, including some that were over 400 feet tall and with speeds in excess of 120 mph, yet I've never ridden one that was as painful and rough as Rip Ride Rockit. With the beating my head and neck took, I'll never ride that one again.

On the other hand, this family from Lancaster, Pennsylvania, thinks Rockit is worth riding:

Our 10-year-old son rode Rip Ride Rockit four times with almost no waiting. This was a ride we hadn't even included in our plan because we thought it would be too scary and the lines not worth the wait. It ended up being a favorite experience of the trip.

This Whalton, England, mom sums up the ride's generational divide:

A fabulous, gut-wrenching coaster that thrilled the socks off my 8- and 9-year-olds. (Mum found it a bit too brutal to repeat.)

TOURING TIPS Rip Ride Rockit's hourly capacity is about 1,500 riders. Because the ride is so close to the USF entrance, it's a crowd magnet, creating bottlenecks from park opening on. Your best chance to ride without a long wait is to be one of the first to enter the park when it opens, or use the single-rider entrance (when available). You'll have to empty your pockets into a free locker and pass through a metal detector before queuing.

Shrek 4-D *(Universal Express)*   ★★★½

**APPEAL BY AGE   PRESCHOOL ★★★½   GRADE SCHOOL ★★★½   TEENS ★★★
YOUNG ADULTS ★★★   OVER 30 ★★★   SENIORS ★★★½**

What it is 3-D movie. **Scope and scale** Major attraction. **When to go** Anytime after experiencing the rides. **Comments** Child swap available (see page 204). The snarkiest 3-D show in town. **Duration of show** 20 minutes.

DESCRIPTION AND COMMENTS An indoor 3-D film with moving theater seating, set between the franchise's first two films, *Shrek 4-D* follows the adventures of Shrek, Donkey, and Dragon as they attempt to rescue Fiona after she's kidnapped by Lord Farquaad. The preshow holding area is themed as Lord Farquaad's dungeon, where the Three Little Pigs and the Gingerbread Man warn riders about the pains and tortures in store for everyone, until the diminutive despot appears to deliver a monologue about his evil plan to reclaim his lost bride. The plan is posthumous because Lord Farquaad ostensibly died in the movie, and it's his ghost making the plans, but never mind.

Inside the main theater, guests don their 3-D glasses and recline in seats that bump and vibrate along with the action, like the D-BOX seats found in local cinemas. The film's 3-D effects aren't bad, but they rely on older polarized glasses. Regardless of what Albert Einstein said, as far as theme parks go, the fourth dimension is water, so guests are subjected to a mild spritz or three during the show, along with tactile effects like leg ticklers.

Technicalities aside, *Shrek 4-D* is a mixed bag. It's frantic, laugh-out-loud funny, and iconoclastic. Concerning the last, the film takes a good poke at Disney, with Pinocchio, the Three Little Pigs, and Tinker Bell (among others) all sucked into the mayhem. But the video quality and 3-D effects are dated by today's ultra-HD standards, the story line is incoherently disconnected from the clever preshow, and the bucking seats swiftly become a pain in the butt. On the upside, in contrast to Disney's *It's Tough to Be a Bug!*, *Shrek 4-D* doesn't generally freak out kids under age 7.

TOURING TIPS Universal claims it can move about 2,400 guests per hour through *Shrek 4-D*, but the show's location at the front of the park and directly across from Despicable Me Minion Mayhem translates to heavy traffic in the morning. If you see lines longer than 20 minutes, try visiting during mealtimes or in the last 2 hours the park is open. There's not much in the film or preshow to scare small children. Stationary seating is available on request. Be aware that *Shrek 4-D* shuts down one of its two theaters in the fall to hold a haunted house for Halloween Horror Nights, greatly increasing wait times during an otherwise slow season.

Transformers: The Ride—3-D *(Universal Express)* ★★★★

What it is Multisensory 3-D dark ride. Scope and scale Super-headliner. When to go First hour the park is open or after 4 p.m. Comments 40" minimum height requirement; child swap available (see page 204); single-rider line available. A breathtaking, deafening blur; not to be missed. Duration of ride 4½ minutes. Loading speed Moderate–fast.

Motion Sickness

DESCRIPTION AND COMMENTS Transformers—those toy robots from the 1980s that you turned and twisted into trucks and planes—have been around long enough to go from commercial to kitsch to cool and back again. Thanks to director-producer Michael Bay's movie series, most recently represented by 2018's *Bumblebee* prequel, "Robots in Disguise" are again a blockbuster global franchise. In 2013 Transformers fans finally received a USF attraction (cloned from earlier rides in Singapore and Hollywood) befitting their pop-culture idols. Recruits to this cybertronic war enlist by entering the N.E.S.T. Base—headquarters of the heroic Autobots and their human allies—beneath a 28-foot-tall statue of Optimus Prime. Inside an extensive, elaborately detailed queue, video monitors catch you up on the backstory. Basically, the Decepticon baddies are after the AllSpark, source of cybernetic sentience. We're supposed to safeguard the shard by hitching a ride aboard our friendly Autobot ride vehicle EVAC, presumably without getting smooshed like a Lincoln in a souvenir penny press every time he shifts into android form. Needless to say, Megatron and his pals Starscream and Devastator won't make things easy, but you'll have Sideswipe and Bumblebee (in his modern Camaro form; look for an old-school Volkswagen Beetle in the final scene) backing you up. For the ride's 4½ minutes, you play human Ping-Pong ball in an epic battle between these Made in Japan behemoths.

To do justice to this Bay-splosion-packed war of good versus evil, Transformers harnesses the same traveling simulator system behind Islands of Adventure's Amazing Adventures of Spider-Man ride, and it ups the ante with photo-realistic high-definition imagery, boosted by dichroic 3-D glasses that produce remarkably sharp, vivid visuals. The plot amounts to little more than a giant game of keep-away, and the uninitiated will likely be unable to tell one meteoric mass of metal from another, but you'll be too dazzled by the debris whizzing by to notice. Fanboys will squeal with delight at hearing original cartoon actors Peter Cullen and Frank Welker voicing the pugilistic protagonists, and then spill into the postride gift shop to purchase armloads of exclusive merchandise, while the rest of us might need a bench on which to take a breather afterward. We'll admit slight disappointment at not getting to see an actual four-story-tall animatronic transform, but the ride's mix of detailed (though largely static) set pieces and video projections was likely a much more maintenance-friendly solution for bringing these colossi to life. Either way, this is one of the most intense, immersive thrill rides found in any theme park. However, Transformers doesn't hold up as well after repeated rides as The Amazing Adventures of Spider-Man, as it lacks the humor, heart, and moving props of its predecessor. Two millennials had, shall we say, a visceral take on Transformers:

The illusion of being smashed through an office building is pretty convincing. If you've ever wondered what it would be like to be eaten, digested, and pooped out of a giant robot, this is the ride for you.

Hopefully, it's also a ride for those who don't exactly see Transformers as a trip down the alimentary canal. Robots poop? Who knew?

TOURING TIPS This ride draws crowds. Your only solace is that The Wizarding World of Harry Potter—Diagon Alley draws even larger throngs. The single-rider line (when available) will get you on board faster, but as singles lines go, this is one of the slower ones and is closed off if it becomes backed up. Finally, it's hard to focus on the fast-moving imagery from the front row; center seats in the second and third rows provide the best perspective.

NEW YORK

THE CITY STREETS OF THE BIG APPLE are re-created in this section of USF. Along with London and Hollywood, New York represents some of the best theming found in the park. Make sure to explore the crooked alleyways behind *The Blues Brothers* stage for some authentic-looking urban backdrops. Trivia note: The statue near the border with San Francisco has the body of Abraham Lincoln and the head of late MCA/Universal mogul Lew Wasserman.

New York has two attractions, one sit-down restaurant, one counter-service restaurant, an arcade, and a Starbucks café. *The Blues Brothers Show* and other musical acts (see page 306) also perform here. First Aid is located in the alley behind Louie's Italian Restaurant.

Race Through New York Starring Jimmy Fallon
(Universal Express) ★★★½

APPEAL BY AGE	PRESCHOOL ★★★½	GRADE SCHOOL ★★★★	TEENS ★★★★
YOUNG ADULTS ★★★½		OVER 30 ★★★½	SENIORS ★★★½

What it is Comedic 3-D simulator ride. Scope and scale Headliner. When to go First 2 hours of the day or according to your Virtual Line return time. Comments May require free Virtual Line reservation (see page 75). 40" minimum height requirement; child swap available (see page 204). Duration of ride 4 minutes. Loading speed Moderate.

DESCRIPTION AND COMMENTS Housed in a replica of NBC's historic 30 Rock offices in Manhattan, Race Through New York offers Virtual Line passes instead of a standby queue. Guests, except for those with Universal Express, are assigned a reservation time via Universal's mobile app or an automated kiosk. When your appointed time arrives, you return to the ride entrance, where you'll be directed to the first lobby of the NBC offices. An NBC page will hand you a color-coded card—hold on to it and take time to enjoy the lobby tributes to the previous hosts of *The Tonight Show:* Steve Allen (1954-1956), Jack Paar (1957-1962), Johnny Carson (1962-1992), Jay Leno (1992-2009 and 2010-2014), and Conan O'Brien (2009-2010).

Once you ascend to the second floor, you await your ride in a fancy lounge outfitted with couches and touch screen tables with video games inspired by *The Tonight Show Starring Jimmy Fallon.* The main attractions, however, are live appearances by some *Tonight Show* regulars: the Ragtime Gals, a male vocal quintet that performs tongue-in-cheek barbershop interpretations of pop hits; and Hashtag the Panda, a dancing fur character (celebrity guests who have worn the costume range from Chris Rock to Miley Cyrus).

Jimmy Fallon's preshow entertainment may be suspended to promote social distancing, allowing guests to skip directly to the simulator ride.

When the color of the lights changes to match the color of your card, it's time to make your way to Jimmy Fallon's studio. The Roots, Fallon's house band, rap the safety instructions before you enter a 72-seat theater with a large screen. Next, you'll don 3-D glasses and race against Fallon in his souped-up Tonight Rider roadster. Starting at the *Tonight Show* studio, the competition sends you careening through the streets and subways of New York and eventually to, yes, the moon. Fans create wind effects, and there are faint pizza smells in addition to the obligatory water spray. (Hey, it's Universal!)

The queueless experience and preshow areas get a lot of points, and the ride itself has some of the sharpest visuals and smoothest movement in the Universal repertoire. But it breaks no new technical ground for the genre, and it relies on recognition of Fallon's stable of characters (like Ew! Girl and Tight Pants Man) for its jokes, which grow stale after several viewings. Race Through New York gets mixed reviews from our readers; this visitor from Crystal Lake, Illinois, represents the majority opinion:

I was surprised with how unimpressed I was with Race Through New York with Jimmy Fallon. Universal has raised the bar so much and has done such an amazing job with everything that I had big hopes for this ride. In the end, it was OK, but not as good as I expected.

But others agree with this family from Vadnais Heights, Minnesota:

We went on it twice, and all the kids loved it. The kids really liked the games they could play before they went on the ride, and they had fun with Hashtag the Panda.

TOURING TIPS   Race Through New York typically opens with a regular standby queue for the first few hours of the day before switching to Virtual Line–only operations. Reserve your Virtual Line pass through the Universal smartphone app for early afternoon, when other attractions generally have their longest lines. You can also grab a ticket from the kiosks outside the attraction after riding Revenge of the Mummy. If return times have run out for the day, check back at the attraction an hour or two before park closing, when walk-ins are usually accepted.

Request a free **studio tour** for a guided glimpse backstage, including a peek into the ride's control room, a visit to the private VIP balcony, and possibly a private audience with Hashtag. Tours are subject to staff availability; try asking at the attraction entrance around 10 a.m. or 4 p.m.

Revenge of the Mummy (*Universal Express*)   ★★★★½

APPEAL BY AGE   PRESCHOOL ★½   GRADE SCHOOL ★★★½   TEENS ★★★★½
YOUNG ADULTS ★★★★½   OVER 30 ★★★★½   SENIORS ★★★★

What it is Combination dark ride and roller coaster. Scope and scale Headliner. When to go The first 2 hours the park is open or after 4 p.m. Comments 48″ minimum height requirement; child swap available (see page 204); single-rider line available. Killer! Not to be missed. Duration of ride 3 minutes. Loading speed Moderate–fast.

Motion Sickness

DESCRIPTION AND COMMENTS Revenge of the Mummy is a high-tech hybrid indoor roller coaster/dark ride based on the *Mummy* flicks starring Brendan Fraser (with no references to the recent Tom Cruise reboot). The ride's premise is that a movie production crew has taken over New York's Museum of Antiquities to film a sequel titled *Revenge of the Mummy*. The queuing area serves to establish the story line: you're in a group touring a set from the *Mummy* films when you enter a tomb where the fantasy world of film gives way to the real thing. You'll notice lots of interactive details built into the queue, including hints that the movie filming isn't going according to plan. By the time you board your clunky, jeeplike ride vehicle, you've learned that the movie's villain, Imhotep, is trying to use the film crew's souls to become immortal. Only the mystical Medjay symbol can save you from certain doom (cue dramatic music).

The ride begins as a slow, very elaborate dark ride, passing through various chambers, including one where flesh-eating scarab beetles descend on you. Suddenly your vehicle stops and then drops backward and rotates. Here's where you're shot at high speed up the first hill of the roller coaster part of the ride. We won't give away any of Mummy's secrets, but here's what you need to know: It's mostly in the dark and there are no loops, inversions, or any kind of upside-downness; there are plenty of tight turns and high-speed drops and a maximum speed of around 45 mph. Though it's a wild ride by anyone's definition, the emphasis remains as much on the visuals, robotics, and special effects as on the ride itself. The special effects are aging but still pretty good: video effects, animatronics, lighting, and enough fire-spewing gas vents to rotisserie a chicken. The endings (yes, plural) are pretty clever.

TOURING TIPS Try to ride during the first 2 hours the park is open. If lines are long, one fallback is to use the singles line, which can cut your wait to a third of the posted wait time and is often more expedient than Universal Express. If you must wait on a hot day, the consolation is that Mummy's air-conditioning system is one of the best in the park.

The front left seat gets the best view of the animatronic effects, while the back corner seats offer the most air time in the coaster sections. Request row three for extra legroom if you found the test seat outside the attraction entrance to be a tight fit. Concerning motion sickness, if you can ride Space Mountain without ill effect, you should be fine on Revenge of the Mummy. Finally, note that the Mummy's queue contains enough scary stuff to frighten little kids all on its own. While most grade-schoolers we surveyed who were plucky enough to ride the Mummy gave it high marks, one father feels the rating for that age group is inappropriate:

> This ride should NOT be recommended for grade-schoolers, for which the ride was rated a 3½. My second-grader (who wasn't scared at all on Space Mountain) was terrified during this ride and cried afterward. I'm really upset I encouraged her to ride it and worried she'll have nightmares. Even I thought it was quite scary, and other adults on our ride echoed the same. You should really consider a warning about the VERY frightening aspects of this ride.

However, this reader thinks we've oversold the Mummy's fright factor:

> We disagree with you about Revenge of the Mummy. We read your description and were anticipating being scared. While the coaster aspect is a fun ride, otherwise it wasn't scary in the slightest.

Ask the greeter out front for a free **production tour;** if it isn't too busy, they may escort you into the maintenance area, where you can watch the coaster cars fly overhead.

SAN FRANCISCO

UNIVERSAL'S TRIBUTE TO Baghdad by the Bay is a bit too abbreviated to leave your heart in, but the designers did manage to squeeze in an attraction, along with a number of eateries and shops, into only a couple of blocks of brick and boardwalk. Be on the lookout for Bruce the shark; this trophy formerly stood in front of the Jaws ride and was transplanted to the Frisco wharf once that attraction sailed away.

Fast & Furious: Supercharged (Universal Express; seasonal)
★ ★ ★

APPEAL BY AGE   PRESCHOOL ★ ★   GRADE SCHOOL ★ ★ ★   TEENS ★ ★ ★
YOUNG ADULTS ★ ★ ★   OVER 30 ★ ★ ½   SENIORS ★ ★ ½

What it is Car chase motion simulator. Scope and scale Headliner. When to go After experiencing the other headliners. Comment 40" minimum height requirement; child swap available (see page 204); single-rider line available; optional Virtual Line reservations available (see page 75). Duration of ride 5 minutes. Loading speed Fast.

DESCRIPTION AND COMMENTS Based on the $5.9 billion box office behemoth, the Fast & Furious experience starts in the elaborate industrial queue (inspired by San Francisco's historic Oriental Warehouse) where you can check out some of the high-performance automobiles seen in the films. Gearheads will weep with envy, while anyone who isn't into exotic cars may feel like they're stuck in their local garage waiting for a lube job. The latter can amuse themselves by hunting for hidden references in the queue to the *Beetlejuice* and *Disaster* attractions that previously occupied the area.

Next, two preshows, featuring live hosts awkwardly interacting with prerecorded clips of Jordana Brewster (Mia Toretto) and Chris "Ludacris" Bridges (Tej), establish the backstory for anyone who hasn't yet seen all—or any—of the nine (and counting) *Furious* films.

After boarding specially designed 48-passenger tramlike "party buses," you're taken to an underground club, where a postrace rave party is in full swing until the feds crash the party, searching for a crucial crime witness hiding among the guests. Series stars Vin Diesel (Dominic "Dom" Toretto), Dwayne Johnson (Luke Hobbs), Michelle Rodriguez (Letty Ortiz), and Tyrese Gibson (Roman Pearce) appear in holographic form to rescue you from Luke Evans (Owen Shaw), the bad guy from *Fast & Furious 6*. In the attraction's climax, a 360-degree projection tunnel—filled with hydraulic platforms, 400-foot-long screens, and excessive sprays of smoke and water—make it appear as if your ride vehicle is in the midst of a high-stakes car chase, speeding at 100-plus mph through a West Coast urban jungle.

Fast & Furious: Supercharged is similar to Skull Island: Reign of Kong in Islands of Adventure, but without the immersive 3-D or impressive animatronics. The dialogue and visual effects are shockingly cheesy even by theme park standards (some consider this part of the appeal). It all goes by in such a nitro-fueled blur that it may not matter to fans of the flicks, but this reader from Nebraska City agrees with our negative assessment:

You warned us that the Fast & Furious ride was bad, but we had to try it once. You were right; it is stunningly, laughably bad. So bad! Plus it was hard to see the screens, so we missed what little did happen.

TOURING TIPS The free Virtual Line system for Supercharged kicks in a couple hours after park opening on busier days, letting you select your ride time via the smartphone app or by grabbing a ticket from the ride's kiosks, but due to the queue arrangement, you'll only save time if the standby wait is more than 30 minutes. Standard standby, Universal Express, and single-rider lines are also available; as a bonus, single riders bypass the embarrassing preshows.

The best views are from the center/right seats in the first bus; stay to the left when the queue splits before the loading dock. Though less scary than the King Kong ride, Supercharged has a slightly higher height requirement. Luckily, the custom slot car racing game in the child swap room may be more fun than the actual attraction.

Supercharged was shut down in the fall of 2020, marking the fastest fall from grace for a major theme park attraction since Disney California Adventure's Superstar Limo. The attraction is officially listed as operating seasonally, but rumors suggest it may never reopen in its original form.

THE WIZARDING WORLD OF HARRY POTTER— DIAGON ALLEY

WHEN UNIVERSAL OPENED The Wizarding World of Harry Potter at IOA, it created a paradigm shift in the Disney–Universal theme park rivalry. Not only did Universal trot out some groundbreaking ride technology, but it also demonstrated that it could trump Disney's most distinctive competence: the creation of infinitely detailed and totally immersive themed areas. To say that The Wizarding World was a game changer is an understatement of the first order.

It was immediately obvious that Universal would build on its Potter franchise success—but how and where? Universal isn't sitting on 27,000-plus acres like Disney, so real estate was at a premium. If Potterville was going to grow, something else had to go.

It just so happened that a substantial chunk of turf at USF was occupied by the aging Jaws ride and its contiguous Amity-themed area. The space allowed for substantial development. Plus, its isolated location—in the most remote corner of the park—was conducive to creating a totally self-contained area where Potter themes could be executed absent any distraction from neighboring attractions.

Two London sites that figure prominently in the Potter saga brim with attraction possibilities: Diagon Alley, a secret part of London that is a sort of sorcerers' shopping mall; and the King's Cross railroad station, where wizarding students embark for the train trip to Hogwarts.

Following much deliberation and consultation with Warner Bros. and author J. K. Rowling, the final design called for a London waterfront street scene flanking the lagoon in Universal Studios. The detailed facades, anchored by the **King's Cross railroad station** on the left and including **Grimmauld Place** and **Wyndham's Theatre,** recall West London scenes from the books and movies. **Diagon Alley,** secreted behind the London street scene, is accessed through a secluded entrance in the middle of the facade. Like Hogsmeade at IOA, Diagon Alley features shops and restaurants in addition to three attractions and live entertainment.

Diagon Alley covers nearly 7 acres—about half the area as the Hogsmeade original—but offers significantly more pedestrian space because it doesn't have space- (and people-) eating outdoor roller coasters. With only one high-capacity ride (**Harry Potter and the Escape from Gringotts**), along with an enlarged version of the **Ollivanders** wand-shop experience in Hogsmeade and the **Hogwarts Express** train connecting the two Wizarding Worlds, the area's increased elbowroom is somewhat offset by a relatively reduced hourly attraction capacity.

Diagon Alley in Detail

Once you're in the London area, take a moment to spot Kreacher (the house elf regularly peers from a second-story window above 12 Grimmauld Place); dial MAGIC (62442) in the red phone booth for a message from the Ministry of Magic; poke your head in the back door of the triple-decker purple Knight Bus; and chat with the Knight Bus conductor and his Caribbean-accented shrunken head. For some Easter eggs from the attraction designers—including the first of several tributes to Jaws, the original occupant of this area—inspect the record albums in the music store window. You'll also find a couple of cabmen's shelters selling snacks (jacket potatoes, British crisps, and hot dogs in cylindrical buns) and London souvenirs, along with an exacting replica of the towering Shaftesbury Memorial Fountain from Piccadilly Circus.

Now enter Diagon Alley next to the Leicester Square marquee in the approximate center of the building facades. As in the books and films, the unmarked portal is concealed within a magical brick wall ordinarily reserved for wizards and the like. (Unfortunately, the wall doesn't actually move, due to safety concerns.) The endless parade of Muggles (also known as plain old humans) in shorts and flip-flops will leave little doubt where that entryway is, and just in case you're completely clueless, during peak periods Universal positions attendants outside to obtrusively point the way.

Once admitted, look down the alley to the rounded facade of **Gringotts Wizarding Bank,** where a 40-foot fire-breathing Ukrainian Ironbelly dragon (as seen in *Harry Potter and the Deathly Hallows: Part 2*) perches atop the dome. The dragon doesn't move, but about every 10 minutes (weather permitting), he unleashes a jet of flame; get your camera ready when you hear him growl. To your left is the **Leaky Cauldron,** the area's flagship restaurant, serving authentically hearty British pub fare.

Intersecting Diagon Alley near the Leaky Cauldron is **Knockturn Alley,** a labyrinth of twisting passageways where the Harry Potter bad guys hang out. A covered walk-through area with a projected sky creating perpetual night, it features spooky special effects in the faux shop windows—don't miss the creeping tattoos and crawling spiders! Finally, to the right of Gringotts is **Carkitt Market,** a canopy-covered plaza where short live shows are staged every half hour or so. All the sections of Diagon Alley are crammed with elaborate signage, animated window displays, and endless hidden details to discover.

Discover is an important word in Diagon Alley because this overwhelmingly intricate area actually feels like a place you can explore and get lost in, much like, say, Epcot's Morocco Pavilion or Disneyland's New Orleans Square. We can't overstate how seamlessly Diagon's designers have rendered the illusion of a living world, topping even Disney California Adventure's Cars Land. *Immersion* is an often-overworked buzzword in themed entertainment, but this Wizarding World exemplifies it, enveloping fans in Potter's world to a degree that far exceeds Hogsmeade's high standards. And even if you aren't a follower of the franchise, you may find yourself falling for the fictional universal after experiencing Universal's incarnation.

Diagon Alley Attractions

Harry Potter and the Escape from Gringotts
(Universal Express) ★★★★★

APPEAL BY AGE   PRESCHOOL ★★½   GRADE SCHOOL ★★★★½   TEENS ★★★★½
YOUNG ADULTS ★★★★★   OVER 30 ★★★★½   SENIORS ★★★★½

What it is Super-high-tech 3-D dark ride with roller coaster elements. **Scope and scale** Super-headliner. **When to go** First thing during early entry or in the late afternoon. **Comments** 42″ minimum height requirement; child swap available (see page 204); single-rider line available. The ultimate realization of "Ride the Movies"; not to be missed. **Duration of ride** 4½ minutes. **Loading speed** Moderate–fast.

DESCRIPTION AND COMMENTS Owned and operated by goblins, Gringotts is the Federal Reserve of the wizarding economy, as well as the scene of memorable sequences from the first and final Potter installments. It's known for its toppling column facade, chandelier-adorned lobby, and bottomless caverns (and the heart-stopping carts running through them). The theme park adaptation is the centerpiece of Diagon Alley and is the ultimate expression of the virtual reality rides that Universal has been refining since IOA opened.

Like Forbidden Journey at IOA, Harry Potter and the Escape from Gringotts incorporates a substantial part of the overall experience into its elaborate queue, which (like Hogwarts Castle) even nonriders should experience. You enter through the bank's lobby, where you're critically appraised by glowering animatronic goblins. Your path takes you to a "security checkpoint," where your photo will be taken (to be purchased afterward as an identity lanyard in the gift shop, natch), and past animated newspapers and office windows where the scenario is set up.

Unlike Forbidden Journey, Gringotts doesn't rush you through its queue but rather allows you to experience two full preshows before approaching the ride vehicles. In the first, goblin banker Blordak and Bill Weasley (Ron's curse-breaking big brother) prepare you for an introductory tour of the underground vaults. Then you're off for a convincing simulated 9-mile plunge into the earth aboard an "elevator" with a bouncing floor and ceiling projections. All this is before you pick up your 3-D glasses and ascend a spiral staircase into the stalactite-festooned boarding cave where your vault cart awaits.

> Due to social distancing, the photo capture, office preshow, and elevator ride may all be bypassed.

Also unlike Forbidden Journey, and indeed all the rest of The Wizarding World, Gringotts is not set in a nebulous "moment frozen in time," where incidents from various stories simultaneously coexist. Instead, visitors enter the bank at the exact moment Harry, Ron, Hermione, and Griphook have arrived to liberate Helga Hufflepuff's Cup Horcrux from Bellatrix Lestrange's vault. Only in this retelling of *Harry Potter and the Deathly Hallows: Part 2*'s iconic action scene, you (as Muggles opening new bank accounts) are ingeniously integrated into the action. Familiar film moments featuring the vaults' guardian dragon play out in the ride's background as Bellatrix and Lord Voldemort appear to menace you with snakes and sinister spells, whereupon the heroic trio pauses its quest to save your hapless posteriors. The storytelling, which is much more coherent than Forbidden Journey's hodgepodge approach, may disorient scholars of the Potter canon, but it's an intelligent way to allow fans to relive a favorite adventure without merely rehashing the plot.

Gringotts's ornately industrial ride vehicles consist of two-car trains, each holding 24 people in rows of four. The ride merges Revenge of the Mummy's indoor coaster aspects with The Amazing Adventures of Spider-Man's seamless integration of high-resolution 3-D film (the finale dome completely surrounds your cart) and massive sculptural sets (some of the rockwork inside is six stories tall), while adding a few new tricks, such as independently rotating carts and motion-simulator bases built into the track.

The result is a ride that, though it doesn't break completely new ground as Forbidden Journey and Spider-Man did, combines favorite innovations from its predecessors in an exhilarating new way. The visuals are sometimes murky and the dialogue difficult to discern. And it's slightly disappointing that no animatronic figures, moving set pieces, or actual pyrotechnics appear in the ride, though you will get spritzed with water, blasted with warm air, and sprayed with fog—this is Universal, after all. Finally, though Helena Bonham Carter and Ralph Fiennes reprised their screen roles, Daniel Radcliffe and Emma Watson did not. Harry and pals' computer-generated image stand-ins look OK, as they're never seen up close, but Hermione's voice double is dreadful.

Nitpicks aside, whether Escape from Gringotts is *the* greatest themed thrill ride of all time or merely *one* of the greatest can be happily debated by park fans until the next great leap forward comes along. To these New England honeymooners, there's not much to debate:

> *Gringotts is a terrific ride! Less intense than the Forbidden Journey but still full of surprises.*

TOURING TIPS Though the interior line is gorgeous and air-conditioned, the mostly unshaded outdoor extended queue holds 4,000 guests—you don't want to be at the end of it. If you're a Universal resort guest and you qualify for early entry, use it; Express Passes aren't valid during early entry, so the line moves swiftly. Otherwise, try the attraction around lunchtime or in the late afternoon; wait times usually peak after opening but become reasonable later in the day. Be warned that, as with any ride this advanced, Gringotts can be expected to experience some downtime almost daily. Most operational interruptions are brief and resolved within 10 or 15 minutes.

As far as physical thrills go, Gringotts falls somewhere between Disney's Seven Dwarfs Mine Train and Space Mountain, with only one short (albeit unique) drop and no upside-down flips. It was designed to be less intense (read: less nauseating) than Forbidden Journey and therefore more appealing to families, with fewer height, weight, and size restrictions. The restraints are similar to Revenge of the Mummy's, with bars across your lap and shins, but slightly more restrictive. Use the test seat to the left of the front entrance if you're unsure, and request the third or sixth row for additional legroom.

The ride feels noticeably different depending on the row in which you're seated. The front is closest to the action and has the scariest view of the drop; 3-D effects look better farther back. The sixth row gets the most coaster action, especially from the initial fall, but the screens are slightly distorted. The far right seat in row four is the sweet spot.

As is the case with most of Universal's thrill rides, you must leave your bags in a free locker. Universal Express is accepted at this attraction, and the only part of the preshow experience that Express guests miss is the boring outdoor queue. If you don't have bags and don't mind breaking up your group, the singles line will cut your wait to about a third of the posted standby time, but you'll skip all the preshows past the lobby; we don't advise this option until after your first ride.

Hogwarts Express *(Universal Express)* ★★★★½

APPEAL BY AGE PRESCHOOL ★★★★½ GRADE SCHOOL ★★★★½ TEENS ★★★★½
YOUNG ADULTS ★★★★½   OVER 30 ★★★★½   SENIORS ★★★★½

What it is Transportation attraction. **Scope and scale** Headliner. **When to go** Late morning or just before park closing. **Comments** Requires a park-to-park ticket. A moving experience; not to be missed. **Duration of ride** 4 minutes. **Loading speed** Moderate.

DESCRIPTION AND COMMENTS Part of the genius of creating Diagon Alley at USF is that it's connected to Hogsmeade at IOA (see Part Eight) by Hogwarts Express, just as in the novels and films. The counterpart to Hogsmeade Station in IOA is USF's King's Cross Station, a landmark London train depot that has been re-created a few doors down from Diagon Alley's hidden entrance. (Note that King's Cross has a separate entrance and exit from Diagon Alley; you can't go directly between them without crossing through the London Waterfront.)

The passage to Platform 9¾, from which Hogwarts students depart on their way to school, is concealed from Muggles by a seemingly solid brick wall, through which you'll witness guests ahead of you dematerializing. (Spoiler: The Pepper's Ghost effect creates a clever but congestion-prone photo op, but you experience only a dark corridor with whooshing sound effects when crossing over yourself.)

Once on the platform, you'll pass a pile of luggage (including an owl cage with an animatronic Hedwig) before being assigned to one of the three train cars' seven compartments. The train itself looks exactly authentic to the nth degree, from the billowing steam to the brass fixtures and upholstery in your eight-passenger private cabin. Along your one-way Hogwarts Express journey, you'll see moving images projected beyond the windows of the car rather than the park's backstage areas, with the streets of London and the Scottish countryside rolling past outside your window. The screen isn't 3-D, but it's slightly curved to conceal the edges and create a convincing illusion of depth. Even more impressive are the frosted-glass doors you enter through, which turn out to be amazing screens that make it seem as if someone is standing on the other side. You experience a different presentation coming and going, and in addition to pastoral scenery, there are surprise appearances by secondary characters (Fred and George Weasley, Hagrid) and threats en route (bone-chilling Dementors, licorice spiders), augmented by vibration and sound effects in the cars. Note that, as in Escape from Gringotts, two of the lead actors did not reprise their roles, to the ride's detriment, as this Middleton, Delaware, reader reports:

> *Ron sounds like Ron, and Harry is decent, but Hermione sounds like they grabbed a worker's relative and put her in a sound booth. I wish they would change it already.*

Hogwarts Express isn't an adrenaline rush in the same way that Escape from Gringotts is, but for those invested in Potter lore, it may be even more emotionally thrilling. And unlike most Potter attractions, it can be experienced by the whole family, regardless of size.

TOURING TIPS Because taking the train involves park-hopping, passengers need a valid park-to-park ticket. Disembarking passengers must enter the second park and, if desired, queue again for their return trip. You'll be allowed to upgrade your one-park Base Ticket at the station entrance.

Lines rarely exceed 15 minutes in the morning, though the queue may swell to an hour in midafternoon, or in the evening when one park closes before the other.

The walk from one train station to the other is just under a mile and takes 20 minutes at a moderate pace. If the posted wait is more than 15 minutes, it's typically quicker to walk to the other Wizarding World than to take the train.

Guests exiting in Hogsmeade have a chance to take a photo with the locomotive before it backs out for its next run. Guests departing from Hogsmeade should pose with the static train outside the station before they queue up.

Ollivanders ★★★★

APPEAL BY AGE PRESCHOOL ★★★½ GRADE SCHOOL ★★★★½ TEENS ★★★★½
YOUNG ADULTS ★★★★½   OVER 30 ★★★★   SENIORS ★★★★

What it is Combination wizarding demonstration and shopping op. **Scope and scale** Major attraction. **When to go** After riding Harry Potter and the Escape from Gringotts. **Comments** Audience stands. Enchanting. **Duration of presentation** 6 minutes.

DESCRIPTION AND COMMENTS Ollivanders, which is located in Diagon Alley in the books and films, is represented by both a small branch in IOA (see page 349) and this much larger location in USF. While the original Hogsmeade outpost is a horrendous bottleneck, where guests roast in an unshaded queue, the Diagon Alley version has multiple cleverly concealed choosing chambers, changing it from a popular curiosity into an actual attraction. The actual experience inside both shops is identical in script and special effects.

Every few minutes, following a scene from the Harry Potter books, a wand-selection show takes place, where a random customer (often a child dressed in Potter regalia) is selected to take part in a wand-choosing ceremony. Usually just one person in each group gets to be chosen by a wand, though occasionally siblings are selected together. This is one of the most truly imaginative elements of The Wizarding World: A Wandkeeper sizes you up and presents a wand, inviting you to try it out; your attempted spells produce unintended, unwanted, and highly amusing consequences. Ultimately, a wand chooses you, with all the attendant special effects.

The Celtic zodiac-inspired wands presented in the ceremony are detailed models that interact with shop windows throughout The Wizarding Worlds (see below). After the presentation, guests exit into a greatly enlarged gift shop, where interactive wands are available for purchase, along with noninteractive "famous wizard" replica wands for a vast variety of characters.

TOURING TIPS Free same-day reservations may be required to see the show; visit the wizard outside Globus Mundi in Carkitt Market to sign up. Check out the self-sweeping broom (shades of *Fantasia*?) while waiting for the show. To increase your odds of being picked, be a cute kid, stand up front, and make eye contact. If your young 'un is selected to test-drive a wand, be forewarned that you'll have to buy it if you want to take it home.

Interactive Wands and Spell-Casting Locations in Diagon Alley

Interactive wands ($55) are available in 13 Ollivanders Original styles inspired by the Celtic calendar; interactive wands modeled after those wielded by a variety of characters (including Harry, Hermione, Dumbledore, Sirius Black, and Luna Lovegood) are also available. In addition, nonfunctional replica wands ($49) are sold at both **Ollivanders** outposts and in the smaller selection at **Wands by Gregorovitch** in Diagon Alley.

The widest selection of wands is found in the two Ollivanders shops. Outside The Wizarding Worlds, stores at the entrance of each park, as well as at Universal Studios Stores in CityWalk and resort hotels, carry a limited variety of interactive and noninteractive wands, including toy "learner" wands ($28.95) for li'l wizards. Wands can also be ordered from Universal Orlando's merchandise website.

Medallions embedded in the ground designate a couple dozen locations split between the two Wizarding Worlds, where hidden cameras in storefront windows can detect the waving of these special wands and respond to the correct motions with special effects both projected and practical. You might use the swish and flick of Wingardium Leviosa to levitate an object or the figure-four Locomotor spell to animate another.

It can take some practice to get the hang of spell casting. Wizards wander around the area to assist novices and demonstrate spells (though they can't loan their wands), but queues to trigger certain effects can grow to a dozen deep at peak times. A map provided with each wand purchase details the location and movement for most effects, but there are some secret ones to uncover on your own. (Hint: One is in Scribbulus's window, and another is in the Slug & Jiggers storefront.) Look at your map under the ultraviolet lights in Knockturn Alley for another surprise.

Note that the price of the interactive wands includes unlimited activations of the hidden effects; you don't have to pay to recharge your wand on subsequent visits, or even replace a battery. Damaged wands are cheerfully repaired for free (even without the original box or receipt) at any Ollivanders, and globe-trotting wizards will be happy to know that their wands will also function at The Wizarding Worlds in Hollywood and Japan. If you encounter a spell-casting location with a sign saying CURRENTLY HAS AN ANTI-JINX IN PLACE, just move along to the next one; that's Potter-speak for "it's broken."

We've received positive feedback on the interactive wands, like this praise from a New York family:

We took our interactive wand and explored all the many surprises for well over an hour and had a fantastic time. An interactive wand is highly recommended. Our girls are 12 and 14, and they had a blast making the wand motions and watching the windows come to life.

This Saint Paul, Minnesota, reader says Potter-loving visitors should set aside significant time for the interactive experiences:

I didn't realize how much of the Universal parks were the "experience" of the Harry Potter areas. Wandering around, sightseeing, and using the interactive wands in these areas in both parks were as important (maybe more so, for our family) as hitting the rides. I advise devoting prime time for this, especially early mornings before the lines for each interactive wand area get too long.

On the other hand, a cost-conscious dad from Rigby, Idaho, sends this advice:

> *If you don't want massive pressure from your kid to buy one of Universal's EXPENSIVE wands, don't do the wand ceremony. If you do it anyway, speak to an attendant prior to entering the ceremony room, and advise him or her that your kids ARE NOT to be wanded! Not getting your kid one of Universal's expensive wands will not ruin their lives—honest. And from what we saw, about half of the users couldn't get their wands to work reliably. The kids get very frustrated when the 5-year-old in front of them can make things appear, move, talk, or whatever, but they can't!*

Entertainment in Diagon Alley

An elevated area in **Carkitt Market,** between The Hopping Pot and the Gringotts Money Exchange, comes to life with short shows inspired by Rowling's stories. Though modest in scope, these are some of the best performances found at Universal, and well worth working into your touring plan if you have more than one day at the resort. Showtimes are listed in the smartphone app; performances usually start every 30 minutes on the hour and half hour.

Celestina Warbeck and the Banshees (★★★½) is a live musical showcasing the Ella Fitzgerald–esque Singing Sorceress with her comely backup crew, swinging to jazzy tunes with a 1940s big band feel. With song titles created by Rowling ("You Stole My Cauldron But You Can't Have My Heart," "A Cauldron Full of Hot Strong Love," and "You Charmed the Heart Right Out of Me"), Celestina and her three Banshees perform a lively show. While the songs contain a plethora of references to the Potter books and movies that fans will love, guests who don't know (or care) about the Harry Potter universe will still enjoy the elaborate choreography, fantastic singing, and witty music and lyrics courtesy of Michael Weiner and Alan Zachary, the duo behind Disney Cruise Line's *Twice Charmed: An Original Twist on the Cinderella Story* and *Once Upon a Time*'s musical episode. During the holiday season, a special Christmas version is performed with different songs and costumes. The show runs about 12–13 minutes.

Tales of Beedle the Bard (★★★½) recounts one of two wizard fables—"The Three Brothers" from *Harry Potter and the Deathly Hallows* or "The Fountain of Fair Fortune"—using puppets crafted by Michael Curry (Broadway's *The Lion King, Finding Nemo—The Musical*). The story is chosen "randomly" at the start of each performance. The puppets are gorgeous in a creepy kind of way, and the way the actors perform while maneuvering them is quite clever, though some of the dialogue can be difficult to understand, especially during the "Fountain" tale. Some preschoolers may be scared of the large Death puppet used in "The Three Brothers." The show runs 10–12 minutes.

Shopping in Diagon Alley

Shopping is a major component of Diagon Alley in Potter lore; while Hogsmeade visitors went wild for the few wizardly shops there, Diagon Alley is the planet's wackiest mall, with a vastly expanded array of enchanted tchotchkes to declare bankruptcy over. Shops include:

WEASLEYS' WIZARD WHEEZES is a joke shop with many of the toys also found in Hogsmeade's Zonko's, plus new gags such as Skiving Snackboxes and Decoy Detonators. Look up through the three-story shop's glass ceiling for fireworks.

WISEACRE'S WIZARDING EQUIPMENT, at the exit of Harry Potter and the Escape from Gringotts, sells crystal balls, compasses, and hourglasses.

MADAM MALKIN'S ROBES FOR ALL OCCASIONS stocks school uniforms, Scottish wool sweaters, and dress robes for wizards and witches. The talking mirror will critique your ensemble if you stand in front of it.

MAGICAL MENAGERIE is the place to adopt a plush cat, rat, owl, or hippogriff; the adorable animatronic Kneazle is unfortunately not for sale.

SHUTTERBUTTON'S will film your family in front of a green screen and insert you into a DVD of Potter scenes ($80 in a souvenir case or $50 with a My Universal Photos package). Loaner Gryffindor robes are available (except during periods of social distancing) to pose in, but you'll have to bring your own wardrobe to represent a different Hogwarts house. Be warned that Slytherin-wear can interfere with the green screen effects.

QUALITY QUIDDITCH SUPPLIES sells golden snitches and jerseys for your favorite Hogwarts house teams.

SCRIBBULUS carries quills, notebooks, and similar school supplies.

BORGIN AND BURKES in Knockturn Alley stocks objects from the dark side of magic (watch out for the mummified hand!).

SUGARPLUM'S SWEET SHOP tempts guests with fudge (including an unbearably sweet Butterbeer variety), pastries, no-melt ice cream (also known as a cup of icing), Potter-themed candies, and most of the other treats also found at Honeydukes in Hogsmeade.

GLOBUS MUNDI *(seasonal)* is a small travel agency–inspired shop in Carkitt Market that carries luggage tags, key chains, pins, and the like.

OWL POST *(seasonal)* offers themed package wrapping, free postmarks, and shipping services from a small window near the Diagon Alley exit.

You can pay for all this loot in **Gringotts bank notes,** which you can purchase inside the **Gringotts Money Exchange** overseen by an imperious interactive animatronic goblin, and then spend it anywhere within Universal Orlando; see page 160 for details. Even if you don't want to exchange any of your Muggle money, take a moment to query the proprietor about his age, the current exchange rate, or almost anything you've ever wanted to ask a goblin (but were afraid to ask). In general, Diagon Alley's stores are larger and more plentiful than the tiny shops over in Hogsmeade, with carefully planned external and internal queues to corral waiting customers.

WORLD EXPO

THIS AREA STRETCHES around USF's central lagoon from Diagon Alley to The Simpsons Ride and somewhat clumsily incorporates several competing aesthetics. The World Expo name, as well as the theming of Men in Black Alien Attack in the area's center, is derived from the New York State Pavilion in the 1964 World's Fair. The *Fear Factor Live* stadium, the area's only other attraction, appears to be themed to the style known as ugly warehouse. Though not exactly an attraction, the space-age Coca-Cola kiosk near Men in Black lets you type your name on a digital soda bottle and refill your Freestyle cup.

Fear Factor Live (Universal Express; seasonal) ★★½

APPEAL BY AGE   PRESCHOOL ★★½   GRADE SCHOOL ★★★★   TEENS ★★★½
YOUNG ADULTS ★★★½   OVER 30 ★★★½   SENIORS ★★★

What it is Live version of the gross-out stunt TV show. Scope and scale Headliner. When to go 3–5 shows daily; crowds are smallest at the first and second-to-last shows. Duration of show 30 minutes.

DESCRIPTION AND COMMENTS *Fear Factor Live* is a stage version of the uniquely stomach-turning reality show that originally ran on NBC and was revived for MTV. In the theme park iteration, six volunteers compete for modest prizes, like Universal T-shirts. Contestants must be 18 years or older (with a photo ID to prove it) and weigh at least 110 pounds. Those demented enough to volunteer should arrive at least 75 minutes before showtime to sign papers and complete some obligatory training for the specific competitive events. Anyone who doesn't wish to compete in the stage show itself can sign up for the Critter Challenge or the Food Challenge. With an adult's permission, volunteers as young as age 16 can compete in the latter.

The stage show is performed in a covered theater and consists of three different challenges. Contestants must hang from a bar two-and-a-half stories in the air while heavy-duty fans blast their faces; grab beanbags out of a tank full of eels; and, for the grand finale, scramble up a wall, jump into a car that's lifted in the air, and then hit a target with a rocket launcher. Between rounds, entertainment includes the Desert Hat Ordeal, where a lunatic audience member has spiders, snakes, roaches, or scorpions placed on his or her face; and the Food Challenge, in which volunteers try to chug a smoothie of curdled milk, mystery meat, and various live bugs without vomiting.

The above description may make the show sound more entertaining than it is. It's our duty to confess that this is one of our least favorite shows in any theme park, anywhere, ever. You've been warned.

TOURING TIPS If you've ever wanted a chance to test your mettle (sanity?), *Fear Factor Live* may be your big chance. Participants for the physical stunts are chosen early in the morning and between performances outside the theater, so head there first thing if you want to be a contestant. The contestants for the skeevier stunts, such as the bug-smoothie drinking, are chosen directly from the audience. Sit close to the front and wave your hands like crazy when it comes time for selection. Finally (and seriously), this show is too intense and gross for kids age 8 and under.

An extremely relevant query from two University of Iowa students:

*We're thinking about volunteering to drink the bug smoothie and
want to know if it's better to chew the bugs or just chug the
smoothie and hope they die after crawling around for a while in
your stomach. Also, do you recommend holding your nose?*

We recommend practicing both options at home, preferably while heavily med-
icated and under the supervision of a psychiatrist. *Fear Factor Live* mercifully goes
on hiatus in the fall to turn its stadium over to Halloween Horror Nights.

Men in Black Alien Attack *(Universal Express)* ★★★★

What it is Interactive dark thrill ride. **Scope and scale** Headliner. **When to go** During the
first 2 hours the park is open. **Comments** 42″ minimum height requirement; child swap available (see page 204); single-rider line available. Buzz Lightyear's Space Ranger Spin on ste-
roids; not to be missed. **Duration of ride** 4½ minutes. **Loading speed** Moderate–fast.

DESCRIPTION AND COMMENTS Men in Black Alien Attack brings together Will Smith
and Rip Torn (as Agent J and Men in Black [MIB] director Zed) for an interactive

Motion Sickness

sequel to the hit sci-fi franchise. You'll notice that the ride's building pays
homage to the architecture from the 1964 World's Fair, including the observation towers from the New York State Pavilion that featured in the 1997
film's finale. That theme is carried over to the attraction's preshow, which
perfectly parodies the style of *Walt Disney's Carousel of Progress* before

taking a surprise turn. In the story line you've been recruited as an MIB trainee.
After an introduction warning that aliens "live among us" and articulating MIB's
mission to round them up, Zed expounds on the finer points of alien spotting and
familiarizes you with your training vehicle and your weapon, an alien zapper.

You then load up in a six-passenger spinning ride vehicle and are dispatched
into an innocuous training room, which is a shooting gallery full of plywood targets
shaped like aliens. Your training is cut short when it's revealed that a real alien spaceship has landed in New York and you must save the city. The meat of the ride consists of careening around Manhattan in your MIB vehicle and shooting aliens. There
are more targets than anyone could possibly shoot, and they're presented at a fast
pace. Each ride vehicle is paired with another ride vehicle running on a parallel track,
and both vehicles compete to see who can shoot the most aliens. At a certain point
during the ride, you'll be able to shoot at the "fusion exhaust port" of the opposing
ride vehicle, causing it to spin momentarily. This disorients the other riders and
causes them to lose precious time splatting the aliens. Of course, the other riders
(and some of the aliens!) can shoot at you too.

Men in Black is interactive in that your marksmanship and ability to blast yourself out of some tricky situations will determine how the story ends. You're awarded
both a personal score and a score for your car. There are about three dozen possible outcomes and literally thousands of different ride experiences determined by
your pluck, performance, and, in the final challenge, your intestinal fortitude.
Regardless of your score, all recruits are deemed not ready to join MIB, and everyone's memories of the game are wiped at the end of the ride.

TOURING TIPS Each alien has sensors that activate special effects and respond to
your zapper. Aim for the eyes and keep shooting because you can score repeatedly on the same target. Your gun has auto-fire and unlimited ammo, so just keep
the trigger depressed the whole ride; you'll even get a small number of points for
missed shots. Targets above you score the most points: look for aliens behind

second-story windows. At the ride's climax, listen carefully for Zed to instruct you to "push the red button," and hold it down when he says "push" to score a bonus 100,000 points. If you're good enough, you can max out with 999,999 points—trust us, it can be done.

The ride is packed with Universal in-jokes. Keep a sharp eye out for an alien seated on a park bench, hiding behind a newspaper. The head on a stick that the alien uses as a disguise bears an uncanny resemblance to Steven Spielberg, executive producer of the *Men in Black* films.

Visitors who are susceptible to motion sickness should heed this warning from a Missouri City, Texas, reader:

This ride was WAY TOO MUCH fast spinning for me. I definitely got dizzy on that one.

Avoid a long wait and ride during the first 2 hours the park is open, or try the single-rider line if you don't mind splitting your group. However, the singles and Express queues skip the preshow, which is worth seeing at least once. You can re-ride by following the signs for the child swap at the top of the exit stairs.

If it isn't too busy, ask the attendant out front for a free **immigration tour.** If you're lucky, they'll take you into the large preshow room below the queue, where you can take selfies sitting at an agent's desk and get a close-up look at the animatronic alien twins.

SPRINGFIELD: HOME OF THE SIMPSONS

BUTTING UP AGAINST Men in Black's modernist architecture is Springfield: Home of the Simpsons, the setting of the long-running animated sitcom *The Simpsons*. What started as just The Simpsons Ride and Kwik-E-Mart store was hugely expanded in 2013, with a fabulous re-creation of Moe's Tavern, the Jebediah Springfield statue (emblazoned with A NOBLE SPIRIT EMBIGGENS THE SMALLEST MAN), and other cartoon landmarks.

Kang & Kodos' Twirl 'n' Hurl (Universal Express; seasonal)
★★★

APPEAL BY AGE PRESCHOOL ★★★★ GRADE SCHOOL ★★★½ TEENS ★★★
YOUNG ADULTS ★★★ OVER 30 ★★★ SENIORS ★★★

What it is Spinning ride. Scope and scale Minor attraction. When to go After The Simpsons Ride. Comments Child swap available (see page 204). Rarely has a long wait. The world's wittiest spinner. Duration of ride 1½ minutes. Loading speed Slow.

DESCRIPTION AND COMMENTS The Twirl 'n' Hurl is primarily eye candy for Springfield. Think of it as Dumbo with Bart's sense of humor: guests ride around in little flying saucers while the alien narrators, Kang and Kodos, hold pictures of *Simpsons* characters. Make the characters speak and spin by steering your craft to the proper altitude. All the while, Kang exhorts you (loudly) to destroy Springfield and makes insulting comments about humans. Preschoolers enjoy the ride, while older kids and *Simpsons* fans crack up over the gags.

TOURING TIPS Twirl 'n' Hurl rarely attracts long lines, but (like all rides in this style) it can be very slow loading. If you want to enjoy the jokes without the wait, you can easily hear them all from the sidelines. If you have folks who are hot to ride, get them on whenever there are 50 or fewer guests in line. Try before 11 a.m. It should take awhile for most guests to arrive in Springfield, especially with Diagon Alley, Transformers, and Despicable Me keeping guests busy elsewhere.

Twirl 'n' Hurl may stop running early on nights when the seasonal evening lagoon show starts before park closing, so as not to distract from the show.

The Simpsons Ride (Universal Express) ★★★★

Motion Sickness

What it is Mega-simulator ride. **Scope and scale** Headliner. **When to go** During the first 2 hours the park is open or after 4 p.m. **Comments** 40″ minimum height requirement; not recommended for pregnant women or people prone to motion sickness; child swap available (see page 204). Despicable Me Minion Mayhem with attitude; not to be missed. **Duration of ride** 4½ minutes, plus preshow. **Loading speed** Moderate.

DESCRIPTION AND COMMENTS Another animated film coupled to a motion simulator, The Simpsons Ride is as much a satire of theme parks as it is a high-speed thrill ride through the Fox animated series that is TV's longest-running sitcom. Featuring the voices of Dan Castellaneta (Homer), Julie Kavner (Marge), Nancy Cartwright (Bart), Yeardley Smith (Lisa), and other cast members, the attraction uses a visit to Krustyland—the absurdly unsafe amusement park owned by the show's cantankerous Krusty the Clown—as an excuse to skewer Disney, SeaWorld, and even Universal itself.

The queue area and preshows involve *Simpsons* video clips (both classic and newly created) that help define the characters for guests who are unfamiliar with the TV show and that mock virtually every classic Disney attraction from The Haunted Mansion (here as the Haunted Condo, with "999 unhappy teen employees") to *Hall of Presidents* (redone as *Hall of the Secretaries of the Interior*—wait time 0 minutes). Not even ride-safety videos are spared; The Simpsons's version is an outrageous gore-fest starring Itchy and Scratchy demonstrating how *not* to behave.

The attraction itself recycled the foundations of Universal's former Back to the Future ride; watch the queue video for a time-traveling cameo by Doc Brown. The simulator is similar to Star Tours at Disney's Hollywood Studios and Universal's Despicable Me Minion Mayhem, but with a larger curved screen more like that of Soarin' at Epcot. The ride vehicles hold eight guests in two rows of four.

The story line has the conniving Sideshow Bob secretly arriving at Krustyland and plotting his revenge on Krusty and Bart for sending him to jail. Sideshow Bob gets even by making things go wrong with the attractions that the Simpsons (and you) are riding. While there are dozens of dips, turns, climbs, and drops during the ride, there are probably hundreds of one-liners and visual puns. Like the show on which it's based, The Simpsons Ride definitely has an edge and operates on several levels. There will be jokes and visuals that you'll get but will fly over your children's heads—and most assuredly vice versa.

TOURING TIPS Because the screen you sit in front of is a giant curved dome, anyone sitting outside the central sweet spot gets a distorted view, which may aggravate motion sickness. For the best experience, ask the attendant at the bottom of the ramps for Level 2, and then ask the next attendant you see for Room 6. Taller guests (6 feet or over) should sit in the front row to avoid bumping their heads.

As far as motion simulators go, The Simpsons Ride isn't as sickness-inducing as many. The wider screen seems to help, as this mom from Huntington, New York, said:

I'm not a fan of wild motion simulators, but I was fine on this ride. The field of vision makes it very engrossing, like Soarin'. However, our family still rates Star Tours higher than The Simpsons Ride, as it was most like actually being a character in the original movie!

Though not as rough and jerky as its predecessor, The Simpsons Ride is a long way from being tame. Skip it if you're an expectant mom or prone to motion sickness. Some parents may find the humor too coarse for younger kids.

WOODY WOODPECKER'S KIDZONE

NAMED AFTER THE CLASSIC Walter Lantz cartoon character, Woody Woodpecker's KidZone is situated in a colorful cul-de-sac between Hollywood and World Expo. KidZone holds most of the park's child-themed attractions, including a pint-size roller coaster and several elaborate playgrounds that are currently closed due to COVID-19.

Different family-friendly themes have long been rumored for KidZone's replacement; most recently, the Super Nintendo World originally slated for this plot may end up here following the indefinite delay of Epic Universe. In the meantime, SpongeBob StorePants, the *Animal Actors* stage, and E.T. Adventure appear to be safe, but the rest of the attractions may someday join Jimmy Neutron and Biff Tannen in Universal's retirement home.

Animal Actors on Location! (Universal Express) ★★★½

APPEAL BY AGE	PRESCHOOL ★★★★	GRADE SCHOOL ★★★★½	TEENS ★★★½
YOUNG ADULTS ★★★½		OVER 30 ★★★★	SENIORS ★★★★

What it is Animal tricks and comedy show. Scope and scale Major attraction. When to go After you've experienced all rides. Comment Cute li'l critters. Duration of show 25 minutes.

DESCRIPTION AND COMMENTS *Animal Actors on Location!* is a live show featuring performing dogs, birds, pigs, and a menagerie of other animals in a covered outdoor stadium. This show integrates video segments with live sketches, jokes, and animal tricks performed onstage. A human trainer acts as the host, explaining how the animals are conditioned to execute the tricks. Several of the animal thespians are veterans of TV and movies; many were rescued from shelters. The demonstration usually makes use of audience volunteers (mostly children) in a couple of segments. Sit in the center of the stadium about halfway up for the best chance to be selected.

If you've seen the bird show at Disney's Animal Kingdom, you'll recognize many of the bird routines in *Animal Actors*. What sets *Animal Actors* apart is the use of varied and unusual kinds of animals, as well as the opportunity to see the animals being trained onstage. The animals are trained using only positive reinforcement— that is, rewarding the animal when it performs the correct behavior—and no negative reinforcement (punishing for incorrect behavior).

TOURING TIPS Check the daily entertainment schedule for showtimes. You shouldn't have any trouble getting into the next performance. The stadium is covered but not enclosed, meaning that it's still hot during summer and cold during winter. Come to the front of the stage at the conclusion to snap a photo with some of the furry stars, and keep an eye out for training sessions with new performers in nearby Central Park.

Curious George Goes to Town (temporarily closed) ★★½

APPEAL BY AGE	PRESCHOOL ★★★★	GRADE SCHOOL ★★★★	TEENS ★★½
YOUNG ADULTS ★★		OVER 30 ★★½	SENIORS ★★

What it is Interactive playground. Scope and scale Minor attraction. When to go Anytime. Comment *The* place for rambunctious kids.

DESCRIPTION AND COMMENTS This interactive playground exemplifies the Universal obsession with wet stuff. In addition to innumerable spigots, pipes, and spray guns, two giant roof-mounted buckets periodically dump a thousand gallons of water on unsuspecting visitors below, as this Seattle father found out:

> *My 10- and 18-year-olds went into Curious George and stood under an eve spraying kids and then got totally soaked when a bucket of water dumped underneath the roof! Stay out unless you're wearing a poncho or a swimsuit.*

Kids who want to stay dry can mess around in the foam-ball playground, also equipped with chutes, tubes, and ball blasters.

TOURING TIPS Visit after you've experienced all the major attractions.

A Day in the Park with Barney *(Universal Express; seasonal)* ★★★

APPEAL BY AGE PRESCHOOL ★★★★ GRADE SCHOOL ★★★½ TEENS ★★
YOUNG ADULTS ★½ OVER 30 ★★½ SENIORS ★★

What it is Live-character stage show. Scope and scale Major children's attraction. When to go Scheduled showtimes. Comment A great hit with preschoolers. Duration of show 20 minutes, plus 5-minute preshow and character greeting after the show.

DESCRIPTION AND COMMENTS Barney—the cuddly purple dinosaur of public-TV fame—leads his sidekicks Baby Bop and BJ in an audience sing-along of toddler classics, including "If You're Happy and You Know It" and "I Love You, You Love Me." A short preshow featuring a live actor playing Mr. Peek-a-boo gets the kids lathered up before they enter Barney's Park (the theater). The characters are supplemented with props—including cartoon cows, pigs, ducks, and skunks—during some of the songs. Interesting theatrical effects include wind, falling leaves, clouds and stars in the simulated sky, and faux snow.

After the show, Barney sometimes hangs out for a brief postshow dance party, where you can snap a selfie with the whole dino herd. On other days, Barney and a pal can be found posing for photos with parents and children in the indoor playground at the theater exit or on a stage outside the venue.

TOURING TIPS If your child likes Barney, this show is a must. There's also a great indoor play area nearby, designed especially for wee tykes. In the weeks around Christmas, this show becomes *A Barney Holiday Show,* featuring a cameo from Frosty the Snowman.

E.T. Adventure *(Universal Express)* ★★★½

APPEAL BY AGE PRESCHOOL ★★★★ GRADE SCHOOL ★★★½ TEENS ★★★
YOUNG ADULTS ★★★½ OVER 30 ★★★½ SENIORS ★★★★

What it is Indoor adventure ride based on the beloved movie. Scope and scale Major attraction. When to go Within 30 minutes of ride opening or late afternoon. Comments 34" minimum height requirement; child swap available (see page 204). A long, strange, happy trip. Duration of ride 4½ minutes. Loading speed Moderate.

DESCRIPTION AND COMMENTS Inspired by Steven Spielberg's classic 1982 film (and the not-so-classic 1985 sequel novel *Book of the Green Planet*), this is the only ride at Universal that's remained essentially unchanged since opening day. Guests board bicycle-like ride vehicles (suspended from the ceiling) on an adventure to return everyone's favorite extra-terrestrial to his dying home planet.

After a brief video introduction from Spielberg himself, guests provide their first name to an attendant and receive a credit card–size interplanetary passport (more on this later) before wending their way through a dark forest of tall pine trees; this is one of the most evocative indoor ride queues in any park. As the ride itself starts, you're weaving through the woods, evading the moon-suited scientists and earthly law enforcement officials trying to capture E.T. As in the film, you're airborne soon enough, flying over Los Angeles (a lovely tableau) and into a warp tunnel to E.T.'s home planet. You arrive just in time to allow E.T.'s healing touch to save everything, and the ride ends in a mash-up of colorful flowers, lighting, and aliens. Concerning the latter, where E.T. is reunited with family and friends, Len Testa likens it to *The Wizard of Oz*'s Technicolor transition, only restaged with a cave full of naked mole rats. (C'mon, Len, where's the love?)

Before you return home, E.T. bids each rider farewell by name, thanks to those passports you received earlier. E.T. can say more than 20,000 names, though he misidentifies riders more often than not. A Baton, North Carolina, reader with perhaps too much time on his hands got to wondering:

Why do the inhabitants of E.T.'s home planet, who presumably have never visited Earth, speak better English than he does?

The preshow and passport system may be bypassed to promote social distancing.

While the attraction's premise is good, its sophistication has lost some luster over its 30-year run. The human animatronics in the first half look laughably like dime-store dummies, and some of E.T.'s pals in the acid-soaked second act are downright disturbing with their out-of-sync facial animation. Even so, because E.T. is one of Universal's only family-friendly dark rides that relies on sets and robotics instead of screens—a type of attraction the resort could use more of—we hope it sticks around for a long time to come.

TOURING TIPS Most preschoolers and grade-school children love E.T. We think it's worth a 20- to 30-minute wait, but no longer than that. The ride often doesn't open until 10 a.m., and lines build quickly within 30 minutes of opening; waits can reach 2 hours on busy days. Ride in the morning or late afternoon. On peak days, a time-saving single-rider line is occasionally opened.

A mother from Columbus, Ohio, writes about horrendous lines at E.T.:

The line for E.T. took 2 hours! The rest of the family waiting outside thought we had really gone to E.T.'s planet.

Fievel's Playland *(temporarily closed)* ★★★

APPEAL BY AGE PRESCHOOL ★★★★½ GRADE SCHOOL ★★★★ TEENS ★½
YOUNG ADULTS ★½   OVER 30 ★★★   SENIORS ★★★½

What it is Children's play area with waterslide. Scope and scale Minor attraction. When to go Anytime. Comment A much-needed attraction for preschoolers. Loading speed Slow for the waterslide.

DESCRIPTION AND COMMENTS A great place for the little ones to blow off some steam. The idea behind this whimsical playground is that you've been shrunk to the size of *An American Tail*'s rodent protagonist and let loose to explore the detritus in an Old West town. The playground contains ordinary household items reproduced on a giant scale, as a mouse would experience them. Kids can climb nets, walk through a huge boot or 1,000-gallon cowboy hat, splash in a sardine-can fountain, sway along elevated wooden bridges, seesaw on huge spoons, and clamber onto a cow skull.

Most of the playground is reserved for preschoolers and grade-schoolers, but a combo waterslide and raft ride is open to all ages. The rafts of the three-story waterslide hold two people, so you should start faking that old war/football/child-bearing back injury to other adults in your group as soon as you get near the playland. You will get wet.

TOURING TIPS Most of Fievel's Playland requires no waiting, so you can visit anytime and stay as long as you want. Most of the play sets are designed for kids old enough to run, climb, and slide by themselves.

The extremely slow-loading waterslide carries only 300 riders per hour. During warmer months, it's possible for the waterslide to develop a wait of 20-30 minutes, and Express Passes are not honored. We don't think the 16-second ride is worth that kind of wait. If riding the slide is important to your child, try visiting right after lunch or dinner, when many other families are still eating.

Lack of shade is a major shortcoming of the entire attraction—the playground is scorching during the heat of the day.

Woody Woodpecker's Nuthouse Coaster
(Universal Express) ★★½

APPEAL BY AGE	PRESCHOOL ★★★★½	GRADE SCHOOL ★★★★	TEENS ★★★
YOUNG ADULTS ★★★		OVER 30 ★★★	SENIORS ★★★½

What it is Kids' roller coaster. Scope and scale Minor attraction. When to go Anytime. Comments 36" minimum height requirement; children 36"–48" must be accompanied by a supervising companion; child swap available (see page 204). A suitable starter thrill ride. Duration of ride 1 minute. Loading speed *Slooow.*

DESCRIPTION AND COMMENTS Woody Woodpecker's Nuthouse Coaster is a short, relatively low roller coaster designed to introduce small children to this kind of amusement park ride. The Nuthouse Coaster is small enough for kids to enjoy but sturdy enough for adults, though its moderate speed might unnerve some smaller children (the minimum height to ride is 36 inches). The entire ride lasts about a minute, and at least 20 of those 60 seconds is spent cranking the train up the first (and only) lift hill. There are several tight turns, but the ride doesn't go upside down or even come close.

TOURING TIPS Visit after you've experienced all the major attractions. If your young child has never before experienced a roller coaster, this would be an appropriate first attempt.

HOLLYWOOD

THE HOLLYWOOD AREA RE-CREATES the glamour and energy of Southern California from the 1930s through the 1950s. Several areas surrounding Hollywood, including Beverly Hills and the Hollywood Hills, are represented. The faux Garden of Allah Villas (famed home of F. Scott Fitzgerald, Marlene Dietrich, and other Hollywood golden age legends) contain the **NBC Media Center** (see page 269).

The Bourne Stuntacular (Universal Express) ★★★★½

APPEAL BY AGE	PRESCHOOL ★★	GRADE SCHOOL ★★★★	TEENS ★★★★½
YOUNG ADULTS ★★★★½		OVER 30 ★★★★½	SENIORS ★★★★

What it is Live-action stunt show. Scope and scale Headliner. When to go Scheduled showtimes; after you've experienced all rides. Comments Not to be missed. May frighten young children. Duration of show 25 minutes.

DESCRIPTION AND COMMENTS This replacement for the revered *Terminator 2: 3-D* show (which closed in 2017) once again blurs the boundary between stage and screen with spectacular results. Housed within the facade of an Art Deco office building, the *Stuntacular* starts in a polished concrete and stainless steel queue featuring static displays that document Jason Bourne's cinematic career, including a couple of vehicles seen in his on-screen adventures. If you're having trouble recalling the Bourne franchise's byzantine plot—which spans a trilogy launched with 2002's hit *The Bourne Identity,* plus a 2012 spin-off, 2016's soft reboot, and a short-lived TV prequel—don't worry. After walking through a "security scanner," viewers are welcomed into a standing-room-only preshow, where Julia Stiles's plucky undercover operative Nicky Parsons (presumably murdered in the most recent movie, but looking hale and hearty here) provides a 6-minute briefing on Bourne's backstory. Basically, he's a brainwashed assassin with a heart of gold, who is always exposing corrupt Homeland Security conspiracies and getting beat down or blown up for his troubles. All you really need to know is that the hero is the guy in the hoodie, and anyone who gets between him and his goal is going to wish they'd stayed home. (Matt Damon appears on the ultrawide screen here in clips from the films, but the main show features voice and body doubles.)

This time around, Bourne's objective is Project Rubicon, a top-secret list held by shady CIA Secretary Collins, who intends to terminate the troublesome spy with extreme prejudice, and their lieutenant Director Dixon, who claims to want to capture Bourne without killing him. Audiences assume the role of "situation analysts," tasked with observing Bourne's activities via a unique "virtual surveillance observation room," which looks suspiciously like a 700-seat theater. Bourne's action sprints from the rooftops of Tangier to the suburban streets of Washington, D.C., and finally climaxes in midair amid Dubai's skyscrapers, with mercifully brief expository interludes from CIA headquarters bridging the locations. The stunts themselves range from bare-knuckle fisticuffs and gun battles using authentically ear-popping automatic weapons, to aerial acrobatics high above the ground, including a couple of heart-stopping 22-foot free-falls into pits in the stage.

These acts of athleticism—performed by talented stunt professionals from Action Horizons, which also staffs Hollywood's wonderful *WaterWorld* show—would be impressive enough on their own, but it's the merging of old-fashioned stunts with next-generation video technology that makes *The Bourne Stuntacular* more than a mere stunt show. Instead of relying on 3-D glasses like the *Terminator* did, *Bourne* utilizes a mammoth 3,640-square-foot LED screen so sharp and vivid that it defies the eye's ability to determine where the digital world ends and reality begins. For example, unless you're sitting in the front row, it's almost impossible to tell that only a handful of the people in the opening scene's cheering crowd are actually there onstage. Paired with robotic set pieces that slide seamlessly in sync with the video, the 130-foot-wide display transforms the entire theater into a roving movie camera, spiraling skyward around a telescoping tower as Bourne climbs to safety, or swooping alongside a high-speed chase while he clings to the roof of a full-size car. Add in bursts of flame, water, wind, and fog, and you have an experience that sometimes feels more like a simulator ride than a stage show, even without any moving seats.

Fast-paced, faithful to the film franchise, and filled with show-stopping special effects, this is easily the best stunt show in Orlando.

TOURING TIPS Shows start about every 45 minutes according to the performance schedule available in Universal's app, but the theater tends to fill up, so arrive at least 15 minutes prior to the performance you wish to attend. Seats in the front row are great for fight choreography aficionados, but we prefer the view of the screen from the rear. The *Stuntacular* features loud gunfire and brutal violence (including choke holds) but no blood or guts.

Universal Orlando's Horror Make-Up Show
(Universal Express) ★★★★½

APPEAL BY AGE   PRESCHOOL ★★   GRADE SCHOOL ★★★½   TEENS ★★★★
YOUNG ADULTS ★★★★   OVER 30 ★★★★   SENIORS ★★★★½

What it is Theater presentation on the art of makeup. **Scope and scale** Major attraction. **When to go** Scheduled showtimes; after you've experienced all rides. **Comments** May frighten young children. A gory knee-slapper; not to be missed. **Duration of show** 25 minutes.

DESCRIPTION AND COMMENTS The *Horror Make-Up Show* is a brief but humorous look at how basic monster-movie special effects are done. The show includes onstage demonstrations of effects, such as blood-spurting fake knives and rubber limbs, plus how mechanical effects are combined with latex masks to transform human heads into wolf-shaped skulls. The hosts pay tribute to Universal makeup pioneers such as Lon Chaney, Jack Pierce, Tom Savini, and Rick Baker, while also poking fun at some of the studio's less successful spooks. Film clips are interspersed throughout the presentation, showing how computer-generated special effects are blended into live-action films like Tom Cruise's 2017 reboot of *The Mummy.* The finale involves an audience volunteer and a remote-controlled creature that isn't all he appears.

This may be Universal's most entertaining live show. While there's plenty of fake blood thrown around, the script is much more funny than scary funny. The hosts keep everything moving along at a fast pace (except when they start to improv and crack each other up like the old Carol Burnett show), and their running commentary about horror-filmmaking is interspersed with plenty of pop-culture jokes for the kids, along with some surprisingly subversive stabs at the hand that feeds them; after offering a dry towel to a damp volunteer, they'll demand cash, smiling, "Welcome to Orlando!"

TOURING TIPS The *Horror Make-Up Show* is the sleeper attraction at Universal, and one of the only theme park comedy shows we can watch over and over again. Its humor and tongue-in-cheek style transcend the gruesome effects, and most folks (including preschoolers) take the blood and guts in stride. But it's the exception that proves the rule, as this reader relates:

> My 7- and 9-year-olds were scared by the Horror Make-Up Show (despite me telling them that the guy wasn't really cutting anyone's arm off!). We ended up leaving before the show was over.

And from a New Orleans family:

> My husband and I really enjoyed the humor; it was just corny enough. The special effects with the audience member were pretty cool, and we thought the whole thing was fun. My kids were not quite as taken with this show. My son (5) hid his face against my arm most of the time, and my daughter (10) had her hands over her eyes a lot. The video montage of horror clips was especially upsetting to them. As we were leaving the theater, they both commented that the show was really scary, and they didn't like it.

A good test is to take your child into the theater lobby between shows, where display cases filled with bloody props and monster masks act as a mini-museum of Universal horror history from *The Hunchback of Notre Dame* to Halloween Horror

Nights. If the static severed heads here send your kid into hysterics, the show itself may have you paying therapy bills for decades to come. (The lobby may be off-limits due to social distancing.)

Look for the second-story windows to the left of the theater marquee for a touching tribute to victims of the Pulse nightclub tragedy.

LIVE ENTERTAINMENT *at* UNIVERSAL STUDIOS FLORIDA

IN ADDITION TO THE SHOWS profiled previously, USF offers two major daily outdoor entertainments, along with a wide range of smaller street performances.

Costumed comic book and cartoon characters (Shrek and Donkey, SpongeBob SquarePants, Transformers) pose for guests at organized meet and greets marked on the park maps. Others, like Scooby-Doo, along with look-alikes of movie stars (both living and deceased), roam the Hollywood and Front Lot areas for photo ops. See page 205 for more character information.

In New York and San Francisco several small-scale shows entertain the crowds. **The Blues Brothers Show** (★★★½) is a 12-minute rhythm and blues concert. Held on the corner of the New York area, across from the lagoon, *The Blues Brothers Show* features Jake and Elwood performing a few of the hit songs from the classic 1980 movie musical, including "Soul Man" and "Shake a Tail Feather." The brothers are joined on stage by Jazz the saxophone player and Mabel the waitress, who belts an Aretha Franklin cover to start the show.

Blues Brothers is one of the better musical performances in the Studios. The singers have captured many of the movie's dance moves and vocal styles, and the music's tempo keeps everyone's toes tapping. The concert is a great pick-me-up, and the short running time keeps the energy high. During the holiday season, a special *Blues Brothers Holiday Show* is performed, featuring songs such as "Blue Christmas" and "Run Rudolph Run," sung around a festive tree festooned with beer cans and cigarette packs. It's even better than the regular show.

Marilyn Monroe and the Diamond Bellas (★★½) perform a 4-minute song and dance routine (anachronistically lip-synched to the *Moulin Rouge* cover of her signature song) in front of the *Horror Make-Up Show*'s facade, followed by a photo op; during the holiday season, "Santa Baby" joins the set list. The **Beat Builders** (★★★) are a quartet of beefy guys who hang out on the scaffolding outside Louie's Italian Restaurant and turn their construction equipment into percussion instruments, in the tradition of *Stomp*.

All of these shows have performance times listed in the app's show schedule, and most are not worth going out of your way for. If you aren't on a tight touring plan and see one starting as you walk by, stop and watch until you get bored, but don't be surprised if some have been retired by the time you read this.

Universal Orlando's Cinematic Celebration (seasonal)
★★★★

What it is Fireworks, dancing fountains, and movies. Scope and scale Major attraction.
When to go 1 show a day, usually at park closing. Comment Presented seasonally, when
the park is open after dark. Duration of show 19 minutes.

DESCRIPTION AND COMMENTS This is USF's big new nighttime event, shown on the
lagoon in the middle of the Studios. The presentation pays tribute to favorite
franchises featured around Universal's parks, including *Jurassic World*, *Despicable Me*, *Transformers*, and *Fast & Furious*. The scenes are projected onto multiple enormous "screens" made by spraying water from the lagoon into the air
(similar to *World of Color* at Disney California Adventure), which are augmented
by more than 120 illuminated fountains.

Highlights of the show include Harry Potter defeating a pack of Dementors
with his Patronus, E.T.'s spaceship blasting into space, and a joyful Justin Timber-
lake tune from *Trolls*. (References to *Kung Fu Panda* and *How to Train Your
Dragon* may be hinting at future attractions.) Each film series is showcased for a
few minutes, before Gru and his Minions kick off a grand finale, gathering all of the
characters together. Fireworks are deployed sparingly, in deference to the residen-
tial neighborhood across the street, but projection mapping (which makes the
New York building facades appear to freeze or burst into flames) is used to good
effect, as are moving lights and lasers.

Cinematic Celebration is easily the best nighttime show USF has offered in this
century, and it's well worth sticking around until closing time to see it. While it isn't
as breathtaking as Magic Kingdom's *Happily Ever After*, it's more exciting and better paced than Disney's Hollywood Studios' *Fantasmic*.

TOURING TIPS The terraced Central Park across the lagoon from San Francisco is the
primary viewing location for this show, with additional viewing between Mel's
Drive-In and Transformers and near Duff Brewery. No reservations are required,
and you should be able to get a good view by arriving at least 15 minutes before
showtime. The grassy field in the rear of Central Park provides the best perspective on the wide-screen presentation but is sometimes reserved for VIPs or special events. Even if you don't stick around for the evening entertainment, keep an
ear out for unscheduled daytime demonstrations of the fountains' capabilities,
synchronized to classic Universal film scores.

Universal's Superstar Parade (temporarily suspended) ★★★

What it is Parade with animated characters. Scope and scale Major attraction. When to
go Check daily entertainment schedule for parade and showtimes. Comment Colorful but
inconvenient. Duration of presentation 15-20 minutes.

DESCRIPTION AND COMMENTS Universal's Superstar Parade features dancers and
performers, four large and elaborate floats inspired by cartoons, and a very mixed
bag of street-prowling Universal characters. The highlighted franchises include
Dora the Explorer (with acrobatic monkeys swinging from her float); *SpongeBob
SquarePants* (accompanied by a phalanx of in-line skating fish); Max, Duke, and
their furry friends from *The Secret Life of Pets* movies (riding in a New York City
apartment–size float filled with animatronic animals); and Gru's whole *Despicable*

Me crew, from his adopted daughters to the adorable yellow Minions. The parade isn't very long, but it stops twice—once in New York near Louie's Italian Restaurant and Revenge of the Mummy and again in Hollywood between the Hello Kitty store and Mel's Drive-In—for a highly choreographed ensemble number. Though impressive in its scope and coordination, the performance is well-nigh impossible to take in from any given viewing spot.

The parade route, marked in the park map, begins at the Esoteric Pictures gate in Hollywood between *Universal Orlando's Horror Make-Up Show* and Cafe La Bamba. It turns right, then immediately makes a hard left around Mel's Drive-In, and follows the waterfront past Transformers toward San Francisco. From there it turns left at Louie's Italian Restaurant and proceeds along Fifth Avenue, past Revenge of the Mummy. At the end of Fifth Avenue, the parade takes a left onto 57th Avenue/Plaza of the Stars and heads toward the front of the park, where it makes another left onto Hollywood Boulevard, from whence it disappears backstage through the gate where it entered.

The same floats used in the parade are trotted out individually to the Character Party Zone (in Hollywood at the corner near Mel's Drive-In) at scheduled times in the late morning and early afternoon for mini-shows and character meet and greets. These are a much better opportunity than the parade itself for your kids to get a photo of their favorite character. Character parties are still scheduled even when the parade itself is not performed.

TOURING TIPS The best viewing spots are along Fifth Avenue, on the front steps of faux buildings in New York. The wheelchair viewing area is in front of the Macy's facade. If you miss part of the parade in the New York area, you can scoot along the waterfront to Mel's Drive-In and catch it as it comes down Hollywood Boulevard. If, after watching the parade on the New York streets, you plan to leave the park, you can use the same route to access Hollywood Boulevard and the park exit before the parade arrives.

SPECIAL EVENTS *at* UNIVERSAL STUDIOS FLORIDA

BEYOND ITS YEAR-ROUND OFFERINGS, USF also hosts some of the best seasonal events in the theme park industry, and most of them are included with any regular admission (including annual passes). For those events that aren't—Rock the Universe and Halloween Horror Nights—you'll need to purchase a separate ticket, and daytime Universal Express Passes (including those offered with hotel rooms) won't be honored.

ROCK THE UNIVERSE *(late January)*

UNIVERSAL ORLANDO BILLS Rock the Universe, its annual weekend of fist-pumping praise-rock and roller coasters, as "Florida's biggest Christian music festival." This hard-ticket after-hours event attracts hordes of church youth groups, who get access to the parks starting at 4 p.m. and keep boogying for the Lord until 1 a.m. It was most recently held January 24–25, 2020. While the 2021 edition of Rock the Universe has been postponed, the event is expected to return in late January 2022.

Concerts take place across three stages inside USF and start after the park closes to day guests at 6 p.m. Past acts have included Switchfoot, Newsboys, Lecrae, TobyMac, Chris Tomlin, We Are Messengers, Lauren Daigle, and Casting Crowns. The headliners perform on the Music Plaza stage, drawing a large percentage of the event's attendees to their hour-plus-long sets. The audiences for these shows rival those at Mardi Gras concerts in size and enthusiasm (if not inebriation), so be sure to show up early if you want a close-up view of your favorite band. Coca-Cola sponsors a Fanzone that features autograph sessions, where attendees can meet and greet all of the headlining artists on a first-come, first-serve basis. Most of the park's thrill rides operate during Rock the Universe, and Hollywood Rip Ride Rockit offers Christian rock songs through its "secret" menu (see page 279) under code numbers 772–796. There's also a Saturday night candle-lighting ceremony just before midnight and a Sunday morning worship service in the Blue Man Group theater.

Single-night tickets start around $72, while two-night tickets cost about $112; annual pass holders can attend for as little as $28. Attendees can buy discounted Rock Your Weekend tickets that combine both event nights with daytime park tickets. Three-park access Friday–Sunday goes for about $128 ($173 for park-to-park). Universal Express Passes run an additional $20 per night for one-time use per ride, or $30 for unlimited use. Youth group leaders get a free ticket for every 10 their charges purchase, plus free access to Universal Express ride queues and lounges with free snacks. Learn more at rocktheuniverse.com.

MARDI GRAS *(early February–mid-April)*

YOU ARE NO DOUBT FAMILIAR with the gigantic Mardi Gras celebration in New Orleans, or at least the idea of it. Well, USF has a yearly festival as well that celebrated its silver anniversary in 2020. Sure, it's not quite as bawdy as its French Quarter compatriot, but it is exceedingly fun and probably a better event to bring the kids along.

Mardi Gras originated in the religious observation of Fat Tuesday (the literal translation of the name), which is the day before Ash Wednesday on the Catholic calendar and the start of Lent's 40 days of dietary restrictions. People bid "farewell to flesh" with a carnival where they indulge in the meat and drink they're about to forswear. Mardi Gras is the New Orleans variation on this tradition—which is echoed in other cities from Venice to Rio de Janeiro.

Over the centuries, the religious significance has been stripped away, and most Mardi Gras revelers attend for strictly secular reasons—namely, epic quantities of booze, beads, and bare breasts. Universal took a look at the festivities and said, "This will make a fine family-friendly event"—minus the bare breasts, of course—and amazingly it is. But that doesn't mean it's inauthentic. Universal engages Kern Studios, the same company that's been building floats for the real deal since 1932, to create the park's parade platforms. And musicians and recipes imported from the Big Easy add to the French Quarter feel. Of course, the real Bourbon Street doesn't have concerts from big-name recording artists after the parade (on select nights), much less a high-speed roller coaster cruising by in the background.

In addition to the parade and headliner concerts, Universal carves a miniature Bourbon Street out of its New York back lot. Chef Steven Jayson and his culinary team pride themselves on the authentic N'awlins flavors they bring to the French Quarter Courtyard, an area between Revenge of the Mummy and Transformers, with temporary food and beverage booths that open at 4 p.m. each Mardi Gras concert night. The jambalaya, andouille sausage, and beignets are all pretty good; save money on bites and beer with a prepaid sampler lanyard. You can eat to the beat and enjoy live blues and zydeco musicians from Louisiana busking on the French Quarter corners. Universal started this tradition more than a decade ago to support New Orleans artists in the wake of Hurricane Katrina.

COVID *tip*
In 2020 the good times were supposed to roll every evening February 1–April 2, but the party ended prematurely due to the pandemic. Event dates for 2021 had not been announced at press time.

Viewing of the parade and concerts are included with any valid admission, and all annual pass holders are admitted in the evening, except Seasonal Pass holders who are blocked out on concert nights. For more information, visit tinyurl.com/unimardigras.

Mardi Gras Parade

Universal's version of a Mardi Gras parade includes the crazy characters of the New Orleans version but is much more compact. Floats are updated every year with new themes—2020 featured "Treasures of the Deep," like the Lost City of Atlantis and Shipwreck Island—but you can always count on the massive King Gator float and multistory Riverboat to roll down Universal's boulevards. The floats are each accompanied by dozens of strolling performers and stilt walkers, while costumed revelers ride upon them and toss colorful plastic beads to the crowds below.

The parade typically follows the same route as the daily Superstar Parade but in reverse, starting and ending at Hollywood's Esoteric Pictures gate near the *Horror Make-Up Show* and traveling clockwise around New York and the waterfront.

Viewing Tips: The parade takes about 15 minutes to pass by any one spot, and it lasts around 45 minutes. The parade generally begins at 7:30 or 7:45 p.m., but it may step off as early as 5:15 p.m. on certain nights. Times may vary with operating hours, so check the park map for details. You can find good viewing anywhere along the parade route, and unless you insist on standing right up front, there's no need to save your spot more than 10 or 15 minutes in advance.

Special reserved viewing areas are also available for annual pass holders (near Mel's Drive-In), American Express card holders (in front of *The Bourne Stuntacular*), guests with disabilities (near Macy's in New York), and young Little Jesters and their families (in front of the Brown Derby).

If you really want to get in on the action, it's possible to volunteer as a bead-tossing float rider. Annual pass holders can sign up for themselves and a guest online; you must RSVP at least one week in advance. Slots are also saved for on-site resort guests; watch Universal's website for preregistration or inquire at your hotel's Ticket Center. If space is available, additional riders may be recruited from park guests in the afternoon. Use the Universal Orlando smartphone app to secure a Virtual Line reservation time, which is available a few hours before the parade on a first-come, first-serve basis. Riding the float as you fling beads is a blast but takes 2–3 hours, and you'll probably miss the beginning of the concert if you participate. All riders must be at least 18 years old (or accompanied by an adult) and 48 inches tall; space is limited and availability is not guaranteed.

Mardi Gras Live Concerts

Every Saturday night (and select Sundays) during the Mardi Gras event, after the parade concludes (approximately 45 minutes after it begins), a big-name concert kicks off on Music Plaza Stage underneath Hollywood Rip Ride Rockit. The concerts are a definite highlight of Universal's Mardi Gras celebration. With dozens of great musical acts entertaining the crowd at no extra cost, there is really no downside to these fantastic concerts, other than the extraordinary crowds that popular artists can draw. To get an idea of the quality of the acts, performers in recent years have included heavyweights from the past—Kool & the Gang; Earth, Wind & Fire; Diana Ross; the Steve Miller Band; REO Speedwagon; and Bell Biv DeVoe—and present, such as Pitbull, Fifth Harmony, Macklemore, The Roots, Karol G, and Luis Fonsi. In addition to the headliners, Universal also imports authentic New Orleans musicians to perform near the French Quarter stalls before the big show. (Musicians and limited food options are still offered on non-concert event nights.)

Viewing Tips: There is no additional charge for Mardi Gras concerts; they are included with park admission. All concerts are standing-room only and first come, first served. Crowds can be enormous, and folks sometimes start lining up shortly after park opening for the hottest acts. There is no extra-cost VIP area available, but there is an ADA-accessible viewing section near the Race Through New York restrooms. Large video screens broadcast the stage to those standing in the far back, so consider watching from the New York Battery Park area if you aren't an überfan of the artist.

HALLOWEEN HORROR NIGHTS
(early September–early November)

THE GODFATHER (or is that gorefather?) of all Universal Orlando seasonal events, Halloween Horror Nights (or HHN, as it's known to its legions of bloodthirsty fans) is recognized as the nation's most popular and industry-awarded haunted theme park event. Originally a locals-friendly filler during a normally slow season, USF's Halloween celebration started in 1991 as a single weekend of Fright Nights. Since then, HHN has grown so famous that the eight-week-long scare-abration can provide a significant percentage of USF's annual attendance statistics. Much like visiting any of Orlando's theme parks during a peak holiday season, an evening at HHN can be tremendous fun if you go in with a solid plan and sane expectations. Without those things . . . well, you might be better off eaten by zombies! This reader, who traveled all the way from Belgium to attend the event, summarizes the sentiments of many haunt fans:

> *Halloween Horror Nights is truly the world's premier Halloween event. I recommend it to any adult or teen who is a Halloween fan. I've been twice and will certainly do it again; it's worth the money!*

We've been attending HHN every year since 1996, and it has become one of our favorite after-dark activities in any park, but it isn't for everybody. Before attending, make sure that Universal's brand of Halloween is right for you; this ain't Mickey's Not-So-Scary Halloween Party. HHN is a gory, gruesome bacchanalia of simulated violence and tasteless satire, marinated with a liberal dose of alcohol and rock-and-roll. In other words, it's a heck of a party as long as you know what you're getting into. If the idea of copious blood, guts, and booze doesn't appeal to you, we advise staying far, far away. Needless to say, it's not appropriate for young children, though you will likely see many there.

COVID *tip*

Halloween Horror Nights was canceled in 2020 and replaced with a limited celebration that allowed daytime guests to experience select haunted houses with regular admission.

The three basic elements of each year's event are haunted houses (or mazes), outdoor scare zones, and theater shows. Universal also makes many of its regular rides available during HHN, including Harry Potter and the Escape from Gringotts (though not the Hogwarts Express) in The Wizarding World of Harry Potter—Diagon Alley.

Planning for Halloween Horror Nights

Even more so than daytime touring, a successful HHN visit requires a careful date selection. In 2020 HHN was originally scheduled for 40 select nights September 10–November 1; visit orlando.halloweenhorror nights.com for the calendar. In short, you want to avoid all Saturdays (especially the final three Saturdays leading up to Halloween) like the plague. Fridays in October—particularly the last two Fridays before Halloween—aren't much better. Wednesdays are usually the least crowded, followed by Thursdays (especially the first two) and Sundays (especially the first, but excluding the last). Opening weekend brings out all the local fans, so your best bets are the last two weeks of September or the first week of October. Halloween night itself and any nights after it are often extremely quiet. The price of Express Passes on a given night (as listed at tinyurl.com/HHNExpress) is your best guide to how busy it will be: the larger the cost, the larger the crowds.

If you walk up to the box office on the night of the event, you'll pay $119.99—a frightening sum for as little as 6½ hours in the park—and likely wait in a ridiculously long line for the privilege. Instead, study the myriad online ticket options in advance and purchase before you leave home.

Deep discounts (up to $52 off) are offered on advance purchases of date-specific tickets. You need to know what night you want to attend when purchasing online because prices range from $67.99 for a Wednesday in September up to $93.99 on October's busiest Saturday. Annual pass holders are entitled to even deeper price breaks (up to $58 off advance tickets) and early event entry during pass-holder parties on select nights during the opening weekends. In the summer, look for early bird "buy one night, get one free" offers for $84.99. If you already have daytime admission to a Universal park, you can purchase an add-on ticket at the park that allows you to remain through the evening's event for a discounted price, depending on the night.

unofficial **TIP**
You can buy a Rush of Fear ticket and upgrade it to an Ultimate Frequent Fear ticket on or before its expiration date.

Finally, if you are a hard-core haunt fan and are spending more than a night in the area, you'll want a Frequent Fear (valid every Sunday–Thursday event night, with Fridays included in the Plus version for an extra fee) or Rush of Fear (valid every event night through the first three weekends) multiday pass. Universal also offers an Ultimate Frequent Fear Pass valid every event night, in case you feel like spending more than the cost of an annual pass for a few weeks of scares. Multiday passes cost about $20 less online than at the gate and are even cheaper for annual pass holders. If you come for an evening and like what you see, any single-night ticket (except the free one included with Premier Annual Passes) can be upgraded to a seasonal pass before you depart.

Universal Orlando's paid line-skipping service is a welcome luxury during the day but an absolute lifesaver at night. On peak event nights, queues for the haunted houses will approach 3 hours, and even on the slowest nights, they'll hit 60 minutes. HHN Express Passes reduce that wait to 25%–33% of what it would otherwise be, which can make the difference between experiencing two or three houses in a night to visiting seven or more. The only catch is that Express starts at $89.99 per person and goes up to more than $159 depending on the night. Express is also available as an add-on for Rush of Fear or Frequent Fear multinight passes. Express Passes often sell out and may be more expensive or unavailable inside the park, so if you do want them, buy in advance. On off-peak nights it's possible to experience all the haunted houses and at least one show without Express, if you arrive early and stay until closing. On peak nights it's virtually impossible to do the same without Express Passes, and can be challenging even with them.

If you're feeling particularly flush and are fed up with any kind of queue, the **RIP guided tour** will whisk you to the head of every line for $199.99–$369.99 depending on the night, admission not included; half-night tours may be available for half price. A private RIP tour for you and up to nine of your friends starts at $1,799 and goes up to $3,999 (again, admission not included). When money is no object, the RIP tours are highly recommended. Call ☎ 866-346-9350 or email vipexperience@universalorlando.com for pricing and reservations.

For the superfans with extra spending money, Universal offers a choice of in-depth HHN experiences. Join one of Universal's designers on daytime lights-on trips through three houses on each of the two **Unmasking the Horror behind-the-scenes tours** ($79.99 and up for one tour, $129.99 for both). On event nights, ticket holders can start their night with a $49.99 Scareactor dinner, which includes an all-you-can-eat buffet and monster meet and greet. These upgrades can be booked online at tinyurl.com/HHNExtras.

To arm yourself with knowledge before braving HHN, visit the official website (orlando.halloweenhorrornights.com), along with the fan-run websites horrornightnightmares.com, hhncrypt.com, hhn rumors.com, and hhnunofficial.com.

Halloween Horror Nights Touring Tips

Please note that the following information is based on 2019's Halloween Horror Nights event and assumes the event returns to its traditional format in 2021.

The event officially begins each evening at 6:30 p.m., but the front gates typically open as early as 6 p.m. If you have an HHN ticket but not daytime admission, you'll want to be outside the park gates, ticket in hand, by 5:45 p.m. at the latest on slow nights, and as early as 5 p.m. on peak nights. Be sure to leave ample time for I-4 traffic and parking, which is full price until 10 p.m. Valet parking is available, but remember that the usual annual pass discounts on valet parking don't apply on event nights.

After navigating the security screening in the parking hub, your goal is to secure a spot as close to the USF turnstiles as possible; don't be shy about lining up at the temporary entry scanners at the center gate. On-site hotel guests also get their own exclusive entrance near the Blue Man Group theater. (Note that the Express Unlimited access included with some resort rooms is not valid during HHN.) Early arrivals may also get a view of a gate-opening performance, which usually occurs just inside the main entrance. Don't worry if you miss this minor event; it's a nice touch but not essential.

Better yet, get a jump on the general public outside the gates by being inside the park before they open. The park closes to daytime guests at 5 p.m. on event nights, but anyone holding a ticket for that night's HHN is allowed to remain inside the park in designated holding areas. Anyone can access this opportunity if they have any valid daytime park ticket, including annual pass holders, or you can add a $25 Scream Early option onto your HHN ticket to enter the park between 3 and 5 p.m.

Note that the park is officially open for regular operations until 5 p.m., but you'll want to enter before 4:30 p.m. to avoid dealing with the arriving evening crowds. Between the park's closing and reopening, guests remaining in the park are confined to one of the following locations:

- The **Springfield** section near Fast Food Boulevard offers priority access to the first two haunted houses that open each evening. Guests in this area can queue for the two houses with entrances in Woody Woodpecker's KidZone between 5:30 and 5:45 p.m. Guests are released from the area around 6 p.m. and can be the first to queue for the houses near the MIB Gear shop. A limited selection of Simpsons food and drink is available here after daytime guests have exited. Note that on select September weekends, this area is restricted to annual pass holders who have registered online for an exclusive pass-holder event, during which three houses are opened as early as 5:30 p.m.

- The **New York** holding area includes Finnegan's Bar and Grill, which offers a full bar and table-service food, though reservations aren't accepted and tables are virtually impossible to secure on event afternoons. Guests here are released around 5:30 p.m., giving them first crack at the most popular soundstage houses.

- A small overflow holding area is located in **Hollywood** near the Hello Kitty shop. There is no food or beverage available here, but you do get early access to the maze closest to the park entrance.

- Finally, **Diagon Alley** is not a holding area for HHN, and the Hogwarts Express train stops running in both directions as soon as USF's closing time arrives.

The 10 haunted houses are the signature attractions at HHN and quickly develop wait times ranging from moderate to absolutely ridiculous. Four haunted mazes are housed in the huge production soundstages behind Hollywood Rip Ride Rockit; four are located in warehouses and large sprung tents erected backstage behind Springfield and World Expo; one is wedged between Men in Black and the *Fear Factor Live* stadium; and one takes over one of the two theaters inside *Shrek 4-D*. Each year, due to theme or location, some houses seem to attract longer queues than others. Typically, the houses near the front entrance and

unofficial **TIP**
Houses that don't open until after 6:30 p.m. will accumulate a large backlog of guests before they begin operating, so save them for the end of the night. Instead, enjoy short waits at the mazes that are operating.

those based on films and TV shows (such as *Beetlejuice, The Haunting of Hill House,* and *Bride of Frankenstein*) have been the most popular, while the original-concept mazes in the rear of the park draw shorter lines than average. Keep this in mind when deciding whether to bite the bullet and queue up for a particular maze.

Even the least popular houses, however, will have peak waits of 30 minutes or more, even on less busy nights. Your first hour at the event is therefore essential to making the most of the evening, and your initial plan of attack is determined by which location you start your night from:

- **SPRINGFIELD HOLDING AREA:** If you're among the first inside the Springfield holding area, queue up for the first available house as soon as allowed. The exit of that house should lead directly to the entrance of the second house to open. Alternatively, if you're late entering the holding area, the queue for the first house may already be posted at an hour or more. In that case, do the second house first, saving the first for later in the early-entry period (the wait should diminish rapidly) or late in the evening. Guests should be released from the Springfield area around 6 p.m. and can line up for the tent houses near MIB Gear, or cross the park to the open soundstage houses.

- **FINNEGAN'S BAR AND GRILL HOLDING AREA:** Enter the New York holding area between 4 and 5 p.m. (the earlier the better, especially if you want to get food or drink), and relax in the holding pen for your pick of the designated early-entry mazes. You'll be walked to the soundstage queues around 5:30 p.m., with the scares starting up around 5:45 p.m. Once the general public is admitted through the front gates (as early as 6 p.m.), queues at the soundstage houses will swiftly build. See as many as you can until waits exceed 30 minutes, and then proceed to the houses in the back of the park.

- **HOLLYWOOD HOLDING AREA:** Check into the holding area outside the Hello Kitty shop before park closing, and work your way through the plaza as close to Despicable Me Minion Mayhem as possible. Guests will be released shortly before the front gates open, when they can make a mad dash to the nearest maze entrance. By the time the first holding area guests exit the haunted house, the line behind them may be an hour or more, so you should head toward Springfield immediately afterward.

- **GENERAL ADMISSION:** If you're among the first folks through the gates when they open around 6 p.m., head straight to the open soundstage houses and jump in line if the wait is still 15 minutes or less. Otherwise, the majority of guests will mob the four houses in the soundstages near the front of the park. You should avoid the horde by heading in the opposite direction, toward Springfield, which should have processed the majority of guests who were already in the park by now. You can also continue through Springfield to the houses outside MIB Gear and in the Men in Black extended queue.

This reader from Highlands Ranch, Colorado, followed our Halloween touring advice with great success:

> *Being a day guest at the park gave us a tremendous head start on Halloween Horror Nights. Using the recommendations in the guide, we waited in the Springfield holding area, which gave us access to several of the houses that opened before the official 6:30 start. We were thus able to see four houses in roughly an hour and still catch the first show.*

After the haunted houses, the live comedy and dance shows, held inside the *Fear Factor Live* stadium, are the top draws. The first and last performances of the night are always the least crowded, but you shouldn't have trouble finding a seat if you show up 15–20 minutes in advance of any showing.

After the sun sets (around 7:30 p.m.) and the waits for the houses become unbearable, begin exploring the scare zones, which have evolved from open-air haunted mazes (minus the conga line queues) into social media–friendly selfie opportunities. Just as much fun as getting scared yourself is finding a vantage point to stand still and see others getting spooked; this is some of the best people-watching you'll ever find. Be on the lookout for staged scenes, in which actors attack planted "victims" within the crowd.

By the midpoint of the evening, standby waits for all the houses will be substantial, and lines for the rides will be astronomical on Saturdays, but experiencing several top attractions should still be manageable using single-rider queues. Men in Black Alien Attack, Revenge of the Mummy, Harry Potter and the Escape from Gringotts, Transformers: The Ride–3-D, and Fast & Furious: Supercharged all have fairly efficient single-rider operations. Hollywood Rip Ride Rockit has a single-rider line, but it's often as long as the standby queue. On off-peak nights, you may find ride queues shockingly short; just be aware that most rides shut down an hour or two before the event ends.

Another HHN must-see is the seasonal lagoon show, which features footage of your favorite film fiends projected on massive water fountains. The 10-minute show, which is repeated hourly after sunset, lacks pyrotechnics, but the pulsating lasers and pumping soundtrack make it even more exciting than the standard lagoon show. You should be able to walk up shortly before the second or third performance; see the *Cinematic Celebration* profile on page 307 for viewing tips.

Even on a slow night, Horror Nights crowds can drive you to drink, and many of your fellow guests will doubtlessly be imbibing. Temporary bars serve beer and overpriced premixed cocktails on seemingly every spare square foot of sidewalk, but for serious in-park boozing, we prefer Finnegan's Bar in New York or Duff Brewery in Springfield. Better yet, if the park is open past 1 a.m., get out of Dodge for an hour or so and retreat to CityWalk. Most HHN passes include admission to CityWalk's clubs, or you can grab a drink at Antojitos or NBC Sports Grill & Brew without a cover charge.

While alcohol is easily obtainable, actual edibles can be harder to find; Universal advertises exclusive gut busters like pizza fries, but the open food locations are often overwhelmed, as this New York reader observed:

> The one complaint we had is the lack of savory meal options and the long waits at the normal counter-service restaurants. There were virtually no savory food item carts. The counter-service restaurants were open but severely understaffed, which resulted in long waits for food. By comparison, every specialty beverage and beer pop-up tent was staffed by at least five people.

As the evening's event approaches its final hour, wait times at the haunted mazes drop dramatically. If you're interested in the headliner show and didn't catch an earlier showing, arrive 15–20 minutes before the last performance on peak nights (or 5–10 minutes before showtime off-peak). Otherwise, use the final hours to catch up on the houses you missed earlier. The last 30–60 minutes before park closing is the best time to hit the most popular houses. If you didn't see the popular mazes at the start of the night, step into line for one of them about 15–20 minutes before closing; you should be allowed to stay in the queue until you're through, barring technical difficulties.

Unless you leave significantly before closing time, you're best off dawdling in the park or CityWalk on the way out. The parking garage exits will be at a standstill, so you might as well grab a seat outside and relax rather than breathing fumes in a traffic jam.

HOLIDAYS AT UNIVERSAL STUDIOS
(early December–early January)
UNIVERSAL ORLANDO CELEBRATES the holiday season every year from the first Friday of December through the Saturday after New Year's. Universal Orlando holidays might not have quite the nostalgic lure of Mickey's merrymaking, but its options are every bit as expertly produced and have the benefit of all being included with regular park admission (unlike the extra-cost hard-ticket nighttime parties at the Magic Kingdom).

USF's holiday festivities feature seasonal decoration on the front archway and throughout the park, holiday songs broadcasting from speakers in the streets, and a giant tree that is ceremoniously lit every evening at sunset. Several park attractions, such as *The Blues Brothers Show,* get into the spirit with special versions tied to the season. Universal also celebrates the holidays Harry Potter style with **Christmas in The Wizarding World.** Holiday decor adorns Diagon Alley's streets and shops, and the Leaky Cauldron serves seasonal snacks. But the star of the holidays at Universal Studios is undoubtedly **Universal's Holiday Parade Featuring Macy's.**

USF has been bringing elements of Macy's famous New York parade down to Orlando for a post-Thanksgiving encore every December for two decades. In 2017 Universal renamed and revamped the procession, adding elaborate new floats showcasing characters from *Shrek, Madagascar,* and *Despicable Me.* But Macy's balloons are still a big part of the fun: while the largest balloons you've seen sailing through Manhattan on TV can't make it down the narrower streets of USF, several of the smaller ones are paraded through both productions, and more of the classic king-size inflatables (such as Garfield and Grover) can be seen on stationary display around the park.

Universal's Holiday Parade begins each evening around 5 p.m. (subject to change; check the show schedule in your park map) near the *Horror Make-Up Show,* continues down Hollywood Boulevard toward the park entrance, travels past Despicable Me Minion Mayhem and *Shrek 4-D* toward New York, and then turns near Revenge of the Mummy and again past Transformers, exiting through the gate it originally entered.

You can get a good view of the parade from anywhere along the route, but ideal viewing spots are near Mel's Drive-In at the beginning of the route and near the large tree in New York toward the end. Reserved viewing areas are marked on the park map for guests with disabilities (in front of Macy's in New York), for annual pass holders (near Mel's Drive-In), and for young Little Stars and their families (near Hollywood's Brown Derby).

If you've always fantasized about guiding a giant inflatable animal down Fifth Avenue, you can volunteer to participate in the parade as a balloon handler for free. Volunteers must be 18 years or older, at least 48 inches tall and 125 pounds, English speaking, and able to walk the mile-long route for up to an hour. Sign-up is held daily 2 hours before the parade starts in Woody Woodpecker's KidZone near E.T. Adventure. A limited number of spots are available for guests each day, and you'll have to sign a waiver to participate.

After the parade on select nights, USF's Music Plaza Stage hosts live concerts by **Mannheim Steamroller.** The electrified orchestra usually performs its amped-up holiday classics on the first two Saturdays and Sundays of the season. These shows can be popular, so arrive at least 45 minutes early if you want a close-up view.

UNIVERSAL STUDIOS FLORIDA TOURING PLANS

OUR STEP-BY-STEP touring plans are field-tested for seeing *as much as possible* in one day with a minimum amount of time wasted in lines. They're designed to help you avoid crowds and bottlenecks on days of moderate to heavy attendance. Understand, however, that there's more to see at USF than can be experienced in one day during peak season. If you're visiting on days of lighter attendance (see "Trying to Reason with the Tourist Season," page 36) or using Universal Express (see page 69), our plans will save you time but won't be as critical to successful touring as on busier days.

In general, most visitors find that they can be far more flexible with their touring plans at Universal than at Disney and still see everything they want to see. But if you're at the parks on a busy day, you'll want to stick to the script, at least until you get the most popular attractions out of the way. Afternoon touring at USF is largely dependent on the park's ever-shifting show schedule, so check showtimes on the park map as soon as you arrive and shuffle the steps accordingly.

Before using any of our Universal Orlando touring plans, first become familiar with Universal's park-opening procedures, as described on page 63. Purchase your admission ahead of time, and call ☎ 407-363-8000 or check universalorlando.com the day before you go to verify official operating hours. If you're eligible for Early Park Admission (see page 65), arrive at USF 90–120 minutes before the official park opening time. If you're not eligible for early entry, arrive at the park 30–45 minutes prior to opening time.

If you're using TouringPlans' Lines smartphone app, you can select any of the following premium touring plans, copy it to your list of personalized plans, and optimize the plan steps to your preferences. Once you arrive at the park, select the appropriate plan in the app to make it active, and track your progress during the day by marking each attraction as complete after exiting. Optimize the plan repeatedly during the day to refine it with the latest wait-time information. If you're following a two-park plan, a link to part two will appear at the top of the plan; switch to the second part when moving to the second park, and then return to part one when you return to the original park.

Once you're admitted into the park, move quickly from attraction to attraction, following your chosen touring plan. If you're not interested in an attraction it lists, simply skip that attraction and proceed to the next. When you encounter a very long line at an attraction that the touring plan calls for, skip the attraction in question and go to the next step, returning later to retry. Don't worry that other people will be following the plans and render them useless. Fewer than 2 in every 100 people in the park will have been exposed to this info.

CHOOSING THE APPROPRIATE TOURING PLAN

WE PRESENT THREE USF touring plans:

- One-Day Touring Plan for Adults
- One-Day Touring Plan for Parents with Small Children
- One-Day Touring Plan for Seniors

In addition, we have three Universal Orlando touring plans that combine both USF and IOA, for guests with park-to-park admission:

- Universal Orlando Highlights One-Day/Two-Park Touring Plan
- Wizarding World One-Day/Two-Park Touring Plan
- Universal Orlando Comprehensive Two-Day/Two-Park Touring Plan

If you have two days at Universal Orlando, the Comprehensive Two-Day/Two-Park Touring Plan is by far the most relaxed. The two-day plan takes advantage of early morning, when lines are short and the park hasn't filled with guests. This plan works well year-round and eliminates much of the extra walking required by the one-day plans. No matter when the park closes, our two-day plan guarantees the most efficient touring and the least time in lines. The plan is perfect for guests who wish to explore the attractions and the atmosphere of USF and IOA, with an emphasis on both Wizarding Worlds.

If you have only one day to visit USF and don't have park-to-park tickets, then use the One-Day Touring Plan for Adults. It's exhausting, but it packs in the maximum. If you have one-day park-to-park passes, the Universal Orlando Highlights Touring Plan will help you pack in all of the best thrill rides at USF and IOA, including The Wizarding

World ones, at the expense of most shows and a lot of shoe leather. Alternatively, Harry Potter superfans who have one-day park-to-park passes and zero interest in anything at Universal outside Hogsmeade and Diagon Alley (a mistake in our estimation, but it's your money) can follow the Wizarding World One-Day/Two-Park Touring Plan to maximize their magical immersion.

If you have young ones in tow, adopt the One-Day Touring Plan for Parents with Small Children. It's a compromise, blending the preferences of younger children with those of older siblings and adults. The plan includes many children's rides but omits roller coasters and other attractions that frighten young children or are off-limits because of height requirements greater than 40 inches. Or use the One-Day Touring Plan for Adults and take advantage of child swap, a technique whereby children accompany adults to the loading area of a ride with age and height requirements but don't board (see page 204).

If you have three days at Universal Orlando, use the Comprehensive Two-Day/Two-Park Touring Plan on the first two days, and use the Universal Orlando Highlights One-Day/Two-Park Touring Plan or Wizarding World Touring Plan on your last day. With four or more days, you can pretty much explore the parks at your leisure, using any of the plans as a general guideline.

ONE-DAY TOURING PLAN FOR ADULTS *(page 395)*

THIS PLAN IS FOR GUESTS without park-to-park tickets and includes every recommended attraction at USF. If a ride or show is listed that you don't want to experience, skip that step and proceed to the next. Move quickly from attraction to attraction, and if possible, hold off on lunch until after experiencing at least six rides.

ONE-DAY TOURING PLAN FOR PARENTS WITH SMALL CHILDREN *(page 396)*

THIS PLAN IS FOR GUESTS without park-to-park tickets and eliminates all rides with a minimum height requirement greater than 40 inches. The plan includes a midday break of at least 2 hours back at your hotel.

ONE-DAY TOURING PLAN FOR SENIORS *(page 397)*

THIS PLAN IS FOR GUESTS without park-to-park tickets and is specifically designed for seniors and grandparents, taking walking distances and attraction ratings from this group into account. This plan focuses on shows and family-friendly attractions and avoids thrill rides.

UNIVERSAL ORLANDO HIGHLIGHTS ONE-DAY/ TWO-PARK TOURING PLAN *(pages 401–402)*

THIS PLAN IS FOR GUESTS with park-to-park tickets who wish to see the highlights of USF and IOA in a single day. The plan uses Hogwarts Express to get from one park to the other and back again; you can walk back for the return leg if the line is too long. The plan includes lunch at Mythos (make reservations before your visit) and dinner at the Leaky Cauldron. During holiday periods, you may need to substitute a quick-service snack for one or both meals to fit in all of the plan's attractions.

WIZARDING WORLD ONE-DAY/TWO-PARK TOURING PLAN *(pages 403–404)*

THIS PLAN IS FOR GUESTS with one-day park-to-park tickets who wish to experience The Wizarding Worlds of Harry Potter to the exclusion of everything else Universal has to offer. The plan uses Hogwarts Express to get from one park to the other and then back again; you can walk back to the first park for the return leg if the line is too long. The plan includes lunch at Three Broomsticks and dinner at the Leaky Cauldron. During holiday periods, you may need to substitute a quick-service snack for one or both meals to fit in all of the plan's attractions.

UNIVERSAL ORLANDO COMPREHENSIVE TWO-DAY/ TWO-PARK TOURING PLAN *(pages 405–408)*

THIS PLAN IS FOR GUESTS with multiday park-to-park tickets who wish to explore USF and IOA in-depth over two days. The plan includes one Hogwarts Express trip between parks per day. Incidentally, all the water rides are concentrated in the morning of the first day, so if bad weather is in the forecast, consider flipping the plan days.

PART EIGHT

UNIVERSAL'S ISLANDS *of* ADVENTURE

UNIVERSAL STUDIOS FLORIDA HAD BARELY opened before planning began on Project X, the second theme park that would provide Universal with enough critical mass to actually compete with Disney. Originally envisioned as Cartoon World, with areas devoted to DC Comics superheroes and *Looney Tunes* characters, the concept evolved into **Islands of Adventure** (IOA), a fully themed fantasy park inspired by family-friendly literature.

From its very inception, IOA was designed to directly compete with Disney's Magic Kingdom. The park has kid-friendly rides and cartoon characters (like Fantasyland), thrill rides in a sci-fi city (like Tomorrowland), and a jungle river with robot creatures (like Adventureland). Its layout—a central entry corridor leading to a ring of connected lands—even mimics the classic Disneyland model, with one major exception: instead of a hub and castle in the center, Universal built a large lagoon, whose estuaries separate the park's thematically diverse "islands" (actually peninsulas).

IOA debuted in 1999 as a state-of-the-art park competing with a Disney park decades older, but it didn't initially do gangbuster business, thanks partly to a botched marketing rollout and Universal's failure to add any major attractions during IOA's first decade. That all changed in 2010, which marked IOA's coming-out party. In one of the greatest seismic shifts in theme park history, Universal opened the first Harry Potter–themed area within the park. Harry P. is possibly the only fictional character extant capable of trumping Mickey Mouse, and Universal went all out to create a setting and attractions designed to be the envy of the industry.

> *unofficial* **TIP**
> Thrill rides at Islands of Adventure are the real deal—not for the faint-hearted or for little ones.

BEWARE OF THE WET AND WILD

THOUGH WE'VE DESCRIBED IOA as a direct competitor to the Magic Kingdom, know this: whereas most Magic Kingdom attractions are designed to be enjoyed by guests of any age, attractions at IOA are created largely for an under-40 population. The roller coasters at Universal are serious with a capital *S*, making Space Mountain and Big Thunder Mountain Railroad look about as frightening as Dumbo. In fact, seven of the top nine attractions at IOA are thrill rides; of these, three will not only scare the crap out of you but will also drench you with water. And about that water: It ain't exactly Evian, as a reader from New York learned the hard way:

> *The amount of water dumped on us at Popeye & Bluto's Bilge-Rat Barges was incredible, and the chlorine was so bad that one of us couldn't see.*

After your chemical baptism, you may be tempted by the heated full-body drying booths strategically positioned near the exit of each drenching attraction, but this Pennsylvania reader has a warning:

> *The People Dryers are a waste of $5. We used one and were no drier than before, just poorer.*

If you get soaked, you're better off just walking off the wetness in warm weather, or packing a change of clothes if it's cool.

For families, there are three interactive playgrounds as well as six rides or shows without height restrictions that young children can enjoy. Of the thrill rides, only The Amazing Adventures of Spider-Man, Skull Island, and the two in Toon Lagoon (described later) are marginally appropriate for little kids, and even on these rides, your child needs to be fairly hardy.

GETTING ORIENTED *at* UNIVERSAL'S ISLANDS *of* ADVENTURE

LAID OUT MUCH LIKE Epcot's World Showcase—arranged in a large circle surrounding a lagoon—IOA evinces the same thematic continuity present in the Magic Kingdom. Each "land," or "island" in this case, is self-contained and visually consistent in its theme.

You first encounter **Port of Entry,** a mélange of Middle Eastern and Asian architecture, where you'll find Guest Services, lockers, stroller and wheelchair rentals, ATM banking, Lost and Found, and shopping. From the Port of Entry, moving clockwise around the lagoon, you access **Marvel Super Hero Island, Toon Lagoon, Skull Island, Jurassic Park, The Wizarding World of Harry Potter—Hogsmeade, The Lost Continent,** and **Seuss Landing.** There is no in-park transportation to move you between lands.

As you enter IOA, lockers and rentals are to your left, and First Aid and Guest Services are to your right. Before bolting through Port of Entry to your first adventure—or at least on your way out before leaving—take a few moments to appreciate the details that Universal lavished on this area, from the fountain made of giant leaves, to the sounds of gamblers from an upstairs casino, to the jail that's been broken and the fire station that burned down. Also listen for the original background music, which is synchronized throughout the park and changes as you move from island to island. Port of Entry doesn't have any attractions, but it does have dining (including a Starbucks) and shopping options.

UNIVERSAL'S ISLANDS *of* ADVENTURE ATTRACTIONS

MARVEL SUPER HERO ISLAND

THIS ISLAND, WITH ITS FUTURISTIC and retro-future design and comic book signage, offers shopping, dining, and two of Orlando's best thrill rides, all based on Marvel Comics characters. The architecture, which some fault as flat, seeks to re-create the Pop Art look of comic book backgrounds; some buildings have Chrome Illusion paint that changes colors depending on the angle of sunlight. Look for the meteor impact sculpture covered in hundreds of Marvel characters, as well as communication booths delivering messages from S.H.I.E.L.D.

Several times a day on a published schedule, Marvel heroes parade in on all-terrain vehicles and take over the streets greeting guests; the activity can make it tough to navigate through the area. Between the roar of The Incredible Hulk Coaster and the bass beats surrounding The Amazing Adventures of Spider-Man building, Super Hero Island is also one of the loudest sections of the park; seek refuge along the water behind Captain America Diner.

In case you were curious: Yes, Disney now owns Marvel Comics, but Universal locked up the theme park rights to certain character groups—the Avengers, Spider-Man, the Fantastic Four, and X-Men—in perpetuity on the East Coast. You may see Black Panther, Iron Man, and Captain America in Disneyland or in Mickey's international parks, but they are exclusive to IOA in Orlando (and Universal Studios Japan) for

continued on page 328

Universal's Islands of Adventure

Attractions

1. The Amazing Adventures
   of Spider-Man UX ☑
2. Camp Jurassic
3. Caro-Seuss-el UX
4. The Cat In The Hat UX
5. Doctor Doom's Fearfall UX
6. Dudley Do-Right's Ripsaw Falls UX
7. Flight of the Hippogriff UX
8. Hagrid's Magical Creatures Motorbike
   Adventure ☑ VL
9. Harry Potter and the Forbidden Journey UX ☑
10. The High in the Sky Seuss Trolley Train Ride! UX
11. Hogwarts Express: Hogsmeade Station UX ☑
12. If I Ran The Zoo
13. The Incredible Hulk Coaster UX ☑
14. Jurassic Park Discovery Center

15. Jurassic Park River Adventure UX ☑
16. Jurassic World VelociCoaster (opening 2021)
17. Me Ship, The Olive
18. Ollivanders
19. One Fish, Two Fish, Red Fish, Blue Fish UX
20. Popeye & Bluto's Bilge-Rat Barges UX ☑

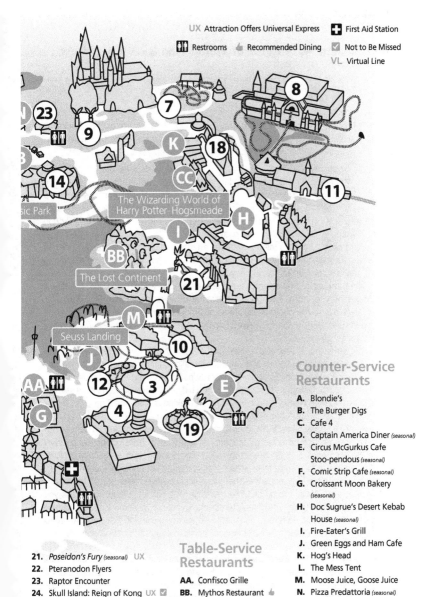

UX Attraction Offers Universal Express   ✚ First Aid Station

🚻 Restrooms   🍴 Recommended Dining   ☑ Not to Be Missed

VL Virtual Line

The Wizarding World of Harry Potter-Hogsmeade

Jurassic Park

The Lost Continent

Seuss Landing

Counter-Service Restaurants

A. Blondie's
B. The Burger Digs
C. Cafe 4
D. Captain America Diner *(seasonal)*
E. Circus McGurkus Cafe Stoo-pendous *(seasonal)*
F. Comic Strip Cafe *(seasonal)*
G. Croissant Moon Bakery *(seasonal)*
H. Doc Sugrue's Desert Kebab House *(seasonal)*
I. Fire-Eater's Grill
J. Green Eggs and Ham Cafe
K. Hog's Head
L. The Mess Tent
M. Moose Juice, Goose Juice
N. Pizza Predattoria *(seasonal)*
O. Thunder Falls Terrace 🍴
P. Wimpy's *(seasonal)*

21. *Poseidon's Fury (seasonal)* UX
22. Pteranodon Flyers
23. Raptor Encounter
24. Skull Island: Reign of Kong UX ☑
25. Storm Force Accelatron *(seasonal)* UX

Table-Service Restaurants

AA. Confisco Grille
BB. Mythos Restaurant 🍴
CC. Three Broomsticks (counter service) 🍴

continued from page 325

the indefinite future. The Guardians of the Galaxy, who are getting their own roller coaster at Epcot, are an exception to this restriction.

The Amazing Adventures of Spider-Man *(Universal Express)*
★★★★★

What it is Indoor adventure 3-D simulator ride. Scope and scale Super-headliner. When to go During the first 40 minutes the park is open. Comments 40" minimum height requirement; child swap available (see page 204); single-rider line available. One of the best attractions anywhere; not to be missed. Duration of ride 4½ minutes. Loading speed Moderate–fast.

DESCRIPTION AND COMMENTS Widely regarded as one of the best theme park attractions in Orlando, and one of our favorite rides anywhere in the world, The Amazing Adventures of Spider-Man remains near the top of IOA's must-do list more than two decades after its debut. The attraction moves a spinning, tilting ride vehicle through 13 scenes (covering 1.5 acres) of mayhem, which fuse 4K 3-D digital projections almost seamlessly with actual sets and props, accompanied by special effects including fog, water, and fire. In many instances guests cannot tell until the action begins whether they're looking at a movie screen or an actual brick wall.

The total package is astonishing—frenetic yet fluid, and visually rich. The ride is wild yet very smooth. Though the attraction opened more than 20 years ago, Spider-Man is still technologically ahead of almost everything at Walt Disney World outside Pandora: The World of Avatar or Star Wars: Galaxy's Edge—which is to say that it will leave you in awe.

The story line is that you're visiting the *Daily Bugle* newspaper (where Peter Parker, also known as Spider-Man, works as a mild-mannered photographer) when crime reports start coming in. The Sinister Syndicate—consisting of Spidey's archenemies Doctor Octopus, Hobgoblin, Electro, Hydro-Man, and Scream—have used an antigravity gun to steal (we promise we're not making this up) the Statue of Liberty. You're drafted on the spot by cantankerous editor J. Jonah Jameson to get the story. You board a 12-passenger SCOOP vehicle—a mobile open-top motion simulator identical to the cars used in Universal Studios Florida's (USF's) Transformers—and follow the "Spider Signal" straight into an epic battle between the web-slinger and his foes.

The Amazing Adventures of Spider-Man combines your ride vehicle's motion so smoothly with the film sequences that you quickly believe you're part of the action. Without giving away too much of the surprise, one part of the attraction has you raised high above the city skyline. After speeding around, you experience a 400-foot sensory drop from a skyscraper roof all the way to the pavement. The blending of 3-D film and pitching of the ride car is so convincing that, during our first ride, we were sure that we were being lifted inside the building; we had to ride a second time, with our glasses off, to see how the effect was done while keeping the car on the ground.

Even though Spidey's cybertronic sibling in USF has proven popular, the original 3-D dark ride has held its ground as the first and still favorite in its genre. It's less frantic and frenetic than Transformers and features more dialogue and humor. And despite using similar systems, some folks who get motion sick on Transformers find that they can tolerate this ride better.

The late Marvel Comics founder Stan Lee made cameo appearances in nearly every film featuring the characters he helped create, and The Amazing Adventures of Spider-Man ride is no exception. Lee appears as the truck driver who swerves to miss your SCOOP vehicle early in the ride, outside the theater as Spidey and Doc Ock duke it out, in the street after your vehicle falls to the ground, and finally with the cops as the stolen Statue of Liberty is being flown back into place. He is also the voice who bids you farewell before disembarking.

TOURING TIPS If you were on hand for Early Park Admission, ride after experiencing The Wizarding World and Skull Island: Reign of Kong. If you elect to bypass The Wizarding World congestion, ride after Hulk.

Seats in the first row are the most immersive, but we find that the 3-D effects focus better from a row or two back. The rear corners get the most movement, while the center of the second row is the most stable. There is an on-ride photo, but the camera is in an odd position, so everyone comes out facing the wrong way.

The standby and Express queues both wind through portions of the *Daily Bugle* newsroom; Express cuts through Peter Parker's darkroom (look for Spidey's glowing handprints on the ceiling), while standby passes by J. J.'s trophy case, with hidden tributes to the designers. The single-rider option, when available, bypasses most of the buildup but can greatly cut your wait as long as the line doesn't reach the stroller parking area.

Doctor Doom's Fearfall *(Universal Express)* ★★★

APPEAL BY AGE	PRESCHOOL ★½	GRADE SCHOOL ★★★½	TEENS ★★★★
YOUNG ADULTS ★★★½		OVER 30 ★★★½	SENIORS ★★★

What it is Tower launch and free fall. Scope and scale Major attraction. When to go During the first hour the park is open or after 3 p.m. Comments 52" minimum height requirement; child swap available (see page 204); single-rider line available. More bark than bite. Duration of ride 40 seconds. Loading speed Slow.

DESCRIPTION AND COMMENTS Here you are (again), strapped into a seat with your feet dangling, blasted 200 feet up in the air, and then allowed to partially free-fall back down. Imagine the midway game where a macho guy swings a sledgehammer, propelling a metal sphere up a vertical shaft to ring a bell—on this ride, you're the metal sphere.

That prospect sounds worse than it actually is. The scariest part of the ride is the apprehension that builds as you sit, strapped in, waiting for the ride to launch. Blasting up and falling down are actually pleasant, with one exhilarating, fleeting moment of negative-gravity air time at the top. Riders in chambers three and four get a great view of the park, while those in one and two look out over I-4 and International Drive.

TOURING TIPS We've seen glaciers that move faster than the line for Doctor Doom's Fearfall, though the ominous queue and satirical propaganda films compensate slightly. If you want to ride without investing half a day, be one of the first to ride. If you're on hand at opening time, being among the first isn't too difficult (mainly because The Wizarding World, Hulk, and Spider-Man attractions are bigger draws). Alternatively, the ride often has no wait near the end of the operating day, and the view is especially nice at night.

Fortunately, Doctor Doom also has a singles line (when available); look for the stairwell to the left of the ride's entrance.

The Incredible Hulk Coaster *(Universal Express)* ★★★★½

APPEAL BY AGE	PRESCHOOL ★	GRADE SCHOOL ★★★★½	TEENS ★★★★★
YOUNG ADULTS ★★★★★		OVER 30 ★★★★½	SENIORS ★★★★

What it is Roller coaster. Scope and scale Super-headliner. When to go During the first 40 minutes the park is open or after 3 p.m. Comments 54" minimum height requirement;

child swap available (see page 204); single-rider line available. A coaster-lover's coaster; not to be missed. Duration of ride 2¼ minutes. Loading speed Moderate–fast.

DESCRIPTION AND COMMENTS The Incredible Hulk's towering loops are some of the most iconic elements of the IOA skyline. The big green guy's 3,700-foot-long track, which was rebuilt from scratch in 2016, pulses with illuminated 32-passenger trains that flash to a synchronized soundtrack composed by Fall Out Boy's Patrick Stump. The entryway stars a statue of the Hulk himself holding a coaster car overhead—the marquee is made of salvaged track from the original version—and the queue building features dramatic lighting and the world's largest plasma display. (Ask a team member for a **gamma tour** to examine the Marvel Comics Easter eggs hidden along the line.) The story line sees guests volunteering for General Thaddeus "Thunderbolt" Ross's experimental attempt to create super-soldiers via gamma ray bombardment. (We're pretty certain it's not covered by Obamacare.) The story falls apart almost as soon as the ride starts, but you'll be too scared to notice.

What you need to know about this attraction is simple. You'll be shot like a carrier-launched jet from 0 to 40 mph in 2 seconds, flung upside down into a zero gravity barrel roll 100 feet off the ground (which will, of course, induce weightlessness), and then thrown immediately into a pair of cobra rolls and a vertical loop of more than 100 feet, into a belowground tunnel, no less! Two more rolls and another loop follow, for a total of seven upside-down experiences in a ride of a little more than 2 minutes. At the end of the ride, you may be just as green as the Hulk.

Seriously, the Hulk is a great roller coaster, one of the best in Florida, providing a ride comparable to that of Kumba or Montu (Busch Gardens) with the added thrill of an accelerated launch, instead of the old-fashioned uphill crank. While still a far cry from the side-to-side shaking of Hollywood Rip Ride Rockit next door, Hulk has developed a tendency toward head-banging, so be mindful of the horse-collar shoulder restraints. We're also a little sad to see the famously hollow steel filled with sand, muting the track's once-mighty roar, though a recorded growl now blares with every launch. The video screen in the launch tube doesn't make much impact, and the audio from the in-seat speakers is sometimes too low to understand, but the driving orchestral rock soundtrack successfully makes the ride feel faster than ever.

TOURING TIPS Our advice is to skip The Wizarding World attractions in the early morning and ride The Incredible Hulk Coaster first thing. Alternatively, if you insist on going to Hogsmeade at rope drop (or if you're eligible for Early Park Admission), you should ride Hulk immediately after you've enjoyed the Harry Potter attractions or save it for late in the day.

Universal provides electronic lockers near the entrance of The Incredible Hulk Coaster to deposit any items that might depart your person during the ride. Use the lockers for anything—and we mean anything—that could be dislodged during your ride: hats, glasses, cell phones, camera bags, and toupees. The only thing you have to hold on to is your park ticket (in your pocket or on a lanyard) in order to reopen your locker afterward. The lockers are free for the duration of your wait, and use of these lockers is enforced. Be prepared to pat down your pockets for loose change, or you'll be pulled aside for a TSA-style wanding after triggering the metal detectors.

If you get to Hulk early enough and the line is short enough, opt for the special front-row line near the boarding area. It's worth waiting an extra 5 or 10 minutes to get a spectacular, brief view of the park. The back left seat gets the best zero gravity effect from the opening inversion.

Storm Force Accelatron *(Universal Express; seasonal)*   ★★½

What it is Covered spinning ride. Scope and scale Minor attraction. When to go Anytime. Comments Child swap available (see page 204). Duration of ride 1½ minutes. Loading speed Slow.

DESCRIPTION AND COMMENTS Storm Force Accelatron is a spiffed-up version of Disney's nausea-inducing Mad Tea Party. In Storm Force Accelatron, up to five people are seated in a round plastic ride vehicle that has a metal wheel mounted in the center. Turning the metal wheel causes the ride vehicle to spin on its central axis. While that's happening, each ride vehicle is part of a group of three similar vehicles, also spinning around a common axis. And the entire group of 12 ride vehicles is simultaneously spinning around the Accelatron's center.

In Universal's take on this carnival classic, you spin to the accompaniment of a simulated thunderstorm. Flashing lights and loud music either really enhance the experience or make it much, much worse, depending on your stomach. A story line involving the X-Men heroine Storm loosely ties this midway-type ride to the Marvel Super Hero Island area, but it's largely irrelevant and offers no advice on keeping your lunch down.

Young children, teens, and masochists like to lure the unsuspecting onto the ride, and then turn the wheel like maniacs. The ride is effective for determining if you've recently developed any kind of inner-ear disorder.

TOURING TIPS Storm Force is hidden behind Hulk's locker banks and is largely overlooked by the crowds. During the off-season, the ride is typically a walk-on, and even on the busiest days, the wait rarely tops 20 minutes. If you're prone to motion sickness, keep your distance.

TOON LAGOON

WHIMSICAL AND GAILY COLORED, with rounded and exaggerated lines, Toon Lagoon translates cartoon art into real buildings and settings. King's Row and Comic Strip Lane, the main drags of Toon Lagoon, are the domains of such vintage Sunday-funnies favorites as *Beetle Bailey, The Family Circus,* and *Blondie*—in other words, intellectual property that Universal could get for cheap. Across a bridge lies Sweethaven, home to Popeye and Olive Oyl, and a mountain dedicated to Dudley Do-Right looms around the corner.

The island's King Features Syndicate and Jay Ward comic characters, though classic, are probably unrecognizable to anyone born after 1980, but that doesn't stop kids from enjoying the resort's two wettest water rides, both of which are found here. Entering Toon Lagoon from Marvel Super Hero Island, you'll have to pass a midway of barely themed carnival games and an enormous amphitheater that sits empty 99% of the time, making this transition the biggest eyesore in an otherwise exquisite park. There are some great photo ops here, especially the sideways sign where you can snap a gravity-defying shot with Marmaduke the Great Dane.

If your kids want to get wet but are too small for the water rides (or you don't want to wait in line), send them to the splash pads at either entrance to Toon Lagoon. A few minutes frolicking in fountains of sulfurous water should satisfy them.

Dudley Do-Right's Ripsaw Falls *(Universal Express)*   ★★★½

APPEAL BY AGE   PRESCHOOL ★½   GRADE SCHOOL ★★★★½   TEENS ★★★★½
YOUNG ADULTS ★★★★   OVER 30 ★★★★   SENIORS ★★★★

What it is Flume ride. **Scope and scale** Headliner. **When to go** Before 11 a.m. **Comments** 44″ minimum height requirement; child swap available (see page 204). **Duration of ride** 5 minutes. **Loading speed** Moderate.

Motion Sickness

DESCRIPTION AND COMMENTS Dudley Do-Right's Ripsaw Falls features characters spun off from the old Rocky and Bullwinkle TV show. Dudley is a cheerfully incompetent Canadian Mountie who pursues Snidely Whiplash, his nemesis, throughout the Great White North. Snidely inevitably tries to kidnap Nell, the girl of Dudley's dreams, and Dudley (with trusted horse, Horse) rescues her, usually in spite of himself. The original cartoons parodied everything from the implausible plots of early silent movie melodramas to the "friendly Canadian" trope, complete with really bad Quebecois accents. We think this attraction may have been inspired by Dudley's "Saw Mill" cartoon circa 1962.

Story line aside, IOA's tribute to the cartoon is a flume ride similar to the Magic Kingdom's Splash Mountain. Riders sit single file in loglike boats and bob along a man-made river, floating past mostly static scenes telling the story of Snidely kidnapping Nell, with Dudley's eventual rescuing.

As far as log flume rides go, Ripsaw Falls is pretty good. There are several medium-size drops during the 5-minute ride, and a heart-stopping 75-foot one near the end. Universal claims this is the first flume ride to "send riders plummeting 15 feet below the surface of the water"; you're just plummeting into a tunnel, but it's a nifty effect. The ride queue and loading area have some visual gags that would make the original show's writers proud, and the on-board ride audio is also good.

That being said, the theming and visuals of Ripsaw Falls aren't in the same league as Disney's Splash Mountain, to which everyone inevitably compares it. Most of Ripsaw Falls's effects are nonmoving statues, whereas Splash Mountain is loaded with moving animatronics, water effects, and gorgeous scenery. Dudley's defects are partly intentional, in keeping with the cartoon's satirical spirit, like an exposed view of backstage following the "scenic overlook" that's cheekily labeled "overlooked scenery." But the flaws are mostly due to the ride's rushed completion (it opened a year earlier than originally scheduled), resulting in a potential classic that was never properly finished.

TOURING TIPS This ride will get you wet, but on average not as soaked as on Popeye & Bluto's Bilge-Rat Barges. If you want to stay dry, however, arrive prepared with a poncho; however, no poncho can protect your feet, as this Seattle reader observed:

It's a conundrum that you have to wear shoes on all rides, but your feet get soaked on Ripsaw Falls. I saw one mother putting small plastic bags over her kids' shoes—it looked funny but perhaps it worked.

If you're going to ride both Ripsaw Falls and Bilge-Rat Barges, see them one after another during the morning (if it's sunny enough to dry you off) or at the end of the day before slogging back to your hotel. After riding, take a moment to gauge the timing of the water cannons that go off along the exit walk. This is where you can really get drenched. Ride this after experiencing all the Marvel Super Hero rides.

This is one of the few single-file log flumes that uses lap bar restraints, and it makes for a mighty tight fit. Make sure you try the test seat outside the queue before waiting in line. If you don't want to ride, you can pump quarters into the water sprayers along the bridge leading to Skull Island and amuse yourself by dousing guests who just survived the big drop.

Me Ship, *The Olive* (temporarily closed)   ★★★

APPEAL BY AGE PRESCHOOL ★★★★½ GRADE SCHOOL ★★★★ TEENS ★★★
YOUNG ADULTS ★★½   OVER 30 ★★★   SENIORS ★★★½

What it is Interactive playground. **Scope and scale** Minor attraction. **When to go** Anytime. **Comment** Colorful and appealing for kids.

DESCRIPTION AND COMMENTS *The Olive* is Popeye's beloved boat coming to life as a three-floor interactive playground. *The Olive* offers a chance for kids to run around and expend some of the energy they've pent up in lines. Besides slides, stairs, and climbing platforms, kids can play with props, including the ship's wheel, bell, and throttle. Those who climb to the second floor will find water cannons that can reach riders on the nearby Bilge-Rat Barges. A separate play area, called Swee'Pea's Playpen, is available for smaller children.

TOURING TIPS Usually opens an hour after the park opens. If you're into the big rides, save this for later in the day. Also, take a few minutes to explore the shoreline pathways behind the ship; you'll find some punny Popeye props and a little peace and quiet.

Popeye & Bluto's Bilge-Rat Barges *(Universal Express)*
★★★★

APPEAL BY AGE PRESCHOOL ★★★ GRADE SCHOOL ★★★★½ TEENS ★★★★½
YOUNG ADULTS ★★★★½   OVER 30 ★★★★½   SENIORS ★★★★

What it is Whitewater rapids raft ride. **Scope and scale** Headliner. **When to go** Before 11 a.m. **Comments** 42″ minimum height requirement; child swap available (see page 204). Bring your own soap; not to be missed. **Duration of ride** 4½ minutes. **Loading speed** Moderate-fast.

DESCRIPTION AND COMMENTS Hands down our favorite whitewater raft ride on the East Coast, Bilge-Rat Barges is only bested in its genre by Grizzly River Run at Disney California Adventure. Bilge-Rat Barges seats 10 riders at a time on a circular raft down a man-made canyon of gushing rapids, waterfalls, twists, turns, and dips. Some of the scenery is visually interesting, such as the 18-foot octopus crammed into a cave two sizes too small, but the minimally moving props along the side don't quite make for an immersive story line.

TOURING TIPS If you didn't drown on Dudley Do-Right, here's a second chance. You'll get a lot wetter from the knees down on this ride, so use your poncho or garbage bag and ride barefoot with your britches rolled up. Each raft has a covered center console into which you can place backpacks, socks, and shoes; lockers or zip-top bags are strongly suggested for anything electronic. If you don't believe us, listen to this reader from Kinross, Scotland:

> *I had seen people coming off the ride soaked but had no clue that every rider gets saturated to the skin!*

This ride usually opens an hour later than the rest of the park. Experience the barges in the morning after the Marvel Super Hero attractions and Dudley Do-Right.

Some people ride Bilge-Rat Barges and Ripsaw Falls consecutively, right before leaving the park, to avoid sloshing around in wet clothes most of the day.

Some children may be frightened more by the way the rapids look, and by the screams coming from the ride as it passes through Toon Lagoon, than by the roughness of the ride itself. These are screams of laughter. If your child is apprehensive about riding, take them to any of the platforms overlooking the ride to see how much fun everyone is having.

SKULL ISLAND

WE'RE NOT ENTIRELY SURE how Skull Island qualifies as its own land on IOA's map when it consists of a single attraction and a couple of kiosks, but that's a question for Universal's crack cartographers. While it's the smallest stand-alone section of this (or perhaps any) park, Skull Island makes a big visual impact on guests passing through to Jurassic Park, with which it shares an aesthetic kinship.

Skull Island: Reign of Kong *(Universal Express)* ★★★★

What it is Indoor-outdoor truck safari with 3-D effects. **Scope and scale** Super-headliner. **When to go** Immediately after park opening or just before closing. **Comments** 36" minimum height requirement; child swap available (see page 204); single-rider line available. Too dark and scary for small children; not to be missed. **Duration of ride** About 6 minutes; 4 minutes when exterior is bypassed in inclement weather. **Loading speed** Fast.

Motion Sickness

DESCRIPTION AND COMMENTS Skull Island: Reign of Kong is both an attraction and an entire "island" unto itself, located between Toon Lagoon's Dudley Do-Right's Ripsaw Falls and the Thunder Falls Terrace restaurant in Jurassic Park. This attraction isn't exactly based on the 2005 *King Kong* remake (though director Peter Jackson did consult on the design), nor is it directly tied to the *Kong: Skull Island* film released in 2017. Rather, the ride is an original adventure set in the 1930s, casting guests as explorers with the Eighth Wonder Expedition Company, which has set up its jungle base camp in an ancient temple inhabited by a hostile Kong-worshipping indigenous tribe. That may seem like a foolish place to pitch your tent, but it makes for a phenomenal queue experience, featuring both lifelike animatronic figures and projection effects that startle unwitting guests.

The winding skeleton-strewn path eventually leads to your transportation: an oversize 72-seat open-sided "expedition vehicle" that superficially resembles Disney's Animal Kingdom's Kilimanjaro Safari trucks. It's helmed by one of five different animatronic tour guides, each with a unique personality and backstory, which lends the attraction additional re-ridability. Your ride begins with a short loop outside through the jungle (which may be bypassed in inclement weather, abbreviating the experience by almost 2 minutes), ending at the massive torch-framed doors in the center of Skull Island's imposing stony facade. The doors open, allowing you passage into a maze of caves. There, you're swiftly assaulted by all manner of icky prehistoric bats, bugs, and beasties, brought to gruesome life through a mix of detailed physical effects and razor-sharp 3-D screens (even better than the ones in Harry Potter and the Escape from Gringotts and Transformers). After barely surviving a preliminary series of multisensory near misses, you're thrust into the center of a raging battle between vicious *V. Rex* dinosaurs and the big ape himself, in a climactic sequence similar (though not identical) to the *King Kong 360 3-D* attraction on Universal Studios Hollywood's (USH's) tram tour. Finally, just when you think it's all over, you'll have one last face-to-face encounter with the "eighth wonder of the world," only this time in the fur-covered flesh.

Although it's still among the top half dozen rides in IOA's impressive lineup, some creative missteps made Kong's long-awaited return fall somewhat short of the world-beating game changer his faithful fans may have expected. The atmospheric queue's muffled radio reports do an inadequate job of establishing the plot before boarding, and the initial scenes introduce characters that are completely abandoned mid-ride. The 360 centerpiece, while noticeably upgraded since its original USH incarnation, doesn't coherently connect to the opening. And the coda's animatronic Kong seems anticlimactically passive, despite his stunningly fluid facial expressions. As a result, the attraction feels oddly brief despite being (at nearly 6 minutes) one of the longest in the resort.

TOURING TIPS Skull Island: Reign of Kong is epic in every sense, from the monumental exterior to the extensive lines it attracts. On the plus side, Kong draws some guests away from The Wizarding World of Harry Potter, helping rebalance the park. Hit Skull Island first thing in the morning after the Marvel rides, or immediately following the Hogsmeade attractions if you're using Early Park Admission. A single-rider queue can help cut your wait, but it misses all the pre-show elements and closes intermittently.

Kong's minimum height requirement is just 36 inches—one of the lowest in the resort—and the ride is designed to be physically accessible to most people. However, on a sensory and psychological level, it's extremely intense; the standby queue alone is enough to reduce fearful kids to tears, though the Express line bypasses most of the scares. If you or your little one has a fear of darkness, insects, or man-eating monsters, you may want to forgo the monkey. A child swap room (with benches and a TV showing clips of the 2005 film) is available, but you're directed to navigate the scary standby queue to reach it. If needed, ask a team member if you can access it via the accommodation line instead. And you don't have to be a small fry for Skull Island to leave you shaken, as this honest reader admitted:

> *Being the grown-up I am, I wasn't expecting to be scared by any rides. However, Reign of Kong was absolutely terrifying. When you're sitting on the very edge and a 3-D dinosaur looks like it's going to eat you, you lose all the bravery you realize you never had.*

For those brave enough to board, the experience is far better in the back half of the truck (ideally, rows seven, eight, or nine), with guests on the right side getting the best view of the finale. If directed to one of the first few rows, politely ask to wait for the next truck so you can sit toward the rear. Sitting at either end of a row reveals the edges of the screens, so sacrifice the enjoyment of your friend or family member by forcing them to sit in the outside seat. The ride uses the same 3-D glasses as Spider-Man and Transformers; don't put them on until you enter the first interior scene, and remove them after the 360 projection tunnel to best appreciate the ending's animatronic.

Plexiglass dividers installed between the trucks' rows to promote social distancing may diminish the 3D effect, especially from center seats.

Ask at the entrance for a **temple tour** to learn technical details about the ride's self-driving trucks, hear about tributes hidden in the queue, and (if you're lucky) skip the standby line.

JURASSIC PARK

JURASSIC PARK IS A STEVEN SPIELBERG film franchise about a theme park with real dinosaurs. Jurassic Park at IOA is a real theme park (or at least a section of one) with fictitious dinosaurs. The iconic visitor center from the original film is one of the first things guests will see across the lagoon after walking through Port of Entry. The amount of space within Jurassic Park is deceptively large, and the entire area is completely immersive as you walk through it (except where Harry Potter's Hogwarts intrusively pokes above the trees).

There are two main entrances to this island, one from Toon Lagoon via Skull Island and another from The Wizarding World of Harry Potter. A third way in is the bridge between Lost Continent and Jurassic Park, which allows guests to bypass Hogsmeade on busy days.

After a decade of watching its wizarding neighbor get all the attention, IOA's Jurassic Park is finally receiving a much-needed update. Construction is well underway on the Jurassic World VelociCoaster, which will stretch from the former Triceratops Encounter to the waterfront behind the Discovery Center and back again. Thrill seekers will salivate over the spaghetti-bowl track's multiple inversions, high-speed launches, and towering top hat when the ride debuts in 2021. In addition, an upgraded Raptor Encounter opened in 2020, and the *Jurassic World* upgrades made to the River Adventure's Californian cousin could come to Orlando, along with a general refurbishment of the rest of the island.

Camp Jurassic *(temporarily closed)* ★★★½

APPEAL BY AGE PRESCHOOL ★★★★½ GRADE SCHOOL ★★★★½ TEENS ★★★ YOUNG ADULTS ★★★   OVER 30 ★★★   SENIORS ★★★

What it is Interactive play area. Scope and scale Minor attraction. When to go Anytime. Comments Creative playground; confusing layout.

DESCRIPTION AND COMMENTS Camp Jurassic is the most elaborate kid's play area at Universal, and one of the best theme park playgrounds you'll find anywhere. A sort of dinosaur-themed Tom Sawyer Island (minus the rafts), it allows kids to explore lava pits, caves, mines, and a rain forest. Explore and you'll find an echo cavern, bat caves, amber-bound bugs, and dilophosaurus heads that double as water blasters. The playground is big enough for many kids to spend a solid hour just running around. You may end up having to go into Camp Jurassic just to get the little nippers out, if you can find them. A parent from Rugby, Indiana, wrote in praise of the playground:

> For kids up to age 11 (depending on size and maturity), Camp Jurassic is an absolutely WONDERFUL experience! It was hilarious to see the 4-year-old enjoying shooting BIG water cannons at people, and his utter incredulity when they started shooting back! The (very!) high rope bridges were adventurous yet safe for all ages. The caves, hidden places, and twisting paths added mystery to the experience. If you have kids 10 and under, this is the place to let them go crazy, as they can safely experience everything.

Most of CJ is accessible to wheelchairs, excepting the ropes and higher platforms. Even the cave paths were navigable for a powered scooter. There are very few sitting spots inside CJ, so adults may want to wait outside in the nice, mostly shaded sitting area at CJ's front entrance. However, there are a couple of hard-to-find-but-there ways in and out, and if your child is easily disoriented, younger, or prone to panic if they lose their adults, they may need an adult to stay with them.

TOURING TIPS Camp Jurassic will fire the imaginations of the under-13 set. If you don't impose a time limit on the exploration, you could be here awhile. The layout of the play area is confusing and intersects the queuing area for Pteranodon Flyers. It's easy for kids and parents to get disoriented. If you think your children may get lost, you may end up having to climb, crawl, and slide along with them. Your chiropractor will thank you.

Jurassic Park Discovery Center *(temporarily closed)*   ★★½

APPEAL BY AGE   PRESCHOOL ★★★★   GRADE SCHOOL ★★★★   TEENS ★★★
YOUNG ADULTS ★★★½   OVER 30 ★★★   SENIORS ★★★

What it is Interactive natural history exhibit. Scope and scale Minor attraction. When to go Anytime. Comment Definitely worth checking out.

DESCRIPTION AND COMMENTS This interactive educational exhibit mixes fiction from the *Jurassic Park* movies, such as using fossil DNA to bring dinosaurs to life, with skeletal remains and other paleontological displays. The best exhibit here lets guests watch an animatronic raptor being hatched, with a young witness getting to name the newborn. You never know quite when one will emerge, but ask an attendant if you should stick around. Other exhibits allow you to digitally "fuse" your DNA with a dinosaur's to see what the resultant creature would look like, play a cheesy game show with dino trivia, or "be a saurus" by seeing through the eyes of a life-size animatronic (if they happen to be working).

TOURING TIPS The center usually opens later than the rest of the park and may close earlier as well; typical hours are 10 a.m.–5 p.m. Cycle back after experiencing all the rides or on a second day. Most folks can digest this exhibit in 10–15 minutes. Behind the Discovery Center is a gorgeous waterfront terrace where you can get away from the crowds—at least when it isn't being used for a special event or as a Hogsmeade holding area. If it isn't busy, ask a lab assistant for a **nursery tour** to go inside the raptor hatchery and get an up close look at props that were used in the films.

Jurassic Park River Adventure *(Universal Express)*   ★★★★

APPEAL BY AGE   PRESCHOOL ★★★   GRADE SCHOOL ★★★★   TEENS ★★★★
YOUNG ADULTS ★★★★   OVER 30 ★★★★   SENIORS ★★★★

What it is Indoor-outdoor river-raft adventure ride. Scope and scale Headliner. When to go Before 11 a.m. Comments 42" minimum height requirement; child swap available (see page 204); single-rider line available. Aging but still exciting; not to be missed. Duration of ride 6½ minutes. Loading speed Fast.

DESCRIPTION AND COMMENTS One of IOA's original headliner attractions, Jurassic Park River Adventure is inspired by a scene in author Michael Crichton's original *Jurassic Park* novel. Guests board tour boats for an aquatic ride through the grounds of Jurassic Park. Everything is tranquil as the tour begins, as the boat floats among large herbivorous dinosaurs such as ultrasaurus and stegosaurus, along with prehistoric-looking plants and the occasional geyser.

To no one's surprise, something goes horribly wrong, and your tour boat is nudged off course by a dinosaur at exactly the most inopportune time: just as you're floating past the vicious raptor enclosure, whose gates have been mysteriously unlocked and left open. Before you have time to ask what OSHA's inspectors really do during the day, your boat is climbing through the inside of the raptor facility amid the destruction and carnage wrought by the escaped animals. Your first face-to-face encounter with a *T. Rex* is also your last, as you find rescue by plunging 85 feet (the tallest water descent in the world when it was built) into the river below.

The drop is a doozy; the scenery, background music, and ride narration are all done well; and Jurassic Park River Adventure is overall one of the more immersive attractions in the entire resort. But the dinosaurs look increasingly arthritic, especially in comparison to this ride's California cousin, which was rethemed to the *Jurassic World* franchise in 2019.

TOURING TIPS Riders don't get as wet on River Adventure as they do on Bilge-Rat Barges or Ripsaw Falls. Though the boats make a huge splash at the bottom of the 85-foot drop, you can stay relatively dry if you're sitting in an interior seat; sitting behind a larger person and keeping your arms down can help. Still, bring a poncho or plastic bag if you want to keep as dry as possible. Paid lockers are located inside the queue. There's a viewing area to the left of the ride's final, big drop, where you can see how wet riders are getting before you decide to ride.

A Honolulu reader thinks Jurassic Park doesn't pass the smell test:

The Jurassic Park ride is a lot of fun—so fun, in fact, that you won't realize how truly HEINOUS the water that drenches you during the climactic splashdown is until much later. We sat in the front row for the ride and got soaked. Three hours later, my girlfriend and I realized that we reeked.

Young children must endure a double whammy on this ride. First, they're stalked by giant, salivating (sometimes spitting) reptiles, and then sent catapulting over the falls. Unless your children are fairly hardy, wait a year or two before you spring the River Adventure on them.

Because the Jurassic Park section of IOA is situated between The Wizarding World of Harry Potter—Hogsmeade and Skull Island: Reign of Kong, the boat ride may experience heavy crowds earlier in the day. Try to ride before 11 a.m., or use the single-rider queue, which often has little to no wait.

Jurassic World VelociCoaster   *(opening summer 2021)*

What it is Roller coaster. Scope and scale Super-headliner. When to go Immediately after park opening or just before closing. Duration of ride About 2 minutes.

DESCRIPTION AND COMMENTS In the summer of 2021, IOA will launch the Veloci-Coaster, Universal Orlando's most extreme roller coaster to date. The new attraction, which dramatically altered IOA's skyline by framing the iconic Jurassic Park Discovery Center, blurs the line between the original film franchise and its *Jurassic World* follow-ups with queue cameos from Chris Pratt (Owen Grady), Bryce Dallas Howard (Claire Dearing), and BD Wong (Dr. Henry Wu). Apparently, none of them have paid attention to the movies in which they starred, because they're offering guests scenic tours of the maximum-security paddocks where Blue and her carnivorous pals camp out. What could possibly go wrong?

Riders will board 24-passenger trains to experience two high-speed launches, an 80-degree dive down a towering 155-foot-tall "top hat," and close encounters with realistic rockwork and animatronic dinosaurs, all while being secured by nothing more than a lap bar (and Newtonian physics). With a top speed of 70 mph and an astounding 12 seconds total of weightless air time (including a first-of-its-kind zero-g inverted stall), VelociCoaster boasts the kind of statistics that make coaster nerds salivate. However, you merely need to look at how the Intamin-built track barrel-rolls and batwings along the waterfront to know that this will be one of the most intense scream machines in town.

TOURING TIPS When it debuts in summer 2021, we expect the VelociCoaster to quickly overtake The Incredible Hulk Coaster as the hard-core thrill junkies' favorite ride. If open, hit it first thing in the morning, or make it your last ride of the night. The entrance is on the lower level behind the Discovery Center and is not directly accessible from Jurassic Park's main pathway; take the bridge from Lost Continent for the most direct route from the park entrance. You can get a preview of the ride's launch by peeking through the wall across from the Raptor Encounter entrance. Even if you aren't brave enough to ride, the illuminated trains make for a beautiful sight after sunset.

Pteranodon Flyers ★★★

APPEAL BY AGE	PRESCHOOL ★★★★½	GRADE SCHOOL ★★★★	TEENS ★★★
YOUNG ADULTS ★★½		OVER 30 ★★★	SENIORS ★★

What it is Kiddie suspended coaster. Scope and scale Minor attraction. When to go In the first or last 30 minutes of the day, or use Virtual Line. Comments 36" minimum height requirement; adults and older children must be accompanied by a child 36"–56" tall. All sizzle, no steak. Duration of ride 1¼ minutes. Loading speed Slower than a hog in quicksand.

DESCRIPTION AND COMMENTS This two-seater kiddie coaster dangles you on a swing below a track that passes over a small part of Jurassic Park. The queue moves at a glacial pace, and the ride itself lasts barely 75 seconds, but you get a gorgeous view of the island's greenery, and the swinging cars deliver a surprisingly satisfying snap as they negotiate the track's curves.

TOURING TIPS This attraction is designed for children 36–56 inches in height. An adult or older child over 56 inches in height must accompany a child meeting the 36- to 56-inch height requirement.

For years, we've suggested skipping Pteranodon Flyers due to its low capacity and paltry length. But recent re-rides, and letters like this one from a Baltimore, Maryland, mom, made us reconsider:

> Even my thrill-riding, 55-inch-tall 10-year-old loved this one! I feel bad for the ride operators who spend the entire day turning people away who don't have a child in the right height range to go. Greatly underrated ride, but you were spot on with the lines by midday.

We still don't think Pteranodon Flyers is worth a long wait, and Universal Express isn't valid on the attraction. If your children insist on riding and abject bribery fails, get in line as quickly as possible after opening, or look for Virtual Line kiosks outside Camp Jurassic that dispense timed-return tickets for Pteranodon Flyers (not available through the Universal app). When in use, you must retrieve a return ticket to ride; the total wait time before your turn arrives won't be much shorter than under the old system, but at least your kids can play in the caves instead of stewing in the standby line. If all return tickets run out for the day, the ride usually reverts to a regular standby queue 2 hours before the park closes.

Raptor Encounter ★★★½

APPEAL BY AGE PRESCHOOL ★★★½ GRADE SCHOOL ★★★★ TEENS ★★★★½
YOUNG ADULTS ★★★★½ OVER 30 ★★★★½ SENIORS ★★★★½

What it is Photo op with lifelike dinosaur. Scope and scale Minor attraction. When to go Before noon. Comments Clever girl! Sure to scare the spit out of small kids. Duration of encounter About a minute. Queue speed Very slow.

DESCRIPTION AND COMMENTS Just when everyone thinks Disney has a lock on the meet and greet market, Universal does the impossible—breeds a live velociraptor and makes it pose for pictures! OK, it isn't actually a real dinosaur on display. In fact, it's an amazingly realistic puppet, created by Michael Curry (who created designs for Disney's *Lion King* and *Finding Nemo* musicals, as well as Diagon Alley's *Tales of Beedle the Bard* show) and brought to life by talented performers.

Blue, *Jurassic World*'s semitame saurian star, makes regular appearances in her paddock next to the River Adventure. A game warden briefs one family at a time regarding proper safety procedures (convey calm assurance, move in slowly, and try not to smell like meat) before they step up for a photo. Don't peer too closely over the edge of the raptor enclosure; you'll spot the cleverly camouflaged legs of the puppeteer inside and spoil the illusion. A Universal photographer will take your picture with his or her camera (included with My Universal Photos packages), and selfies are also encouraged—just don't be surprised if the dino snaps when you say, "Smile!"

Raptor Encounter isn't among IOA's major attractions, and the queue can move at a crawl, but this crew from Calgary, Canada, says you shouldn't overlook it:

I was really intrigued by the Raptor Encounter. We probably would have missed it if it hadn't been for the guide. It was one of the highlights of our day! Blue the raptor tried to eat [my 15-year-old son's] hat. It was super fun.

TOURING TIPS The Raptor Encounter has become quite popular, so ask a team member stationed outside the paddock entrance approximately how long your wait will be before queuing. Don't try to touch the raptor, or you may come home minus a hand; surreptitiously feeding your offspring to the dinosaurs is also discouraged by management. When the full-grown Blue needs a break, an adorable (but equally deadly) handheld baby velociraptor may take her place.

THE WIZARDING WORLD OF HARRY POTTER—HOGSMEADE

THE ORIGINAL WIZARDING WORLD OF HARRY POTTER is an amalgamation of landmarks, creatures, and themes that are faithful to the films and books. You access the area through an imposing gate that opens onto **Hogsmeade,** depicted in winter and covered in snow. This is The Wizarding World's primary shopping and dining venue. Exiting Hogsmeade, you first glimpse the towering castle housing **Hogwarts School of Witchcraft and Wizardry,** flanked by the **Forbidden Forest** and **Hagrid's Hut.** The grounds and interior of the castle contain part of the queue for the super-headliner **Harry Potter and the Forbidden Journey.**

Universal went all out on the castle, with the intention of creating an icon even more beloved and powerful than Cinderella Castle at Disney's Magic Kingdom, and very nearly succeeded—if only they'd added a bit more brick and rockwork to conceal the big honking soundstage that holds the land's groundbreaking ride.

Hogsmeade in Detail

The Wizarding World of Harry Potter—Hogsmeade is in the northwest corner of IOA, between The Lost Continent and Jurassic Park. From the IOA entrance, the most direct route there is through Port of Entry and then right, through Seuss Landing (staying to the left of Green Eggs and Ham) and The Lost Continent, to the Hogsmeade main gate. The alternative route is to cross the bridge connecting The Lost Continent with Jurassic Park, and then turn right after entering the latter area. Note that the bridge is closed on slower days.

For the moment, though, let's begin our exploration at The Wizarding World's main entrance, on The Lost Continent side. Passing beneath a stone arch, you enter the village of **Hogsmeade.** The **Hogwarts Express** locomotive sits belching steam on your right. The village setting is rendered in exquisite detail: stone cottages and shops have steeply pitched slate roofs, bowed multipaned windows, gables, and tall, crooked chimneys.

Your first taste—literally—of the Harry Potter universe comes courtesy of **Honeydukes.** Specializing in Potter-themed candy such as Acid Pops (no flashbacks, guaranteed), Tooth Splintering Strong Mints, and Fizzing Whizbees, the sweet shop offers no shortage of snacks that administer an immediate sugar high. There's also a small bakery inside. While we recommend avoiding the prepackaged Cauldron Cakes, which look much better than they taste, the big draw is the elaborately boxed Chocolate Frogs. The chocolate inside isn't anything special, but the packaging looks as if it came straight from a *Harry Potter* film, complete with a random lenticular wizard trading card; buy one in a collectible tin to get all five cards.

Next door to Honeydukes and set back from the main street is **Three Broomsticks,** a rustic tavern serving English staples. To the rear of the tavern is the **Hog's Head pub,** which serves a nice selection of beer as well as The Wizarding World's signature nonalcoholic brew, Butterbeer (see page 219).

Roughly across the street from the pub is the entrance to **Hagrid's Magical Creatures Motorbike Adventure** roller coaster, as well as benches in the shade at the **Owlery,** where animatronic owls (complete with lifelike poop) ruffle and hoot from the rafters. Next to the Owlery is the **Owl Post,** where you can have mail stamped with a Hogsmeade postmark before dropping it off for delivery (an Orlando postmark will also be applied by the real USPS). The Owl Post also sells stationery, toy owls, and magic wands. Here, once again, a nice selection of owls preens on the timbers overhead. You access the Owl Post in either of two ways: through an interior door following the wand-choosing demonstration at **Ollivanders** (see page 349) or through **Dervish and Banges,** a magic-supplies shop that's interconnected with the Owl Post.

At the far end of the village, the massive **Hogwarts Castle** comes into view, set atop a rock face and towering over Hogsmeade and the entire Wizarding World. Follow the path through the castle's massive gates to the entrance of Harry Potter and the Forbidden Journey. Below the castle and to the right, at the base of the cliff, are the **Forbidden Forest, Hagrid's Hut,** and the **Flight of the Hippogriff** children's roller coaster. Also beneath Hogwarts, at Forbidden Journey's exit, is **Filch's Emporium of Confiscated Goods,** which offers all manner of Potter-themed gear, including Quidditch clothing, magical-creature toys, film-inspired chess sets, and, of course, Death Eater masks (breath mints extra).

In keeping with the stores depicted in the Potter films, the shopping venues in Hogsmeade are small and intimate—so intimate, in fact, that they feel congested when they're serving only 12–20 shoppers. Because the stores are so jammed, IOA sells some Potter merchandise, including wands, through street vendors and in Port of Entry shops.

At the end of the village and to the left is the bridge to **Jurassic Park,** the themed area contiguous to The Wizarding World. This is the best vantage point to get your photo with Hogwarts Castle in the background, as the hordes of people posing in the middle of the walkway will attest.

Entertainment in Hogsmeade

Hogsmeade raised "retail theater" in theme parks to unprecedented levels, as nearly every shop space and storefront window sport some sort of animatronic or special effects surprise. At **Dervish and Banges,** the fearsome *Monster Book of Monsters* rattles and snarls at you as Nimbus 2001 brooms strain at their tethers overhead. At the **Hog's Head** pub, the titular porcine part, mounted behind the bar, similarly thrashes and growls when the barkeep receives a gratuity.

Two brief street entertainments are staged in a raised outdoor alcove at the Forbidden Journey end of Hogsmeade. Showtimes are listed in the smartphone app; performances alternate, usually starting every 30 minutes on the hour and half hour.

The *Frog Choir* (★★★) is composed of four singers, two of whom are holding large amphibian puppets sitting on pillows. Inspired by a brief scene in *Harry Potter and the Prisoner of Azkaban,* the group sings a cappella three or four wizard-related songs, including "Hedwig's Theme" and "Something Wicked This Way Comes." The 10-minute show is followed by a photo op. Though cute, the *Frog Choir* isn't much more than filler for IOA's attraction list and probably isn't worth going out of your way for. A special set of Yuletide tunes is performed during the annual Christmas in The Wizarding World celebration.

The *Triwizard Spirit Rally* (★★★) showcases a group of three men, who perform martial arts–type moves including jumps, kicks, and simulated battle with sticks; and a group of four women, who perform simple rhythmic gymnastic moves with ribbons. After each 6-minute show, the students of Beauxbatons Academy of Magic and the Durmstrang Institute are available for group photos. Though marginally more exciting than the *Frog Choir,* this is only a must-do for major Potter fans.

On select evenings throughout the year, *The Nighttime Lights at Hogwarts Castle* show (★★★½; temporarily suspended) brings the

Forbidden Journey facade to life with colorful spells and magical creatures cavorting to John Williams's stirring film score, all thanks to the Muggle miracle of digital projection mapping. Powerful video projectors (some cleverly disguised as owl roosts) are hidden around Hogsmeade, all pointing at Hogwarts and the mountain on which it sits, and twinkle lights in the trees change colors to complement the castle. While the Sorting Hat narrates, each of the school's four houses gets a chance to unfurl its banners and show off its mascot; watch out for Slytherin's snapping snake. The brief 5-minute celebration is capped with a quick burst of pyrotechnics.

In the fall of 2019, Universal imported the **Dark Arts at Hogwarts Castle** show from Hollywood and ran it during the Halloween season. Using the same projection technology as the original *Nighttime Lights,* this 10-minute show features all of The Wizarding World's wickedest characters, from Aragog to Dementors to Trolls, and finally Lord Voldemort himself. Fortunately, just when all seems lost, a familiar Patronus gallops in to put things right. With clouds of spooky fog and surprising bursts of flame, this version of the castle light show is more frightening for young children and more exciting for older ones. Watch out for a pack of Death Eaters, who stalk Hogsmeade Village starting 30 minutes before the first show.

During the holiday season's Christmas in The Wizarding World event, a special **Magic of Christmas at Hogwarts** version of the projection show is presented. About 7 minutes long, it features additional fan-favorite characters like the Weasley twins, who transform the castle's turret into a big Boggart Banger. It's well worth seeing even if you've already experienced the other versions.

The best viewing area for the castle shows is in front of the *Frog Choir* stage or on the bridge to Jurassic Park. The show is repeated every 15–20 minutes from sunset to park closing. The first couple showings are the most crowded, and the last is the least attended. Prior to showtime, the bridge to Jurassic Park is restricted to exiting traffic only, and guests entering Hogsmeade through The Lost Continent are held in front of Ollivanders (where there is no view of the show) once the courtyard around the castle is full. Our recommendation is to make your way into Hogsmeade shortly before the first performance, and enjoy Forbidden Journey and Flight of the Hippogriff during the first couple showings. You'll be able to access the rides via designated walkways, and lines should be nonexistent. Then wait for the crowd to begin exiting after a show, and grab a good spot for one of the later runs.

Flight of the Hippogriff *(Universal Express)* ★★★

APPEAL BY AGE PRESCHOOL ★★★★ GRADE SCHOOL ★★★★ TEENS ★★★½
YOUNG ADULTS ★★★½   OVER 30 ★★★½   SENIORS ★★★½

What it is Kiddie roller coaster. Scope and scale Minor attraction. When to go First 90 minutes the park is open or after 4 p.m. Comments 36" minimum height requirement; child swap available (see page 204). A good beginner coaster. Duration of ride 1 minute. Average wait in line per 100 people ahead of you 6½ minutes. Loading speed Slow.

DESCRIPTION AND COMMENTS Below and to the right of Hogwarts Castle, next to Hagrid's Hut, the Hippogriff is short and sweet but not worth much of a wait. An outdoor, elevated coaster designed for children old enough to know about Harry Potter but not yet tall enough to ride Forbidden Journey, the ride affords excellent views of the area within Wizarding World and of Hogwarts. The theming is also very good, considering that this isn't a major attraction. As a children's coaster only slightly taller and longer than the Magic Kingdom's Barnstormer, it has no loops, inversions, or rolls. It's just one big hill and some mild turns, and almost half of the 1-minute ride time is spent going up the lift hill. Unfortunately, Orlando's Hippogriff has become increasingly rough in recent years, and it's not as pleasant to ride as the identically named coaster at Universal Studios Hollywood.

For fans of Harry Potter, there are two gorgeous items in this attraction that you'll want to see. The first is a faithful re-creation of Hagrid's Hut in the queue (complete with the sound of Fang howling), while the second is an incredible animatronic of Buckbeak that you pass by while on the ride. Remember that when Muggles encounter hippogriffs such as Buckbeak, proper etiquette must be maintained to avoid any danger. Hippogriffs are extremely proud creatures; show them the proper respect by bowing to them and waiting for them to bow in return.

TOURING TIPS Have your kids ride soon after the park opens while older siblings enjoy Forbidden Journey.

Hagrid's Magical Creatures Motorbike Adventure ★★★★★

APPEAL BY AGE PRESCHOOL ★★   GRADE SCHOOL ★★★★½   TEENS ★★★★★
YOUNG ADULTS ★★★★★   OVER 30 ★★★★★   SENIORS ★★★★½

What it is Indoor-outdoor roller coaster. Scope and scale Super-headliner. When to go Use Virtual Line, or get in line midday or an hour before closing. Comments 48" minimum height requirement; child swap available (see page 204); single-rider line available; not to be missed. Duration of ride About 3 minutes. Loading speed Moderate.

Motion Sickness

DESCRIPTION AND COMMENTS In September 2017 Universal Orlando decommissioned the Dragon Challenge inverted roller coasters (originally known as the Dueling Dragons) in favor of a new family-friendly thrill ride themed around everyone's favorite half-giant groundskeeper. The replacement, which opened in 2019, is a highly themed roller coaster without huge hills or upside-down loops. Instead, it focuses on multiple high-speed launches through the heavily forested terrain during outdoor segments, and close encounters with animatronic beasties inside and between the ride's indoor show buildings.

Riders begin with a walking tour of the gardens behind Hagrid's Hut (whose front side is seen from Flight of the Hippogriff's queue) before entering the moss-covered ruins on the fringe of the Forbidden Forest, where Hagrid holds his Care of Magical Creatures classes. A projected preshow similar to the one in Harry Potter and the Escape from Gringotts succinctly establishes the premise: Arthur Weasley has cloned a Muggle motorcycle, so your class can take a field trip to see Hagrid's latest pet, the never-before-seen fire crab. The preshow, which is bypassed by the Express and single-rider queues, isn't as essential as the setups in the other Potter headliners, and the meandering queue that follows, although decorated with Easter eggs referencing the books and films, mostly consists of monotonous stone walls.

Upon finally arriving at the boarding station, you'll discover that the 14-passenger trains from Intamin indeed resemble Hagrid's vintage motorbike, complete with low-slung sidecars. At nearly a mile long, the track is the longest of any coaster in Florida, and a record-setting multiplicity of magnetic launches propels riders along its curvy course. Highlights of the adventure include a vertical spike that leads into a backward helix, followed by a dropping track in the darkness. Fantastic beasts and familiar figures from the Potter world, including the flying Ford Anglia, Fluffy the three-headed dog, and old Hagrid himself (an impressively lifelike animatronic), make appearances during your experience.

If you think Universal's attractions are too dependent on video screens and simulated movement, Hagrid is here to answer your prayers with richly detailed scenery, spectacular practical effects, and accelerated air time that's exhilarating but not too extreme for tweens and parents to enjoy together. While the coaster's 50-mph top speed might not sound terribly swift, it feels far faster when you're navigating ground-hugging twists and turns through a grove of 1,200 real trees. Move over, Expedition Everest, and step aside, Seven Dwarfs Mine Train: Hagrid's is the best "story coaster" in Orlando, and a strong contender for the best ride at Universal Orlando.

TOURING TIPS The word is out about how good Hagrid's is, and the ride receives a huge rush of guests every morning at rope drop. If you're swift enough to be among the very first guests in line, your wait should be brief (assuming the ride begins running on time), but you'll probably be rushed past the preshow. However, if you're even a few hundred people behind the leading wave, you'll find yourself slowly snaking through a queue that extends into the former *Sindbad* stadium.

Exacerbating the attraction's limited carrying capacity is its tendency to frequently shut down due to bad weather or mechanical issues, which can sometimes take hours to resolve. And to top it off, the queue is sometimes cut off prior to park closing. To mitigate the wait times, Virtual Line may be offered on busier days; use Universal's smartphone app to check the ride's operational status starting a half hour before park opening, and secure a return time (if available) as soon as you set foot on Universal property; see page 75 for further details. If Virtual Line is not in use, your best options are to check the queue in early afternoon (wait times tend to dip briefly around lunchtime) or in early evening, especially after a late-afternoon rainstorm has passed; the effects look especially magical after sunset. While we consider the Motorbike Adventure not to be missed, we hesitate suggesting you spend several hours standing in line for it, especially if you're only spending one day in the park. A mom from Teaneck, New Jersey, echoes our conflicting feelings:

> *Hagrid's was amazing—a true physical experience with incredible theming and heart. I hope they can eventually get that ride to operate for most of the park's operating hours. Getting on it was a frustrating and risky experience in terms of time.*

Hagrid's does not currently offer Universal Express access, but it may in the future. A single-rider queue is sometimes available, but it isn't very efficient.

Each of the coaster's two seating options provides a slightly different experience. The sidecar sits lower but closer to the effects, so every rider gets a good view. Larger guests (over 40-inch waists) should test the sample seats before lining up and request the motorbike seat to enjoy a little more breathing room than the cramped sidecar.

Harry Potter and the Forbidden Journey *(Universal Express)*
★★★★★

APPEAL BY AGE PRESCHOOL ★★ GRADE SCHOOL ★★★★½ TEENS ★★★★½
YOUNG ADULTS ★★★★½ OVER 30 ★★★★½ SENIORS ★★★★

What it is Motion-simulator dark ride. Scope and scale Super-headliner. When to go Immediately after park opening or in the last hours before closing. Comments 48" minimum height requirement; child swap available (see page 204); single-rider line available. Marvelous for Muggles; not to be missed. Duration of ride 4¼ minutes. Loading speed Fast.

DESCRIPTION AND COMMENTS This ride provides the only opportunity at Universal Orlando to come close to Harry, Ron, Hermione, and Dumbledore as portrayed by the original actors. Half the attraction is a series of preshows, setting the stage for the main event, a thrilling dark ride. The characters are incorporated into the queue and serve as an important element of the overall experience, not merely something to keep you occupied while you wait for the main event.

From Hogsmeade you approach the castle's imposing Winged Boar gates and progress along a winding path. Guests enter the castle on a lower level and walk through a sort of dungeon festooned with various icons and prop replicas from the Potter flicks, including the Mirror of Erised from *Harry Potter and the Sorcerer's Stone,* before touring the Hogwarts greenhouses, which compose the larger part of the Forbidden Journey's standby queuing area; despite some strategically placed mandrakes, there isn't much here to amuse. If you're among the first in the park and in the queue, you'll move through this area pretty quickly. Otherwise . . . well, we hope you like plants. The greenhouses are not air-conditioned, but fans move the (hot) air around. Blessedly, there are water fountains but, alas, no restrooms.

Having finally escaped horticulture purgatory, you enter the castle, moving along its halls and passageways. One chamber you'll probably remember from the films is a multistory gallery of portraits, many of whose subjects come alive when they take a notion. You'll see for the first time the four founders of Hogwarts: Helga

unofficial **TIP**

Even if your child meets the height requirement, consider carefully whether Forbidden Journey is an experience he or she can handle. Because the seats on the benches are compartmentalized, kids can't see or touch Mom or Dad if they get frightened.

Hufflepuff holding her famous cup, Godric Gryffindor and Rowena Ravenclaw nearby, and the tall, moving portrait of Salazar Slytherin straight ahead. The founders argue about Quidditch and Dumbledore's controversial decision to host an open house at Hogwarts for Muggles (garden-variety mortals). Don't rush through the gallery—the effects are very cool, and the conversation is essential to understanding the rest of the attraction.

After you've navigated some more passages, you'll enter Dumbledore's office, where the wizard principal appears on a balcony (thanks to Musion Eyeliner high-definition "hologram" technology) and welcomes you to Hogwarts. After his welcoming remarks, Dumbledore dispatches you to the Defence Against the Dark Arts classroom to hear a presentation on the history of Hogwarts.

As you gather to await the lecture, Harry, Ron, and Hermione pop out from beneath an invisibility cloak. They suggest you ditch the lecture in favor of joining them for a proper tour of Hogwarts, including a Quidditch match. After some repartee among the characters and a couple of special effects surprises, it's off to the Hogwarts Official Attraction Safety Briefing and Boarding Instructions Chamber—OK, it's actually the Gryffindor Common Room, but you get the picture. The briefing and instructions are presented by animated portraits, including an etiquette teacher. Later on, even the famed Sorting Hat gets into the act. All this leads to the Room of Requirement, where hundreds of candles float overhead as you board the ride.

After all the high-tech stuff in your queuing odyssey, you'll naturally expect to be wowed by your ride vehicle. Surely it's a Nimbus 3000 turbo-broom, a phoenix, a hippogriff, or at least the Weasleys' flying car. But no, what you'll ride on one of America's most technologically advanced theme park attractions is . . . a *bench*? Yep, a bench.

A bit anticlimactic, perhaps, but as benches go, this one's a doozy, mounted on a Kuka robotic arm. When not engaged in Quidditch matches, a Kuka arm is a computer-controlled robotic arm similar to the kind used in heavy manufacturing. In Forbidden Journey, the arm moves the ride vehicle through a series of live sets and action scenes projected all around you. The movement of the arm is synchronized to create the motion that corresponds to what's happening in the film. When everything works right, it's mind-blowing.

High-tech hijinks aside, is the attraction itself ultimately worthy of the hype? In a word, *yes*! Your 4¼-minute adventure is a headlong sprint through the most thrilling moments from the first few Potter books: you'll soar over Hogwarts Castle, narrowly evade an attacking dragon, spar with the Whomping Willow, get tossed into a Quidditch match, and fight off Dementors inside the Chamber of Secrets. Scenes alternate between enormous physical sets (complete with animatronic creatures), elaborate lighting effects, and high-definition video-projection domes that surround your field of view, similar to Soarin' or The Simpsons Ride. Those Kuka-powered benches really do "levitate" in a manner that feels remarkably like free flight, and while you don't go upside down, the sensation of floating on your back or being slung from side to side is certainly unique.

The seamless transitions between screens and sets, and the way the domes appear to remain stationary in front of you while actually moving (much like Dreamfinder's dirigible in the original Journey into Imagination at Epcot), serve to blur the boundary between actual and virtual better than any attraction before it. The greatest-hits montage plotline may be a bit muddled, but the ride is enormously effective at leaving you feeling as though you just survived the scariest scrapes from the early educational career of The Boy Who Lived.

To understand the story line and get the most out of the attraction, you really need to see and hear the entire presentation in each of the preshow rooms. This won't happen unless you just park yourself and watch a full run-through of each preshow. Try to find a place to stop where you can let those behind you pass and where you're as far away from any staff as possible. As long as you're not creating a logjam, the team members will leave you alone as often as not.

Another gripe: The dialogue in the preshows is delivered in British accents of varying degrees of intelligibility, and at a very brisk pace. Add an echo effect owing to the cavernous nature of the preshow rooms, and it can be quite difficult for Yanks to decipher what's being said. This is especially evident in the staccato repartee between Harry, Ron, and Hermione in the Defence Against the Dark Arts classroom.

TOURING TIPS While much of the attention has turned toward Hagrid's coaster, the best way to ride Forbidden Journey with a reasonable wait is still to be one of the first through the turnstiles in the morning, use Universal Express, or visit in the final hours of the evening, especially during the projection show (when scheduled).

Universal warns you to secure or leave behind loose objects, which most people interpret to mean glasses, purses, hats, and the like. However, the ride makes a couple of moves that will empty your trousers faster than a master pickpocket—ditto and worse for shirt pockets. When these moves occur, your stuff will clatter around like quarters in a slot machine tray. It's much better to use the small compartment built into the seat back for keys, coins, phone, wallet, and pocket Bible. Be prepared, however: team members don't give you much time to stow or retrieve your belongings.

The single-rider line is not clearly marked, so relatively few guests use it. To get there, enter the attraction's Express queue, and stay to the right upon entering the castle. Whereas on most attractions the wait in the singles line is one-third the wait in the standby line, at Forbidden Journey it can be as much as one-tenth. Because the individual seating separates you from the other riders whether your party stays together or not, the singles line (when available) is a great option, as this wife from Edinburgh, Scotland, discovered:

Trust me—sitting next to hubby on Forbidden Journey, romantic though it may be, is not as awesome as having to wait only 15 minutes as a single rider.

If you see a complete iteration of each preshow in the queue and then experience the ride, you'll invest 25–35 minutes even if you don't have to wait. Universal Express users get to see all the important preshow elements, only bypassing the greenhouses and some minor statues. If you elect to skip the preshows (the Gryffindor Common Room, where you receive safety and loading directions, is mandatory) and use the singles line, you can get on in about 10–25 minutes at any time of day. At a time when the posted wait in the regular line was 2 hours, we rode and were out the door in 15 minutes using the singles line.

Forbidden Journey is one of our favorite rides in the world, and it's a big hit with our readers, like this mother of three from Crystal Lake, Illinois:

I was in awe from the minute I stepped into line, [and] from the minute I began "flying," I was like a little kid. The integration of movement, video screens, and real scenery was so seamless that I truly felt like I was part of the movie. Here I was, a 40-year-old woman, and I literally walked off the ride with tears in my eyes and happiness in my heart. It was the most amazing ride I'd ever been on, and I believe any ride would be hard-pressed to bring about the same feeling of joy!

But much as we enjoy Forbidden Journey, it behooves us to pass along this warning from a mom in St. Louis:

A security person at Universal told me that Harry Potter and the Forbidden Journey is THE most motion sickness–inducing ride in the two Universal parks. My husband and daughter went on the ride, and then somehow convinced me to try it. I should have listened to the security person!

As well as this, from a reader in Ann Arbor, Michigan:

The Forbidden Journey ride scared me a lot, and I am not a wimp. I loved Gringotts and Hagrid's Motorbike, loved Spider-Man, but Forbidden Journey was just too much.

The ride's videos were upgraded in 2018 to 4K, 120 frames per second, creating a smoother, sharper image that's easier to watch for those with a weak stomach. Universal has also toned down the Kuka programming since the ride opened and added fans to each seat that blow cool air on rider's foreheads in a somewhat successful effort to reduce motion sickness. We nonetheless recommend that you not ride with a full stomach. If you start getting queasy, fix your gaze on your feet and try to exclude as much from your peripheral vision as possible.

In response to many larger guests being denied rides when Harry Potter and the Forbidden Journey first opened, the end seats on each flying bench were redesigned to accommodate a wider variety of body shapes and sizes. Though these modified seats allow many more people to ride, it's still possible that guests of size can't fit in them. The best way to figure out whether you can fit in a regular seat or one of the modified ones is to sit in one of the test seats outside the queue or just inside the castle. After you sit down, pull down on the safety harness as far as you can. One of three safety lights will illuminate: A green light indicates that you can fit into any seat, a yellow light means that you should ask for one of the modified seats on the outside of the bench, and a red light means that the harness can't engage enough for you to ride safely.

In addition, IOA team members select guests of all sizes "at random" to plop in the test seats, but they're really looking for large people or those who have a certain body shape. Team members handle the situation as diplomatically as possible, but if they suspect you're not the right size, you'll be asked to sit down for a test. For you to be cleared to ride, the overhead restraint has to click three times; once again, it's body shape rather than weight (unless you're over 300 pounds) that's key. Most team members will let you try a second time if you don't achieve three clicks on the first go. Passing the test by inhaling sharply is not recommended unless you can also hold your breath for the entire 4-plus minutes of the ride.

Hogwarts Express *(Universal Express)* ★★★★½

APPEAL BY AGE PRESCHOOL ★★★★½ GRADE SCHOOL ★★★★½ TEENS ★★★★½
YOUNG ADULTS ★★★★½ OVER 30 ★★★★½ SENIORS ★★★★½

What it is Transportation attraction with special effects. **Scope and scale** Headliner. **When to go** Immediately after park opening until midafternoon. **Comments** Requires park-to-park admission. A moving experience; not to be missed. **Duration of ride** 4 minutes. **Loading speed** Moderate.

DESCRIPTION AND COMMENTS The counterpart to USF's King's Cross is Hogsmeade Station, which sits on the border between IOA's Hogsmeade and Lost Continent. See Part Seven, page 291, for a full review of the Hogwarts Express experience.

TOURING TIPS Because the Hogsmeade Station doesn't include the cool Platform 9¾ effect found at the King's Cross end, you'd expect waits for the one-way trip to be shorter here. Surprisingly, lines can be longer here than at USF on slower days, though King's Cross is the busier end during peak periods. Lines are usually less than 20 minutes through the morning but can build later in the day. Hogsmeade Station also lacks other King's Cross amenities, such as air-conditioning and an in-queue snack stand.

If you wish to experience the train, do so before the queue builds in mid-afternoon.

Ollivanders ★★★★

APPEAL BY AGE PRESCHOOL ★★★★ GRADE SCHOOL ★★★★½ TEENS ★★★★½
YOUNG ADULTS ★★★★½ OVER 30 ★★★★ SENIORS ★★★★½

What it is Combination wizarding demonstration and shopping op. **Scope and scale** Minor attraction. **When to go** In the first or last hours of the day. **Comments** Audience stands; identical to USF version but with a much slower line. Enchanting but inefficient. **Duration of presentation** 6 minutes.

DESCRIPTION AND COMMENTS Next to the Owl Post is Ollivanders, a musty little shop stacked to the ceiling with boxes of magic wands. Inside you'll find the same intimate wand-choosing ceremony found in the Diagon Alley attraction of the same name (see page 292). It's great fun, but the tiny shop can accommodate at most only 24 guests at a time. After the show, the whole group is dispatched to the Owl Post and Dervish and Banges to make purchases.

The wand experience is almost as popular as the Potter rides. Lines build quickly after opening, and there's little to no shade. If you're just looking to buy a wand without seeing the ceremony, a cart is set up near the *Frog Choir* stage, usually with little to no wait.

TOURING TIPS Due to its very low capacity (fewer than 150 guests per hour), long waits for the show at Ollivanders can form, and you may need to sign up for a free same-day reservation outside the shop. If you need to see this show, and you can't go to the USF branch, go first thing in the morning or as late as possible.

You don't need to see the wand-selection show to purchase a wand at Ollivanders—just enter the store directly rather than waiting in the long outdoor queue. Interactive wands and other Harry Potter merchandise are also available online and at an outdoor cart near the *Frog Choir* stage, as well as at Islands of Adventure Trading Company.

Interactive Wands and Spell-Casting Locations in Hogsmeade

Interactive wands sold in either park come with a map that shows Diagon Alley spell-casting locations on one side and Hogsmeade locations on the other. All of the spells in Hogsmeade are found in the central village, not near Hogwarts Castle or Hogwarts Express. Effects aren't as numerous or as elaborate in Hogsmeade as they are in Diagon Alley, and several are adaptations of older effects that previously ran automatically. There are also no hidden effects in Hogsmeade (as far as we know). On the other hand, there usually aren't quite as many kids trying to trigger effects here. If you're only visiting IOA, it probably isn't worthwhile to buy an interactive wand, but if you're visiting both parks, make sure to test out your purchase from USF's Ollivanders here.

THE LOST CONTINENT

ONCE AMONG IOA'S LARGEST AREAS, The Lost Continent surrendered its medieval Merlinwood section to be turned into The Wizarding World of Harry Potter—Hogsmeade, leaving only the Arabian and Ancient Greek portions intact. What's left of Lost Continent is extremely well themed and features the park's only environments that aren't tied to a licensed intellectual property. Lost Continent can be reached directly from Hogsmeade or Seuss Landing, or on busy days via a bypass bridge to Jurassic Park.

The Lost Continent was home to *The Eighth Voyage of Sindbad Stunt Show,* which set sail for uncharted shores in September 2018, with no imminent plans announced for a replacement; the stadium's courtyard currently serves as a holding pen for hopeful riders of Hagrid's Magical Creatures Motorbike Adventure. *Poseidon's Fury,* the island's only headliner, is only open seasonally. Proposals have been floated to turn the entire land into Hyrule (from *Legend of Zelda*) or a Pokémon attraction, and there are always advocates for expanding The Wizarding World. More recently, characters from *Madagascar* and *Kung Fu Panda* have been making appearances here, but we predict that Universal will direct its efforts elsewhere for at least a few years.

The best (and often only) attraction in Lost Continent may be the **Mystic Fountain,** an interactive talking fountain. A team member behind the scenes controls the fountain and is able to talk to and hear from anyone who approaches. Many kids seem mesmerized by it. Parents can grab a quick snack or drink while the little ones are entertained by the fountain mere steps away. The park's second First Aid station is also located here, behind the coin vendor.

Poseidon's Fury (Universal Express; seasonal)   ★★★½

APPEAL BY AGE	PRESCHOOL ★★	GRADE SCHOOL ★★★	TEENS ★★★
YOUNG ADULTS ★★★½	OVER 30 ★★★		SENIORS ★★★½

What it is High-tech theater attraction. **Scope and scale** Headliner. **When to go** After experiencing all the rides. **Comments** Audience stands throughout. Dumb but dazzling. **Duration of show** 17 minutes, including preshow.

DESCRIPTION AND COMMENTS Greek god Poseidon dukes it out with an evil wizardlike guy—named Lord Darkenon, of all things—with Poseidon as the heavy. The two fight with fire, water, lasers, and smoke machines.

As you might have inferred, the story is somewhat incoherent, but the special effects are still amazing, as is the theming of the preshow area. The plot unfolds in installments as you pass through a couple of antechambers and finally into the main theater. Though the production plods a bit at first, it wraps up with quite an impressive flourish.

TOURING TIPS Catch *Poseidon* after getting your fill of the rides. When the attraction is open, tours begin 1 or more hours after the rest of the park and end 30 minutes or more before park closing.

If you're still wet from Dudley Do-Right's Ripsaw Falls, Popeye & Bluto's Bilge-Rat Barges, or the Jurassic Park River Adventure, you might be tempted to cheer the evil wizard's flame jets in hopes of finally drying out. Our money, however, is on Poseidon—it's legal in Florida for theme parks to get guests wet, but setting them on fire is frowned upon.

While most of the action takes place on movie screens, *Poseidon's Fury* can frighten many small children. The entire theater is thrown into total darkness many times during the show, and several of the special effects involve fire, loud noises, and flashing lights.

As impressive as the facade of *Poseidon's Fury* is, this Massachusetts mom of a family of four thinks the attraction itself is a letdown:

The one attraction we wished we'd skipped was Poseidon's Fury. *The posted wait time was 10 minutes. After waiting 30 minutes, we were ushered into a series of rooms with no chairs to watch a set of poorly executed special effects. I'm 5 feet tall and saw none of it because everyone was standing, and the floor was poorly slanted. At the end, we were all tired and wanted to go home.*

This family from Cincinnati also weren't fans:

We were looking for a place to get out of the sun, and standing for 25 minutes with Express Pass made for a long and boring 25 minutes. Voted least favorite attraction from everyone in our party.

Finally, from a woman in New York State:

The show was really annoying. I'm short and couldn't see anything.

SEUSS LANDING

THIS 10-ACRE THEMED AREA is based on Dr. Seuss's famous children's books. Buildings and attractions replicate a whimsical, brightly colored cartoon style with exaggerated features and rounded lines. The odd-shaped facades were carved from Styrofoam and sprayed with concrete, and the impossibly bent palm trees were salvaged from Hurricane Andrew, resulting in a land without a single straight line or right angle.

Featuring many of Dr. Seuss's most beloved characters (including the Lorax, the Grinch, Thing 1 and Thing 2, Sam-I-Am, and the Cat in the Hat), *Oh! The Stories You'll Hear!* (★★★) is a fun singing and dancing show staged in an outdoor area between Circus McGurkus Cafe Stoo-pendous and All the Books You Can Read. After each 9-minute show, the characters separate for individual meet and greets and autographs. Showtimes are listed in the park map. During inclement weather, the show may relocate within the Circus McGurkus Cafe Stoo-pendous restaurant nearby.

Look for a photo op with top-hatted dignitaries outside the Mulberry Street Store; the figure with the beard and glasses is Dr. Theodor "Seuss" Geisel himself.

Caro-Seuss-el *(Universal Express)* ★★★

APPEAL BY AGE PRESCHOOL ★★★★½ GRADE SCHOOL ★★★½ TEENS ★★★
YOUNG ADULTS ★★★   OVER 30 ★★★   SENIORS ★★★½

What it is Merry-go-round. Scope and scale Minor attraction. When to go Anytime. Comments Child swap available (see page 204). Ride is outside but covered. Wonderfully whimsical. Duration of ride 2 minutes. Loading speed Slow.

DESCRIPTION AND COMMENTS Totally outrageous, this full-scale, 56-mount merry-go-round is made up entirely of Dr. Seuss characters, each of which has an interactive effect (wagging tongues, blinking eyes) that the rider can control. While you turn, a Seussian orchestra of ridiculous instruments plays like a cacophonous calliope.

TOURING TIPS A gentle ride, even for the smallest children. If you are too old or don't want to ride, Caro-Seuss-el is still worth an inspection. If you do want to ride, waits are usually not too long, even in the middle of the day.

The Cat in the Hat *(Universal Express)* ★★★½

APPEAL BY AGE PRESCHOOL ★★★★½ GRADE SCHOOL ★★★★ TEENS ★★★
YOUNG ADULTS ★★★   OVER 30 ★★★½   SENIORS ★★★★

What it is Indoor cartoon dark ride. Scope and scale Major attraction. When to go Before 11:30 a.m. or after 4 p.m. Comments 36" minimum height requirement; child swap available (see page 204). Dr. S. would be proud. Duration of ride 3¾ minutes. Loading speed Moderate.

DESCRIPTION AND COMMENTS Universal's answer to Disney's vintage Fantasyland dark rides, this indoor, sit-down attraction recounts the entire *Cat in the Hat* story from beginning to end in a little less than 4 minutes. Guests ride on "couches" through 18 different sets inhabited by animatronic Seuss characters. Of course, mayhem ensues when Cat brings Thing 1 and Thing 2 over to play, as the beleaguered goldfish tries to maintain order in the midst of bedlam, but the entire mess is cleaned up just before Mom gets home.

The audio narration is clear, and each scene is crammed with the kind of crazy furniture and bizarre housewares found in the book. The ride is straightforward enough, but we wish it had more sophisticated animatronics and better effects.

TOURING TIPS This is fun for all ages. Try to ride early, or ride late in the day after families with young children have started to depart.

We think there's almost nothing here to frighten small children beyond some loud noises. A father of three from Natick, Massachusetts, disagrees:

The Cat in the Hat ride has quite the fright potential. My wife took my fairly advanced 3½-year-old daughter on the ride, and she was screaming her head off. Nearly two years later, she still reminds me of the scary Cat in the Hat ride (it hasn't affected her love for the books, though!).

The High in the Sky Seuss Trolley Train Ride!
(Universal Express) ★★★½

APPEAL BY AGE PRESCHOOL ★★★★½ GRADE SCHOOL ★★★½ TEENS ★★★
YOUNG ADULTS ★★★   OVER 30 ★★★½   SENIORS ★★★★

What it is Elevated train. Scope and scale Major attraction. When to go Before 11:30 a.m. or just before closing. Comments 36" minimum height requirement; child swap available (see page 204). A relaxed look at the park. Duration of ride 3½ minutes. Loading speed Molasses.

DESCRIPTION AND COMMENTS An elevated train ride through and around the buildings in Seuss Landing, the Trolley Train putters along elevated tracks while a voice reads a Dr. Seuss story over the train's speakers. As each train makes its way through Seuss Landing, it passes a series of simple animatronic characters in scenes that are part of the story being told.

The slow ride around Seuss Landing is pleasant and affords great views of most of the park, including Marvel Super Hero Island. Little tunnels and a few mild turns make this a charming attraction, but a high minimum height requirement (recently reduced to 36") means that many in the trolley's target demographic are banned from riding.

Note that you can choose from two different train tracks at the boarding station. As you face the platform, to your left is the Beech track, which is aquamarine; to your right is the Star track, which is purple. If you're riding with a large group, keep your group together if you all want the same experience because the track on each side offers different visuals and two randomly selected ride soundtracks.

TOURING TIPS The line for this ride is much less charming than the attraction. The trains are small, fitting about 20 people, and the loading speed is glacial. Save High in the Sky for the end of the day or ride first thing in the morning. There is no on-ride photo, but a photo op is sometimes available in the standby queue.

If I Ran the Zoo *(temporarily closed)* ★★★

APPEAL BY AGE PRESCHOOL ★★★★½ GRADE SCHOOL ★★★★ TEENS ★★½
YOUNG ADULTS ★★½   OVER 30 ★★★½   SENIORS ★★★½

What it is Play area. Scope and scale Diversion. When to go Anytime. Comments Kids may get wet. A nice break for parents.

DESCRIPTION AND COMMENTS This interactive play area and outdoor maze, themed to Dr. Seuss rhymes, is filled with fantastic animals and gizmos from the stories.

TOURING TIPS Tour anytime. Note that much of the play area is unshaded. Bring a drink and hat for the little ones.

One Fish, Two Fish, Red Fish, Blue Fish
(Universal Express) ★★★

APPEAL BY AGE PRESCHOOL ★★★★½ GRADE SCHOOL ★★★★ TEENS ★★★
YOUNG ADULTS ★★★   OVER 30 ★★★½   SENIORS ★★★½

What it is Wet version of Dumbo the Flying Elephant. **Scope and scale** Minor attraction. **When to go** Before 11:30 a.m. **Comments** Child swap available (see page 204). Plan on getting wet. Who says you can't teach an old ride new tricks? **Duration of ride** 2 minutes. **Loading speed** Slow.

DESCRIPTION AND COMMENTS Imagine a mild spinning ride similar to Disney's Magic Carpets of Aladdin, TriceraTop Spin, and Dumbo rides, only with Seuss-style fish for ride vehicles, and you have half the story. The other half involves yet another opportunity to drown.

Guests board a fish-shaped ride vehicle mounted to an arm attached to a central axis, around which the vehicles spin. Guests can raise and lower their fish 15 feet in the air while traveling in circles and trying to avoid streams of water sprayed by other fish mounted to squirt posts around the ride's perimeter.

You can avoid most of the spray by going up or down at the right time. If you pay attention to the color of your vehicle and listen to the song played in the background, you can (eventually) figure out when to move your fish.

TOURING TIPS We don't know what it is about this theme park and water, but you'll get wetter than at a full-immersion baptism. Lines can build in the afternoon, so ride early while you'll still have time to dry off.

SPECIAL EVENTS *at* UNIVERSAL'S ISLANDS *of* ADVENTURE

IOA DOESN'T HOST NEARLY AS MANY special events throughout the year as USF, but the one it has is first-rate and included with standard admission.

HOLIDAYS *(mid-November–early January)*

YOU'LL FIND CHRISTMAS DECOR throughout IOA's Port of Entry, and Hogsmeade celebrates **Christmas in The Wizarding World** with festive ornamentation, holiday treats, and a spectacular light show on Hogwarts Castle (see page 342). But the epicenter of the holiday at IOA is obviously Seuss Landing. The star, naturally, is the Grinch, the iconic icky-green grump who famously stole Christmas from the Whos, only to return it when his undersized heart finally grew.

The Grinch is normally represented in the park by a masked representation of the cartoon character, but during Grinchmas, a speaking actor wearing professional prosthetic makeup impersonates Jim Carrey's live-action film incarnation. The Grinch meets and greets guests during the day inside the All the Books You Can Read store; he takes time to interact before each photograph, usually to hilarious effect, which results in a very slow-moving line. If meeting the Grinch is a priority, make this your first stop in the morning.

In addition to greeting guests, the Grinch stars in his own *Grinchmas Who-liday Spectacular,* a 30-minute musical performed six to eight times each day inside a soundstage behind Circus McGurkus Cafe Stoo-pendous. The show, which blends the original book and cartoon with elements from the Carrey flick and musical accompaniment arranged by Chip Davis of Mannheim Steamroller, is a must-see for Grinch fans. It features a first-rate cast (some of whom have appeared on Broadway), expansive set, and even an appearance by a live canine as the Grinch's faithful pet, Max.

Showtimes are listed in the park map and typically begin between 10:45 a.m. and noon and continue until around 6 p.m. Line up near the One Fish, Two Fish ride a minimum of 30–45 minutes before showtime, as performances fill to capacity early on busy days. You will be directed to a seat once inside, but the venue is shallow enough that even the back row has an acceptable view.

The **Grinch character breakfast** is held in Circus McGurkus Cafe Stoo-pendous on select mornings during November and December. It costs $34.99 (plus tax and gratuity) for adults, $20.99 for kids age 9 and under. Theme park admission is required; see "Character Meals" on page 213 for information.

UNIVERSAL'S ISLANDS *of* ADVENTURE TOURING PLANS

DECISIONS, DECISIONS

WHEN IT COMES TO TOURING IOA efficiently in a single day, you have two basic choices, and as you might expect, there are trade-offs. The Wizarding World of Harry Potter—Hogsmeade sucks up guests like a Hoover vacuum and is quickly overrun by crowds on days of moderately heavy attendance. Even on slow days, Hagrid's Magical Creatures Motorbike Adventure can attract an hour-plus wait within minutes after opening. Because of Harry Potter and the Forbidden Journey's several preshows, it takes about 25 minutes to experience, even if you don't have to wait, which compounds the challenge of creating an optimal touring plan.

If you're intent on experiencing **Hagrid's Magical Creatures Motorbike Adventure** and **Harry Potter and the Forbidden Journey** first thing, be at the turnstiles waiting to be admitted at least 30–60 minutes before the park opens. The park's gates will open 15–30 minutes before the appointed hour, with Potter-bound guests racing counterclockwise from Port of Entry to Seuss Landing. The left path through Seuss Landing past Green Eggs and Ham Cafe is the most direct, but the right route toward Cat in the Hat (where day guests are corralled during Early Park Admission, or EPA) is usually less congested when EPA is not offered. Once you're permitted, move as swiftly as possible to The Wizarding World and then ride Hagrid's Magical Creatures, followed by Forbidden Journey and Flight of the Hippogriff, in that order.

If the rides operate as designed, you're golden. You can get Hogsmeade out of the way in about an hour and a half, and be off to other must-see attractions before the park gets crowded. Then come back to The Wizarding World late in the day to explore Hogsmeade and the shops. If, on the other hand, the rides suffer technical difficulties, you may be stuck in line a long while, during which time the crowds will have spread to other areas of IOA. By the time you exit, there will be long lines for all of the park's other popular attractions.

Unless you have Early Park Admission (EPA) privileges at IOA, a much better choice (and the path we follow in our recommended touring plans) is to skip Potterville first thing. Instead, enjoy other attractions in IOA, starting at Marvel Super Hero Island and Skull Island. The good news is that The Wizarding World usually clears out in the afternoon, and its queues are often empty in the last hour, even on busy days. If you aren't an early bird, around lunchtime or late afternoon are the best times to try the Motorbike Adventure; be sure to check the Universal app throughout the day for Virtual Line return times. You can usually ride Forbidden Journey with a minimal wait if you step in the queue shortly before closing time.

Even if you do take advantage of early entry, Forbidden Journey frustratingly runs only a small fraction of its available benches during the EPA hour, often making what should be a nominal wait stretch to 30 minutes or more. As a consequence, Forbidden Journey's wait is sometimes longer during EPA than it will be later that same afternoon. If the queue is backed up beyond the talking portraits, save Forbidden Journey until after it has been brought up to full speed. Otherwise, you'll waste your entire early-entry hour standing in the Gryffindor Common Room and risk missing the opening rush toward Jurassic Park and Skull Island.

ONE-DAY TOURING PLAN FOR ADULTS *(page 398)*

THIS TOURING PLAN IS FOR GUESTS without park-to-park tickets and is appropriate for groups of all sizes and ages. It includes thrill rides that may induce motion sickness or get you wet. If the plan calls for you to experience an attraction that doesn't interest you, simply skip it and go to the next step. Be aware that the plan calls for some backtracking. If you have young children in your party, customize the plan to fit their needs and take advantage of child swap at thrill rides.

ONE-DAY TOURING PLAN FOR PARENTS WITH SMALL CHILDREN *(page 399)*

THIS PLAN IS FOR GUESTS without park-to-park tickets and eliminates all rides with a minimum height requirement greater than 40 inches. The plan includes a midday break of at least 2 hours back at your hotel.

ONE-DAY TOURING PLAN FOR SENIORS *(page 400)*

THIS PLAN IS FOR GUESTS without park-to-park tickets and is specifically designed for seniors and grandparents, taking walking distances and attraction ratings from this group into account. This plan focuses on shows and family-friendly attractions and avoids thrill rides.

Also see pages 321–322 in Part Seven for descriptions of our multi-day and multipark touring plans.

PART NINE

UNIVERSAL'S VOLCANO BAY

UNIVERSAL ORLANDO DESCRIBES **Volcano Bay**'s 28 acres as "a lush, tropical oasis that unfolds before you, instantly transporting you to a little-known Pacific isle." Unlike the former Wet 'n Wild, whose only themes appeared to be concrete and plastic, Volcano Bay showcases a scenic, man-made mountain and a colorful atmosphere that goes toe to toe with those of Disney's water parks.

The park looks like an upscale resort in the South Pacific, with lush palm trees, thatched roofs, and tiki carvings (created by some of the same craftsmen behind Trader Sam's bar at Disney). As long as you're at ground level, you'll hardly guess that there's a busy interstate only yards away. The beautifully landscaped park contains many of the small details and inventive technology expected from the Universal theme park division, but it's not substantially different from any other water park in style, no matter what the marketing suggests.

Volcano Bay has an elaborate backstory (detailed at tinyurl.com /waturi) based on the fictional Waturi tribe, an ancient Polynesian people who set out on their outrigger canoes to find a new home with the mantra "Water Is Life. Life Is Joy." The Waturi visited many Polynesian islands, drawing elements from each culture, until they caught sight of the legendary fish Kunuku playing in the waves of Volcano Bay and settled there. The Waturi legend also influenced the unpronounceable names of most of the attractions, but that's about as far as the theming goes on the slides—don't expect any animatronics or elaborate effects.

Nomenclature notwithstanding, no one can deny that Universal opened Volcano Bay before it was really ready for prime time. The park premiered in a semi-incomplete state, and guests who paid full price for an unfinished attraction loudly lambasted Volcano Bay on websites like Yelp and TripAdvisor. Today, the park has worked out most (but not all) of its operational quirks and offers a good variety of activities. If you're staying on-site (or if you temper your attraction-riding expectations) and can relax into the park's immersive atmosphere, Volcano Bay may just be your slice of paradise alongside I-4.

Universal's Volcano Bay

Attractions

1. Honu Slide
2. ika Moana Slide
3. Kala & Tai Nui Serpentine Body Slides
4. Ko'okiri Body Plunge
5. Kopiko Wai Winding River
6. Krakatau Aqua Coaster
7. Maku Round Raft Ride
8. Ohyah and Ohno Drop Slides
9. Puihi Round Raft Ride
10. Puka Uli Lagoon
11. Punga Racers
12. The Reef
13. Runamukka Reef
14. Taniwha Tubes: Tonga & Raki
15. TeAwa the Fearless River
16. Tot Tiki Reef
17. Vol's Caverns
18. Waturi Beach

Restaurants

A. Bambu
B. The Feasting Frog
C. Kohola Reef Restaurant & Social Club
D. Whakawaiwai Eats

First Aid Station   Restrooms   Cabanas

A Seattle family wrote to us comparing Volcano Bay with Disney's aquatic offerings:

Typhoon Lagoon really suffered in comparison to Volcano Bay. Slides at VB were faster, longer, and more fun overall, and I cannot overstate the convenience of not having to carry your own tubes up the stairs.

A family from Grafton, Massachusetts, shared their feelings:

We all agreed it's the best water park we've ever been to. The variety of activities, the park layout, the food—everything was wonderful. The early issues with TapuTapu seem to have been ironed out; the system worked great both days we were there.

GETTING ORIENTED
at VOLCANO BAY

ONCE DROPPED OFF at Volcano Bay's bus plaza, guests are ushered through an ornate underground tunnel (seemingly hewn from stone) before ascending an escalator into the park. At the entryway, fountains burble beside an Easter Island–style statue that occasionally speaks; you'll also find more prosaic objects like an ATM, lockers, and Guest Services window outside the park's turnstiles.

Volcano Bay is divided into four primary areas (also known as lands), each with a unique theme, but because all of the areas sport the same lush South Seas scenery, it's impossible to tell where one section ends and another begins without a map. Guests enter the park at **Wave Village,** which is dominated by the **Waturi Beach** multidirectional wave pool and **The Reef** leisure pool. Paths from there lead clockwise to **Rainforest Village,** home to the park's densest collection of thrill rides, including **TeAwa the Fearless River,** and counterclockwise to **River Village,** which has family-friendly attractions like the signature **Krakatau Aqua Coaster** and **Kopiko Wai** lazy river. The heart of the park puts **The Volcano** in Volcano Bay: 200-foot-tall **Krakatau,** home to hidden caverns with cascading waterfalls and special effects triggered by your TapuTapu band (see next section).

 COVID *tip*
At press time, Volcano Bay was not operating on Tuesdays or Thursdays, and park capacity has been limited to promote social distancing. The park was also closed November 2020–February 2021.

While there are signposts throughout the park, the winding walkways can make it confusing to find your way. Blissfully, many of the cement sidewalks are cooled by sprinklers, so at least you won't burn your bare feet while wandering in circles.

TAPUTAPU AND VIRTUAL LINES

UNIVERSAL BOASTS THAT IT HAS eliminated the biggest hassles at water parks—standing in long lines for slides—by replacing queues with a Virtual Line mandatory reservation system. Where it differs from Universal Express or Disney's FastPass+ is that there is no standby line at all; all guests save their places in line with their TapuTapu wearables, allowing them to do other things as they await their turns.

Every visitor is issued a waterproof TapuTapu wristband (think a slightly bulkier Apple Watch with a rubber wristband) that you use to claim your place in the Virtual Lines, as well as reserve and open lockers, and make payments throughout the park. The TapuTapu bands also trigger special effects throughout Volcano Bay, such as controlling streams of water in Tot Tiki Reef or shooting water cannons at other guests who are enjoying the Kopiko Wai Winding River.

To enter Volcano Bay, you must first register a ticket with an online account and assign it to your name; setting up a credit card charge account (with a secure PIN and custom spending limits for each family member) is optional. Attendants will assist you with this at the turnstiles, but your entry will be far smoother if you set everything up ahead of time through universalorlando.com or the official Universal mobile app when purchasing your tickets in advance.

Every attraction that uses Virtual Lines has a tiki totem outside its entrance with a digital display. For the first hour or so after opening, most slides will show "Ride Now," indicating that there is little to no wait to ride. Once its queue begins to build, each attraction activates its Virtual Line, and the totem displays a wait time; by 11 a.m., most slides will report at least an hour virtual wait.

Tap your TapuTapu band against the glowing symbol below any of the touch screens surrounding the tiki, and you'll be assigned an approximate time when you can return. Your actual return time may be earlier than expected if other guests skip their return times, or later if the attraction temporarily closes due to weather or technical problems; TapuTapu will notify you of any changes. You can hold a reservation for only one ride at a time, and TapuTapu will alert you when it's time to return with a minimal wait—typically 5–15 minutes, but we've experienced waits of more than 30 minutes during technical difficulties.

Reservations don't expire once they become active, so you don't have to rush to ride, but you can't get in another Virtual Line until you use or cancel your first ride. You may, however, jump into any queue displaying "Ride Now" without losing your place in a Virtual Line. Conversely, if a tiki says "Ride Full," all the day's reservations are claimed, but don't lose hope; closed Virtual Lines often reopen in the hours before closing as other guests exit, abandoning their spots.

In theory, Volcano Bay's Virtual Line system should allow guests to enjoy wait-free attractions like the wave pool and lazy river instead of standing in hot queues. In *reality,* guests who don't enter early spend a lot of time baking on the beach and may get to ride only four or five slides on a busy day. We love the idea of the Virtual Line and being able to relax while waiting our turn. TapuTapu's implementation has made great strides since opening day, and we were able to experience everything we wanted to during recent visits. That said, the system still doesn't feel completely seamless, so we recommend visiting with measured expectations of how many slides you'll ride in a day.

One final hitch: though the TapuTapu wristband has two snaps and a rubber ring to hold it more securely, it has a habit of coming loose, especially in TeAwa the Fearless River. If your TapuTapu takes a swim, swing by Guest Services for a free (though time-consuming) replacement.

Volcano Bay Universal Express Passes, which bypass the Virtual Lines and provide immediate access to the slides' boarding queues, are sold in advance online and inside the park at the concierge huts; quantities are limited and sell out on busy days. Express at Volcano Bay is not free for anyone—even those staying in the top three on-site hotels—and it's available only for one-time use, not unlimited. However, it's cheaper than purchasing Express at the theme parks, especially if you go for the version valid only on select slides. See page 72 for details.

CABANAS AND PREMIUM SEATING

YOU CAN UPGRADE YOUR VISIT with reserved padded loungers ($49.99 and up per pair), 6-person cabanas ($199.99 and up), or 16-person Family Suite cabanas ($599.99 and up). While they're not a necessity, we recommend the private loungers for their included shade canopy, locking storage box, and attendant to deliver food and drink orders. The locker's mechanism can only be activated by one TapuTapu at a time and is frustratingly finicky; carefully align your wristband with the sensor, and firmly push down until you hear it click.

The cabanas get all the same perks, plus towel service, fruit and bottled water, the ability to order upscale appetizers (such as conch fritters and coconut shrimp) that aren't offered on the regular menus, and a private kiosk for making TapuTapu reservations. Note, however, that many cabanas don't offer much privacy, and the attendants get mixed reviews on their attentiveness, making them a dubious value.

The private loungers and cabanas are yours to use all day, even if you exit and return to the park, but they sell out early. Call ☎ 877-489-8068 (for loungers) or 877-801-9720 (for cabanas) up to 60 days in advance for reservations, and bring a printout of your confirmation to the park. When selecting a seat location, keep in mind that Wave Village is nearest to the entrance and gets the most morning sun; River Village is closest to the kids' playgrounds and smoking areas; and Rainforest Village is right up against the interstate. Upon arriving, head to a concierge hut to be checked in and walked to your reserved area; most guests make a beeline to the concierge closest to the entrance, while there's rarely a wait at the one in River Village.

LOCKERS AND TOWELS

RESTROOM AND CHANGING FACILITIES with large banks of lockers are located around the park; the ones in Wave Village closest to the park entrance are always the most crowded, while the ones at the back of the park in River Village are rarely busy. Lockers come in three sizes and cost between $9 and $16. (Note that you'll need a credit card—either in hand or linked to your TapuTapu account—to rent directly at the locker; see an attendant to pay with cash or a hotel key.) Lockers are yours for the full day and are opened and closed with your TapuTapu. Up to four other members of your party can also be assigned access to your locker; follow the prompts on the locker kiosk's touch screen to add additional authorized users.

A bank of large all-day lockers ($16) is located immediately outside the park, but we don't recommend using them because you must return your TapuTapu and forfeit any Virtual Line reservations each time you exit.

Towels are not provided free (as they are at some other water parks), but you can rent one for $6 at any concierge hut. You'll have to dry it in the sun between swims because that fee doesn't include swapping out wet towels (unless you luck into a sympathetic employee). Souvenir towels are also sold for around $25.

UNIVERSAL'S VOLCANO BAY ATTRACTIONS

THE BULK OF VOLCANO BAY'S SLIDES are hidden from the view of guests as they enter behind the mountain's blown-out back side. Attractions range from mild family-friendly raft rides (all with convenient conveyer belts that carry your raft uphill for you) to heart-seizing drop slides from the caldera's summit. Read the posted warnings carefully before you climb 20 stories to the top, and be prepared for a discreet weigh-in before most slides to ensure your safety.

THE VOLCANO

THE 200-FOOT VOLCANO **Krakatau** lies at the center of the park. Inside, guests can explore hidden caverns with cascading waterfalls.

Vol's Caverns ★★★

APPEAL BY AGE	PRESCHOOL ★★★	GRADE SCHOOL ★★★★½	TEENS ★★★
YOUNG ADULTS ★★½		OVER 30 ★★★½	SENIORS ★★★

What it is Interactive walk-through. Scope and scale Diversion.

The volcano contains a network of caverns concealed behind waterfalls and curtains of steam; look for entrances near the queues for Krakatau Aqua Coaster, Ko'okiri Body Plunge, and Kala & Tai Nui Serpentine Body Slides. Once inside, you'll find colorful fountains surrounding Vol, the spirit of the mountain who converses with guests through a digital projection, similar to the Mystic Fountain in Islands of Adventure. Ask Vol to tell you the legend of Volcano Bay's discovery, and make sure you trigger the light display depicting Kunuku, the mythical fish, on the cave wall.

RAINFOREST VILLAGE

THIS VILLAGE HOUSES the park's densest collection of thrill rides. Note that several of this area's attractions—including Maku and Puihi,

Punga Racers, and Taniwha Tubes—may not open in the mornings until the end of the Early Park Admission hour.

Kala & Tai Nui Serpentine Body Slides ★★★★½

APPEAL BY AGE PRESCHOOL ★★½ GRADE SCHOOL ★★★★½ TEENS ★★★★½ YOUNG ADULTS ★★★★½   OVER 30 ★★★★   SENIORS ★★★½

What it is Two extreme twisting body slides. Scope and scale Headliner. Comments 48″ minimum height requirement; 275-pound maximum weight requirement per rider. Duration of ride About 25–30 seconds.

After falling through a drop door, two riders go down 124-foot body slides simultaneously. Their paths cross several times as they hurtle down translucent intertwining tubes. The blue Kala slide is intense enough, but the green Tai Nui side is like The Incredible Hulk Coaster of slides: it starts fast and gets even faster as it goes. These slides are sometimes "Ride Now" even when other attractions have long virtual waits, perhaps because they are so intimidating. Note that you must climb more than 200 steps to reach the top of these slides.

Maku Round Raft Ride ★★★

APPEAL BY AGE PRESCHOOL ★★★½ GRADE SCHOOL ★★★★ TEENS ★★★★½ YOUNG ADULTS ★★★★½   OVER 30 ★★★★½   SENIORS ★★★★

What it is Mild family raft ride. Scope and scale Major attraction. Comments 42″ minimum height requirement; 48″ minimum height requirement if riding alone; 1,050-pound maximum weight requirement per raft. Duration of ride About 30–40 seconds.

Maku and Puihi mean "wet" and "wild," respectively, in the fictional Waturi language, making this pair of group raft slides a subtle tribute to Volcano Bay's predecessor. North America's first "saucer ride," the six-person Maku round raft plunges riders through bowl-like formations that are surrounded by erupting geysers before ending in a pool. Unfortunately, the advertised fountains usually fail to deliver on the slide's name, making it one of the park's bigger busts. On the plus side, there's rarely a long wait for Maku, and the tower it shares with Puihi has one of the park's only elevators, for those unable to climb stairs.

Ohyah and Ohno Drop Slides ★★★½

APPEAL BY AGE PRESCHOOL ★★ GRADE SCHOOL ★★★★½ TEENS ★★★★½ YOUNG ADULTS ★★★★½   OVER 30 ★★★★   SENIORS ★★★½

What it is Two twisting body slides with drop endings. Scope and scale Minor attraction. Comments 48″ minimum height requirement. Duration of ride About 15 seconds.

Two short but intense twisting slides launch guests 4 and 6 feet above the water at the end, guaranteeing that splashdown sends water straight up your sinuses. Ohno is the taller of the two and typically has a longer wait; the extra 2 feet of free fall isn't worth an additional 20 minutes.

Puihi Round Raft Ride ★★★★½

APPEAL BY AGE PRESCHOOL ★★★ GRADE SCHOOL ★★★★ TEENS ★★★★½ YOUNG ADULTS ★★★★½   OVER 30 ★★★★½   SENIORS ★★★

What it is Thrilling family raft ride. Scope and scale Major attraction. Comments 42″ minimum height requirement; 48″ minimum height requirement if riding alone; 850-pound maximum weight requirement per raft. Duration of ride About 45 seconds.

Maku's mate, Puihi, is the far more frightening slide of the pair: a six-person raft launches down a dark, winding tunnel before shooting up a banked curve; riders glimpse the highway below and momentarily experience zero gravity prior to sliding back down. Among the park's family raft slides, this is second only to Honu for making riders scream in terror.

Puka Uli Lagoon ★★½

APPEAL BY AGE PRESCHOOL ★★★★ GRADE SCHOOL ★★★★★ TEENS ★★★
YOUNG ADULTS ★★★★ OVER 30 ★★★★ SENIORS ★★★

What it is Kiddie pool with fountains. Scope and scale Diversion.

This shallow pool near the Ohyah and Ohno Drop Slides is framed by towering tikis and windmill-like contraptions that spray water when TapuTapu sensors are activated. The area around Puka Uli is a great spot to set up camp if you're keeping an eye on young kids, but not so much if you're looking for peace and quiet.

Punga Racers ★★★½

APPEAL BY AGE PRESCHOOL ★★★ GRADE SCHOOL ★★★★ TEENS ★★★★
YOUNG ADULTS ★★★★ OVER 30 ★★★★ SENIORS ★★★½

What it is Side-by-side mat slides. Scope and scale Minor attraction. Comments 42" minimum height requirement; 48" minimum height requirement if riding alone; 300-pound maximum weight requirement per rider. Duration of ride About 20 seconds.

Guests go feet first down enclosed body slides across four lanes and through "underwater sea caves" (that is, plastic tubes). The orange slide in the center feels the fastest, while the two outside tubes are twistier; tuck your elbows in on the turns or you may be bruised. Punga Racers originally featured racing mats that guests rode while facing forward, but after several guest injuries, the ride was redesigned without mats and with a safer splashdown landing.

Taniwha Tubes: Tonga & Raki ★★★★

APPEAL BY AGE PRESCHOOL ★★★ GRADE SCHOOL ★★★★ TEENS ★★★★
YOUNG ADULTS ★★★★½ OVER 30 ★★★★ SENIORS ★★★★

What it is Four intertwined two-passenger raft slides. Scope and scale Major attraction. Comments 42" minimum height requirement; 48" minimum height requirement if riding alone; 300-pound maximum weight requirement per rider; 450-pound maximum weight requirement per raft. Duration of ride About 25-30 seconds.

One tower sports four Easter Island–inspired waterslides with rafts for single or double riders, who sit single file bobsled-style. The slides are similar but not identical—bear left to Tonga (the green slides) with more open-air sections if you get claustrophobic, or go right to Raki (the blue ones) if you like enclosed slides with lots of twists. The best thing about Taniwha Tubes is that they're almost always "Ride Now," and you'll rarely wait more than a few minutes for your turn, so you can try out all four slides to find your favorite.

TeAwa the Fearless River ★★★★½

APPEAL BY AGE PRESCHOOL ★★½ GRADE SCHOOL ★★★★½ TEENS ★★★★½
YOUNG ADULTS ★★★★½ OVER 30 ★★★★½ SENIORS ★★★★

What it is Rapids river. Scope and scale Headliner. Comments 42" minimum height requirement; 48" minimum height requirement if riding alone; every rider must wear an approved life vest.

On this racing-torrent river, guests hang ten in their mandatory life vests amid roaring whitewater rapids as they surf beneath the slides inside Krakatau. This is the best attraction of its kind that we've experienced outside of the Atlantis resort in the Bahamas, but if you're looking for a lazy river, this ain't it! A tip for hopeful surfers: paddle upstream as you exit from under the volcano long enough to catch a curl from the wave generator.

RIVER VILLAGE

NAMED AFTER THE WATERWAY that winds through it, River Village features family-friendly attractions.

Honu Slide   ★ ★ ★ ★ ★

APPEAL BY AGE PRESCHOOL ★ ★ ★ ½ GRADE SCHOOL ★ ★ ★ ★ ½ TEENS ★ ★ ★ ★ ½
YOUNG ADULTS ★ ★ ★ ★ ½   OVER 30 ★ ★ ★ ★ ½   SENIORS ★ ★ ★ ★ ½

What it is Extreme family raft ride. Scope and scale Headliner. Comments 42" minimum height requirement; 49" minimum height requirement if riding alone; 700-pound maximum weight requirement per raft. Duration of ride About 35–40 seconds.

Honu and ika Moana are two separate slides attached to the same tower, where guests board multiperson animal-themed rafts (a sea turtle and a whale, respectively) before speeding down into a pool. Honu is a blue raft slide that sends two to five riders vertically up two giant sloped walls before sliding back down, giving a terrifying taste of what skateboarders call hang time at the top. It's the scariest group raft ride in the park, and our pick as the best. It's also the most popular, along with Krakatau Aqua Coaster, so make it one of your top priorities on arrival.

ika Moana Slide   ★ ★ ★

APPEAL BY AGE PRESCHOOL — GRADE SCHOOL ★ ★ ★ ½ TEENS ★ ★ ★ ★ ½
YOUNG ADULTS ★ ★ ★ ★ ½   OVER 30 ★ ★ ★ ★ ½   SENIORS ★ ★ ★ ★

What it is Moderate family raft ride. Scope and scale Major attraction. Comments 42" minimum height requirement; 48" minimum height requirement if riding alone; 750-pound maximum weight requirement per raft. Duration of ride About 45 seconds.

Though both are boarded from the same platform, don't confuse ika Moana with its neighbor, Honu. Ika Moana (no relation to the Disney princess) is a much gentler journey in and out of twisting green tunnels, on a raft that's supposed to spray water from its center. Much like Maku and Puihi, ika Moana isn't necessarily a bad ride; it's simply upstaged by its sibling.

Kopiko Wai Winding River   ★ ★ ★ ★

APPEAL BY AGE PRESCHOOL ★ ★ ★ ★ GRADE SCHOOL ★ ★ ★ ★ TEENS ★ ★ ★ ★
YOUNG ADULTS ★ ★ ★ ★   OVER 30 ★ ★ ★ ★ ½   SENIORS ★ ★ ★ ★ ½

What it is Lazy river. Scope and scale Headliner. Comments Children under 48" must wear an approved life vest and be accompanied by a supervising companion.

This gentle lazy river passes through the water park's landscape and into the volcano's hidden caves. The highlight of the ride is Stargazer Cavern, a mist-filled grotto with constellations of pinpoint lights blanketing the rocky ceiling. Beware of spots where guests on dry land can soak you by triggering TapuTapu-activated fountains. You're allowed to swim along without an inner tube, but snag one anyway for maximum relaxation.

Krakatau Aqua Coaster ★★★★★

What it is Roller coaster–style family raft ride. Scope and scale Super-headliner. Comments 42″ minimum height requirement; 48″ minimum height requirement if riding alone; 700-pound maximum weight requirement per raft. Duration of ride 1½ minutes.

Guests board a specially designed canoe that seats up to four. The ride uses linear induction motor technology, which launches the canoe uphill as well as downhill as you twist and turn around the volcano's blown-out interior. It's similar to Crush 'n' Gusher at Disney's Typhoon Lagoon but far longer and more thrilling, delivering delightful moments of air time like a real coaster. It's a shame that Universal didn't make Krakatau a full-blown dark ride by including indoor scenes or special effects, but this is still the best waterslide we've ever been on. Krakatau is the park's starring headliner and can only service about 700 guests per hour, so either take advantage of "Ride Now" at rope drop or get your Virtual Line reservation as early as possible.

Runamukka Reef ★★★½

What it is Wet playground. Scope and scale Minor attraction. Comments 48″ maximum height requirement for slides.

This three-story water playground for older children inspired by the coral reef includes twisting slides, sprinklers, and more. Even though it's intended for kids, parents will want to clamber around the structure too.

Tot Tiki Reef ★★½

What it is Infant splash area. Scope and scale Diversion. Comments 48″ maximum height requirement for slides.

This small toddler play area has spraying Maori fountains, slides, and a kid-size volcano. Visually imaginative but hardly expansive, this is little more than a glorified splash pad, but it's entertaining enough for the swim-diaper set. Speaking of which, swim diapers are mandatory for all babies and may be bought at Whakawaiwai Eats.

WAVE VILLAGE

LOCATED AT THE BASE of Krakatau, Wave Village contains wave and leisure pools, as well as the park's largest beach.

Ko'okiri Body Plunge ★★★★½

What it is High-speed vertical drop slide. Scope and scale Headliner. Comments 48″ minimum height requirement; 300-pound maximum weight requirement per rider. Duration of ride About 20 seconds.

Hop on this 125-foot slide, featuring a drop door with a 70-degree-angle descent, straight through the heart of the mountain. Drumbeats building up to the drop get your heart pounding, but the plunge itself is over before you have time to scream. You won't be able to see much with all the water in your face, but other guests can watch your splashdown through a clear tube located between Waturi Beach's wave pool and The Reef pool. As with all body slides, cross your ankles, fold your arms across your chest, and arch your back for the best ride. Ko'okiri commands the longest waits of the extreme body slides, so daredevils should make it their first stop. Note that you must climb more than 200 steps to reach the top of this slide.

The Reef   ★ ★ ★

APPEAL BY AGE PRESCHOOL ★ ★ ★ ★   GRADE SCHOOL ★ ★ ★ ★   TEENS ★ ★ ★ ★
YOUNG ADULTS ★ ★ ★   OVER 30 ★ ★ ★ ★   SENIORS ★ ★ ★ ★

What it is Calm pool with a view. Scope and scale Minor attraction. Comments Children under 48" must wear an approved life vest.

Relax in this leisure pool with calm waters and its own waterfall, and watch braver souls shoot down the Ko'okiri Body Plunge through a clear tunnel where the pool meets Waturi Beach.

Waturi Beach   ★ ★ ★ ★

APPEAL BY AGE PRESCHOOL ★ ★ ★   GRADE SCHOOL ★ ★ ★ ★½   TEENS ★ ★ ★ ½
YOUNG ADULTS ★ ★ ★ ★   OVER 30 ★ ★ ★ ★   SENIORS ★ ★ ★ ★

What it is Wave pool. Scope and scale Super-headliner. Comments Children under 48" must wear an approved life vest.

The central swimming lagoon at Volcano Bay, situated at the foot of Krakatau Lagoon and fed by waterfalls cascading off the volcano's peak, contains a cutting-edge wave pool capable of cycling through different types of surf. A musical fanfare sounds every 10 minutes as the sign above the pool rotates, indicating a shift in the seas: from calm waters, to moderate multidirectional chop, to powerful unified breakers.

UNIVERSAL'S VOLCANO BAY TOURING STRATEGY

DUE TO THE NATURE of the Virtual Line system, it's impossible for us to provide a precise touring plan for Volcano Bay as we do for other parks. We can, however, share basic strategies to maximize the number of attractions you can experience during your visit, which worked out well for these readers from Lee's Summit, Missouri:

We followed the touring advice exactly. The park closed due to capacity, but we did everything and didn't feel like it was too hard to ride things. We were done and chilling out when it got busy.

Just remember that your enjoyment of Volcano Bay isn't dictated by the quantity of slides you ride. Simply vegetating in a lounge chair or lazy river all day is perfectly valid:

1. Purchase your admission in advance, and create an online account at universalorlando.com or through the Universal Orlando mobile app to register your tickets and members of your party. You can also set up a credit card for charging purposes if you wish.

2. Arrive at Volcano Bay as early as possible, at least 60–75 minutes before the park's official opening, leaving extra time for parking and transportation.

3. Upon entering, secure seats and a locker, if needed. The loungers on Waturi Beach are the first to be claimed, but you'll find plenty of options around the rear side of the volcano until midmorning. Families with toddlers should claim chairs near Tot Tiki Reef.

4. Tackle the most popular slides while the queues are in "Ride Now" mode, starting with Krakatau Aqua Coaster, Honu, and Ko'okiri Body Plunge (for thrill seekers only), in that order.

5. Circle counterclockwise from River Village to Punga Racers; ride a couple of times if there's no line, then tackle Puihi in Rainforest Village.

6. By now you've experienced the majority of the popular slides, and the Virtual Line system has probably been activated. Get a return time for Ohyah or Ohno (whichever is sooner). While waiting, ride Kala & Tai Nui (if you're brave and they still show "Ride Now") or relax in the Puka Uli Lagoon.

7. After using your Ohyah or Ohno return time, backtrack clockwise to experience Maku, which should still say "Ride Now."

8. Cross the park back to River Village and ride Ika Moana. Check one of the park's wait time boards while walking there; if Ika Moana is "Ride Now," you can use TapuTapu to get a return time for your second ride on Krakatau Aqua Coaster, Ko'okiri Body Plunge, or Honu along the way.

9. You've now conquered all of the park's slides save for Taniwha Tubes, which you can experience at any time. Virtual Line waits may be in the triple digits by now, so enjoy the wave pool, Fearless and Winding Rivers, and any other slides still showing "Ride Now" while waiting for your next return time. Also take time to explore the volcano's caverns and search for interactive TapuTapu effects.

10. Lines for food at Volcano Bay build early and move slowly. Order an early lunch before 11 a.m. or wait until after 3 p.m. It's important to stay hydrated, so feel free to visit the bars early and often. Restaurants begin to shutter 2 hours prior to park closing; Kohola Reef and Dancing Dragons typically stay open the latest.

11. During the summer, you can count on a thunderstorm sweeping through in midafternoon. Everyone is ushered out of the water as soon as lightning strikes within 5 miles, and many guests flee for the parking buses once a downpour starts. Sit tight; Orlando showers are usually short-lived, and you'll have the slides to yourself once the all clear is given.

12. As closing time approaches, Virtual Line waits begin to drop, and some queues that were formerly full may reopen, so secure your last re-rides on any favorites.

13. Try to stay in the park past sunset to see the volcano erupt with crimson water. Don't forget to return your TapuTapu wristbands on your way out.

PART TEN

UNIVERSAL ORLANDO CITYWALK

A SHOPPING, DINING, AND ENTERTAINMENT VENUE, City-Walk doubles as the entrance plaza for Universal Studios Florida and Islands of Adventure. Situated between the parking complex and the theme parks, CityWalk is heavily trafficked all day but truly comes alive at night. The complex is arrayed in a crescent shape around the waterway that connects Universal's two theme parks with the resort's top three hotels. Along its streets, CityWalk offers a number of nightclubs to sample, and many of those entertainment and restaurant venues depend on well-known brand names. You'll find a **Hard Rock Cafe** and concert hall; **Jimmy Buffett's Margaritaville;** a **Bubba Gump Shrimp Co.;** a branch of New Orleans's famous **Pat O'Brien's** club; an **NBC** sports bar; and a reggae club that celebrates the life and music of Bob Marley. Places that operate without big-name tie-ins include the **Red Coconut Club,** a lounge and nightclub; **The Groove,** a high-tech disco; **Toothsome Chocolate Emporium,** a fanciful chocolate-themed restaurant; and **City-Walk's Rising Star,** a karaoke club with a live backup band.

Another CityWalk distinction is that most of the clubs are also restaurants, or alternatively, several of the restaurants are likewise clubs. Though there's a lot of culinary variety, restaurants and nightclubs are different animals. Room configuration, acoustics, intimacy, sight lines, and atmosphere—important considerations in a club—are not at all the same in a venue designed to serve meals. Though it's nice to have all that good food available, the club experience is somewhat dulled.

COVID *tip*
At press time, City-Walk is shutting down nightly at 10 p.m. (midnight on select weekends), and many CityWalk venues are temporarily closed or operating on reduced schedules.

Red Coconut Club, The Groove, and City-Walk's Rising Star are more nightclub than restaurant, whereas Margaritaville is more restaurant than club. Bob Marley's and Pat O'Brien's are about half-and-half. The Hard Rock Cafe, Antojitos, Bigfire, Vivo,

continued on page 372

Universal Orlando CityWalk

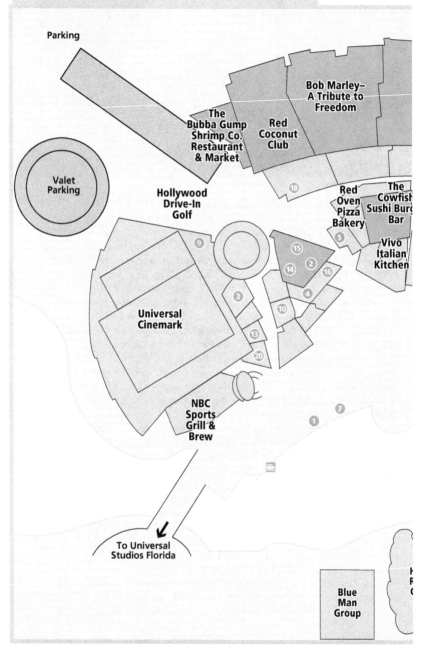

Parking

Valet Parking

The Bubba Gump Shrimp Co. Restaurant & Market

Red Coconut Club

Bob Marley– A Tribute to Freedom

Hollywood Drive-In Golf

Red Oven Pizza Bakery

The Cowfish Sushi Burg Bar

Vivo Italian Kitchen

Universal Cinemark

NBC Sports Grill & Brew

To Universal Studios Florida

Blue Man Group

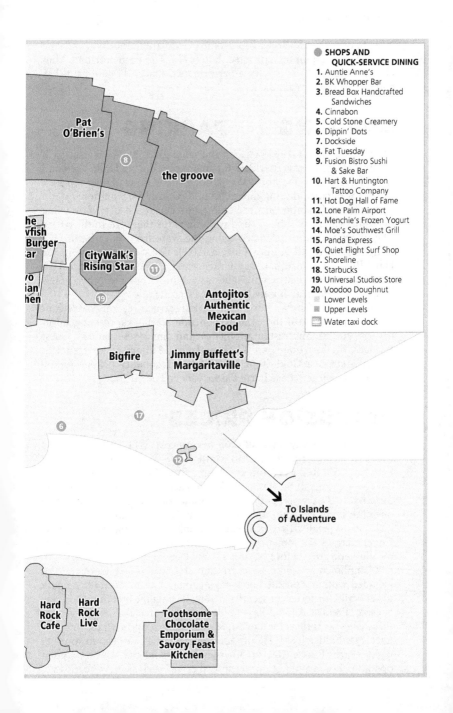

SHOPS AND QUICK-SERVICE DINING

1. Auntie Anne's
2. BK Whopper Bar
3. Bread Box Handcrafted Sandwiches
4. Cinnabon
5. Cold Stone Creamery
6. Dippin' Dots
7. Dockside
8. Fat Tuesday
9. Fusion Bistro Sushi & Sake Bar
10. Hart & Huntington Tattoo Company
11. Hot Dog Hall of Fame
12. Lone Palm Airport
13. Menchie's Frozen Yogurt
14. Moe's Southwest Grill
15. Panda Express
16. Quiet Flight Surf Shop
17. Shoreline
18. Starbucks
19. Universal Studios Store
20. Voodoo Doughnut
- Lower Levels
- Upper Levels
- Water taxi dock

continued from page 369

NBC Sports Grill & Brew, Toothsome Chocolate Emporium, and The Cowfish are restaurants, profiled in Part Six. The venue for Blue Man Group (page 376) is strictly a performance space, though a full bar and snack food are available.

ARRIVING *and* PARKING

CITYWALK VISITORS PARK in the same garage as Universal park guests. Self-parking is free after 6 p.m. (except during Halloween and special events); prime and valet parking are also available. See Part Three for detailed driving directions and parking information.

Universal Orlando on-site hotel guests can reach CityWalk using the same water taxis, buses, and walking paths that lead to the parks. The water taxi hub is located along the waterfront path before the bridge to Universal Studios Florida (USF). Guests walking from the Hard Rock and Portofino Bay Hotels enter CityWalk closest to USF near Hard Rock Cafe, while guests walking from the other hotels enter CityWalk near Jimmy Buffett's Margaritaville.

As you enter CityWalk from the parking structure, you'll see a concierge kiosk beneath the escalator outside Starbucks, offering information, guide maps, restaurant menus, and dining reservations. Guest Services, the restrooms, an ATM, and First Aid are all to your left, immediately past Cold Stone Creamery. A secondary ticket window where you can purchase Party Passes is near The Groove.

ADMISSION PRICES

CITYWALK'S **Party Pass All-Club Access** costs $11.99 plus tax and gets you into all the clubs: Bob Marley, The Groove, Margaritaville, Pat O'Brien's, Red Coconut, and Rising Star. You can pay an individual cover charge of $7 (tax included) at each club. Given that, getting the all-access pass makes the most sense if you plan to visit more than one club in an evening, though if you arrive before the cover charge kicks in (typically 10 p.m.), you can enjoy your first club for free. Cover charges are sometimes waived entirely on slower nights; ask at the club entrance before buying a Party Pass.

Complimentary admission to the aforementioned clubs is also included with any on-site hotel stay or multiday Universal theme park ticket (valid for seven consecutive nights, starting the first time the ticket is used). Premier Annual Pass holders also get free club admission for themselves, as well as for a guest, Sunday–Thursday. Preferred and Premier Pass holders get 20% off additional Party Passes (up to four per night). Party Passes (free or otherwise) are valid only during regular operating hours and not during special events such as New Year's Eve.

Nightclubs not enough for you? If you're hungry for more, City-Walk's concierge desk offers a number of combination tickets that could save you a few dollars, providing you choose carefully. For $29.95 (tax and gratuity included), the **Meal & Movie Deal** includes cinema admission with dinner at Vivo Italian Kitchen, Red Oven Pizza Bakery, The Cowfish, Toothsome, NBC Sports Grill & Brew, Antoji-tos, Bob Marley, Fusion Bistro Sushi, Margaritaville, or Pat O'Brien's. The **Meal & Party Deal**, which trades the cinema admission for a City-Walk Party Pass, is only $27.95 (tax and gratuity included) and offers the same dining options. Likewise, the **Meal & Blue Man Group Deal** combines—what else?—dinner at the same restaurants, with a ticket to see Blue Man Group (see page 376) for $26.50 more than the seat's face value. With all of these deals, you get an entrée and soft drink but must order from a limited menu. If you like Jamaican curry, fish sand-wiches, spicy tuna rolls, or jambalaya, the meal portion of these deals can save you about $5–$10 on dinner, depending on what you order.

CONTACTING CITYWALK

CONTACT CITYWALK GUEST SERVICES at ☎ 407-224-2691, or visit its website at citywalk.com/orlando. CityWalk personnel may not be up on individual club doings, so your best bet may be to contact specific clubs directly when you reach the Orlando area.

CITYWALK CLUBS

THE FOLLOWING NIGHTCLUB VENUES are mostly located along the elevated curv-ing pathway that sits behind and above City-Walk's central plaza. At most of these venues, you must be 21 or older (passport or photo ID required) to enter after 10 p.m.

COVID *tip*
Some CityWalk venues may be closed and entertainment may be canceled to promote social distancing. Cover charges will not be collected when clubs close at 10 p.m.

Bob Marley—A Tribute to Freedom

What it is Reggae restaurant and club. Hours Friday-Sunday, 5-10 p.m.; closed Monday-Thursday. Cuisine Jamaican-influenced appetizers and main courses. Entertainment Live reggae bands and DJ in the outdoor gazebo every night. Cover $7 after 10 p.m. nightly (more for special acts).

This club is a re-creation of Marley's home in Kingston, Jamaica, and contains a lot of interesting Marley memorabilia. The open-air courtyard is the center of action. Must be age 21 or older after 9 p.m. Sunday is Ladies Night, with no cover charge for women before midnight and drink specials.

CityWalk's Rising Star *(open select weekends)*

What it is Karaoke club with live band and backup singers Tuesday-Saturday (Sunday-Monday, sing to recorded tracks with live backup singers). Hours At press time,

Friday–Sunday, 5 p.m.–midnight; closed Monday–Thursday. Cuisine Pizza and bar snacks. Entertainment Karaoke. Cover $7 (no extra charge to sing).

With live musicians backing you up, you can pretend that you've hit the big time at this opulent karaoke. The good news is that, instead of a canned "tiny orchestra," Rising Star gives you a live host and backup singers to perform with, plus a full live backing band on select nights (typically Tuesday–Saturday, prior to the pandemic). The bad news is that the song list is rather short, with only a little more than 200 options instead of the thousands you may be used to back home. Even so, this is an extremely popular karaoke spot, so be sure to put in your selections as early in the evening as possible if you want to get on stage. While waiting your turn, you can get your courage up with one of its supersweet specialty cocktails; pizza, hot dogs, and sweets are available if stage fright makes you hungry. Guests age 18 and older are welcome Sunday–Thursday, but the club is normally restricted to those age 21 and up on Friday and Saturday.

The Groove *(temporarily closed)*

What it is High-tech disco. Hours Closed at press time; previously, nightly, 9 p.m.–2 a.m. Cuisine No food. Entertainment DJ plays dance tunes. Cover $7 after 10 p.m.

Guests must be age 21 or older to enter this *très chic* club designed to look like an old theater in the midst of restoration. There are seven bars and several themed cubbyholes (the ultramodern Blue Room, laid-back Green Room, and brothel-like Red Room) for getting away from the thundering sound system. Dancers are barraged with strobes, lasers, and heaven knows what else. Friday nights feature DJ Chino, and DJ M-Squared spins every Saturday. VIP reserved tables with premium bottle service is available for those with money and liver cells to burn; call ☎ 407-224-2166 to book your party. Attire is casual chic with no hats or tank tops permitted for men.

Jimmy Buffett's Margaritaville

What it is Key West–themed restaurant and club. Hours Daily, 11 a.m.–10 p.m. Cuisine Caribbean, Florida fusion, and American. Entertainment Live rock and island-style music. Cover $7 after 10 p.m. (select nights only).

Margaritaville is a big place with three bars that turns into a nightclub after 10 p.m. Jimmy Buffett covers are popular (no surprise), as are island music and light rock. If you eat dinner here, you'll probably want to find another vantage point when the band cranks up on the main stage around 9 p.m. There's always an acoustic guitarist strumming on the Porch of Indecision from 5 p.m. daily. If you're already inside the restaurant eating dinner before the cover charge kicks in, you won't be kicked out when the band kicks off.

Pat O'Brien's Orlando

What it is Dueling-piano sing-along club and restaurant. Hours Friday–Sunday, 5–10 p.m.; closed Monday–Thursday. Cuisine Cajun. Entertainment Dueling pianos and sing-alongs. Cover $7 after 10 p.m. for piano bar only.

At this clone of the famous New Orleans club of the same name, a solo pianist starts playing a little after 5 p.m.; he or she is joined by a second starting around 9 p.m. These are some of the most talented singing musicians in town and will happily handle nearly any request you throw at them (even—*gasp!*—Disney tunes) as long as you write it on a generous gratuity. You can dine in the courtyard or on the terrace without paying a cover. You must be age 21 or older to hang out here after 10 p.m.

Red Coconut Club *(temporarily closed)*

What it is Modern lounge and nightclub. Hours Closed at press time; previously, nightly, 8 p.m.–2 a.m. Cuisine Appetizers; Red Oven Pizza delivery available after 10 p.m. Entertainment Lounging and dancing, with live music on Friday and Saturday. Cover $7 after 10 p.m.

This nightspot is billed as a nightclub and ultra-lounge, advertising talk for "hip place to be seen." The eclectic mix of decor—part 1950s, part tiki—and three bars on two levels would make it a great latter-day hangout for the Rat Pack, if Frank and Dean happened to be resurrected in Orlando. There is a dance floor, and the bar serves signature martinis and mojitos. An evening here can quickly add up, with VIP bottle service starting at $100 (call ☎ 407-224-2425 for reservations), but a nightly happy hour (Sunday–Thursday, 8–10 p.m.; Friday–Saturday, 6–9 p.m.) offers $6 cocktails and appetizers. On weekends, a live band swings with Latin music and Top 40 covers 8 p.m.–midnight, after which a DJ closes out the night.

CITYWALK ENTERTAINMENT

BEYOND THE NIGHTCLUBS, CityWalk's attractions include an array of separately ticketed entertainment venues. Note that none of the following attractions are included in basic Party Passes or park tickets.

UNIVERSAL CINEMARK 20 WITH XD

IF YOU WANT TO TAKE A BREAK from "riding the movies" inside Universal's parks and just want to watch one instead, the 20-screen Universal Cinemark at CityWalk has you covered. The Cineplex had faded under AMC's management, but Cinemark took over in late 2018 and began a full refurbishment. All 20 screens were outfitted with La-Z-Boy–like Luxury Loungers, featuring oversize cupholders and motorized footrests. All screens also have digital projection and surround sound, as well as stadium seating. An upgraded snack bar serves hot foods (along with the usual overpriced cinema standards, including Coke Freestyle sodas) and alcohol.

The Cinemark's digital XD theater was added by retrofitting a wall-to-wall screen into an existing room, along with new multichannel speakers and an advanced projector that generates 35 trillion colors. It's bigger than the standard screens and delivers more impact in 3-D films but isn't ginormous like the true IMAX screen at Pointe Orlando on I-Drive.

Tickets for showings starting after 6 p.m. (4 p.m. on Saturday, Sunday, and holidays) cost $11.25 for adults; 3-D films cost $3.50 extra, XD films cost $3 extra, and 3-D XD costs $5 extra. Early-bird matinees starting before 1 p.m. cost $7.75 for everyone, and all shows between 1 and 6 p.m. (4 p.m. on Saturday, Sunday, and holidays) are $9.75. Tickets for kids ages 1–11, seniors age 62 and up, and all Universal seasonal and Annual Pass holders cost $8.25 at all times. On Discount Tuesday, all showings are just $5.50 (not valid on holidays or opening day of new films). Revivals of classic films are only $5 ($3 for kids). Note that children under age 6 are not permitted to attend

R-rated films after 6 p.m., thanks to Cinemark's distraction-free environment policy.

You can get reimbursed for standard self-parking at the Universal Orlando garage with the same-day purchase of two matinee movie tickets; be sure to bring your parking receipt with you to the box office (see page 154 for details).

Visit cinemark.com/florida/universal-cinemark-at-citywalk-and-xd or use Cinemark's mobile app to see showtimes and buy tickets, or call ☎ 407-354-3374 to hear a recording of what's playing. Tickets can be retrieved from automated kiosks located to the right of the box office. You can save the $1–$2 online service fee and get a free standard movie ticket each month, along with a 20% discount on concessions, by joining Cinemark's Movie Club for $9.99 (cinemark.com/movieclub).

BLUE MAN GROUP *(temporarily closed)*

NO PIECE OF ENTERTAINMENT better encapsulates the "Universal Difference" than the Blue Man Group's nightly performances at City-Walk. Blue Man Group, now owned by Cirque du Soleil, is intimate, offbeat, and occasionally ornery, with elements of avant-garde performance art that are as likely to provoke a loud "WTH?" as applause.

The three blue men of the Blue Man Group are just that—blue—and bald and mute. Wearing black clothing and skullcaps slathered with bright-blue grease paint, they deliver a fast-paced show that uses music (mostly percussion) and multimedia effects to make light of contemporary art and life in the information age. The Universal act is just one expression of a franchise that started with three friends in New York's East Village. Now you can catch their zany, wacky, smart stuff in New York, Las Vegas, Boston, Chicago, and Berlin, among other places. The 1-hour, 45-minute Orlando production reflects cultural changes in the use of technology in daily life; it includes some segments similar to those seen in other cities but isn't identical.

Funny, sometimes poignant, and always compelling, Blue Man Group pounds out vital, visceral tribal rhythms on complex instruments (made of PVC pipes) that could pass for industrial intestines, and makes seemingly spontaneous eruptions of visual art rendered with marshmallows and a mysterious goo. The weekly supplies include 25½ pounds of Cap'n Crunch, 60 Twinkies, 996 marshmallows, and 9½ gallons of paint. If all this sounds silly, it is, but it's also strangely thought-provoking and deals with topics such as the value of modern art, the ubiquity and addictive nature of tablet devices, the way rock music moves you, and how we're all connected. (*Hint:* It's not the internet.)

A live percussion band backs Blue Man Group with a relentless and totally engrossing industrial dance riff. The band resides in long, dark alcoves above the stage. At just the right moments, the lofts are lit to reveal a group of pulsating neon-colored skeletons.

Audience participation completes the Blue Man experience. The blue men often move into the audience to bring guests onstage. At the end of the show, giant glowing balloons drop from the rafters for the audience to bat around like beach balls. And a lot of folks can't help standing up to dance and laugh. Magicians for the creative spirit that resides in us all, Blue Man Group makes everyone a coconspirator in a joyous explosion of showmanship.

This show is decidedly different and requires an open mind to be appreciated. It also helps to be a little loose because, like it or not, everybody gets sucked into the production and leaves the theater a little bit lighter in spirit. If you don't want to be pulled onstage to become a part of the improvisation, avoid sitting in the first half-dozen or so rows.

The Blue Man Group Box Office (☎ 888-340-5476 or 407-BLUE-MAN [258-3626]) is open 7 a.m.–7 p.m. EST, or you can buy tickets online at bluemanorlando.com. Advance tickets at the Universal Orlando website run $60–$110 for adults, $30–$57 for children ages 3–9; tickets purchased at the box office cost $10 more. The show isn't recommended for kids under age 3, but they may attend without a ticket if they sit on a lap. AAA members get a 10% discount at the box office or up to 25% off online, and all annual pass holders (even seasonal pass holders) save 20% on up to six tickets. If you're also eating at CityWalk or visiting the theme parks, you can save a few bucks on the bundle with a Blue Man Group combo ticket (see page 373). All Blue Man Group tickets include free CityWalk club admission after the show. Blue Man Group also partners with Autism Speaks to offer periodic sensory-friendly shows with modifications such as reduced sound and light levels; visit blueman.com/autismspeaks for details.

A VIP option ($199 for adults, $149 for children) combines premium poncho seating for the show with a guided backstage tour of the theater, starting 1 hour prior to the performance, and a meet and greet with the Blue Man Group after the show.

The show is staged in the Sharp Aquos Theatre, which was originally the Nickelodeon soundstage (look for "green slime" tiles in the outside restrooms). It can be accessed from CityWalk by following the path between Hard Rock Cafe and Hollywood Rip Ride Rockit, or by exiting Universal Studios Florida through the side gate near Despicable Me Minion Mayhem. Center seats in rows B–F go for a premium price; we recommend center seats in rows G–L, at least 11 rows back from the stage.

CITYWALK STAGE

AT VARIOUS TIMES OF THE YEAR, Universal offers free concerts and DJ performances on a stage located in the plaza at CityWalk. The stage may be positioned in front of the water feature between Vivo and the Universal Studios Store or it may be located closer to the waterline at the bottom of the amphitheater. Performances are almost exclusively at night, though the space has been used for live tapings of morning talk shows. When *Ant & Dec's Saturday Night Takeaway* taped its 2018 finale here, they drew huge crowds, but there's normally no problem getting a view. The entertainment is usually free, but on New Year's Eve and a few other occasions, the entire area is reserved for those purchasing special-event tickets.

HARD ROCK LIVE

ACROSS THE LAGOON from most of CityWalk, adjoining the Hard Rock Cafe and separate from the Hard Rock Hotel, this theater hosts concerts, contests, and various private events. Musical acts, both nationally known and up-and-coming, as well as stand-up comedians, appear regularly. Recent shows have run the gamut from Alice Cooper and Elvis Costello to *So You Think You Can Dance* and *Mystery Science Theater 3000*. Great acoustics, comfortable seating (for up to 3,000), and good sight lines make this the best concert venue in town.

The hours vary with live shows; performances usually begin 7–9:30 p.m. Ticket prices vary depending on the act, ranging from $24 to more than $200. There is a full liquor bar, and (depending on the event) you can order food from the restaurant's kitchen. Floor viewing is from removable chairs, or sometimes standing-room only depending on the act, while guests in the VIP balcony can get cocktail service delivered to their leather armchairs. Annual pass holders save $5 on tickets to the Classic Albums Live series, where talented studio musicians re-create records from the 1970s through 1980s note for note; their renditions of Queen and Pink Floyd are flawless.

Be sure to leave plenty of time for parking and security. You'll be inspected again before entering the venue, and the line can be agonizingly slow. Also note that there's normally no reentry allowed once you exit the venue.

For information and an events calendar, call ☎ 407-351-7625 or see hardrock.com/live/locations/orlando/calendar.aspx. To purchase tickets for an event at Hard Rock Live, call ☎ 407-351-LIVE (5483) or visit ticketmaster.com/Hard-Rock-Live-Orlando-tickets-Orlando /venue/278539. (*Warning:* Exorbitant service fees apply.)

HOLLYWOOD DRIVE-IN GOLF

SO THIS IS WHAT MONEY and imagination can do. On one edge of the CityWalk entertainment complex, these 18-hole courses are awash in elaborate settings, props, and even audio. The theme is a drive-in movie showing two features: *Invaders from Planet Putt* and *The Haunting of Ghostly Greens*. Players can choose a single (18 holes) or double (36 holes) feature.

The *Invaders from Planet Putt* course entertains with nonfrightening statues and props such as rocket ships and little green men; a pretend newspaper box shows the *Roswell* [New Mexico] *Register* of July 8, 1947, with the blaring headline UFO SIGHTINGS CONTINUE.

The *Haunting of Ghostly Greens* course features a giant spider, a graveyard, and a basement-lab scene. This course is particularly nice at night but may creep out younger golfers. At various holes, the sound effects are a mooing cow, a chain saw, and a ray gun.

The courses are quite easy, and the greens are in superb condition. We rank Hollywood Drive-In as the best minigolf in Orlando, along with Disney's Fantasia Gardens and Congo River in Kissimmee. Note that one of the courses is fully wheelchair accessible, while the other requires navigating some stairs.

Hollywood Drive-In is located at the entrance to CityWalk, between the Universal Cinemark and the valet parking loop. As you exit the parking garages and moving sidewalks, Hollywood Drive-In Golf is on your immediate right, down one level.

The course is open daily, 9 a.m.–2 a.m. For 18 holes, it costs $16.99 for adults, and $14.99 for children ages 3–9. For 36 holes, it costs $30.98 for adults, and $26.98 for children ages 3–9. Preferred and Power Annual Pass holders, Florida residents, military, adults age 62 and older, and AAA members all save 10% on 18 holes for up to five players; Premier Pass holders save 15%. You can purchase online at hollywooddriveingolf.com in advance, saving up to 10%, but online tickets aren't refundable if unused.

COVID *tip*
Only one of the two minigolf courses may be available during your visit. All clubs and balls are sanitized in between players.

Before 6 p.m., you must pay the usual parking fee to play at Hollywood Drive-In, which drastically boosts the price of playing these courses if you aren't already visiting Universal Orlando.

Call ☎ 407 802-4848 or visit the website above for more information. You can download a free scorecard app for iOS and Android in preparation for your putting.

APPENDIX

READERS' QUESTIONS TO THE AUTHORS

Question:

When you do your research, are you admitted to the parks for free? Do the Universal people know you're there?

Answer:

We pay the regular admission, and usually the Universal people don't know we're on-site. Similarly, both in and out of Universal Orlando, we pay for our own meals and lodging.

Question:

How often is The Unofficial Guide *revised?*

Answer:

We publish a new edition once a year in the late fall.

Question:

Where can I find information about what's changed at Universal Orlando in between published editions of The Unofficial Guide?

Answer:

We post important information online at theunofficialguides.com and touringplans.com.

Question:

Do you write each new edition from scratch?

Answer:

We do not. When it comes to a destination the size of Universal Orlando, it's hard enough to keep up with what's new. Moreover, we put a lot of effort into communicating the most useful information in the clearest possible language. For future editions, if an attraction or hotel hasn't changed, we're reluctant to tinker with its coverage for the sake of freshening the writing.

Question:

How many people have you surveyed for your age-group ratings regarding the attractions?

Answer:

Since the first *Unofficial Guide* containing Universal coverage was published in 1992, we've interviewed or surveyed thousands of Universal

Orlando patrons. Even with such a large survey population, however, we continue to find that certain age groups are underrepresented. Specifically, we'd love to hear more from seniors about their experiences with coasters and other thrill rides.

READERS' COMMENTS

OUR READERS LOVE TO SHARE TIPS. An Iowa City, Iowa, couple offers this observation about being in touch with your feelings:

We didn't build rest breaks into our plans but were willing to say, "OK, I'm just not having fun right now—we should leave the park," and go on to something else (like a water park, hotel pool, or shopping trip). This is a skill I would like to see more people develop. I can't count the number of people I saw who were obviously not having fun.

A Norwalk, Ohio, mom searched for happy feet:

On the subject of footwear, support is just as important as comfort. On one trip I wore Keds—big mistake. My shins ached unbelievably before the end of the second day. From then on I was a die-hard tennis shoe girl, until I discovered FitFlops [go to fitflop.com for stores]. You get the support of a tennis shoe with the comfort of a flip-flop.

A woman from Mount Gretna, Pennsylvania, had some questions about theme park attire:

There wasn't a section that addressed whether you could wear dresses on rides. Quite a few amusement parks have security straps or bars that come up between one's knees, making it very difficult and immodest to wear dresses or skirts. Many women want to wear dresses for convenience, comfort, or cultural/religious convictions. I was concerned as I was packing whether this would limit any rides I could get on. I was quite pleased that it did not.

A Columbia, Missouri, woman offers advice for wives with anxious husbands:

A smartphone is the best thing in the world for keeping your husband busy in line. As long as mine had that phone, he could check email, check dinner plans, and take and send pictures of the kids to family back home. He never complained about waiting in line, ever.

All for the love of Mom, writes a woman from Haddon Heights, New Jersey:

I was traveling with my mother, who has an artificial knee, a herniated disc, and bad feet. My mantra was, "Try not to kill your mother." Without the book, I would have undoubtedly come home an orphan.

Finally, a Somerville, Alabama, woman is succinct if nothing else:

Everything, other than my husband, was perfect.

And so it goes. . . .

INDEX

Note: Page numbers in **bold** indicate main entry.
IOA = Islands of Adventure **USF** = Universal Studios Florida **VB** = Volcano Bay

Universal Studios Florida

UNIVERSAL STUDIOS FLORIDA ONE-DAY TOURING PLAN FOR ADULTS

1. Buy admission in advance. Call ☎ 407-363-8000 the day before for the official opening time.

2. Arrive at USF 90–120 minutes before the official opening time if Early Park Admission is offered and you're eligible, or 30–45 minutes before opening if you're a day guest. Check Universal's app for daily showtimes, and look for Virtual Line reservations for select attractions starting 15–30 minutes before park opening.

3. Early-entry guests should visit Ollivanders (**3a**) and ride Harry Potter and the Escape from Gringotts (**3b**). If Gringotts isn't operating, enjoy the rest of Diagon Alley but don't get in line.

4. Before early entry ends, ride Despicable Me Minion Mayhem. Day guests should begin their tour here.

5. Ride Hollywood Rip Ride Rockit.

6. Experience Transformers: The Ride 3-D.

7. Ride Revenge of the Mummy in New York (using Virtual Line if available).

8. Ride Race Through New York Starring Jimmy Fallon, or get a Virtual Line return time for early afternoon if the standby entrance isn't available.

9. Experience Men in Black Alien Attack in World Expo.

10. Ride The Simpsons Ride in Springfield.

11. Try Kang & Kodos' Twirl 'n' Hurl (open seasonally).

12. Ride E.T. Adventure in Woody Woodpecker's KidZone.

13. Eat lunch at Fast Food Boulevard.

14. Work in *Animal Actors on Location!* around lunch, according to the daily entertainment schedule.

15. Experience Race Through New York Starring Jimmy Fallon according to the Virtual Line reservation you made, if you didn't ride earlier.

16. See *Universal Orlando's Horror Make-Up Show* (**16a**) and *The Bourne Stuntacular* (**16b**) according to the daily entertainment schedule.

17. See *Shrek 4-D* in Production Central.

18. Chat with the Knight Bus conductor and his shrunken head outside of Diagon Alley. Also look for Kreacher in the window of 12 Grimmauld Place, and dial MAGIC (62442) in the red phone booth.

19. See *Celestina Warbeck and the Banshees*.

20. See the wand ceremony at Ollivanders, and buy a wand if you wish.

21. See *Tales of Beedle the Bard*.

22. Tour Diagon Alley. Browse the shops, explore the dark recesses of Knockturn Alley, and discover the interactive effects. If you're hungry, try the Leaky Cauldron or Florean Fortescue's Ice-Cream Parlour.

23. Ride Harry Potter and the Escape from Gringotts.

24. Revisit favorite attractions, if time permits.

25. If it's scheduled, watch *Universal Orlando's Cinematic Celebration* from Central Park (between Hollywood and Woody Woodpecker's KidZone).

UNIVERSAL STUDIOS FLORIDA ONE-DAY TOURING PLAN
FOR PARENTS WITH SMALL CHILDREN

1. Buy admission in advance. Call ☎ 407-363-8000 the day before for the official opening time.

2. Arrive at USF 90–120 minutes before the official opening time if Early Park Admission is offered and you're eligible, or 30–45 minutes before opening if you're a day guest. Check Universal's app for daily showtimes, and look for Virtual Line reservations for select attractions starting 15–30 minutes before park opening. Rent a stroller if needed.

3. Early-entry guests should ride Harry Potter and the Escape from Gringotts, and use child swap or exit after the elevators. Or just enjoy Diagon Alley.

4. Before early entry ends, ride Despicable Me Minion Mayhem. Day guests should wait in the Front Lot until permitted to ride Despicable Me.

5. See *Shrek 4-D* in Production Central.

6. Experience Transformers: The Ride 3-D if your kid can handle the noise and explosions.

7. Ride Race Through New York Starring Jimmy Fallon, or get a Virtual Line return time for midafternoon if the standby entrance isn't available.

8. Ride E.T. Adventure.

9. Ride The Simpsons Ride in Springfield.

10. Try Kang & Kodos' Twirl 'n' Hurl (open seasonally).

11. See *Animal Actors on Location* (**11a**) and *A Day in the Park with Barney* (**11b**; open seasonally) according to the entertainment schedule. Get a snack on Fast Food Boulevard while waiting for the shows to start.

12. Between shows, work in Woody's Nuthouse Coaster (**12a**) and time in Fievel's Playland (**12b**)

and Curious George Goes to Town (**12c**), if available.

13. Take a break from the park for at least 2 hours, depending on how late the park is open. If staying nearby, return to your room for a nap. Otherwise, take a rest at CityWalk or a resort hotel.

14. Return to the park a couple hours before the Superstar Parade and use your Virtual Line reservation for Race Through New York, if you didn't ride earlier.

15. If your kids are brave, see *Universal Orlando's Horror Make-Up Show* (**15a**) and/or *The Bourne Stuntacular* (**15b**) according to the daily entertainment schedule.

16. Greet characters such as Shrek, SpongeBob, and the Transformers at locations shown on the park map.

17. See the late afternoon Superstar Parade (if scheduled) from New York near Revenge of the Mummy.

18. On your way into Diagon Alley, chat with the Knight Bus conductor and his shrunken head. Also look for Kreacher in the window of 12 Grimmauld Place, and dial MAGIC (62442) in the red phone booth.

19. See the *Celestina Warbeck and the Banshees* and *Tales of Beedle the Bard* shows.

20. See the wand ceremony at Ollivanders.

21. Tour Diagon Alley. If you're hungry, try the Leaky Cauldron or Florean Fortescue's Ice-Cream Parlour.

22. Ride Harry Potter and the Escape from Gringotts from the standby queue (if you didn't ride earlier), and use child swap or exit after the elevators.

23. Revisit any favorite attractions, time permitting, and (if scheduled) watch *Universal Orlando's Cinematic Celebration* from Central Park.

Universal Studios Florida

The Wizarding World
of Harry Potter–
Diagon Alley

New York

San
Francisco

Production
Central

7th Ave.

World
Expo

Springfield:
Home of the
Simpsons

Hollywood

Woody
Woodpecker's
KidZone

Main Entrance

UNIVERSAL STUDIOS FLORIDA ONE-DAY TOURING PLAN FOR SENIORS

1. Buy admission in advance. Call ☎ 407-363-8000 the day before for the official opening time.

2. Arrive at USF 90–120 minutes before the official opening time if Early Park Admission is offered and you're eligible, or 30–45 minutes before opening if you're a day guest. Check Universal's app for daily showtimes, and look for Virtual Line reservations for select attractions starting 15–30 minutes before park opening. Rent a wheelchair or ECV if needed.

3. Early-entry guests should ride Harry Potter and the Escape from Gringotts. Exit after the elevators if you don't wish to experience a mild roller coaster. Or enjoy the rest of Diagon Alley.

4. Before early entry ends, hotel guests should exit Diagon Alley and then ride Despicable Me Minion Mayhem. Day guests should wait in the Front Lot until permitted to ride Despicable Me. Stationary seating is available on request.

5. See *Shrek 4-D* in Production Central. Stationary seating is available on request.

6. Experience Race Through New York Starring Jimmy Fallon. If simulated motion bothers you, enjoy the preshow but exit before the ride.

7. Ride E.T. Adventure in Woody Woodpecker's KidZone.

8. Ride Kang & Kodos' Twirl 'n' Hurl (open seasonally) in Springfield if 50 or fewer people are in line.

9. Ride Men in Black Alien Attack in World Expo if you can tolerate some moderate spinning.

10. Have an early lunch at Leaky Cauldron.

11. See the *Celestina Warbeck and the Banshees* and *Tales of Beedle the Bard* shows.

12. See the wand ceremony at Ollivanders, and purchase a wand if you wish.

13. Tour Diagon Alley. Browse the shops, explore the dark recesses of Knockturn Alley, and discover the interactive effects. If you're still hungry, try Florean Fortescue's Ice-Cream Parlour.

14. Experience Harry Potter and the Escape from Gringotts via the standby queue (if you didn't earlier), and exit after the elevators if you don't wish to experience a mild roller coaster.

15. Chat with the Knight Bus conductor and his shrunken head. Also look for Kreacher in the window of 12 Grimmauld Place, and dial MAGIC (62442) in the red phone booth.

16. See *The Blues Brothers Show* (**16a**) and *Animal Actors on Location!* (**16b**) according to the daily entertainment schedule. If time is short, skip *Animal Actors*.

17. See the late afternoon Superstar Parade (if scheduled).

18. See *Universal Orlando's Horror Make-Up Show* (**18a**) and/or *The Bourne Stuntacular* (**18b**) according to the daily entertainment schedule.

19. Have an early dinner inside the park at Fast Food Boulevard, Finnegan's Bar, or Lombard's Seafood.

20. Revisit any favorite attractions, time permitting, and (if scheduled) watch *Universal Orlando's Cinematic Celebration* from Central Park (between Hollywood and KidZone).

Universal's Islands of Adventure

The Lost Continent

Seuss Landing

Port of Entry

Jurassic Park

Marvel Super Hero Island

Toon Lagoon

Skull Island

UNIVERSAL'S ISLANDS OF ADVENTURE ONE-DAY TOURING PLAN FOR ADULTS

1. Buy admission in advance. Call ☎ 407-363-8000 the day before for the official opening time.

2. Arrive at IOA 90–120 minutes before the official opening time if Early Park Admission is offered and you're eligible, or 30–45 minutes before opening if you're a day guest. Check Universal's app for daily showtimes, and look for Virtual Line reservations for Hagrid's Magical Creatures Motorbike Adventure starting 15–30 minutes before park opening; get an early afternoon return time if available.

3. Early-entry guests should ride Hagrid's Magical Creatures Motorbike Adventure in Hogsmeade.

4. Ride Flight of the Hippogriff (**4a**), followed by Harry Potter and the Forbidden Journey (**4b**), if at least 30 minutes remain in early entry.

5. If time remains before official opening, ride The Incredible Hulk Coaster (**5a**). Otherwise, early-entry guests should enter Jurassic Park as soon as allowed and ride the Jurassic World VelociCoaster (**5b**; opening 2021).

6. Ride The Amazing Adventures of Spider-Man. Day guests should start with Spider-Man (**6a**), followed by Skull Island: Reign of Kong (**6b**). Early-entry guests may ride Reign of Kong (**6b**) on their way to Spider-Man (**6a**) if walking from Jurassic Park. Both early-entry and day guests continue as follows.

7. Take the Jurassic Park River Adventure. Put your belongings in a pay locker here and leave them through the next two rides.

8. Ride Dudley Do-Right's Ripsaw Falls in Toon Lagoon.

9. Ride Popeye & Bluto's Bilge-Rat Barges. Retrieve your property from Jurassic Park.

10. Eat an early lunch. A good sit-down choice is Mythos. Make reservations at zomato.com.

11. Ride Hagrid's Magical Creatures Motorbike Adventure in Hogsmeade.

12. See the wand ceremony at Ollivanders, and buy a wand if you wish.

13. See the *Frog Choir* perform on the small stage outside Hogwarts Castle.

14. Ride Harry Potter and the Forbidden Journey.

15. See the *Triwizard Spirit Rally* on the small stage outside Hogwarts Castle, time permitting.

16. Ride Flight of the Hippogriff (if you haven't already).

17. Explore the Jurassic Park Discovery Center.

18. Meet Blue at the Raptor Encounter.

19. In Lost Continent, see *Poseidon's Fury* (open seasonally).

20. Chat with the Mystic Fountain.

21. Experience The High in the Sky Seuss Trolley Train Ride! in Seuss Landing.

22. Ride One Fish, Two Fish, Red Fish, Blue Fish.

23. Enjoy the Caro-Seuss-el.

24. Experience The Cat in the Hat.

25. In Marvel Super Hero Island ride Doctor Doom's Fearfall.

26. Ride Storm Force Accelatron (open seasonally).

27. Ride The Incredible Hulk Coaster.

28. Have dinner at Three Broomsticks in Hogsmeade.

29. Get in line for the Jurassic World VelociCoaster (**29a**; opening 2021) or Hagrid's Magical Creatures Motorbike Adventure (**29b**) at least 1 hour before the park closes. Then watch the last Hogwarts Castle light show (if scheduled) before closing, or revisit any favorite attractions.

Universal's Islands of Adventure

UNIVERSAL'S ISLANDS OF ADVENTURE ONE-DAY TOURING PLAN FOR PARENTS WITH SMALL CHILDREN

1. Buy admission in advance. Call ☎ 407-363-8000 the day before for the official opening time.

2. Arrive at IOA 90–120 minutes before the official opening time if Early Park Admission is offered and you're eligible, or 30–45 minutes before opening if you're a day guest. Check Universal's app for daily showtimes. Rent a stroller if needed.

3. Ride Flight of the Hippogriff (**3a**), see the wand ceremony at Ollivanders (**3b**), and tour the queue (but exit before boarding) at Harry Potter and the Forbidden Journey (**3c**).

4. Early-entry guests can exit Hogsmeade into Jurassic Park as early entry ends and ride Skull Island: Reign of Kong (**4a**) as soon as it opens (if your kids are brave enough), then continue to Marvel Super Hero Island to ride The Amazing Adventures of Spider-Man (**4b**). Guests without early entry should start at this step with Spider-Man.

5. Ride Storm Force Accelatron (open seasonally).

6. Experience Skull Island: Reign of Kong if you dare (and haven't already).

7. Continue to Jurassic Park. Get a timed-return ticket for Pteranodon Flyers if your child is 36–56 inches tall.

8. Let the kids explore the Jurassic Park Discovery Center (**8a**) and play in Camp Jurassic (**8b**) until their time comes to ride Pteranodon Flyers.

9. Meet Blue at the Raptor Encounter.

10. Return to Toon Lagoon. Explore Me Ship, *The Olive*.

11. Take a break from the park for at least 2 hours, depending on how late the park is open. If staying

nearby, return to your room for lunch and a nap. Otherwise, take a rest at CityWalk or a resort hotel.

12. Return to the park. See the next scheduled show of *Oh! The Stories You'll Hear!* in Seuss Landing.

13. Explore If I Ran the Zoo while waiting for the show.

14. Ride The Cat in the Hat.

15. Ride One Fish, Two Fish, Red Fish, Blue Fish.

16. Enjoy the Caro-Seuss-el.

17. Ride The High in the Sky Seuss Trolley Train Ride.

18. See *Poseidon's Fury* (open seasonally) in The Lost Continent.

19. Chat with the Mystic Fountain.

20. Enter The Wizarding World of Harry Potter–Hogsmeade, and see the *Frog Choir* or *Triwizard Spirit Rally* perform on the small stage outside Hogwarts.

21. Ride Flight of the Hippogriff (if you didn't earlier).

22. If you didn't already, walk through the queue of Harry Potter and the Forbidden Journey.

23. See the wand ceremony at Ollivanders if you didn't earlier, and buy a wand if you wish.

24. See the stage show you didn't see earlier. Snap a picture of the Hogwarts Express conductor, and explore the shops and interactive windows around Hogsmeade.

25. Have dinner at Three Broomsticks.

26. Watch the Hogwarts Castle light show (if scheduled), or revisit any favorite attractions.

Universal's Islands of Adventure

UNIVERSAL'S ISLANDS OF ADVENTURE ONE-DAY TOURING PLAN FOR SENIORS

1. Buy admission in advance. Call ☎ 407-363-8000 the day before for the official opening time.

2. Arrive at IOA 90–120 minutes before the official opening time if Early Park Admission is offered and you're eligible, or 30–45 minutes before opening if you're a day guest. Check Universal's app for daily showtimes. Rent a wheelchair or ECV if needed.

3. Early-entry guests should explore the shops of Hogsmeade (**3a**), see the wand ceremony at Ollivanders (**3b**), and walk through the queue at Harry Potter and the Forbidden Journey (**3c**) (ask for the exit before boarding).

4. Exit Hogsmeade before early entry ends, and head to Seuss Landing to ride The Cat in the Hat. Guests without early entry should start at this step.

5. Ride One Fish, Two Fish, Red Fish, Blue Fish.

6. Enjoy the Caro-Seuss-el.

7. Ride The High in the Sky Seuss Trolley Train Ride!

8. Experience *Poseidon's Fury* (open seasonally) in The Lost Continent.

9. Chat with the Mystic Fountain.

10. Enter Hogsmeade and walk through the queue of Harry Potter and the Forbidden Journey (if you didn't earlier).

11. See the *Frog Choir* or *Triwizard Spirit Rally* perform on the small stage outside Hogwarts.

12. See the wand ceremony at Ollivanders (if you didn't earlier), and buy a wand if you wish.

13. Have lunch at Three Broomsticks (**13a**) or Mythos (**13b**).

14. After lunch, see the stage show you didn't see earlier. Snap a picture of the Hogwarts Express conductor, and explore the shops and interactive windows around Hogsmeade. Make sure you sample (or at least smell) some sweets at Honeydukes.

15. Cross the bridge to Jurassic Park and see the exhibits in the Jurassic Park Discovery Center.

16. Meet Blue at the Raptor Encounter.

17. Ride Skull Island: Reign of Kong, or at least request a temple tour through its elaborate queue.

18. Walk counterclockwise around the park, paying attention to the quiet paths along the waterfront in each island.

19. Revisit any favorite attractions, or remain in Hogsmeade to watch the Hogwarts Castle light show (if scheduled). Or exit the park for an early dinner in CityWalk.

The Wizarding World
of Harry Potter–
Diagon Alley

New York

San
Francisco

Production
Central

World
Expo

Springfield:
Home of the
Simpsons

Woody
Woodpecker's
KidZone

Hollywood

Main Entrance

UNIVERSAL ORLANDO HIGHLIGHTS ONE-DAY/
TWO-PARK TOURING PLAN: PART ONE *(Assumes: 1-Day Park-to-Park Ticket)*

1. Buy admission in advance. Call ☎ 407-363-8000 the day before for the official opening time.

2. Arrive at USF 90–120 minutes before the official opening time if Early Park Admission is offered and you're eligible, or 30–45 minutes before opening if you're a day guest. Check Universal's app for daily showtimes, and look for Virtual Line reservations for Hagrid's Magical Creatures Motorbike Adventure starting 15–30 minutes before park opening; get an early afternoon return time if available. **Alternative:** If only IOA is open for Early Park Admission and you're eligible, arrive at IOA 90–120 minutes before official opening. Ride Hagrid's Magical Creatures Motorbike Adventure (**2a**), Harry Potter and the Forbidden Journey (**2b**), and Flight of the Hippogriff (**2c**). Then take the first Hogwarts Express (**2d**) of the morning to USF, and continue at the next step. *(See the next page for the map of the previous four steps.)*

3. Early-entry guests should head to Diagon Alley to visit Ollivanders (**3a**) and ride Harry Potter and the Escape from Gringotts (**3b**). If Gringotts isn't operating, enjoy the rest of Diagon Alley but don't get in line.

4. Return to the front of the park to ride Despicable Me Minion Mayhem. Day guests should begin here.

5. Ride Hollywood Rip Ride Rockit.

6. Experience Transformers: The Ride 3-D in Production Central.

7. Ride Revenge of the Mummy in New York.

8. Ride Race Through New York Starring Jimmy Fallon if the standby entrance is open.

9. Ride Men in Black Alien Attack in World Expo.

10. Experience The Simpsons Ride in Springfield.

11. Ride E.T. Adventure in Woody Woodpecker's KidZone.

12. Ride Hogwarts Express to IOA. Have your park-to-park ticket ready.

Tour Islands of Adventure using Part Two of this plan (see next page); then return to USF and resume at step 23 below.

23. See *Universal Orlando's Horror Make-Up Show* (**23a**) and/or *The Bourne Stuntacular* (**23b**) according to the daily entertainment schedule.

24. Chat with the Knight Bus conductor outside of Diagon Alley. Also look for Kreacher in the window of 12 Grimmauld Place and dial MAGIC (62442) in the red phone booth.

25. See *Celestina Warbeck and the Banshees* or *Tales of Beedle the Bard* in Diagon Alley.

26. See the wand ceremony at Ollivanders, and buy a wand if you wish.

27. Eat dinner at the Leaky Cauldron.

28. Tour Diagon Alley. Browse the shops, explore the dark recesses of Knockturn Alley, and discover the interactive effects.

29. Ride Harry Potter and the Escape from Gringotts.

30. If scheduled, watch *Universal Orlando's Cinematic Celebration* from Central Park (between Hollywood and Woody Woodpecker's KidZone).

(continued on next page)

The Lost Continent

Seuss Landing

Port of Entry

Jurassic Park

Marvel Super Hero Island

Toon Lagoon

Skull Island

UNIVERSAL ORLANDO HIGHLIGHTS ONE-DAY/TWO-PARK TOURING PLAN: PART TWO

(continued from previous page)

13. Experience Hagrid's Magical Creatures Motorbike Adventure using your Virtual Line reservation (if available).

14. Ride Harry Potter and the Forbidden Journey.

15. Ride Flight of the Hippogriff if the wait isn't too long.

16. Break for lunch. We suggest Green Eggs and Ham Cafe in Seuss Landing (**16a**) for a quicker meal or Mythos (**16b**) in Lost Continent for sit-down dining.

17. Ride The Cat in the Hat in Seuss Landing.

18. Ride The Incredible Hulk Coaster on Marvel Super Hero Island.

19. Ride The Amazing Adventures of Spider-Man.

20. Ride Skull Island: Reign of Kong.

21. Ride the Jurassic World VelociCoaster (**21a**; opening 2021) or take the Jurassic Park River Adventure (**21b**).

22. Return to USF via Hogwarts Express, or walk back to the other park if the posted wait exceeds 20 minutes.

Resume Part One starting with step 23 (see previous page).

WIZARDING WORLD ONE-DAY/TWO-PARK TOURING PLAN: PART ONE
(Assumes: 1-Day Park-to-Park Ticket. Excludes: All non-Potter attractions.)

1. Buy admission in advance. Call ☎ 407-363-8000 the day before for the official opening time.

2. Arrive at USF 90–120 minutes before the official opening time if Early Park Admission is offered and you're eligible, or 30–45 minutes before opening if you're a day guest. Check Universal's app for daily showtimes, and look for Virtual Line reservations for Hagrid's Magical Creatures Motorbike Adventure starting 15–30 minutes before park opening; get an early afternoon return time if available. **Alternative:** If IOA is open for Early Park Admission and you're eligible, arrive at IOA's turnstiles 90–120 minutes before the official opening time (**2a**). Ride Hagrid's Magical Creatures Motorbike Adventure (**2b**) and then Harry Potter and the Forbidden Journey (**2c**). Ride Flight of the Hippogriff (**2d**) as well if you have time. Take the first Hogwarts Express of the morning to King's Cross Station (**2e**), and continue at the next step. *(See the next page for the map of the previous five steps.)*

3. Early-entry guests should ride Harry Potter and the Escape from Gringotts. If Gringotts isn't operating, enjoy the rest of Diagon Alley but don't get in line.

4. See the wand ceremony at Ollivanders, and buy a wand if you wish. Gringotts may have a long line by the time the park officially opens if Early Park Admission was offered, so day guests should begin with Ollivanders if the posted wait time for Gringotts is more than 30 minutes.

5. Have breakfast at the Leaky Cauldron or Florean

Fortescue's Ice-Cream Parlour (hey, you're on vacation!).

6. Tour Diagon Alley. Browse the shops, explore the dark recesses of Knockturn Alley, and discover the interactive effects.

7. See one of the two *Tales of Beedle the Bard* shows.

8. Exit Diagon Alley and ride the Hogwarts Express from King's Cross Station to IOA. Have your park-to-park ticket ready.

Tour Islands of Adventure using Part Two of this plan (see next page); then return to USF and resume at step 15 below.

15. Chat with the Knight Bus conductor and his shrunken head. Also look for Kreacher in the window of 12 Grimmauld Place, and dial MAGIC (62442) in the red phone booth.

16. Reenter Diagon Alley and catch the *Tales of Beedle the Bard* show that you didn't see earlier.

17. Ride Harry Potter and the Escape from Gringotts.

18. See the *Celestina Warbeck and the Banshees* show.

19. Have dinner at the Leaky Cauldron, or just eat dessert from Florean Fortescue's Ice-Cream Parlour or Sugarplum's Sweet Shop.

20. Stay in Diagon Alley (**20a**) until closing time, enjoying the atmosphere. The fireworks of the nighttime show look fantastic over the Gringotts dragon. Alternatively, take Hogwarts Express (**20b**) back to IOA and watch the light show on Hogwarts Castle (**20c**) (performed seasonally).

(continued on next page)

WIZARDING WORLD ONE-DAY/TWO-PARK TOURING PLAN: PART TWO
(Assumes: 1-Day Park-to-Park Ticket. Excludes: All non-Potter attractions.)

(continued from previous page)

9. Enter Hogsmeade and ride Harry Potter and the Forbidden Journey.

10. See the *Frog Choir* or *Triwizard Spirit Rally* perform on the small stage outside Hogwarts.

11. Ride Flight of the Hippogriff (**11a**), followed by Hagrid's Magical Creatures Motorbike Adventure (**11b**) using your Virtual Line reservation (if available).

12. Have lunch at Three Broomsticks.

13. After lunch, see the stage show you didn't see earlier. Snap a picture of the Hogwarts Express conductor, and explore the shops and interactive windows around Hogsmeade. Make sure you sample (or at least smell) some sweets at Honeydukes.

14. Return to USF via Hogwarts Express.

Resume Part One starting with step 15 (see previous page).

UNIVERSAL ORLANDO COMPREHENSIVE TWO-DAY/TWO-PARK TOURING PLAN: DAY ONE
(Assumes: Multiday Park-to-Park Ticket)

1. Buy admission in advance. Call ☎ 407-363-8000 the day before for the official opening time.

2. Arrive at IOA 90–120 minutes before the official opening time if Early Park Admission is offered and you're eligible, or 30–45 minutes before opening if you're a day guest. Check Universal's app for daily showtimes, and look for Virtual Line reservations for Hagrid's Magical Creatures Motorbike Adventure starting 15–30 minutes before park opening; get a midday return time if available.

3. Early-entry guests should ride Hagrid's Magical Creatures Motorbike Adventure (**3a**), followed by Harry Potter and the Forbidden Journey (**3b**). Ride Flight of the Hippogriff (**3c**) if you have time.

4. Early-entry guests can exit Hogsmeade before early entry ends and ride The Incredible Hulk Coaster in Marvel Super Hero Island. Guests without early entry should start at this step with the Hulk.

5. See The Amazing Adventures of Spider-Man.

6. Experience Skull Island: Reign of Kong.

7. Take the Jurassic Park River Adventure. Put your belongings in a pay locker here and leave them through the next two water rides.

8. Reverse course to ride Dudley Do-Right's Ripsaw Falls in Toon Lagoon.

9. Ride Popeye & Bluto's Bilge-Rat Barges. Now that you've achieved maximum soakage, retrieve your property from Jurassic Park.

10. Get your photo taken at the Raptor Encounter if the wait isn't overwhelming.

11. Ride Hagrid's Magical Creatures Motorbike Adventure using your Virtual Line reservation (if available) if you didn't ride earlier.

12. Stop and chat with the Mystic Fountain (**12a**) on your way to experience *Poseidon's Fury* (**12b**; open seasonally) in The Lost Continent.

13. Eat lunch at Mythos in Lost Continent (**13a**) or Three Broomsticks in Hogsmeade (**13b**).

14. After lunch, take the Hogwarts Express from Hogsmeade Station to USF, or walk to the other park if the posted wait exceeds 20 minutes. Have your park-to-park ticket ready.

(continued on next page)

UNIVERSAL ORLANDO COMPREHENSIVE TWO-DAY/TWO-PARK TOURING PLAN:
DAY ONE (continued)
(Assumes: Multiday Park-to-Park Ticket)

(continued from previous page)

15. Retrieve a Virtual Line reservation for Race Through New York Starring Jimmy Fallon (if available) or ride standby if the wait is short.

16. Work in *The Blues Brothers Show* around your Jimmy Fallon return time according to the daily entertainment schedule.

17. See *Shrek 4-D* in Production Central.

18. See *Universal Orlando's Horror Make-Up Show* (**18a**) and *The Bourne Stuntacular* (**18b**) according to the daily entertainment schedule.

19. If you have time, see the late afternoon parade (if scheduled).

20. On your way into Diagon Alley, chat with the Knight Bus conductor and his shrunken head. Also look for Kreacher in the window of 12 Grimmauld Place, and dial MAGIC (62442) in the red phone booth.

21. See the *Celestina Warbeck and the Banshees* and *Tales of Beedle the Bard* shows.

22. See the wand ceremony at Ollivanders, and buy a wand if you wish.

23. Tour Diagon Alley. Browse the shops, explore the dark recesses of Knockturn Alley, and discover the interactive effects. If you're hungry, try the Leaky Cauldron or Florean Fortescue's Ice-Cream Parlour.

24. Ride Harry Potter and the Escape from Gringotts.

25. Revisit a favorite attraction, or browse the Williams of Hollywood prop shop.

26. If scheduled, watch *Universal Orlando's Cinematic Celebration* from Central Park (between Hollywood and Woody Woodpecker's KidZone).

(Day Two is on the next two pages.)

UNIVERSAL ORLANDO COMPREHENSIVE TWO-DAY/TWO-PARK TOURING PLAN: DAY TWO
(Assumes: Multiday Park-to-Park Ticket) (Day One is on previous pages.)

1. Buy admission in advance. Call ☎ 407-363-8000 the day before for the official opening time.

2. Arrive at USF 90–120 minutes before the official opening time if Early Park Admission is offered and you're eligible, or 30–45 minutes before opening if you're a day guest. Check Universal's app for daily showtimes, and look for Virtual Line reservations for Hagrid's Magical Creatures Motorbike Adventure starting 15–30 minutes before park opening; get an evening return time if available.

3. Early-entry guests should ride Harry Potter and the Escape from Gringotts. If Gringotts isn't operating, enjoy the rest of Diagon Alley but do not get in line.

4. Before early entry ends, hotel guests should exit Diagon Alley and ride Despicable Me Minion Mayhem. Day guests should wait in the Front Lot until permitted to ride Despicable Me.

5. Ride Hollywood Rip Ride Rockit.

6. Experience Transformers: The Ride 3-D in Production Central.

7. Ride Revenge of the Mummy in New York.

8. Experience Fast & Furious: Supercharged (open seasonally). Virtual Line reservations shouldn't be necessary, but use the single-rider line if the standby wait time exceeds 20 minutes.

9. Walk past the London Waterfront to ride Men in Black Alien Attack in World Expo.

10. Ride The Simpsons Ride in Springfield.

11. Ride Kang & Kodos' Twirl 'n' Hurl (open seasonally) if 50 or fewer people are in line.

12. Ride E.T. Adventure in Woody Woodpecker's KidZone.

13. Work in *Animal Actors on Location!* around lunch (we recommend Fast Food Boulevard), according to the daily entertainment schedule.

14. Ride the Hogwarts Express from King's Cross Station to IOA. Have your park-to-park ticket ready.

(continued on next page)

Universal's Islands of Adventure

The Lost Continent

Seuss Landing

Port of Entry

Jurassic Park

Marvel Super Hero Island

Toon Lagoon

Skull Island

UNIVERSAL ORLANDO COMPREHENSIVE TWO-DAY/TWO-PARK TOURING PLAN:
DAY TWO *(continued)*
(Assumes: Multiday Park-to-Park Ticket)

(continued from previous page)

15. Ride The High in the Sky Seuss Trolley Train Ride! in Seuss Landing.
16. Enjoy the Caro-Seuss-el.
17. Ride One Fish, Two Fish, Red Fish, Blue Fish.
18. Experience The Cat in the Hat.
19. Cross through Port of Entry to Marvel Super Hero Island and ride Storm Force Accelatron (open seasonally).
20. While in Marvel, ride Doctor Doom's Fearfall.
21. Walk through Toon Lagoon to Jurassic Park and explore Camp Jurassic.
22. Check out the exhibits in the Jurassic Park Discovery Center.
23. Enter Hogsmeade, and see the *Frog Choir* or *Triwizard Spirit Rally* perform on the small stage outside Hogwarts.
24. Ride Flight of the Hippogriff.

25. Have dinner at Three Broomsticks.
26. After dinner, see the stage show you didn't see earlier. Snap a picture of the Hogwarts Express conductor, and explore the shops and interactive windows around Hogsmeade. Make sure you sample (or at least smell) some sweets at Honeydukes.
27. Try to ride Hagrid's Magical Creatures Motorbike Adventure around sunset using your Virtual Line reservation (if available).
28. Ride Harry Potter and the Forbidden Journey during the first Hogwarts Castle nighttime light show (performed seasonally).
29. Get in line for the Jurassic World VelociCoaster (opening 2021) at least 1 hour before the park closes.
30. Watch the last Hogwarts Castle light show before closing, or revisit any favorite attractions.